THE LAWS OF INNKEEPERS

—For Hotels, Motels, Restaurants, and Clubs

THE
LAWS OF INNKEEPERS

—For Hotels, Motels, Restaurants, and Clubs

JOHN H. SHERRY

CORNELL UNIVERSITY PRESS

ITHACA AND LONDON

First published 1972 by Cornell University Press.
Published in the United Kingdom by Cornell University Press Ltd., 2–4 Brook Street, London W1Y 1AA.

Second printing 1973

International Standard Book Number 0-8014-0702-8
Library of Congress Catalog Card Number 76-37780

PRINTED IN THE UNITED STATES OF AMERICA
BY VAIL-BALLOU PRESS, INC.

Librarians: Library of Congress cataloging information appears on the last page of the book.

Contents

Contents

Preface

This book is the culmination of years of teaching the "Laws of Innkeepers" in the School of Hotel Administration at Cornell University. The invitation to teach a course in hotel law came to me as a practicing attorney, specializing in the hotel field, from the late Howard B. Meek, Dean of the School, who believed that instruction in law was essential to the training of executives responsible for making decisions in the complex and diverse operations of modern hotels, motels, and restaurants.

In organizing the material for the course, I had the benefit of the classic work of the late Joseph Henry Beale, Jr., Bussey Professor of Law at Harvard University. Professor Beale was attracted to the subject of hotels as part of his over-all interest in public service corporations. He found that the law of innkeepers was the earliest, simplest, and clearest formulation of those fields of law concerned with the various public service callings. His book, published in 1906, has been regarded by the legal profession as the authority on the subject for more than half a century, has been cited by the courts in innumerable decisions, and has molded legal thought in the development of the law of innkeepers. I have made full use of Professor Beale's text and retained with little or no change, by permission of Mrs. Beale, the many sections of permanent value. Whatever merit this book may have is due in large part to Professor Beale, and I gratefully acknowledge my indebtedness to him.

The book has been planned to serve three purposes: first, as a textbook for use in collegiate schools of hotel and restaurant administration; second, as a reference manual for use by hotel, motel, restaurant, and club operators and executives; third, as a tool for attorneys in the general practice of law who encounter legal problems in the public hospitality field.

The text covers the applicable basic common-law principles throughout the United States. Since it would have been impracticable to include in the book statutory material for all the states, the coverage has been restricted to New York. To make the book adaptable for use in all states, a pocket is appended to the back cover, so that the statute laws of any state, keyed to the basic text, can be kept with the book.

The sections, or portions of sections, that have been incorporated into the present text from Beale's *The Law of Innkeepers and Hotels* are accounted for in the cross-reference table at the end of the text.

In preparing the manuscript for the press, I have enjoyed the good fortune of much valuable assistance. My associates, John F. Gilligan, Esq., and John E. H. Sherry, Esq., have greatly increased the value of the book by contributions and critical reading and suggestions.

Leonard G. Miller, Esq., then a senior in the Columbia Law School, now a member of the Ohio Bar, read the manuscript and checked the citations, and made valuable corrections and additions to the text.

Joseph T. McLaughlin, Esq., then a senior in the Cornell Law School, now a member of the New York Bar, assisted in selecting and digesting materials for the book.

Mr. James Rosenblatt, now a senior in the Cornell Law School, has assisted in the final preparation of the manuscript for the press.

Mrs. Mary Mignano, a secretary in the Cornell Law School, rendered valuable assistance in the final typing of the manuscript.

My secretary, Mrs. Miriam Paress, has given unstintingly of time and patience to help me focus attention on the manuscript.

Grateful thanks are due to the Statler Foundation and its wise and perceptive trustees, Peter J. Crotty, Esq., Dr. Harry Seeberg, and the late Judge Ward B. Arbury, for assistance in the form of a grant to Cornell University toward the expenses of preparing the manuscript for publication.

I am especially indebted to Professor Robert A. Beck, Dean of the Cornell Hotel School, without whose interest, assistance, and encouragement this book would not have been possible.

I am also grateful to the many clients whose problems have afforded me much practical experience in this field.

A word of appreciation is in order also to the staff of Cornell University Press for many valuable suggestions in editing and preparing the manuscript.

Last, but not least, I happily acknowledge my indebtedness to my wife, Marguerite Horwath Sherry, whose patience, forbearance, and tactful prodding moved the manuscript through to publication.

JOHN H. SHERRY

New York City
April 1972

THE LAWS OF INNKEEPERS
—For Hotels, Motels, Restaurants, and Clubs

CHAPTER 1

Historical Introduction

1:1 *Inns in the Ancient and Medieval World*

Houses of public entertainment have been maintained in all countries from early times. In the ancient world we hear of inns and taverns in all civilized countries: in Egypt, in Asia, in Palestine, in Greece, and in Italy. The beerhouses or taverns of ancient Egypt were furnished with mats, stools, and armchairs upon which customers sat side-by-side, fraternally drinking beer, wine, palm brandy, cooked and perfumed liquors. Slaves and maidservants served and entertained the customers and strived to maintain an atmosphere of ease and conviviality. The taverns of Babylon and Nineveh were owned by wealthy merchants who employed women managers, sold liquor on credit, and received payment in grain, usually after the harvest.

Inns and taverns were found throughout the Holy Land. A tavern in a town was in contrast with the caravanserai (unfurnished overnight resthouse) of the open road. The forerunners of the Greek inns were public places, lesches, where people gathered for gossip and amusement.

In ancient Rome publicans and their houses were held in general contempt just as they were in Greece. The Romans were a proud race who held that the business of conducting a tavern was a low form of occupation, and the running of such establishments was usually entrusted to slaves. The inns along the highways were of questionable reputation. Landlords were predatory and robberies of travelers were common. On the great highways leading to Rome, posthouses were located at various stages where horses could be baited and fresh ones obtained. These posthouses were great government inns used by the military as halting places where provender for men and beasts of the legions was provided. Officials were assigned to them for purposes of inspection and for the apprehension of dangerous or un-

[1]

desirable characters. Before any service could be obtained therein, it was necessary to present credentials.[1]

Throughout the Middle Ages the use of such houses continued all over the world. Travel abroad was much more common during the Middle Ages than we often realize; and the traveler returning to England might have brought home with him information about the trade of the innkeeper and suggested its establishment in his own land. But there is no reason to suppose that the English inns were not of indigenous growth; certain it is that they were noted as the cleanest, the best supplied, and the most attractive inns in the world. We must turn to the habits and needs of travel in medieval England to explain the origin, the nature, and the legal position of English inns.

1:2 *Study of History of English Inns to Understand the Law*

The laws regulating the rights and duties of an innkeeper are not in all respects what one might have looked for as applying to the innkeeper of today. The innkeeper occupies in our law a peculiar and apparently anomalous position: while not technically a bailee of the goods of his guests, he is held to the strictest responsibility which any bailee is under; and while apparently a mere individual householder with no corporate or other franchise specially granted, he is compelled, like the great railroad corporations, to receive and entertain strangers whether he will or not. These and other duties and responsibilities of the innkeeper will be considered at length later, but in order that we may understand the reason for the apparently peculiar doctrine of the law regulating the rights and liabilities of innkeepers, in order that we may learn the extent of their responsibilities and understand their limitations, we must examine briefly the early history of innkeeping in England, the character and nature of inns, and the functions which they performed in the social life of the English people at the time when the law of innkeepers was forming, that is, during the fourteenth and fifteenth centuries. The nature of the English inn in the Middle Ages determined the English law of innkeepers, and the principles thus established form the basis of the law of innkeepers in every place where the common law prevails.

---

[1] For a general discussion, see W. Firebaugh, *The Inns of Greece and Rome,* 2d ed. (Chicago, 1928).

1:3 *Conditions of Travel in Medieval England*

There was a surprising amount of traveling in England in the Middle Ages. The roads, to be sure, were very bad and in general were impassable for loaded wagons, and the transportation of goods from place to place was therefore almost impossible. While one portion of the country was well supplied with food, another portion not so far away might be in the throes of famine without a chance of relief so far as land transportation was concerned. Yet, in spite of this, the roads were sufficient for foot passengers or for lightly loaded horses, and they were used by multitudes of people on foot and on horseback. Carriers of goods existed, but they transported their goods in packs by means of horses.

The roads were not only bad, but they were infested with outlaws and robbers of all sorts. Between the villages there were long stretches of forest, and these forests were the refuge of the outlaws who formed a considerable proportion of the population of the country. They might at any time attack travelers by day, but that was unusual. Since it usually happened that travelers proceeded in companies, there was not much danger of attack during daylight hours; but at night the danger increased considerably.

1:4 *Houses of Accommodation for Travelers*

Such being the conditions of traveling, two results followed: a traveler had to carry the lightest weight baggage possible, and he had to secure protection at night from thieves and outlaws. He could not conveniently carry with him food for his journey, and he therefore had to find entertainment along the road. He could not safely sleep in the open and thus had to find some house which would offer him protection as well as entertainment for the night. These needs led naturally to the establishment of a course of business which should supply the demand. At the proper place on every main road of travel, houses were devoted to the business of furnishing food, drink, and safe lodging to hungry and weary travelers. Thus, out of the needs of the wayfarer and as an incident of travel from place to place, grew the English inn. It was established to supply the needs of the traveler along his journey, to wit, to furnish food and drink for man and beast and rest and safety for the night.

Inns were intended for the middle class: merchants, small landowners, itinerant packmen, etc. A certain number of beds were placed in one room. . . . Each man bought separately what he wished to eat, chiefly bread, a little meat, and some beer. Complaints as to the excessive prices were not much less frequent then than now. . . . The people petitioned Parliament and the King interfered accordingly with his accustomed useless goodwill. Edward III [1312–1377] promulgated, in the twenty-third year of his reign [1350], a statute to constrain "hostelers et herbergers" to sell food at reasonable prices; and again, four years later, tried to put an end to the "great and outrageous cost of victuals kept up in all the realm by innkeepers and other retailers of victuals, to the great detriment of the people travelling through the realm." [2]

The inn was not the only accommodation which weary travelers might find in the course of their journey. The religious houses practiced hospitality and freely received certain classes of people. The nobles and magnates habitually resorted to them for refreshment and were received both in consideration of their own bounty and as representatives of the class to which the community owed its foundation and its wealth. The very poor also were received out of mere charity, for hospitality to the poor was one of the first requirements of religion as it was understood in the Middle Ages. To the houses of the friars, therefore, rich and poor resorted for entertainment; but the great middle class, the men who were able to pay their way, were not welcome there. If they had the means to pay for accommodation and were without special claim to favor, they had to go to those whose business it was to care for them. The great houses of nobles and gentry were also open to travelers who were in need of entertainment, but there, too, it was as a rule only the rich and the poor who were expected to avail themselves of the private hospitality. Anyone lost or benighted would of course be received; but the lord of the manor had no desire to compete with the innkeeper who had to make his livelihood from the wayfarer.

Besides these private houses and the inn for necessary entertainment,

[2] J. Jusserand, *English Wayfaring Life in the Middle Ages*, 4th ed., trans. L. Smith (New York, 1961), p. 61.

the alehouse or tavern supplied incidental refreshment of the traveler though generally intended to serve another purpose. This house primarily supplied the wants of the inhabitants of the place, for there the native found rest, heat, companionship, and beer. He could stay until the stroke of curfew, and then was turned out to find his way home as best he might, quarreling and fighting by the way, using his knife freely, or falling from his horse into a convenient stream, easy prey for enemies and robbers. "The law would not have a tavern haunted out of season," and the nighttime was out of season. The difference between the inn and the tavern is therefore obvious. The one was instituted for the weary traveler, the other for the native; the one furnished food that the traveler might continue his journey, the other furnished drink for the mere pleasure of neighbors; the one was open to the traveler for protection at night, the other turned its guest out at the very moment when he most needed protection, and left him to find it, if his remaining senses permitted him to do so, in his own home. A tavern, then, is not an inn, and the innkeeper's duties do not extend to the tavernkeeper.

1:5 *Development of Inns from Private Houses*

Such being the course of life among wayfarers in medieval England, the inn was a natural outgrowth of the conditions. The inn, the public house of entertainment, was evolved from the private house. Any householder might receive a stranger for the night, as indeed in rural communities many householders are still apt to do. If in the course of time one such householder came, either through the superiority of his own accommodation or by reason of the lack of competition, to receive all persons who in that village needed accommodation he would thereby have become an innkeeper. He would have done it perhaps gradually, without any distinct change marking the transition from private householder to public innkeeper; nor would the accommodation he offered be different in kind from the accommodation that would be offered by the private householder furnishing occasional accommodation to a transient guest. The inn was an outgrowth of the private house, and the kind of house employed and the general conduct of life in the house would be the same in the early inn and the private house of the same period. In order to discover the nature of the accommodation afforded by the inn, it is, therefore, worthwhile to examine the plan of life in the ordinary dwelling of the time.

The English houses of the thirteenth and fourteenth centuries differed greatly, of course, in size and in elegance, but the plan of life in all houses had certain common features. Indoor living centered about the great hall, the principal part of the house, to which other parts were added as they might be required. In the hall the days were spent, so far as they were spent indoors, meals were eaten, and at nighttime the tables were removed and the beds were spread. The mistress, to be sure, had a small room of her own, the bower, into which she could retire at any time, and the master of the house had a separate chamber in which he slept. But the retainers, the servants, and the ordinary guests slept together in the common hall. The house of a man who was well-to-do might have an additional chamber for guests, and a stable was usually attached to the hall at one end. The hall was warmed and lighted by a great fire. In each chamber there was a small fireplace for heat, and light was supplied by a candle.

The inn was undoubtedly built on this same plan, even when a building was built especially for an inn; in most cases, however, the inn had been built for an ordinary dwelling house. The weary traveler coming to the inn at nightfall would have his supper at the great table, and his bed would then be spread in the hall itself. Heat and such light as was necessary he would have from the hall fire. If he brought a horse and paid for his keep we are told he paid no extra charge for his bed, but the foot traveler paid a small sum for his lodging. A traveler of better estate would pay for and receive accommodation in a small chamber. There he would be served with food, and his bed would be spread; he would be charged not merely for the food and lodging, but also for his fire and candle. Even there he would not be likely to occupy the chamber alone, or even a bed alone; the king himself on his travels was expected to have a bedfellow, and a private person would be fortunate if he had only one. Still he was traveling in luxury if he shared with two or three others a private chamber, a private bed, and a private fire.

As time went on and the business of the innkeepers increased, especially in the great towns, buildings were built as inns, the number of chambers being greatly increased. In the sixteenth century we hear of inns in London which could accommodate one hundred guests. It must be clear that with so many guests the common hall would be needed for the reception and for the general table, and the guests must have all been put into special chambers for sleeping, but most of these were undoubtedly still common chambers, in which travelers were put as they happened to come, sharing not merely the chamber but the bed with strange bedfellows.

1:6 Development of the Law

Such being the business and such the customs of innkeepers, their responsibility, which through modern eyes seems anomalous, is easily explained. They undertake as a business to furnish food, protection, and shelter to the wayfaring guest. Having undertaken such a public business, and the public need being concerned, the innkeeper must supply his service to all; and in order to perform his undertaking he must furnish not merely sufficient food and a tight roof, but sufficient protection against the dangers of country traveling. To refuse shelter, to fail to provide food, or to permit robbers from outside to enter the inn would be a breach of his obligation and would render him liable to action. But this is not the limit of his obligation. If he puts a stranger into a common room with other strangers and bids him sleep, the innkeeper must undertake his care and protection during the night, not merely against persons outside but against strange bedfellows within the inn. It is interesting to notice how history repeats itself in this case. A much later invention, the sleeping car, brought back to modern life some of the obsolete features of the life of the Middle Ages. A number of persons, strangers to one another, were received to sleep in a common room open to persons from outside. The existence of the same conditions imposed a similar responsibility, and the proprietor of the sleeping car, like the innkeeper in the Middle Ages, was obliged to protect his guests as well as he could against danger from within and from without. The innkeeper's liability did not exist in the case of a private chamber, into which only the guest who engaged it or friends brought into it by himself were allowed to enter. If a man engaged a room and was put in exclusive control of it, and was given the key, the protection which the innkeeper was obliged to furnish him was, therefore, merely against outsiders who might be permitted to break into the room without right. Against the inmates the guest had no right to call upon the innkeeper for protection. This is the reason of the stress laid in the old cases upon the fact that the innkeeper has given the guest the key of his room; this gift of key marked and symbolized the fact that the room was no longer in the innkeeper's disposal, that he could quarter no stranger in it, and that the guest and his friends alone could enter, and, therefore, against those who rightly entered the innkeeper undertook no responsibility.

The business of innkeeper having been carried on in this way, the distinctive features of the law are easily accounted for. The principles of the innkeeper's liability once being established have continued unchanged until the present day, and the hotelkeeper in the great cities of the United States derives his rights and traces his responsibilities to the host of the humble village inn of medieval England.

CHAPTER 2

The Nature of an Inn

2:1   *The Inn Is a Public House*

From the earliest times the fundamental characteristic of an inn has been its public nature. It is a public house, a house of public entertainment, or, as it is legally phrased, a common inn, a house kept "publicly, openly and notoriously, for the entertainment and accommodation of travellers and others, for a reward." [1]

The whole system of travel and communication in rural England, at the time the law of inns was in the making, required that the weary traveler should find, at convenient places beside the highway, houses of entertainment and shelter to which he might resort during his journey for food, rest, and protection. The ordinary laws of supply and demand would lead to the establishment of such houses by the roadside at places which would sufficiently serve the public convenience, but those laws could not be trusted to secure to each individual the benefit of the food and shelter therein provided. The desire for gain is not the only passion which moves men, innkeepers or others. Hatred, prejudice, envy, sloth, or undue fastidiousness might influence an innkeeper to refuse entertainment to a traveler, even though he could pay his score. The supply of food and shelter to a traveler was a matter of public concern, and the house which offered such food and shelter was engaged in a public service. The law must make injustice to the individual traveler impossible; the caprice of the host could not be permitted to leave a subject of the king hungry and shelterless. In a matter of such importance the public had an interest, and must see that, so far as was consistent with justice to the innkeeper, his inn was carried on for the benefit of the whole public, and so it became in an exact sense a public house.

[1] *State* v. *Stone*, 6 Vt. 295, 298 (1834).

[9]

2:2 *Innkeeper Professes a Public Business*

It follows from the nature of the inn that an innkeeper is one who professes to serve the public by keeping an inn. The most striking characteristic of his employment, that which distinguishes his employment from that of an ordinary person's, is the fact that his calling is a public one. He is a "common innkeeper," who, in the quaint language of Lord Holt "has made profession of a trade which is for the public good, and has thereby exposed and vested an interest of himself in all the King's subjects that will employ him in the way of his trade." [2] Whether a man is an innkeeper depends, therefore, in the first place upon whether he makes a profession of serving the public needs, whether his regular business is entertaining travelers.

2:3 *Distinction between Innkeeper and Private Host for Hire*

In many places where there are no inns, private householders occasionally, and even frequently, take in and accommodate travelers and receive compensation, but merely as a matter of accommodation, and without making a business of the practice. They receive the stranger and traveler out of mere hospitality or from motives among which gain is merely incidental, and their livelihood is not derived from their hospitality. Such persons, though they receive compensation for the accommodation they furnish, are not innkeepers.[3]

Thus in *Howth* v. *Franklin*,[4] it was shown that a man had a house on the high road, much visited by travelers, who were uniformly entertained and charged; these facts were notorious and relied on by travelers. On the other hand, he often declared that he did not keep an inn, he refused to take boarders, and often entertained his friends and countrymen free of charge. The court held that the question

---

[2] *Lane* v. *Cotton*, 88 Eng. Rep. 1458, 1464 (K.B. 1701).

[3] *Lyon* v. *Smith*, 1 Iowa 184 (1843); *Goodyear Tire & Rubber Co.* v. *Altamont Springs Hotel Co.*, 206 Ky. 494, 267 S.W. 555 (1924); *Kisten* v. *Hildebrand*, 48 Ky. (9 B. Mon.) 72 (1848); *State* v. *Steele*, 106 N.C. 766, 11 S.E. 478 (1890); *State* v. *Mathews*, 19 N.C. 424 (1837); *Howth* v. *Franklin*, 20 Tex. 798 (1858); *Southwestern Hotel Co.* v. *Rogers*, 183 S.W.2d 751 (Tex. Civ. App. 1944), *aff'd*, 143 Tex. 343, 184 S.W.2d 835 (1945).

[4] 20 Tex. 798 (1858).

whether he was or was not an innkeeper was for the jury and that the jury might on this evidence find him an innkeeper. In the course of his opinion Judge Roberts said:

There are numerous farmers situated on the public roads of the country, who occasionally, and even frequently, take in and accommodate travellers, and receive compensation for it, who are not innkeepers, and are not liable as such. It is not their business or occupation, nor do they prepare and fit up their establishments for it. They yield to the laws of hospitality, in receiving and entertaining the stranger and the traveller, yet they cannot afford to do so without some compensation. This view of the subject the Court also presented to the minds of the jury, by telling them in substance, that if [the] defendant only occasionally entertained travellers for compensation, when it suited his own pleasure, he did not thereby become an innkeeper.[5]

Similarly, in *Lyon* v. *Smith*,[6] it was proved that the person alleged to be an innkeeper had entertained several individuals at his house overnight and been paid a compensation for his care and attentions, but there was no proof that he held himself out in any manner as a common innkeeper, or that he was so regarded by the public. In the course of his opinion Chief Justice Mason said:

To render a person liable as a common innkeeper, it is not sufficient to show that he occasionally entertains travelers. Most of the farmers in a new country do this, without supposing themselves answerable for the horses or other property of their guests, which may be stolen, or otherwise lost, without any fault of their own. Nor is such the rule in older countries, where it would operate with far less injustice, and be less opposed to good policy than with us. To be subjected to the same responsibilities attaching to innkeepers, a person must make tavern-keeping, to some extent, a regular business, a means of livlihood [*sic*]. He should hold himself out to the world as an *innkeeper*. It is not necessary that he should have a sign, or a license, provided that he has in any other manner authorized the general understanding that his was a public house, where strangers had a right to require accommodation. The person who occasionally entertains others for a reasonable compensation is no more subject to the extraordinary responsibility of an innkeeper than is he liable as a common carrier, who in certain special cases carries the property of others from one place to another for hire.[7]

---

[5] *Id.* at 802–803.   [6] 1 Iowa 184 (1883).   [7] *Id.* at 186.

If, however, the housekeeper does as a matter of fact receive every member of the public who applies for entertainment, as a regular course of business, he is an innkeeper, though he may claim that his house is still a private one.[8]

The question whether a house where a guest is entertained is a public inn or a private house is a question of fact, to be determined, like any fact, upon all the evidence. In determining the question, the facts may lead to a presumption against a party. Thus if a housekeeper does an act which he could not legally do unless he is an innkeeper he will be presumed, in the absence of evidence to the contrary, to be an innkeeper. Thus in *Korn v. Schedler*,[9] it was held that when a man has applied for a license to sell liquor as a hotelkeeper, he cannot later deny liability for the loss of a guest's property on the ground that he does not keep a hotel.

2:4 *Innkeeper Serves Transient Guests*

The person whose needs the innkeeper undertakes to serve is the weary traveler, a person who stays with him merely for a short time in the course of his journey. The inn is therefore primarily provided for transient guests, and one who does not profess to serve transient guests is not an innkeeper. (For this reason it was held necessary in the old cases to allege, in an action by a guest against an innkeeper, that the plaintiff was "transient.")

This characteristic of an innkeeper is the distinguishing feature between an inn and a boardinghouse. A boardinghouse is for the entertainment not of transient guests, who must find food and shelter at once, but of more or less permanent occupants, who may at their leisure make bargains with their host. The boarder being in this position, the housekeeper may exercise the same liberty. If the boarder may select and bargain for his boarding place, so the housekeeper may select and bargain with his guests. The distinction and the reason for it were brought out very neatly in *Bonner v. Welborn*, an early Georgia case.[10] The defendant, who was proceeded against on a statute affecting innkeepers, was the keeper of a hotel at a country

[8] *Jaquet v. Edwards*, 1 Jamaica 70 (1867).
[9] 11 Daly (N.Y.) 234 (Ct. C.P. N.Y. Co. 1882).   [10] 7 Ga. 296 (1849).

watering place, who undertook, either in his hotel or in cottages near it which he rented, to entertain visitors for a season. In holding that he was not an innkeeper Judge Nesbet said:

It is because inns and innkeepers have to do with the travelling public—strangers—and that for brief periods, and under circumstances which render it impossible for each customer to contract for the terms of his entertainment, that the law has taken them so strictly in charge. And it is because of the compulsion innkeepers are under, to afford entertainment to anybody, that the law has clothed them with extraordinary privileges. Now, under this (it is submitted), correct legal view of innkeepers, was the plaintiff in this case, an innkeeper? Was that his business? His business was, to rent his houses to families or persons who might contract with him for their occupancy. They are not his guests, they are beyond dispute, his tenants, and he their landlord. His business was, to furnish board, lodging and attention. But to whom? To the wayfaring world? No. But to persons who might resort to his healthful fountains and salubrious locality, for a season, that is, for the fall and summer months. They were not his guests for a day, or night, or week, but his lodgers or boarders for a season. They were not chargeable according to any tariff of rates, fixed by law, but according to contract, varied, beyond doubt, according to time, amount of accommodation, and other circumstances. These are not the characteristics of the business of innkeeping, but indicate a boarding house. As well might every private boarding house in the State, be adjudged an inn or a tavern, as this party's establishment. The object for which people are stated in the declaration, to have visited the springs, necessarily forbids the idea of their being travellers, and of plaintiff's house being a tavern. It was health, in the use of the medicinal waters. That object indicates abiding—permanency of location, for a season, at least. These waters cannot cure by seven draughts; or like the waters of Jordan, by seven washings.[11]

But the fact that a person receives those who are not transient guests does not prevent his being an innkeeper. Though in its origin the business of an innkeeper was to supply the needs of travelers, yet once in the business an innkeeper will naturally be quite willing to do a profitable business with other persons. An innkeeper will ordinarily receive and care for any proper person who applies, even though, not being a traveler, he could not demand such reception as a legal right; and such reception of guests does not work a change of employment.

[11] *Id.* at 307–308.

One who keeps a house of entertainment for travelers is not the less an innkeeper because he also receives other persons.[12]

Even if the innkeeper caters to permanent guests, and makes his inn attractive for them, he is none the less an innkeeper if he professes also to supply the needs of travelers, as most hotelkeepers do. Thus the fact that a house stands upon enclosed grounds which are reserved for the exclusive use of guests, that the gates are closed at night, and that the house is thus rendered attractive as a pleasure resort and guests are thereby induced to remain a considerable time, does not prevent the house from being an inn if it is held out as a place of entertainment for travelers.[13]

And even in a case where the chief attraction of a hotel was a mineral spring connected with it, and it did not appear that persons resorted to the hotel except such as desired to use it as a watering place, it was assumed without argument that the hotel was an inn.[14]

The function and purpose of hotels change with the period, methods of travel and conditions of society. [Citation omitted.] Now hotels are often devoted to the entertainment of guests seeking rest, recreation and pleasure. They are located in the mountains and at the seaside, where guests may go in the summer; or they may be located where there is a warm climate, to attract guests who wish to escape the rigors of winter. They differ in the main from purely commercial hotels only in respect to the greater attention they give to features of recreation and amusement, and in the usual duration of stay of the guests.[15]

2:5 Innkeeper Supplies the Needs of a Traveler

The innkeeper supplies all the entertainment which the weary traveler actually needs on the road, which in simplest terms are food, shelter, and protection. If the keeper of a house of entertainment does not undertake to furnish either food or shelter, he is not a common

[12] *Wintermute* v. *Clark,* 5 Sand. (N.Y.) 242 (Super. Ct. 1851).

[13] *Fay* v. *Pacific Improvement Co.,* 93 Cal. 253, 26 P. 1099 (1892); *Powers* v. *Raymond,* 197 Cal. 126, 239 P. 1069 (1925).

[14] *Willis* v. *McMaham,* 89 Cal. 156, 26 P. 649 (1891); *Perrine* v. *Pavlos,* 100 Cal. App. 2d 655, 224 P.2d 41 (Dist. Ct. App. 1950).

[15] *Friedman* v. *Shindler's Prairie House, Inc.,* 224 App. Div. 232, 236–237, 230 N.Y.S. 44, 50 (3d Dep't), *aff'd mem.,* 250 N.Y. 574, 166 N.E. 329 (1928).

innkeeper, and this requirement distinguishes inns from many similar houses of public entertainment. Thus a house which does not supply lodging is not an inn, and this rule excludes from among inns a restaurant or eating house. On the same principle a coffeehouse or a bar and grill is not an inn. And for the same reason a house that furnishes only lodging without food, like a lodginghouse, or an apartment hotel, or a sleeping car, is not an inn.

If all elements of entertainment required by a traveler are furnished him by the host the house may be an inn, notwithstanding they are independently furnished and separately charged. Thus a hotel is no less an inn though it is conducted on the so-called European plan; the fact that the food is separately obtained and paid for, and the guest may procure his food elsewhere if he chooses, does not alter the legal character of the house.

In the case of such a hotel it usually happens that food is supplied in a restaurant, connected with the hotel but open to everyone, not merely to guests of the hotel. It is this connection of the restaurant with the hotel as part of the same establishment that makes the hotel an inn.

The hotelkeeper cannot avoid the responsibility of an innkeeper by proving that the restaurant is in fact conducted by an independent person. If the hotel is held out to the public, as having a restaurant connected with it and forming part of it, it is an inn, and not a mere lodginghouse.

In *Johnson* v. *Chadbourn Finance Co.*[16] the court held that the establishment in question was a hotel even though it had no dining room or café since there was an independently operated café in the building to which there was access from the offices and sleeping quarters without going out of doors. Moreover the establishment itself was known as the Hotel Vendome and on its letterhead it was stated that there was a first-class café in connection with the hotel. Thus the Vendome, by its name and practices, masqueraded as a hotel and this was sufficient for the court to classify it as a hotel.

But, on the other hand, if there is no holding them out as parts of the same establishment, the fact that an independent restaurant is con-

[16] 89 Minn. 310, 94 N.W. 874 (1903). See also *Asseltyne* v. *Fay Hotel*, 222 Minn. 91, 23 N.W.2d 357 (1946).

ducted under the same roof and is resorted to by lodgers, does not make a lodginghouse an inn,[17] nor does the fact that the keeper of the lodginghouse is in the habit of sending out to procure cooked food for his guests at their request.[18]

The common-law concept of an "inn" which requires that food and shelter both be furnished to travelers still prevails in New York and in the majority of jurisdictions. However, there is a strong minority trend toward relinquishing food service as a necessary requisite to innkeeping. Most state legislatures have enacted statutes governing the construction, maintenance, and operation of hotels, and the rights and duties of hotelkeepers to their guests and the public. Statutory definitions of hotels vary from state to state, depending upon the public policy of the state as well as upon the subject matter to which the statute applies. For example, hotels are defined in building codes, in fire regulations, in alcoholic beverage licensing laws, in labor laws, in public health codes, in penal statutes, in statutes limiting the liability of hotelkeepers for money or other property in their custody, and so forth. Nor are statutory definitions necessarily uniform even within a single jurisdiction.

2:6 *Innkeeper Defined*

The innkeeper is the person who on his own account carries on the business of an inn. In other words, he is the proprietor of the establishment. The person actually employed as manager, though he has the whole direction of the enterprise, is not an innkeeper if he is acting on behalf of someone else. Thus the salaried manager of a hotel owned or operated by a corporation is not to be held responsible as an innkeeper; the corporation is the innkeeper. Note, however, that, by statute, hotel managers and employees are often held personally liable for violations of, for example, liquor laws, labor laws, and sanitary codes. Note also the distinction between the *owner* of the physical hotel property, land, buildings, and equipment, and the *operator* of the hotel who is very often a lessee or managing or operating agent.

[17] *Cromwell* v. *Stephens,* 2 Daly (N.Y.) 15, 3 Abb. Prac. (n.s.) 26 (Ct. C.P.N.Y. Co. 1867).

[18] *Kelly* v. *Excise Comm'rs of New York,* 54 How. Pr. (N.Y.) 327 (Ct. C.P. 1877).

While in such cases the one in actual charge of the conduct of the hotel business is the innkeeper, the owner of the property may also be held responsible by statute for the safe condition of the building.

It has been held, however, that a hotel owner, not in possession of the premises leased by him to a lessee operator, is not liable as insurer for the loss of a guest's personal property.[19]

The profession of readiness to serve the public need not be made in any particular way; it is enough that by word or act the innkeeper makes public his intention to become such. It has been usual, particularly in former times, to advertise his house by hanging out a sign; but it is not essential to a man's being an innkeeper that he should do so. If he in fact carries on the business publicly as innkeeper he will be held as such, although he never displayed a sign. The profession may be made by any method of soliciting the patronage of the public, as by advertising, by keeping a public register, by running a coach to a railroad station, and so forth.

What acts are sufficient to justify a finding that a man is an innkeeper is a question which has often been a subject of judicial decision. In a California case, the keeper of the "What Cheer House" insisted that his house was a lodginghouse and not an inn because, he said, the eating department was distinct from the lodging department. It appeared that in the basement of the "What Cheer House," and connected with it by a stairway, there was a restaurant, which was conducted by the defendant and two other persons jointly, and that the three shared the profits. The court held that the "What Cheer House" was an inn.[20] In the course of his opinion Judge Rhodes said:

Where a person, by the means usually employed in that business, holds himself out to the world as an innkeeper, and in that capacity, is accustomed to receive travellers as his guests, and solicits a continuance of their patronage, and a traveller relying on such representations goes to the house to receive such entertainment as he has occasion for, the relation of innkeeper and guest is created, and the innkeeper cannot be heard to say that his professions were false, and that he was not in fact an innkeeper. The rules regulating the respective rights, duties and responsibilities of innkeeper and guest have their origin in consideration of public policy, and were designed mainly for the protection and security of

[19] *Cohen* v. *Raleigh Hotel Corp.*, 153 N.Y.L.J. No. 71, 18 (Sup. Ct. 1965).
[20] *Pinkerton* v. *Woodward*, 33 Cal. 557 (1867).

travellers and their property. They would afford the traveller but poor security if, before venturing to intrust his property to one who by his agents, cards, bills, advertisements, sign, and all the means by which publicity and notoriety can be given to his business, represents himself as an innkeeper, he is required to inquire of the employés as to their interest in the establishment, or take notice of the agencies or means by which the several departments are conducted. The same considerations of public policy that dictated those rules demand that the innkeeper should be held to the responsibilities which, by his representations, he induced his guest to believe he would assume. We think the jury were fully warranted by the evidence in finding that the "What Cheer House" was an inn.[21]

In a later case in the same state, the court dealt with a similar question as follows:

We think the evidence in this case is full and complete to the point that the Hotel Del Monte was a public inn. It not only had a name indicating its character as such, but it was also shown that it was open to all persons who have a right to demand entertainment at a public house; that it solicited public patronage by advertising and in the distribution of its business cards, and kept a public register in which its guests entered their names upon arrival, and before they were assigned rooms; that the hotel, at its own expense, ran a coach to the railroad station for the purpose of conveying its patrons to and from the hotel; that it had its manager, clerks, waiters, and in its interior management all the ordinary arrangements and appearances of a hotel, and the prices charged were for board and lodging. These facts were certainly sufficient to justify the court in finding, as it did, that the appellant was an innkeeper.[22]

2:7 Carrying on Other Business

An innkeeper may at the same time and on the same or neighboring premises carry on a different business, which though similar to that of the innkeeper is not identical with it. For instance, an innkeeper may maintain and operate an independent garage. In the same way, an innkeeper may establish under the same roof as his inn a restaurant for the accommodation of persons who are not his guests. If the restaurant is entirely distinct from the rooms proper to the inn, a per-

---

[21] *Id.* at 597.

[22] *Fay* v. *Pacific Improvement Co.*, 93 Cal. 243, 259–260, 26 P. 1099, 1100 (1892).

son who resorts merely to the restaurant is not a guest. So where an innkeeper had the refreshment bar at the side of his building with a separate entrance it was held that one served there was not a guest.[23] On this principle one who, not being a lodger in the hotel on the European plan, resorts to the restaurant connected with the hotel for food is not a guest.[24] By the same token, a mere customer at a bar, a restaurant, a barbershop, or newsstand operated by a hotel is not a guest.[25]

2:8 Inn and Hotel Defined

CROMWELL v. STEPHENS
2 Daly (N.Y.) 15, 3 Abb. Prac. 26 (Ct. C.P. N.Y. Co. 1867)

[Application for an injunction prohibiting defendants, composing the Croton Aqueduct Board, from cutting off the Croton water from a building owned by plaintiff. The board, upon the assumption that plaintiff's building was a hotel, imposed a special tax applicable to hotels only. Plaintiff contends that he is operating a cheap lodging-house. The question presented is whether the building is a "hotel."]

DALY, J.: ". . . Ordinarily, in a legal inquiry, it is sufficient to refer to some approved lexicographer to ascertain the precise meaning of a word. But this is a word of wide application, and as the meaning which is to be attached to it in this country, has been the subject of much discussion upon the argument, it may be well to refer to its origin and past history, as one of the means of determining its exact signification. The word is of French origin, being derived from *hostel,* and more remotely from the Latin word *hospes,* a word having a double signification, as it was used by the Romans both to denote a stranger who lodges at the house of another, as well as the master of a house who entertains travelers or guests. Among the Romans it was a universal custom for the wealthier classes to extend the hospitality of their house, not only to their friends and connections when they came to a city, but to respectable travelers generally. They had inns, but they were kept by slaves, and were places of resort for the lower orders, or for the accommodation of such travelers as were not in a condition to

[23] *Regina v. Rymer,* [1877] 2 Q.B.D. 136, 46 L.J.M.C. 108.
[24] *Krohn v. Sweeney,* 2 Daly (N.Y.) 200 (Ct. C.P. N.Y. Co. 1867).
[25] *Wallace v. Shoreham Hotel Corp.,* 49 A.2d 81 (D.C. Mun. Ct. App. 1946).

claim the hospitality of the better classes. On either side of the spacious mansions of the wealthy patricians were smaller apartments, known as the *hospitium,* or place for the entertainment of strangers, and the word *hospes* was a term to designate the owner of such a mansion, as well as the guest whom he received. [Citation omitted.] This custom of the Romans prevailed in the earlier part of the middle ages. From the fifth to the ninth century, traveling was difficult and dangerous. There was little security, except within castles or walled towns. The principal public roads had been destroyed by centuries of continuous war, and such thoroughfares as existed were infested by roving bands, who lived exclusively by plunder.

"In such a state of things there could be little traveling, and consequently the few inns to be found were rather dens to which robbers resorted to carouse and divide their spoils, than places for the entertainment of travelers. [Citation omitted.] The effect of a condition of society like this was to make hospitality not only a social virtue but a religious duty, and in the monasteries, and in all the great religious establishments, provision was made for the gratuitous entertainment of wayfarers and travelers. Either a separate building, or an apartment within the monastery, was devoted exclusively to this purpose, which was in charge of an officer called the hostler, who received the traveler and conducted him to this apartment, which was fitted up with beds, where he was allowed to tarry for two days, and to have his meals in the refectory, while, if he journeyed upon horseback, provender was provided by the hostler for his beast in the stables. [Citation omitted.] In many countries this apartment, or guest hall, of a monastery retained the original Latin name of *hospitium,* but in France the word was blended with *hospes* and changed into *hospice,* and it afterward underwent another change. As civilization advanced, and the nobility of France deserted their strong castles for spacious and costly residences in the towns, they erected their mansions upon a scale sufficiently extensive to enable them to discharge this great duty of hospitality, as is still, or was very recently, the custom among the nobility and wealthier classes in Russia, and in some of the northern countries of Europe. Borrowing, by analogy, from an existing word, and to distinguish it from the guest house of the monastery, every such great house or mansion was called a *hostel,* and by the mutation and attrition to which these words are subject in use, the *s* was gradually dropped from the word, and it became *hôtel.* As traveling and intercourse increased, the duty upon the nobility of entertaining respectable strangers became too onerous a burden, and establishments in which this class of persons could be entertained by paying for their accommodation sprung up in the cities, towns, and upon the leading public roads, which, to distinguish them from the great mansions or hotels of the wealthy, and at the same time to denote that they were superior to the *auberge* or *cabaret*, were called *hotelleries*, a name which has been in use in France for several centuries, and is still in use to some extent as a common term for inns of the better class, while the word hotel, in France, has long ceased to be confined to its original signification, and has become a word of a most extensive meaning. It is the term for the mansion of a prince, nobleman, minister of state, or of a person of distinction, or of celebrity. It is applied to a hospital, as Hôtel Dieu; or to a town hall, as Hôtel de Ville; to the residence of a judge, to certain public offices, and to any house in which furnished apartments are let by the day, week, or month. [Citation omitted.]

"The word, though so long in use in France, is of comparatively recent introduction into the English language. The Saxon word *inn*, was employed to denote a house where strangers or guests were entertained, down to the time of the Norman invasion; and, under the Norman rule, it was, in the popular tongue, the word for the town houses in which great men resided when they were in attendance on court, several of which became afterward legal colleges, under the well known titles of inns of court. [Citation omitted.] In all legal proceedings, however, and wherever the Norman French was spoken, the word *hostel* was the term for all such establishments. The places where entertainment could be procured for a compensation, to distinguish them from the inns, or great houses, where it was furnished gratuitously, were called in English common inns; while in Norman French, by a change analogous to that which had occurred in France, they were called first *hostelleries*, and afterward *hostries*. . . . To 'host,' was to put up at an inn; and 'hostler,' before referred to as the title of the officer in the monastery who was charged with the entertainment of guests, was the Norman word for innkeeper, and was in use until about the time of Elizabeth, when, the keeping of horses at livery becoming a distinct occupation, it was the term for the keeper of a livery stable [citation omitted], and afterward of the groom who has charge of the stables of an inn. [Citation omitted.]

". . . [T]he word hotel came into use in England by the general introduction in London, after 1760, of the kind of establishment that was then common in Paris, called an *hôtel garni,* a large house, in which furnished apartments were let by the day, week, or month. [In some early dictionaries,] . . . hotel is given as the proper pronunciation of *hostel,* an inn; [later,] . . . it is incorporated as an English word, and is defined in the latter to be 'an inn, having elegant lodgings and accommodations for gentlemen and genteel families. . . .'

"The word was introduced into this country about 1797. Before that time houses for the entertainment of travelers in this city were at first called inns, and afterward taverns and coffee-houses. In 1794, an association organized upon the principle of a tontine, erected in Wall Street what was then a very superior house for the accommodation of travelers, called the Tontine Coffee-house; the success of which led to the formation of another company for the erection of one upon a still more extensive scale in Broadway. This structure, which was called the Tontine Tavern, was built about 1796, upon the site of what had been a famous tavern or coffee-house in colonial times, and from the extensive accommodation it afforded, and the superior character of its appointments, it was then, and for many years afterward, the most celebrated establishment of the kind in the country. There was at that period a rage for everything French. The city was filled with refugees from France and from the French West India possessions, whose residence among us produced a great change in our social habits, amusements, and tastes, . . . while a fierce party strife prevailed between those who advocated the principles of the French Revolution and those who condemned them. The French national airs were sung in the streets; men mounted the tri-color cockade; and the proprietors of the new tavern, falling in with the popular current, gave a French name to their establishment, by changing it from the Tontine Tavern to the City Hotel. The new word was afterward adopted by the proprietors of other houses for the entertainment of travelers in this and neighboring cities, and, becoming general, found its way into American dictionaries. . . .

"It is to be deduced from the origin and history of the word, and the exposition that has been given to it by English and American lexicographers, that a hotel, in this country, is what in France was known as a *hotelerie,* and in England as a common inn of that superior class usually found in cities and large towns. A common inn is defined by Bacon to be a house for the entertainment of travelers and passengers, in which a lodging and necessities are provided for them and for their horses and attendants. . . . In *Thompson* v. *Lacy* (3 B. & A. 283), Justice Bayley declares it to be 'a house where a traveler is furnished with everything which he has occasion for while upon his way,' and in the same case, Best, J., says it is 'a house, the owner of which holds out that he will receive all travelers and sojourners who are willing to pay a price adequate to the sort of accommodation provided, and who come in a situation in which they are fit to be received.' But a more practical idea of what was understood at the common law as common inns, may be gathered from Hollingshed's description of them, as they existed in the days of Elizabeth. 'Every man,' says that quaint chronicler, 'may in England use his inn as his own house, and have for his monie how great or how little varietie of vittals and whatsoever service himself shall think fit to call for. If the traveler have a horse, his bed doth cost him nothing, but if he go on foot, he is sure to pay a pennie for the same. Each comer is sure to be in clean sheets wherein no man hath been lodged since they came from the laundress, or out of the water wherein they were washed. Whether he be horseman or footman, if his chamber be once appointed, he may carry the key with him as of his own house as long as he lodgeth there. In all our inns we have plenty of ale, biere, and sundrie kinds of wine; and such is the capacity of some of them that they are able to lodge two hundred or three hundred persons and their horses at ease, and with very short warning (to) make such provision for their diet as to him that is unacquainted withall may seem to be incredible' (Hollingshed's Chronicle—Description of England). . . .

"In the above-mentioned case of *Thompson* v. *Lacy*, the defendant kept a house in London called the Globe Tavern and Coffee-house, where he furnished beds and provisions to those who applied. No stage, coaches, or wagons stopped there, nor were there any stables belonging to the house. The question was whether this was an inn, and it was held that it was. 'The defendant does not charge,' said Best, J., 'as a mere lodging-house keeper, by the week or month. . . . A lodging-house keeper, on the other hand, must make a contract with every man that comes, whereas an inn-keeper is bound, without making any special contract, to provide lodging and entertainment for all at a reasonable price.' In *Doe* v. *Lansing* (4 Camp. 76), decided before the above, Lord Ellenborough held that a coffee-house in London, where persons from the country lodged, was not an inn; and in an earlier case (*Parkhurst* v. *Foster*, 1 Salk. 387), it was held that an establishment at a watering-place, where persons were taken to lodge, in which dressed meat was furnished to them at fourpence per joint, and small beer at twopence per mug, and to whom stables were let to their horses, was not an inn. Neither of the cases are [*sic*] fully reported, and if maintainable, it must be upon the ground that these were not houses for the general reception of travelers, but places where either a lodging or certain articles of food, or the stabling of a horse, could be procured by paying for each, in contradistinction to the general entertainment which an inn supplied to all travelers or guests at a reasonable charge. . . .

"It follows from these authorities, that an inn is a house where all who conduct themselves properly, and who are able and ready to pay for their entertainment, are received, if there is accommodation for them, and who, without any stipulated engagement as to the duration of their stay, or as to the rate of compensation, are, while there, supplied at a reasonable charge with their meals, their lodging, and such services and attention as are necessarily incident to the use of the house as a temporary home."

CRAPO *v.* ROCKWELL
48 Misc. 1, 94 N.Y.S. 1122 (Sup. Ct. 1905)

COCHRANE, J.: "The primary and fundamental function of an inn seems clearly to have been to furnish entertainment and lodging for the traveler on his journey. This at all times seems to have been its distinguishing feature. This idea has been expressed in the literature of ages, in history, sacred and profane, in fiction and in poetry. So true is this that the term 'inn' seems always to have been used in connection with the corresponding notion of travelers seeking the accommodation and protection of the inn. Thus the Christian era dawned on a Judean scene, where travelers away from home who had gone up to be taxed pursuant to the decree of the Roman emperor, sought refuge in a manger 'because there was no room for them in the inn.' Sir Walter Scott characterizes the inn of the old days of

Merry England as 'the free rendezvous of all travelers' of which the
bonny Black Bear of Cumnor village, not conducted merely, but
'ruled by Giles Gosling, a man of a goodly person,' as landlord, was
a typical instance. And so the most illustrious bard of England says,
referring to the time of approaching twilight, with the west glimmer-
ing with streaks of day, 'now spurs the lated traveler apace to gain
the timely inn.'"

KRAUS v. BIRNS
39 Misc. 2d 562, 241 N.Y.S.2d 189 (Sup. Ct. 1963)

[Plaintiff sues for a declaratory judgment declaring the Hotel Sherman to be a hotel and for an injunction restraining the Building Com-
missioner from prosecuting plaintiff for operating a rooming house
without a license.]

MANGAN, J.: "The court is called upon to determine whether the
subject premises is a rooming house requiring a permit under section
D26-3.22 of the Administrative Code of the City of New York, or a
hotel which is not subject to the control or jurisdiction of the Department of Buildings of the City of New York.

"On the precise issue whether the subject premises is a hotel or a
rooming house, the plaintiffs contend that the certificate of occupancy
issued to it for 'Multiple Dwelling Class B—Furnished Rooms' does
not preclude its use as a hotel, asserting that the use as stated in the
certificate applies to hotels as well as rooming house accommodations
and that factually the subject premises is a hotel and not a rooming
house.

"Defendant contends that the certificate of occupancy is controlling,
and since it states the use of the premises to be for 'furnished rooms',
the legal use is a rooming house and not a hotel, and, further, that
factually the subject premises is a rooming house and not a hotel.

". . . [T]he subject premises does not serve food and . . . defendant contends that is a necessary characteristic of an inn or hotel.
. . . At common law an inn meant a place where a traveler would be
furnished food, lodging and entertainment. Food was a necessary
service for hotels classified as 'Inns' in the days of poor transportation.
Because of changing times, food is no longer an essential service
[citations omitted]. All that is essential is that the establishment be

commonly known as a hotel and be engaged in the business of providing customary hotel service to transients [citations omitted].

". . . In order for the subject premises to be legally constituted a hotel under section D26-3.22 [of the Administrative Code of New York City], it must (A) be a multiple dwelling; (B) be used for single-room occupancy; (C) be commonly regarded as a hotel in the community in which it is located; (D) provide the customary services of a hotel as therein contained.

"(A-B) The subject premises is a multiple dwelling used for single-room occupancy. (C) On the evidence adduced it is regarded as a hotel in the community in which it is located, being listed in the telephone directory as a hotel, maintaining electric neon signs with the inscription 'Hotel Sherman,' having a canopy bearing the legend 'hotel,' being a member of the Hotel Association in the City of New York, having registered as a hotel with the Office of Housing Expediter, Temporary State Housing Rent Commission, New York City Rent Commission, and paying hotel tax to the City of New York. (D) On the evidence, it is shown that the customary services set forth in said section are being furnished. Forty percent of gross receipts are used for payroll, and the following are the customary services being rendered to the guests: (1) daily maid service; (2) room service; (3) 24-hour desk service; (4) porter service; (5) bellboy service; (6) intercom telephone service; (7) coin-box telephone service; (8) television upon request and coin-operated radio in every room; (9) linens changed daily; (10) owns and uses own linen; (11) call sheets for guests; (12) daily laundry delivery; (13) daily watchman service; (14) registration cards numbered consecutively; (15) resident manager living on premises; (16) control board for all rooms; (17) sprinkler system in all rooms; (18) fire alarm system; (19) owns all furniture and fixtures used in operation of premises; (20) rates on a daily and weekly basis; (21) no cooking permitted.

"The word 'hotel' is not one with a fixed and unalterable meaning; in fact, whether a place is or is not a hotel in a given instance may depend on the particular statute involved or the circumstances of the individual case. . . . It is easier to tell what does not constitute a hotel than what it is. A rooming house and a hotel have much in common, and to differentiate for the purposes intended, one must look to the facts and to statutory law.

". . . On all the evidence, the court finds and declares that the subject premises fall within the Administrative Code definition of hotel under section D26-3.22; and a permit for a rooming house should not be required of plaintiffs."

2:9 Motel Defined

The word "motel" is of comparatively recent origin. It is a modern coined word derived from, and an abbreviation of, the words "motorist's hotel." The word "motel" generally denotes a small hotel where lodgings are available for hire, with a minimum of personal service being furnished by the proprietor.

[W]ith the great use of automobiles, there has been a tremendous development throughout the entire United States in the construction of buildings which furnish lodging accommodations for transients and which buildings are denominated motels. . . . These motels have filled a required need for housing accommodations . . . quite generally more conveniently located for access by the general public than the normal hotel, and having greater facilities or accommodations for parking of automobiles immediately adjacent to the building itself. The mode of operation of the average motel results . . . in a great deal of "self-service" on the part of the guests and a reduction in the cost to the guest by way of gratuities. [26]

Hotels and motels are in point of fact of the same genus, differing only in style, design, appearance, location, and the type of service. They are both service establishments furnishing lodging, with or without meals, and a variety of other services to transients. A place which would otherwise be an inn or hotel does not lose its character as such because of its mode of construction, the name applied to it, or the fact that food or drink cannot be obtained therein. The same rules of law have been applied in cases of injuries to guests in motels as in hotels. Legal distinctions between hotels and motels, where they exist, are statutory, as in zoning ordinances, alcoholic beverage licensing laws, building codes, and other local ordinances.

[26] *Schermer* v. *Fremar Corp.*, 36 N.J. Super. Ct. 46, 50–51, 114 A.2d 757, 760 (1955).

CHAPTER 3

Houses of Public Entertainment Other Than Hotels

3:1 *Other Public Houses Not in Public Calling*

Similar in many respects to inns are other houses maintained for use of the public; but none of them ministers to any absolute public necessity, and none of them, therefore, is regarded as engaged in a public calling. No part of the law of public callings, therefore, applies to these establishments. Furthermore, the law regulating the extent of liability of innkeepers is, as we shall see, in many respects peculiar and does not apply to keepers of other public houses. Nor does any keeper of such a house have a lien at common law though, as will be seen, a lien has been given to some of them by statute. But in other respects the same principles of law apply to these houses of entertainment as to inns.

3:2 *Apartment Hotels*

The phrase "apartment hotel" originated about 1900, and has been used interchangeably with the words "family hotel" or "residential hotel" to describe hotels which made a practice of renting apartments, furnished or unfurnished, for fixed periods, the lessees or guests being treated in other respects like the transient guests of the house. The apartments are usually provided with kitchenettes or serving pantries for light housekeeping by the tenants. Section 181 of the New York Lien Law defines an apartment hotel as a "hotel wherein apartments are rented for fixed periods of time, either furnished or unfurnished, to the occupants of which the keeper of such hotel supplies food, if required." In addition to food service, apartment hotels generally pro-

[28]

vide other customary hotel services, such as maid service, linen service, secretarial and desk service, and bellman service.

3:3 *Rooming Houses, Boardinghouses, and Lodginghouses*

A "rooming house" is a building or a portion of a building in which nonhousekeeping furnished rooms are rented on a short-term basis of daily, weekly, or monthly occupancy to more than two paying tenants, not members of the landlord's immediate family.[1] A rooming house is not necessarily a place of public accommodation to which any well-behaved person of means can go and demand lodging as a matter of right as he can do at a hotel. Subject to the provisions of applicable civil rights laws, the keeper of a rooming house may receive whom he will, reject whom he will, and usually makes special contracts with each of his guests concerning compensation and length of stay.

In the city of New York the operation of a rooming house requires a municipal permit.[2]

The only material difference between a rooming house and a "boardinghouse" is that a boardinghouse furnishes meals, in addition to lodging.

A "lodginghouse" differs from an inn or rooming house, in that it is a house in which persons are housed for hire for a single night, or for less than a week at one time.

Section 181 of the New York Lien Law accords rooming, boarding, and lodginghouse keepers a lien for unpaid charges on the property of their guests on the premises.

3:4 *Apartment Houses*

The term "apartment house" came into use about 1880. The term designates a multiple dwelling which is either rented, leased, or hired out for occupancy as the residence or home of three or more families living independently of each other. "An 'apartment' is that part of [an apartment house] consisting of one or more rooms con-

---

[1] Rent and Eviction Regulations of the New York State Housing Rent Commission, Part I, Section 3–(6).

[2] Administrative Code, Section D26–3.22.

taining at least one bathroom arranged to be occupied by [the] members of a family, which room or rooms are separated and set apart from all other rooms within [the building]." [3]

3:5 Restaurant Defined

A "restaurant" is a public establishment where food is prepared, served, and sold for consumption on the premises. The term includes, but is not limited to, buffets, lunchrooms, lunch counters, cafeterias, grill rooms and hotel dining rooms.

An "eating place" is an establishment, other than a restaurant, where food is prepared, served, and sold on the premises. It is of a more private character than a restaurant. The term includes, but is not limited to, dining rooms of clubs or associations, school lunchrooms, and eating places in factories or offices for personnel employed in such places.[4]

A "coffeehouse" is often used to refer to a popularly priced hotel dining room, while the term "café" is synonymous with restaurant. An "ordinary" is an eating house where regular meals are served at fixed prices.

The term "tavern" has come to be restricted to an eating and drinking place with limited kitchen facilities. In times past, the term was frequently used synonymously with inn or hotel, but the use of the word in this sense has become obsolete (see also 1:4). There is a similarity between a tavern and a "bar and grill", which is an establishment where the food volume is less than one-third of the entire volume of business.

A restaurant is not an inn and a restaurant keeper is not engaged in a public employment in the sense that a carrier or innkeeper is. The distinctions between the duties and obligations of a restaurant keeper and an innkeeper will be pointed out in subsequent chapters.

3:6 Steamboats and Sleeping Cars

A "steamboat" is not an inn though it supplies board and lodging as well as transportation. However, the relations that exist between a

---

[3] New York Multiple Dwelling Law, Section 4.
[4] New York City Health Code, Section 87.01.

steamboat company and its passengers who have procured staterooms for their comfort during the journey differ in no essential respect from those that exist between an innkeeper and his guests.[5]

A "sleeping car" (Pullman) is a place for the reception and entertainment of travelers, but it is not an inn. It differs from an inn in many important particulars. In brief, the inn affords necessary protection and accommodation to travelers while they rest from their journey; the sleeping car offers a single accommodation—a bed—to passengers while they continue their journey. The sleeping car does not afford needed personal protection—the carrier is obliged to protect the passenger even if he rides in the ordinary coach. Nor does the sleeping-car company provide food; the passenger may get his meals on the train in a dining car, or in the sleeping car itself in a buffet, but this is not a necessary part of the undertaking of the car company. It is the duty of the carrier, not of the car company, to provide facilities for meals. Furthermore, the sleeping-car company does not undertake to serve all travelers, but only those whom the carrier will allow to ride in the car. For these reasons the sleeping car is almost universally held not to be an inn.

[5] *Adams* v. *New Jersey Steamboat Co.*, 151 N.Y. 163, 45 N.E. 369 (1896).

CHAPTER 4

The Public Duty of Innkeeping

4:1 Law of Public Callings

From the very beginning of our law it has been recognized that some kinds of business were of special importance to the public, and that all persons engaged in such business owed the public certain duties. No one could be compelled to enter upon the employment, but if he chose to do so, he thereby undertook the performance of the public duties connected with it. The property which he devotes to the public employment is "affected with a public interest" and ceases to be *juris privati* only.[1]

Property does become clothed with a public interest when used in a manner to make it of public consequence, and affect the community at large. When, therefore, one devotes his property to a use in which the public has an interest, he, in effect, grants to the public an interest in that use, and must submit to be controlled by the public for the common good, to the extent of the interest he has thus created. He may withdraw his grant by discontinuing the use; but, so long as he maintains the use, he must submit to the control.[2]

The duty placed upon one exercising a public calling is primarily a duty to serve every man as a member of the public. This primary duty involves for its complete performance that the service should be adequate, that only a reasonable price should be charged for it, and that all members of the public should be served equally and without discrimination.

4:2 Innkeeper Is in Public Employment

The innkeeper has from the earliest time been recognized as engaged in a public employment and, therefore, as subject to the duty

[1] Lord Hale, *De Portibus Maris*, 1 Harg. Law Tracts 78.
[2] Waite, C. J., in *Munn v. Illinois*, 94 U.S. 113, 126 (1876).

of one engaged in such an employment. Professor Bruce Wyman adds the following to what has already been said as the reason for holding that an innkeeper's calling is a public one:

When the weary traveller reaches the wayside inn in the gathering dusk, if the host turn him away what shall he do? Go on to the next inn? It is miles away, and the roads are infested with robbers. The traveller would be at the mercy of the innkeeper, who might practise upon him any extortion, for the guest would submit to anything almost, rather than be put out into the night. Truly a special law is required to meet this situation, for the traveller is so in the hands of the innkeeper that only an affirmative law can protect him.[3]

4:3 *Duty to Receive Guests*

The first public duty of the innkeeper, in which his calling differs from the analogous callings of rooming, boarding, and lodginghouse keepers, and restaurant proprietors, is his duty to receive travelers as his guests. This duty will be examined at length in the following chapter.

4:4 *Duty to Provide Adequate Facilities*

Not only must the innkeeper be willing to receive travelers as his guests, he must be prepared to shelter and entertain them. An innkeeper without a roof to cover the heads of his guests or without sufficient food to appease their hunger would be as little regardful of the public obligation under which he acts as the innkeeper who refused admittance to his inn to the weary traveler. It is apparent, therefore, that from the duty to receive necessarily follows the duty to provide adequate facilities. Such facilities include an inn in proper repair and of sufficient size to supply the demand, sufficient stores of wholesome food and comfortable furniture, and a sufficient number of servants to perform the requirements of service and protection to the guest. The innkeeper's duty in these particulars will be considered at greater length in Chapter 13.

[3] "The Law of the Public Callings as a Solution of the Trust Problem," 17 *Harv. L. Rev.* 156, 159 (1903).

4:5 *Duty to Refrain from Discrimination*

It is clear that the innkeeper can perform his duty to the public only by refraining from discrimination in his treatment of guests. If he gives to one man better service in the line of his business than to another, or serves him at a lower price, he is to that extent fostering the interest of an individual against that of the whole public. Each traveler who applies for admittance to an inn does so as a representative of the public, into whose service the innkeeper has entered, and each person equally represents that public, and is equally entitled to all the service which the innkeeper owes. It is only when he steps outside his public calling and performs services not included in the business of innkeeping that he is entitled to act from motives of private interest or friendship. Two early cases show the tenor of judicial precedent concerning discrimination:

> The public right is a common right, and a common right signifies a reasonably equal right. . . .
> . . . Equality, in the sense of freedom from unreasonable discrimination, being of the very substance of the common right, an individual is deprived of his lawful enjoyment of the common right when he is subjected to unreasonable and injurious discrimination in respect to terms, facilities, or accommodations. . . . [W]hether unreasonableness of terms, facilities, or accommodations operates as a total or a partial denial of the right; and whether the unreasonableness is in the intrinsic, individual nature of the terms, facilities, or accommodations, or in their discriminating, collective and comparative character,—the right denied is one and the same common right, which would not be a right if it could be rightfully denied, and would not be common, in the legal sense, if it could be legally subjected to unreasonable discrimination, and parcelled out among men in unreasonably superior and inferior grades at the behest of the servant from whom the service is due.
> The commonness of the right necessarily implies an equality of right, in the sense of freedom from unreasonable discrimination. . . . What kind of a common right of carriage would that be which the carrier could so administer as to unreasonably, capriciously, and despotically enrich one man and ruin another? [4]

----

[4] Doe, J., in *McDuffee* v. *Portland & Rochester R.R.*, 52 N.H. 430, 448 (1873).

. . . [A] service for the public necessarily implies equal treatment in its performance, when the right to the service is common. Because the institution, so to speak, is public, every member of the community stands on an equality as to the right to its benefit, and therefore, the carrier cannot discriminate between individuals for whom he will render the service. In the very nature, then, of his duty and of the public right, his conduct should be equal and just to all.[5]

These vigorous opinions were delivered in cases where discrimination by common carriers was in question; but the same public duty which was the foundation of the obligation in these cases binds the innkeeper, and the language used is as applicable to the one employment as to the other. Innkeepers too are forbidden to discriminate between guests. ". . . [A]s they cannot refuse to receive guests, so neither can they impose unreasonable terms on them."[6]

Discrimination on account of race, creed, color, or national origin is specifically proscribed by the federal Civil Rights Act of 1964, as amended, and by state civil rights acts wherever they exist. These statutes will be more fully treated in subsequent chapters.

4:6 What Amounts to Unreasonable Discrimination

Equality of service does not mean identity of service; and if one guest gets service that is reasonably and substantially equivalent to that furnished to another guest, he cannot complain. Some difference is of course necessary. If all the guest chambers in an inn are properly equipped, no one can legally complain because the room assigned to another has more tasteful furniture, or a more attractive outlook from the window; nor can a guest object because he is not assigned to the same table in the dining room as another, or because a particular employee is assigned to another guest rather than to himself.

Even if there is discrimination, it may in some circumstances be justified. A guest might for his own fault, in order to secure the comfort or the safety of other guests, be obliged to be content with inferior accommodations. This principle is expressed by Judge Doe with his usual clearness and vigor:

[5] Bedle, J., in *Messenger* v. *Pennsylvania R.R.*, 37 N.J. 531, 534 (1874).
[6] Lord Kenyon, C. J., in *Kirkman* v. *Shawcross*, 101 Eng. Rep. 410, 412 (K.B. 1794).

A certain inequality of terms, facilities, or accommodations may be reasonable, and required by the doctrine of reasonableness, and, therefore, not an infringement of the common right. It may be the duty of a common carrier of passengers to carry under discriminating restrictions, or to refuse to carry those who, by reason of their physical or mental condition, would injure, endanger, disturb, or annoy other passengers; and an analogous rule may be applicable to the common carriage of goods. Healthy passengers in a palatial car would not be provided with reasonable accommodations, if they were there unreasonably and negligently exposed, by the carrier, to the society of small-pox patients. Sober, quiet, moral, and sensitive travellers may have cause to complain of their accommodations, if they are unreasonably exposed to the companionship of unrestrained, intoxicated, noisy, profane, and abusive passengers, who may enjoy the discomfort they cast upon others. In one sense, both classes, carried together, might be provided with equal accommodations; in another sense, they would not. The feelings not corporal, and the decencies of progressive civilization, as well as physical life, health, and comfort, are entitled to reasonable accommodations. [Citation omitted.] Mental and moral sensibilities, unreasonably wounded, may be an actual cause of suffering, as plain as a broken limb; and if the injury is caused by unreasonableness of facilities or accommodations (which is synonymous with unreasonableness of service), it may be as plain a legal cause of action as any bodily hurt, commercial inconvenience, or pecuniary loss. To allow one passenger to be made uncomfortable by another committing an outrage, without physical violence, against the ordinary proprieties of life and the common sentiments of mankind, may be as clear a violation of the common right and as clear an actionable neglect of a common carrier's duty, as to permit one to occupy two seats while another stands in the aisle.[7]

4:7 *Duty to Make Reasonable Charges*

Another rule clearly following from the general principle that the innkeeper must receive all travelers as his guests is that he is limited to a reasonable compensation for his services; for if he could charge what he pleased, he could make anyone's right to be received valueless by requiring the payment by way of accommodation of a prohibitive amount. The question of what compensation the innkeeper is entitled to recover will be discussed in Chapter 27.

[7] *McDuffee* v. *Portland & Rochester R.R.*, 52 N.H. 430, 451–452 (1873).

4:8 *Duty to Receive Strangers*

Under some circumstances the innkeeper in the course of his public service may be obliged to admit to the inn persons who are not and do not intend to become guests. The nature and extent of this duty will be examined later.

CHAPTER 5

Innkeeper's Public Duty
to Receive Guests

5:1 Duty to Admit the Public

The fundamental duty of the innkeeper to the public, as a person engaged in a public employment, is to receive for entertainment in his inn all travelers, that is, transients, who properly apply to be admitted as guests. This duty is symbolized by the traditional ceremony on the occasion of dedicating a new hotel or motel to the public of throwing away the key to the inn, thus to proclaim to the world that the door to the hospitality of the inn never will be locked and all weary travelers always will be welcome. This duty is not absolute, but subject to lawful excuses, it binds every innkeeper from the time he opens his doors to the public.

This public duty of the innkeeper is owed to travelers only, and no one who is not a traveler can demand, as a matter of law, to be received at an inn. For, as the court said in *Calye's Case*,[1] ". . . [C]ommon inns are instituted for passengers and warfaring men . . . [a]nd therefore if a neighbour who is no traveler, as a friend, at the request of the innholder lodges there and his goods be stolen, etc., he shall not have an action. . . ."

5:2 Who Is a Traveler?

In early times, the courts construed the word "traveler" strictly to mean persons engaged in a journey. The tendency of the modern cases is to be very liberal in regarding one who calls at a hotel for admission as a traveler. It has been said that "[a] townsman or

[1] 77 Eng. Rep. 520, 521 (K.B. 1584).

neighbor may be a traveler, and therefore a guest at an inn, as well as he who comes from a distance, or from a foreign country." [2] In general, the guest is a transient who receives accommodations at an inn for compensation. It is the transient character of the visit, that is, its indefinite, temporary duration, that distinguishes a guest from a lodger, boarder, or tenant in the hotel.

5:3 *Duty to Receive Persons Incapable of Contracting*

The innkeeper's obligation to receive is not confined to the reception of guests with whom he can make a binding contract. Thus, an innkeeper has been held legally bound to receive an infant (a person under twenty-one years of age) apparently responsible and of good conduct, who applies for admission as a guest; the mere fact of infancy alone would not justify refusal to admit him.

It should be noted that while the innkeeper is under duty to admit infants and other travelers incapable of making contracts, provided they come in a proper condition and are able to pay for their charges, he can collect only for "necessaries" furnished. What necessaries are depends on the circumstances of each case, such as the character of the hotel, the infant's station in life, the goods and services furnished, and the like. It has been held that money, although it buys most necessities, is not itself a "necessary." An infant may, therefore, repudiate an obligation to reimburse the innkeeper for cash advances. [3]

5:4 *Reception May Be Demanded at Night*

While it is clear that an inn may be closed at reasonable hours during the night, [4] it seems also clear that a traveler actually reaching the inn while it is closed may wake the innkeeper and demand admittance.

[2] *Walling* v. *Potter*, 35 Conn. 183, 185 (1868).
[3] *Watson* v. *Cross*, 63 Ky. (2 Duv.) 147 (1865).
[4] *Commonwealth* v. *Wetherbee*, 101 Mass. 214 (1869).

REX *v.* IVENS
7 Car. & P. 213, 173 Eng. Rep. 94 (1835)

[Indictment against an innkeeper for not receiving one Williams as a guest at his inn, and also for refusing to take his horse. Plea, not guilty.

It appeared that Williams, a law clerk of Newport, applied for admission at the Bell Inn, at Chepstow, kept by defendant. The day was Sunday and the hour a few minutes before midnight. The inn was closed, the defendant and his wife retired for the night. Williams tapped at the door. Mrs. Ivens went to the window and asked for the caller's name. The answer was, "What is that to you about my name." Mrs. Ivens said, "At such a late hour I want to know your name and where you come from." Williams replied, "If you must know my name, it is Williams, and I come from Newport; and now you are as wise as you were before, and be damned to you." Mrs. Ivens then shut the window and refused to admit Williams.]

COLERIDGE, J. (In summing up): "The facts in this case do not appear to be much in dispute; and though I do not recollect to have ever heard of such an indictment having been tried before, the law applicable to this case is this:—that an indictment lies against an innkeeper, who refuses to receive a guest, he having at the time room in his house; and either the price of the guest's entertainment being tendered to him, or such circumstances occurring as will dispense with that tender. This law is founded in good sense. The innkeeper is not to select his guests. He has no right to say to one, you shall come into my inn, and to another you shall not, as everyone coming and conducting himself in a proper manner has a right to be received; and for this purpose innkeepers are a sort of public servants [*sic*], they having in return a kind of privilege of entertaining travelers, and supplying them with what they want. It is said in the present case, that Mr. Williams . . . conducted himself improperly, and therefore ought not to have been admitted into the house of the defendant. If a person came to an inn drunk, or behaved in an indecent or improper manner, I am of the opinion that the innkeeper is not bound to receive him. You will consider whether Mr. Williams did so behave here. It is next said that he came to the inn at a late hour of the night, when probably the family were gone to bed. Have we not all knocked at inn doors at late hours of the night, and after the family have retired to rest, not for the purpose of annoyance, but to get the people up? In this case it further appears, that the wife of the defendant has a conversation with the prosecutor, in which she insists on knowing his name and abode. I think that an innkeeper has no right to insist on knowing those particulars, and certainly you and I would think an innkeeper very impertinent, who asked either the one or the other of any of us. However, the prosecutor gives his name and residence; and supposing that he did add the words 'and be damned to you,' is that a sufficient reason for keeping a man out of an inn who has travelled till midnight? I think that the prosecutor was not guilty of such misconduct as would entitle the defendant to shut him out of his house. It has been strongly objected against the prosecutor . . . that he had been travelling on a Sunday. To make that argument of any avail, it must be contended that travelling on a Sunday is illegal. It is not so, although it is what ought to be avoided whenever it can be. . . . With respect to the non-tender of the money by the prosecutor, it is now a custom so universal with innkeepers to trust that a person will pay before he leaves an inn, that it cannot be necessary for a guest to tender money before he goes into an inn; indeed, in the present case, no objection was made that Mr. Williams did not make a tender; and they did not even insinuate that they had any suspicion that he could not pay for whatever entertainment might be furnished to him. I think, therefore, that that cannot be set up as a defense. It however remains for me next to consider the case with respect to the hour of the night at which Mr. Williams applied for admission; and the opinion which I have formed is, that the lateness of the hour is no excuse to the defendant for refusing to receive the prosecutor into his inn. Why are inns established? For the reception of travellers, who are often very far distant from their own homes. Now, at what time is it most essential that travellers should not be denied admission into the inns? I should say when they are benighted, and when, from any casualty, or from the badness of the roads, they arrive at an inn at a very late hour. Indeed, in former times, when the roads were much worse, and were much infested with robbers, a late hour of the night was the time, of all others, at which the traveller most required to be received into an inn. I think therefore, that if the traveller conducts himself properly, the innkeeper is bound to admit him, at whatever hour of the night he may arrive. The only other question in this case is, whether the defendant's inn was full. There is no distinct evidence on the part of the prosecution that it was not. But I think the conduct of the parties shews that the inn was not full; because, if it had been, there could have been no use in the landlady asking the prosecutor his name, and saying, that if he would tell it, she would ring for one of the servants.

"Verdict—Guilty."

5:5 *Refusal to Receive Guests Made a Misdemeanor*

As we have seen, the refusal of an innkeeper, *without just cause or excuse*, to receive and entertain a guest, was an indictable offense at common law. The refusal is also a civil wrong, for which damages are recoverable in a civil action.[5]

In the state of New York, the refusal has been made a misdemeanor by Section 40-e of the Civil Rights Law (formerly Section 513 of the Penal Law), which reads as follows:

A person, who, either on his own account or as agent or officer of a corporation, carries on business as innkeeper, or as common carrier of passengers, and refuses, without just cause or excuse, to receive and entertain any guest, or to receive and carry any passenger, is guilty of a misdemeanor.

In *People* v. *McCarthy*,[6] the defendant innkeeper was prosecuted for keeping a bawdy house. The proof disclosed that on the night in question the twenty-two rooms in the hotel were rented thirty-three times, making it obvious that some of the rooms at least were used by more than one patron or patrons during the same night, and that similar occurrences happened upon repeated prior occasions. The defendant's instructions to the desk clerks were to admit any couple to a room in the hotel if they looked "over age" and if they merely stated that they were married, without any offer or inquiry to substantiate the fact. The defendant relied for his defense on Section 513 of the Penal Law (now Section 40-e of the Civil Rights Law)

---

[5] *Cornell* v. *Huber,* 102 App. Div. 293, 92 N.Y.S. 434 (2d Dep't 1905).
[6] 204 Misc. 460, 119 N.Y.S.2d 435 (Magis. Ct. 1953).

arguing in effect that he was duty bound, under penalty of the law, to admit all who applied. Said the court:

> The court is aware of the provisions of section 513 of the Penal Law which make it a misdemeanor for an innkeeper to refuse to receive guests "without just cause or excuse." It certainly would not be without cause or excuse to make a fair inquiry to ascertain whether the couple that desires accommodations are in fact married to each other; nor would it be a violation of section 40 of the Civil Rights Law to make such an inquiry.[7]

5:6 Discrimination against United States Uniform

Section 40-g of the New York Civil Rights Law provides:

> A person who excludes from the equal enjoyment of any accommodation, facility or privilege furnished by innkeepers or common carriers, amusement or resort, any person lawfully wearing the uniform of the army, navy, marine corps or revenue cutter service of the United States, because of that uniform, is guilty of a misdemeanor.

5:7 Discrimination against Sightless Persons Accompanied by Seeing-Eye Dogs

Section 40-h of the New York Civil Rights Law provides:

> A person, who, either on his own account or on behalf of any partnership, association or corporation, excludes from the equal enjoyment of any accommodation, facility or privilege furnished by innkeepers or common carriers, or by owners, managers or lessees of theaters, restaurants, hotels or other public places of amusement or resort, except motion picture theaters, any sightless person accompanied by a seeing-eye dog, because of that fact, unless the admission of such person and dog would tend to create a dangerous situation, is guilty of a *misdemeanor*.

[7] *Id.* at 437–438.

CHAPTER 6

Discrimination in Places
of Public Accommodation:
Civil Rights

6:1 Civil Rights Defined

A "civil right" may be defined as one which appertains to a person by virtue of his citizenship in a nation for the purpose of securing to him the enjoyment of his means of happiness. It includes the right to buy, sell, and to own property, freedom to make contracts, trial by jury, and the like. In another sense, the term also refers to certain rights secured to citizens of the United States by the Thirteenth, Fourteenth, and Fifteenth Amendments to the Constitution, and by various statutes, state and federal, commonly known as civil rights acts.

A principal object of such acts has been the securing of equal rights in places of public accommodation to all citizens without discrimination on account of race, creed, color, or national origin. It is in this latter sense that innkeepers and other public hosts throughout the nation are concerned with the subject.

6:2 Innkeeper's Common-Law Duty to Admit All Who Apply

We have already seen that at common law, a person engaged in a public calling, such as an innkeeper or public carrier, was held to be under a duty to the general public and was obliged to serve without discrimination all who sought service, whereas proprietors of purely private enterprises were under no such obligation, the latter enjoying an absolute power to serve whom they pleased.[1]

[1] *Madden* v. *Queens County Jockey Club, Inc.,* 296 N.Y. 249, 72 N.E.2d 697, *cert. denied,* 332 U.S. 761 (1947).

6:3 *Restaurant Keeper's Common-Law Duty to Receive Members of the General Public*

Whether a restaurant keeper, as distinguished from an innkeeper, is legally required to admit members of the general public has not been conclusively decided. In *Madden* v. *Queens County Jockey Club, Inc.,* the Court of Appeals decided that places of amusement and resort, as distinguished from those engaged in a public calling, such as inns or common carriers, enjoy an absolute power to exclude those whom they please, subject only to the legislative restriction that they not exclude one on account of race, creed, color, or national origin. The court upheld the right of a race track to exclude Madden even though the exclusion was without cause.

In *Noble* v. *Higgins,*[2] the plaintiff was refused service in defendant's restaurant on purely personal grounds. He sought to recover damages, basing his action on Sections 40 and 41 of the Civil Rights Law (see below, 6:8–6:11). The court dismissed the complaint on the merits on the authority of *Grannan* v. *Westchester Racing Association,*[3] as extended and applied in *Woollcott* v. *Shubert,*[4] stating: "It may be conclusively determined after an examination of the last-quoted authorities that 'the legislature did not intend to confer upon every person all the rights, advantages and privileges in places of amusement or accommodations, which might be enjoyed by another. Any discrimination not based upon race, creed or color does not fall within the condemnation of the statute.'"[5] The court then added: "It would seem then that the common-law right still remains with those not engaged as common carriers, or in like occupations, to discriminate between persons according to rules established where the person applying for accommodation is objectionable for some reason. Otherwise, persons unclean, untidy, intoxicated or affected by disease might claim the same attention in a crowded restaurant or other public place as those against whom no objection could be urged. *Brandt* v. *Mink,* 38 Misc. Rep. 750. [38 Misc. 750, 78 N.Y.S. 1109 (Sup. Ct. 1902).]"

[2] 95 Misc. 328, 158 N.Y.S. 867 (Sup. Ct. 1916).
[3] 153 N.Y. 449, 47 N.E. 896 (1897).   [4] 217 N.Y. 212, 111 N.E. 829 (1916).
[5] 95 Misc. 329, 158 N.Y.S. 868.

In the *Brandt* case, plaintiff was refused service in defendant's restaurant because he wore no collar. His action was predicated on Sections 40 and 41 of the Civil Rights Law. The defense was that the defendant had established a rule in his restaurant not to serve any man who did not wear a collar. The court held that this rule was a reasonable one, applicable alike to all citizens of every race, creed, and color and, therefore, would come within the exception in the Civil Rights Law. The judgment was reversed but for some reason unexplained by the court a new trial was ordered.

In the recent case of *Moore* v. *Wood*,[6] plaintiff sued for damages for mental anguish and humiliation and exposure to public ridicule for defendant's refusal to serve plaintiff luncheon in his restaurant. Defendant's motion for summary judgment, dismissing the complaint, was denied. There was no issue of civil rights raised in the case; plaintiff relied instead on the common-law liability of an innkeeper for injury to plaintiff's feelings as a result of humiliation for wrongful refusal of service. The court in denying defendant's motion for summary judgment ruled that plaintiff had stated a cause of action sufficient to entitle him to a trial on the issues: (1) whether defendant's refusal to serve plaintiff was because of some established rule of the defendant restaurant; (2) whether the rule was reasonable; and (3) whether plaintiff did, in fact, fail to comply therewith; and if those issues are decided in the negative, to determine: (4) the extent of plaintiff's damages, if any.

Defendant subsequently moved for reargument. The court granted the motion to reargue, but upon reconsideration adhered to its original decision. Judge Stanislaw, sitting in Supreme Court, Suffolk County, had the following to say in disposing of defendant's motion:

It is movant's contention that the court overlooked the distinction between the duty to the public of an *innkeeper* and that of a place of *public amusement*, in that the former may not discriminate and arbitrarily refuse persons service and accommodation, while the latter is privileged to serve only those whom it pleases (*Madden* v. *Queens County Jockey Club*, 296 N.Y. 249; *Aaron* v. *Ward*, 203 N.Y. 351). The court has considered that contention. But we do hold, as movant urges that a public restaurant in this day and age is entitled to the same immunities heretofore afforded a place of public amusement (*Matter of Sled Hill Cafe* v. *Hostetter*, 22 N.Y. 2d 607).

[6] 160 N.Y.L.J. No. 73, 17 (Sup. Ct. 1968).

The thrust of this law suit is that defendants' deliberate refusal to serve plaintiff in a public restaurant resulted in damage to the latter's reputation. As very recently stated by the Court of Appeals: " 'Society has a persuasive and strong interest in preventing and redressing attacks upon reputation,' and the courts are delegated with the responsibility of protecting that right (*Rosenblatt* v. *Baer*, 383 U.S. 75, 86)" (*William* v. *William and McCuaig*, _____ N.Y. _____).

The question is not so much whether there is precedent to maintain this action "but whether defendant inflicted such a wrong upon the plaintiff as resulted in lawful damages [for] the law will not suffer an injury and a damage without a remedy" (*Kuzek* v. *Goldman*, 150 N.Y. 176, 178, 179, 44 N.E. 773, 774). In view of the strides made in recent years by our courts, as well as the Legislature, to protect the dignity of man, it would be unlawful and unjust to dismiss this action at this stage of the proceeding. "Even though the past furnishes no current declaration of the right to maintain such an action, neither reason nor logic dictates that it must be held that no such action exists. The declaration of legal rights arises when the occasion presents itself for such a declaration, when social and economic progress commands that such a one be made" (*Rozell* v. *Rozell*, 281 N.Y. 106, 114, 22 N.E. 2d 254, 258). The determination of the question presented should, we believe, be reserved for trial.

The writer has been informed that upon trial, plaintiff was denied recovery.[7]

6:4 *Civil Rights Amendments to the Federal Constitution*

The great constitutional amendments following the Civil War fundamentally affected civil rights. The Thirteenth Amendment (December 18, 1865) abolished slavery. The Fifteenth Amendment (March 30, 1870) guaranteed to all citizens the right to vote. It is the Fourteenth Amendment (July 28, 1868) which is most relevant for our purposes. It reads, in part:

All persons born or naturalized in the United States and subject to the jurisdiction thereof, are citizens of the United States and of the State wherein they reside. No State shall make or enforce any law which shall abridge the privileges or immunities of citizens of the United States; nor shall any State deprive any person of life, liberty or property, without due process of law; nor deny to any person within its jurisdiction the equal protection of the laws.

[7] *Letaiyo* v. *Wood*, 161 N.Y.L.J. No. 77, 26 (Sup. Ct. 1969).

6:5 *"Separate but Equal Doctrine" Applied to Innkeepers*

In 1875, the Congress, in order to implement the Fourteenth Amendment, enacted a federal Civil Rights Act, and imposed penalties for violating its provisions. The application of the act to innkeepers was made an early issue and was resolved by Judge Dick in his charge to the grand jury in North Carolina.[8] The public accommodations section of the Civil Rights Act of 1875 was struck down by the Supreme Court in the *Civil Rights Cases*.[9] In his charge, Judge Dick had this to say:

The law only requires innkeepers, common carriers, etc., to furnish accommodations to colored men, equal to those provided for white men, when the same price is paid. Innkeepers may have separate rooms and accommodations for colored men, but they must be equal in quality and convenience to those furnished white men. . . . Both races are alike entitled to receive convenient and comfortable accommodations in inns and public conveyances, and neither a white man nor a colored man has a right to say that the innkeeper shall put them in the same room without their mutual consent. . . . If the innkeeper tenders such accommodations, and the guest refuses them, he may compel the guest to quit the inn, and seek for accommodations elsewhere.[10]

This interpretation established the "separate but equal" doctrine in relation to innkeeping. It was understood, of course, that if the innkeeper maintained no separate accommodations for colored men, he felt at liberty to exclude them; and, absent local civil rights legislation, innkeepers felt under no compulsion to provide dual accommodations in the same establishment for the benefit of colored men.

6:6 *State Civil Rights Laws*

Following the Civil War, state legislatures in response to popular sentiment, particularly in the Northern states, enacted civil rights laws, outlawing discrimination in places of public accommodation on

[8] *Charge to the Grand Jury,* 30 F. Cas. 999 (No. 18,258) (C.C.W.D.N.C. 1875).

[9] 109 U.S. 3 (1883).

[10] 30 F. Cas. 999, 1001 (No. 18,258) (C.C.W.D.N.C. 1875).

account of race, creed, color, or national origin. Today, the majority of states have civil rights statutes of their own applicable to places of public accommodation, including hotels, motels, restaurants, theatres, barbershops, and a variety of other places.

6:7 Equal Rights in Places of Public Accommodation According to the New York Civil Rights Law

New York was one of the first states to legislate on the subject of civil rights. Section 40 of the Civil Rights Law, originally enacted in 1895, provides that all persons are entitled to the full and equal accommodations, advantages, facilities, and privileges of any "place of public accommodation, resort or amusement," subject only to conditions and limitations established by law and applicable alike to all persons. The law further provides that no person shall refuse, withhold from, or deny to any person such accommodations or privileges by reason of *race, creed, color, or national origin*. A place of public accommodation is defined to include inns, hotels (including resort hotels), taverns, roadhouses, restaurants, barrooms, barbershops and beauty salons, and many other places.

6:8 Restriction on Advertising and Business Solicitation According to the New York Civil Rights Law

Section 40 also prohibits the use of any circulars or advertisement, or the mailing of any written or printed matter which contains any statement, express or implied, that any of the accommodations, facilities, or privileges will be refused or denied on account of race, creed, color, or national origin, or that any person is unwelcome, not acceptable, not desired, or not solicited because of race, creed, color, or national origin.

6:9 Penalties According to the New York Civil Rights Law

Section 41 of the Civil Rights Law fixes a penalty for a violation of Section 40 at not less than $100 nor more than $500 and gives the person who has been aggrieved the right to bring a *civil action* for such amount. In addition, the violation is made a *misdemeanor* and is punishable by a fine of not less than $100 nor more than $500, or imprisonment of not less than thirty days nor more than ninety days, or both.

6:10 *Protecting Civil and Public Rights According to the New York Civil Rights Law*

The protection of Section 40 applies to *any person,* irrespective of his citizenship or residence. Section 44-a (formerly Section 514 of the Penal Law) makes it a misdemeanor for a person to exclude by reason of race, color, creed, national origin, or previous condition of servitude, a citizen of New York State, from the equal enjoyment of any accommodations, facilities, or privileges furnished by innkeepers or common carriers, or, to deny or aid another in denying to any other person, because of race, creed, color, or national origin the full enjoyment of the accommodations, etc., of any hotel, inn, tavern, restaurant, or other place of public resort or amusement.

This section was originally enacted to secure to citizens of African descent equal rights with white persons to the facilities furnished by carriers, innkeepers, taverns, restaurants, and places of public resort or amusement. It is similar in import to Section 40.[11]

6:11 *Cases Interpreting Sections 40 and 41 of the New York Civil Rights Law*

There is a difference between a "place of public accommodation" and a "place of public amusement." Theatres and concert halls are places of public amusement; restaurants and hotels are places of public accommodation.[12]

Section 40 of the Civil Rights Law does *not* apply to a family or residential hotel, in which apartments are arranged in small suites, differing in no essential respect from those in an ordinary apartment house.[13]

Nor does the section apply to a private club, the facilities and

---

11 *People* v. *King,* 110 N.Y. 418 (1888).
12 *People* v. *Keller,* 96 Misc. 92, 161 N.Y.S. 132 (Ct. Gen. Sess. 1916).
13 *Alsberg* v. *Lucerne Hotel Co.,* 46 Misc. 617, 92 N.Y.S. 851 (Sup. Ct. 1905).

privileges of which are available to members only. A club is not a place of public accommodation but rather an institution of a distinctly private nature. Complaint by members based on ejection and use of language describing plaintiffs in derogatory manner but which failed to allege discrimination on account of "race, creed, color" was held defective.[14]

Application of the American Labor Party for a temporary injunction to enjoin the Hotel Concourse Plaza in New York City from canceling a contract for the use of the hotel's grand ballroom was denied, since the cancellation was not based on race, creed, color, or national origin. The contract in question contained the following provision: "The hotel reserves the right to cancel engagements at any time where rules are not observed, or where functions are of a nature not acceptable to the hotel." The hotel canceled the contract when it learned that the ballroom was to be used for a rally to confer upon Paul Robeson the International Peace Award for which he was cited by the Warsaw World Peace Congress.[15]

In an action for recovery of a penalty under Sections 40 and 41 of the Civil Rights Law, the defense that the defendant was out of food at the time was rejected as sham and unworthy of belief.[16]

The employer was not guilty of violating Sections 40 and 41 of the Civil Rights Law when a waiter refused to serve a colored customer in violation of his employer's instructions to serve white and colored customers alike, without discrimination.[17]

A rule in a restaurant, applicable alike to all citizens, that a person who did not wear a collar would not be served is a reasonable rule and is not within the proscription of the statute.[18]

Refusal to serve an unescorted female patron at the bar, although willing to serve her at a table near the bar, has been held not a violation of Sections 40, 40-c, or 40-e of the New York Civil Rights Law.[19]

[14] *Garfield* v. *Sands Beach Club, Inc.*, 137 N.Y.S.2d 58 (Sup. Ct. 1954).
[15] *American Labor Party* v. *Hotel Concourse Plaza*, 200 Misc. 587, 102 N.Y.S.2d 413 (Sup. Ct. 1950).
[16] *Wilson* v. *Razzetti*, 88 Misc. 37, 150 N.Y.S. 145 (Sup. Ct. 1914).
[17] *Hart* v. *Hartford Lunch Co.*, 81 Misc. 237, 142 N.Y.S. 515 (Sup. Ct. 1913).
[18] *Brandt* v. *Mink*, 38 Misc. 750, 78 N.Y.S. 1109 (Sup. Ct. 1902).
[19] *DeCrow* v. *Hotel Syracuse Corporation*, 59 Misc. 2d 383, 298 N.Y.S.2d 859 (Sup. Ct. 1969).

NOBLE *v.* HIGGINS

95 Misc. 328, 158 N.Y.S. 867 (Sup. Ct. 1916)

DAVIS (ROWLAND L.), J.: "On December 10, 1915, the plaintiff entered the restaurant of the defendants in the city of Oneonta, and asked to be served with certain food, offering at the same time to pay therefor. His request was refused and he was ordered to leave the premises. The plaintiff commenced an action to recover from the defendants a penalty pursuant to the provisions of chapter 6 of the Consolidated Laws, known as the Civil Rights Law, as amended by chapter 265 of the Laws of 1913.

"The evidence was brief, simple and practically undisputed. At the close of the evidence both sides moved for the direction of a verdict, and the jury was formally directed at the time to find a verdict for the plaintiff, which they did, assessing the penalty at $100. All proceedings after the entry of the verdict were stayed until the court could consider the legal questions involved in the controversy.

"The refusal to serve the plaintiff was apparently on purely personal grounds. The refreshment asked for by the plaintiff was not refused, withheld from or denied to him on account of race, creed, or color. Therefore, it seems that the interpretation of the Court of Appeals in *Grannan* v. *Westchester Racing Association,* 153 N.Y. 449 (1897), as extended and applied under the present statute in *Woollcott* v. *Shubert,* 217 N.Y. 212, forbids the application of the statute to the state of facts recited here.

"It may be conclusively determined, after an examination of the last-quoted authorities that 'the legislature did not intend to confer upon every person all the rights, advantages, and privileges in places of amusement or accommodation, which might be enjoyed by another. Any discrimination not based upon race, creed or color does not fall within the condemnation of the statute.'

"It would seem then, that the common-law right still remains with those not engaged as common carriers, or in like occupations, to discriminate between persons according to rules established where the person applying for accommodation is objectionable for some reason. Otherwise, persons unclean, untidy, intoxicated or affected by disease might claim the same attention in a crowded restaurant or other public place as those against whom no objection could be urged. *Brandt* v. *Mink*, 38 Misc. Rep. 750.

"Whether or not plaintiff had a remedy at common law for any indignity or humiliation caused by the act of the defendants need not be considered here, although some of the authorities cited on [sic] the plaintiff's brief discussed that question. The action is brought solely on the theory that the plaintiff is entitled to recover a penalty or forfeiture given under the Civil Rights Act where a violation occurs." [Complaint dismissed on the merits.]

In *Cohn* v. *Goldgraben*,[20] plaintiff, a white person, in company of a colored person, entered defendant's restaurant catering to a colored patronage in Harlem. Plaintiff was refused service for the reason that it was "against the rules of the house to serve a mixed party." Plaintiff's action for damages for violation of Sections 40 and 41 of the Civil Rights Law was dismissed. Said the court, per Whitaker, J.:

I do not think the refusal to serve "mixed parties," white and colored, at the same table when there is a willingness to serve the same people at separate tables should be construed as a violation of the statute.

The rights granted to the citizen by the statute are strictly personal and the statute may only be invoked when the refusal is based upon the ground personal to the plaintiff. The plaintiff was not refused service solely upon his own color but upon the fact that his companion had a different color. Had the plaintiff been alone or had he separated himself from his companion he would have been served.

The judgment should be affirmed, with twenty-five dollars costs.[21]

Mr. Justice Bijur, in a vigorous dissent, disagreed with the majority, and held that defendant's refusal to serve plaintiff was in plain violation of the statute:

The Civil Rights Law . . . provides that no owner of a restaurant "shall directly or indirectly refuse, withhold from or deny to any person any of the accommodations, advantages or privileges thereof . . . on account of race, creed or color." It seems to me to be clear that plaintiff was, on the occasion in question, denied the privileges of defendant's restaurant because he was white. The defendant virtually said to plaintiff: "If you were colored and came here with Williams, you would be served; *but*

[20] 103 Misc. 500, 170 N.Y.S. 407 (Sup. Ct. 1918).
[21] *Id.* at 501–502 and 408.

being white, we will not serve you." The law naturally does not undertake to define or even to indicate which if any race or color may be regarded as superior. Its sole and manifest purpose is to prevent discrimination on that account. [Emphasis in original.] [22]

HOBSON *v.* YORK STUDIOS, INC.
208 Misc. 888, 145 N.Y.S.2d 162 (N.Y. Mun. Ct. 1955)

[The plaintiffs, Raymond S. Hobson, a Negro, and his wife, a white woman, seek to recover statutory redress under Section 41 of the Civil Rights Law, alleging that when they applied for a room in the defendant's hotel, they were rejected by reasons of their race. . . .

It appeared that on May 6, 1953, Mrs. Hobson, a white woman, personally called at defendant's hotel, obtained a reservation for herself and her husband, paid a deposit of $5.00 and obtained a receipt.

The next day both husband and wife appeared to claim their reservation and to pay the balance due. Instead of admitting them, the desk clerk told Mr. Hobson that the hotel did not want "white and colored" living together in view of the tendency of another interracial couple, who had resided there previously, to fight all the time. The desk clerk then returned the plaintiff's deposit.]

WAHL, J.: "I have accepted the testimony of the plaintiffs, seemingly, respectable and worthy citizens, and I am convinced that both of them were discriminated against because of their race. The *post litem* contention that Mr. Hobson was offensive and abusive and that that was the basis of the refusal to give the plaintiffs accommodations is not convincing, nor was it pleaded as a matter of affirmative defense. It is natural that a defendant accused of racial discrimination will seek avoidance of statutory penalties therefor through 'explanations.' . . .

"Since no corporate officer of the defendant testified, it does not appear that the defendant gave any instructions to its desk clerk not to discriminate racially. If nothing was said to employees about refusing admission to persons of the colored race, then the acts of the desk clerk are chargeable to the corporation. [Citation omitted.] Once the accusation is made of a racial rejection by a place of public accommodation, a corporate defendant is bound to come forward

[22] *Id.* at 502 and 408–409.

with proof that the discrimination which is offensive to the statute has been forbidden by specific instructions to corporate employees. [Citations omitted.] On this point the defendant elected to remain mute.

"I now come to an aspect of this case which is not free of difficulty: If the white plaintiff, Rose Hobson, was discriminated against because of her race, may she be given relief under the Civil Rights Law? . . .

"The principal case cited in support of strict construction of Section 40 is *Cohn* v. *Goldgraben* (103 Misc. 500). It is also often cited for the proposition that the refusal by a place of public accommodation to serve a 'mixed couple,' *i.e.*, Negro and white, does not offend the statute. It should be noticed that *Cohn* v. *Goldgraben* (*supra*) where only the white member of the 'mixed couple' sued, represents a now antiquated view of the law and that, further, the decision appears to have turned upon a refusal by a restaurant to serve a Negro and a white man at the same table. There, the question was one of services, not one of public accommodations, such as a lodging. Hotels and inns have long enjoyed a special statute in the law and restaurants have never been subjected to the liability of innkeepers. [Citations omitted.] . . .

"The words 'any person' [in the statute] . . . when given their usual meanings, must include protection for white persons as well as Negroes who are rejected because of race. To all but the naive, it is clear that a white woman may be the butt of a racial discrimination because she has elected to marry a Negro. I am convinced that both plaintiffs were rejected by the defendant because Mr. Hobson is a Negro and his wife is a white woman. Such a refusal, as applied to Mrs. Hobson, is a rejection of her because of her color. . . .

"The modern view of New York's civil rights legislation is found in the acute insight of Mr. Justice Bijur's dissenting opinion in *Cohn* v. *Goldgraben* (*supra*). There, a colored waiter in the defendant's restaurant located in Harlem claimed he could not serve a 'colored and white person *together*.' . . .

"Judge Bijur would have given the white plaintiff relief under the Civil Rights Law. . . .

"In effect, what the defendant's desk clerk said to Mrs. Hobson was that if she had been married to a white man, her reservation for a room would have been honored. If the rejection was based upon some private theory of 'social acceptability,' where Negroes and whites are in intimate association, it is still offensive to the law. . . .

"The credible testimony confirms a racial discrimination against each of the plaintiffs. The Law Against Discrimination states its purpose to be 'the protection of the public welfare, health and peace of the people of this state' (Executive Law, §290) [Laws of 1955, Ch. 340, Sec. 1]. This is inclusive of *all* people, white as well as Negro. The old cases which would limit the application of the Civil Rights Law to Negroes only are clearly negatived by recent legislative enactments. This legislation is remedial in concept and liberal in its scope; it represents the public policy of the State which applies to the entire public.

"For all of the foregoing reasons, I direct that the plaintiffs have judgment against the defendant in the amount of $100 each."

MOON *v.* GETTY REALTY CORP.
203 Misc. 273, 118 N.Y.S.2d 784(Sup. Ct. 1952)

[Civil action to recover a penalty for alleged violation of the Civil Rights Law.

The defendant Getty Realty Corporation, through William M. Willy, its banquet manager, made an agreement with the plaintiff over the telephone to permit her to hold a summer party on the roof of the Hotel Pierre. The dates first proposed were one of the following: July 20, 21, 27, or 28, 1951, but they finally decided definitely on the 20th of July, 1951. Mr. Willy assured the plaintiff that the roof was available on that date. The plaintiff informed Mr. Willy that the party was to be held under the name of an unincorporated association known as the Urban League Guild, of which she was president. Mr. Willy suggested that she come down to the office of the Hotel Pierre on May 22, 1951, at five-thirty P.M. for the purpose of signing a contract and making arrangements.

On May 22, 1951, at about five-thirty P.M., the plaintiff arrived at the Hotel Pierre and had a conversation with Mr. Rama, who introduced himself as Mr. Willy's assistant. She explained her mission to Mr. Rama and asked to see Mr. Willy. He excused himself for a moment, went into another office and came back and told her she could not see Mr. Willy because Mr. Willy was a busy man, and then told her the hotel roof garden was not available.

The court below held that plaintiff was an aggrieved person and that the fact that she acted for others, including herself, was immaterial, and granted judgment for plaintiff in the sum of $200 against each of the defendants, the Hotel Pierre, Willy and Rama.]

PER CURIAM: "This court has held that the right under the statute is strictly personal, and that the statute, penal in nature, must be strictly construed; the plaintiff must clearly bring himself within its terms (*Cohn v. Goldgraben,* 103 Misc. 500). Section 41 of the Civil Rights Law provides that recovery may be had against any 'agency, bureau, corporation or association . . . by the person aggrieved thereby,' while Section 40 provides that all 'persons within the jurisdiction of this state shall be entitled to the full and equal accommodations,' etc. This would indicate that it was the legislative intent that the recovery be only in a person; it is apparent from the record that the plaintiff was not acting as an individual in her dealings with the defendants and therefore the defendants did not refuse the reservation to the plaintiff personally.

"The judgment should be reversed, with $30 costs, and complaint dismissed, with costs." [All concur.]

6:12 *Federal Civil Rights Act of 1964*

The Civil Rights Act of 1964 became law on July 2, 1964. It is the first federal legislation in civil rights, other than voting, in ninety years. It is nationwide in its application and fills a void in the protection of civil rights in states which failed to legislate on this subject. Title II of the act prohibits racial and religious discrimination in places of public accommodation. Title VII of the act prohibits similar discrimination in employment.

6:13 *Injunctive Relief against Discrimination in Places of Public Accommodation—Title II*

The following definitions are given in Section 201 of Title II:

Section 201. *Establishments Covered*

(a) All persons shall be entitled to the full and equal enjoyment of the goods, services, facilities, privileges, advantages, and accommodations of any place of public accommodation, as defined in this section, without discrimination or segregation on the ground of race, color, religion, or national origin.

(b) Each of the following establishments which serves the public is a place of public accommodation within the meaning of this title if its operations affect commerce, or if discrimination or segregation by it is supported by State action:

(1) any inn, hotel, motel, or other establishment which provides lodging to transient guests, other than an establishment located within a building which contains not more than five rooms for rent or hire and which is actually occupied by the proprietor of such establishment as his residence;

(2) any restaurant, cafeteria, lunchroom, lunch counter, soda fountain, or other facility principally engaged in selling food for consumption on the premises, including, but not limited to, any such facility located on the premises of any retail establishment; or any gasoline station;

(3) any motion picture house, theater, concert hall, sports arena, stadium or other place of exhibition or entertainment; and

(4) any establishment (A) (i) which is physically located within the premises of any establishment otherwise covered by this subsection, or (ii) within the premises of which is physically located any such covered establishment, and (B) which holds itself out as serving patrons of such covered establishment.

(c) The operations of an establishment affect commerce within the meaning of this title if (1) it is one of the establishments described in paragraph (1) of subsection (b); (2) in the case of an establishment described in paragraph (2) of subsection (b), it serves or offers to serve interstate travellers, or a substantial portion of the food which it serves, or gasoline or other products which it sells, has moved in commerce; (3) in the case of an establishment described in paragraph (3) of subsection (b), it customarily presents films, performances, athletic teams, exhibitions, or other sources of entertainment which move in commerce; and (4) in the case of an establishment described in paragraph (4) of subsection (b), it is physically located within the premises of, or there is physically located within its premises, an establishment the operations of which affect commerce within the meaning of this subsection. For purposes of this section, "commerce" means travel, trade, traffic, commerce, transportation, or communication among the several States, or between the District of Columbia and any State, or between any foreign country or any territory or possession and any State or the District of Columbia, or between points in the same State but through any other State or the District of Columbia or a foreign country.

(d) Discrimination or segregation by an establishment is supported by State action within the meaning of this title if such discrimination or segregation (1) is carried on under color of any law, statute, ordinance, or regulation; or (2) is carried on under color of any customer or usage required or enforced by officials of the State or political subdivision thereof; or (3) is required by action of the State or political subdivision thereof.

(e) The provisions of this title shall not apply to a private club or other establishment not in fact open to the public, except to the extent that the facilities of such establishment are made available to the customers or patrons of an establishment within the scope of subsection (b).

The inns, hotels, motels, and other places serving transient guests are covered, except "Mrs. Murphy's boardinghouse," that is a building with not more than five rooms for transient guests and which is also occupied by the proprietor himself.

On the other hand, a restaurant is covered only if it serves or offers to serve interstate travelers, *or* a substantial portion of the food or beverage which it serves has moved in interstate commerce. In the *Ollie's Barbecue Case*,[23] a family-owned restaurant in Birmingham, Alabama, purchased some $150,000 worth of food in a year, of which some 46 per cent was meat purchased from a local butcher who in turn procured it from outside the state. The restaurant was held to be subject to the Act.

A hotel or motel restaurant which serves transient guests who move in interstate commerce is subject to the Act.

A hotel or motel barbershop, beauty salon, cigar stand, flower shop, laundry, Turkish bath, ticket agency, shoeshine parlor, or any other similar facility which serves transient out-of-town guests, is subject to the Act, even though a barbershop across the street serving local people only may not be.

Bona fide private clubs or other establishments not in fact open to the public are specifically excepted from the Act's coverage. But the Act would seem to cover a so-called club admitting anyone upon signing an application and paying a nominal admission charge.

[23] *Katzenbach* v. *McClung*, 379 U.S. 294 (1964).

The Act does not force proprietors of covered establishments to accept undesirable customers. Persons who come in an improper condition to be received, those who are drunk, disorderly, filthy, inappropriately dressed, rude, or otherwise undesirable on legitimate grounds other than race or religion may be excluded.

A hotel barber, for example, may not refuse to cut a Negro guest's hair solely because the guest is a Negro, but he may refuse him service if his skin is infected, or if he is drunk or disorderly.

Section 202 of the Act nullifies all state or local laws requiring or prescribing discrimination on grounds of race or religion, such as the Greenville, South Carolina, ordinance in *Peterson* v. *Greenville*.[24] The ordinance made it unlawful for a hotel, restaurant, etc., to furnish meals to white persons and colored persons in the same room, or at the same table, or at the same counter.

Section 203 of the Act forbids the intimidation, coercion, or the threatening or punishing of any person for exercising or attempting to exercise his rights under the Act.

6:14   *Discrimination on Account of Sex: Refusal to Serve Unescorted Women at Hotel or Restaurant Bars*

Refusal of an innkeeper or restaurant keeper to serve unescorted women at a stand-up bar is not a violation of the Civil Rights Act of 1964.

In *DeCrow* v. *Hotel Syracuse Corporation*,[25] the Federal District Court for the Northern District of New York (Port, D.J.) dismissed, on defendant hotel's motion, a complaint which stated that on December 20, 1967, the hotel refused service to plaintiffs at its bar in the Rainbow Lounge, a restaurant in the Hotel Syracuse, in keeping with its established policy of not serving an unescorted woman at its bar "[a]lthough she was sitting quietly and in no way disturbing any other patrons."

Said the court:

The conduct of hotels and restaurants is governed by section 201(a) of said Act (42 U.S.C.A. §2000(a)). The full and equal enjoyment of public accommodations without discrimination on account of *"race, color, religion,*

24 373 U.S. 244 (1963).   25 288 F. Supp. 530 (1968).

or national origin" (emphasis added), including the right to be served at a bar, has been guaranteed by Congress. No such guarantee has been made on account of *sex*. This court should not gratuitously do what Congress has not seen fit to do. Mrs. Kennedy's complaint should be addressed to Congress.

The court similarly dismissed plaintiff's contention that the complaint stated a claim under 42 U.S.C.A. §§1983 and 1985 in that plaintiffs were deprived of their rights, privileges, or immunities secured by the Constitution and laws and that defendant conspired to deprive plaintiffs of the equal protection of the laws or of equal privileges and immunities under the laws. Judge Port had this to say in disposing of plaintiffs' contention: "The short answer, so well established as not to require citation of authorities, is that these sections, like the Equal Protection Clause of the 14th Amendment, are only directed at State action, which is nowhere alleged in the complaint."

In *Seidenberg* v. *McSorley's Old Ale House, Inc.*,[26] plaintiffs, members of the National Organization for Women, sought to enjoin defendants, operators of a bar primarily engaged in serving alcoholic and nonalcoholic beverages, from continuing its 114-year practice of catering only to men. The defendant moved for an order dismissing the complaint for failure to allege sufficient facts to state a valid claim under 42 U.S.C.A. §1983.

The Federal District Court for the Southern District of New York, (Tenney, D.J.) held that the court had jurisdiction of the action and that the complaint stated a claim for relief on the grounds that since a state license was required to operate a bar, there was sufficient state involvement to make the acts of the licensee those of the state itself and that the discrimination against women was unreasonable. "Bars or taverns, though a species of private property, are clearly in the public domain, 'affected with a public interest' and subject to more extensive State supervision than the lunch counters in *Garner* and *Lombard*,"[27] said Judge Tenney.

Once we assume, for the purposes of defendant's motion, that its policy of excluding women may properly be considered the acts of the State, the Court must then determine whether such discrimination is founded in

[26] 308 F. Supp. 1253 (1969).
[27] *Garner* v. *Louisiana*, 368 U.S. 157 (1961); *Lombard* v. *Louisiana*, 373 U.S. 267 (1963).

reason and thus a permissible classification within the meaning of the Fourteenth Amendment.

. . . To adhere to practice supported by ancient chivalristic concepts, when there may no longer exist a need or basis therefor, may only serve to isolate women from the realities of everyday life, and to perpetuate, as a matter of law, economic and sexual exploitation. While members of each sex may at times relish the opportunity to withdraw to the exclusive company of their own gender, if it be ultimately found that the State has become significantly involved in a policy which mandates such seclusion, then considerable question is presented as to whether, for the purposes of the Fourteenth Amendment, this discrimination is founded upon a basis in reason.[28]

6:15 Penalties for Violation of Title II

There are no criminal penalties for violation of Title II. Enforcement is by suit, by the person affected. The aggrieved person must bring a civil action for injunction in his own behalf. If he is unable to bring the suit himself because of lack of funds, or because of intimidation, the court in its discretion may permit the Attorney General to intervene, if he certifies that the case is of general public importance. But the Attorney General is denied the right to initiate suits in behalf of individuals.

The prevailing party in a suit may be allowed, at the discretion of the court, reasonable attorney's fees, as part of his costs.

In the words of the then Senator (later Vice-President) Humphrey:

If the alleged discrimination occurs in a State or locality that has a public accommodations law covering the practice alleged, the individual cannot . . . bring his suit in Federal court until 30 days after he has registered a complaint with the proper State or local authorities. If these authorities

---

[28] *Seidenberg* has not been tried and no appeal has been taken from the District Court's order. 317 F. Supp. 593 (1970). On motion for summary judgment the District Court held that provision of Civil Rights Act of 1964 guaranteeing to all persons the full and equal enjoyment of public accommodations without discrimination on account of race, color, religion, or national origin applies neither to discrimination on basis of sex nor to discrimination in a bar or tavern whose principal business is the sale of alcoholic beverages rather than food. But the court further held that refusal of the ale house, which was primarily a bar serving alcoholic and nonalcoholic beverages and which was subject to extensive and pervasive state regulation, to serve women denied women equal protection.

then initiate enforcement proceedings under the State or local law and such proceedings have not been completed by the time suit is filed in Federal court, the Federal court may at its discretion stay the suit until such proceedings are terminated.

If the alleged discrimination has occurred in a State or locality without a public accommodations law, the individual who is aggrieved may bring suit in Federal court immediately. The court may refer such a case to the Federal Community Relations Service for efforts to settle the dispute by voluntary methods. The Service is authorized to investigate the case for that purpose. The time limit on such a referral to the Community Relations Service is 60 days, although, upon expiration of this period, the court may extend the referral for up to another 60 days, if it still believes there is a reasonable possibility of obtaining voluntary compliance.

Since the experience in States that have public accommodations laws is that most complaints can be settled by voluntary procedures, it is expected that discretionary referral under these provisions will further the purposes of the title without requiring Federal court orders in many cases.

At the same time . . . State and local officials [are given] a greater responsibility and a greater opportunity to achieve voluntary compliance without Federal action. The intent . . . is to preserve the power of the Federal courts as a last rather than a first step.

The Attorney General has two roles to play in public accommodations suits. One of these is to intervene, at the discretion of the court, in suits brought by aggrieved individuals. . . .

While the Attorney General would not have power to initiate suits in individual cases, he would have authority to initiate legal action on his own under Title II when "he has reasonable cause to believe that any person or group of persons is engaged in a pattern or practice of resistance to the full enjoyments of any of the rights secured by this title." In such cases the Attorney General need not refer the complaint to the Community Relations Service, although he could if he wanted to. Nor is there any requirement for exhaustion of State or local remedies beforehand. If the Attorney General files a certificate that the case is of general public importance, a three-judge court with a mandate to act expeditiously would be appointed. Provision is also made for expedited proceedings in cases filed by the Attorney General in which he does not ask for a three-judge court.

In short, where the Attorney General believes that a suit brought by an individual under title II is important—because, for example, the points of law involved in it are of major significance or because the particular decision will constitute a precedent for a large number of establishments—

he may request intervention, in order to present the Government's point of view. And where he believes there is a pattern or practice designed to perpetuate discrimination, he may sue directly.

It is expected that this power of the Attorney General will be an important aid to maintaining public order in cases in which repeated discrimination in public accommodations has given rise to demonstrations and public violence. Since these are among the most explosive and disruptive instances of discrimination, [Congress] felt that the Attorney General had to have power to act quickly and decisively in the interest of public peace and harmony.

Legal assistance [is provided] to persons aggrieved: [Section 204 of the act] authorize[s] the court, in such circumstances as it deems just, to appoint an attorney for a person aggrieved and to permit his suit to be filed without the payment of fees, costs, or security. Relief would be possible for persons experiencing denial of their rights under title II, who, for financial or other justifiable reasons, are unable to bring and maintain a lawsuit.[29]

Section 206 gives the Attorney General the right to bring an action for preventive relief only if he has reasonable cause to believe and pleads that a person or group of persons is engaged in a pattern or practice of discrimination intended to deny the full exercise of the rights under Title II.

6:16 Supreme Court Holds Act Constitutional

In the test case of *Heart of Atlanta Motel* v. *United States*,[30] the Supreme Court, speaking through Mr. Justice Clark, unanimously sustained the constitutionality of the act. Although Congress had purported to act under both the commerce clause and Section 5 of the Fourteenth Amendment, the majority opinion relied solely upon the commerce clause to sustain the statute. (Justice Douglas wrote a concurring opinion urging that the statute should have been upheld simply on the basis of the Fourteenth Amendment. Justice Goldberg, also concurring, was content to rest upon the commerce clause but argued that the Fourteenth Amendment was a source more consonant with the act's basic purposes: what was involved, he stressed, was "the vindication of human dignities and not mere economics." [31] Clark

[29] 110 *Cong. Rec.* 12712–12713 (1964).   [30] 379 U.S. 241 (1964).
[31] *Id.* at 291.

found that Congress had a rational basis for finding that racial discrimination by motels and hotels adversely affected interstate commerce and that the means selected to eliminate that evil were reasonable and appropriate. He noted that the American people had become increasingly mobile; that Negroes in particular had been the subject of discrimination in transient accommodations and often had been unable to obtain any; that these exclusionary practices were nationwide and hence significantly impaired the Negro traveler's pleasure; and that the net result of these factors was that interstate travel by a substantial portion of the Negro community was impeded and discouraged.

Although the Heart of Atlanta Motel served a substantial number of interstate travelers, in a companion case decided the same day, *Katzenbach* v. *McClung*,[32] the court held the act constitutional as applied to a restaurant that neither solicited nor catered to interstate travelers but came within the act only because a substantial portion of the food served therein had moved in interstate commerce.

[32] 379 U.S. 294 (1964).

CHAPTER 7

Reception of the Guest

7:1 *Payment May Be Demanded at Time of Admission*

The innkeeper is not bound to receive the guest until the price of the accommodation is tendered, that is to say, he may demand payment in advance. Insistence on advance payment may be, and usually is, waived in practice. Thus, if a traveler enters an inn and makes his desire to become a guest known to the innkeeper, the latter must request advance payment if he means to insist on it as a condition of receiving the guest.

7:2 *Duty to Receive Baggage or Luggage with Guest*

The cases clearly establish that an innkeeper is under duty to admit not only the person, but the baggage of his guest as well. It is also clear, however, that not all goods which the guest may bring with him can be considered "baggage." In this connection, it has been held that

[l]uggage and baggage are essentially the bags, trunks, etc., that a passenger takes with him for his personal use and convenience with reference to his necessities or to the ultimate purpose of his journey, and in this connection it has been held that, within limits, the same include such jewelry as may be adapted to the tastes, habits and social standing and be necessary for the convenience, use and enjoyment of the traveler either while in transit or temporarily staying at a particular place.[1]

[1] *Waters v. Beau Site Co.*, 114 Misc. 65, 68, 186 N.Y.S. 731, 732 (N.Y. City Ct. 1920).

7:3 Innkeeper May Not Investigate Ownership of Guest's Luggage

In order to demand admittance for the luggage he brings, the guest is not bound to prove that it is his own. A guest may come to an inn with the goods of another, and the ownership of the goods is no business of the innkeeper.

He has not to inquire whether the goods are the property of the person who brings them or of some other person. If he does so inquire, the traveller may refuse to tell him, and may say, "What business is that of yours? I bring the goods here as my luggage, and I insist upon your taking them in"; or he may say "They are not my property, but I bring them here as my luggage, and I insist upon your taking them in"; and then the innkeeper is bound by law to take them in.[2]

The innkeeper may undoubtedly refuse to receive goods known to him to be stolen when they are brought to the inn by the thief; but in the ordinary case he need not and cannot investigate the question of title.

If the traveler brought something exceptional which is not luggage —such as a tiger or a package of dynamite—the innkeeper might refuse to take it in; but the custom of the realm is that, unless there is some reason to the contrary in the exceptional character of the things brought, he must take in the traveler and his goods.

Whether an animal which is not dangerous, like a dog, could be refused on the ground that there are no facilities at the inn to prevent the dog from becoming a nuisance to the guests is more doubtful. It could not be restrained from annoyance by a regulation, like a piano; and on the whole it would seem that unless the inn has, or considering the nature of its business, ought to have, peculiar facilities for caring for animal pets they may be excluded from the inn.

7:4 Innkeeper Must Have Notice of Traveler's Intention to Be Received

The burden appears to be on the applicant to give notice to the innkeeper that he desires to be received as a guest. Thus where a

---

[2] Lord Esher, M.R., in *Robins* v. *Gray*, [1895] 2 Q.B. 501, 504.

person was traveling at night, and came to an inn after it was shut up for the night, and knocked, it was held that the innkeeper must, in order to be liable for not admitting the guest, have heard the knocking, and in addition must reasonably have concluded that the person was a bona fide guest. Parke, B., said, in charging the jury:

> There is no doubt that the law is, that a person who keeps a public inn is bound to admit all persons who apply peaceably to be admitted as guests. You will therefore have to say whether you are satisfied that the noise made by yon plaintiff's brother was really heard by the defendant; and if so, whether you think that she ought to have concluded from it that the persons so knocking at the door were persons requiring to be admitted as guests, or whether she might have concluded that they were drunken persons, who had come there to make a disturbance. You will take the case into your consideration, and find, by your verdict, whether you think that the noise made at the door implied that the persons who made it wanted to be admitted as guests or not.[3]

The requirement of giving notice of intention to become a guest has been held satisfied by a request for accommodation or entertainment and by furnishing same in the customary manner. "The traveler receiving lodging without food, or food without lodging, or any other form of refreshment which the innkeeper publicly professes to serve in the usual and customary way in which travelers are entertained, thereby becomes a guest."[4]

In *Langford v. Vandaveer,*[5] one of the men in a party of four, consisting of two men and two women, asked for overnight accommodation for "four oil men" in defendant's motor court. Defendant was unaware that two members in the party were women, the register having been signed by one of the men as "C. P. Howe and party." Plaintiff, one of the women, was seriously injured by a gas heater explosion in the cabin assigned to and occupied by the party. She predicated her right of recovery on defendant's negligence in the maintenance of the heater, and claimed that she was a "lawful guest for pay." Defendant took the position that plaintiff was a trespasser. The trial court instructed the jury

---

[3] *Hawthorne* v. *Hammond*, 174 Eng. Rep. 866, 869 (1844).
[4] *Hill* v. *Hotel Co.*, 124 Tenn. 376, 380–381, 136 S.W. 997, 998–999 (1911).
[5] 254 S.W.2d 498 (Ky. 1953).

that plaintiff was a guest as a matter of law. On appeal, judgment for plaintiff was reversed. Said the court:

In the case at bar, the intention of the young lady to become a guest in the legal sense is apparent. The question is whether or not she was intentionally or knowingly received as such by the proprietor of the motor court. Generally, an innkeeper, though the conductor of a semipublic institution, is not under obligation to receive as a guest everyone who applies. He has the right to reject or expel persons whom he reasonably deems objectionable. [Citations omitted.] Under this rule of law a person may not impose himself upon the proprietor and become a guest without his knowledge or intention to receive him. One becomes a guest only if he is received to be treated as a guest and the intention to become such must be communicated to the innkeeper or his agent. This is a fact to be proved by evidence, definite or circumstantial. [Citations omitted.] [6]

[6] *Id.* at 501.

CHAPTER 8

Innkeeper's Duty to Persons Who Are Not Guests

8:1 *Duty to Admit Strangers Not Seeking Accommodations or Service: "Lobby Lizards"*

One who is not a guest or intending immediately to become a guest, has, generally speaking, no right to enter or remain in the inn against the objection of the innkeeper.[1] There are, to be sure, in every inn, "public rooms," and persons not guests are often in the habit of resorting to such rooms; but they are admitted to them only by the consent of the innkeeper. If that consent is withdrawn, one who is not a guest has no more right to enter a public room in an inn than he has to enter the private room of a guest. "[B]arring the limitation imposed by holding out inducements to the public to seek accommodation at his inn, the proprietor occupies it as his dwelling-house, from which he may expel all who have not acquired rights, growing out of the relation of guest." [2]

The same idea was vigorously expressed by Judge Parsons in *Commonwealth* v. *Mitchell:* [3]

If it should be held, as was contended on the argument, that because a man keeps a public house all who choose have a right to enter and occupy the hall or bar-room, or even the public parlour in a hotel, and that the proprietor has not a right to request them to leave, and if they do not, and he gently lays his hands on one to lead him out, he is guilty of an assault and battery but few persons would be found as lodgers in public houses. For where is the distinction to be drawn? If one may enter the inn and tarry there, all may. The pickpocket, the burglar, gambler and horse-thief,

---

[1] *State* v. *Whitby*, 5 Harr. (5 Del.) 494 (Ct. Gen. Sess. 1854).
[2] Avery, J., in *State* v. *Steele*, 106 N.C. 766, 783, 11 S.E. 478, 484 (1890).
[3] 2 Parsons 431, 435 (Pa. Ct. C.P. 1850).

can come and take his seat by the side of the most virtuous man in the community in the gentleman's common parlour at the hotel, and the proprietor cannot eject him (no matter how annoying it may be to the guest) without being indicted for an assault and battery. Nor would the line of distinction be drawn here—the filthy and unclean would claim the same right. It is only necessary to state such a proposition to show its absurdity.

8:2 Stranger Coming to Inn for Convenience of Guest

While the general principle just stated is unquestioned, there are certain cases in which a stranger may desire to enter the inn, not merely for his own pleasure or business, but because the convenience of a guest of the inn calls him there. While no right to enter the inn can be based on his own claim, he can under certain circumstances claim to be exercising a right of the guest. It must be borne in mind, however, that in order to show a right of admittance he must base his claim on a right of the guest whom he comes to see.

Even in such a case there is some authority for saying that he cannot legally enter the inn against the objection of the innkeeper. Judge Parsons, in *Commonwealth* v. *Mitchell,* was of the opinion that a person desiring to call upon a guest, even if he had been sent for by the guest, could not legally resist exclusion by the innkeeper, and that the innkeeper might use any force that was necessary to exclude him without being liable to an action for assault and battery, though he might be liable to an action on the case for refusal. This opinion, however, is probably incorrect. If, either in his own right or the right of a guest, the party is permitted by the law to enter the inn, the innkeeper can probably not justify the use of force to exclude him.

8:3 Stranger Coming for Social Call on Guest

Though there is no direct authority in favor of such a right, it seems that a stranger coming to make a social call upon the guest at the guest's request would have a right to be admitted for that purpose. Any other rule would deprive the guest of one privilege necessary for his comfort while at the inn. If, however, the guest has not previously requested the stranger to call, it seems clear that the stranger cannot object if he is denied admittance to the inn and the guest is not informed of his presence.

8:4 Stranger Coming by Appointment to Do Business with Guest

In the ordinary case it is tolerably clear that a stranger who comes by appointment to do business with a guest has a right to be admitted. "It is conceded," said Parker, J., in *Markham* v. *Brown*,[4] "that he may be bound to permit the entry of persons who have been sent for by the guest." And even those courts which are most reluctant to permit the entrance of a stranger, do in fact, concede the right to such persons. To be sure, if the visitor misconducts himself after his entrance he may be excluded. As Judge Avery said in *State* v. *Steele*:

If it be conceded that the prosecutor went into the hotel, at the request of a guest, for the purpose of conferring with the latter on business, still, in any view of the case, if, after entering, he engaged in "drumming" for his employer when he had been previously notified to desist, in obedience to a regulation of the house, the defendant had a right to expel him, if he did not use more force than was necessary. . . . The guest, by sending for a hackman, could not delegate to him the right to do an act for which even the guest himself might lawfully be put out of the hotel.[5]

And Judge Parsons said forcibly in *Commonwealth* v. *Mitchell*, "Can it be said [that] . . . the proprietor is bound to let every felon in the city enter his house, find access to his chambers, to visit a guest who happens to lodge there, and, who has thus sought the lodging to enable his associates in crime to enter the house for the purpose of robbing the other guests, or stealing the valuables from the hotel? Such a thing could not be tolerated." [6]

As to the general right of the guest to have a proper person visit him at the inn on business, the same learned justice in the same case appears to recognize it, while qualifying it by his doctrine, already stated, that the innkeeper might lawfully use force to keep the visitor from making use of this right.

When a guest has been admitted to a hotel and has taken a room, if any one calls to see him upon business, fair dealing would seem to require that the proprietor should communicate the intelligence to the guest, and

---

[4] 8 N.H. 523, 529 (1837).   [5] 106 N.C. 766, 784, 11 S.E. 478, 485 (1890).
[6] 2 Parsons 431, 437 (Pa. Ct. C.P. 1850).

if he consented to see the visitor, let him enter. But this, I apprehend, would be more by courtesy than a sheer claim of right. And if the proprietor of the house should refuse to suffer the visitor to come in, or if he had entered should request him to depart, and on his refusal, gently lead him out, I am not prepared to say who would be guilty of an assault and battery for so doing. That the proprietor would be liable to an action, both to the guest and the visitor for any injury either might sustain in consequence thereof, I have no doubt. And probably might be liable to an indictment upon the same principle he would be for refusing to entertain a traveller when he had room. But because one should allege he had business with a guest, and the guest desire to see a visitor that was obnoxious to the keeper of the house, and therefore any one can enter the hotel on such a pretext and stay as long as he pleases without the proprietor possessing the power to remove him, is a principle which cannot be sanctioned on any clear legal ground.

The guest is but an occupier of his lodgings at the will or sufferance of the proprietor, and necessity requires that he who has charge of that house should determine whether visitors who may desire to call upon a lodger are proper persons to be admitted within his chambers; otherwise, under such a pretext, thieves and robbers might gain admittance and rob his other guests of much that is valuable. Any different rule would expose every hotelkeeper to an imminent risk.[7]

8:5 Stranger Coming to Solicit Business from Guest

Where a stranger seeks admittance to an inn for the purpose of soliciting the patronage of guests, he may clearly be excluded from the inn. Indeed, as is pointed out in State v. Steele,[8] it may under some circumstances be the innkeeper's duty to exclude such a person, for he is bound to protect the guest against troublesome tradesmen. The innkeeper is certainly under no obligation to furnish his inn as a free place of business for all tradesmen who wish to use it for that purpose. If the privilege of carrying on business in the inn is a valuable one, there is no reason why the innkeeper should not secure for himself that benefit. Accordingly, the innkeeper may either conduct himself, or make an exclusive contract with another to conduct a barbershop, newsstand, or other business in the inn.

[7] Id. at 436.   [8] 106 N.C. 766, 11 S.E. 478 (1890).

8:6 *Public Carriers Coming to Solicit Guest's Patronage*

There is, however, one case in which the right of the innkeeper to exploit the privilege of using the inn for his own benefit may, it seems, be limited. In any business not connected with travel he may do as he pleases and the guest has no right to complain; but as the inn is established for the comfort and safety of travelers, and the innkeeper is under a public duty to secure that comfort and safety, he owes a fiduciary protection toward his guest in all that concerns traveling, and he is, therefore, not permitted to do anything which might bring his own private interests into competition with the interest of his guest in any matter that is connected with the guest's journey. The departure from the inn, in continuation of the guest's journey, is, therefore, a matter in which the innkeeper must act solely for the benefit of the guest, and cannot permit his own interest in any way to come into competition with the guest's interest. Any arrangement, therefore, by which he permits one carrier to enter the inn and solicit the patronage of the guest, in connection with his departure, and refuses to permit other competing carriers to do the same, is not permitted to him; for the guest, finding his patronage solicited by a carrier, will naturally conclude that he must deal with that carrier if he is to get away from the inn, and even if he knows that there is another competing carrier he will be under an inducement to deal with the first carrier owing to the greater convenience of so doing. This advantage extended by the innkeeper to one carrier over another will enable the favored carrier to obtain a larger compensation for his services from the guest than he could get if the competition were equal, and this is detrimental to the interest of the guest. It is true that the favored carrier is obliged to carry the guest at a reasonable rate, but that reasonable rate is not a rate that is rigidly fixed; and a rate considerably higher than a competitive rate may nevertheless be reasonable. If, as may usually be the case, the carrier is obliged to pay the innkeeper a certain sum for his privilege, he will be entitled to have the amount so paid included in the rate he may charge, since it seems a part of his legitimate expenses. Since, therefore, the innkeeper in giving the exclusive privilege of soliciting patronage to one carrier is acting to the detriment of his guest in a matter which concerns the continuation of his journey, the innkeeper's action is illegal, and the competing carrier has a right to demand admittance for the purpose of soliciting the patronage of the guests. This right, it will be noticed, is based upon the right of the guest not to be subjected to a monopoly, and the carrier, therefore, will have no right to demand admittance if all carriers are equally excluded from the inn.

The leading case on this point is *Markham* v. *Brown*,[9] in which it was held that an innkeeper who admitted to his inn the representative of one line of stagecoaches which passed through the town could not lawfully exclude the representative of another competing line.

8:7 *Right of Stranger Forfeited by Misconduct*

It is clear that this right, like the right of the guest himself, may be forfeited by the misconduct of the visitor, and may even be denied because of the bad character or bad intentions of the visitor. The language of Judge Parsons to this effect has already been quoted (8:4) and to the same effect is the opinion of the New Hampshire Supreme Court in *Markham* v. *Brown:*

[T]he defendant might forfeit this right by his misconduct, so that the plaintiff might require him to depart, and expel him; and if, by reason of several instances of misconduct, it appeared to be necessary for the protection of his guests or of himself, the plaintiff might prohibit the defendant from entering again, until the ground of apprehension was removed. Thus if affrays or quarrels were caused through his fault, or he was noisy, disturbing the guests in the house—interfered with its due regulation—intruded into the private rooms—remained longer than was necessary, after being requested to depart—or otherwise abused his right, as by improper importunity to guests to induce them to take passage with him; the plaintiff would have a right to reform that, and, if necessary, to forbid the defendant to enter, and treat him as a trespasser if he disregarded the prohibition.

So, if, after a lawful entry of the defendant, he committed an assault upon the plaintiff, or any trespass upon his property; the plaintiff might treat him as having entered for the unlawful purpose, and as a trespasser *ab initio*. [Citations omitted.] [10]

[9] 8 N.H. 523 (1837).   [10] *Id.* at 531.

When a person otherwise having a right to enter is refused admittance because it is suspected that he intends to do wrong after he enters, or because he is a person of bad character or reputation, the responsibility of the innkeeper is evidently large. So far as the authorities go, the innkeeper may undoubtedly justify exclusion on such a ground. Yet it is a difficult matter to establish a mere evil intention; and in the ordinary case it is the wiser course to admit the applicant, subject to the rules of the inn, and eject him when he violates a rule or does any act justifying exclusion.

8:8 *Stranger Entering to Make Inquiry*

In one class of cases, however, one who is neither a guest nor a person having business with a guest may enter an inn. One may have occasion to make inquiry at the office of an inn either into some matter connected with the business of the inn or even for a letter or message addressed to himself. If all inns had the same accommodations and charged the same prices, persons who desired accommodation would not need to make inquiry before deciding which inn to patronize; or if in each place there was but a single inn there would be no object in such an investigation. But wherever more than one inn is found in a town, the traveler needs information before he can choose which inn to patronize. It must be his right, therefore, before deciding to become a guest, to enter and inquire what room he can get and what price will be charged, and to make such other investigation as is possible. While no decided case has been found in which this subject is discussed, the right is believed to be beyond question; and in the analogous case of a common carrier it has been so held. A person going to a railroad station in order to get a timetable, but not at that time to take a train, has been held to have a right on the premises.[11]

It is the custom of inns to receive letters and telegrams addressed to strangers and to keep them a reasonable time to be called for. While, of course, an innkeeper cannot be compelled to accept such communications, still if he makes a practice of doing so (as in fact is true of most innkeepers) it seems to be clear that he must admit to the office bona fide persons coming to make inquiries for such communications. This is of course not a duty placed upon the innkeeper by

[11] *Bradford* v. *Boston & Maine R.R.*, 160 Mass. 392, 35 N.E. 1131 (1894).

reason of any provision of the law of innkeepers; but it results necessarily from the practice of innkeepers, as it has just been described. An illustration of the importance of this right may be found in the English case of *Strauss* v. *County Hotel and Wine Co., Ltd.*[12] In that case a person came to an inn intending to stay overnight, and found waiting for him a telegram summoning him to another city. If the innkeeper as a matter of good business policy consents to receive such messages, he leads travelers to depend upon being admitted to inquire for them; and he cannot therefore refuse to admit them.

[12] [1883] 12 Q.B.D. 27.

CHAPTER 9

Legal Excuses for Refusal
to Receive a Guest

9:1 *Refusal to Receive Guest Because of Lack of Accommodation*

When the innkeeper's accommodations are exhausted, he may refuse to receive an applicant as a guest. If all his sleeping rooms are occupied, he need not admit a guest to sleep in a sitting room or (in modern times) to share the bedroom of another guest. In an English case, an applicant who had been refused admission to an inn because the inn was full sued the innkeeper and proved that the coffee room was unoccupied, and that there was room, without overcrowding, for the applicant to sleep in a room with another guest. The court held, nevertheless, that he had been rightly refused admission.[1] Lord Alverston, C.J., was of the opinion that even if the applicant had asked to occupy the coffee room, he might legally have been refused. Darling, J., said:

No doubt an innkeeper is bound to provide accommodation for travellers, but he is not bound to do so at all risks and all costs. He is only bound to provide accommodation so long as his house is not full; when it is full he has no duty in that respect. The question then arises, when an innkeeper's house may properly be said to be full. I do not think that the old cases can help one very much, because in olden times people were in the habit of sleeping many in one room, and several in one bed. People who were absolutely unknown to each other would sleep in the same room, as is done in common lodging-houses at the present time. Therefore, if we got a definition of "full" in one of the old cases, I should not be surprised to find that what was called "full" then we should now call "indecent overcrowding." It is the habit now of people to occupy separate bedrooms, and, having regard to the ordinary way of living at the present

[1] *Browne* v. *Brandt*, [1902] 1 K.B. 696.

[78]

time, I think an inn may be said to be full for the purpose of affording accommodation for the night if all the bedrooms are occupied. There might have been a difficulty here if the plaintiff had said, "I will take your sitting room. I do not want to go to bed. I will sit up all night." But that difficulty does not arise on the facts of this case. The county court judge has found that the house was full having regard to modern ways of living. He referred to Chaucer and the Canterbury pilgrims. One need only look at the "Sentimental Journey" to see how people's habits have altered since the time of Laurence Sterne. I am of opinion that the county court judge's decision was right.[2]

It might be added that rooms held under reservations for incoming guests can be said to be occupied, and that rooms "out of order" and thus not available for occupancy are not to be counted.

Excluding a traveler on the ground that "the house is full" is an affirmative defense and the burden of pleading and proving it rests on the innkeeper.[3]

9:2 Refusal to Receive Persons of Objectionable Character or Condition

An innkeeper holds out his house as a public place to which travelers may resort, and, of course, surrenders some of the rights which he would otherwise have over it. Holding it out as a place of accommodation for travelers, he cannot prohibit persons who come under that character, in a proper manner and at suitable times, from entering, so long as he has the means of accommodation for them.

However, an innkeeper is not obliged to make his house a common receptacle for all comers, whatever may be their character or condition. He is not obliged to receive one who is not able to pay for his entertainment,[4] and there are considerations of greater importance than this. He is indictable if he usually harbors thieves,[5] and he is answerable for the safekeeping of the goods of his guests,[6] and is not

<hr>

[2] Id. at 698.

[3] Jackson v. Virginia Hot Springs Co., 209 F. 979 (W.D.Va. 1913).

[4] Thompson v. Lacy, 106 Eng. Rep. 667 (K.B. 1820).

[5] M. Bacon, A New Abridgement of the Law (Philadelphia, 1852), vol. 5, p. 226.

[6] See generally J. Story, Commentaries on the Law of Bailments, 9th ed. (Boston, 1878), pp. 429–456.

bound to admit one whose notorious character as a thief furnishes good reason to suppose that he will purloin the goods of the guests or of the innkeeper himself. So he is also liable if his house is disorderly, and he cannot be held to wait until an affray has begun before he interposes, but may exclude common brawlers, as well as any one else who comes with the intent to commit an assault or make an affray. He may also prohibit the entry of one whose misconduct in other particulars, or whose filthy condition, would subject his guests to annoyance. He has the right to prohibit common drunkards and idle persons from entering, and to require them, and others before mentioned, to depart if they have already entered. And any person entering not for lawful purpose, but to do an unlawful act—as to commit an assault upon one lawfully there—must be deemed a trespasser in entering for such unlawful purpose.[7]

An innkeeper may exclude a person who is widely publicized in the public press as a common gambler, a "gangster," a "mobster," a "tinhorn punk," an ex-convict, or a person who is habitually picked up by the police for questioning, and whose presence in the inn would injure the good reputation of the innkeeper and his house, and would tend to keep desirable clientele away from it.[8]

Mere unconventionality of costume would not, however, be a ground for refusal to receive a guest, so long as the costume is decent. In *Regina v. Sprague*,[9] a lady traveler in "rational dress," which happened to be a cycling costume, was refused by the defendant innkeeper permission to lunch in the coffee shop of the inn, but was offered refreshment in the bar parlour. She refused service in the bar and had the innkeeper indicted for unlawfully and wilfully neglecting and refusing to supply her as a traveler with refreshment without sufficient cause. The jury returned a verdict of not guilty, fully vindicating the innkeeper.

Whether an innkeeper might exclude a woman appearing in a miniskirt is not wholly free from doubt. Exclusion may be justified if, because of physical characteristics, shape, age, manners, etc., her appearance would create a commotion and result in unfavorable comments by other guests in the house. A rule requiring decent, conven-

[7] *Markham v. Brown*, 8 N.H. 523 (1837).
[8] *Goodenow v. Travis*, 3 Johns. (N.Y.) 427 (Sup. Ct. 1808).
[9] 63 J.P. 233 (Surrey Quarter Sessions 1899).

tional dress in the public rooms of the inn would seem to be a reasonable rule, enforceable by the innkeeper.

9:3 Restriction of Accommodation to Certain Classes

It is uncertain on the authorities how far an innkeeper may consent to receive only a certain class of guests. It is no doubt competent for an innkeeper to fix the character of his entertainment so high that his reasonable charges will shut out all but wealthy or well-to-do patrons. "[H]e does not absolutely engage to receive every person who comes to his house, but only such as are capable of paying a compensation suitable to the accommodation provided." [10] If, however, a person applies for such accommodation and is prepared to pay the price demanded, the innkeeper could hardly refuse to receive the guest on the ground that he was a poor man and ought not to afford such an entertainment.

In *Johnson v. Midland Railway Co.*,[11] Baron Parke said, "A man may keep an inn for those persons only who come in their own carriages." This doctrine seems doubtful, but it would seem competent for an innkeeper to maintain a house for the accommodation of men, or women, or elderly persons only.[12]

9:4 Refusal to Receive One Whose Companions Have Acted Improperly

An innkeeper cannot refuse to receive a guest or other person otherwise admissible because companions of the applicant have previously misconducted themselves.[13] Thus in a leading case an innkeeper refused to serve an applicant because he belonged to the militia and wore its uniform, and other members of the militia wearing the same uniform had previously misconducted themselves. The innkeeper alleged that he was unable to discriminate between them, and took them all as parties who came there to create a disturbance in the house. This excuse was held insufficient.[14] Emery, J., said:

[10] *Thompson v. Lacy*, 106 Eng. Rep. 667 (K.B. 1820).
[11] 154 Eng. Rep. 1254 (Ex. 1849).　　　　[12] *Id.* at 1256.
[13] *Markham v. Brown*, 8 N.H. 523 (1837).
[14] *Atwater v. Sawyer*, 76 Me. 539 (1884).

[T]he offered testimony would not be admissible unless it logically tended to prove a reasonable cause for such belief. The bill of exceptions states, that some eighty or a hundred men, members of two militia companies, and clad in the uniform of the Maine militia arrived in town on the day named; that "more or less" of them (how many is not stated) went to the defendant's inn, and there behaved in a disorderly and insulting manner. These plaintiffs though members of the militia companies, were not of this disorderly party, nor with them. It is not claimed that the plaintiffs were otherwise than sober, orderly and respectable. The only connection shown between them and the disorderly ones was their membership of the same militia companies. It is not even shown they were of the same company. The only similarity in appearance was in the uniform. Such membership was honorable, and there was not in that any reasonable cause to believe the plaintiffs intended insult. The uniform was honorable and the rightful wearing it by the plaintiffs was no reasonable cause for apprehension of insult. We do not know how many of the organization had misbehaved. We have no right to assume the number was large. We ought rather to assume the number was small. It would be illogical and unjust to say, there was reasonable cause to believe that every member of those companies meditated misconduct because a small number of them had already misconducted. Yet if there was reasonable cause to fear insult from the plaintiffs, there was equal cause to fear it from every member.

The defendant's claim that he could not distinguish between the plaintiffs and the others, cannot be admitted against the plaintiffs' right to entertainment. The plaintiffs were not with the others. Their rights cannot be abridged by the similarity in appearance to other persons not present. It was the defendant's duty to discriminate.[15]

9:5 *Refusal to Receive One Who Brings an Animal*

We have seen earlier that an innkeeper is under legal obligation to receive not only the person of a guest, but the luggage or baggage that he brings with him, as well. If the guest insists on bringing animals, the innkeeper has the choice of admitting or refusing them. If the animals are dangerous or, by reason of size or disposition, likely to frighten or harm other guests in the house, exclusion would be proper.

[15] *Id.* at 541–542.

In an English case, it appeared that a person who had been in the habit of bringing one or more dogs with him to an inn, to the annoyance of guests, had been forbidden by the innkeeper to come to the inn with a dog. Notwithstanding this, he demanded admittance, having with him a large dog in leash. The innkeeper refused to admit him and was indicted for the refusal. The court held that the refusal was justifiable.[16] In the course of his opinion, Chief Baron Kelly said:

I do not lay down positively that under no circumstances could a guest have a right to bring a dog into an inn. There may possibly be circumstances in which, if a person came to an inn with a dog, and the innkeeper refused to put up the dog in any stable or outhouse, and there were nothing that could make the dog a cause of alarm or annoyance to others, the guest might be justified in bringing the dog into the inn. But it is not necessary to decide any such question. In this case, looking at the previous facts, the number of dogs previously brought, and their kind and behavior, the nature of the right claimed by the prosecutor in his letter [To "follow his inclinations" in bringing dogs, when they were not wet and dirty], and the size and class of the dog, I think the defendant would have had ample ground for his refusal.[17]

Mr. Justice Manisty added that, in his opinion, "a guest cannot, under any circumstances, insist on bringing a dog into any room or place in an inn where other guests are." [18]

The control of domestic animals, particularly dogs, is often regulated by municipal ordinances. In the city of New York, Section 161.05 of the New York City Health Code provides: "A person who owns, possesses or controls a dog shall not permit it to be in any public place or in any open or unfenced area abutting on a public place unless the dog is effectively restrained by a leash or chain not more than six feet long."

Section 161.03 of the code further provides: "A person who owns, possesses or controls a dog, cat or other animal shall not permit the animal to commit a nuisance on a sidewalk of any public place, on a floor, wall, stairway or roof of any public or private premises used in common by the public, or on a fence, wall or stairway of a building abutting on a public place."

---

[16] *Regina* v. *Rymer,* [1877] 2 Q.B.D. 136, 46 L.J.M.C. 108.
[17] *Id.* at 140.   [18] *Id.* at 141.

A violation of the above sections of the code is made an offense punishable by a fine of $25.00 or ten (10) days in jail or both.[19]

In the event it should be desirable to admit a domestic animal, be it a dog or a cat, the innkeeper may insist, as a condition of admittance, that a guest sign an agreement accepting full responsibility for any damage to person or property by the animal and agreeing to remove the animal in the event its behavior should become objectionable.

9:6 Exclusion of Persons Traveling without Baggage

It is well settled that an innkeeper is under legal obligation to admit not only the person of the traveler, but also the baggage he brings with him. But what about the person who applies for admission who has no baggage in his possession? The possession of baggage at the time of applying for admission to the inn prima facie identifies the applicant as a bona fide traveler. It also serves as security for the extension of credit. Absence of baggage may, therefore, be a just cause for inquiry. Such inquiry should, of course, be made tactfully, with due regard to the rights of those involved, and should not denote suspicion, hostility, or an undisguised assumption of unlawful or immoral intent. There may be valid reasons for the absence of baggage, as where a suburbanite is stranded in town or weather conditions impede travel. A more sensitive situation arises, as is illustrated in the case below, where couples of the opposite sex apply without baggage. Payment in advance in any appropriate case may always be demanded in a no-baggage situation.

9:7 Identification May Be Required of Couples of the Opposite Sex Applying for Admission without Baggage

COQUELET v. UNION HOTEL CO.
139 Md. 544, 115 A. 813 (1921)

[Action for slander.]

STOCKBRIDGE, J.: [Plaintiff, Henriette Coquelet, went from Washington to Baltimore accompanied by her husband, Lieutenant Henri Coquelet. They spent the afternoon in Baltimore, visited a motion picture house and, after the show, decided to get some food. Strolling,

[19] New York City Inferior Criminal Courts Act, Section 95.

they passed the Caswell Hotel, operated by defendant, where they dropped in to the grillroom for supper.]

"Before the supper was over Lieutenant Coquelet found himself feeling worse, and proposed to his wife that they remain in Baltimore over night, to which she assented. He accordingly left the table, went to the office of the hotel, and registered as Henri Coquelet and wife. Having registered, he inquired the price of rooms, was told the price of the rooms and, according to the testimony of Madame Coquelet, was told, after the clerk had learned that they had no baggage, that they could not be accommodated at the hotel with a room. He returned to the grill room, where he reported the substance of the interview he had just had to his wife, and at the conclusion of their repast both of them entered the office, and Madame Coquelet went to the clerk in charge, F. G. Murray, and asked for the reason that they were refused lodging for the night.

"According to Madame Coquelet's own testimony, she was attired in a 'fluffy French dress and picture hat and some other things,' and the clerk declined to give any reason for his refusal to give them a room. . . . [The assistant manager in charge upheld the conduct of the clerk and plaintiff and her husband left and found accommodation elsewhere.]

". . . [D]efendant's eighth prayer, . . . was to the effect that there was an established rule of the hotel that persons would not be assigned to a room there who were without baggage, in the absence of proper identification. This rule was one entirely reasonable in its character. When Lieutenant Coquelet registerd [sic], there is nothing to show that he was in any manner identified to the receiving clerk of the hotel except such as the receiving clerk might have inferred from his appearance."

[Judgment for defendant affirmed.]

9:8 *Exclusion of Business Competitors*

CHAMPIE v. CASTLE HOT SPRINGS CO.
27 Ariz. 463, 233 P. 1107 (1925)

[Suit in equity by Castle Hot Springs Co., an innkeeper, to enjoin defendant from unlawfully coming upon plaintiff's premises for the purpose of competing with plaintiff's livery business. The court below granted an injunction.]

LOCKWOOD, J.: "Has an innkeeper the right to refuse a competitor access to his premises, for the purpose of competition, when the presence of the latter is requested by one of the former's guests? Counsel for defendant urged most strenuously that to hold with plaintiff would be to establish a monopoly and make the guests practically prisoners, and that public policy denies to innkeepers unlimited rights over their own property, imposing on them certain duties to the general public.

"There is, of course, nothing to the statement that the guests are deprived of their freedom. They can come and go at will. It is true that the injunction does tend to establish a monopoly. But of what? Private property is, in its nature and purpose, a monopoly. The very essence thereof is that I may do as I will with my own, provided always that I do not interfere with the legal rights of others. One of the most cherished principles of our common law, to use the old phrase, is that 'a man's house is his castle, from which he may exclude any and all persons at will, even to the slaying of the invader.'

"No doubt innkeepers have some duties to the general public greater than that of ordinary property owners, but, so far as we are advised, it has never been held that they must furnish their private facilities for the use of a competitor in business. Cases involving the same general principles as the one at bar have frequently arisen, and it has been held almost invariably that the owner of the premises is within his rights in excluding a competitor therefrom. . . ." [Judgment affirmed.]

It may be doubtful whether an innkeeper can justify the refusal to receive a bona fide traveler merely because he intends to act in the interest of a rival inn. If that is his sole purpose in coming to the inn, he is not a bona fide traveler, and may be refused admittance on that ground; if he is a genuine guest the innkeeper must receive him but may prevent him from soliciting custom while a guest. The innkeeper unquestionably has such power and by the exercise of it he may sufficiently protect himself.

9:9 *Innkeeper's Monopoly of Business with Guests and Patrons within the Inn*

How far may an innkeeper go in his refusal to make his private facilities available to tradesmen who have legitimate contracts with guests or patrons of the inn? May he exclude a florist hired by a patron to decorate a function room for a wedding on the ground that the innkeeper has an exclusive contract with a florist concessionaire? It has been held:

An inn-keeper has, unquestionably, the right to establish a news-stand or a barber-shop in his hotel, and to exclude persons who come for the purpose of vending newspapers or books, or of soliciting employment as barbers and, in order to render his business more lucrative, he may establish a laundry or a livery-stable in connection with his hotel, or contract with the proprietor of a livery-stable in the vicinity to secure for the latter, as far as he legitimately can, the patronage of his guests in that line for a *per centum* of the proceeds or profits derived by such owner of vehicles and horses from dealing with the patrons of the public house. After concluding such a contract, the inn-keeper may make, and, after personal notice to violators, enforce a rule excluding from his hotel the agents and representatives of other livery-stables who enter to solicit the patronage of his guests, and where one has persisted in visiting the hotel for that purpose, after notice to desist, the proprietor may use sufficient force to expel him if he refuses to leave when requested, and may eject him, even though, on a particular occasion, he may have entered for a lawful purpose, if he does not disclose his true intent when requested to leave, or whatever may have been his purpose in entering, if he, in fact, has engaged in soliciting the patronage of the guests. . . .

. . . . The proprietors of the public house might legitimately share in the profits of any such incidental business, as furnishing carriages, buggies, or horses to the patrons, and for that purpose had as full right to close their house against one who attempted to injure the business in which they had such interest, as the owner of a private house would have had, and this view of the case is inconsistent with the doctrine enunciated in *Markham v. Brown*.[20]

That an innkeeper may lawfully forbid his guests or patrons from bringing into the inn food or beverages for consumption in the house,

[20] Avery, J., in *State v. Steele*, 106 N.C. 766, 783, 11 S.E. 478, 484 (1890).

thus lowering the innkeeper's business is beyond doubt. The privilege of doing so, if granted, may be made subject to a special charge, such as a "corkage charge."

Whether the innkeeper's common-law monopoly would constitute an unlawful restraint of trade in violation of State antimonopoly statutes has not been the subject of judicial decision. In New York, Section 340 of the General Business Law, commonly known as the Donnelly Act, provides in relevant part that "every contract, agreement, arrangement or combination whereby . . . competition or the free exercise of any activity in the conduct of any business, trade or commerce or in the furnishing of any service in this state is or may be restrained . . . is hereby declared to be against public policy, illegal and void."

In *Eagle Spring Water Co.* v. *Webb & Knapp, Inc.*,[21] the defendant, landlord of a commercial building in New York City, contractually barred all tenants from accepting, for use in the premises, drinking water and other services from any persons not authorized by the landlord. The plaintiff sued for and obtained injunctive relief against the defendant. The court found that the landlord itself was not in the water supply business, nor was it seeking to protect the interests of any tenant so engaged. The arbitrary choice of exclusive tradespeople to be used by tenants was solely for economic advantage to the landlord and completely unrelated to the protection of any legitimate interest in the property.

However, the facts in the *Eagle* case are readily distinguishable from the usual hotel or catering situation. The decoration of a function room, the food and beverages served at a function, the music performed, and the services rendered all combine to create a "package," an atmosphere which is a vitally important part of the character and of the image of the house and which the innkeeper may legitimately protect by either providing the services himself or by selecting exclusive concessionaires to do so.

21 236 N.Y.S.2d 266 (Sup. Ct. 1962).

CHAPTER 10

Innkeeper's Right to Evict One Who Has Been Admitted to the Inn

10:1 *Right to Eject in General*

Even after one has been admitted to an inn as a guest he may be ejected for proper cause. By his admission as a guest he is perhaps in a better position to demand the services of the innkeeper than when he first applied for admission, but probably this advantage is merely tactical. While the burden is on one who applies for admission to prove himself entitled to demand it, once he has been received as a guest the burden is placed on the innkeeper to justify the act of ejecting him. But as far as substantive rights go, it is doubtful that the guest gains any by securing admission to the inn. If, after his admission, circumstances occur which would have justified the innkeeper in refusing to admit him had they existed when he applied for admission, they will equally justify the innkeeper in ejecting him.

10:2 *Ejection for Misconduct*

If the guest after being received misconducts himself so as to annoy the other guests, he may for that cause be ejected from the inn. Thus, a guest who persists in annoying other guests by soliciting their custom in his business may be ejected. So one may be ejected who becomes obnoxious to other guests or to the innkeeper by reason of intoxication. Also, a guest may be ejected who makes a disturbance or engages in disorderly conduct in the inn. "If a man comes into a public-house, and conducts himself in a disorderly manner, and the landlord requests him to go out, and he will not, the landlord may turn him out. There is no doubt that a landlord may turn out a person who is making a disturbance in a public-house, though such a disturbance does not amount to a breach of the peace." [1]

10:3 *Ejection for Illness*

If a guest in the inn becomes ill, it is the duty of the innkeeper to treat him with the consideration due to a sick man. In the discharge of his duty, the innkeeper may call a physician to examine the sick guest and, if so requested by the guest, to treat him. If the guest refuses treatment or medical services and if, in the opinion of the physician who examined him, the guest's condition is serious, the guest may be removed to a hospital. In the event the diagnosis is one of contagious disease, this must be done promptly, under medical supervision, to protect the other guests in the house and for the preservation of public health.

In *Levy* v. *Corey,*[2] the plaintiff alleged that while his wife was confined to her room in the defendant's hotel, dangerously ill with typhoid fever, the defendant at three o'clock in the morning made noisy preparations, declaring it his intention to remove her from the hotel to an outhouse where the servants slept, unless the plaintiff paid twenty-five hundred dollars. The plaintiff, having paid the money, was suing to recover it on the ground that it was paid under duress. Chief Judge McAdam, of the City Court of New York, in charging the jury, stated the applicable law thus:

. . . [W]here a guest is taken ill at a hotel, with a contagious disease, likely to be communicated to others, the proprietor, after notifying the sick guest to leave, has the right to remove such guest in a careful and becoming manner, and at an appropriate hour, to some hospital or other place of safety, provided the life of the guest be not imperiled thereby. This is not only a right inherent in the hotel-keeper, but a duty owing to the other guests, and to the preservation of the public health.

Second. If the hotel-keeper exercises these rights at an improper time, or in an illegal and unbecoming manner, he is liable, therefor, on the ground of negligence, or for the abuse of authority.

[1] *Howell* v. *Jackson,* 172 Eng. Rep. 1435, 1436 (N.P. 1834).
[2] 1 City Ct. Rep. Supp. 57 (1884).

Third. The hotel keeper has the right, under the circumstances before detailed, to make any reasonable arrangement for extra compensation, the amount of which is left largely to the mutual agreement of the parties in interest, and when they mutually agree in respect thereto, the law will infer, that the price agreed upon is fair and just, and the burden of proving the contrary is on him who alleges imposition, or undue advantage. The agreement, to be legal, however, should be voluntary, and the result of mutual assent in respect to which the minds of both parties should meet.

Fourth. If, however, the hotel-keeper, not content to join in an agreement founded on mutual assent, determines to take advantage of the misfortune which has occurred in his house, makes threats to remove the guest when not in a condition to be removed, or threatens to remove such guest at a time or in a manner not warranted by the circumstances, and by force of such threats exacts from such guest, or her husband, a sum of money arbitrarily named by him, and not fixed by voluntary assent, nor warranted by the exigencies of the occasion, he commits a wrong which the law will not tolerate; he has exacted the money so obtained by duress, and acquires no title to it, and it can be recovered back by the person from whom it was wrongfully exacted.

McHUGH v. SCHLOSSER
159 Pa. 480, 28 A. 291 (1894)

WILLIAMS, J.: "The defendants are hotelkeepers in the city of Pittsburgh. McHugh was their guest and died in an alley appurtenant to the hotel on the second day of February, 1891. Mary McHugh the plaintiff is his widow, and she seeks to recover damages for the loss of her husband, alleging that it was caused by the improper conduct of the defendants and their employees. . . . McHugh came to the Hotel Schlosser late on Friday night, January 30th, registered, was assigned to and paid for a room for the night, and retired. On Saturday and Sunday he complained of being ill and remained most of both days in bed. A physician was sent for at his request, who prescribed for him. He also asked for and obtained several drinks during the same time, and an empty bottle or bottles remained in his room after he left it. During the forenoon of Monday he seemed bewildered and wandered about the hall on the floor on which his room was. About the middle of the day the housekeeper reported to Schlosser that he

[McHugh] was out of his room and sitting half dressed on the side of the bed in another room. Schlosser and his porter both started in search of McHugh, and Schlosser seems to have exhibited some excitement or anger. He was found and the porter led him to his room. While this was being done Schlosser said to him 'You can't stay here any longer'; to which McHugh replied 'I'll git.' The porter, on reaching his room, put his coat, hat and shoes on him and at once led him to the freight elevator, put him on it, and had him let down to the ground floor. He then took him through a door, used for freight, out into an alley some four or five feet wide, that led to Penn avenue. Rain was falling, and the day was cold. A stream of rain water and dissolving snow was running down the alley. McHugh was without overshoes, overcoat or wraps of any description. When the porter had gotten him part way down the alley he fell to the pavement. While he was lying in the water and the porter standing near him, a lady passed along the sidewalk on Penn avenue and saw him. She walked a square, found Officer White, and reported to him what she had seen. He went to the alley to investigate; and when he arrived McHugh had gotten to his feet, but was leaning heavily against the wall of the hotel, apparently unable to step. The porter was behind him with his hands upon him, apparently urging him forward. What followed will be best told in the officer's own words. He says: 'I asked what's the matter with this man, Mr. Powers? He says, he's sick. I says he ought to have something done for him, and at that time he fell right in the alley on his back. He had his coat open, no vest, and his shoes were untied. He had strings in his shoe, but not tied.' The officer was asked if the man spoke, after he reached the place where he was; and he replied thus: 'He spoke to me. Somebody said he was drunk. He rolled his eyes up and he says, "Officer, I am not drunk; I am sick; I wish you would get an ambulance and have me taken to the hospital." Then I ran to the patrol box.' It required about twenty minutes to get an ambulance on the ground. During all this time the man continued to lie on the pavement in the alley. At length, after an exposure of about half an hour in the storm and on the pavement, the ambulance came. He was placed on the stretcher, lifted into the ambulance and taken to police headquarters and thence to the hospital but all signs of life had disappeared when he was laid on the hospital floor. The postmortem examination disclosed the fact that the immediate cause of death was valvular disease of the heart. The theory of the plaintiff was that the shock from exposure to wet and cold in the alley had, in his feeble and unprotected condition, brought on the heart failure from which he died; and as the exposure resulted from the conduct or directions of the defendants, they were responsible for his death.

"Three principal questions were thus raised: First, what duty does an inn keeper owe to his guest? Second, what connection was there between the defendants' disregard of their duty, if they did disregard it in any particular, and the death of Mr. McHugh? Third, if the plaintiff be entitled to recover, what is the measure of her damages?

". . . [As to the first of these questions the trial judge, in charging the jury, had stated the rule thus:] 'If [the annoying acts] . . . were the result of sickness, although they might under certain circumstances remove him, such removal must be in a manner suited to his condition.' This was saying that if McHugh was intoxicated, and the disturbances made by him were due to his intoxication, he might be treated as a drunken man; but if he was sick, and the disturbances caused by him were due to his sickness, he must be treated with the consideration due to a sick man. This is a correct statement of the rule. In the delirium of a fever a sick man may become very troublesome to a hotelkeeper, and his groans and cries may be annoying to the occupants of rooms near him, but this would not justify turning him forcibly from his bed into the street during a winter storm. What the condition of the decedent really was, went properly to the jury for determination. If they found the fact to be that he was suffering from sickness, then the learned judge properly said that, if his removal was to be undertaken, it should be conducted in a manner suited to one in his condition.

"[Second] . . . The question which the defendants were bound to consider before putting the decedent out in the storm, was not whether such exposure 'would' surely cause death, but what was it reasonable to suppose might follow such a sudden exposure of the decedent in the condition in which he then was? What were the probable consequences of pushing a sick man, in the condition the decedent was in, out into the storm without adequate covering, and when he fell from inability to stand on his feet, leaving him to lie in the stream of melting ice and snow that ran over the pavement of the alley, for about half an hour in all, in the condition in which officer White found him?

"[Third] . . . The true measure of damages is the pecuniary loss suffered, without any solatium for mental suffering or grief; and the pecuniary loss is what the deceased would probably have earned by his labor, physical or intellectual, in his business or profession, if the injury that caused death had not befallen him, and which would have gone to the support of his family. In fixing this amount, consideration should be given to the age of the deceased, his health, his ability and disposition to labor, his habits of living and his expenditures." [Judgment for plaintiff reversed and a new trial ordered.]

10:4   *Ejection for Refusal to Pay*

As the innkeeper may refuse to admit a traveler at the beginning unless he will pay in advance, so he may eject him if after admission he falls into arrears and fails on demand to pay the amount due the innkeeper. The hotel bill accrues and is due day-by-day (*de die in diem*) on demand (that is, a separate demand may be made for each day's bill as it accrues). The innkeeper is not required to provide food or service for a guest who refuses to pay a proper charge. The innkeeper may refuse food or service even if he does not eject the guest from the premises. Refusal of service may cause many a headstrong guest to leave and save the innkeeper the problem of physical ejection.

MORNINGSTAR v. LAFAYETTE HOTEL CO.
211 N.Y. 465, 105 N.E. 656 (1914)

[Appeal from a judgment of the Appellate Division of the Supreme Court in the fourth judicial department, entered May 11, 1912, affirming a judgment in favor of defendant entered upon a verdict.

The nature of the action and the facts, sofar as material, are stated in the opinion.]

CARDOZO, J.: "The plaintiff was a guest at the Lafayette Hotel in the city of Buffalo. He seems to have wearied of the hotel fare, and his yearning for variety has provoked this lawsuit. He went forth and purchased some spareribs, which he presented to the hotel chef with a request that they be cooked for him and brought to his room. This was done, but with the welcome viands there came the unwelcome addition of a bill or check for $1, which he was asked to sign. He refused to do so, claiming that the charge was excessive. That evening he dined at the café, and was again asked to sign for the extra service, and again declined. The following morning, Sunday, when he presented himself at the breakfast table, he was told that he would not be served. This announcement was made publicly, in the hearing of other guests. He remained at the hotel till Tuesday, taking his meals elsewhere, and he then left. The trial judge left it to the jury to say whether the charge was a reasonable one, instructing them that if it was, the defendant had a right to refuse to serve the plaintiff further, and that if it was not, the refusal was wrongful. In this, there was no error. An innkeeper is not required to entertain a guest who has refused to pay a lawful charge. Whether the charge in controversy was excessive, was a question for the jury.

"The plaintiff says, however, that there was error in the admission of evidence which vitiates the verdict. In this we think that he is right. He alleged in his complaint that the defendant's conduct had injured his reputation. He offered no proof on that head, but the defendant took advantage of the averment to prove what the plaintiff's reputation was. A number of hotel proprietors were called as witnesses by the defendant, and under objection were allowed to prove that, in their respective hotels, the plaintiff's reputation was that of a chronic faultfinder. Some of them were permitted to say that the plaintiff was known as a 'kicker.' Others were permitted to say that his reputation was bad, not in respect of any moral qualities, but as the guest of a hotel. The trial judge charged the jury that they must find for the defendant if they concluded that the plaintiff had suffered no damage, and this evidence was received to show that he has suffered none.

"It is impossible to justify the ruling. The plaintiff, if wrongfully ejected from the café, was entitled to recover damages for injury to his feelings as a result of the humiliation [citations omitted]; but his reputation as a faultfinder was certainly not at issue. The damages recoverable for such a wrong were no less because the occupants of other hotels were of the opinion that he complained too freely. In substance, it has been held that the plaintiff might be refused damages for the insult of being put out of a public dining room because other innkeepers considered him an undesirable guest." [Judgment reversed and a new trial granted.]

10:5 *Ejection of Husband from Wife's Bedroom*

WARREN *v.* PENN-HARRIS HOTEL CO.
91 Pa. Super. 195 (1927)

"Trespass to recover damages for alleged unlawful treatment by employees of a hotel. [Judgment for plaintiffs from which defendant appealed.]

KELLER, J.: "Both actions were based on averments that the plaintiffs—who were husband and wife—had been received by the defendant as guests in the hotel operated and maintained by it and that in violation of the rights due them as such guests they had been humiliated, insulted, disturbed and inconvenienced by the unwarranted acts and conduct of the defendant's employees, as set forth in the several statements of claim.

"There is no doubt that Mrs. Warren was received as a guest of defendant's hotel, and assigned a room for her use and occupancy; but the evidence, on careful reading . . . shows that he [Dr. Warren, her husband] was not a guest of the hotel, in the sense that a room had been assigned him for his use, but that, on the night in question, without the knowledge or acquiescence of the defendant and its responsible agents, he was occupying, in company with his wife, a single room which had been assigned for her sole use and occupancy. The fact that he ate some supper in the coffee room conducted by the hotel did not make him a guest with the right to occupy a room of the hotel; nor did the mere fact that his wife was a guest of the hotel, in occupancy of a room assigned to her, authorize him to share such room and sleep there that night without the knowledge and consent of the defendant, acting through its duly constituted agents. . . .

"Mrs. Warren testified that travelling by herself by train from St. Louis she arrived at Harrisburg between nine and ten o'clock on the morning of August 11th and went directly to the hotel, and had breakfast there. She did not then engage a room, but made use of the waiting room, ladies room and parlor. She inquired at the desk whether there was any message for her from her husband, Dr. Warren, of New York, whom she had expected to meet her and was awaiting

word from him, as an emergency might have detained him. . . .
Around two o'clock in the afternoon, not having heard from her
husband and concluding he was on his way by automobile, she
registered and was assigned a single room. . . .

"Late in the afternoon she told the clerk she was expecting her
husband, Dr. Warren, and if he came she would be in the dining
room; but she did not register for him nor notify the clerk that, if
he came, he intended to spend the night there and occupy her room.
When Dr. Warren arrived at the hotel and inquired for his wife, he
was given the message she had left for him; but he did not register
himself nor inform the clerk that he would spend the night in the
hotel and share the room assigned to his wife. There was, therefore,
no notice of any kind to the hotel authorities that Mrs. Warren's room
would also be occupied by her husband, and the additional charge
made by the hotel for an extra person sleeping in an assigned room
was not imposed.

"When, therefore, the house detective making his regular rounds
between eleven o'clock and midnight to see that things about the
hotel were as they should be, heard a man talking to a woman in a
dark room which his records showed had been assigned to a woman
alone, and after satisfying himself by communicating with the office
downstairs that his records were correct, knocked on the door but
received no answer, he was justified in opening the door and asking
who the man was and what he was doing there; and on being informed that the man was Dr. Warren, the husband of the registered
occupant, he was within his authority and violated no rights of Dr.
Warren in demanding that if the latter was the husband of the occupant of the room, he should so register. Such measures and precautions are taken for the benefit not only of the hotel but of the other
guests as well. A hotel which knowingly permits couples of different
sexes to occupy the same rooms without registering as husband and
wife is correctly regarded as a disorderly house, and those in charge
of it may be prosecuted for maintaining such a house, and persons
frequenting it are affected by its character. Hence a hotel is required
to be careful in such matters for the protection of its guests no less
than on its own account.

"As before stated, Dr. Warren was not a guest of the hotel and no
duty was owing to him as such guest; hence the averment on which

his cause of action was based cannot be sustained and judgment should have been entered in his action for the defendant notwithstanding the verdict. . . .

"Mrs. Warren's case is in a different situation. She was a guest and was entitled to the protection and treatment due a guest. While her husband had no right to occupy her room with her without notifying the hotel clerk of his intention to do so, and registering if requested, there is nothing in the case to show that she knew he had not registered or informed the clerk of his intention to share the room with her. Hence it was not shown that she knew she was violating the rules of the hotel. Nevertheless there was such a violation, and had the house detective done nothing more than open the door when he knocked and received no reply, and inquire who the man was and what he was doing there, and upon being informed that it was her husband, insist on his being registered as such, we would enter judgment for the defendant in her case also. But there is some testimony that the detective became abusive and insulting. . . . [I]f after she had explained that her companion was her husband, the detective, without investigating the truth of her declaration, called her names impugning her chastity, or subsequently when the Warrens were leaving the hotel he again assailed her with like epithets, he went too far and made his employer who had committed this line of work to him as part of his duties liable in damages for the injury inflicted. . . .

"Judgment [for Mrs. Warren] reversed, with a new venire."

BOYCE v. GREELEY SQUARE HOTEL CO.
181 App. Div. 61, 168 N.Y.S. 191 (2d Dep't), aff'd, 228
N.Y. 106, 126 N.E. 647 (1917)

[The plaintiff, accompanied by her husband and daughter, went to the Hotel McAlpin on September 21, 1915, at about 7 o'clock in the evening. Plaintiff's husband informed defendant's room clerk that he wanted a room for his wife and daughter, whom he registered as "Mrs. Alexander R. Boyce and Miss Florence Boyce." A room was assigned to them on the fifteenth floor and defendant's clerk explained that plaintiff's husband would be given permission to visit her and to give her treatments. The next day plaintiff's husband called about

5 P.M. while plaintiff was out shopping, and obtained her room key from the floor clerk. When plaintiff returned, all three had dinner and while plaintiff's daughter remained downstairs plaintiff and her husband went up to the room. There, behind locked doors, plaintiff undressed put on her night robe, and lying on the bed prepared for a treatment. A douche pan was placed under her and her husband proceeded with the treatment. When he was about half finished, there was a knock on the door, and a demand that it be opened or it would be broken in. Plaintiff's husband, after inquiring who was there and receiving no reply, went to the door, which he unlocked and opened. The defendant's head house officer, Denniston, and his assistant, Brazier, were standing in the hall. Mr. Boyce inquired: "Who are you? What do you want?" Denniston replied: "I am the hotel detective. You are prostituting this hotel. You are using this place for a whore house." Plaintiff's husband said: "This lady is my wife; I am giving her douches." Denniston replied: "So much the worse, you are under arrest; come along with us." Mr. Boyce replied: "You wait until I get through what I am doing. I will show you in a moment who I am. I have got commutation, and I have got letters." Plaintiff testified that in addition to the conversation mentioned, Denniston called her a prostitute. Plaintiff's husband accompanied the detectives to the office and upon his return found his wife in hysterics and suffering pain, which she has suffered "ever since."]

RICH, J.: "While an innkeeper has the right to make and enforce proper rules to prevent immorality, or any other form of misconduct tending to injure the reputation of his house, or which violates the recognized moralities and proprieties of life, and has the right of access to the room of a guest under reasonable and proper circumstances and at proper times, such rule has no application to the facts presented by the record in the case at bar, and does not furnish a defense to the plaintiff's cause of action, for the reason that the defendant had notice that the plaintiff and the man who accompanied her to the hotel and to the room assigned her were husband and wife, and the further fact that she was an invalid requiring treatment at times, which had to be given her by her husband; a room was given her on the fifteenth floor for the express purpose of permitting her husband to visit her therein, and he was informed that he might do so. If any permission was required, it was given. Furthermore, there was concededly a telephone in plaintiff's room, and the house detectives admitted that they knew that fact and that they could have ascertained the relation of the parties occupying the room and for what purpose the plaintiff's husband was in her room, without going to the room at all. They testified that their purpose in going there was to learn from the man and woman who the man was and for what purpose he was there.

". . . No authority to which our attention is directed sustains the appellant's contention that the damages which are recoverable in this action are not such as would fully compensate the plaintiff for the pain, suffering, humiliation and impaired health which she suffered and which were the direct result and consequence of the defendant's breach of duty. Plaintiff's recovery in the case at bar was expressly limited by the trial court to compensatory damages. Every other element of damages, including punitive damages and the alleged slander, were excluded, and the verdict represents actual damages, the direct result and consequence of defendant's breach of duty, and is compensatory only. . . .

"It is contended that the verdict is excessive. Twelve men of affairs have assessed plaintiff's damages at $8,000, and the learned and experienced justice who presided at the trial has found that it is not excessive. In these circumstances, any lingering doubt as to whether the verdict was excessive should be resolved in favor of defendant's innocent victim." [Affirmed.][3]

[3] One of the issues at the trial related to the admissibility of a certain letter from defendant's manager to plaintiff's husband, written a week after the occurrence upon which the action was founded: September 30, 1915. Mr. Alexander R. Boyce, Long Island City, L.I.—Dear Mr. Boyce: We would like to have our Mr. Denniston, who so unfortunately gave you offense in the manner he handled the unusual incident of your recent stay at the McAlpin, call to apologize. We hope that you will be so lenient as to permit this, and we sincerely trust you will be willing to accept the apology. We feel that Mr. Denniston was overzealous and very mistaken in his attitude toward you. The only extenuation is in our rigid policy of protecting the good name and repute of this hotel in the way explained to you by the writer. If you will kindly take this into consideration, and accept Mr. Denniston's apology, we hope you will then feel everything possible in the way of reparation has been done. With deep regret that you should have suffered so unfortunate an annoyance, we are, Very truly yours, Merry & Boomer, Managers, L. M. Boomer.

Defendant objected to the admission in evidence of the letter on the ground

10:6 *Ejection of Woman of Bad Reputation*

RAIDER *v.* DIXIE INN
198 Ky. 152, 248 S.W. 229 (1923)

SAMPSON, C. J.: "Appellant Thelma Raider applied to the Dixie Inn, at Richmond, for entertainment and paid her board and lodging for a week in advance, saying that her home was in Estill County and she had come to Richmond, at the expense of her mother, to take treatments from a physician. At the end of the week she paid in advance for another week, and so on until the end of a month, when she went down town, and on returning was informed by the proprietor and his wife, who are appellees in this case, that she no longer had a room at that hotel, and remarked to her that no explanation was due her as to why they had requested or forced her removal. Alleging that she was mortified and humiliated by the words and conduct of the proprietors of the hotel, appellant Raider brought this action to recover damages in the sum of $5,000.00. Appellees [denied in their answer the use of harsh or improper conduct] but admitted that they had required appellant to vacate her room and to leave the hotel and gave as their reason for so doing that she was a woman of bad character, recently an inmate of a house of prostitution in the city of Richmond and had been such for many years next before she came to the inn, and was in said city a notoriously immoral character; that appellees did not know her when she applied for entertainment at their hotel, but immediately upon learning who she was and her manner of life had moved her belongings out of the room into the lobby of the hotel, and kindly, quietly and respectfully asked her to leave; that they had in their hotel several ladies of good reputation who were embarrassed by the presence of appellant in the hotel and

---

that it was written after the happening of the events in the hotel and therefore not binding on the defendant.

The court, in overruling defendant's objection, held that in writing the letter, the manager was engaged in the business of his principal and in the performance of his duty and his act was within the scope of his authority and in any event the letter did no harm to defendant.

who declined to associate with her and were about to withdraw from the hotel if she continued to lodge there; that appellant had not been of good behaviour since she had become a patron of the hotel. . . . [Thereafter, plaintiff amended her original petition, by] adding the following paragraph:

" 'Plaintiff says that she is advised that these defendants (the Dixie Inn) had a legal right to remove her and that she does not question that right but that she was removed as a guest for hire from said Dixie Inn at a time that was *improper* and in a *manner* that was *unduly disrespectful* and *insulting* and that she was greatly *mortified* and *humiliated* thereby and suffered indignity because of the wrongful manner in which she was removed from said Dixie Inn as herein set out and complained of.'

"To the petition as amended the appellees demurred generally. This the court sustained and on the failure of appellant to further plead, dismissed her petition, and she appeals.

"As a general rule a guest who has been admitted to an inn may afterwards be excluded therefrom by the innkeeper if the guest refuses to pay his bill, or if he becomes obnoxious to the guests by his own fault, is a person of general bad reputation, or has ceased to be a traveller by becoming a resident. [Citation omitted.]

"It appears, therefore, fully settled that an innkeeper may lawfully refuse to entertain objectionable characters, if to do so is calculated to injure his business or to place himself, business or guests in a hazardous, uncomfortable or dangerous situation. The innkeeper need not accept anyone as a guest who is calculated to and will injure his business [citation omitted]. A prizefighter who has been guilty of law breaking may be excluded. *Nelson* v. *Boldt*, 180 Fed. 779. Neither is an innkeeper required to entertain a card sharp, *Watkins* v. *Cope*, 84 N.J.L. 143; a thief, *Markham* v. *Brown*, 8 N.H. 523; persons of bad reputation or those who are under suspicion, *Goodenow* [sic] v. *Travis*, 3 John's [sic] (N.Y.) 427 [citation omitted]; drunken and disorderly persons, *Atwater* v. *Sawyer*, 76 Maine 539; one who commits a trespass by breaking in the door, *Goodenow* v. *Travis, supra;* one who is filthy or who subjects the guests to annoyance, *Pidgeon* v. *Legge*, 5 Week. Rep. 649 [citation omitted].

"It, therefore, appears that the managers of the Dixie Inn had the right to exclude appellant from their hotel upon several grounds without becoming liable therefor, unless the means employed to remove her were unlawful. . . . The averments of the petition show she was not present at the time they took charge of her room and placed her belongings in the lobby of the hotel, where they were easily accessible to her; that when she came in they quietly told her that they had taken charge of her room and placed her belongings in the lobby of the hotel, where they were easily accessible to her; that when she came in they quietly told her that they had taken charge of her room, but gave no reason for doing so. We must believe from the averments of the petition that . . . the whole proceeding was very quiet and orderly. As they had a right to exclude her from the hotel they were guilty of no wrong in telling her so, even though there were other persons present in the lobby at the time they gave her such information, which is denied. . . .

"Judgment affirmed."

10:7 *Ejection of Homosexuals*

Homosexuals, in a desire to seek out one another, are accustomed to congregate in large numbers and tend to frequent hotel and restaurant bars as places of rendezvous. Innkeepers in New York City and San Francisco in particular are confronted by a social condition that is less acute in smaller communities, since quantities of such persons seek the anonymity afforded by life in a metropolis. They are often difficult to identify; their proclivities may remain dormant for long periods of time and be disclosed only momentarily.

The responsibility of management concerning what to do with homosexuals is very great indeed. The result of excluding patrons on suspicion, without sufficient ability to prove the point, may be an ugly suit for slander, assault, or malicious prosecution. Even a lawyer might be puzzled concerning what to do when confronted with such patronage. Since the innkeeper or restaurant keeper may be charged with suffering or permitting his premises to become disorderly and thus subject his liquor license to revocation (see Section 106(6) of the Alcoholic Beverage Control Laws of New York) the following suggestions are submitted for guidance:

1. Instruct the headwaiters, captains, waiters, and, in particular, the bartenders, to observe the conduct of patrons. If from actions or

conversation it becomes apparent that the premises are being used as a rendezvous, the matter should be reported to top management.

2. Offending patrons can and should be refused service and should be made aware that their patronage is not welcome.

3. In acute situations, a call upon the commanding officer of the local police precinct may be advisable to enlist his cooperation and to head off affirmative police action.

4. Legal counsel should be consulted at the outset for determining an appropriate course of action.

10:8 *Ejection of Discharged Employee*

A discharged employee who refuses upon request to leave the premises or who, not being a guest or patron, insists on reentering against the wishes of the innkeeper, may be lawfully ejected.[4]

10:9 *Ejection of Nonguests*

JENKINS *v.* KENTUCKY HOTEL, INC.
261 Ky. 419, 87 S.W.2d 951 (1935)

[Action to recover damages for an alleged assault claimed to have arisen from a request of the house detective that plaintiff leave the hotel.

It appeared that plaintiff, Ellen Jenkins, was sitting at about 9 P.M., in the lobby of the hotel waiting for her sister-in-law who was attending a meeting on the fourth floor of the hotel. While thus seated, the house detective approached her and asked her what she was doing there. She told him the purpose and object of her visit and she says that the detective told her in a rude and insulting manner that no such meeting was held in the hotel, and ordered her to leave the premises. She says his manner and demeanor were so threatening that she was afraid he would use force to evict her and she therefore left the hotel and returned later and joined her sister on the fourth floor.]

STITES, J.: "It is admitted that appellant was at most a mere licensee,

---

[4] *Hill* v. *Greeley Square Hotel Co.*, 175 App. Div. 421, 161 N.Y.S. 1085 (1st Dep't 1916).

and if she had been requested in a proper manner to leave the lobby and had failed to do so, reasonable force could lawfully have been used to eject her. It is contended, however, that the rude and insulting manner accompanying the request to leave was an assault. With this we cannot agree. Howsoever culpable may have been the words or attitude of the detective, there was no unlawful injury by force. . . . He had the right to eject appellant if she refused to leave as requested. Bad manners are not actionable. . . . There was no breach of any legal duty owed to appellant.

"Judgment affirmed."

A licensee is a person who is privileged to enter or to remain on the premises of another only by virtue of the possessor's consent. Consent may be given by words, either written or spoken, or it may be manifested by acts other than words. In determining whether a particular course of action is sufficient to manifest consent, account must be taken of customs prevailing in the community. If hotel-keepers in a city generally permit members of the public to enter the lobby and public halls and places in the hotel, persons, whether local residents or others, are justified in regarding the failure of the hotel-keeper to object to their presence as sufficient manifestation of a willingness to admit and permit them to remain.

When the consent express or implied is withdrawn, the license to remain terminates. One who thereafter persists in remaining on the premises over the objections of the hotel-keeper becomes a trespasser and may be removed as such.

It should be remembered that a hotel is a private place and the fact that visitors invited by guests and others may come and go in and out of the hotel by the thousands each day does not change the legal status of the hotel. The term "public place" is relative; indeed what is a public place for one purpose is not for another.[5]

10:10 *Eviction of Guest Who Has Overstayed Agreed Term*

An innkeeper may, particularly in times of unusual demand for accommodations, require that the guest agree to limit his stay to a

[5] *People ex rel. DuBois* v. *Thorpe,* 198 Misc. 462, 101 N.Y.S.2d 986 (Magis. Ct. 1950).

specified period, such as five days. The agreement limiting the stay should be in writing, duly signed by the guest. Innkeepers have adopted the practice of printing or stamping the limitation on the registration card. The guest who overstays the agreed time limit may be required to leave. If he refuses, he may be evicted in a reasonable manner not inflicting unnecessary injury or undue humiliation upon the guest. The usual method is to remove the guest's luggage from his room during his absence and to double-lock the room so as to deny him reentry.

10:11   *Ejection of Roomer, Lodger, or Boarder: Lockout*

As a guest may be ejected for neglecting or refusing to pay his bill when due, so the innkeeper may eject a roomer, lodger, or boarder (but not a tenant) for nonpayment of rent and other charges without resort to summary dispossess proceedings. The ejection is ordinarily done by making demand upon the guest, roomer, lodger, or boarder for payment of the bill within a specified time, and requesting that he leave the premises if the bill is not paid. If the demand is not met, the defaulting individual may be evicted. This is accomplished by double-locking the room and detaining the baggage under the lien law for the unpaid bill. If the defaulting individual refuses to leave the room, the innkeeper has the right physically to evict him, using reasonable force for the purpose.

Tenants, as distinguished from guests, roomers, lodgers, and boarders, may not be ejected by the innkeeper for nonpayment of rent and incidental charges. As will be seen in a subsequent chapter, a tenant has a legally recognized interest in the premises he occupies. As a condition of the tenant's ejection, this interest must first be terminated in a legal proceeding and an order directing eviction must first be obtained. The order is then executed by an officer of the court issuing the order, such as a sheriff or a marshal.

In some states statutes have been enacted for the benefit of persons unlawfully ejected from real property. An example of such a statute is Section 853 of the New York Real Property Actions and Proceedings Law (formerly Section 535 of the Real Property Law) which provides as follows: "If a person is disseized, ejected, or put out of real property in a forcible manner, or, after he has been put out, is held and kept out by force or by putting him in fear of personal violence, he is entitled to recover treble damages in an action therefor against the wrong-doer."

HENNIG v. GOLDBERG
188 Misc. 609, 68 N.Y.S.2d 698 (N.Y. City Ct. 1947)

[Action for forcible entry or detainer by Elsie Hennig against Solomon Goldberg and others.]

BYRNES, C.J.: "There was, in this case, no relation of landlord and tenant between plaintiff and defendants. Defendants were innkeepers, and plaintiff occupied a room in their hotel. She was, therefore, not in possession of real property, and for that reason she was not 'disseized, ejected, or put out of real property' or 'held and kept out' (within the meaning of [Section 535] Real Property Law), when defendants, in her absence changed the lock of the room which she occupied, so that upon her arrival at the hotel in the early morning of February 20, 1946, and again in the early afternoon of February 25, 1946, she was unable to gain admittance.

"No case under section 535 of the Real Property Law involving innkeeper and guest has come to my attention, and that statute seems not to have been applied in the past to such relationship.

"Furthermore, I find that plaintiff occupied the room—which had been assigned to one Bihovsky, who had dwelt in it for some time and had paid the February, 1946, rent in advance and in full—without permission from defendant Margolin or any one representing the hotel, that she had not registered as a guest and that the permission to use the room which she had obtained from the guest Bihovsky gave her no lawful right to the room and did not even put her in possession inasmuch as Bihovsky's rights as a guest were not assignable or transferable.

"So that plaintiff was not even a guest of defendants and in no sense did she have possession of any real property. One who is not in possession of real property is not 'put out' or 'kept out.' Obviously section 535 of the Real Property Law was never intended to make it necessary for an innkeeper to resort to court proceedings (even to squatter proceedings) to remove from his inn, or from a room in his inn, one who came in without his permission, express or implied. This is simply a case in which defendants found plaintiff in a room in which she did not belong and changed the lock so that she could not again gain access to that room. In so doing defendants were within their strict legal right, although I think it probable that they acted as they did because they wished to rent the room to someone who would pay a daily rather than a monthly rate. I do not wish it to be understood that anything I have said is a recommendation of defendants as I have no wish to express any approval of their conduct, but they acted lawfully and are not answerable in damages to plaintiff." [Complaint dismissed.]

LANDRY v. ALLERTON NEW YORK CORPORATION
83 N.Y.S.2d 774 (Sup. Ct. 1948)

McNally, J.: "This is a motion to strike out the defense and partial defense contained in the amended answer for alleged insufficiency.

"The first cause of action alleges, inter alia, that although plaintiff, a guest at defendant's apartment hotel, had paid the stipulated rent in advance for the week commencing April 18, 1948, the defendant during her absence from her room and without her knowledge or consent had forcibly and wrongfully entered the room and adjusted the lock so that she could not get into the room. It is further alleged that defendant refused to permit plaintiff to enter the room unless and until she paid the defendant the sum of $75, the amount of two checks which defendant had cashed for one Muller, which plaintiff had endorsed, and which had been returned by the bank for insufficient funds.

"The answer admits that plaintiff had paid the stipulated rent in advance for the week commencing April 18, 1948. It attempts to justify defendant's conduct by alleging as a defense that the checks had been cashed at plaintiff's request for plaintiff's escort, Muller, and that the checks were dishonored both by Muller and by plaintiff, the endorser. It may be assumed, without deciding, that defendant has a lien under Section 181 of the Lien Law upon plaintiff's baggage and other property brought by her on the premises, on the theory that the cashing of the checks for plaintiff's escort at plaintiff's request constituted the furnishing of an 'extra' within the meaning of that statute. It does not follow, however, that defendant had the right to exclude plaintiff from the room, notwithstanding the fact that she had paid the stipulated rent therefor, in advance, for a period beyond the date of exclusion. Nor is the case of *Morningstar* v. *Lafayette Hotel Co.*, 211 N.Y. 465 [citations omitted] in point. That case would be authority, perhaps, for defendant's refusing to serve plaintiff with a meal in the dining room or to render similar services to her. The case does not, however, go so far in its language or in its reasoning as to justify an innkeeper, who had contracted to permit a guest to occupy a specific room for a specified period for a stipulated consideration, in ousting or excluding the guest from the room during that period, when she had paid the stipulated consideration for the use of the room for a period beyond the ouster or exclusion.

"In the court's opinion the complete defense is insufficient.

"The partial defense is, however, sufficient. It alleges facts which are at least material and relevant for the purpose of mitigating the treble damages claimed by plaintiff as the result of the defendant's alleged violation of Section 535 of the Real Property Law. The allegations may also be material and relevant for the purpose of reducing any punitive damages which plaintiff may claim by reason of exclusion from her room and the charges concerning her character made by defendant.

"The motion is granted to the extent of dismissing the complete defense and otherwise denied."

In the subsequent trial to a jury of the above case, plaintiff recovered a verdict and moved for treble damages. Her motion was denied. Said the court: "[T]his does not appear to be a case for treble damages, since the evidence falls short of establishing that physical force against plaintiff's person was used or threatened." [6]

10:12 *Ejection of One Who Has Ceased to Be a Traveler*

If by lapse of time the guest has ceased to be a traveler and has become a resident, he no longer has a right to demand entertainment, and the innkeeper may exclude him. In an English case, it appeared that the plaintiff went to an inn in Brighton, was given rooms, and

---

[6] *Landry* v. *Allerton New York Corporation*, 194 Misc. 925, 88 N.Y.S.2d 293 (Sup. Ct. 1949).

stayed there for a period of ten months. It was then intimated to her that the manager wished her to leave, but this she refused to do. Notice was then given her requiring her to leave, and as she still refused, advantage was taken of her being out of the hotel, and her things were brought down and put outside, and on her return she was refused admittance. She then sued the innkeeper for wrongfully excluding her from the inn. The court held that she was lawfully excluded.[7]

Lord Esher, M.R., delivering the opinion of the court, said:

The question is whether it is the law that if a person goes to an inn in the character of a traveller that person retains the same character for any time however long. If so, the law would be contrary to the truth; and I will never submit, unless compelled by an Act of Parliament, to say that a thing shall be deemed to be that which it is not. Therefore, the question whether a person has ceased to be a traveller seems to me again to be a question of fact, and mere length of residence is not decisive of the matter, because there may be circumstances which shew [sic] that the length of the stay does not prevent the guest being a traveller, as, for instance, where it arises from illness; but it is wrong to say that length of time is not one of the circumstances to be taken into account in determining whether the guest has retained his character of traveller.[8]

But though the innkeeper may lawfully exclude an inmate after he has ceased to be technically a guest, his justification for such exclusion depends upon his being able to affirmatively show that the former guest has ceased to have that character. This was the ground of decision in a Canadian case. A traveler came to an inn, was received as a guest, and remained six weeks, paying for her board by the week; at the end of that time she was ejected by the innkeeper. She was held to be entitled to damages.[9]

It was proved that the plaintiff came to [the] inn as a traveller or guest, and was received as such. If she did pay by the week as was alleged, and if she was charged for board by that name, that would not certainly show that she was there under any special contract inconsistent with the common law relation between an innkeeper and his guest. She had been there about six weeks. If she had rented a certain apartment as tenant for any certain term, she would have been no longer a guest; but what

---

[7] *Lamond* v. *Richard,* [1897] 1 Q.B. 541.   [8] *Id.* at 546.
[9] *Whiting* v. *Mills,* 7 U.C.Q.B. 450 (Ontario 1849).

is shown is that she came to the inn as a guest; that she was so received, stayed there six weeks, and had paid for her board by the week two days in advance.

Under these facts, we think the defendant, for all that appears, had his privilege of lien on the plaintiff's goods, if she had attempted to depart without paying; and that she, on the other hand, had her rights as a guest, and could not be rudely or abruptly turned out without some cause to justify it; and no such cause was shown, nor was any pleaded.

If the relation of guest had, before the occasion complained of been put an end to, we can only say that it was not proved to be so upon the trial.[10]

10:13 Eviction of Restaurant Patrons

The innkeeper's right to evict a guest for cause extends to restaurant and bar patrons as well. It has been held that it is the duty of a restaurant keeper to accord protection to his patrons from insult or annoyance while they are in his restaurant. In putting a stop to the annoyance, he may eject the person guilty of the offense and in so doing may use all necessary force.[11]

10:14 Ejection of Unauthorized Intruders: Criminal Trespass

The modern inn is not only a home for the traveler away from home; it is a center for community affairs, social and business functions, exhibits, conferences, entertainment, a magnet that attracts people from all walks of life, desirable and undesirable as well. Among the undesirables are the daily intruders, who, in the mistaken belief that the inn is a public house open to all, arrogate to themselves the right to remain in the public areas of the house without invitation or permission and challenge the innkeeper to put them out.

The New York State Legislature recognized the seriousness of unauthorized intrusions upon hotel premises and made the same an offense, known as criminal trespass, in the Revised Penal Law, which became effective September 1, 1967. Every innkeeper, and indeed every restaurant keeper, should be familiar with the provisions of this statute.

[10] *Id.* at 452.   [11] *Chase v. Knabel*, 46 Wash. 484, 90 P. 642 (1907).

Criminal trespass consists of three degrees, which are defined in Sections 140.05, 140.10, and 140.15 of the Penal Law. The basic or lowest degree of offense is:

Section 140.05. *Criminal Trespass in the Third Degree*

A person is guilty of criminal trespass in the third degree when he knowingly enters or remains unlawfully in or upon premises.

Criminal trespass in the third degree is a violation.

If the premises constitute a "building" the offense is of a more aggravated nature and becomes:

Section 140.10. *Criminal Trespass in the Second Degree*

A person is guilty of criminal trespass in the second degree when he knowingly enters or remains unlawfully in a building or upon real property which is fenced or otherwise enclosed in a manner designed to exclude intruders.

Criminal trespass in the second degree is a Class B misdemeanor.

If the invaded premises constitute a dwelling, then the offender is guilty of:

Section 140.15. *Criminal Trespass in the First Degree*

A person is guilty of criminal trespass in the first degree when he knowingly enters or remains unlawfully in a dwelling.

Criminal trespass in the first degree is a Class A misdemeanor.

The term "premises" includes the term "building" and the term "building" is any structure used for overnight lodging of persons, or used by persons for carrying on business therein.

The term "dwelling" means a building which is usually occupied by a person lodging therein at night.

"Night" means the period between thirty minutes after sunset and thirty minutes before sunrise.

A person "enters or remains unlawfully" in or upon premises when he is not licensed or privileged to do so. A person who regardless of his intent, enters or remains in or upon premises which are at the time open to the public does so with license and privilege unless he defies a lawful order not to enter or remain, personally communicated to him by the owner of such premises or other authorized person. A license or privilege to enter or remain in a building which is only partly open to the public is not a license or privilege to enter or remain in that part of the building which is not open to the public (Section 140.00).

The innkeeper in possession or control of the premises of the inn, is justified, by the provisions of Section 35.20 of the Penal Law, in using physical force upon an intruder when and to the extent that he reasonably believes it necessary to prevent or terminate the commission or attempted commission of a criminal trespass in or upon the premises.

It would seem important to limit the application of the foregoing sections of the Penal Law to those undesirables whose presence in the inn is or may become harmful to the guests or to the security of the house. In this class are any known prostitutes who find hotel lobbies favorite places of resort, homosexuals, known to be such, using the inn for rendezvous, and the class of obnoxious persons known as "lobby lizards" who spend nothing but time at the inn. If, after a polite but firm request to leave, any such undesirable individual persists in remaining in the inn, police assistance may be called, and an arrest on a complaint (under Section 140.10 if the premises in question are public areas; under Section 140.15 if the intruder is in a private guest room) may be made. Needless to add, by way of caveat, the innkeeper or his security officer should, whenever possible, consult legal counsel before making an arrest.

CHAPTER 11

Relationship of Innkeeper and Guest

11:1 *Innkeeper's Obligation to Care for Guest*

The obligation of an innkeeper to care for his guest is imposed by law, and necessarily results from the admittance of the guest to the inn. There is no need of a contract between the parties. As soon as the relation of host and guest is established, the rights and duties of both parties to the relation are at once fixed. This is, to be sure, a consensual obligation; the consent of the innkeeper as well as that of the guest is needed to create it. If the innkeeper refuses to receive the guest, though his refusal is wrongful,[1] or if the guest enters the inn without the knowledge of the innkeeper, and without his consent,[2] the obligation does not arise. But though consent to receive the guest is required, and the obligation is a consensual one, it is not in any sense contractual, and it is not necessary to seek the elements of a contract in the relation between the parties.

11:2 *Capacity to Contract Not Required*

For this reason it is not necessary to find in a guest the capacity to make a contract. The relationship may be as well established with a person under incapacity, an infant, a married woman, or an insane person as with a person entirely *sui juris*. The innkeeper is obliged to receive and entertain the guest, and he is obviously bound by the obligations and entitled to the rights flowing from the relation. As he

[1] *Bennett* v. *Mellor*, 101 Eng. Rep. 154 (K.B. 1793); *Bird* v. *Bird*, 123 Eng. Rep. 47, 337 (C.P. 1558).

[2] *Gastenhofer* v. *Clair*, 10 Daly (N.Y.) 265 (C.P. 1881).

is compelled to receive, "[i]t would be a legal absurdity to compel a man to make a contract, and, at the same time, permit the other party, who is the instrument of compulsion, to avoid such contract." [3] (The court is, of course, using the word *contract* in a broad and non-technical sense.)

On the other hand, when a man has become and remains an innkeeper, a supervening incapacity on his own part will not protect him from responsibility. So in an old English case where an innkeeper was sued for failure to keep safely the goods of his guest, he pleaded that at the time the guest lodged with him he was sick and of non sane memory. On demurrer, this was held not to be a good plea. "For the defendant, if he will keep an inn, ought at his peril to keep safely his guest's goods and although he be sick, his servants then ought carefully to look to them. And to say he is of non sane memory it lieth not in him to disable himself." [4]

11:3 *Guest Need Not Be the Party Bound to Pay*

It is not necessary even that the guest should be personally obliged to pay. If, for instance, a man goes with his family to an inn, each member of the family is a guest, though the head of the family alone is responsible for payment of the innkeeper's charges. And in general everyone who is received and entertained as a guest at an inn is a guest, though his bill is paid by another.[5]

11:4 *What Law Governs the Obligation?*

Since the obligation of the innkeeper to his guest is created by the law, and not by the will of the parties, the nature of the obligation depends upon the law that creates it; since laws vary in different jurisdictions, it becomes important to determine what law creates and governs the relation. The law of the place in which the guest is received by the innkeeper will determine the nature of the obligation created by such reception.[6]

[3] *Watson v. Cross,* 63 Ky. (2 Duv.) 147, 148 (1865).
[4] *Cross v. Andrews,* 78 Eng. Rep. 863 (K.B. 1598).
[5] *Fisher v. Bonneville Hotel Co.,* 55 Utah 588, 188 P. 856 (1920); *Read v. Amidon,* 41 Vt. 15 (1868); *Kopper v. Willis,* 9 Daly (N.Y.) 460 (C.P. 1881).
[6] *Holland v. Pack,* 7 Tenn. 151 (1823).

11:5 Reception of Traveler Establishes Relation of Host and Guest

When a traveler comes to an inn and is received by the innkeeper for the purpose of entertaining him during his journey, the relation of host and guest is thereby established.[7] No lapse of time is required for the establishment of this relation; if the guest presents himself for entertainment and is accepted, the relation "is instantly established between them." [8]

11:6 Notice to Innkeeper of Traveler's Intention to Become Guest

To become the guest of an inn, the traveler must first give the innkeeper an opportunity to receive or to reject him. No person can make himself a guest without the innkeeper's assent. The required assent may be and is usually given by an employee entrusted with the duty of receiving or rejecting travelers, such as the desk clerk or assistant manager if the traveler seeks room accommodations, or the headwaiter or other person in charge of the dining room if he visits the inn for food or refreshments. There need be no formal bargain, for the acceptance of a traveler as a guest will be implied when a room is assigned to him, or when food or refreshments are furnished to him, at his request.

In the case of *Gastenhofer* v. *Clair*,[9] the plaintiff was invited by his uncle to dinner in defendant's hotel. Not finding his uncle on arrival, plaintiff had dinner alone; having finished his meal, he met his uncle in the lobby and went with him to the dining room. Plaintiff left his overcoat on a chair near the entrance to the dining room where there was no attendant. The coat having disappeared through no fault or negligence on defendant's part, it was incumbent on plaintiff to prove

[7] *Pinkerton* v. *Woodward*, 33 Cal. 557 (1867); *Healey* v. *Gray*, 68 Me. 489 (1878); *Norcross* v. *Norcross*, 53 Me. 163 (1865); *Ross* v. *Mellin*, 36 Minn. 421, 32 N.W. 172 (1887).

[8] *Norcross* v. *Norcross*, 53 Me. 163 (1865); *accord, Ross* v. *Mellin*, 36 Minn. 421, 32 N.W. 172 (1887).

[9] 10 Daly (N.Y.) 265 (C.P. 1881).

that he was a guest. In this he failed. The court held that he was not a guest. Said Judge Daly:

It is not the fact that a person does or does not take lodgings or partake of refreshments in the inn that makes him a guest. It is the motive with which he visits the place: whether to use it even for the briefest period or the most trifling purpose as a public house or not; and I think it will be long before the courts will be disposed to hold landlords liable for the property of persons who call to visit their guests, and incidentally enjoy the hospitality of the house. The taking of the dinner without notice to the proprietor or the clerk no more constituted plaintiff a guest than his sitting in the parlor, using the reading-room or writing-room, etc. for any period, while waiting for his host to appear.[10]

In the case of *Hill* v. *Memphis Hotel Co.*,[11] plaintiff, a resident of Oklahoma, motoring en route to New Orleans, stopped at the Gayoso Hotel in Memphis, Tennessee. Without registering or speaking with the clerk on duty, he went directly to the hotel restaurant, had a meal there, then relaxed for awhile in the hotel lobby where he bought a cigar. Plaintiff was held to be a guest. He was a traveler; he was assisted upon arrival by the hotel doorman who placed plaintiff's baggage in the lobby; he was seated and served in the dining room and paid his check in the customary manner; it was not incumbent upon him to give notice to the desk clerk or some particular officer or agent of the hotel company in order to become a guest.

A traveler may, however, enter a public room at an inn without at once presenting himself as a guest; in such case, the relation of host and guest is not established between the innkeeper and himself. So a traveler who enters a public room of an inn for a temporary purpose, without intending to lodge or be otherwise entertained at the inn, is not a guest.[12]

As soon as the relation is established, the guest must compensate the innkeeper for his services; however, it must be clear that one who enters an inn does not by that mere fact become liable to pay the inn-keeper's charges. Bearing this in mind, we can agree in the correctness of the decision in an English case where it appeared that a traveler went to an inn and gave his luggage to a porter, intending to stay at

---

[10] *Id.* at 267.   [11] 124 Tenn. 376, 136 S.W. 997 (1911).
[12] *Bernard* v. *Lalonde*, 8 Leg. News 215 (Can. 1885).

the inn, but upon being handed a telegram which had been sent there for him, he decided not to stop, but to continue his journey at once. It was held that he had not become a guest.[13]

11:7   Refusal of Innkeeper to Accept Guest

Not only must the guest communicate his intention to the innkeeper; the latter must consent to receive him as a guest. If the innkeeper refuses to receive a person as a guest, whether the refusal is legal or illegal, the relation is not established. Therefore when an innkeeper refuses to receive a guest (whether justifiably because his house is full, or unjustifiably), such person cannot, by placing his property in the inn, make the innkeeper liable for it.[14]

If the refusal is wrongful, the remedy is by action for the refusal; if it is lawful, the applicant has no right to force the obligation on the innkeeper. Thus, where the innkeeper having said his inn was full, the applicant nevertheless placed his goods in the inn, and induced a guest to share his bed with him, without the consent of the innkeeper, it was held that the latter was not responsible for the goods as innkeeper.[15]

So where an innkeeper refused to accept a guest because he was going to serve on a jury next morning, and the traveler at his request received the keys to look out for himself, the relation of host and guest was not established.[16]

11:8   Reception in Another Capacity Than as Guest

A person may be received in an inn by the innkeeper, but in another capacity than as guest. He may, for instance, come to the inn on the invitation of the innkeeper as his friend, and not on the footing of a paying guest.[17] Or, he may be a prospective employee hired to commence employment at some future date but, having arrived

---

[13] *Strauss* v. *County Hotel and Wine Co., Ltd.*, [1883] 12 Q.B.D. 27.

[14] *Bennett* v. *Mellor*, 101 Eng. Rep. 154 (K.B. 1793); *Bird* v. *Bird*, 123 Eng. Rep. 47, 337 (C.P. 1558).

[15] *Bird* v. *Bird*, 123 Eng. Rep. 47, 337 (C.P. 1558); *White's Case*, 73 Eng. Rep. 343 (K.B. 1558).

[16] *Y.B. Anon. 11 Hen. 4*, f. 45, pl. 18 (1409).

[17] *Anonymous*, 1 Rolle's Abr. 3, pl. 4; *Taylor* v. *Humphreys*, 142 Eng. Rep. 519 (C.P. 1861).

earlier, admitted to occupy a room in the inn prior to the commencement of his employment.[18] The relation of host and guest is not established in such cases, and the responsibility of the innkeeper does not come into existence.

[18] *Powers* v. *Raymond,* 197 Cal. 126, 239 P. 1069 (1925).

CHAPTER 12

Who Is a Guest?

12:1 *Guest Need Not Resort to Inn for Both Food and Lodging*

It is not necessary, in order that one received at an inn should become a guest there, that he should resort to the inn for both food and lodging. The inn must be prepared to supply both, at the traveler's need, but the traveler may stop on his way at an inn merely for food and drink, or for either one of them, and proceed on his journey the same day, or he may arrive at the inn late at night, needing lodging only, and leave the inn early in the morning without stopping for breakfast. In either case he is a guest.

So it has been held that a traveler resorting to an inn for food and drink only is a guest.[1] Upon this principle, where a person came to an inn in the afternoon, intending to leave by a late train that night, and therefore took no room, but remained in the public room of the inn, waiting for his train, and intending to get supper there, it was held that he was a guest.[2] And so where one called at an inn for the purpose of dining only, and was supplied with dinner in the dining room, he was held to be a guest.[3] Even if he resorts to the inn for drink only, he may thereby become a guest.[4] "Of course, a man could not be said to be a traveller who goes to a place merely for the purpose of taking refreshment. But, if he goes to an inn for refreshment in the course of a journey, whether of business or of pleasure, he is entitled to demand refreshment."[5] So in an English case where the servant of the plaintiff,

---

[1] *Hill* v. *Memphis Hotel Co.*, 124 Tenn. 376, 136 S.W. 997 (1911); *Read* v. *Amidon*, 41 Vt. 15 (1868); *Kopper* v. *Willis*, 9 Daly (N.Y.) 460 (C.P. 1881); *McDonald* v. *Edgerton*, 5 Barb. (N.Y.) 560 (Sup. Ct. 1849).

[2] *Overstreet* v. *Moser*, 88 Mo. Ct. App. 72 (1901).

[3] *Read* v. *Amidon*, 41 Vt. 15 (1868); *Orchard* v. *Bush & Co.*, [1898] 2 Q.B. 284.

[4] *McDonald* v. *Edgerton*, 5 Barb. (N.Y.) 560 (Sup. Ct. 1849).

[5] Cockburn, C.D., in *Atkinson* v. *Sellers*, 141 Eng. Rep. 181, 183 (C.P. 1858).

having the plaintiff's goods, asked if he could leave the goods until next week, and upon the innkeeper's saying he could not yet tell whether he would have the room to keep them, the servant set down the goods and had some liquor, and while he was drinking the goods were stolen, it was held that the relationship of host and guest had been established and the innkeeper had become liable for the goods.[6]

12:2 Whether Guest Must Be Personally Entertained

Whether, in order to be a guest, a traveler must be personally entertained at the inn is somewhat doubtful on the authorities. In several jurisdictions, it has been held that a traveler who comes to town and himself lodges in a private house is not a guest, though he sends his servant or his horse to the inn. If, under such circumstances, the horse dies in the night, through no negligence of the innkeeper, it is held that the latter is not liable.[7]

But by another view it is held in such a case that the innkeeper is liable as such if he receives a horse, although the owner does not lodge at the inn, for he receives the horse and is paid for it in the course of his business as innkeeper. The majority of the court of Queen's Bench so held, against the opinion of Lord Holt; [8] and this opinion has been followed in Massachusetts [9] and Delaware.[10] In the Delaware opinion, Chief Justice Comegys said:

The law makes the owner a guest because of the compensation charged by the innkeeper. The liability of the traveler for that (which attaches upon the reception of the beasts) constitutes this relation of host and guest. It is his property that is nourished, while upon his journey, and that in law is the same as if he had been in his own person the actual recipient of entertainment. It would be otherwise entirely of dead or inanimate things, left at the inn by such traveler, as to which nothing would be paid to the innkeeper. The existence of an inn involves in legal contempla-

[6] *Bennett* v. *Mellor*, 101 Eng. Rep. 154 (K.B. 1793).

[7] *Healey* v. *Gray*, 68 Me. 489 (1878); *Ingallsbee* v. *Wood*, 33 N.Y. 577 (1865); *Neale* v. *Croker*, 8 U.C.C.P. 224 (1858).

[8] *Yorke* v. *Grenaugh*, 92 Eng. Rep. 79 (K.B. 1703). "[F]or the inn-keeper gains by the horse, and therefore that makes the owner a guest, though he was absent. *Contra* of goods left there by a man, because the inn-keeper has no advantage by them" (*Id.* at 80).

[9] *Mason* v. *Thompson*, 26 Mass. (9 Pick.) 280 (1830).

[10] *Russell* v. *Fagan*, 12 Del. 389, 8 A. 258 (1886).

tion a stable attached to it also; and travelers with horses and carriages are not to be presumed to put them up at the inn to be kept there otherwise than as in inn-stables strictly; whereas, those not travelers in the sense I have been employing, but merely putting up their teams at the inn stable as a livery (as is the case with persons residing near towns who use such stables as mere conveniences) are not to be considered in the light of guests, and entitled to the same degree of protection as travelers are.[11]

The Vermont authorities appear to take the same view, though the point is not finally determined. In the leading case of *McDaniels* v. *Robinson*, it appeared that the plaintiff left his horse at the defendant's inn, and took a room in the inn and left goods in the room; he took only part of his meals there, and did not use his room every night. Some of the goods were lost. The innkeeper was held liable as such, on all the facts, and the court intimated that putting the horse up was alone enough to make the plaintiff a guest.[12] On a new trial, however, the plaintiff was not proved to have been a guest personally; and the leaving of the goods which were lost had nothing to do with the stabling of the horse. For this reason (without denying that the innkeeper would have been liable as such for injury to the horse) the court gave judgment for the defendant.[13]

In the case of *Ticehurst* v. *Beinbrink*,[14] the plaintiff recovered a judgment against the defendant, an innkeeper, for the value of a horse, which was stolen while in the defendant's stable. The plaintiff, a veterinary surgeon, intending to drive his horse from Oyster Bay, Long Island, to New York City, decided, when he reached Hollis, Long Island, not to go any further with his horse at that time. He stopped at the hotel or inn of the defendant. He tied his horse under a shed, and he went into the inn, and asked the person whom he found in charge if he could leave his horse at the inn-stable during the night, as he intended to return to the borough of Brooklyn. The person in charge of the inn said, "We don't board no horse here, and don't keep no livery stable," but finally consented that the horse might be left there during the night. While in the inn, the plaintiff received and paid for a drink of whisky and a cigar. The horse was unharnessed and put in the

11 *Id.* at 394.   12 *McDaniels* v. *Robinson*, 26 Vt. 316 (1854).
13 *McDaniels* v. *Robinson*, 28 Vt. 387 (1856).
14 72 Misc. 365, 129 N.Y.S. 838 (Sup. Ct. 1911).

stable attached to the inn. The plaintiff returned to the inn, and after waiting at the inn about twenty minutes boarded a trolley car and rode to Jamaica, where he took a train for the borough of Brooklyn, New York City. During that night the horse was stolen from the stable of the defendant.

The evidence failed to establish any negligence on the part of the defendant, and the sole question before the court was whether he was liable as an innkeeper whose liability, as such, arises only when the relation of host and guest exists.

The court, in reversing the judgment in favor of the plaintiff, held that plaintiff was not a guest and not entitled to recover. Said the court, after review of the leading authorities:

"A guest is a transient person who resorts to, or is received at, an inn for the purpose of obtaining the accommodations which it purports to offer." [Citation omitted.]

A guest may be such actually or constructively.

The real or presumed intention to become a guest is a controlling factor in determining whether one is in fact to be considered as a guest.

If a guest leave the inn intending to return, the relation of host and guest is, in the absence of evidence to the contrary, deemed to continue in the interim as to animate but not as to inanimate property, because the innkeeper gains a profit from the former but none from the latter.

Where one makes a contract with an innkeeper to stable and care for his horse, but does not become or intend to become a guest, the innkeeper is not liable as such for the loss of the horse.

The fact that one making such a contract received refreshments at the inn, under a contract separate and distinct from that under which the horse is cared for, does not of itself constitute such person a guest.

In *Adler* v. *Savoy Plaza*,[15] it appeared that plaintiff was accustomed to staying at defendant's hotel whenever she visited New York and had been a guest of the hotel many times. She and her husband had requested reservations for May 15, 1946. Upon their arrival at ten o'clock that morning, they were advised that their reservation was for the following day, but that the hotel would try to accommodate them, so they registered hoping that a room might be assigned during the day. At the same time, they delivered their luggage to the bell captain, and it was deposited in a section of the lobby set aside for luggage of

[15] 279 App. Div. 110, 108 N.Y.S.2d 80 (1951).

arriving and departing guests. Plaintiff's husband attended to business during the day while plaintiff was in and out of the hotel. When both returned to the hotel in the afternoon, they found that a room was still not available, so they whiled away some time in the lounge bar and had dinner in the room of a friend who was a guest of the hotel.

All during the day defendant's manager was seeking accommodations for the couple but was unable to locate them in the hotel. He finally secured accommodations for them for the night at the Sherry Netherlands Hotel where they registered at about 8:00 P.M., taking with them two suitcases and a cosmetic case, and leaving the suitcase with the valuables and two matching cases at defendant's hotel.

When plaintiff returned to defendant's hotel the next morning, to take up a residence for two or three weeks, and requested delivery of her luggage, the large suitcase was missing. During the night the suitcase had been delivered by the night manager of the hotel to an impostor.

The circumstances of this delivery are not altogether clear as the night manager was deceased at the time of the trial. Whether there was some complicity on the part of one or more of the hotel employees, as plaintiff suggests, we are not called upon to surmise. It is quite apparent that defendant was negligent, probably grossly negligent, and if the case would be determined simply on a question of negligence, plaintiff would be entitled to recover the amount of her loss.

The court ruled, *as a matter of law,* on the admitted facts, that plaintiff was a guest in defendant's hotel, notwithstanding that at the time of the loss she was registered and resided at the Sherry Netherland.

12:3 *Entertainment of Servant or Child as Making Master or Parent a Guest*

Where a man's servant (or minor child) with his property is received at an inn, it has been said that the master (or father) is a guest, and has the rights of such.[16] It is clear, however, that the servant or child who is personally present at the inn is himself a guest, even if the master or parent accompanies him and pays the bill; [17] a fortiori if he

[16] *Epps* v. *Hinds,* 27 Miss. 657 (1854); *Coykendall* v. *Eaton,* 55 Barb. 188 (N.Y. Sup. Ct. 1869); *Robinson* v. *Waller,* 81 Eng. Rep. 599 (K.B. 1617).
[17] See Chap. 11:3.

is not present. It would seem that since there is but one person present obtaining entertainment and as but one guest is paid for, there is but one guest; and the absent master or father is therefore not properly a guest. The point actually decided in the cases is therefore that the innkeeper is directly liable to the master or parent, as owner, for a loss of the goods; and the true reason for the decision is doubtless that in the mind of the court in *Robinson v. Waller*,[18] when it distinguished the case from that where the goods were taken to the inn by a bailee on the ground that in the case under discussion "the absolute property" is in the owner. In other words, the father or master being in legal possession of the goods while they are in the hands of the servant or member of his family, he may sue the innkeeper directly, as the person whose possession has been infringed.

12:4 Resorting to Inn to Attend Banquet or Other Function

Where a banquet or a ball is held at an inn, a guest at such banquet or ball is not a guest of the innkeeper, and the latter is not liable, in the absence of negligence, for any goods lost by the guest.[19] In such a case Judge Blodgett said:

. . . [A]s to the banquet where the loss occurred, and which they attended on the invitation and at the expense of the club, the plaintiffs are justly to be regarded as its guests, and not of the defendant, as innkeeper or otherwise, who simply provided the banquet as caterer under a contract with the club, without any lien or claim for compensation against its guests, and with no right or power to exclude anybody from participating in its festivities whom the club might properly invite.

Neither by contract nor by operation of law was the defendant acting in the character of innkeeper as to the club, and still less as to its guests, who would have had no right whatever to attend except upon its invitation. Both the club and its guests came not as ordinary travelers to an inn, but as to a banquet, for the purpose of participating in and enjoying its festivities.[20]

The fact that the innkeeper himself supplies the banquet, so that the persons present are being furnished entertainment by him for

[18] 81 Eng. Rep. 599 (K.B. 1617).
[19] *Carter v. Hobbs*, 12 Mich. 52 (1863); *Amey v. Winchester*, 68 N.H. 447, 39 A. 487 (1895).
[20] *Amey v. Winchester*, 68 N.H. 447, 39 A. 487 (1895).

hire, does not alter the case. On this point Judge Blodgett said aptly, in *Amey* v. *Winchester:*

[T]he fact that the defendant chanced to be keeping an inn and served the banquet there makes his liability no greater than that of any other person, not an innkeeper, who might have taken and executed the contract either at the inn or elsewhere. One may be an innkeeper without being a club caterer, or he may be a club caterer without being an innkeeper, or he may be both; but if he is, the two employments are so far separate and distinct in respect of duties and liabilities as not to make him responsible in the one capacity for liabilities incurred in the other.[21]

The case is the same even if the guest at the ball or banquet deals in other ways directly with the innkeeper, as by buying liquor, or putting up his horse in the stable of the inn.[22]

Nor is the case altered even if the innkeeper is himself the person who gives the entertainment and invites the public to be present. So, where an innkeeper gave a ball and furnished food and drink to a person attending the ball, he was held not to be an innkeeper in so doing, though one who resorted to him as an innkeeper and was provided with the same refreshment would become a guest. In this case the innkeeper, the court said, was in the position of any owner of a ballroom who should do the same. It is not the amount of refreshment but the character under which the person buys it that makes him a guest.[23]

In *Amey* v. *Winchester,*[24] a person who was apparently a guest at the inn, attended such a banquet, leaving his hat at the door of the supper room, and it was lost during the banquet. The court held that the owner was not a guest at the time, and the innkeeper was not liable. It may be doubted whether in this case the court did not go too far; for it is difficult to see how the guest ceased to be such by attending the banquet at his inn.

In the more recent case of *Ross* v. *Kirkeby Hotels, Inc.,*[25] the plaintiffs, husband and wife, were to be married in the Hotel Warwick in

21 *Id.* at 449.
22 *Carter* v. *Hobbs,* 12 Mich. 52 (1863); *Fitch* v. *Casler,* 17 Hun. (N.Y.) 126 (Sup. Ct. 1879).
23 *Fitch* v. *Casler,* 17 Hun. (N.Y.) 126 (Sup. Ct. 1879).
24 68 N.H. 447, 39 A. 487 (1895).
25 8 Misc. 2d 750, 160 N.Y.S.2d 978 (Sup. Ct. 1957).

New York City. The husband arrived at the hotel in his car on the morning of his wedding day. He issued specific instructions to place the car in the hotel garage. Instead the doorman left it on the street, where it was broken into and the contents carried off.

In an action against the hotel for the recovery of the loss, the issue was whether plaintiffs were guests of the hotel at the time of the loss. If they were guests, the hotel was entitled to the statutory limitation of liability for the loss of the property of guests; absent innkeeper-guest relationship, the plaintiffs were entitled to the full value of their loss.

The court held that plaintiffs were not guests, ruling that a person renting hotel facilities solely for a wedding is not a guest within the meaning of Section 201 of the General Business Law, the New York statute limiting a hotelkeeper's liability for the property of guests.

12:5 One Not Entitled to Admittance Received as Guest

Even a person not entitled to demand admittance, not being a bona fide traveler, will become a guest and entitled to all the rights of a guest if he is received voluntarily in the inn upon the same footing as a guest. The innkeeper has a right to refuse to receive him, but that right may be waived by consenting to receive the guest. Thus it is usually stated that one who lives in the same town with the innkeeper cannot be a guest, since he is not a traveler seeking entertainment during a journey. While it is true that such a person is often received to be entertained out of friendship alone, and therefore is not a guest, yet if he is really received on the footing of a guest the relation of host and guest is thereby established.[26]

12:6 Guest at Inn for Illegal Purpose

Where a person went to an inn with a prostitute and took a room which he occupied with her, it was held that on account of his misconduct he did not become a guest, any more than would a thief who took a room in order to steal from the guests.[27] It is clear in this case,

[26] *Walling* v. *Potter*, 35 Conn. 183 (1868); *Orchard* v. *Bush & Co.*, [1898] 2 Q.B. 284.
[27] *Curtis* v. *Murphy*, 63 Wis. 4, 22 N.W. 825 (1885).

as the court says, that if the innkeeper had been aware of the party's purpose in applying for the room, he might have refused to receive him; and even after the applicant had been received, he could have been ejected, upon his purpose becoming known. It does not follow, however, as the court appeared to hold, that therefore he was not a guest. The court says that if he had been a guest, "he could not have been turned into the street, though his profligate conduct was outraging all decency and ruining the reputation of the hotel." [28] This dictum can hardly be supported; for, as has been seen, the innkeeper would certainly have a right to turn out a guest under such circumstances (see 10:2). And although the innkeeper would have been justified in refusing to receive the applicant as a guest, it by no means follows that if he was received the applicant did not occupy the exact position of a guest. The innkeeper can doubtless waive his right to refuse admittance and accept an applicant as his guest; though it is equally clear that he may, if he chooses, accept him on such terms that he will not be a guest (see 12:5). In this case the applicant was received as a guest. He, however, was guilty of fraud in asking for accommodation for himself and wife; and the decision may probably best be supported on the ground that the guest was precluded from recovery in the case because of his fraud.

As Mr. Justice Kennedy said in *Orchard* v. *Bush & Co.*,[29] "[I]f a man is in an inn for the purpose of receiving such accommodation as the innkeeper can give him, he is entitled to the protection the law gives to a guest at an inn." [30]

12:7 *Guest at Inn as Result of Illegal Act*

However it may be with the guest who is acting illegally while in the inn, it is clear that he is none the less a guest because he may have been guilty of an illegal act in coming to the inn, if his illegal conduct has ceased. Thus, in a similar case to the one just discussed, where the man remained after the woman had left the inn, and lost his goods, it was held that he might recover from the innkeeper. Even assuming that such misconduct would have barred him while the misconduct continued, the loss here happened after his misconduct ceased,

[28] *Id.* at 8.   [29] 2 Q.B. 284 (1898).   [30] *Id.* at 289.

and his previous immorality could not affect his subsequent status as a guest.[31]

On the same principle, in a case where it appeared that the defendant was received at the inn on Sunday, and that to reach the inn on that day he had broken the statute which forbade traveling on Sunday, he was held to be a guest nevertheless, since the relationship was established by acts not necessarily connected with traveling on Sunday.[32]

In *Cramer* v. *Tarr*,[33] plaintiffs falsely registered in defendant's lodginghouse as husband and wife. A fire broke out and plaintiffs were injured while escaping from their room. They sued to recover damages for personal injuries which they alleged resulted from defendant's negligence. Defendant moved for summary judgment for dismissal of the complaint on the theory that plaintiffs, not being married, were trespassers by reason of their unlawful purpose, and that no duty of reasonable care was owed them.

The court denied defendant's motion. Said the court:

In the absence of any showing of a causal connection between plaintiffs' alleged statutory violation and their injuries, it is the considered opinion of this Court that neither false registration nor an illegal or immoral purpose in occupying a room in the defendant's boarding house would affect the status of these plaintiffs as guests to whom the defendant owed the duty of reasonable care. It follows, therefore, that plaintiffs would not be barred from maintaining these actions even if false registration for an illicit purpose could be inferred. . . .

In accord with the general principle thus stated and applied by the Maine court, the better view of the law and the greater weight of authority is specifically to the effect that false registration in an inn or lodging house for an immoral or illegal purpose will not preclude recovery for injuries resulting from the innkeeper's negligence where there is no showing of a causal connection between the illegality and the plaintiff's injuries. . . . To the extent that *Curtis* v. *Murphy*, 1885, 63 Wis. 4, 22

[31] *Lucia* v. *Omel*, 46 App. Div. 200, 61 N.Y.S. 659 (2d Dep't 1900). The facts differed from the Wisconsin case (which was distinguished in the opinion) in two important particulars: In the Wisconsin case, the plaintiff was a resident of the same town, which does not seem to have been true in this case; and the innkeeper had wrongfully refused to take charge of the property before its loss.
[32] *Cox* v. *Cook*, 96 Mass. (14 Allen) 165 (1867).
[33] 165 F. Supp. 130 (D. Me. 1958).

N.W. 825, and related cases express views in conflict with the foregoing, they are considered by this Court to be unsound.

The Court is of the opinion, therefore, that even if false registration for the purpose of fornication were established, these plaintiffs would yet be guests to whom the defendant owed a duty of reasonable care for their safety and the defendant would not be entitled to judgment as a matter of law.[34]

In *Meador* v. *Hotel Grover*,[35] plaintiff sued, as administrator of the deceased, to recover damages for the deceased's death. It appeared that the deceased went to defendant's hotel for the purpose of sexual intercourse with a prostitute who was a guest in defendant's hotel at the time. The complaint alleged that defendant was negligent in that the elevator operator failed to bring the elevator to a stop upon discovering that the plaintiff was caught between the elevator floor and the door on the second floor and was being crushed. Judgment dismissing the complaint was reversed and the case was remanded, the court stating:

For a plaintiff to be barred of an action for negligent injury under the principle of public policy implicit in the maxim ex dolo malo non oritur actio, his injury must have been suffered while and as a proximate result of committing an illegal act. The unlawful act must be at once the source of both his criminal responsibility and his civil right. The injury must be traceable to his own breach of the law and such breach must be an integral and essential part of his case. Where the violation of law is merely a condition and not a contributing cause of the injury, a recovery may be permitted. [Citations omitted].

The mere status of the plaintiff as a lawbreaker at the time of his injury is not sufficient of itself to bar him from resort to the courts.[36]

A different view was taken by the Supreme Court of North Carolina in *Jones* v. *Bland*.[37] The court in that case held that an innkeeper owes no duty to a person going to the room of a guest, upon the latter's invitation, for the purpose of gambling, except not willfully or intentionally to injure him. The court's theory appears to have been that the innkeeper's duty does not extend to wrongdoers who come upon the premises for an unlawful purpose, and that even though invited by a

---

[34] *Id.* at 132.   [35] 193 Miss. 392, 9 So. 2d 782 (1942).   [36] *Id.* at 405.
[37] 182 N.C. 70, 108 S.E. 344 (1921).

guest of the inn, such person has the status of a trespasser in his relation with the innkeeper.

In any event, the guest's misconduct should be set up by the innkeeper as an affirmative defense, as was pointed out in *Rapee* v. *Beacon Hotel Corp.*[38] In that case, plaintiff and his fiancée registered at defendant's hotel as husband and wife under an assumed name. While in the hotel, plaintiff was injured as a result of falling into the pit at the bottom of an elevator shaft, the door having been left open through the negligence of the defendant. Defendant claimed that plaintiff's fraudulent misrepresentation of his personality made him a trespasser on the hotel premises. The Court of Appeals refused to assent to defendant's argument: "Foremost on the defendant's part was an intention to contract with the man and the woman who had put signatures on the register and, that being so, the plaintiff became a guest of the hotel, though the defendant may perhaps have been deceived as to his identity." [39] Plaintiff's trickery was not set up as an affirmative defense and thus was of no avail to defendant on appeal.

12:8 *Registration as Establishing the Relation of Host and Guest*

While registration is the customarily recognized method of establishing the innkeeper-guest relationship, it has been held that one may become a guest at an inn without registering.

MOODY v. KENNY
153 La. 1007, 97 So. 21 (1923)

[Action against the defendants, owners of the Monteleone Hotel in New Orleans to recover the sum of $10,000 for damages. Verdict and judgment for $5,000, from which defendant appeals.

One Mr. Bradley was a guest of the Hotel Monteleone in New Orleans. His friends, Mr. and Mrs. Moody, arrived at the hotel but could obtain no rooms. Bradley then offered them his room and he went to lodge elsewhere. Bradley spoke about this arrangement to the day clerk of the hotel, but this clerk forgot to say anything about it to the night clerk.

The Moodys retired in their room for the night when the house

[38] 293 N.Y. 196, 56 N.E.2d 548 (1944).   [39]*Id.* at 199.

officer passing by heard Mrs. Moody's voice inside. This particular section of the hotel was reserved for men, so the house officer reported
the presence of a woman to the clerk on duty, who checked the register
and found the room assigned to Mr. Bradley; he then called the room
on the phone. Not having received a reply, he sent up the house officer
to investigate. The latter verified the facts and reported back to the
clerk who sent him back to the room with the night watchman. The
testimony differs as to what happened; Moody and his wife claiming
that they were grossly insulted and ejected, dragged down to the
front office for explanation, while the house officer testified that he
merely asked for an explanation of the lady's presence in the room.

It was admitted that neither Moody nor his wife were registered as
guests at the hotel. The defense of the hotel was that the plaintiffs not
being guests, the hotel was justified in making inquiry of their presence
in a room assigned to another man.]

LAND, J.: "While a mere guest of the registered occupant of a room
at a hotel, who shares such room with its occupant without the knowledge or consent of the hotel management, would not be a guest of the
hotel, as there would be no contractual relations in such case between
such third person and the hotel proprietor; at the same time, when the
registered occupant of a room, with the knowledge and consent of the
hotel management, turns his room over to another person, and the
hotel clerk delivers the key of the room to that person, he becomes an
accepted guest of the hotel and is not a mere licensee. The fact that
such person fails to register, or is not required to register, is immaterial; as the registration of guests at a hotel is no part of the contract
between the hotel proprietor and the guest, but the purpose of a
register is to keep track of the number of people in the house and to
keep the books straight. A register is kept solely for the benefit and
convenience of the hotel proprietor.

"A guest may be accepted at a hotel, without registration, by the
mere delivery to him of the key to the room by the clerk. There is no
law in this state requiring a guest to sign a hotel register as the
evidence of a contract between the parties. Such contracts are mere
matters of oral consent, and are legal without further formality."
[Judgment reduced to $500 and affirmed as so amended.]

O'NIELL, C. J. (dissenting): "I respectfully dissent from the statement in the majority opinion in this case that a hotel register is kept
solely for the benefit and convenience of the proprietor. A hotel register

is as necessary to protect a guest in his exclusive right to occupy a particular room, as it is necessary to protect the proprietor in his right to collect what the guest owes for occupying the room.

". . . I do not know how the clerks who hand out the room keys to the guests in large hotels identify the guests and avoid the mistake of giving a key to one who is not entitled to it. I imagine it would cause much embarrassment if the key clerks should require the guests to be identified every time one of them asks for the key to his room. For that reason, I suppose that the key clerks in the large hotels must rely upon their judgment of the honesty of the men who ask for keys to their rooms. . . .

". . . [W]hatever mistake was made by the hotel clerk, or by the house detective, in this instance, was a pardonable mistake . . . [and] I am not in favor of allowing damages for a pardonable mistake, when the injury . . . cannot be measured in dollars and cents and the condemnation therefore would be very much like an infliction of punishment. I do not know how the management of the large hotels can maintain their respectability if they cannot with impunity inquire into the right of a strange man and woman to occupy a room where another man is registered as a guest of the hotel."

12:9 *Statutes Requiring the Keeping of Hotel Registers*

At common law an innkeeper is not required to keep a register of guests in the house. However, statutes in New York and several other states now mandate the keeping of registers. The New York statute is Section 204 of the General Business Law, which reads as follows:

The owner, lessee, proprietor or manager of any hotel, motel, tourist cabins, camp, resort, tavern, inn, boarding or lodging house shall keep for a period of three years a register which shall show the name, residence, date of arrival and departure of his guests. Such record may be kept within the meaning of this section when reproduced on any photographic, photostatic, microfilm, microcard, miniature photographic or other process which actually reproduced the original record.

In addition to the requirements of Section 204 of the General Business Law, the Election Law, in order to prevent frauds at elections, imposes certain duties on innkeepers. Section 61(1) provides:

Every keeper of a hotel, lodging house, boarding house or rooming house in a town or city, shall cause to be kept for a period of one year a record showing the name and residence and the date of arrival and departure of his guests or lodgers and the room, rooms or bed occupied by them, which record shall have a space in which each guest or lodger shall sign his name. The keeping of but one person as a guest or lodger in any building shall not constitute such building either a boarding house or a rooming house within the meaning of this section.

Section 61(2) further provides that in cities of over five thousand inhabitants the police captain of each precinct shall furnish to the board of elections a complete list of the hotels, lodginghouses, boardinghouses, and rooming houses in his precinct, not less than forty nor more than sixty days before each general election. The board of elections, at least thirty-five days before the election, shall furnish to the hotel, etc., keeper a blank report form to be filled out by him. The hotel, etc., keeper must fill out the report form and deliver it or send it, by registered mail, to the board of elections at least twenty-nine days before the election. The report form indicates the information to be furnished and sworn to by the hotel, etc., keeper. It includes a description of the premises, names of the guests or lodgers and employees residing in the premises, the length of time they have lived there, and the sex and age of each such person.

Section 60 of the Election Law which applies only to hotels, lodging, boarding, and rooming houses of less than fifty rooms, located anywhere in the state, empowers the local board of elections to require a special report by the keepers of such hotels, etc., at any time, giving the names, length of residence, and other information of every resident over twenty-one years of age in the house. A misstatement in such report is punishable by a civil penalty of one thousand dollars.

12:10 *Preregistration: Must Guest Register Personally?*

In the interests of greater efficiency and better service, some innkeepers have adopted the practice of preregistering incoming guests. The registration card is completed by the hotel personnel in advance of the guest's arrival, so as to save him the time and inconvenience of registering in person. In New York, there is no legal prohibition against this practice. The risks involved therein are, of course, obvious, in terms of identifying those in the house, in the collection of charges, and in matters of security.

12:11 *True-Name Registration*

A number of states have enacted so-called true-name registration statutes, the purpose of which is to aid law enforcement agencies to trace and identify individuals charged with criminal offenses. As an example, in Massachusetts (General Laws, Chap. 140, §§27–29), every innholder and every lodginghouse keeper, etc., is required to keep, in permanent form, a register in which shall be recorded the true name or name in ordinary use and the residence of every person engaging or occupying a private dining room not containing a bed or couch, or opening into a room containing a bed or couch, for any period of the day or night in any part of the premises controlled by the licensee, together with the true and accurate record of the room assigned to such person and of the day and hour when such room is assigned. The guest is required to sign his own name and shall not be allowed to occupy any room in the house without so registering. The register shall be kept for a period of one year from the date of the last entry therein. The violation of the law is punishable by a fine of from $100 to $500 or by imprisonment for not more than three months, or both.

The Massachusetts law further provides that no person shall write or cause to be written, or if in charge of a register knowingly permit to be written, in any register in any lodginghouse or hotel any other or different name or designation than the true name or name in ordinary use of the person registering or causing himself to be registered therein. No person occupying such room shall fail to register or fail to cause himself to be registered. Violation of the law is punishable by a fine of from $10 to $25.

Indiana and New Jersey have also enacted compulsory registration laws.

12:12 *Patron of Hotel Restaurant as Guest of Hotel*

ALPAUGH *v.* WOLVERTON
184 Va. 943, 36 S.E.2d 906 (1946)

[Proceeding by notice of motion for judgment based on the refusal of defendant, a hotel and restaurant keeper, to serve food and drink to plaintiff. Dismissed and plaintiff brings error. Affirmed.

Plaintiff alleged that he was a member in good standing of the Manassas, Va., Chamber of Commerce; that the defendant was the owner and operator of a certain hotel and restaurant in said town; that defendant entered into an arrangement to furnish lunch, food and drink to members of said Chamber of Commerce on Tuesdays of each week and that although plaintiff was a member in good standing of said organization and tendered the price of the meal, yet the defendant, in utter disregard of his "duties and obligations" to the plaintiff, "wilfully, wickedly, wantonly and maliciously" refused to serve plaintiff with food and drink on Tuesday, October 31, 1944, while plaintiff was seated at the dining table of the "hotel" along with other members of said organization, thereby maliciously humiliating him and bringing him into ridicule, disrespect and disgrace.

The second count is identical with the first, except that it charges defendant with refusal to serve plaintiff at a Kiwanis dinner on Friday, November 10, 1944.]

EGGLESTON, J.: "The defendant filed a demurrer which, in substance, challenged the sufficiency of the notice of motion . . . [in that] it failed to allege that the defendant had violated any legal duty which he owed to the plaintiff. . . .

"The plaintiff insists that the allegations of the notice of motion for judgment are sufficient to show that in furnishing and agreeing to furnish the meals, under the circumstances stated, the defendant was a hotel operator or an innkeeper; that, as such, he 'was not entitled to say whom he would serve and whom he would not so serve,' but that 'he was legally bound to entertain and serve each and every one requesting such service and entertainment,' whether he be a local resident or a traveler from a distance.

"The defendant, on the other hand, insists that the allegations show that the relation established, or sought to be established, between the parties was not that of innkeeper and guest, but merely that of a restaurateur and customer, and that under the latter relation there was no common-law duty on the part of the defendant to serve the plaintiff, or any other customer, with meals.

[After stating the duties of an innkeeper in relation to guests the court continued:] ". . . The proprietor of a restaurant is not subject to the same duties and responsibilities as those of an innkeeper, nor is he entitled to the privileges of the latter. [Citations omitted.] His rights and responsibilities are more like those of a shopkeeper. [Citations omitted.] He is under no common-law duty to serve everyone who applies to him. In the absence of statute, he may accept some customers and reject others on purely personal grounds. [Citations omitted.]

"Everyone patronizing or seeking to patronize the facilities of a hotel or inn does not necessarily become a 'guest' of the establishment within the technical meaning of that term. It is well settled that the proprietor of a hotel may be a technical 'innkeeper' as to some of his patrons and a 'boarding housekeeper' as to others. . . .

"No one would seriously contend that a casual patron of a barbershop located in a hotel, or one who purchases a newspaper or cigar from a hotel newsstand, or one who uses the pay-telephone in the hotel lobby, by virtue of such patronage alone, thereby became a 'guest' of the hotel in a technical sense.

"And so, too, where a hotel operator operates a restaurant for the accommodation both of its guests and of the public in general, he may be an innkeeper as to some of his patrons and a restaurateur as to others. Clearly, one who goes into a restaurant, to which the general public in invited, for a meal, should be entitled to no greater privileges and subject to no greater liabilities because the establishment is operated by one who also operates a hotel, rather than by one who furnishes only food to his customers. In either case the customer seeks only restaurant service.

"We do not mean to imply that the relationship of innkeeper and guest may not arise where the patron partakes of a single meal at the hotel. . . . But in these cases there were other circumstances which indicated an intent to create the relationship.

"Indeed, the controlling factor in determining whether the relationship of innkeeper and guest has been established is the intent of the parties. [Citations omitted.]

"Applying these principles to the case before us, it is clear that the allegations of the notice of motion do not show the establishment of the relation of innkeeper and guest between the parties. On the contrary, they show merely the relationship of restaurateur and patron.

"There is no allegation that the plaintiff sought or intended to seek to become a guest of the hotel, or that he, or the proprietor, or the latter's servants or employees, did anything to indicate the intention to create such relation. There is no allegation that the plaintiff sought any of the other accommodations furnished by the establishment. On the contrary, it is clear that he sought merely to patronize the restaurant, as such. The allegation is that the defendant had entered into an 'arrangement and agreement' with two social clubs, under the provisions of which the defendant was to serve certain meals on certain days to the members of these clubs, including the plaintiff. It was while the plaintiff was seated at a table in the restaurant, pursuant to these arrangements, that he sought and was refused service of meals on two occasions.

"Since the notice of motion for judgment charges the defendant with the breach of no legal duty, the demurrer thereto was properly sustained. The judgment is *affirmed*."

One who is merely a customer at a bar, a restaurant, a barbershop, or newsstand operated by a hotel does not thereby establish the relationship of innkeeper and guest.[40]

12:13 *Deposit of Chattels with Innkeeper*

When the baggage of a transient is received by the innkeeper and the transient thereafter accepts some service for which he pays, or obligates himself to pay, such transient will be considered a guest of the innkeeper from the time the baggage was received.[41]

FREUDENHEIM *v.* EPPLEY
88 F.2d 280 (3d Cir.), appeal dismissed, 302 U.S. 769 (1937)

[Action by J. Freudenheim & Sons, a partnership, against the receivers of the Pittsburgh Hotels Corporation to recover damages suffered by the alleged negligence of the defendant in failing to safely keep some $40,000 worth of its diamonds deposited with defendant by Sol J. Freudenheim, one of the partners, who was an alleged guest of the hotel. On trial, a verdict was had for the plaintiff for $41,893.13. The court below entered judgment in favor of the defendant n.o.v. (judgment notwithstanding the verdict) on the ground that plaintiff was not a guest of the defendant's hotel at the time of the deposit,

40 *Wallace* v. *Shoreham Hotel Corp.*, 49 A.2d 81 (D.C. Mun. Ct. App. 1946).
41 *Burton* v. *Drake Hotel Co.*, 237 Ill. App. 76 (1925).

that the deposit was a gratuitous bailment, and that there was no proof of gross negligence on the part of defendant. This is an appeal by plaintiff from said judgment.]

BUFFINGTON, C.J.: ". . . [T]he uncontradicted facts in the case showed that Freudenheim was the traveling salesman of his diamond firm, and . . . was accustomed to visit . . . Pittsburgh. . . . [He was accustomed, when trade justified, to stay] at hotels which had vaults for the deposit of valuables and he left his bag containing diamonds in their vaults. Prior to 1922–23, he had stopped at other hotels in Pittsburgh, but since then had stopped at the William Penn. Prior to 1930 he came to Pittsburgh eight or nine times a year and stayed at the William Penn two, three, or four days at a time, depending on trade conditions. In 1933 he was twice in Pittsburgh, received his mail at the hotel, but did not stay overnight. On every one of his trips to Pittsburgh he used the vault at the William Penn. On the morning of December 5, 1933, after visiting other cities, he arrived in Pittsburgh from Cincinnati before 7:00 A.M. After checking his personal bag at the railroad station, he went to the hotel. His proof was: 'I intended to stay . . . as long as I could do business here.' He arrived at the hotel around 7:00 o'clock, but the cashier's office, where the hotel had vaults, was not open, and the cashier, Schaller, had not arrived. . . . [Around 7:30, he again went back to the cashier's cage and Schaller there greeted him, saying, "I suppose you want a box." He knew Freudenheim quite well. He took a set of two keys from a board and handed Freudenheim an interlocking printed check used at the hotel for vault service.] One [part of this check] was the stub check given to Freudenheim, in form following:

WILLIAM PENN HOTEL
VAULT CHECK
C 6306

Checked by _____
Room _____

"The other [part] was a corresponding numeral, 6306, signed by Freudenheim and retained by the hotel. . . . [The cashier then inserted one of the two keys in the metal box in the safe, turned it and withdrew it. Freudenheim then inserted the other key, opened the box, and put his brief case with the merchandise in it right inside that box, closed the door, and went downstairs.] . . . From these facts, could an inference be reasonably drawn that Freudenheim was a guest of the hotel?

"In the first place, we have the fact that Freudenheim was known to the hotel as a past guest and that there was the possibility of his lodging at the hotel if trade warranted such stay. There was, therefore, in the minds of both parties that the hotel would have Freudenheim as a guest. He was recognized by the cashier; inquiry was made whether he wanted a box; he was given the box; his merchandise was deposited; and the operation recognized by both parties by the corresponding vault checks with similar numbers. This was a service or accommodation which the hotel had extended before and Freudenheim had enjoyed before.

". . . Now it is clear that vault service for valuables is a customary hotel accommodation and that it was the intention of both parties that Freudenheim should have that accommodation, and the relation of guest and hotel being once established, the doctrine in *Wright* v. *Anderton,* 1 K.B. 209, applies, viz.: 'The responsibility of an innkeeper for the safety of a traveller's property begins at the moment when the relation of guest and host arises, and that relation arises as soon as the traveller enters the inn with the intention of using it as an inn, and is so received by the host. It does not matter that no food or lodging has been supplied or found up to the time of the loss. It is sufficient if the circumstances show an intention of the one hand to provide and on the other hand to accept such accommodation.'

"Moreover, later on, and before he left, Freudenheim . . . did take his dinner in the general dining room of the hotel. It is true he did not take a room and register, but his omission to do so does not put him out of guest protection. See *Moody* v. *Kenny,* 153 La. 1007, 97 So. 21, 22, 29 A.L.R. 474, wherein it is said: 'The fact that such person fails to register, or is not required to register, is immaterial; as the registration of guests at a hotel is no part of the contract between the hotel proprietor and the guest, but the purpose of a register is to keep track of the number of people in the house and to keep the books straight. A register is kept solely for the benefit and convenience of the hotel proprietor.'

"This is in accord with cases cited in 14 Ruling Case Law, 518, which says: 'It is not necessary that a traveller shall register at an inn as a guest in order to become such, but it is sufficient if he visits the inn for the purpose of receiving entertainment and is entertained accordingly.'

"The jury having found a verdict in favor of the plaintiff, and the court having erred in holding as a matter of law that Freudenheim was not a guest, the judgment below is vacated, and the record is remanded, with instruction to the court to enter judgment on the verdict in favor of the plaintiffs."

[Rehearing denied March 23, 1937. Petition for certiorari dismissed. 302 U.S. 769.]

ARCADE HOTEL CO. *v.* WIATT
44 Ohio 32, 4 N.E. 298 (1886)

[Action to recover the sum of $2,195 which plaintiff alleged he deposited with the defendant on October 14, 1882, while a guest at the hotel, for safekeeping in its safe, and which it refused to return or repay to him.

The defendant below denied that plaintiff was a guest of the hotel, and that he deposited, or it received, any money from him for safekeeping. The plaintiff below recovered judgment for the amount claimed.

One of the questions before the court was whether plaintiff was a guest of the hotel at the time of the alleged deposit. So far as the evidence upon this issue is reviewed by the court, it is presented in the opinion.]

OWEN, J.: "Was Wiatt a guest of the hotel at the time he delivered to the clerk the package containing the money involved in suit? This is the vital issue in the case. . . .

"Wiatt testified that he entered the hotel about ten minutes after two o'clock in the morning, accompanied by his friend Mullen, and applied to the clerk for accommodations.

"He says: 'I asked for accommodations that night; I says to him: "How are you fixed for accommodations?" He says: "Very well, as we have not been doing very much since the Exposition." I says: "Very good, let me have a room, and I will stop with you to-night." He says:

"All right, I will just take your name. I am busy now making up my night account. I will just take your name." I says: "Very well, I have been eating something and I do not care about retiring now, I will be back in perhaps a half an hour." ' . . . 'I then produced this package of money. I said: "I would like to leave this with you." '

"He delivered the package to the clerk and received, as a check for it, a slip of paper with his name written thereon by the clerk. He says: 'I then passed out through the west end of the Arcade; . . . I was going up as far as . . . The Turf Exchange . . . I left there in the neighborhood of five o'clock . . . [and went] [d]irect from there to the Hotel Emery.'

"[Upon his return to the hotel,] the clerk and the money were missing; he soon became concerned for his money, and these, with other circumstances, may sufficiently account for his failure to take a room for the balance of the night, or morning.

"[On cross-examination, the plaintiff testified that he was engaged in operating a gambling room up under Gilligan's place; that he was a married man keeping house in the city of Cincinnati, that] . . . '[a]fter attending to my business, it being rather late, and the neighborhood being rather a disreputable one, as everybody knows that is familiar with it, I did not care to carry this amount of money with me, and go home and not find anybody there; and I told my wife I would stop down at the hotel to-night. . . . I had no intention of going home that night.'

". . . At the time the clerk took charge of his money, Wiatt had not registered his name; it was not entered upon any of the books of the hotel; no room had been assigned him; and while it is not necessary to contend that all, or any, of these facts were necessary to constitute him a guest of the hotel, they are valuable aids in determining, in the light of the other proof in the case, whether that relation in fact existed. There is proof which may account for his failure to register. Still, if he had registered, and this is shown to have been for the purpose of securing a safe depository for his money, it would not avail him.

"It will not do to contend that the deposit of his money contributed to constitute him a guest. Unless he was a guest, the clerk had no authority to bind his principal by receiving the money." [Judgment reversed.]

It would seem, therefore, that to entitle a person visiting an inn to be treated as a guest, and to hold an innkeeper responsible for money deposited with him for safekeeping, it must appear that such visit was for the purposes which the common law recognizes as the purposes for which inns are kept; and where such visit is made by one who does not require the present entertainment or accommodations of such inn, but whose purpose is simply to deposit his money for safekeeping, he is not a guest of the inn or hotel.

12:14 *Length of Stay as Affecting Status of Guest*

One who seeks accommodations in an inn with a view to permanency, so as to make the inn his home, is not a guest. The length of stay, however, is not ordinarily decisive for he will continue to be a guest as long as he retains his transient status. The question whether a person receiving accommodations at an inn is a guest or a lodger, boarder, or tenant, is one of fact.[42]

In *Holstein* v. *Phillips*,[43] the plaintiff, a resident of South Carolina, stopped at defendant's hotel and was charged ten dollars per week for board. She was to stay two or three weeks, but no agreement was made for any particular time. In an action to recover for the loss of valuables, the defense was that plaintiff was not a guest. (It appeared that defendant failed to comply with the statute limiting his liability as innkeeper.) Judgment for plaintiff was affirmed, the court stating:

She came to the hotel from her home in South Carolina for a short stay; she was a stranger to the parties defendant, and entered as a guest, so far as appears, without any prearrangement as to terms or time, but on the implied invitation held out to the public generally. She was there for no definite time, and, in our opinion, she was transient in every sense of the term and within every reason that gave her the right to the protection on which she insists. And, where this is true, all the authorities—certainly those having the better reason—are to the effect that the mere fact that she was to pay board by the week, or even at a reduced rate, does not alter her position as guest or deprive her of the right to hold defendants as insurers.[44]

[42] *Hancock* v. *Rand*, 94 N.Y. 1 (1883).
[43] 146 N.C. 366, 59 S.E. 1037 (1907).   [44] *Id.* at 372.

In *Pettit* v. *Thomas*,[45] plaintiff sued for the loss of her property destroyed by fire in defendant's hotel. The defense was that plaintiff was not a guest and that defendant was therefore not liable as innkeeper for the loss. It appeared that plaintiff paid her bills weekly and received a special rate, but that there was no agreement as to how long she would stay. The lower court had instructed the jury as follows:

1. You are instructed that the distinction between a boarder and a guest is made by the contract. A boarder is one who contracts for board and entertainment for a definite period and for a fixed sum. One who stays at a hotel for an indefinite period is not a boarder, but a guest.

2. If you believe from the evidence that the plaintiff resided in Louisville, Kentucky, and, desiring to come to Hot Springs for her health, arranged to stop at defendant's hotel at so much per week and that her proposed stay was for an indefinite period subject to be terminated by the plaintiff at will, and that she was received into the said hotel on these terms and conditions, then you will find the plaintiff was a guest of the defendant and was not a boarder.[46]

Judgment for plaintiff was affirmed on appeal, the court stating:

[T]he fact that a person had been at a hotel for more than a week, and paid the reduced weekly rate, does not make him a boarder, rather than a guest, in the absence of an agreement as to the time he would remain at the hotel. Neither does the fact that one makes an arrangement to pay a reduced rate per meal, or per day, or per week, take away his character as a guest, where there is no agreement as to the time he will remain at the hotel. And the question whether one is a boarder or guest is one of fact, to be determined by the jury under proper instructions from the court.[47]

In *Kaplan* v. *Stogop Realty Co.*,[48] it was held that a person who occupied a suite in defendant's hotel for a period of eleven months, paying rent on a monthly basis, the defendant furnishing maid service, linens, towels, soap, light, and telephone service, was not a transient person and, therefore, not a guest. And in the later case of *Mason* v. *Hotel Grand Union*,[49] a person who resided in the hotel from August 1, 1940 to May 30, 1942, when he was robbed, and

[45] 103 Ark. 593, 148 S.W. 501 (1912).   [46] *Id.* at 596.
[47] *Id.* at 600.   [48] 133 Misc. 611, 233 N.Y.S. 113 (Sup. Ct. 1929).
[49] 41 N.Y.S.2d 309 (N.Y. City Ct. 1943).

who paid on a monthly basis and had no other home or residence, was a tenant, and not a guest.

12:15 Employee as Guest

An employee residing in a hotel pursuant to his contract of employment is not a guest.[50] An employee, discharged at a late hour of the day, and permitted to occupy a room for the night, because of the lateness of the hour of her discharge, is not a guest.[51]

12:16 Lodgers, Boarders, and Tenants Distinguished from Guests

The nature and extent of the legal obligations of an innkeeper to persons in the inn depend on their relationship to the innkeeper. At common law, he is an insurer of the property of his guests in the house subject to exceptions and limitations; for the property of lodgers, boarders, and tenants his responsibility depends upon the exercise of reasonable care. He has a lien on the property of guests, (and by statute) lodgers, and boarders, but not of tenants. He owes a high degree of care for the personal comfort and safety of guests, to whom he owes a duty of courtesy as well. He may lock out a guest, lodger, or boarder for nonpayment of his reasonable charges, but must resort to legal process to dispossess a tenant. It is, therefore, important, in ascertaining legal rights and obligations, to understand the distinction between guests and nonguests. The determination is not an easy one, and where there is any doubt as to the status of a person, particularly in cases of lockout, the innkeeper should seek legal advice before taking action.

BRAMS v. BRIGGS
272 Mich. 38, 260 N.W. 785 (1935)

[Replevin by Brams against Briggs and another for office equipment, personal apparel and furniture held under a lien by virtue of 2 Comp. Laws 1929, §8791. Judgment for defendant. Plaintiff appeals.]

[50] *Powers* v. *Raymond*, 197 Cal. 126, 239 P. 1069 (1925).
[51] *Morrison* v. *Hotel Rutledge Co.*, 200 App. Div. 636, 193 N.Y.S. 428 (1st Dep't 1922).

BUTZEL, J.: "On November 7, 1929, Samuel S. Brams on registering at the Briggs Hotel in Detroit was assigned to room 1208. His registration card stated that he was to pay at the rate of '$90' but it is undisputed that actually a rate of $85 per month was fixed by arrangement with the late Lester Briggs, then proprietor of the hotel. The building was operated as a permanent residence hotel, the nature of the lay-out of the rooms being such that people remained there for months and years at a time. The record leaves it uncertain as to whether Brams rented the room furnished, and substituted his own furniture for that of the hotel. At any rate he did install his own furniture, including a large safe, desk, couch, chairs, etc. The hotel supplied the wall bed or beds. Plaintiff used the room as his business headquarters, and also slept there when in town and in the vicinity of the hotel. Although he made frequent trips away from Detroit, his furniture remained in the room and he continued to pay rent. He kept the key to his room at all times, and did not have to call at the desk in order to be allowed to get into the room. The hotel furnished maid service for the room, and also provided bell boys for the convenience of the guests.

"Brams became delinquent in his payments, and on May 8, 1930, his room was locked by the hotel management and his goods were seized on account of an unpaid bill of $242.10 for charges incurred during his stay. He thereupon brought a replevin action with a count for conversion, against Lester Briggs, the hotel, and one of its employees. Defendants claim a lien on the goods detained. . . .

". . . The sole question on appeal is whether plaintiff's relationship with the Hotel Briggs was one of guest, boarder or lodger in a hotel, inn, boarding or lodging house, so as to give defendants the right to the statutory or common-law lien. From the facts appearing in the meagre record, it does not seem that there was the relation of innkeeper and guest which gave rise to the innkeeper's lien under the common law.

". . . [W]e believe that if plaintiff was not a guest in a hotel, he was at least a lodger and thus came under the purview of the statute.

"In *McIntosh* v. *Schops*, 92 Ore. 307 (180 Pac. 593), plaintiff rented rooms in the Standish Hotel, which furnished accommodations to transients and permanent roomers. He paid rent at the rate of $12 per month for a period of over two years. The court held that since plaintiff's occupancy was of a permanent nature, at a fixed rental per week or month, he was *prima facie*, in the absence of evidence to the contrary, a lodger or boarder rather than a guest, and defendant was therefore not liable to him as an insurer for the loss of his goods. . . .

"In *Fox* v. *Windemere Hotel Apartment Co.*, 30 Cal. App. 162 (157 Pac. 820), plaintiff, who had rented three rooms in the Windemere Hotel Apartments at the rate of $55 a month, was held to be a 'lodger' within the meaning of the California statute giving a lien to hotel, inn, boarding house and lodging housekeepers upon the goods of guests, boarders or lodgers. The evidence showed that the building contained 58 apartments or suites; that defendant resided on the premises and at all times had control and supervision over the same; that it had a hotel keeper's license; that defendant retained keys to all suites or apartments and had access to them at all times to keep them in order. The court stated: 'Where, as here, the testimony shows that the house was under the direct control and supervision of the owners, that the rooms were furnished and attended to by them, and that they or their servants retained the keys thereto, a person renting such a room makes himself a lodger and not a tenant.'

". . . In the instant case plaintiff obtained his room by special arrangement with the proprietor, Mr. Briggs, at a certain fixed rate, and his stay was of a permanent nature. It also appears from the record that plaintiff had merely the use of his room, the hotel management retaining the general control and furnishing maid service, etc. Under this state of facts, we believe that plaintiff's relation with defendant was that of a lodger, and defendant is therefore entitled to a lien under the statute." [The judgment is affirmed.]

MARDEN v. RADFORD
229 Mo. App. 789, 84 S.W.2d 947 (Kansas City Ct. App. 1935)

[Action to recover damages for personal injuries sustained by plaintiff in a fall in a kichenette apartment, in the Claremont Hotel, in Kansas City. Judgment for $3000 for plaintiff from which defendant appeals.

It appeared that plaintiff rented from defendant a kitchenette apartment in said hotel; that defendant furnished plaintiff gas, electricity, water, linens, dishes, silverware, telephone, and all furniture; that defendant cleaned all the windows, and maintained employees to care for plaintiff's suite or apartment, and otherwise retained control and supervision over plaintiff's apartment.

The action has been brought on the theory of negligence consisting in the maintenance of a drainboard in the kitchen of plaintiff's apartment in a weak and rotted condition, which, when plaintiff took hold of it in an attempt to switch on the light, gave way and precipitated plaintiff to the floor, injuring her severely.

The answer contained a general denial and a plea of contributory negligence on plaintiff's part.]

REYNOLDS, C.: "The plaintiff was permitted to recover below upon the theory that she was a lodger in defendant's building in her occupancy of the apartment therein and that her relation to defendant was that of a lodger and that defendant was therefore bound to keep the apartment in an ordinarily reasonable state of repair for plaintiff's use and occupancy thereof and was therefore liable to plaintiff for damages sustained by her by reason of his not so keeping it in such state of repair.

". . . There was no written contract or agreement between the parties clearly defining the relationship between them. . . . The contract was entirely oral. There was very little said by the contracting parties at the time that the apartment was engaged. Defendant's manager showed the apartment and announced the price at which the use thereof might be had; and, thereupon, plaintiff's daughters engaged the apartment; and, afterward, plaintiff with her daughters entered and occupied the same.

". . . The issue being thus, from the position of the parties, made to depend upon whether the plaintiff was a lodger or a tenant, it becomes important to find a true basis of distinction between the two.

"The relation of landlord and tenant arises from contract between the parties, either express or implied, by which the exclusive possession and control or the right thereto of the rented premises is passed to the tenant.

". . . The authorities agree, as essential to such relationship, that there must be a reversion in the landlord; the creation of an estate in the tenant, at will or for a term less than that for which the landlord holds the same; the transfer of the exclusive possession and control of the premises to the tenant; and, generally speaking, a contract, either express or implied, between the parties.

". . . A lodger lodges with someone who has control over the place where he lodges. When the owner of a house takes a person to reside in part of it, such person has no exclusive right to the rooms appropriated to him. In order to constitute one a lodger, that one must be lodging with such other in the house of the other. Where the premises and the control thereof are given up by the proprietor to another, such other person is not a lodger but ordinarily a tenant.

". . . The chief distinction between a tenant and a lodger apparently rests in the character of the possession. A tenant has the exclusive legal possession of the premises, he and not the landlord being in control and responsible for the care and condition of the premises. A lodger, on the other hand, has merely a right to the use of the premises, the landlord retaining the control and being responsible for the care and attention necessary and retaining the right of access to the premises for such purpose.

". . . Moreover, the case at bar presents a personal contract between defendant and plaintiff, to furnish a variety of services which included plaintiff's right to occupancy of an apartment in defendant's building. There was more involved than a mere occupancy of the apartment. All of the fixtures and equipment were owned by the defendant. He owned the silverware and the linens and furnished the gas, the light, the heat, the water, and the telephone lines. When a person thus in the possession of the building lets to another a room or rooms and furnishes to such other the gas, the light, the water, the heat, and the telephone service and maintains in the building a lobby, an office and a staff of servants to furnish various services to the occupants of the various units and remains personally or through his manager in general possession and control of the entire building, such a relationship may be constituted between such a person and that other as to require the determination of the character thereof to be left to the jury.

". . . The same establishment may be operated as an inn, a hotel, a rooming or lodging house, an eating house, and an apartment, as separate institutions or in combination and under the same management. Such operation does not make the occupants of the building of one class—guests, roomers or tenants. The relationship of the proprietor with some might be that of an inn or hotel-keeper and guest; with others, that of landlord and tenant; with still others, that of landlord or lodging-housekeeper and guest—depending upon the contract with each particular guest and the character of each particular occupancy." [Judgment affirmed.]

In *Shearman* v. *Iroquois Hotel and Apartment Co.*,[52] the plaintiff's furniture was in an apartment, under written lease to her husband, in defendant's hotel. Defendant contended that it had a lien on this furniture to the amount of the husband's hotel bill. The apartment was rented unfurnished, and plaintiff's furniture was brought in to make the place habitable. By the terms of the written lease, the absolute right of use and occupation of the apartment was given to the husband as a dwelling for himself and family, and the defendant had no right of entry upon the premises, except for repairs and alterations.

The plaintiff's husband was held to be a tenant and not a lodger in defendant's hotel. That being so, the defendant had no lien on the plaintiff's furniture.

In general, the following facts should be ascertained in determining the distinction between guests and tenants:

1. Whether the person has any other home or legal residence.

2. Whether he votes from the hotel.

3. Whether he has steady employment in the city in which the hotel is situated.

4. Whether he has a written lease covering a fixed period of time.

5. Whether the rent is paid on a daily, weekly, monthly, or annual basis.

6. Whether there has been any expression of intention to leave the hotel at any particular future date for the purpose of going elsewhere.

12:17 *Dispossession of Tenants by Summary Proceedings*

Since the distinction between a lodger and a tenant is often a shadowy one, in case of any doubt, it would seem best to assume that a person who has resided in the hotel on a weekly or monthly rate basis for over thirty days is a tenant, and to proceed against him

[52] 42 Misc. 217, 85 N.Y.S. 365 (Sup. Ct. 1903).

accordingly. This view is reinforced by the provisions of Section 711 of the New York Real Property Actions and Proceedings Law, which became effective September 1, 1963, and which reads, in part, as follows: "An occupant of one or more rooms in a rooming house in a city having a population of one million or more, who has been in possession for thirty consecutive days or longer is a tenant under this article; he shall not be removed from possession except in a special proceeding."

12:18 *Termination of the Relation of Innkeeper and Guest*

The general rule is that when the guest pays his bill and departs, the strict liability does not cease at once, but continues for a reasonable time within which to remove the baggage; and if the host undertakes to deliver the baggage to a common carrier thereof, strict liability continues until the delivery is made.[53]

The relation, with its strict liability, may and does continue during the mere temporary absence of the guest from the inn. The length of time during which the absence may continue without terminating the relation is not fixed by law; the question of this duration in a given case is important only as evidence to determine whether the relation of host and guest continues in the interim. In order for this relation to continue during the guest's absence from the inn, however, the law does prescribe certain conditions which must be fulfilled:

1. There must be on the part of the guest an animus revertendi, which must be known to the innkeeper, or he must be properly chargeable therewith.

2. The intent must be to return within a reasonable time.

3. The liability to compensate the innkeeper, on the part of the guest, must continue during the absence. The right of the host to charge the guest is the criterion of the former's strict liability as host to the latter.[54]

In *Watkins* v. *Hotel Tutwiler Co.*, plaintiff had checked out of defendant's hotel and paid his bill in full. He left some of his trunks in the hotel's baggage room, intending to return in a few days. He also

[53] *Kaplan* v. *Titus*, 64 Misc. 81, 117 N.Y.S. 944 (Sup. Ct. 1909), aff'g 140 App. Div. 416, 125 N.Y.S. 397 (1st Dep't 1910).
[54] *Watkins* v. *Hotel Tutwiler Co.*, 200 Ala. 386, 388, 76 So. 302, 304 (1917).

deposited for safekeeping the sum of $1,900 and obtained a receipt from an individual behind the desk whom plaintiff believed to be the hotel clerk, but who in fact was not employed by the hotel and merely volunteered his services in assisting and looking after mail, checking baggage for the guests, and like services in expectation of such gratuities as guests might offer him. Upon returning to the city, plaintiff spent the night at his apartment without checking in at defendant's hotel. The next day, when he called for his trunks, they were properly delivered to him, but he never received his money. The individual behind the hotel desk to whom plaintiff delivered his money made off with it; he was subsequently convicted of larceny.

The court held that plaintiff was not a guest at the time of the loss of his money, or indeed, at the time he deposited it.

The trial court . . . properly instructed the jury that under all the evidence the relation of host and guest had terminated before the deposit was made. The mere fact that plaintiff and defendant both contemplated renewing that relation within a few days, and that the latter received the goods or money to keep until the relation should be renewed, would not be sufficient to charge defendant as an innkeeper, but only as a gratuitous bailee.[55]

The same result was reached in the earlier case of *DeLapp* v. *Van Closter*.[56] In that case, plaintiff, a bartender, checked into defendant's hotel in Kansas City. The next morning, plaintiff went down to the desk, asked the clerk for an envelope, placed $580 therein, and handed it to the clerk for safekeeping. The clerk in turn handed plaintiff a slip on which was written "6-17-07, DeLapp," and placed the package in the desk drawer. Later in the afternoon plaintiff surrendered his key and checked out. Three weeks later when plaintiff returned for his money, it was not to be found. The plaintiff was not entitled to recover. When he surrendered the key to his room and left without returning, he ceased to be a guest of the inn. "The fact that he did not intend to return and did not in fact do so, it seems to us, is conclusive on that question." [57]

In the Ohio case of *Hotels Statler Co.* v. *Safier*,[58] plaintiff was a guest in defendant's hotel each week for about four days. Each time he left the hotel, he had his trunk delivered to the hotel storage

[55] *Id.* at 390.   [56] 136 Mo. App. 475, 118 S.W. 120 (1909).
[57] *Id.* at 480.   [58] 103 Ohio St. 638, 134 N.E. 460 (1921).

room; upon his return it was redelivered to him. About August 1, 1917, when plaintiff returned again, he was told that his trunk and contents had been lost. The plaintiff, while technically a guest when the arrangement for storage was made, was not a guest during the period of storage. The statutory limitation of liability for the guest's property was not available to the hotel.

Courts in New York and Kentucky have taken a different view of liability for property remaining in the hotel after a guest's departure. In *Dilkes* v. *Hotel Sheraton*,[59] upon facts substantially similar to those found in the *Safier* case, the limitation of liability for the property of guests was held to remain in full force and effect after departure of the guest, the court stating:

The fact that the goods are permitted to remain in the hotel baggage room as a matter of accommodation with the expectation, or even mere hope, on the part of the hotel that the guest will return and resume residence does not, it seems to us, create a different relationship with respect to the stored goods, at least in the absence of some express agreement. Nor would the fact that residence was not resumed by the guest alter the relationship in which the goods were held or remove the limitation of liability. If this were not so, the hotel would be afforded protection under the statute when it was receiving the benefit of the guest's patronage, and lose the protection when it was accommodating the guest without remuneration. We think that the Legislature intended to give a broader protection. . . . [W]e find nothing in the present evidence to warrant a different rule of liability than that applied to innkeeper and guest.[60]

In *Kentucky Hotel* v. *Cinotti*,[61] the statutory limitation of liability was held to apply to property lost subsequent to the guest's departure from the hotel. "As the absence was to be temporary and the guest intended to return shortly and secure personal accommodations, the relationship of innkeeper and guest continued during the interval insofar as liability for the safekeeping of the property is concerned." [62]

12:19 *Penalty for Charging Guest after Departure*

The New York statute, Section 206 of the General Business Law, which mandates innkeepers to post "a statement of the charges or rate of charges by the day and for meals furnished and for lodging" also

---

[59] 282 App. Div. 488, 125 N.Y.S.2d 38 (1st Dep't 1953).   [60] *Id.* at 489.
[61] 298 Ky. 88, 182 S.W.2d 27 (1944).   [62] *Id.* at 91.

provides a penalty for charges made after the guest's departure, that is to say, after the termination of the innkeeper-guest relationship. The pertinent part of the statute reads:

No charge or sum shall be collected or received by any such hotel keeper or innkeeper for any service not actually rendered or for a longer time than the person so charged actually remained at such hotel or inn, nor for a higher rate of charge for the use of such room or board, lodging or meals than is specified in the rate of charges required to be posted by the last preceding sentence; provided such guest shall have given such hotel keeper or innkeeper notice at the office of his departure. For any violation of this section the offender shall forfeit to the injured party three times the amount so charged, and shall not be entitled to receive any money for meals, services or time charged.

12:20 Penalty for Charging Guest for Services Not Actually Rendered

Section 206 of the General Business Law is designed to penalize the innkeeper for charging the guests for services they do not actually receive. Included in this category would be blanket charges for services which some guests receive but which other guests do not.

STATE OF NEW YORK v. WALDORF-ASTORIA
67 Misc. 2d 90, 323 N.Y.S.2d 917 (Sup. Ct. 1971)

BAER, J.: "Petitioner brings this special proceeding under subdivision 12 of section 63 of the Executive Law to permanently enjoin and restrain the respondents from conducting and transacting their business in a 'persistently fraudulent and illegal manner,' and to direct restitution to all consumers of the amount charged for services not rendered, plus triple damages, pursuant to section 206 of the General Business Law.

"The General Business Law does require every hotel to post 'a statement of the . . . charges by the day and for meals furnished and for lodging.' It further provides that 'No charge or sum shall be collected or received by any such hotel keeper or inn keeper for any service not actually rendered.'

"Between December 2, 1969 and May 21, 1970 the respondents did add to each bill of each customer a 2% charge for sundries. The respondents contend that this was a proper charge because of the peculiar needs of their clientele, and the capital cost and maintenance cost of their internal communications system. They also contend that counsel for the New York State Hotel and Motel Association, of which they are members, advised of the propriety of such charges. This latter contention is not borne out by an advisory letter dated April 17, 1970, wherein respondents were advised that it was 'Improper to charge guests for interior calls or interior service other than through his room rent.' They were advised in the same communication that such charges should be 'included in the room rent' or 'if separately stated, should be clearly identified.'

"The respondents' plea in defense or amelioration is grossly mistaken. Of course, they could charge more for the room but it was fraudulent and deceitful to add to each billing after the room charge 'Sund's' without any explanation, itemization or identification.

"Respondents argue that there was no violation of section 206 of the General Business Law because that section only prohibits charges 'for any service not actually rendered' and that message services in fact were rendered. However, even respondents admit that all of their customers did not receive special, costly messenger service. They contend that 77% did receive such service but admit that 23% did not. None of their customers received any explanation or itemization of the charge for sundries. All of them were charged this 2% during the period in question.

"In any event, the practice was fraudulent within the meaning of subdivision 12 of section 63 of the Executive Law, wherein fraud is defined as 'any device, scheme or artifice to defraud and any deception, misrepresentation, concealment . . . or unconscionable contractual provisions.' [Citation omitted.] Although the 2% charge was discontinued after an inquiry by the petitioner, this in no way restricts the court from restraining the practice. [Citations omitted.]

" 'The business of an innkeeper is of a *quasi* public character, invested with many privileges and burdened with correspondingly great responsibilities.' [Citation omitted.] The charge for message services delineated as sundries was fraudulent and unconscionable. Accordingly, petitioner's application is granted to the extent that respondents are permanently enjoined from engaging in the fraudulent and illegal acts and practices complained of herein.

"The amount of money to be refunded is admitted. The petitioner, by its Bureau of Consumer Frauds and Protection, investigated the records of the respondents and claims that the 2% charge for sundries during the period in question involved 64,338 customers and amounts to $113,202.83. Frank A. Banks, vice-president and manager of respondent, in an affidavit of June 10, 1971, states that during the period in question transient room sales amounted to $6,329,484. The 2% charge would therefore be over $126,000. However, the exact amount is not important, as the respondents are ordered to refund to each and every customer during the period in question all charges for unexplained sundries. These refunds are to be made within 60 days of the date of service of the judgment herein with notice of entry. Within 30 days thereafter canceled vouchers or copies thereof will be exhibited to the petitioner. If payment cannot be made to any customer for any reason, the amounts thereof will be deposited with the petitioner, who will deposit same with the court if restitution cannot be made (Abandoned Property Law, §600). Petitioner may suggest another method of creating a fund to assure restitution upon settlement of judgment, if so advised.

"If there be disagreement as to the amount involved in the restitution herein ordered, either party may submit an order at the time of settling judgment, for an assessment of damages.

"The demand for treble damages is denied. The Executive Law provides for restitution only. The General Business Law provides for treble damages to the injured parties. The injured parties may seek such punitive damages but the petitioner may only obtain restitution for them. The petitioner, in addition to one bill of costs against respondents, is granted an allowance of $2,000 against the respondent Hotel Waldorf-Astoria Corporation (CPLR 8303, subd. [a], par. 6)."

CHAPTER 13

Duty of Courteous and Considerate Treatment for Protection and Care of Guest's Person

13:1 Common-Law Duties of Innkeeper to Guest

The common-law duties of the innkeeper to his guests may be divided into three classes: he must furnish (1) shelter, (2) protection, and (3) food. He is therefore called upon to provide safe premises, to protect the guest against personal harm, and to furnish a sufficient quantity of wholesome food.

13:2 Innkeeper's Right of Access to Guest's Room

It is a basic legal principle which governs the relationship of innkeeper and guest that the innkeeper holds himself out as able and willing to entertain guests for hire, and, in the absence of a specific contract, the law implies that he will furnish such entertainment as the character of his inn and reasonable attention to the convenience and comfort of his guests will afford.

If the guest is assigned to a room upon the express or implied understanding that he is to be the sole occupant thereof during the time that it is set apart for his use, the innkeeper retains a right of access thereto only at such proper times and for such reasonable purposes as may be necessary in the general conduct of the inn or in attending to the needs of a particular guest. If, for instance, there should be an outbreak of fire, a leakage of water or gas, or any other emergency calling for immediate action in a room assigned to a guest, the innkeeper and his servants must necessarily have the right to enter without regard to the time of day or night and without consulting the wish or convenience of the guest. It is equally clear that for the purpose of enabling the innkeeper to fulfill his express or implied contract to furnish his guest with such convenience and comfort as the inn affords, he and his servants must have such access to the room at all such reasonable times as will enable him to fulfill his duty in that behalf. It is obvious that as to this general right of entry no hard and fast rule can be laid down, for what would be reasonable in a case where a room is occupied by two or more guests, or where access to one room can be had only through another, might be highly unreasonable where a separate room is assigned to the exclusive use of a single guest. It is also manifestly proper and necessary that an innkeeper should have the right to make and enforce such reasonable rules as may be designed to prevent immorality, drunkenness, or any form of misconduct that may be offensive to other guests, or that may bring his inn into disrepute, or that may be radically inconsistent with the generally recognized proprieties of life. To these reserved rights of the innkeeper the guest must submit.

Should an emergency arise, calling for immediate and unpremeditated action on the part of the innkeeper or his employees, in securing the safety or protection of the guests or of the building in which they were housed, the usual rules of decency, propriety, convenience, or comfort might be disregarded without subjecting the innkeeper to liability for mistake of judgment or delinquency in conduct; but for all other purposes any occasional or regular entries into a guest's room are subject to the fundamental consideration that it is for the time being *his* room, and that he is entitled to respectful and considerate treatment at the hands of his host. Such treatment necessarily implies an observance by the innkeeper and his employees of the proprieties as to the time and manner of entering the guest's room, and of civil deportment toward him when such an entry was either necessary or proper.[1]

Whether the innkeeper is legally entitled to enter a guest's room solely for the purpose of appraising the nature or value of the guest's property as a measure of extending credit, has not been the subject of judicial determination. It would seem that an entry for such a purpose would not be proper without notice to the guest and appraising him of the purpose. Moreover, there are other means of evaluating

[1] *DeWolf* v. *Ford,* 193 N.Y. 397, 86 N.E. 527 (1908).

baggage for credit purposes. The bellmen should be trained to observe the quality and quantity of incoming baggage and report "light baggage" to the credit office. Later, after the guest has been roomed, it should be the task of the house-keeping staff to report promptly conditions in the room, such as "sleepouts," no baggage, firearms, and the like. In any event, if an entry is to be made into a guest's room during his absence therefrom, for any purpose, it should be made in the presence of a witness, such as a security officer or a floor house-keeper.

13:3 *Exclusive Right of Guest to Use and Possession of His Room*

The guest also has affirmative rights which the innkeeper is not at liberty willfully to ignore or violate. When a guest is assigned to a room for his exclusive use, it is his for all proper purposes and at all times until he gives it up. This exclusive right of use and possession is subject to such emergent and occasional entries as the innkeeper and his servants may find it necessary to make in the reasonable discharge of their duties, but these entries must be made with due regard to the occasion and at such times and in such manner as are consistent with the rights of the guest. One of the things which a guest for hire at a public inn has the right to insist upon is respectful and decent treatment at the hands of the innkeeper and his servants. That is an essential part of the contract whether it is express or implied. This right of guest necessarily implies an obligation on the part of the innkeeper that neither he nor his servants will abuse or insult the guest, or indulge in any conduct or speech that may unnecessarily bring upon him physical discomfort or distress of mind. The innkeeper, it is true, is not an insurer of the safety, conveniences, or comfort of the guest. But the former is bound to exercise reasonable care that neither he nor his servants shall by uncivil, harsh, or cruel treatment destroy or minimize the comfort, convenience, and peace which the latter would ordinarily enjoy if the inn were properly conducted, due allowance being always made for the grade of the inn and the character of the accommodation which it is designed to afford.[2]

2 *Id.*

13:4 *Damages for Unlawful Intrusion into Guest's Room*

In *Newcomb Hotel Co.* v. *Corbett*,[3] the plaintiff sued for damages for unlawful intrusion by an employee into plaintiff's guest room while she was a guest in defendant's hotel.

Plaintiff was alone in the room to which she had been assigned in defendant's hotel, having retired and gone to bed for the night. She was aroused by the night watchman of the hotel, who was accompanied by a police officer who demanded admission. Plaintiff phoned the clerk on duty and asked for protection against the threatened intrusion, but to no avail. The night watchman accused plaintiff of having a man in her room, and over plaintiff's protest opened the door with a pass key, entered, searched the room, and discovered the suspicion unfounded.

It appeared, in defense against an action for unlawful intrusion upon her privacy by plaintiff, that defendant's hotel clerk upon examining plaintiff's signature on the registration card drew the inference that plaintiff was a male, since plaintiff failed to indicate by a prefix to her name that she was a female. The clerk thus believed that plaintiff entered the room of a male guest without authority; hence the search of the room.

The jury found for plaintiff and returned a verdict for $5,500. On appeal, the judgment was affirmed.

The court reasoned as follows: Since a hotelkeeper has an opportunity of seeing his guests when he receives them, he is chargeable with knowledge as to what guests are assigned to particular rooms in the hotel, and therefore he has no right to assume that a guest who is occupying a room to which he has been assigned is any other than the guest properly entitled to occupy the room. While, in order to facilitate his business in handling his guests, a hotelkeeper may require his guests, when applying for accommodations at his hotel, to register their names in a register, he is nevertheless not thereby relieved, by any false inference he may draw from the register, from the duty resting upon him of knowing to what rooms the various guests are assigned. Thus, where a female guest has applied for lodging at a hotel and has signed her name upon the register, without any prefix to her

3 27 Ga. App. 365, 108 S.E. 309 (1921).

signature or other indication that her signature is that of a female, and is assigned to a certain room in the hotel, the hotelkeeper is charged with notice that the particular room is occupied by the female guest, and he has no right to assume, from any false inference which he may afterwards draw from the character and handwriting of her signature on the register, that the person entitled to occupy the room is a man, and that the female guest properly occupying the room is an intruder, and not entitled to it. That the hotelkeeper, possessing actual knowledge of this fact, may, when acting through another and different clerk, having drawn such false inference from the character of the guest's signature, is not a defense to a suit against him by the guest for unlawfully entering her room for the purpose of ascertaining if immoral conduct is being practiced therein.

Where a guest of a hotel is occupying his room, and is neither engaged in nor permitting improper conduct therein, nor affording any just ground to suspect such, it is an unjustified intrusion upon the guest, and a trespass upon his rights incident to his occupancy of the room for the hotelkeeper to effect an uninvited and unpermitted entry into the room for the purpose of ascertaining whether improper conduct on the part of the guest or anyone is transpiring therein.

In *McKee* v. *Sheraton-Russell, Inc.,*[4] the plaintiff, June McKee, sought to recover for injuries she alleged she had sustained when her room in defendant's hotel was invaded.

Shortly after midnight of Saturday, September 4, 1954, plaintiff, who had reached New York that evening from Detroit, arrived at the Sheraton-Russell, registered, and was assigned a room with bath on the seventh floor.

She testified that when she retired on Sunday night, September 5, she locked her door and attached a "Do Not Disturb" sign to the outside doorknob. About 6:45 A.M. on September 6, she arose and went to her bathroom. Reentering her bedroom she discovered, crouched near the end of her bed, the bellboy who upon her arrival at the hotel had shown her to her room. Plaintiff was undressed and, attempting to cover herself, tried to get the bellboy to leave. He remained, however, for some twelve to twenty minutes, making remarks which the court regarded as suggestive; and, near the end of his stay, he advanced upon her with hands outstretched. She finally managed

4 268 F.2d 669 (2d Cir. 1959).

to get him out of the room without being physically touched by him but shortly thereafter he returned and attempted to persuade her not to tell anyone what had happened. She suffered fright and shock, and also proffered evidence tending to show that this occurrence had aggravated a preexisting urinary ailment.

The bellboy, who was called to the witness stand by the court, corroborated the plaintiff's story that he was in fact in her room that morning. He testified, however, that he was not on duty, that he believed Miss McKee had checked out and that her room was unoccupied, that he wanted to take a radio from there to the locker room for his own use, and that he was not in Miss McKee's room in the course of, or in furtherance of, the business of the hotel. He stated that he had obtained the passkey he used from the hotel desk where room keys were readily accessible to the bellmen. He denied that he was in the room for as long a time as plaintiff claimed, and denied that he was other than respectful to her.

The jury awarded plaintiff $5,000 compensatory and $5,000 punitive damages. The judgment entered on the jury's verdict was reversed on appeal and a new trial ordered. In the new trial the jury again found for the plaintiff for $10,000 compensatory damages, which on defendant's motion, the court reduced to $5,146.25.

In *Dixon* v. *Hotel Tutwiler Operating Co.*,[5] the plaintiff and his wife registered as guests in defendant's hotel. Through an error at the front desk, the registration card, prepared by the clerk, showed the name of the husband alone as a guest. Subsequently, a house officer entered plaintiff's room during the night, interrupting their sleep.

Mere suspicion of improprieties or indecencies will not authorize a violation of the well-recognized rights of a guest, said the court. The grounds should be more than a mere suspicion; they should be reasonable; there should be a proper inquiry for the truth and facts in the premises.

13:5 *Duty to Furnish and Right to Assign and Change Guest Accommodations*

It is the duty of the innkeeper to supply the guest with such accommodations as he needs, due allowance being made for the grade of

[5] 214 Ala. 396, 108 So. 26 (1926).

the inn and its facilities. The inn, though a public house, does not, however, become in any sense the house of the guest; the innkeeper continues to be the housekeeper, and the management of the house remains absolutely and at all times in his hands, subject only to the right of the guest to receive reasonable entertainment.

The assignment of a guest to a room is in no sense a lease; it is a mere revocable license. It follows that the innkeeper, in the course of his management, has the absolute right to assign the guest to any proper room, and he may at will change the room and assign the guest, with or without his consent, to another room.

DOYLE v. WALKER
26 Upper Canada Queen's Bench Rep. 502 (1867)

[Trespass for breaking and entering certain apartments in the possession of the plaintiff and his family, in the American Hotel, in the City of Toronto, and taking plaintiff's goods in the said apartments.

The plaintiff occupied two rooms in the American Hotel kept by defendant, and was charged for his accommodation by the day. On September 18, the plaintiff owed $83.25. He was asked to leave. On the 21st, plaintiff owed $109.15. He asked for the bill which was rendered at 2:00 P.M. that day. But on that morning defendant had gone into the plaintiff's room, no person being in it at the time and he put up some additional beds therein and removed the plaintiff's trunks and property. This was the trespass complained of. Plaintiff was not in the hotel at the time, but was at his office in town, where defendant's clerk had gone to him and demanded payment, when plaintiff said he was going to leave. The bill was not paid until that evening. The jury found for the plaintiff, damages $100.]

DRAPER, C.J.: "The plaintiff neither asserts nor proves any special contract. He rests his case upon what he assumes to be his right resulting from his being a guest in an inn, and the defendant being the innkeeper. He assumes that having been let into possession of a room, he has acquired such an exclusive right of possession as against his landlord, so long as he continues to occupy it, that the latter is liable as a trespasser for entering and removing his trunks out of it.

"We do not so understand the law. The contention appears to us to be inconsistent with the well-settled duties, liabilities, and rights of the innkeeper. Whatever may be the traveller's right to be received as a guest, and to be reasonably entertained and accommodated, the landlord has, in our opinion, the sole right to select the apartment for the guest, and, if he finds it expedient, to change the apartment and assign the guest another without becoming a trespasser in making the change. If, having the necessary convenience, he refuses to afford reasonable accommodation he is liable to an action, but not of trespass. There is no implied contract that a guest to whom a particular apartment has been assigned shall retain that particular apartment so long as he chooses to pay for it. We think the contention on the plaintiff's part involves a confusion between the character and position of an innkeeper and a lodging housekeeper.

"It appears to us further, that although the innkeeper is bound to receive, the guest must not only be ready and willing, and before he can insist as of right to be received that he must offer, to pay whatever is the reasonable charge; and that a guest who has been received loses the right to be entertained if he neglects or refuses to pay upon reasonable demand. The plaintiff's bill accrued due *de die in diem,* and had been in arrears though frequently demanded."

[Rule absolute for new trial.]

In *Hervey* v. *Hart,*[6] the plaintiff applied for accommodations at the Bienville Hotel in Mobile, and was accepted as a guest by the defendant, who assigned him to "Parlor A." While plaintiff continued to occupy said apartment and during his temporary absence from the hotel, defendant moved his baggage, refused to allow him use of said apartment and refused to furnish him with other proper accommodations. In an action by the guest against the innkeeper, the court cited *Doyle* v. *Walker,* with approval and added that the defendant innkeeper was not liable if he offered plaintiff proper accommodations in lieu of the room previously assigned him.

As the innkeeper may assign the guest to any chamber he pleases, so he may serve him with food in any room he pleases, provided it is a decent and proper room; and the guest cannot complain if the innkeeper refuses to serve him in the common dining room. This question was involved in the interesting case of *Regina* v. *Sprague.*[7]

[6] 149 Ala. 604, 42 So. 1013 (1906).
[7] 63 J.P. 233 (Surrey Quarter Sessions 1899).

The suit was an indictment for refusing to supply Lady Harberton with food. Lady Harberton was cycling, clad in the "rational costume," so called, and she stopped for luncheon at the defendant's inn. The defendant refused to serve her in the coffee room unless she put a skirt over the "rational costume," but offered to serve her in a private room behind the bar. On looking into the room Lady Harberton found it was occupied by men, some of whom were smoking, and refused to enter; and thereupon the prosecution was instituted, at the Surrey Quarter Sessions. The defendant urged that no person had a right to choose a particular room; to which Mr. Cave, the chairman, replied, "Suppose a landlord said he would only supply victuals in the coal cellar?" The defendant said that was an extreme case; but would an indictment lie against a landlord because a fastidious lady disliked the smell of smoke? The case ought not to be left to the jury. The chairman, however, left the question to the jury. The question was, he said, whether there was a refusal to supply food in a decent and proper place. The innkeeper could select the room provided it was a decent and proper place. Nor, in his opinion, was a guest entitled to have a room exactly to his or her taste. The jury must judge by the requirement of ordinary and reasonable persons. The chairman then asked the jury to consider whether the bar parlor was a decent and proper room for a guest to have lunch in. The jury brought in a verdict of not guilty. It may be doubted whether an American jury would have been so ungallant; but the action of the chairman was unquestionably correct.

At the same time the innkeeper cannot go further than determine the kind of accommodation to be furnished to the guest; he cannot demand that the guest make any particular use of the accommodation. He may place such reasonable food as he chooses before the guest, but he cannot complain if the guest refuses to eat it; nor can he object if the guest refuses to occupy his bed, but chooses to sit up all night. So in the course of the argument in *Fell* v. *Knight*,[8] Alderson, B., said: "A traveller is not bound to go to bed: he may have business to attend to, which would render it necessary for him to sit up all night. An innkeeper cannot be justified in turning his guest out because he refuses to sleep."

The innkeeper must, of course, provide a reasonable number of

[8] 151 Eng. Rep. 1039, 1041 (Exch. 1841).

common rooms but he may refuse to furnish light and heat for the guest to occupy his chamber as a reading or writing room, or a common room as a sleeping apartment. So where a guest refused to sleep in the chamber assigned to him, and requested that candles should be furnished him that he might sit up all night in a chamber, the innkeeper was justified in refusing, at least where he offered to allow the guest to sit up and have light in the regular reading room. In *Fell* v. *Knight,* Lord Abinger, C.B., said: "I do not think a landlord is bound to provide for his guest the precise room the latter may select. . . . All that the law requires of him is, to find for his guests reasonable and proper accommodation: if he does that, he does all that is requisite." [9]

A landlord is not bound to provide a traveler with a particular room, nor to permit him to occupy a bedchamber as a sitting room if he offers him another room fit and proper for the purpose. He is to provide him with a room affording reasonable accommodation, but not any room which the caprice of guest may lead him to select.

13:6 *Right of Guest to Display Business Signs in Lobby*

One who rents a room in a hotel does not acquire the right to use the hotel for advertising purposes. In *Samuel* v. *Boldt,*[10] plaintiff checked into the Bellevue Stratford in Philadelphia and was given a room on a day-to-day basis to be used as a millinery shop. There was nothing in the agreement about the use of display signs. Shortly after she had taken possession of the room, plaintiff put up signs in the lobby which were immediately removed by the management. She was then given notice to vacate her room. She complained that the management refused to permit her the public display of placards announcing her business and prevented her from operating her shop and finally dispossessed her. The court had no hesitation in directing judgment for the defendant innkeeper.

13:7 *Duty to Furnish Telephone Service*

The innkeeper is under no duty to furnish telephone service to his guests. In point of fact, however, hotel rooms are almost universally

[9] *Id.* at 1042.   [10] 77 Pa. Super. 144 (1921).

provided with telephones for the convenience of guests. A question may well arise, therefore, as to the liability of an innkeeper for damages arising as a result of failure to provide service.

In *Lewis v. Roescher,*[11] the action was brought by an executrix against the owner and operator of a hotel and was based on two counts. The first count alleged that the defendant had furnished her deceased husband with tainted food from which he contracted ptomaine poisoning. The second count stated that the decedent contracted for a room which was equipped with a telephone, that the telephone was defective, or the defendant's clerk was inattentive, that the decedent became desperately ill and was unable to leave his room, and that when his repeated efforts to telephone failed, he was forced to suffer and vomit excessively until the following morning when he finally obtained a physician. The complaint alleged that the defendant breached her contract in failing to provide facilities for communicating the decedent's illness, but there was no allegation of defendant's knowledge of either the defective phone or the guest's illness. The lower court dismissed the complaint. On appeal, the Supreme Court of Arkansas reversed on the first count but upheld the lower court's determination on the second.

The court held as follows: The hotel was under no duty to furnish Lewis with a telephone in his room, and would not be liable because the telephone furnished was defective, or because he was unable to get communication with the clerk. Special damages claimed because of the failure to furnish telephone connection could be recovered only where the hotel had knowledge of the circumstances and conditions. There was no implied warranty that Lewis would be furnished with telephone service, and there was no allegation in the complaint that the hotel had knowledge of the fact that the telephone was defective. Nor was there any allegation that the hotel had knowledge that Lewis was either sick or that he was likely to become sick and suffer.

It would seem that if the innkeeper had knowledge of the circumstances and had negligently failed to provide telephone service and the results to the guest were foreseeable, damages would have been recoverable.

[11] 193 Ark. 161, 98 S.W.2d 956 (1963).

13:8   *Liability for Failure to Furnish Guest with Key and to Awaken Him*

GUMBART *v.* WATERBURY CLUB HOLDING CORPORATION
27 F. Supp. 228 (D. Conn. 1938)

[Plaintiff seeks to recover damages for personal injuries received in a fall while attempting to enter through a window.]

HINCKS, D. J.: "For purposes of this memorandum, I assume throughout that the relationship between plaintiff and defendants was that obtaining between guest and innkeepers.

"The first count, insofar as it is based upon the defendants' failure to supply the plaintiff with a key to the premises, fails to state a cause of action. *Neither common law nor statute require an innkeeper, unrequested, to supply every guest with a key to the inn or to keep the entrance either unlocked or under attendance during the night* [emphasis supplied]. . . .

"The first count also fails to state a cause of action in so far as it is based upon the maintenance of an outside window in the defendants' building. To be sure, it is stated that this window was unprotected and 'open and easily accessible to anyone from the outside'; that inside the window there was a drop of some 25 feet to the floor of the gymnasium; and that the gymnasium was unlighted at the time in question. The complaint, however, fails to show that the defendants invited the plaintiff to enter by the window, either by express invitation or by an invitation which might be implied from a walk leading to the window or from any other features of the lay-out of the premises. A guest's implied invitation of entry may not be expanded to include such a means of entrance. [Citations omitted.] And the same rule is applicable to gratuitous licensees. [Citations omitted.] Since from the facts stated it appears affirmatively that the plaintiff in attempting to enter by a window was neither invitee nor licensee, the remaining facts alleged are insufficient to show the violation of any duty on the part of the defendants. . . .

"The third count also sounds in tort, and must also be held to be insufficient in law. *For I can find nothing in the common law nor any statute which imposes a mandatory duty upon innkeepers to awaken*

guests from their slumbers at a requested hour. [Emphasis supplied.]
Indeed, the proposition is tacitly abandoned in plaintiff's brief.

"Furthermore, this count fails to state facts from which it could be
found that the defendants' alleged negligence was the proximate
cause of the only injury complained of. For if the defendants had
called the plaintiff at 7:30 and had thus learned that he was not in
his room, they would have been under no duty to search for him in
the gymnasium. In other words, the defendants' negligence (assuming it to have been negligence) in failing to call the plaintiff was not
a substantial factor in bringing about the aggravation of the plaintiff's
injuries, and hence not a legal cause thereof." [Citation omitted.]
[Complaint dismissed.]

13:9 *Liability for Failure or Delay in Delivering Messages, Mail, and Telegrams*

There is no common-law or statutory duty imposed on innkeepers
to deliver messages and telegrams addressed to guests. Such duty, if
there be any, is voluntarily assumed by the innkeeper and is contractual in its nature. Liability is the result of breach of promise to perform a service implied from the nature of the business.

The innkeeper is sometimes confronted with claims for special
damages for mental suffering and also for the loss of profits in business transactions which were not consummated because of failure or
delay in delivery of a letter, telegram, or message.

In the majority of jurisdictions damages are not recoverable for
mental suffering consequent on delay in the delivery of a telegraphic
message, nor for sickness and physical suffering resulting from such
mental distress. It is also well settled that a hotelkeeper is not liable
for special damages in the nature of loss of profits in an unconsum-
mated business transaction unless he has knowledge of the fact that
delay or failure of delivery will result in such special damages.

The innkeeper should be intelligently informed about postal regulations applicable to the handling of mail addressed to guests in the
hotel. He should obtain from the local post office a copy of the Official
Postal Guide which contains regulations specially applicable to hotels.
In general, a hotel may be liable for negligence in failing to use reasonable care in the delivery or handling of mail. The duty, the breach

of which may be the foundation of such liability, may be assumed by voluntary agreement, or it may be implied from the custom and service practice of the hotel upon which the aggrieved guest relied or had a right to rely. It is invariably unwise for an innkeeper to commit himself to a guest by agreement to hold mail for any period longer than ten days. In the large transient hotels it might be wise to post a notice in a conspicuous place at the mail desk with respect to the handling of mail after departure. Special care should be used with respect to registered mail, C.O.D. packages, and parcel post.

In *Joslyn* v. *King*,[12] the plaintiff was a letter carrier. He had a registered letter addressed to a guest at defendant's hotel. The plaintiff delivered the letter to the clerk of the hotel who signed for it. The clerk placed the letter in the letter box and then left the desk for six hours to get some sleep. When the clerk returned he discovered that the letter had been purloined. The plaintiff being under a duty to deliver the letter only to the addressee was held liable for the loss. The letter had contained $100 and this amount the plaintiff paid the guest. The plaintiff then sued the hotel owner and the clerk. The defense was twofold: (1) the plaintiff was himself negligent in not delivering the letter to the addressee; and (2) the plaintiff did not communicate the value of the letter to the clerk when he delivered it. The trial court entered judgment for the plaintiff. On appeal, the judgment was affirmed.

The court reasoned: The negligence of the plaintiff in delivering the letter in no way relieved the defendants of their own negligence. The fact that the letter had to be signed for was notice that the letter was of more than ordinary importance and that special care was required. The bailment was voluntarily assumed and care should have been proportionately increased.

There are no reported cases involving innkeepers on the subject of damages recoverable for failure to deliver messages, telegrams, or a trunk or other property, for that matter. Such situations usually involve a negative wrong of failing to perform a usual or ordinary service to which a guest was entitled either because of a promise made to him or because a promise of service was implied from the usual practice of hotelkeepers. In such cases there is no recovery for the results of an unforeseen situation which thereafter arises. The cases

12 27 Neb. 38, 42 N.W. 756 (1889).

which follow, although not arising out of hotel practice, illustrate the applicable law of damages.

KERR STEAMSHIP CO., INC. v. RADIO CORPORATION OF AMERICA
245 N.Y. 284, 157 N.E. 140 (1927)

Cardozo, C.J.: "On May 15, 1922, the plaintiff, Kerr Steamship Company, Inc., delivered to defendant, the Radio Corporation of America, a telegram consisting of twenty-nine words in cipher to be transmitted to Manila, Philippine Islands.

"The telegram was written on one of the defendant's blanks, and is prefaced by the printed words: 'Send the following radiogram via R.C.A., subject to terms on back hereof which are hereby agreed to.'

"The defendant had no direct circuit for the transmission of radiograms to the Philippine Islands. A radiogram could have been sent to London, where by transfer to other companies it might have reached its destination. This was expensive for the customer. To reduce the expense and follow a more direct route, the defendant forwarded its Philippine messages over the line of the Commercial Cable Company, which transmitted them by cable. When messages were thus forwarded, the practice was to send them upstairs to be copied. One copy was then handed to the cable company, and one kept for the defendant's files. That practice was followed in this instance except that the copy intended for the cable company was mislaid and not delivered. As a consequence the telegram was never sent.

"The telegram on its face is an unintelligible cipher. It is written in Scott's code. Translated into English, it remains at best obscure, though some inkling of the transaction may be conveyed to an ingenious mind. Untranslated, it is jargon. The fact is that one Macondray, to whom the telegram was addressed, had called the plaintiff for instructions as to the loading of a ship, *The Blossom*. The instructions were contained in the undelivered message. As a result of the failure to transmit them, the cargo was not laden and the freight was lost. The trial judge directed a verdict for $6,675.29, the freight that would have been earned if the message had been carried. He held that the cipher, though the defendant could not read it, must have been understood as having relation to some transaction of a business nature and that from this understanding without more there ensued a liability for the damages that would have been recognized as natural if the transaction had been known. [The Appellate Division affirmed, and defendant appeals.] The defendant insists that the tolls which the plaintiff was to pay, $26.78, must be the limit of recovery.

"The settled doctrine of this court confines the liability of a telegraph company for failure to transmit a message within the limits of the rule in *Hadley* v. *Baxendale* (9 Exch. 341). Where the terms of the telegram disclose the general nature of the transaction which is the subject of the message, the company is answerable for the natural consequences of its neglect in relation to the transaction thus known or foreseen. [Citations omitted.] On the other hand, where the terms of the message give no hint of the nature of the transaction, the liability is for nominal damages or for the cost of carriage if the tolls have been prepaid. [Citations omitted.]

"We are now asked to hold that the transaction has been revealed within the meaning of the rule if the length and cost of the telegram or the names of the parties would fairly suggest to a reasonable man that business of moment is the subject of the message. This is very nearly to annihilate the rule in the guise of an exception. The defendant upon receiving from a steamship company a long telegram in cipher to be transmitted to Manila would naturally infer that the message had relation to business of some sort. Beyond that, it could infer nothing. The message might relate to the loading of a cargo, but equally it might relate to the sale of a vessel or to the employment of an agent or to anyone of myriad transactions as divergent as the poles. Notice of the business, if it is to lay the basis for special damages, must be sufficiently informing to be notice of the risk. [Citations omitted.]

"The plaintiff makes the point that the action is one in tort for the breach of a duty owing from a public service corporation, and that the rule of *Hadley* v. *Baxendale* does not protect the carrier unless sued upon the contract. . . . Though the duty to serve may be antecedent to the contract, yet the contract when made defines and circumscribes the duty. . . . As it is, there is little trace of a disposition to make the measure of the liability dependent on the form of action. A different question would be here if the plaintiff were seeking reparation for a wrong unrelated to the contract, as *e.g.*, for a refusal to accept a message or for an insistence upon the payment of discriminatory rates. The plaintiff alleges in the complaint that the defendant did accept the message and 'promised and agreed' to transmit it, and that the plaintiff has 'duly performed each and every condition of the agreement' on its part to be performed and is willing to pay the charges. We do not stop to inquire whether such a complaint is turned into one in tort by the later allegation that the defendant was negligent in the performance of its promise. . . ."

[Judgment below reversed; judgment directed in favor of plaintiff for $26.78, to be offset against costs in all courts, which are awarded to defendant. All concur.]

RIVES *v.* AMERICAN RAILWAY EXPRESS CO.
227 App. Div. 375, 237 N.Y.S. 429 (1st Dep't 1929)

O'MALLEY, J.: "The plaintiff, a vaudeville artist, seeks damages for defendant's failure to promptly forward certain trunks containing his theatrical equipment. The question presented is whether he is entitled to recover the sum of $285, which he asserts he would have earned in a subsequent engagement had his trunks arrived at destination in due time.

"Plaintiff completed an engagement at Waltham, Mass., on the evening of August 4, 1928. At about noon of that day he went to the defendant's local office, and told the man in charge that he was *concluding* his performance. He was told that his trunks would be picked up the first thing Monday morning, August sixth. The plaintiff several times admitted that this was all the conversation he had with the person in defendant's office.

"The trunks did not arrive in New York City until August ninth, which is concededly more than a reasonable time required for forwarding from Waltham. Because of this delay, the plaintiff lost an engagement in Buffalo, N.Y., which was to commence on August ninth, and the contract for which engagement provided for a morning rehearsal. In consequence the plaintiff suffered cancellation of this engagement for which he was to receive the sum of $285 net. In addition, he was compelled to pay the sum of $1 for telegrams sent at defendant's suggestion in an endeavor to locate the trunks.

"In the circumstances disclosed, we are of opinion that the plaintiff may not recover the sum lost for the cancelled engagement. It is well-settled that 'damages for breach of contract are only those which are incidental to, and directly caused by, the breach, and may reasonably be presumed to have entered into the contemplation of the parties; and not speculative profits, or accidental or consequential losses.' (*Brown* v. *Weir*, 95 App. Div. 78, 80, 88 N.Y.S. 479, 480 [2d Dep't 1904]). The loss of this engagement was not within the contemplation of the parties at the time the contract was entered into, nor do the circumstances lead to such presumption. Plaintiff's written contract for the Buffalo engagement is dated August seventh, and the record is barren of any evidence that the contract was even in an inchoate state on August fourth. Moreover, there is no evidence that plaintiff communicated in any way to the defendant the fact that any such engagement was in being when the contract of carriage was made, or that such engagement was contemplated. In failure of such proof, a recovery may not be had for the loss of this future engagement. As was stated in *Brown* v. *Weir* [95 App. Div. at 81, 88 N.Y.S. at 481]: 'Whenever special or extraordinary damages, such as would not naturally or ordinarily follow a breach, have been awarded for the nonperformance of contracts, whether for the sale or carriage of goods or for the delivery of messages by telegraph, it has been for the reason that the contracts have been made with reference to the peculiar circumstances known to both, and the particular loss had been in the contemplation of both at the time of making the contract, as a contingency which might follow the nonperformance.' "

[The judgment as entered is reduced to the sum of $1, and as thus modified, affirmed. All concur.]

To sum up, in the vast majority of cases, a hotelkeeper would not be liable for damages to a guest in the nature of "loss of business," loss of commission on some anticipated deal, or loss of compensation for services the guest has been unable to perform by reason of the hotelkeeper's failure to perform some service, such as awakening the guest at a requested hour, or delivering a message, telegram, letter, or the like. The courts usually hold such claims vague, general, and meaningless. The rule with respect to such claims has been succinctly stated in the Pennsylvania case of *Macchia* v. *Megow:* [13]

[13] 355 Pa. 565, 569–570, 50 A. 2d 314, 316 (1947).

Anticipated profits on a resale are not recoverable unless in contemplation of the parties when the original contract was made: [Citations omitted.] "Parties, when they enter into contracts, may well be presumed to contemplate the ordinary and natural incidents and consequences of performance or nonperformance; but they are not supposed to know the conditions of each other's affairs, nor to take into consideration any existing or contemplated transactions, not communicated nor known, with other persons. Few persons would enter into contracts of any considerable extent as to subject-matter or time if they should thereby incidentally assume the responsibility of carrying out, or be held legally affected by, other arrangements over which they have no control and the existence of which are [*sic*] unknown to them": Sutherland on Damages, 4th ed. vol. 1, p. 182, §47.

The exception to the rule is where the hotelkeeper, or his duly authorized representative, being made fully aware of the consequences to the guest of failure to perform the service, nevertheless makes a binding commitment to perform. In this connection, it would seem doubtful that a telephone operator, a mail clerk, or bellman, or even an assistant manager, would have implied authority to commit the hotelkeeper.

13:10 *Damages for Mental Suffering and Anguish Resulting from Breach of Contract*

It is well settled that mental suffering, anguish, and humiliation resulting from breach of contract are generally not compensable. The only exceptions here relevant are where an innkeeper or common carrier has intentionally and wilfully insulted and abused a guest or passenger, or where a patron of a public resort has been publicly and wrongfully ejected by the proprietor thereof.

In *Dalzell* v. *Dean Hotel Co.*,[14] plaintiff and her husband, while attending a convention, were guests in defendant's hotel. The day after their arrival, plaintiff's husband left the room and while he was away, defendant's clerk, honestly but mistakenly believing, because of an error in the checkout records, that plaintiff and her husband had checked out, sold the room to another guest and ejected plaintiff (then in a pregnant condition) from possession. In an action for breach of contract, plaintiff demanded compensatory and exemplary

---

[14] 193 Mo. App. 379, 186 S.W. 41 (1916).

damages. The trial judge instructed the jury that if they found for the plaintiff, they could allow her only nominal damages. The jury thereupon returned a verdict for plaintiff for $5.

The judgment was reversed on appeal on the following grounds: Even though there was no actual malice in the case, in that defendant did not know that it was doing wrong, *legal malice* may be presumed "from gross and culpable negligence in omitting to make suitable and reasonable inquiries." [15] No ill will, or hatred, or personal spite is necessary to create legal malice. The jury might infer legal malice from the fact that plaintiff was refused a chance to prove that defendant was wrong, though plaintiff repeated three times that there was a mistake.

In *Emmke* v. *DeSilva*,[16] plaintiff registered on April 1 at defendant's hotel and was assigned to a room. She told the desk clerk at the time that her husband would arrive in a few days and would be with her at the hotel from time to time, but that his business would require him to be elsewhere on occasion and that he would not be with her constantly.

Plaintiff's husband came to the hotel on April 11, spent the night and day with her and returned to the hotel on the 16th and occupied the room with her that night. About 1 o'clock the next morning, Emmke, president of defendant hotel company and himself a co-defendant, entered plaintiff's room which was then dark, awakened plaintiff and her husband, and according to plaintiff "maliciously and insultingly accused plaintiff of unchastity and in her presence spoke of her husband in loathsome terms of vulgarity, whereby plaintiff suffered nervous strain and mental anguish, was greatly insulted and humiliated."

Defendant objected to the sufficiency of the complaint and to the evidence in support of it on the ground that neither show personal violence or injury to the plaintiff. The jury found for plaintiff for $3,500 as damages, of which $2,000 were stated as actual and $1,500 as exemplary damages.

On appeal, the judgment entered on the jury's verdict was affirmed

---

[15] *Id.* at 401 and 48, Story, J., quoting *Stubbs* v. *Mulholland*, 168 Mo. 47, 77, 67 S.W. 650, 659 (1902), in turn quoting *Wiggin* v. *Coffin*, 29 F. Cas. 1157, 1159 (No. 17624) (C.C.D. Me. 1836).

[16] 293 F. 17 (8th Cir. 1923).

as to the $2,000 actual damages and reversed as to the $1,500 punitive damages. Said the court: "notwithstanding no physical injury was inflicted, plaintiff was entitled to recovery on account of the mental anguish and humiliation to which she was subjected." [17]

In *Gefter v. Rosenthal*,[18] plaintiff sued to recover damages for humiliation and mental suffering he alleged he received because at a dinner celebrating his twenty-fifth wedding anniversary his guests were charged a fifteen-cent tip for each coat checked. Plaintiff had entered into a written agreement with the caterers that he would pay defendants fifteen cents per coat checked, and there would be no tipping for cloakroom services. Plaintiff claimed that defendants' wanton and intentional violation of their written agreement and their charge of fifteen cents per coat checked caused him humiliation and mental suffering to the extent of $15,000, plus $5,000 punitive damages. There was no claim for physical injuries.

The court dismissed plaintiff's amended complaint. "There can be no recovery for humiliation, disappointment, anxiety, or mental suffering, or emotional distress when unconnected with physical injury or physical impact [citations omitted]." [19]

Judge Musmanno did not like "the categorical finality" with which the majority of the court dismissed the complaint. He thought that the question whether the defendants intentionally and wantonly compelled the plaintiff's guests to pay for tips for which the plaintiff had already made provision should have been left to the jury. He concurred in the result, nevertheless, because, as he put it,

. . . no person could in these days reasonably complain, to the extent of being humiliated and anguished, because he was required to pay 15 cents for cloakroom service. If anything he should rejoice that his outlay was so modest a one. I believe we can take judicial notice of the fact that a hat, or a topcoat, if constructed of fairly good wearing material and of such a fashion that it does not fall out of style too soon, ordinarily costs the owner during the period he wears it, an amount in excess of the original cost, simply to get it back from the clutches of check room custodians. The public is so educated and enured to this polite and even pleasant petty brigandage that no one can in his heart really say that he suffers because of it. There would be more apt to be a shock to the hotel

[17] *Id.* at 21.   [18] 384 Pa. 123, 119 A.2d 250 (1956).
[19] *Id.* at 125 and 251.

or restaurant guest if he were suddenly informed that he was *not* required to pay for the redemption of his hat and coat.

Of course, the plaintiff here contends that he had already paid the 15 cents tip for his guests so that when they were also required to pay that amount, the total cost for ransoming each person's headgear and outer garments involved a total expenditure of 30 cents. In a pragmatic appraisement of the little annoyances and grievances which enter into everyday life, I believe that a person should have to be inordinately sensitive to go into a state of anguish because his friends paid a 15 cent fee which he had already liquidated. Certainly the guests who had gathered to celebrate the plaintiff's 25th wedding anniversary could not have been too much exercised over paying 10 cents less than the number of years the host and hostess had enjoyed the bliss of wedded life.

In any event it is farfetched to assume that the guests would regard the plaintiff any less the perfect host because in a public hostelry they were required to expend a nickel and dime to obtain back a wrap which, in previous visits to that same hostelry or to others, undoubtedly cost them as much if not more, per visit.[20]

In *Frank* v. *Justine Caterers, Inc.*,[21] where the dismissal of plaintiff's complaint for mental anguish suffered by reason of poisoned food served by defendant caterer to plaintiff's guests was affirmed on appeal, the court stated: "The alleged cause of action does not come within any exception to the general rule that mental suffering resulting from a breach of contract is not a subject of compensation."

In *New York Hotel Statler Co., Inc.*, v. *Levine*,[22] a dinner dance in honor of the Bar Mitzvah of the defendant's son was held at the Hotel Statler. Upon defendant's failure to pay the bill, plaintiff sued for its recovery. Defendant counterclaimed for $3,000.00 for alleged humiliation, ridicule, and criticism suffered by or directed at her by reason of plaintiff's alleged breach of contract in serving certain non-Kosher foods at the "Kosher-style" dinner she ordered. In addition she alleged that she "has been upset and nervous as a result of plaintiff's breach of contract." The court granted defendant's motion to strike out the counterclaim so as to remove same from consideration of the jury at the trial.

[20] *Id.* at 126 and 251–252.
[21] 271 App. Div. 980, 68 N.Y.S.2d 198 (2d Dep't 1947) (Mem. opinion).
[22] Mun. Court of New York City, Man. 9th Dist., 1957, not officially reported.

CHAPTER 14

Duty to Provide Safe Premises for Protection and Care of Guest's Person

14:1 Innkeeper's Duty of Reasonable Care for Person of Guest

It is the duty of an innkeeper to take reasonable care of the persons of his guests, so that they may not be injured while in the inn by want of such care on his part. He is not, however, an insurer of the guest's safety; his responsibility is limited to the exercise of reasonable care and he may be held liable only for injuries caused by his negligence.

14:2 Negligence as Basis of Liability for Injuries

The standard of care is the care which a reasonably prudent person would exercise under the circumstances to avoid a reasonably foreseeable harm. This is neither the highest care nor the lowest. To choose the highest care would avoid many accidents, but the additional safety would be attained at too great a cost of public convenience. By reducing the maximum rate of speed for automobiles to 20 mph, many accidents would be avoided, but the inconvenience to travelers and the harm to business would be intolerable.

The standard of conduct of a reasonable man may be determined either by legislation as in building codes which prescribe fire exits in hotels, by judicial decisions, or applied to the facts of a case by judge or jury, if there is no statute, regulation, or decision.

While the standard of care remains the same, all circumstances must be taken into account in its application. The care in crossing the street on a summer day differs from the care required in crossing

an icy street in winter. The care with respect to a small child differs
from that with respect to an adult.

The law exacts from each person in his conduct only the care of
a reasonably prudent person *under the same circumstances*. The standard of care for a skilled person and an unskilled person is the same,
but in determining whether in either case ordinary skill has been
exercised, the fact of the profession or nonprofession of skill is a
circumstance that must be considered. Thus, the standard of care
of a. physician is measured by his professional standards. If a person
who holds himself out as skilled in surgery injures his patient in an
operation which he knows he is not competent to perform, he is
negligent even though he does as well as any unskilled person would
have done under the same circumstances. He is responsible because he
professed to have skill when a person of ordinary prudence would
not have made that profession.

The Reasonable Man

"The Common Law of England has been laboriously built about a
mythical figure—the figure of 'The Reasonable Man.' . . .

"It is impossible to travel anywhere or to travel for long in that
confusing forest of learned judgments which constitutes the Common Law of England without encountering the Reasonable Man.
He is at every turn, an ever-present help in time of trouble, and his
apparitions make the road to equity and right. There never has been
a problem, however difficult, which His Majesty's judges have not in
the end been able to resolve by asking themselves the simple question, 'Was this or was it not the conduct of a reasonable man?' and
leaving that question to be answered by the jury.

"This noble creature . . . is one who invariably looks where he
is going, and is careful to examine the immediate foreground before
he executes a leap or bound; who neither star-gazes nor is lost in
meditation when approaching trap-doors or the margin of a dock;
who records in every case upon the counterfoils of cheques such
ample details as are desirable, scrupulously substitutes the word
'Order' for the word 'Bearer,' crosses the instrument 'a/c Payee only,'
and registers the package in which it is dispatched; who never mounts
a moving omnibus and does not alight from any car while the train
is in motion; who investigates exhaustively the *bona fides* of every
mendicant before distributing alms, and will inform himself of the

history and habits of a dog before administering a caress; who believes no gossip, nor repeats it, without firm basis for believing it to be true; who never drives his ball till those in front of him have definitely vacated the putting-green which is his own objective; who never from the year's end to another makes an excessive demand upon his wife, his neighbors, his servants, his ox, or his ass; who in the way of business looks only for that narrow margin of profit which twelve men such as himself would reckon to be 'fair,' and contemplates his fellow-merchants, their agents, and their goods, with that degree of suspicion and distrust which the law deems admirable; who never swears, gambles, or loses his temper; who uses nothing except in moderation, and even while he flogs his child is meditating only on the golden mean. Devoid, in short, of any human weakness, with not one single saving vice, sans prejudice, procrastination, ill-nature, avarice, and absence of mind, as careful for his own safety as he is for that of others, this excellent but odious character stands like a monument in our Courts of Justice, vainly appealing to his fellow-citizens to order their lives after his own example. . . .

"To return, however, as every judge must ultimately return, to the case which is before us—it has been urged for the appellant, and my own researches incline me to agree, that in all that mass of authorities which bears upon this branch of the law *there is no single mention of a reasonable woman.*" [1]

14:3 *Duty to Furnish Safe Premises*

The innkeeper is bound to provide reasonably safe premises. This duty the innkeeper cannot escape by delegating it to another, even though the latter is a skilled and generally careful person. The innkeeper is responsible if his delegate is negligent. Thus, where an innkeeper had his elevator inspected in the usual manner, by competent employees of the elevator manufacturing company which originally installed the elevator, and the latter negligently failed to find a defect, the innkeeper was held liable to a guest who was injured by reason of the defect.[2]

---

[1] A. P. Herbert, *Misleading Cases in the Common Law*, 6th ed. (London, 1931), pp. 9–13. Emphasis in original.

[2] *Stott* v. *Churchill*, 15 Misc. 80, 36 N.Y.S. 476 (Ct. C.P. 1895), *aff'd mem.*, 157 N.Y. 692, 51 N.E. 1094 (1898).

14:4 *Liability by Reason of Defective Premises*

Ceilings

A, a guest in B's hotel, while in the act of dressing in the morning, is struck on the head and is injured by a large piece of plaster which fell from the ceiling. There is no evidence to explain the accident.

B is liable to A. The accident points to a defective condition which B, in the exercise of the care which he owed to A, as a guest, should have discovered. The ceiling was under B's exclusive control; moreover, ceilings maintained in proper condition do not ordinarily fall. The maxim, *res ipsa loquitur* (the thing speaks for itself), applies.[3]

Stairways

A, a guest in B's hotel, walks down the dining room to the lobby. It is a wet day and the marble steps upon which A walks are slippery. A falls and is injured. B is not liable to A.

[In order to recover, it is necessary for A to show] . . . by competent evidence that the presence of such foreign substance, whatever it was, produced a slippery, unsafe and dangerous condition on [the] stair[s]; that such dangerous condition remained long enough to give [B] reasonable notice, actual or constructive, of its existence; that [B], after having such notice, nevertheless negligently failed to remove a danger or warn [A] of its presence; and that such dangerous condition on [the stairway] was the proximate cause of [A's] fall and injury.

. . . All wet marble floors or stairs, just as all polished or oiled wooden floors and stairs, can be said to be slippery to the same extent. But it does not follow necessarily or legally from that fact alone, without any further description or location, that the stair was unsafe and dangerous, nor does such fact alone establish reasonable notice to the defendant of its existence and danger therefrom so as to charge defendant with negligence for failing to remedy the condition or warn the plaintiff of it. If that were not so, it would be negligence *per se* to maintain such stairs or floors at all and the duty of the invitor in such event would become substantially transformed to that of an insurer. However, this is not the law.[4]

[3] *Morris* v. *Zimmerman*, 138 App. Div. 114, 122 N.Y.S. 900 (1st Dep't 1910).
[4] *Ziegler* v. *Providence Biltmore Hotel Co.*, 59 R.I. 326, 330–332, 195 A. 397, 399–400 (1937).

Floors

A, a guest in B's hotel, returns home from work at three o'clock in the morning, at which time the marble floor in the lobby is being scrubbed with water and soap. A walks onto the floor, slips, and falls. B is not liable to A. A is clearly guilty of contributory negligence as a matter of law.

Plaintiff violated the ordinary duty of care required of all persons to look where they are going. Had she been looking into the lobby as she was coming through the door she could not have failed to see the cleaning man who was busily engaged with his mop and bucket just a few feet inside the entrance. Her view was not obstructed by any other person thereabout. . . . The answer must be that the plaintiff was not looking when she entered. Had she seen the wet floor, it is most improbable that she would have fallen. . . .

[A] person may not abandon the duty of ordinary care for his own safety, and, in the event of injury, seek to charge one whose negligence would not in itself have been sufficient had there not been combined therewith the lack of due care on the part of the injured person: [Citations omitted.] [5]

Doors

A, a guest in B's hotel, approached the revolving door at the front entrance from the outside and placed her hand on the outer edge to push the door inward. Someone from the inside coming out suddenly revolved the door, one of the four glass panels of which, being broken, had been replaced with an opaque beaver board. A is knocked on the sidewalk and is injured. B is liable to A.

It well might be found that the opaque beaver board created a danger in the use of the revolving door which made it defective; and called for care in oversight of its use which the defendant failed to provide. The length of time during which the door in its defective condition was permitted to be used was in dispute. Reasonable care might depend upon how long the risk of use while defective was continued. The defendant was not responsible for negligent conduct of others in hurrying through the door [citation omitted]; but the fact that a third person moved the door

[5] *Walker* v. *Broad & Walnut Corp.*, 320 Pa. 504, 507–508, 182 A. 643, 644–645 (1936).

does not necessarily break the causal connection of the defendant, with the injury, if such action should have been anticipated. [Citations omitted.] [6]

SCHUBART v. HOTEL ASTOR, INC.
168 Misc. 431, 5 N.Y.S.2d 203 (Sup. Ct. 1938), aff'd mem., 255 App. Div. 1012, 8 N.Y.S.2d 567 (2d Dep't 1938), aff'd mem., 281 N.Y. 597, 22 N.E.2d 167 (1939)

SMITH (PETER), J.: "The jury returned a verdict of $2,500 in favor of plaintiff. During the trial the court reserved decision on defendant's motion to dismiss made at the end of the plaintiff's case and at the end of the whole case and on defendant's motion to set aside the jury's verdict. These motions were made principally on the ground that as matter of law plaintiff failed to show any negligence on the part of defendant. As to its negligence or freedom from negligence, defendant offered no evidence; it rested on plaintiff's proof. This proof may be briefly summarized:

"On Saturday evening, November 16, 1935, plaintiff, a woman sixty-three years of age, in the company of her son, daughter-in-law and two friends, went to the Hotel Astor (owned and operated by defendant) at Forty-fourth Street and Broadway, Manhattan, for the purpose of attending a banquet tendered by the Danish Society. Plaintiff had almost completed her entrance through the revolving door and was just about to step into the hotel proper; the door was turning slowly. Suddenly 'there was an awful rush' and 'a couple of young fellows . . . without hats and coats' running from inside the hotel lobby or corridor and chasing each other 'came rushing by.' They both entered the same compartment of the revolving door; they virtually 'jumped upon the door' and at the same moment they gave it 'a big' or 'extra hard' push. As a result of this sudden and strenuous push plaintiff was struck by a part of the door and sustained a fractured hip and other injuries.

"On that day the rival teams of Army and Notre Dame had played in this city their football game of the season. The Army faction had selected and used the Hotel Astor as their headquarters. When plaintiff arrived at the hotel there were 'lots of people' . . . in the hotel lobby and corridor; it was crowded beyond normal. 'There was a

[6] Promisel v. Hotels Statler Corp., 286 Mass. 15, 17, 189 N.E. 804, 805 (1934).

large crowd of people' and they were 'laughing, joking, quite gay, hilarious' and 'very noisy.' The door was revolving steadily; it was 'constantly in use.' There were people going out at every section; there were no empty spaces in the door; and 'the people were coming in and going out in great numbers.'

"Despite this condition at the hotel defendant did not maintain a doorman or attendant at or near the door and it did nothing to control its operation or to supervise its use. There was an attendant stationed outside on the sidewalk near the curb, some distance from the door, but he paid no attention to the door and he was concerned only with the safety and well-being of the patrons as they alighted from or entered their automobiles.

"Plaintiff claims that under the circumstances here defendant was remiss in its duty of reasonable care for her safety because it failed to have a doorman present or to take other means and precautions to control the operation of the revolving door and to supervise its use; and so the jury has found. Defendant, on the other hand, takes the position that it was not negligent because as matter of law in the exercise of its duty it was not required to have a doorman present or to take any other means to supervise the use of the revolving door, and that the complaint, therefore, should be dismissed.

"There is no doubt that the owner of an ordinary building, under ordinary circumstances, is not required to have a doorman present or to take any particular action to supervise the use or to control the operation of a revolving door. Here, however, we have neither an ordinary building nor ordinary circumstances. On the contrary they are both, in every sense, extraordinary. The Hotel Astor is a landmark in this city. It is so well known that the court may take judicial notice of the fact that it is one of the most popular hotels in the heart of the most congested part of the most congested metropolis in the world. To it flock people of every kind and every age; to them it is open at all times. Neither can the court ignore the commonly known fact that on Saturday nights this congestion is invariably increased; and that on the day of a great sporting event, such as the Army–Notre Dame football Game, the influx of people from the suburbs and other cities further aggravates this congestion.

"Under these circumstances, and with the hotel as the headquarters of one of the football factions, the court cannot say as matter of law that on that particular Saturday night no duty devolved upon defendant to have a doorman present or to take some other means of precautions to control the operation of the revolving door and to supervise its use. The number of people who congregated in the lobby and corridor was extraordinary, and the majority of them exhibited, in the plain view of those in charge of the hotel, a gay, hilarious and carousing mood. Defendant could not help having notice of the unusual number of people present and of their mood. When an extraordinary number of people, who openly manifest such spirited predilections, which are neither normal nor peaceful for a hotel, take possession of its main lobby or corridor, defendant could readily anticipate that the revolving door would not only be subjected to excessive use but also that it would be likely to receive rough usage and unseemly abuse. Defendant, if it had exercised reasonable care and diligence for the safety of its patrons, could readily have foreseen that unless it took some definite precautions with respect to controlling the use of the revolving door some innocent patron, especially one who no longer has her agility or youth and who did not come to share in the fun and the frolic, might be injured by the unexpected antics or the unrestrained cavorting of some youthful celebrant of this carousing holiday group.

"'The obligation of those who collect numbers of people in one place, for gain and profit, to be vigilant in their efforts to protect such people, has long been recognized.' [Citations omitted.]

"When one assembles a crowd or a large number of people upon his property for purposes of financial gain to himself he assumes the responsibility of 'using all reasonable care to protect the individuals from injury from causes reasonably to be anticipated.' In the exercise of this duty it is incumbent upon him to furnish a sufficient number of guards or attendants and to take other necessary precautions to control the actions of the crowd; and whether the guards furnished or the precautions taken are sufficient is ordinarily a question for the jury to determine under all the circumstances. [Citations omitted.] . . .

"In the Restatement of the Law of Torts the same rule is adopted with respect to the liability of one who holds out his property for the use of the public (§348, pp. 953–956). There it is expressly pointed out that in the exercise of reasonable care, the owner of a public place has 'a duty to police the premises' and to furnish a sufficient number of servants to afford reasonable protection 'if the place is one or the character of the business is such that the utility or other possessor should expect careless or criminal third persons to be thereon either generally or at some particular time' (p. 955)'. As an illustration of the rule showing when liability will be imposed there is cited the case of a football team returning home and the failure of the railroad company to provide sufficient guards at the station to control the conduct of the boisterous crowd who, in fun or jest, cause harm to a passenger (p. 955).

"Of course 'the ability to anticipate' and 'the range of reasonable apprehension is at times a question for the court, and at times, if varying inferences are possible, a question for the jury.' [Citation omitted.] In the instant case, however, under all the circumstances, there can be no question that varying inferences are possible with respect to defendant's 'ability to anticipate' and its 'range of reasonable apprehension,' or, in other words, its failure to perform its duty of reasonable care. Therefore, it was primarily for the jury to determine the proper inference to be drawn; and the court, in its charge, squarely submitted that issue to the jury for their determination.

"Accordingly, defendant's motions to dismiss the complaint and to set aside the jury's verdict are denied."

Elevators

A, a guest in B's hotel, upon passing from his room into the hall makes a wrong turn, walks into the open shaft of a freight elevator, and is severely injured. There is no explanation of why and how the door to the elevator shaft has been left open. B is liable to A.

A guest in a hotel is there on the invitation of the proprietor and for the proprietor's profit; and, while he ought not and cannot be said to be an insurer of the safety of the person of his guest while within the hotel, yet the guest is received upon the implied understanding that while on the premises as a guest his life shall not be imperiled by the rash, inconsiderate, and negligent acts of the proprietor or those who are his servants. By the implied contract between a hotel-keeper and his guest the former undertakes not only to furnish the latter with suitable food and lodging, but there is also implied upon the part of the proprietor the further undertaking that the guest shall be treated with due consideration for his safety. The relation existing between an innkeeper and his guest is much like that existing between a common carrier and its passenger, and, while not an insurer of the personal safety of the guest, the proprietor of the hotel is held, and ought to be held, to the exercise of a very high degree of care for the protection of his guests against the negligent acts of servants employed therein.[7]

"[A] guest of a hotel need not look for pitfalls or dangerous places. He has a right to presume that the keeper of the hotel has exercised reasonable care to make the place safe. It is not like when a person goes to some place which is very dangerous, such as crossing a railroad track, then he must stop, look and listen, to see whether or not a train is coming, and, if he fails to do so and is injured, he cannot recover, but, when a person goes to a hotel where he is a guest, he is not required to look for pitfalls or dangerous places. He has a right to presume that the place where he is going is safe, but the law does require him to exercise reasonable diligence and reasonable care, such as ordinarily prudent persons under like circumstances would exercise." [8]

Where an innkeeper leaves the door to an elevator open or unlocked so that a guest falls into the well and is injured, the innkeeper is in the ordinary case held liable.[9]

This duty of the innkeeper does not arise out of his control of the elevator, but merely out of his duty to guard the guest against harm arising from the construction or operation of the premises. The duty would be the same, though the innkeeper has no control over the elevator and no right to close the door of the elevator well.

Granting that defendant had no control of the elevator shaft, or the small hall leading to it, it was his duty to have maintained a door or barrier at the entrance from the main hall to the small hall which led to the dangerous aperture. To leave the approach from his hall to another which conducted his guest to a pitfall, open and unguarded, was such negligence as would make him liable, in our opinion, and that he had no actual control of the small hall, and the shaft itself, would not relieve him. When the conditions are permitted to be such, in a hotel, that from slight want of attention, or from the confusion or misapprehension that naturally attends a stranger in feeling his way through a dark hall, one may be led up, without meeting door or barrier, to a well hole into which a plunge is taken, it may be to death, the hotel keeper can not escape the charge of

[7] *Trulock* v. *Willey*, 187 F. 956, 958–959 (8th Cir. 1911).

[8] *Id.* at 959–960.

[9] *Hayward* v. *Merrill*, 94 Ill. 349 (1880); *Bremer* v. *Pleiss*, 121 Wis. 61, 98 N.W. 945 (1904).

negligence on the plea that he had no right to close up the well hole itself. He might bar or close up the entrance to a small hall, and thus prevent guests of his house, who were unacquainted with the location and the limits of his possession and control in the halls, from entering the passage to tread which in darkness was dangerous.[10]

But, as in the ordinary case, the guest cannot recover, in spite of the innkeeper's neglect of duty, if he was himself negligent. Thus, where the guest was familiar with the elevator, found the door partly open, pushed it further open and fell in, his recovery was barred by contributory negligence.[11] Said the court:

[W]here the door is fully open and the shaft is dark, the question whether a passenger is guilty of contributory negligence in stepping in without examination is one for the jury. [Citations omitted.] We have found no case, however, holding that where the door to the shaft is only halfway open, so that the passenger is obliged to, and does, open it the rest of the way in order to enter, the question of contributory negligence is a matter of doubt; nor do we see how it could be so held. It seems to us entirely clear that the fact that the door is only partway open is a definite and unequivocal advertisement that something is wrong—certainly not an assurance that the car is there. The use of passenger elevators is now so universal that all know that when an elevator car is brought to a standstill, ready for passenger to enter or leave, the door is always thrown wide open. A door only halfway open is a plain suggestion of some unusual condition—a hint to investigate, not an invitation to enter, or an assurance of safety.

In *Jenkins* v. *Missouri State Life Ins. Co.,*[12] defendant hotelkeeper's elevator operator failed to bring the cab to a proper stop level with the floor and failed to give the plaintiff guest proper warning as she stepped out of the cab. As a result she fell into a dimly lighted corridor and suffered serious injuries. The court in affirming judgment in favor of plaintiff, said:

Defendant's operator provided the means of exit and created the condition which caused plaintiff's injury by his own act in operating the elevator. Stopping the elevator at the third floor and opening the doors to the hallway was an invitation to plaintiff to leave it. [Citation omitted.] It amounted to an assurance by the operator that she could do so in

[10] Morgan, J., in *Mauzy* v. *Kinzel*, 19 Ill. App. 571, 573 (1886)
[11] *Bremer* v. *Pleiss*, 121 Wis. 61, 65; 98 N.W. 945, 946–947 (1904).
[12] 334 Mo. 941, 69 S.W.2d 666 (1934).

safety. Before giving such an invitation and assurance, it was his duty to place the elevator in such a position that plaintiff had a reasonably safe means of leaving it. If he failed to do so, he was negligent and plaintiff could recover for her injuries caused by such negligence, unless barred by her own contributory negligence, which is not claimed here.[13]

In *Gohn* v. *Butte Hotel Co.*, a totally blind hotel guest approached the elevator, found the door partially open, and intending to step into the cab, stepped into an open elevator shaft, seriously injuring himself. In reversing a judgment in favor of defendant entered on a motion for nonsuit, the court said:

"An elevator for the carriage of persons is not, like a railroad crossing at a highway, supposed to be a place of danger, to be approached with great caution; but, on the contrary, it may be assumed, when the door is thrown open by an attendant, to be a place which may be safely entered without stopping to look, listen, or make a special examination. *Tousey* v. *Roberts*, 114 N.Y. 312, 316, 21 N.E. 399 (1889). The open door constitutes an invitation to enter without special investigation, and where darkness prevents discovery of the absence of the elevator cage the question of contributory negligence is one for the jury. [Citations omitted.]

By the decided weight of authority it is the duty of those in charge of a passenger elevator to exercise the highest degree of care in the operation and maintenance thereof, the same as that required of carrier of passengers for hire. (See Note in 2 L.R.A. (n.s.) 744; Webb on Elevators 367 (2d ed.). . . .) And it is not contributory negligence as a matter of law for a passenger incapable of taking care of himself to fail to provide an attendant.[14]

Condition of Room Assigned to Guest

A, a guest in B's hotel, gets up in the morning to answer a knock on the door. As she walks barefoot on the carpeting towards the door, she steps upon a needle which runs into her foot and breaks. There is no proof that the room was cleaned prior to its assignment. B is liable to A. "[T]he proprietor of a hotel is bound to use due care to have a room therein thoroughly cleaned after its occupants have left the hotel and before its assignment to incoming guests." [15]

[13] *Id.* at 949 and 670–671.
[14] 88 Mont. 599, 608–610, 295 P. 262, 264 (1931).
[15] *Nelson* v. *Ritz Carlton Restaurant & Hotel Co.*, 9 N.J. Misc. 1240, 1242, 157 A. 133, 134 (Sup. Ct. 1931).

Bathroom and Bath-Shower

A, a guest in B's hotel, in taking a bath, attempts to move the mixing valve handle regulating the flow of water. The handle is stuck and turns hard, and when it moves slightly, a gush of steam follows, burning A's arms. The shower has been in use for twenty years. B is liable to A. "A shower that would emit steam and a heavy flow of boiling water, when its handle was set for water at a safe temperature, could be found to be a dangerous menace to anyone using the bath. . . . [T]he failure to ascertain its condition and remedy the defect or withdraw [the] shower booth from use [may well be found to constitute negligence]."[16]

A, a guest in B's hotel, while taking a bath, notices hot water leaking from the faucet in the bathtub. She attempts to shut off the hot water with ordinary pressure. The porcelain handle breaks and a portion enters her hand, causing serious injury. A chambermaid testifies that she noticed that the faucet was dripping the morning of the accident and she turned it off. B is liable to A.

B rented the room and the appliances in it and had the duty to provide reasonably safe accommodations. B, as hotelkeeper, retained exclusive control in respect to installation and maintenance, notwithstanding that A had possession and use of the room and the equipment in it while he was a guest.[17]

A, a guest in B's hotel, in taking a shower, turns the cold water off. The hot water valve is stuck, however, and A is momentarily trapped under gushing hot water. A is severely burnt. B is liable to A.

Although innkeepers are not insurers of the safety of the persons of their guests, A's complaint was sufficient to raise a question of negligence for the jury's consideration. "[T]here is respectable authority for the proposition that the furnishing of water overheated to the point that it constitutes a hazard to guests tends to show negligence."[18]

A, a guest in B's hotel, in taking a bath steps into the tub, the bot-

16 *Parsons* v. *Dwightstate Co.*, 301 Mass. 324, 326–327, 17 N.E.2d 197, 198 (1938).

17 *Kane* v. *Ten Eyck Co., Inc.*, 267 App. Div. 789, 46 N.Y.S.2d 251 (3d Dep't 1943), *aff'd mem.*, 292 N.Y. 701, 56 N.E.2d 125 (1944).

18 *Black* v. *Heininger*, 163 So. 2d 3, 6 (Fla. 1964).

tom of which is wet and therefore A slips, falls, and is injured. B is not liable to A.

Plaintiff must have known, since it is a matter of common knowledge—and one which most of us know through painful experience—that a small amount of water in the bottom of a bathtub creates a slippery condition; and we think we may safely say that any reasonably prudent person makes at least a cursory examination of the bathtub before stepping into it.

It does not appear . . . that plaintiff's vision was defective, nor that the "slippery substance" could not have been discovered by "the ordinary use of her senses." . . . [I]t appears that the plaintiff's injuries were the result of her own failure to exercise ordinary care, and under such circumstances the question of negligence was properly decided by the court as a matter of law.[19]

Under Massachusetts law, a guest may not recover damages for injuries suffered in a hotel when the guest fell in a shower, where all it appears is that the tub was smooth and shiny and that the hotel failed to provide a bath mat in the tub. "[N]o duty is owed to a guest, where the conditions are open and obvious to an ordinarily intelligent person, to . . . call attention to dangers which are apparent to the senses of such a person." [20]

Furnishings and Equipment

An innkeeper is liable for injuries to a guest caused by defective furniture, where the innkeeper knew, or should have known, of the defect. In *Lyttle* v. *Denny*,[21] the plaintiff was a guest in defendant's hotel in Johnstown, Pennsylvania. In the room to which he was assigned there was an old-style folding bed, with a wardrobe in the back, and so arranged that the bed portion would fold up so as to leave the bed in an upright position when not in use. The top of the bed was heavy, weighing about 300 pounds. The plaintiff occupied the bed during the night, and early the next morning, as he was about to rise, the top or upright portion of the bed fell forward upon him crushing his head down upon his breast and inflicting severe

[19] *Miller* v. *Shull*, 48 So. 2d 521, 522 (Fla. 1950).
[20] *Kitchen* v. *Women's City Club*, 267 Mass. 229, 232, 166 N.E. 554, 555 (1929), quoted in *La Bart* v. *Hotel Vendome Corp.*, 213 F. Supp. 958, 959 (D. Mass. 1963).
[21] 222 Pa. 395, 71 A. 841 (1909).

injury. At the trial plaintiff was nonsuited; on appeal, reversed and remanded for a new trial. Said the court:

[T]he duty imposed by law upon an innkeeper requires him to furnish safe premises to his guests, and to provide necessary articles of furniture, which may be used by them in the ordinary and reasonable way without danger. . . . The trial judge thought it was incumbent upon the plaintiff to show in detail just what was wrong with the bed, and the reason for its falling; and because this did not appear from the testimony offered by the plaintiff, judgment of nonsuit was entered. We do not agree with his view in this respect. Bearing in mind the duty of an innkeeper to guard with reasonable care the safety of his guests, proof of the happening of such an extraordinary accident casts the burden of explanation at once upon the defendant. The accident was so far out of the usual course that no fair inference can arise that it could have resulted from anything less than negligence upon the part of the management of the hotel. Beds do not usually operate as spring traps to close upon and catch the confiding guest. Yet the bed furnished by the defendant to the plaintiff in this case proved to be just such a dangerous trap. . . . The circumstances under which this accident occurred were certainly such as to call for full explanation by the defendant. The facts indicate a lack of reasonable care upon his part, and it is for him to show why he should be relieved from liability.[22]

In *Seelbach, Inc.* v. *Cadick*,[23] the plaintiff was an eight-month-old child, Gail Cadick, who accompanied her parents to the defendant Seelbach Hotel, in Louisville, Kentucky. Upon checking into the hotel, the father requested a baby bed for the child and was told that none was available. The family was assigned to a room with two double beds. In putting the child to bed, the father pushed one of the double beds against the wall. It did not fit flush against the wall, however, because of a projection connected with a covered radiator which caused an opening a foot long and some eight inches wide. In this open space there was a hot radiator pipe just above floor level. The parents put a light travel case on the bed near the opening. Gail went to sleep on the bed, but during the night she either fell or crawled off into the opening and was severely burned over the neck, shoulders, and face. Judgment entered on a jury's verdict in the sum of $56,500 was, on appeal, affirmed.

[22] *Id.* at 398–399 and 842–843.   [23] 405 S.W.2d 745 (Ky. 1966).

The court held that a hotel owes its guest a duty to provide articles of furniture which may be used by them in the ordinary and reasonable way without danger. Further, it is common knowledge, said the court, that a double bed is not the type of furniture generally utilized as a sleeping place for very young infants able to move about. Furthermore, testimony revealed that the hotel itself recognized this duty to provide proper sleeping accommodations for infants since it had thirty-six beds available upon request. The evidence also showed that a baby bed was available on the night of the accident although for some undisclosed reason it was not furnished.

The court did not decide, however, if the failure to furnish a baby bed standing alone constitutes negligence so as to impose liability on the hotel. It went on to a consideration of the exposed hot radiator pipe in the room. It was an inseparable component that must be taken into account in determining whether the hotel could be found negligent in assigning the infant a room without a baby bed. If there were no baby beds available that night, then the hotel should have taken extra precautions for what was to her a dangerous and hidden hazard. The presence of the hot pipe was certainly a condition that had a material bearing upon the entire negligence question. The necessity for the baby bed becomes more important in the light of this hazard, and conversely, the hazard assumes more importance because of the lack of the baby bed.

The court found that the parents were not the cause of the baby's fall, but that even if the parents had been found negligent, their negligence would not necessarily excuse the hotel from liability. Had the hotel furnished a baby bed, there would have been no problem.

In light of this and other cases, it would seem advisable for innkeepers who accept infant guests to take the extra care suggested by the courts. If a baby bed is requested it should, of course, be supplied. If it is not requested but is available, it should perhaps be suggested to the parents. If no such beds are available, the parents should be advised of this situation, and if they still wish accommodation, the hotel should assure itself that the child has reasonable sleeping accommodations and that no safety hazards exist. The prudent innkeeper may well have a nurse and a baby sitter on call for the convenience of guests traveling with infant children, as well as for his own protection.

In *Polsey* v. *Waldorf-Astoria, Inc.*,[24] plaintiff, while sitting on a sofa in defendant's hotel, was injured by a massive lamp, about seven feet tall, weighing some 200 pounds, which was pushed over by another guest and fell on plaintiff. The lamps were not fastened to the floor. The hotel was held not liable. The court stated:

That it was of massive appearance is not in itself a sufficient ground upon which to predicate a claim of negligence. A floor lamp is an article of common use made for the very purpose of being moved from point to point in the room as occasion may arise. The comparative size and weight of such a lamp does not necessarily require it to be made fast to the floor lest someone might use it for a purpose for which it was not intended. As well might it be contended that a massive chair might induce a hilarious guest to stand on the arm of the chair and, in the event of an accident, attempt to hold the owner for negligence upon the ground that the apparent massiveness of the chair warranted him in climbing upon its arm and thereby led him into a trap. No negligence can be imputed to the defendant, appellant, for a failure to anticipate a misuse by a guest of an article of common use.[25]

In *Nettles* v. *Forbes Motel, Inc.*,[26] plaintiff fell from a dressing-table stool on which she was standing and suffered a fracture of one of her vertebrae. The stool collapsed when plaintiff, wishing to turn on the room air conditioner, which was some eighty-one inches from the floor, stepped on it. Plaintiff was 5'2" tall and weighed 107 lbs.

The stool was purchased unassembled and was assembled by a hotel employee. It was obviously loose, since it collapsed under minimal strain. Such a defect, said the court, should have been discovered in the exercise of reasonable care. Judgment for plaintiff for $7,057.22 was affirmed.

In *Jones* v. *Pinehurst, Inc.*,[27] plaintiff, a guest at a banquet in defendant's hotel, sued to recover for injuries suffered in a fall as she was leaving the speaker's platform at the conclusion of a banquet.

The rear of the platform was located approximately eighteen inches from the wall immediately to the rear of the speaker's table. There was a narrow passageway along the rear of the platform as the only means of egress and ingress to the place settings at the table.

[24] 220 App. Div. 613, 222 N.Y.S. 273 (1st Dep't 1927).
[25] *Id.* at 615 and 275.   [26] 182 So. 2d 572 (La. App. 1966).
[27] 261 N.C. 575, 135 S.E.2d 580 (1964).

As plaintiff was walking from her seat at the table at the conclusion of the banquet, she was looking at the table to her right and not at the floor, following the person immediately ahead of her. Her foot slipped from the edge of the platform and she fell against the wall.

The trial court entered a compulsory nonsuit from which plaintiff appealed. *Held:* Affirmed. Plaintiff was familiar with platforms of the type on which she fell and on this particular occasion she was simply retracing the steps she had taken as she entered. The platform was level and without defects. Plaintiff did not look where she was placing her feet. If she had been at all attentive she could have discovered the eighteen-inch open space between the edge of the platform and the wall behind it.

Where a condition of the premises is obvious, generally there is no duty on the part of the owner to warn of that condition.

14:5 *Violation of Statutory Duty as Negligence*

The standard of conduct of a reasonable man may be established by a statute or by an ordinance. The violation of such a statute or ordinance may be negligence in itself if: (1) the injured party is one of a class of persons whom the statute was intended to protect, and (2) the harm which has occurred is of a type which it was intended to prevent.[28]

In *Pirtle's Administratrix* v. *Hargis Bank & Trust Co.,*[29] the action was to recover damages for the death of a guest in the Combs Hotel, Hazard, Kentucky, who lost his life at the time the hotel was destroyed by fire.

The deceased was occupying a room on the fifth floor of the hotel at the time of the fire. There was no fire escape and in order to reach the exit on the ground floor deceased was compelled to pass from his bedroom through a large room into a hallway which led into another hall, from which he could reach the ground floor by elevator or inside stairway. Deceased was in the bathroom when warned of the presence of fire, the extent of which was not disclosed to him at the time. A few minutes afterwards smoke accumulated and more or less spread throughout the building. It must be presumed that deceased

---

[28] W. Prosser, *Torts,* 3d ed. (St. Paul, Minn., 1964), at 35.
[29] 241 Ky. 455, 44 S.W.2d 541 (1931).

intentionally remained in the building with knowledge of the presence, the whereabouts, and the extent of the fire, and thereby brought about his own death.

It was charged that the defendant negligently failed to equip or provide the hotel, and that, in violation of a Kentucky statute, it was not equipped or furnished, at the time of the fire, with an iron stairway on the outside of the building, not less than two feet wide, with steps with not less than a six-inch tread, connecting each other above the ground with an opening therefrom with a platform landing at each floor, guarded by an iron railing. It was also alleged that, also in violation of the statute, no equipment was provided in the hotel for the purpose of fighting or extinguishing fire therein. A judgment for defendant was reversed and a new trial ordered. Said the court:

> It is a firmly fixed rule that one injured by a violation of a statute may recover from a defendant such damages as he has sustained by reason of a violation of it. It is equally as well established that such violation must be the direct and proximate cause of the injury complained of. A recovery of damages from another may not be sustained merely because such other has violated a statute.[30]

The burden of proving contributory negligence rested upon the defendant.

In *Bell* v. *Daugherty*,[31] it was held that the mere presence of boxes and such rubbish as would ordinarily accumulate about a hotel, in the basement thereof, is not alone sufficient to charge the hotelkeeper with negligence. The guest in this case was awakened at about two o'clock in the morning by smoke which filled her room, called for help, but received no response. She tried to call the office on the telephone but received no response. She thereupon sat on the window sill and called for help; then she leaned out of the window, but saw no one, got frightened, and next thing she remembered she was being picked up by a policeman, having fallen out and received serious injuries. The court held that the hotelkeeper's failure to warn the guest that she was in a place of safety (even though there was much smoke, the fire was confined to some rubbish in the basement and never endangered any part of the hotel) was not negligence; that a degree of care requiring such warning would practically make a hotelkeeper an in-

---

[30] *Id.* at 468 and 546.   [31] 199 Iowa 413, 200 N.W. 708 (1924).

surer, and that this is not the degree of care required by law of hotelkeepers.

Moore v. *Dresden Investment Co.*[32] was an action to recover damages for personal injuries sustained by plaintiff while a guest in defendant's hotel. The action was based on defendant's negligence in failing to maintain adequate fire escapes as required by the laws of the state of Washington and by the ordinances of the city of Seattle, as a result of which plaintiff was severely burned in a fire in defendant's hotel. The Supreme Court of Washington quoted with approval from a treatise on negligence:

[W]here the legislature of the state, or the council of a municipal corporation, having in view the promotion of the safety of the public, or of individual members of the public, commands or forbids the doing of a particular act . . . the general conception of the courts, and the only one that is reconcilable with reason, is that the failure to do the act commanded, or the doing of the act prohibited, is negligence as mere matter of law, otherwise called negligence *per se;* and this, irrespective of all questions of the exercise of prudence, diligence, care or skill; so that if it is the proximate cause of damage or hurt to another, and if that other is without contributory fault, the case is decided in his favor, and all that remains to be done is to assess damages.[33]

14:6   *Standard of Care Required of Innkeeper to Child Guest*

BAKER *v.* DALLAS HOTEL CO.
73 F.2d 825 (5th Cir. 1934)

SIBLEY, C.J.: "Mr. and Mrs. Robert F. Baker sued the Dallas Hotel Company, owners and operators of a hotel in Dallas, Tex., under the Texas death statute, . . . for the death of their infant son, Bobby, who fell from a window of the twelfth story of the hotel. On the evidence, the judge held that no actionable negligence appeared on the part of the defendant and that there was contributory negligence on the part of the plaintiffs, and directed a verdict for the hotel company. Mr. and Mrs. Baker appeal, and assign as the sole error the refusal to permit the jury to pass upon the issues of negligence.

[32] 162 Wash. 289, 298 P. 465, 1258 (1931).
[33] *Id.* at 300–301 and 469 quoting S. D. Thompson, *Commentaries on the Law of Negligence,* 2d ed. (Indianapolis, 1901), vol. 1, sec. 10.

". . . [T]he Bakers, having with them the child 2 years and 5 months old, registered as guests of the hotel and were assigned to a room with adjoining bath on Wednesday. At about 9 o'clock the next Saturday morning Mrs. Baker had just bathed the child and left him playing with his blocks on the floor near the center of the room while she was washing something in the adjoining bathroom. Mr. Baker was in bed, awake, but with his back toward the window a few feet away. The sash was raised, but the opening was covered by a wire window screen which they knew was there, but had never examined. The windowsill was about the height of Bobby's face. In front of it was a radiator which did not extend the whole length of the sill, but left a space on each side. The cut-off valve of the radiator was under one of these spaces, and Bobby could have stepped upon this valve and climbed into the window. Neither Mr. nor Mrs. Baker knew he was near the window until after a short absence she returned from the bathroom and saw him sitting sidewise on the windowsill with his head pressed against the screen, and before she could reach him the screen opened outwards and he fell below and was killed. An examination of the screen showed that it was hinged at the top and was intended to be secured from opening outwards by two spring plungers of metal, one on each side near the bottom of the screen frame, which passed through the frame into holes in the wooden window facing. The screen was old, and the springs had become weak, and the window facing had grooves worn by the ends of the plungers from each hole outwards so that the plungers got but little hold in the facing. A slight pushing of the screen was found by experiment sufficient to open it. The hotel company had employees whose duty it was to inspect windows and screens. This screen had not been reported as out of order to the superintendent, but he did not know whether it had been reported to the housekeeper or carpenter. There were heavy iron grills outside of some of the windows of the hotel, but none on this window.

". . . An innkeeper is not the insurer of the safety of his guests, but owes to them ordinary care to see that the premises assigned to them are reasonably safe for their use and occupancy. [Citations omitted.] When a child of tender years is accepted as a guest, the inexperience and the natural tendencies of such a child become a part of the situation and must be considered by the innkeeper. We do not mean that the innkeeper becomes the nurse of the child, or assumes its

control when accompanied by its parents, but only that he is bound
to consider whether his premises, though safe enough for an adult,
present any reasonably avoidable dangers to the child guest. The
control and general responsibility for the child accompanied by a
parent or nurse is with the latter, who are also bound to exercise
ordinary care to keep the child from harm. As has been stated, when
parents are complaining of the negligence of the innkeeper, their
own negligence which contributes to the injury is a good defense to
their suit. Negligence is not attributable as such to a child of 2½
years. [Citation omitted.] The conduct of such a child being natural,
spontaneous, and instinctive, is like that of an animal, and is similarly
to be anticipated and guarded against by those charged with any
duty in respect to the child. What then should this innkeeper and
these parents have anticipated that this child might do, and what have
they respectively done or failed to do that was negligent? There is no
statutory requirement respecting hotel windows or window screens,
obedience to which would be diligence and failure to comply with
which would be negligence per se. There is no course of decisions
establishing any rule applicable specially to children and hotel windows. The only available standard of care is the conduct of the ideal
person of ordinary prudence, to be judged of by the jury as a question
of fact. A jury should consider whether the defects attributed to this
screen were known to the innkeeper or had existed for such time as
that he is to be charged with knowledge of them, whether he should
in due prudence have anticipated that a child of this age would be
attracted towards the window and would climb to see what was outside and might be led to lean against the insecure screen and be endangered, and whether another room or at least a warning about the
insecurity of this screen was due. On the other hand, the jury ought
also inquire whether the parents should not have anticipated the same
danger and kept better watch over the child or have tested the
screen, and whether they themselves were contributorily negligent
if the innkeeper was negligent. The innkeeper and the parents perhaps
ought equally to have anticipated the danger of a child trying to get
into the window, but the duty of inspecting the screen is not the
same. The responsibility for the premises is primarily on the innkeeper, and the guest may generally assume that they are safe. But
it is argued that the screens are there to keep insects out and not to

keep children in, and there is no duty on the innkeeper to have them safe for the latter purpose, and parents have no right to rely on them for such purposes. [Citation omitted.] But yet if the screen to all appearances, and as screens are usually found, would serve to protect the child, the false appearance of an insecurely fastened screen might easily mislead the parent or even inspire confidence in a child to lean against it. [Citation omitted.] Though there was no original duty to have any screen in the window for the purpose of keeping the child in, the jury might conclude that prudence would as respects this child, have required that it be as securely fastened as screens customarily are, lest it prove a deception and a trap. We agree with the trial judge that the failure to have protecting grills at the windows is not negligence. . . . [Reversed and remanded.]

The reasoning of the court in *Baker* v. *Dallas Hotel Co.* was adopted by the Supreme Court of Appeals of Virginia in *Crosswhite* v. *Shelby Operating Corp.*[34] In that case the testimony indicated that in the early morning of June 24, 1943, Mrs. Fitzgerald accompanied by her two small daughters, the elder of whom was Sheridan Fitzgerald, about three years old, had registered as guests at defendant's hotel, and were assigned to a room on the fourth floor. They went to the room assigned. The mother left Sheridan playing in the bedroom and went into an adjoining bathroom to wet a cloth for use about the toilet of the smaller child. When she came back she saw Sheridan standing on the windowsill with her back to a wire screen. Seeing the danger in which this child stood, she rushed to her rescue, but before she could reach her, the child leaned against this wire screen, which gave way, she fell through the window and was killed.

The child's administrator sought to recover damages from the Shelby Operating Corporation. The trial court dismissed the complaint for failure to state a cause of action. On appeal, the judgment of dismissal was reversed and the case was remanded for trial to a jury on the issue of negligence.

In *Roberts* v. *Del Monte Properties Co., Inc.,*[35] plaintiff, seven-year-old son of a tenant in defendant's hotel building, was playing by jumping and sliding on some mattresses piled in the hall near a

[34] 182 Va. 713, 30 S.E.2d 673 (1944).
[35] 111 Cal. App. 2d 69, 243 P.2d 914 (1952).

window on the fifth floor of defendant's hotel. While plaintiff was on the top mattress, he accidentally tumbled backward toward the open window behind the pile. The screen in the window gave way and the boy and screen fell down into a patio. Plaintiff was seriously injured. There was evidence that the screen was in a weakened and defective condition. Judgment for the plaintiff infant was affirmed.

The court held that the action of playing on such a pile of mattresses would not render plaintiff a trespasser or licensee to whom the hotel operator owed no duty of care except to refrain from overt or intentional acts, and that violation of statute by a seven-year-old child does not constitute contributory negligence on the part of the child as a matter of law and whether violation constituted contributory negligence is for the jury.

In *Waugh* v. *Duke Corp.*,[36] the infant plaintiff, a guest in defendant's motor lodge, walked into a glass panel adjacent to the door of the guest room. The child believed that the panel, running from floor to ceiling, was an open space giving direct access to the courtyard. The glass broke, the broken fragments fell into the room and cut the child about the face, leg, arms, and knee, requiring surgical operation to camouflage a facial scar resulting from the accident.

The court entered judgment for plaintiff, having found as a fact that the defendant was negligent in that it failed to warn the child plaintiff of the existence of the floor to ceiling glass panel, and failed to construct guards around such panel.

14:7 *Vermin, Insects, Animals*

An innkeeper who negligently fails to keep his premises in a clean and safe condition is responsible for injuries to his guests caused by rats, mice, or insects.

In *DeLuce* v. *Fort Wayne Hotel*,[37] plaintiff, an actress, was a guest in defendant's hotel. On the day after her arrival, she was to present a review of a show at the home of a local business executive, and intending to use the pool at her host's home, took along her swim equipment, including hand and foot fins. Upon her return to the hotel that evening, she left her swimming equipment on a chair in the lobby while she was at the desk inquiring for messages that may have been left for her. Someone in the lobby picked up one of her swim

---

[36] 248 F. Supp. 626 (M.D.N.C. 1966).   [37] 311 F.2d 853 (6th Cir. 1962).

fins, hit the top of a radiator in the lobby with it and dropped it behind the radiator. When plaintiff reached down to retrieve it, she felt a sharp bite on her hand. A rat, approximately a foot long, was hanging from her finger. She was given a tetanus antitoxin injection and later developed postencephalitic Parkinsonism.

The trial court instructed the jury that a relevant statute of Michigan made it mandatory for a hotelkeeper to keep his premises free from rats, and that if plaintiff had been bitten by a rat while on the hotel premises, the hotel would be guilty of negligence as a matter of law and plaintiff entitled to recover.

A judgment for plaintiff for $25,000 was set aside and a new trial ordered on the ground that the jury instruction was erroneous. The Seventh Circuit held that the defendant hotelkeeper was liable only if he knew or should have known of the presence of rats on his premises. If, however, the rat in question was on the premises at the time of the accident because of failure to use due care to keep his premises free of rats, the court stated the defendant would be guilty of a violation of the statute, and, therefore, negligent per se.

In *Del Rosso* v. *F. W. Woolworth Co.*,[38] it appeared that while plaintiff was eating her luncheon in defendant's restaurant, she was aroused by outcries of other persons and saw a big rat coming toward her; that it ran directly beneath the table at which she was sitting; that she jumped and fell and received severe injuries; that the rat came from the kitchen of the defendant, went back of a lunch counter, then came upon the restaurant floor and ran back of another lunch counter. A directed verdict in favor of defendant was affirmed on appeal.

There was no evidence, said the court, that the presence of this or other rats on its premises had ever come to the knowledge of the defendant. There was nothing in the record to show circumstances calculated to arouse apprehension that rats were on its premises. The court said:

The rat is commonly recognized as an enemy of mankind. It is offensive from almost every point of view. . . . It is not a domestic animal but is *ferae naturae.* [Citation omitted.] There is nothing in this record to indicate effective and practicable means to keep occupied premises entirely clear of this vermin. The record does not show that the defendant failed to try to preserve its premises free from the pest. . . . The facts here disclosed do not warrant the finding of any act or omission on the

38 293 Mass. 424, 200 N.E. 277 (1936).

part of the defendant in violation of a legal duty owed by it to the plaintiff.[39]

14:8 Condition of Areas outside the Inn

The duty of an innkeeper to maintain his premises in a safe condition extends to areas under his control outside as well as inside the inn.

In *Carter* v. *Davis*,[40] defendants were operators of the LaLoma Motel in Las Vegas. Plaintiff checked into the motel in the afternoon. Snow had been falling all day and the following morning. Defendant swept the area clean immediately in front of the motel and cautioned plaintiff about crossing the street to reach a restaurant for breakfast. As plaintiff stepped out of the motel office, she fell in an area previously swept by defendant. The question was whether the dangerous condition caused by natural elements was equally apparent to the plaintiff as to all others.

The court affirmed judgment in favor of defendant on the ground that the dangerous condition of the accumulated snow was as apparent to plaintiff as it was to defendant.

In *Hill* v. *Hotel Pierre Corp.*,[41] plaintiff, then 69, exiting through a revolving door leading into Fifth Avenue in New York City, caught the heel of her shoe in a perforated metal and rubber mat, and was forcibly precipitated to the sidewalk, sustaining serious and permanent injuries. The mat was about an inch thick, immediately in front of the revolving door, and was placed there by the defendant. No defect in the mat was claimed. The court, affirming a judgment in favor of defendant entered on a jury's verdict, rejected plaintiff's contention that the placing of the mat there was in itself negligence.

A note with respect to *parking lots* should be in order. The construction of a parking lot should afford adequate space for ingress, egress, and maneuverability of cars; the ground surface should be free of potholes and obstructions, strips and barriers should be painted in bright colors and adequate lighting should be maintained for patrons to move about safely at night.

---

[39] *Id.* at 425 and 277–278.   [40] 74 N.M. 443, 394 P.2d 594 (1964).
[41] 28 App. Div. 2d 1104, 284 N.Y.S.2d 403 (1st Dep't 1967) (mem. opinion).

CHAPTER 15

Responsibility with Respect to Swimming Pools

15:1 *General Rule of Liability*

An innkeeper who provides a swimming pool for the comfort and convenience of his guests is not an insurer of the safety of guests who avail themselves of such facilities. His only duty is to use ordinary and reasonable care in the construction, maintenance, and operation of the pool, and to provide an adequate degree of general supervision so as to render the pool reasonably safe for the use of his guests.[1]

15:2 *Duty of Adequate Supervision*

What is adequate supervision? That depends on the circumstances of each case. In *McKeever* v. *Phoenix Jewish Community Center*,[2] a parent sued the defendant club for the death by drowning of a ten-year-old child in the club's pool. The trial resulted in judgment for the club, which was affirmed by the Supreme Court of Arizona.

From the testimony at the trial it appeared that plaintiff and his family were members of the defendant club. On the day of the accident the whole family, including plaintiff, his two sons, and his nine-year-old and ten-year-old daughters were using the pool. The young children were using the shallow end of the pool, which was separated from the deep end by a rope supported by buoys.

Plaintiff's ten-year-old daughter, Mary Agnes, with two young girl friends, moved over to the deep side of the safety rope. In their play

---

[1] *Curcio* v. *City of New York*, 275 N.Y. 20, 9 N.E.2d 760 (1937); *Peterson* v. *City of New York*, 267 N.Y. 204, 196 N.E. 27 (1935).
[2] 92 Ariz. 121, 374 P.2d 875 (1962).

the girls jumped into the deep water and successfully climbed back to jump several times. It seems that none but the nine-year-old sister of Mary Agnes saw these children in this game although there were roughly forty other children and a *lifeguard* at the pool. An older brother of Mary Agnes testified that approximately five minutes passed from the time he saw the three little girls in the shallow part of the water until he knew of the accident. During that period Mary Agnes was left alone at that part of the pool, her two girl friends having returned to other areas. Immediately thereafter, the body of Mary Agnes was discovered at the bottom of the pool by two other swimmers.

The evidence also indicated that the lifeguard was on duty at the time, that he observed the three little children at the deep end of the pool and they appeared reasonably able swimmers to him. The lifeguard got to the scene of the accident as fast as was humanly possible, and made every effort to revive the child without success.

The trial court refused plaintiff's request to instruct the jury as to the doctrine of *res ipsa loquitur*, which is a rule of circumstantial evidence and gives rise to an inference of responsibility for an injury. The doctrine is applied in cases where the instrumentality which produced an injury is within the exclusive possession and control of the defendant charged with negligence, and such person has exclusive knowledge of the care exercised in the control and management of that instrumentality. Evidence of circumstances which show that the accident would not ordinarily have occurred without neglect of some duty owed to the plaintiff is sufficient to justify an inference of negligence and to shift the burden of explanation to the defendant.[3]

Plaintiff's doctor testified that a drowning could result from very little water on the back of a person's throat causing a spasm of the glottis which closes off the airway. This could occur within a matter of seconds. Consequently, several factors other than the defendant's alleged negligence could conceivably be said to have contributed to the child's death. One such factor could have been the parents' leaving her without immediate and direct supervision in an inherently dangerous body of water, where drowning is not only possible but may be expected in the event of misjudgment on the part of the child. Even an unnoticed chance fall by a child from a pool's edge into the

---

[3] *Galbraith v. Busch*, 267 N.Y. 230, 196 N.E. 36 (1935).

water could be the cause. There was no error in the refusal to give the requested instruction regarding the doctrine of *res ipsa loquitur*.

In *Cohen* v. *Suburban Sidney-Hill, Inc.*,[4] the minor plaintiff was an eight-year-old boy whose father was a member of the club operated by defendant. The boy had the privilege of using the pool located on the club premises. There were at least three lifeguards on duty at the pool on the date of the accident. The minor plaintiff was going up on a ladder which led to a high diving board approximately twenty feet above the concrete flooring which extended around the pool. The ladder and the diving board were wet. There were a number of other children trying to climb this ladder to get on the diving board. There were no lifeguards attempting to regulate the number of children going up on this diving board. The minor plaintiff was near the top as other children were climbing up the ladder. He slipped and went over on his back on the concrete flooring around the pool. Upon the conclusion of an opening statement by plaintiff's counsel, the trial judge granted defendant's motion for a directed verdict.

On appeal, the judgment entered on the verdict was affirmed. Said the court:

There is nothing in the opening statement to show or to justify an inference as to what it was that caused the minor to slip and fall from the ladder. It is as likely that he fell simply because he lost his foothold, or because he did not grip the ladder while ascending, or because the ladder was wet, as that he fell because of the lack of supervision by the defendant. . . . The [plaintiff was] required to show that it was more likely that the injury was occasioned by the negligence of the defendant than by a cause for which the defendant was not liable. . . . [The verdict] for the defendant [was] rightly directed.[5]

In *Wagenschnur* v. *Green Acres Recreation Ass'n, Inc.*,[6] the minor plaintiff was a nine-year-old girl who attended a swimming party at defendant's swimming pool. She asked for and received permission to remove from the storeroom, and to play with, certain hard plastic floats. In the course of such play, one of the floats bobbed up far enough out of the water to strike and break a portion of one of her front teeth. There was a lifeguard on duty at or near the pool at the

---

[4] 343 Mass. 217, 178 N.E.2d 19 (1961).   [5] *Id.* at 219 and 21.
[6] 196 A.2d 401 (Del. Super. Ct. 1963).

time the floats were in use but he did not feel it was necessary to give more specific supervision to the plaintiff's use of the floats.

In her action to recover for the damage to her front teeth, plaintiff contended that defendant's lifeguard was negligent in permitting children to use the float and in failing to supervise its use. Judgment for the defendant was affirmed on appeal. Said the court, "[O]ne who participates in an active sport accepts the obvious dangers connected therewith and the operator of the facility in the exercise of reasonable care cannot be held liable for those dangers which are inherent in such activity and are obvious to the participant." [7]

15:3 Death or Injury as Presumption of Negligence

In general, the fact of the death or injury of a swimming-pool patron is not conclusive proof of negligence and does not even raise a presumption of negligence on the part of the pool operator.

In *Rovegno* v. *San Jose Knights of Columbus Hall Association*,[8] a mother sued to recover damages for the death of her nineteen-year-old son, who died in a swimming pool in a building owned by the defendant and used for social and athletic purposes by its members. The action was grounded on alleged negligence by reason of defendant's failure to provide an experienced lifeguard at the pool. The evidence disclosed that young Rovegno and a boy guest went swimming in the pool at a time when no one was present at the pool and no member or officer of defendant had notice or knowledge that the boys intended to swim or that they were swimming in the pool at the time. Notices were posted in the locker rooms and in the pool, reading: "Bathers using pool do so at their own risk."

Rovegno's companion swam across the pool first. When he turned around, Rovegno, who was concededly not a good swimmer, started across. At a point about halfway across the pool, he was seen to jump up and down in deep water. His face was white as could be and bore a frightened look or horrible expression. His companion, being unable to assist him from the pool, went outside for help. Rovegno was found lying at the bottom of the pool at the nine-foot depth, dead. An autopsy revealed that death resulted from a cardiac condition "more than anything else" rather than from "real drowning."

[7] *Id.* at 403.   [8] 108 Cal. App. 591, 291 P. 848 (1930).

The trial court, by granting defendant's motion for nonsuit, took the case from the jury. On appeal, the judgment of nonsuit was reversed and the case remanded for trial to a jury. The court reasoned that whether death occurred by drowning or not was a question for the jury to determine. Just what would have happened had a lifeguard been present was a matter of speculation or of inference and one for the jury and not for the court. It was similarly for the jury to determine whether defendant's negligence was the proximate cause of young Rovegno's death and whether the arrangements made by defendant were such as ordinarily prudent persons, situated as defendant was, would have done.

The court also rejected defendant's contention that the deceased was bound by the notice, "Bathers using pool do so at their own risk," and therefore he assumed the risk of drowning. Said the court, "This action is based upon alleged negligence, while the last suggested defense, if it be a defense, arises from contract. Even though it might have been available against the decedent had he lived and brought suit for damages on account of personal injuries, it cannot operate to defeat his mother's independent statutory right of action." [9]

A contrary result was reached by a New York court in a substantially similar action in the case of *Laut* v. *Brooklyn & Queens Y.M.C.A.*[10] In that case, a mother sued to recover for the death by drowning in defendant's pool of her twenty-three-year-old son. It appeared that the boy went into the pool alone. There were no attendants or supervisors or anyone else there at the time. There were posted rules in the locker rooms and in the pool, reading:

DO NOT SWIM ALONE

NOTIFY THE ATTENDANT BEFORE ENTERING THE POOL

YOU USE THE POOL AT YOUR OWN RISK

PRACTICE SAFETY FIRST

The action was predicated on defendant's alleged negligence in not having an employee present in the pool for lifesaving purposes and for supervision of neophyte swimmers; failing to give the deceased any instructions as to the use of the pool under the circumstances

[9] *Id.* at 598 and 850.

[10] 262 App. Div. 1038, 30 N.Y.S.2d 425 (2d Dep't 1941) (mem. opinion), *aff'd mem.*, 289 N.Y. 593, 43 N.E.2d 722 (1942).

existing at the time of the drowning; failing to supervise the pool's use so as to prevent the deceased from entering, and allowing the deceased to enter the pool knowing that no supervisors were present.

The jury returned a verdict in favor of plaintiff. The judgment entered on the verdict was reversed on appeal. The court found no affirmative evidence of negligence causing the accident, nor any evidence to warrant an inference of negligence.

15:4 *Contributory Negligence of Patron*

The patron of a swimming pool is under a duty to exercise ordinary care for his own safety. Thus, if a patron knew of a particular danger or would have known of it by the exercise of ordinary care, or was duly warned, but nevertheless placed himself in peril, thereby causing or contributing to his injury or death, he is guilty of contributory negligence which in a majority of jurisdictions serves as an absolute bar to the recovery of damages. On the other hand, the patron has the right to assume that the owner or operator has discharged his duty of providing a reasonably safe place for his patrons.

In *Ryan v. Unity, Inc.,*[11] plaintiff, employed as doorman in the Delmonico Hotel in Miami Beach, got off from work at 2:30 A.M. Thereafter, in company with three females, he visited a bar and restaurant. From there he and his girl friends went to the Surrey Hotel, arriving there at about 4:30 A.M. The party then decided to take a swim and while it was still dark and visibility was still low, they all proceeded to the swimming pool. Plaintiff immediately went to the diving board and dove headlong into the swimming pool which contained approximately two feet of water at the deepest end where the diving board was located, and thereby sustained severe head injuries. The pool had been drained for cleaning at the time.

Summary judgment for defendant was affirmed on appeal. Said the court:

From a careful study of the record it appears that appellant failed to exercise ordinary care for his own safety when, during the early morning hour of approximately 5:00 A.M. while it was still dark and visibility was low, he dove headlong into the swimming pool without giving the slightest heed to existing conditions at that particular time. By doing so,

[11] 55 So. 2d 117 (Fla. 1951).

he directly contributed to his own injury and made his own negligent act a concurring proximate cause of his injury.[12]

In *Biltmore Terrace Associates* v. *Kegan*,[13] a minor guest of defendant's hotel and his father sued for injuries to the minor guest who dove from beyond a four-foot wall at the edge of the ocean and was permanently injured when he struck bottom.

The minor was fifteen years old at the time of the accident, and had been a guest of the hotel for twelve days. The defendant operated a patio-pool resort hotel and provided a patio-pool area between the hotel proper and the ocean. This structure was located landward of the mean highwater line, but the tides on occasion brought the water up to the wall and to a depth of several feet. The ocean side of the patio-pool area was enclosed by a wall approximately four feet in height. On the day of the accident, the pool was closed because of bad weather, and no lifeguard was on duty or any person of authority present to oversee the recreation area.

Plaintiff and a young friend climbed over the wall and stood on the slanted ledge on the opposite side of the wall. After waiting for a large wave, plaintiff's friend dived into the ocean. Shortly thereafter, plaintiff took a dive, struck the bottom of the shallow water and suffered a complete and permanent paralysis from the neck down. The jury returned a substantial verdict for the plaintiff. On appeal, the judgment entered on the verdict was reversed by the Supreme Court of Florida, and the complaint was dismissed. The court held that it was the duty of the trial court to direct a verdict for the defendant at the close of the plaintiff's case. Said the court:

It is suggested that the hotel violated this duty [of reasonable care for the safety of its patrons] in one or more of the following ways: 1. It failed to maintain a lifeguard on duty. 2. It failed to maintain a guard rail. 3. It failed to post signs or other warnings against use of the subject wall or the beams protruding therefrom as a means of diving or jumping into the ocean. . . . We think that the plaintiffs, in all of the above contentions, overlook the fact . . . that there was a four-foot wall at the end of the patio area. The plaintiff found it necessary to climb over this wall and assume a precarious position outside of the wall area in order to get

[12] *Id.* at 117–118.

[13] 130 So. 2d 631 (Fla. Dist. Ct. App. 1961, writ of certiorari discharged and cause dismissed, 154 So. 2d 825 (Fla. 1963).

a footing from which to dive. There was no other way by which one could enter the ocean except to climb over the wall. . . . To require a warning under such circumstances would be as ludicrous as requiring a sign on the top of an office building reading "don't jump off here." . . .

In view of our holding that the plaintiffs failed to prove negligence on the part of the defendant, it is not necessary for us to discuss in an extended fashion our holding that the plaintiff was guilty of contributory negligence as a matter of law.[14]

15:5   Duty to Supervise Diving Area

Diving activities involve greater risk of injury than ordinary use of a swimming pool, and supervision should therefore be commensurate with the risks involved.

In *Allon v. Park Central Hotel Co., Inc.*,[15] plaintiff sued the defendant hotel and its pool concessionaire for injuries sustained in the hotel pool. It appeared that plaintiff was swimming down the hotel pool from the shallow end and as he approached the diving board at the deep end somebody did a back dive and they met head-on. As a result, plaintiff sustained rupture of the right ear drum, followed by acute traumatic mastoiditis.

Plaintiff claimed that defendant was negligent in failing to have a sufficient number of employees in the swimming pool to prevent patrons from diving off the diving board at the time when patrons using the pool were immediately below the diving board. Although the court, at defendant's request, charged the jury that "the plaintiff in the exercise of reasonable care was required to adjust his conduct to other persons who were using the pool at the time or who reasonably could be expected to use the pool by right," the jury nevertheless brought in a verdict for plaintiff, which was affirmed on appeal.

In the subsequent case of *Byron v. St. George Swimming Club, Inc.*,[16] plaintiff sustained her injury while diving from the high board in defendant's swimming pool. No one was using the diving section at the time plaintiff jumped, making a swan dive. As she reached the water her head struck a boy who was swimming underneath the water in the diving section, looking for a lost cap. The boy, made codefendant in the action, had no right to be swimming in the diving

[14] *Id.* at 634.   [15] 272 N.Y. 631, 5 N.E.2d 366 (1936) (mem. opinion).
[16] 283 N.Y. 505, 28 N.E.2d 934 (1940) (per curiam).

section, and his presence there was obviously a danger to any person diving from the boards. There were signs in the pool to warn swimmers and divers, reading "Diving at your own risk" and "Look before you dive."

Plaintiff grounded her action on the defendant club's negligence in failing to restrict the diving area to divers and in failing to give warning to plaintiff and others that the rules would be relaxed to allow a nondiver to enter the diving area to search for his cap. The trial court dismissed the action at the end of the plaintiff's case, and the Appellate Division affirmed. But the Court of Appeals reversed and remanded the case for a new trial. Said the court, "The risk of injury from diving under the conditions obtaining at the place and time of the accident was not, as a matter of law, assumed by the plaintiff." [17]

The court also pointed out, as another ground for reversal, the exclusion by the trial court of evidence that it was the uniform custom and practice of the defendant in the maintenance of the pool and in the protection of its diving patrons, to maintain two guards to keep the diving section of the pool free from swimmers when patrons were diving.

15:6 Safety of Pool Premises

A pool operator is under a duty to use ordinary care in maintaining the pool premises in safe condition for the use of patrons. He is not an insurer, however, of the safety of his patrons.

In *Bristol* v. *Ernst*,[18] plaintiff and a friend were guests at defendant's summer hotel. Defendants maintained a swimming pool for the use of their guests. While wading into the pool, plaintiff sustained a severe cut on one foot, caused by a piece of glass on the bottom of the pool. The trial court gave the following instructions on the law to the jury:

"It was the duty of defendants, having held this out as an inducement to the guests, to keep it in a reasonably safe condition. It was their duty to see that there was nothing on the bottom of the pool that would cause injuries to those that were using it in a careful and prudent manner". . . . "[I]t is the duty of the owner or the maintainer of the pool to keep it

[17] *Id.* at 508 and 934.
[18] 261 App. Div. 713, 27 N.Y.S.2d 119 (1st Dep't 1941).

free and clear from any obstructions that would be of a dangerous character." [19]

The jury returned a verdict for the plaintiff. The judgment entered on the verdict was reversed on appeal. The trial court was held to have committed reversible error in its charge to the jury. The Appellate Division held that the law did not impose on the defendants an absolute duty to maintain the pool in a reasonably safe condition, but imposed upon them only the duty to exercise ordinary care in the maintenance of the pool.

In *Fuller* v. *Vista Del Arroyo Hotel*,[20] plaintiff sued to recover for personal injuries at defendant's swimming pool. Plaintiff had been a frequent guest at the hotel for some five years. On the day of the accident, while descending a flight of concrete steps to the walk surrounding the pool, she stepped on the second step which was damp and partly shaded by the shadow of adjacent trees, and slipped and fell, with a resultant broken leg. The step where the accident happened was twelve inches wide and had a slope in such distance of approximately three-eighths of an inch. When constructed, it had been roughed by brushing, the marks on the step where the accident occurred running the width of the step rather than lengthwise, as was the case of marks on other steps in the series. At the time of the accident, the step was slick and smooth. Both defendant and plaintiff knew that the steps were used by bathers and were damp.

A judgment in favor of defendant upon a directed verdict was affirmed on appeal. Said the court:

Viewing the evidence, as we have in arriving at the facts above stated, in the light most favorable to [plaintiff], we are of the opinion that such facts fail to disclose any act or acts of negligence by defendant nor would they support an inference that any negligence of defendant was the proximate cause of the regrettable injury which plaintiff . . . has suffered.[21]

In *Post* v. *Camino Del Properties, Inc.*,[22] plaintiff sued to recover for injuries he suffered when he slipped and fell on the surface of the recreational area around defendant's swimming pool. The area around the pool was of roughened surface concrete. Before reaching the pool

19 *Id.* at 714 and 121.   20 42 Cal. App. 2d 400, 108 P.2d 920 (1941).
21 *Id. at* 401 and 921.   22 173 Cal. App. 2d 446, 343 P.2d 294 (1959).

and sunken below this level was an area of smooth concrete for a distance of twelve to fifteen feet from the pool. A set of two steps twelve to fourteen inches wide with six- or eight-inch risers was constructed between these areas and extended on three sides of the pool. The steps were of black cement and not roughened. The plaintiff walked toward these steps from where he was seated. They were wet from other bathers' dripping suits. Somewhere thereon plaintiff's foot slipped out from under him. His head struck the concrete and knocked him unconscious. He suffered a fracture of the four thoracic vertebrae.

Plaintiff maintained that his injury was the direct result of defendant's negligence in maintaining the surface of the area around the pool in a slippery, hazardous, and unsafe condition. Plaintiff testified that he was familiar with the rough cement area around the pool, but not with the smooth black cement area where he fell. The pool manager, who also doubled as lifeguard, called by plaintiff as witness, stated that, on occasion prior to the accident, he requested his superiors to place stripping along the steps in the vicinity where plaintiff fell, but that his requests were put off; that he applied a wax called "sure grip" about twice a year to the area, but that it would wear off.

The jury returned a verdict for plaintiff. Defendant then moved for judgment notwithstanding the verdict, which was granted. On appeal, the trial court was reversed on its decision on the motion, but was sustained on ordering a new trial.

15:7 Boisterous Conduct

In *Gordon v. Hotel Seville, Inc.*,[23] plaintiff, Ethel Gordon, sued to recover for personal injuries she suffered in defendant's swimming pool. It appeared that a number of boys were engaged in boisterous conduct and horseplay, including pushing or throwing boys into the pool, and that such activities were permitted to go unrestrained for some time.

On the day of the accident, Mrs. Gordon went into the pool at the shallow end. A short time later, while she was swimming there face down, a body landed on her, following which she blacked out or

[23] 105 So. 2d 175 (Fla. Dist. Ct. App. 1958), *cert. denied,* 109 So. 2d 767 (Fla. 1959).

fainted, was assisted from the pool, and became hysterical. A pool attendant rendered first aid and Mr. Gordon, husband of the plaintiff, stated in his deposition that the pool attendant made an admission to him that "these fellows picked one another up bodily and threw him into the pool, and one of them landed on her head."

The trial court granted a motion for summary judgment in defendant's favor. On appeal, the judgment was reversed and the case remanded. The causal connection between the horseplay and the injury was held to be supplied by the admission of the pool attendant, a hotel employee who was in the performance of duties as a pool attendant, that the accident resulted from the horseplay at the pool.

15:8 Comparative Knowledge of Operator and Injured Party as Test of Liability

A swimming-pool operator may be held liable for injuries caused by equipment used at the pool, the dangerous character of which is known to him but is not known to the injured patron.

In *Tucker* v. *Dixon*,[24] the eleven-year-old girl plaintiff and her parents were guests at defendant's motel. Almost immediately after checking in, young Karen went swimming in the motel pool. As she entered the pool, she observed three boys playing with an object in the water which they were throwing back and forth. The boys then left the pool, leaving the object in the water. The accident occurred when Karen surfaced after taking a dive and struck her mouth on a hard plastic float, fracturing two of her front teeth. The float was part of the equipment used for cleaning the pool. It was left lying near the pool, where the boys picked it up, threw it into the pool, and left it in the water just as Karen got there.

The trial court found that defendant was negligent in leaving the cleaning equipment near the pool where the float could be detached and thrown into the water; that defendant's negligence was the proximate cause of Karen's injury and that she was not guilty of contributory negligence. The appearance of the float which was an unknown object to Karen and her parents was such as did not place

[24] 144 Colo. 79, 355 P.2d 79 (1960).

them or any other reasonably prudent person under like circumstances on notice of its weight or possible danger from contact with it, when in the water. Judgment for the plaintiff was affirmed, on appeal. Said the court:

It is to be noted that the comparative knowledge of the parties is the test of liability—that is to say, the knowledge of the defendant as opposed to the knowledge of the person injured. Two conditions must concur, if the possessor of the land is to be held liable: (1) a realization that the condition constitutes an unreasonable risk to the patron; and (2) the absence of reason to believe that the condition will be discovered by the patron or the risk realized by him.[25]

The floats in this case were not playthings; they were part of the cleaning and maintenance equipment of the motel whose employees were fully cognizant of the weight and hardness of the float. Karen, on the other hand, had no idea of its normal use or the danger of striking it. All she knew was that some boys had previously been playing with it. She used that degree of care which ordinarily prudent children of her age and like intelligence would be expected to use under like circumstances.

15:9 *Summary*

A pool operator is not liable for dangers inherent in the use of the pool and obvious to the user.

The law does not impose an absolute duty on the pool operator to maintain the pool in a safe condition. His duty is merely to use ordinary care in the maintenance of the pool.

It has been held negligence for a pool operator to leave equipment around the pool area, the dangerous character of which is known to the operator but not known to the injured patron.

The drowning of a child in a pool does not, in and of itself, raise an inference of negligence by the operator.

Diving activities involve greater risk and call for supervision commensurate with the risk.

[25] *Id.* at 84 and 82, quoting *Webb v. Thomas,* 133 Colo. 458, 465, 296 P.2d 1036, 1039 (1956).

The mere falling of a child from the top of a diving board onto the flooring below does not of itself prove negligence by the pool operator.

An unattended pool should not be left open for use by patrons, particularly not by children. In a majority of jurisdictions contributory negligence, that is failure of a patron to exercise ordinary care for his own safety, bars recovery in case of injury or death.

CHAPTER 16

Responsibility for Conduct of Persons in the Inn

16:1 *Protection against Injury by Third Parties*

The innkeeper, while not an insurer of a guest against personal injury, must protect him against injury from third persons so far as it is within his power to do so. In the early case of *Rommel v. Schambacher*,[1] the plaintiff, a minor, entered defendant's tavern, where he met one Edward Flanagan. They both became intoxicated on liquor furnished them by defendant. While plaintiff was standing on the outside of the bar, engaged in conversation with the defendant, who was on the inside thereof, Flanagan pinned a piece of paper to Rommel's back, and set it on fire. The trial court directed a nonsuit. On appeal, the decision in favor of defendant was reversed and a new trial ordered. Said the court:

There is no doubt that the defendant, from the position occupied, had a full view of the room outside of the bar, and did see, or might have seen, all that was going on in it. If, in fact, he did see Flanagan setting fire to the plaintiff, and did not interfere to protect his guest from so flagrant an outrage, his responsibility for the consequences is undoubted. If, on the other hand, he was guilty of making Flanagan drunk, or if he came there drunk, and Schambacher knew that fact, he was bound to see that he did no injury to his customers. All this is a plain matter of common law and good sense, and does not depend on the act of 1854, or any other statute. Where one enters a saloon or tavern, opened for the entertainment of the public, the proprietor is bound to see that he is properly protected from the assaults or insults, as well of those who are in his employ, as of the drunken and vicious men whom he may choose to harbor.[2]

[1] 120 Pa. 579, 11 A. 779 (1887).   [2] *Id.* at 582 and 779.

In *Malloy* v. *Coletti*,[3] the plaintiff, while a guest in defendant's restaurant, was violently struck on the head by a heavy glass water tumbler thrown by a patron, and was seriously injured. The complaint alleged that the defendant had notice of the continued offensive, boisterous, and unlawful conduct of the patron who injured plaintiff. defendant moved to dismiss the complaint for failure to state a cause of action. Defendant's motion was denied.

In *Hughes* v. *Coniglio*,[4] plaintiff entered defendant's restaurant as a patron about midnight. There were a number of other people in the place at the time and everything was quiet and peaceful. Suddenly, as plaintiff was about to seat himself, two other patrons, without warning, jumped up and began fighting, one cutting the other with a knife. As patrons scurried for protection, someone pushed plaintiff into the path of the fighters and he was stabbed. Defendant's place had no previous history of disorderly conduct by patrons and both the altercation and resulting injury to plaintiff happened suddenly and unexpectedly and without any warning and by the exercise of reasonable care could not either have been discovered or prevented by defendant. Judgment dismissing the action was affirmed on appeal.

The court purported to accept the general rule that the proprietor of a public place of business such as a restaurant is not an insurer of a patron against personal injuries inflicted by other persons on the premises who are in no manner connected with the business but is liable therefor only when he is negligent. However, it quoted with approval the statement in 28 *American Jurisprudence, Innkeepers*: "He is guilty of negligence if he admits to his place or permits to remain there, as a guest, a person of known violent and disorderly propensities, who will probably assault or otherwise maltreat his guests; and he may be liable in damages for the consequences of such negligence." [5]

In *Shank* v. *Riker Restaurant Associates, Inc.*,[6] the plaintiff and his female companion entered the defendant's restaurant and ordered coffee, seating themselves at the counter. Almost immediately they were attacked by three men who had been in the restaurant for the

[3] 114 Misc. 177, 186 N.Y.S. 730 (Sup. Ct. 1921).

[4] 147 Neb. 829, 25 N.W.2d 405 (1946).   [5] *Id.* at 833 and 408.

[6] 28 Misc. 2d 835, 216 N.Y.S.2d 118 (Sup. Ct. 1961), *aff'd mem.*, 15 App. Div. 2d 458, 222 N.Y.S.2d 683 (1st Dep't 1961).

past fifteen to twenty-five minutes. The plaintiff was severely injured in the attack and he sued the defendant owner for damages. A judgment for plaintiff in the sum of $60,000 was affirmed on appeal.

Evidence showed that the manager of the restaurant had witnessed the violent conduct of the man who eventually assaulted the plaintiff for twenty minutes before the plaintiff entered the restaurant. His conduct made it abundantly clear that he constituted a source of physical danger to defendant's patrons. Therefore the manager's negligence was the competent producing cause of the plaintiff's injuries. It was held that the defendant's manager failed to discharge his obligation to reasonably avoid an assault or injury to his patrons.

In *Hibbs v. Brown Hotel Co.*,[7] the plaintiff, a woman of 60, was dining at the defendant hotel where dancing was allowed. She and her escort ventured forth for a sedate waltz and while they were dancing, the plaintiff was struck in the ankle by another patron doing the "jitterbug." Plaintiff returned to her table and waited until the "jitterbug" couple left the floor before attempting another waltz. This time plaintiff was struck in the back by the "jitterbugging" couple, who had returned to the dance floor. She fell, striking her elbow on a post. Her arm became swollen the next day and surgery was eventually required. Plaintiff sued the hotel for not preventing dangerous dancing in their dining room. The trial court directed a verdict for the defendant hotel. The Court of Appeals of Kentucky affirmed, stating:

The "jitterbugs" described in the testimony were active, not rowdyish; enthusiastic, not callous. . . . [T]he dance floor was not so crowded that "jitterbugging" . . . amounted to reckless conduct. . . . [T]he Hotel was not negligent and the risk involved here came within the scope of those ordinarily assumed by devotees of the dance. The Hotel is not an insurer. . . . [I]n the circumstances of the present case we do not find the exercise of the frantic act disorderly conduct or such conduct that the management of the Hotel was required to prevent it.[8] . . .

In *Poulos v. Brady*,[9] plaintiff entered defendant's taproom to get a glass of beer. While in the premises, and before being served, plaintiff asked for and was directed to the men's room. As he was about to enter the room, he was set upon and bitten by defendant's dog. The

[7] 302 S.W.2d 127 (Ky. 1957).   [8] *Id.* at 127–128.
[9] 167 Pa. Super. 150, 74 A.2d 694 (1950).

jury found for plaintiff and the judgment entered on the jury's verdict was, on appeal, affirmed on the authority of *Rommel* v. *Schambacher*.

16:2 *Protection against Injury by Employees*

As the innkeeper must protect the guest against third persons, a fortiori he must protect him against injuries from his own employees. And since the employees are provided, among other things, for the purpose of protecting guests, every injury inflicted upon the guest by an employee, either intentionally or negligently, is a breach of his duty of protection, and renders the innkeeper liable to the guest. The innkeeper's duty, the breach of which by his employee causes the injury, is not the negative duty not to assault the guest, but the affirmative duty to protect him from assault. The employee, in assaulting the guest, is committing the tort for himself, but he is breaching the obligation of protection which rests on the innkeeper, and which the employee has himself been employed to carry out.

CLANCY *v.* BARKER

71 Neb. 83, 98 N.W. 440 (1904), adhered to

on rehearing, 71 Neb. 91, 103 N.W. 446 (1905)

[The plaintiff and his wife with their infant son of about six years of age, were registered at the Barker Hotel in the City of Omaha. At about 8:30 o'clock of the evening of January 15, 1902, the boy left his mother's room and went down the elevator to the first floor of the hotel, as he says, "To get some water." Reaching that floor, he passed by a room where a boy named Lacey, who was employed as a porter or bellboy at the hotel, was playing a harmonica. The door being ajar, he entered his room, apparently to satisfy his childish curiosity; another boy, who sometimes ran the elevator, was also in the room; both of these employees seem to have been off duty at the time and engaged in amusing themselves in a room not occupied by any of the guests of the house. As the Clancy boy entered the room, young Lacey said to him apparently in jest, "See here, young fellow, if you touch anything, this is what you get," at the same time pointing a pistol at him. The pistol was at that instant accidentally discharged, the ball striking the young Clancy boy in the head, destroying one of his eyes and inflicting other injuries upon him which, however, did not prove fatal. This action was brought by the father to recover damages alleged to have been sustained by him by reason of these facts.

At the close of the plaintiff's case, the court directed a verdict for the defendants, and from a judgment rendered on such verdict, the plaintiff appeals.]

ALBERT, C. [after stating the facts]: "The defendants insist, that the plaintiff, having failed to allege that the servant wilfully or maliciously inflicted the injury, it was incumbent on him to show that the injuries were the result of negligence on the part of the servant in the performance of some duty . . . which the defendants owed the plaintiff. We think they overlook the theory upon which this action was brought and prosecuted. The plaintiff by his petition and evidence obviously intended to commit himself unreservedly to the theory that his cause of action is *ex contractu*. A contract is alleged in the petition, the wrongful acts of the servant, which resulted in injury to the boy are alleged, not for the purpose of stating a cause of action *ex delicto*, but for the purpose of showing a breach of contract and consequent damages.

"This brings us at once to the question, whether the act of the servant, resulting in the injuries complained of, constitutes a breach of the implied contract between the plaintiff and the proprietors of the hotel for the entertainment of the former and his family. By the implied contract between a hotel keeper and his guest, the former undertakes more than merely to furnish the latter with suitable food and lodging. There is implied on his part the further undertaking that the guest shall be treated with due consideration for his safety and comfort. [Citations omitted.] . . .

"If then the defendants were under a contractual obligation that the plaintiff and his family should be treated with due consideration for their comfort and safety, the act of the servant, resulting in the injuries complained of, obviously amounts to a breach of contract. That the wrongful act was committed by a servant is wholly immaterial. The rule which requires that a guest at a hotel be treated with due consideration for his comfort and safety would be of little value if limited to the proprietor himself. As a rule he does not come in contact with the guests. His undertaking is not that he personally shall treat them with due consideration, but that they shall be so treated while inmates of the hotel as guests; and if they be not thus treated there is a breach of the implied contract, whether the lack of such treatment is the result of some act or omission of the proprietor himself, or of his servant or servants.

"Neither do we deem it material whether the servant, at the time of the injury, was actively engaged in the discharge of his duty as servant or not. He was a servant of the proprietor and an inmate of the hotel; his duty as to the treatment to be accorded the guests of the hotel was a continuing one and rested upon him wherever, within the hotel, he was brought in contact with them. To hold otherwise, would be to say that a guest would have no redress for any manner of indignity received at a hotel, so long as it was inflicted by a servant not actively engaged in the discharge of some duty. . . .

"It is equally immaterial to this case, . . . whether the shooting was accidental or wilful. The servant in pointing a loaded gun at the boy committed a trespass, and as a result of such trespass inflicted serious and permanent injuries on the child. His acts, therefore, constituted a breach of the implied undertaking of his employers to treat the plaintiff and his family with due consideration for their safety and comfort, for which breach his employers are liable in damages. . . ."

[Judgment reversed and the cause remanded for further proceedings according to law. On rehearing the court adhered to its former judgment, with one judge dissenting.]

It is to be noted that in the foregoing action in the State Courts of Nebraska it was the injured boy's father who sued for damages he suffered as a result of the injury to his son.

In a separate action which he commenced in the federal court, the father sued the same defendant on the same cause of action on behalf of his minor son. In this action, the decision was in favor of the defendant hotelkeeper. The federal court found a marked difference between the relation of a common carrier to a passenger, on the one hand, and of an innkeeper to a guest on the other hand.

A minority of states, including New York, follow the Nebraska rule, while the majority of states, including California and Pennsylvania, follow the rule articulated by the federal court below.

CLANCY v. BARKER
131 F. 161 (8th Cir. 1904)

[The facts of this case are stated in *Clancy* v. *Barker*, decided by the Supreme Court of Nebraska].

SANBORN, Cir. J.: "[C]ounsel for the plaintiff in error asserts a right of recovery against the defendants on two grounds: First, he contends that by receiving the boy and his parents as guests at the hotel the proprietors of the hotel undertook, like a common carrier of passengers, to protect him against injuries occasioned by the negligence or wilful misconduct of their employés in and about the hotel, and that this contractual obligation of the defendants was violated. In the second place, counsel contends that when Lacey, the porter, pointed the pistol at the boy, he was guilty of a wrongful and negligent act; that he was engaged at the time in the performance of one of his duties as servant; and that on this ground the defendants are liable. It is argued that it was a part of Lacey's duty as a servant, when the child entered the room where he was playing the harmonica, to see that he did not disturb or handle any articles in the room; that a jury might well infer that the act which occasioned the injury was done by Lacey in the performance of this duty; and that the ordinary rule, 'Respondeat superior,' applies to the case.

"We entertain no doubt that the act in question was in fact wrongful and negligent, but the difficulty which we encounter in upholding this latter theory is that the evidence fails to show that Lacey had been charged with the duty of guarding such articles as may have been in the room where the accident occurred. . . . So far as the evidence warrants an inference, the inference is that Lacey was not engaged at the time in the discharge of any duty for and in behalf of the defendants; that he was temporarily, at least, off duty, engaged in amusing himself; and that he pointed the pistol at the child in sport, to see how he would act, rather than to prevent him from touching or intermeddling with anything in the room. The act in question seems to have been prompted by a momentary impulse, . . . and to have been in no wise connected with the discharge of any duty or with the performance of any task that had been devolved upon [Lacey] by the defendants. Under these circumstances we are of opinion that the proprietors of the hotel cannot be held accountable for the act in question on the second ground above stated, since it is too well settled to require the citation of any authority that the master is not responsible ordinarily for the negligent acts of his servant, unless they are committed while the servant is rendering some service for and in behalf of the master.

"But counsel for the plaintiff insists that, although the defendants were not negligent in the employment of their servant, the bellboy, and although he was not acting in the course or within the actual or apparent scope of his employment when he discharged the pistol, yet the defendants are liable for the injury he inflicted, because it is a part of the contract between an innkeeper and his guest that the former will insure the safety of the person of the latter against injury from every act or omission of his servants. The crucial question here, therefore, is whether or not an innkeeper is an insurer of the safety of the person of his guest while the latter remains in his hotel against the negligent and willful acts of his servants, when they are acting without the course and without the actual or apparent scope of their employment. . . .

"Counsel for the plaintiff insists that the liability of the innkeepers should be extended in the case at bar even beyond that of common carriers, so that the defendants should be held liable for the injuries inflicted by the willful or careless act of their servant when he was not acting within the course or scope of his employment. The argument in support of this contention is that common carriers are liable for the negligent or willful acts of their servants to whom they intrust the care, custody, and control of the passengers they transport, and that the liability of innkeepers to their guests is similar to that of carriers to their passengers.

". . . [T]here is a marked difference in the character of the contracts of carriage on a railroad or steamboat and of entertainment at an inn, and a wide difference in the relation of the parties to these contracts. In the former, the carrier takes and the passenger surrenders to him the control and dominion of his person, and the chief, nay, practically the only, occupation of both parties is the performance of the contract of carriage. For the time being all other occupations are subordinate to the transportation. The carrier regulates the movements of the passenger, assigns him his seat or berth, and determines when, how, and where he shall ride, eat, and sleep, while the passenger submits to the rules, regulations, and directions of the carrier, and is transported in the manner the latter directs. The contract is that the passenger will surrender the direction and dominion of his person to the servants of the carrier, to be transported in the car, seat, or berth and in the manner in which they direct, and that the latter will take charge of and transport the person of the passenger safely. The logical and necessary result of this relation of the parties is that every servant of the carrier who is employed in assisting to transport the passenger safely, every conductor, brakeman, and porter who is employed to assist in the transportation, is constantly acting within the scope and course of his employment while he is upon the train or boat, because he is one of those selected by his master and placed in charge of the person of the passenger to safely transport him to his destination. Any negligent or willful act of such a servant which inflicts injury upon the passenger is necessarily a breach of the master's contract of safe carriage, and for it the latter must respond. But the contract of an innkeeper with his guest, and their relations to each other, are not of this character. The innkeeper does not take, nor does the guest surrender, the control or dominion of the latter's person. The performance of the contract of entertainment is not the chief occupation of the parties, but it is subordinate to the ordinary business or pleasure of the guest. The innkeeper assigns a room to his guest, but neither he nor his servants direct him when or how he shall occupy it; but they leave him free to use or to fail to use it, and all the other means of entertainment proffered, when and as he chooses, and to retain the uncontrolled dominion of his person and of his movements. The agreement is not that the guest shall surrender the control of his person and action to the servants of the innkeeper, in order that he may be protected from injury and entertained. It is that the guest may retain the direction of his own action, that he may enjoy the entertainment offered, and that the innkeeper will exercise ordinary care to provide for his comfort and safety. The servants of the innkeeper are not placed in charge of the person of the guest to direct, guide, and control his location and action, nor are they employed to perform any contract to insure his safety; but they are engaged in the execution of the agreement of the master to exercise ordinary care for the comfort and safety of the visitor. The natural and logical result of this relation of the parties is that when the servants are not engaged in the course or scope of their employment, although they may be present in the hotel, they are not performing their master's contract, and he is not liable for their negligent or willful acts. . . ."

[The judgment below, directing a verdict in favor of defendants on the conclusion of the plaintiff's testimony was affirmed.]

THAYER, Cir. J. (dissenting): "If a servant of a hotel, when off duty, should meet a guest outside of the hotel, and not on the premises, and there assault him, it is doubtless true—although the case at bar requires no decision on that point—that the innkeeper could not be charged with responsibility for the servant's conduct; and it is probably true that the innkeeper would not be responsible for an assault committed on one of his guests within the hotel by a stranger, provided he has taken all reasonable precautions to prevent such occurrences by excluding disorderly persons from his premises. But in my opinion the law casts on the innkeeper an obligation to see to it that his guest is not injured, while within the hotel, by the wrongful, inconsiderate, or negligent acts of those who are his servants. . . .

"Now it is true that a hotel is an immovable structure and does not run on wheels like a train of cars; but in all other respects the relation existing between an innkeeper and his guest is like that existing between a carrier and passenger, and this fact has always been recognized, as shown by the cases above cited. An innkeeper, like a carrier, is engaged in a quasi public service. When he embarks in the business of keeping a hotel, he is bound to provide entertainment for all travellers who seek a place of rest and refreshment, provided they come to him in a fit condition to be entertained as guests, and are able to pay the customary charges. . . . [T]he innkeeper, like the carrier, has the exclusive right to select all of the persons who are to aid him in the discharge of his quasi public functions. I have been unable, therefore, to discover any sufficient reason why he should not be held responsible to his guests for the consequences of any wilful and wrongful acts of his servants, committed within the hotel, to the same extent that the carrier is responsible to his passengers for like wrongful acts of its servants; and within the authorities above cited a carrier would be clearly responsible to one of its passengers for an injury inflicted by one of its employés under such circumstances as those disclosed in the present case. . . .''

This case was decided under the doctrine of *Swift* v. *Tyson*,[10] which allowed the federal court exercising diversity jurisdiction to exercise an independent judgment as to what the common law of the state was —or should be. This doctrine prevented uniformity in the administration of the laws of the state and was rejected on that ground in *Erie R.R.* v. *Tompkins*.[11] Except in matters governed by the federal Constitution or by the acts of Congress, the law to be applied in any case is the law of the state. The federal court is now bound by the substantive law of the state whether it is declared by the legislature in a statute or by the highest court of the state in order to promote uniformity and to discourage the type of forum shopping which obviously occurred in the *Clancy* case.

In *Ledington* v. *Williams*,[12] plaintiff, a guest in defendant's hotel, sued to recover damages for personal injuries he suffered when a porter employed by defendant, provoked by some remark made by the plaintiff, attacked and badly wounded and cut him with a razor. The trial court instructed the jury that if they believed that plaintiff was a guest and defendant's porter was not acting in self-defense, they should find for the plaintiff.

On appeal, it was reversed. The court reviewed and considered both *Clancy* v. *Barker* cases, and decided to adopt the "federal" rule, supported by the weight of authority. Under such rule, the general test of the innkeeper's liability for a willful or malicious act of his employee, causing injury to a guest, is whether or not, at the time the act was done, the servant was acting in pursuance of his duties as such employee and in behalf of his employer, or was acting for himself from motives or for a purpose with which his duties as an employee were not related, or that the master had failed to exercise ordinary care for his guests' safety or had with knowledge of servant's bad and quarrelsome character employed or afterwards retained him as an employee.

In *Crawford* v. *Hotel Essex Boston Corp.*,[13] plaintiff was a registered guest in defendant's hotel. One evening he entered the hotel about

---

[10] 41 U.S. (16 Pet.) 1 (1842).   [11] 304 U.S. 64 (1938).

[12] 257 Ky. 599, 78 S.W.2d 790 (1935).   [13] 143 F. Supp. 172 (D. Mass. 1956).

midnight in company of a fellow guest. The two entered the elevator simultaneously with a man and woman who were unknown to them. Before the door closed, defendant's house officer approached the elevator and asked who was the woman's escort and whether she was registered, suggesting that she was with the plaintiff. The third man said she was his wife but admitted she was not registered. The officer then asked if plaintiff was registered, to which the plaintiff replied that he was. The officer told the plaintiff to wait and that he would speak to him after he had arranged for the other man to register his wife. Plaintiff went up on the elevator to the ninth floor, where his room was located, but before he could enter his room the house officer caught up with him, and said, "I thought I told you to wait downstairs. I'm going to throw you out," and without more ado punched him in the face, breaking his jaw, and then departed.

The jury found for plaintiff. Defendant's motion for judgment notwithstanding the verdict was denied. The plaintiff was a registered guest in the hotel. This gave him contractual rights greater than those of a usual business invitee. He was entitled to "immunity from rudeness, personal abuse and unjustifiable interference, whether executed by the defendant or his servants, or those under his control." [14]

16:3 *Employee's Abusive Conduct*

In *Arky* v. *Leitch*,[15] plaintiff and her friend failed to receive a room with private bath in defendant's hotel, but were assigned to a room with a connecting bath. They suffered great inconvenience and embarrassment by having their bathroom entered by someone from the other room connected therewith. When they laid their grievance to the clerk in charge, he treated them in an offensive and insulting manner. In an action for the recovery of damages for the offensive treatment, the testimony tended to establish willfulness or gross inattention to duty by the defendant, sufficient to go to the jury. There was no evidence of pecuniary damage. A verdict for $1,000 in plaintiff's favor was reduced to one-half on appeal.

[14] *Id.* at 174, quoting *Frewen* v. *Page*, 238 Mass. 499, 503, 131 N.E. 475, 476 (1921).
[15] 131 Miss. 14, 94 So. 855 (1922).

16:4 *Employee's Inattention to Duty*

SHERIDAN *v.* HOTELS STATLER CO., INC.
282 Mass. 456, 185 N.E. 33 (1933)

[Action for personal injuries, based on negligence. Plaintiff, in leaving defendant's hotel, desired to take a taxicab. The doorman opened the cab door for her and stood holding the door while she entered.]

"The plaintiff had got in, faced about, and, with her hand brushing the door or the side of the cab near the hinges of the door, which were toward the rear of the vehicle, she was seating herself, when the doorman shut the cab door. Her finger was caught in the hinge and was injured. [The jury found for the plaintiff.] The only questions are whether there was sufficient evidence of negligence by the doorman or of lack of due care by the plaintiff to justify submitting those issues to the jury.

WAIT, J.: "A majority of the court think that there was. It could be found that the duty of the doorman was to use reasonable care to make sure that those upon whom he was attending were so arranged within the cab that the door could be closed without injury to them, and that, in closing it while looking elsewhere, he was not performing that duty. It could also be found that while it was the duty of the plaintiff to use due care to see that her fingers were not in a place of danger when the door was closed, and although she had seen the doorman looking elsewhere and attending to some extent to another than herself as he was closing the door, she still might rely upon him to give his whole attention to her and to allow her to be fully seated in safety before completing the closing. Exceptions overruled. . . ."

In *Giles* v. *Pick Hotels Corp.*,[16] plaintiff was injured while he and a bellboy employed by defendant were engaged in removing luggage from plaintiff's car in front of defendant's hotel in Detroit. While the bellboy was taking luggage out of the rear seat of the car, plaintiff reached into the front seat to remove a brief case. In doing so, he

---

[16] 232 F.2d 887 (6th Cir. 1956) (per curiam).

supported himself by placing his left hand on the center pillar to which the rear door was hinged, with his fingers in a position to be injured if the rear door was closed. The bellboy closed the rear door, and as a result a part of plaintiff's left index finger had to be amputated.

The trial judge found plaintiff guilty of contributory negligence as a matter of law and directed a verdict for defendant. On appeal, affirmed. "Ordinarily a door jamb or crack is not the place for fingers," said the court.[17]

SMITH v. JEFFERSON HOTEL CO., INC.
48 Ga. App. 596, 173 S.E. 456 (1934)

[Action for damages against the Jefferson Hotel on account of the alleged conduct of the servant and agent of the defendant toward plaintiff while she was a guest in the hotel.

Plaintiff alleged that she was in the habit of staying at the defendant's hotel as guest on Saturday nights. On the night of March 11, 1933, which was a Saturday night, she applied for a room at defendant's hotel. While standing at the desk, the clerk informed her that there had been a telephone call for her and after receiving the desired room, she seated herself in the lobby waiting for a repetition of the telephone call. While reading her paper there, two detectives arrested her and although she asked for assistance from the hotel clerk who was a witness of the whole occurrence, he failed to respond. Plaintiff further alleged that while she was seated in the hotel lobby, the clerk on duty received information over the telephone that a woman was wanted by the police and the desk informed the officers that the woman wanted was at the hotel and the officers arrested her on the identification of the clerk. It was shown that the arrest was illegal and plaintiff was dismissed from the custody without any explanation.

Plaintiff's complaint was dismissed.]

PER CURIAM: . . . "One conducting a hotel is not under a duty to prevent the arrest of a guest of the hotel by officers of the law who are seemingly acting within their authority. There is no duty on the part of a hotel company the violation of which will make it liable in dam-

---

[17] Id. at 888, quoting (a bit inaccurately) Abent v. Michigan Cab Co., 279 Mich. 617, 618, 273 N.W. 289, 290 (1937).

ages because it has not investigated and determined for itself whether or not such an arrest, within the apparent scope of the officers' authority, is legal.

". . . There can be no question that if the hotel company or its agents in charge of its guest wilfully and wantonly made false statements to the police as to the identity of a guest and thus caused his or her arrest illegally, the hotel company would be liable. . . .

"Judgment affirmed."

[Dissenting opinion omitted.]

16:5 Injuries to Guests by Independent Contractors— Malpractice of House Physician

An innkeeper is not responsible for the negligence of a physician, lawyer, pharmacist, or shopkeeper conducting independent professional practice or doing business on premises in the inn.

In *Barry v. Merriman*,[18] plaintiff, a guest in defendant's hotel, met with an accident in front of the hotel and injured her knee. She returned to the hotel, spoke to the employees of her injury and was referred to defendant Merriman, an osteopath physician, who had an office for the practice of his profession in the hotel. Plaintiff complained that the treatment was negligent and sued the doctor for malpractice and the hotel for recommending him. The hotel was held not liable. The Appellate Division stated:

There have been many changes in the method of conducting the ancient business of the innkeeper. The inns in the cities, and especially in New York city and the larger centers of population throughout the country, have developed into immense structures, accommodating thousands of guests. Comforts and conveniences for their guests are provided by the individuals and corporations conducting these establishments never dreamed of in the old days. But the measure of the duty of the innkeeper to his guest has not been substantially altered. When the hotel employs and furnishes these conveniences as a part of its duty to its guest, or voluntarily, it may be that it would be responsible for the negligence of its agent or employee in performing the work he was employed to do as the representative of his employer, the hotel company. But when we find stores and offices in hotel buildings which, while they may be a convenience to the guest at the hotel, are entirely apart from any duty which the hotel owes

[18] 215 App. Div. 294, 214 N.Y.S. 66 (2d Dep't 1926).

to its patrons, it seems to me there is no relation of *respondeat superior* between the hotel company and these outside enterprises. We find physicians and lawyers conducting offices in hotels; brokers, florists, milliners, drug stores in the hotel buildings, saving the steps of the guests if they desire to patronize them. Most of the larger hotels have in their establishments telegraph offices for the convenience of their patrons. But, it seems to me, there is not authority in law or reason for holding the hotel company responsible for the alleged negligence of these outside conveniences, whether they be brokers, lawyers, physicians, telegraph companies, milliners or haberdasheries. The relation of master and servant does not exist between the hotel company and these guests or tenants. Because a hotel clerk or porter or bellboy may recommend them to a guest at the hotel, it does not follow that the hotel is responsible for the alleged negligence of the physician or the lawyer, drug store clerk or the salesman in the boot and shoe shop. When the plaintiff, injured by her fall, . . . returned to the hotel asking for a doctor, what was more natural, humane and proper than the information given to her that the defendant physician had an office in the hotel and the suggestion and advice to her as alleged in the complaint that he was fit and proper and able to treat her, and the request or alleged direction to the defendant physician to treat her. A woman claiming that she had met with an accident, asking for a physician, was the hotel to refuse to assist her and order her away to a hospital in an ambulance, with the alternative risk of responsibility for her medical treatment? Such a claim seems to me to be very unreasonable. I think the responsibility of the Hotels Corporation to the plaintiff was to exercise reasonable care for her safety, comfort and entertainment while she was a guest at the hotel. What constitutes reasonable care depends upon the circumstances of the case. [Citation omitted.] The Hotels Corporation was not an insurer of the safety of her person. *Clancy* v. *Barker*, 131 F. 161 [citation omitted]. It has been said that the liability of an innkeeper is the same as that of common carriers and similar institutions, but Judge Sanborn in the case last cited points out that while the duties of an innkeeper to his guests may be similar to the duty of a carrier to the passenger, the limit of their liability is not the same. . . . [I]n the matter of supplying medical attention to the passenger it has been held that the duty of the carrier is "to select a reasonably competent man for that office, and it is liable only for a neglect of that duty. . . . It is responsible solely for its own negligence and not for that of the surgeon employed. . . . If in plaintiff's case he erred in his treatment it does not prove that he was incompetent, or that it was negligence to appoint him." [Citations omitted.] [19]

[19] *Id*. at 296–298 and 68–70.

16:6 *Protection against One Who Has Right to Remain in the Inn*

Where an innkeeper is so situated that he is unable to exclude a certain person from the inn or to control that person's actions, he is not liable for injury done by such person, in the absence of negligence. Thus, where a married woman kept an inn, and her husband, who lived in the inn, injured a guest, the innkeeper was held not to be liable in the absence of negligence.[20] The court pointed out that the wife could not control, direct, or discharge her husband, who had a right of homestead in the premises; and that even though he acted as her servant about the inn, she could not be liable for his act.

16:7 *Restaurant Keeper's Duty to Protect Patrons*

SCHELL *v.* VERGO

166 Misc. 839, 4 N.Y.S. 2d 644 (Rochester City Ct. 1938)

[This is an action for assault. Defendant Vergo was the owner of a barroom and restaurant. Plaintiff, while a patron of defendant's place of business, was assaulted by the defendant McGillicuddy, an employee of Vergo's. He seeks a recovery herein against both defendants.]

TOMPKINS, J.: "The evidence shows that about one A.M. on the morning of December tenth, the plaintiff, homeward bound, stopped at the defendant Vergo's place of business; entered that part where the defendant has a bar. The plaintiff purchased a glass of beer, paid for it, and then proceeded to experiment with a machine sometimes termed a 'pin ball' machine. Not satisfied that the machine correctly reported the results of his skill or luck, he complained to McGillicuddy, who had served him the beer in question. McGillicuddy failed to show interest. Shortly after plaintiff again complained to McGillicuddy and asked for return of the nickel or nickels he had fed into the machine. The bartender was still unsympathetic. The plaintiff then turned from where he had been talking to the bartender, with the intention of leaving. Before, however, he had taken more than a step or two he felt the impact either of McGillicuddy's fist or of something wielded by him, upon the left side of his face and jaw. The plaintiff's

[20] *Curtis v. Dinneen,* 4 Dak. 245, 30 N.W. 148 (1886).

knees wobbled, but he saved himself from completely falling to the floor. He then left defendant's place of business and proceeded homeward to find solace in such applications as his unprofessional efforts might suggest. That he must have suffered pain is evident from his photograph taken next day, which showed an oversized cheek unbeautiful to the eye. Not only did the plaintiff suffer acute pain, but he was also, being a lawyer, subject to humiliation on appearance in public and among sympathetic but curious friends, with a cheek swollen most noticeably beyond its natural regular proportions. This condition continued for several days. At the time of the trial, the plaintiff's appearance had entirely regained its usual dignified expression.

"May the owner of a saloon or barroom, where malt liquors are sold, be held liable for his servant's willful assault upon a guest? Plaintiff was a guest. McGillicuddy, who served plaintiff with beer, was Vergo's servant.

"The general rule is that a master is not responsible for the torts of his servant unless committed in the conduct of his business. [Citations omitted.] There are exceptions to this rule. They grow out of the duty owing by the master to the person injured. Among the oldest of these exceptions are common carriers and innkeepers. [Citations omitted.] The duty of the master here grows out of his relation to the passenger or guest, and is created or, perhaps, to be exact, defined by law. Recovery for its breach may be had in tort as well as on contract. [Citations omitted.]

"By . . . section 40 of the Civil Rights Law 'a place of public accommodation' now includes restaurants, saloons, barrooms, and places where malt liquors are sold. If the inclusion of bathhouses in this enumeration of 'places of public accommodation' is sufficient to place the same responsibility on their proprietors as attaches to common carriers and innkeepers in relation to their liability for a breach of duty by their servants to guests or passengers, then why, being 'a place of public accommodation,' is not a similar duty owed by the proprietor of a saloon to his guests, the duty to protect them from the torts of his servants? Both logic and common sense asserts that should be so. He invites generally. He may not exclude because of race, creed or color. Those who accept his invitation, become his guests when they partake of what he offers. They should be entitled to protection from the willful trespass of those he employs to serve them.

"In 15 Ruling Case Law, under the topic of 'Intoxicating Liquors' it is said (at p. 428), referring to the duty and liability of a saloon keeper to patrons on the premises, 'the greater number of decisions and the better reason appear to favor placing on the proprietor the duty of seeing to it that the patron is not injured, either by those in his employ or by drunken or vicious men whom he may choose to harbor. . . . and where such an act was done by the defendant's servant left in charge of the saloon, such was held to present even a stronger case against the defendant.' *McKeon* v. *Manze* (157 N.Y.S. 623) is directly in point. The defendant Manze was the proprietor of a saloon operated in connection with a hotel or lodging house. The plaintiff McKeon visited the saloon for the purpose of purchasing a beer. The defendant Taft, Manze's employee, engaged in an altercation with a guest called 'Happy,' threw a beer glass at 'Happy,' which unhappily landed in the plaintiff's face, inflicting a bad cut. The plaintiff recovered in the City Court of Buffalo. On appeal the recovery was affirmed, the court holding that even though Manze did not sustain towards the plaintiff the technical relation of an innkeeper, nevertheless, 'substantially the same duties and obligations exist as to such persons. The same rules apply quite generally to places which the public are invited to patronize.' The case seems to me to be a salutary application of the extension of the obligations of an innkeeper to safeguard his guests to the proprietor of a saloon, which is now, by the provisions of section 40 of the Civil Rights Law, a place of 'public accommodation.'

"Judgment in favor of the plaintiff, against each defendant, in the sum of $100, as damages for his pain, suffering and humiliation."

16:8 *Injuries to Strangers by Objects Falling from Hotel Windows*

The innkeeper's duty of reasonable care extends to areas outside the inn and to persons other than guests. He may be liable for injuries to passers-by on the street adjoining the inn inflicted by objects permitted to fall from window sills or thrown by unruly and boisterous guests. His liability in either case is predicated on negligence.

In *Wolk* v. *Pittsburgh Hotels Co.*,[21] the plaintiff, a jewelry clerk,

[21] 284 Pa. 545, 131 A. 537 (1925).

was seated in his automobile parked on the side of the street near the William Penn Hotel, a twenty-story structure in Pittsburgh, operated by defendant. Between 9 and 10 o'clock at night, a pint bottle crashed through the top of the car and struck him on the head. It appeared that milk bottles, jars, flower vases, and grapefruits had been seen frequently on the window sills of the hotel. It was plaintiff's contention that the defendant was negligent in permitting such articles as had been mentioned to be placed on the window sills, in not erecting protective guards, and for failure to inspect the condition of the property.

The jury found for the plaintiff. On appeal, the judgment entered on the verdict was reversed, and judgment entered for the defendant notwithstanding the verdict.

The court said, that an innkeeper

could no more be held responsible for the consequences of his guests' wilful acts in throwing articles to the street unless he could prevent it, than he would be for the wrongful act of his servants outside the scope of employment. Nor would he be liable for the result of articles placed on the window sill falling to the street unless he knew, or had reason to know, the thing placed there was of a dangerous nature, or likely to fall to the street. The proprietor is under no duty to inspect for such articles; they do not come within the class of objects likely to get out of order by use. Nor has it been shown that guards on the windows were customary, indeed they might become, through carelessness, an instrument of great danger. [Citation omitted.] The fact that bottles were placed on other window sills is not sufficient to charge him with notice as to the windows of transient guests, the other sills being in use by the occupants of apartments as above stated. These circumstances do not give rise to an implication of knowledge.

. . . [W]here a transient guest places bottles or things of like nature on a window sill, the proprietor is not liable for injury through their falling until he knows or should have known of such act, and then only, if he fails to take immediate steps to remedy the danger. Beyond this he cannot be held liable for acts not detrimental in themselves to the building, the business, the patrons or anything connected therewith, but are solely acts affecting a stranger off the premises.

. . . There was no evidence to show that room 722, where the mark was found, was occupied as an apartment for light housekeeping or by a guest or otherwise. This was not difficult of proof. The hotel register or other books would show it, or the party who afterwards visited the room could state whether it had the appearance of having been occupied.[22]

If the room had been unoccupied at the time when the bottle fell, the defendant could have been held liable, since he would then have been in effective control of the room. Since plaintiff was unable to prove that defendant innkeeper was in effective possession and control of the room at the time of the accident, he failed on one of the two key issues in the case.

The plaintiff similarly failed on the issue of notice. The innkeeper must know or have reason to know that the articles placed on a window sill were of a dangerous nature or that it was likely they would fall to the street. This is true whether the room is used by a transient guest or not. The evidence in the case did not connect the defendant innkeeper with the injury.

An innkeeper who rents apartments to tenants or permanent guests is like the landlord of an apartment building who would not be liable for the negligent condition of his tenant's window sills since the tenant is in complete control and would himself be liable to third parties for injuries caused by an object thrown or falling from his window. The mere presence of bottles on some sills was not enough to render the hotel liable since these sills might well belong to permanent guests who were permitted to use their sills in this fashion at their own risk. The rule was extended to transient guests in this case because the defendant would have no notice that transient guests were using their window sills for storage of bottles. The basic conclusion of the court on the point of notice was that the owner must know or have reason to know that the articles placed on the sill were of a dangerous nature or that it was likely they would fall to the street. The question arises, however, as to whether some future court might find that in the interest of public safety any article placed on a window sill by a transient guest is of a potentially dangerous nature. Also in a hotel where there were virtually no permanent guests the court would presumably not be able to dismiss the prolonged presence of articles on the window sills by attributing them to permanent guests. A further question which arose in this case was the difficulty of prov-

22 *Id.* at 552–553 and 540–541.

ing that the bottle really did fall from the hotel in question. There was also the possibility that the bottle might have been thrown from the room, in which case the owner would not be liable unless he could have prevented the guest from doing such an act.

The final question considered was the burden on the innkeeper to protect against such accidents. There was evidence to show that it was not the custom to erect guards on the window sills to protect those passing below from falling objects. The court also mentioned the possibility of placing a warning poster in a conspicuous place directing the guests not to place objects on their sills, but it did not decide whether or not this would be sufficient to exempt the owner from liability.

The case would seem to stand for the proposition that there must be a causal connection between the fall of the object and the acts of the innkeeper, his servants, or persons for whose acts he may be held responsible. The innkeeper who rents to permanent guests is not generally liable to strangers for injuries caused when an object falls or is thrown from the window of such a guest. As regards transient guests, the innkeeper is not liable to strangers under similar circumstances unless he knows, or should have known, that the articles were on the window sills and fails to take immediate steps to remedy the danger. Of course, if the room is vacant when the accident occurs, the innkeeper would be liable, since he is in possession and control of a vacant room. The innkeeper is also liable for injuries which occur due to conditions which exist in that part of the premises which he occupies or that which is occupied by all the tenants jointly. The key to such liability is found in the concept of possession.

In *Darrah* v. *Wilkinsburg Hotel Co.*,[23] the plaintiff was attending a dance in the defendant hotel's ballroom where he was struck on the head by a flowerbox which fell from the balcony over the dance floor. This case deals with one of the possibilities mentioned in *Wolk* where the innkeeper is in possession and control of the site from which the object fell. The innkeeper exercised sufficient control over the balcony to be responsible for a dangerous condition which was allowed to exist there. Testimony showed that it was the custom to anchor such boxes to the floor to prevent any danger and that the innkeeper here had ignored the custom. Citing *Wolk* the court pointed

[23] 318 Pa. 511, 178 A. 669 (1935).

out that in those parts of the hotel occupied by the innkeeper or transient guests, care must be exercised to prevent articles from being placed in a position where slight carelessness may be disastrous. An interesting fact in this case was that the flowerbox had not fallen over the balcony, but rather had been kicked over by accident by an innocent third party. The court declared that one who creates a dangerous situation cannot escape liability even though the act of an innocent third party contributes to the final result. The situation is again different than *Wolk* in that the plaintiff was a guest in the hotel, not a stranger outside the hotel, and the object causing the injury was placed in position by the innkeeper or his servant, not by a tenant. Nevertheless the court repeated the necessity of finding either possession by the owner of the site from which the object fell, or knowledge by the owner-innkeeper (actual or constructive) of the presence of the object and its inherent danger. Here the court found both requirements and the verdict was for the plaintiff.

16:9 *Injuries to Strangers by Objects Thrown from Hotel Windows*

GORE *v.* WHITMORE HOTEL CO.
229 Mo. App. 910, 83 S.W.2d 114 (Kansas City Ct. App. 1935)

CAMPBELL, C.: "The plaintiff, about eleven o'clock on the night of September 2, 1931, while walking on the sidewalk along the north side of the Muehlebach Hotel building, in Kansas City, was suddenly and violently pushed by other persons on the sidewalk into the street and against the side of a moving taxicab and severely injured. The persons who pushed the plaintiff were endeavoring to escape being struck by a large paper bag containing water which had been thrown from a window of said hotel. Plaintiff brought this suit to recover for his injuries, obtained a judgment in the sum of $1,500 from which the defendant has appealed.

". . . The evidence discloses that the Veterans of Foreign Wars began its three-day convention on Sunday, August 31, 1931; that 250 to 300 of them were guests of the Muehlebach Hotel, which hotel was in the possession of the defendant and being operated by it. Beginning on the afternoon of August 31, placards, feathers, telephone books, pillows, paper sacks, large and small, containing water and large laundry bags filled with water were thrown from the windows of the hotel to the sidewalks below. The 'bombardment' continued until about 4:30 o'clock of the next morning and then for a time there was a lull. The throwing was resumed on the afternoon of Monday and continued into the night and was resumed on Tuesday afternoon and continued until plaintiff was hurt. The defendant's night manager testified that the condition 'continued the full time of the convention.'

"No witness in giving his testimony estimated the number of objects thrown from the windows of the hotel but it may reasonably be inferred that the objects were numerous. The defendant's day manager, Mr. Osborne, testified that from time to time there was a 'regular deluge' of bags containing water falling and that at other times a single bag was falling; that he 'saw bags being thrown out of the windows, with water in them, and saw water poured out of pitchers, on the sidewalks, whenever a passer-by would pass down the street, they would try to throw water on them'; that he made no effort to stop the throwing 'except probably' to go to the house officer 'and see who these people were. . . .'

". . . It is plaintiff's theory that a public nuisance was created and thereafter existed for three days in the hotel building; that defendant, though it knew of the condition, failed to exercise due care to abate it, and that such failure resulted in injury to plaintiff.

"The defendant contends that the court erred in refusing its request to direct verdict in its favor. In support of this insistence the defendant argues that the only negligence charged was that defendant knew or in the exercise of due care could have known that the particular bag, the falling of which resulted in injury to the plaintiff, was likely to be dropped or thrown from a room in the hotel 'in time, thereafter, by the exercise of ordinary care, to have prevented the occurrence. . . .' Considering all the allegations of the petition, we think it is not subject to the construction placed upon it by the defendant. [Citations omitted.]

"The defendant further contends that the throwing of objects prior to the particular object did not cause the injury to plaintiff. True, the objects which were thrown prior to the particular one did not hurt the plaintiff. The evidence, however, shows that objects of the same general character were thrown from windows on both the north and east frontages of the hotel. This was sufficient to allow the jury to find that the defendant's offending guests were acting in concert both in creating and maintaining the nuisance and that the throwing of the particular object was merely one of the acts in the continuance of the wrong. . . .

"The evidence further shows that the defendant was aware of the creation and maintenance of the nuisance and that damage was likely to result therefrom, or at least the jury could so find. When the defendant became aware of the existence of the nuisance it was its duty to exercise reasonable care to abate the condition and if it could by the exercise of such care have abated the nuisance prior to the time plaintiff was injured and negligently failed to do so then it is liable for the resulting damages. The defendant argues that the legal relations existing between it and its offending guests precludes recovery. Each guest to whom the defendant assigned a room was entitled to courteous treatment at the hands of the defendant and its employees and if the guest properly demeaned himself the defendant did not have the right of access to the room of the guest save for the purpose of caring for it or for other purposes not necessary here to state. [Citations omitted.] The guest was also under the duty not to engage in unlawful or disorderly conduct which endangered other guests or strangers and a wilful violation of that duty forfeited the right of the guest to possession of the room.

"There was no evidence identifying any particular room from which any of the objects were thrown nor was there evidence identifying any of the offenders. Nevertheless, the defendant as a matter of law was under the duty to exercise reasonable care to identify the offenders and the rooms used by them in the perpetration of the wrong. . . .

"The defendant had the right to cause one of its employees to go into the several rooms each day for the purpose of servicing them. Having that right the jury could find that the defendant had the means at hand to ascertain the rooms from which pillows, laundry bags and telephone books were absent. . . .

"The mere failure of defendant to exercise ordinary care to identify the rioters was not sufficient to fix liability upon it. The defendant was not liable unless it could by the exercise of ordinary care have abated the condition in time to have prevented the injury to plaintiff. The evidence was sufficient to allow the jury to find that the defendant, though he had the right to evict the wrongdoers, negligently failed to identify them, and hence, never attempted to exercise such right. Having the legal right to evict the offenders, this court cannot say as a matter of law that the defendant could not by the exercise of reasonable care have enforced this right prior to the time plaintiff was injured. The question was one for the jury. . . ."

PER CURIAM: "The foregoing opinion of Campbell, C., is adopted as the opinion of the court. The judgment is affirmed. All concur."

In *Holly* v. *Meyers Hotel & Tavern, Inc.*,[24] plaintiff sued to recover for personal injuries inflicted upon her by a bottle thrown from a room in defendant's hotel. Said room was occupied by five Canadian sailors who became noisy. When guests in adjoining rooms complained about them, the clerk on duty warned them on the telephone and twenty minutes later went to their room and told them to pipe down or be ejected. Nothing significant happened until two hours later when plaintiff, while walking on the sidewalk alongside the hotel, was struck by a Coca-Cola bottle thrown out of a window in the sailors' suite.

The trial court granted defendant's motion for the dismissal of the complaint, on the theory that although defendant owed the plaintiff a duty of care, yet defendant was not put on any notice which would require it to take any further or more drastic action than it did. The clerk warned the people in the room, they promised to become quiet, and the defendant heard nothing further about it until after the accident. The Appellate Division reversed and held that the factual issue as to whether the clerk acted with reasonable prudence should have been submitted to the jury.

The New Jersey Supreme Court reversed the Appellate Division and reinstated the judgment of dismissal. In the court's view, there was no occasion for affirmative action on the clerk's part during the two-hour period between his warning to the sailors and plaintiff's injury and under the admitted circumstances no inference of fault or neglect might reasonably be drawn from his inaction. The contrary view, the court suggested, would tend to ignore the real relation between the hotel and its transient guests and the limited extent of control or

24 9 N.J. 493, 89 A.2d 6 (1952).

supervision which may properly be exercised by the former over the latter.

CONNOLLY v. NICOLLET HOTEL
254 Minn. 373, 95 N.W.2d 657 (1959),
order denying motion for new trial aff'd,
258 Minn. 405, 104 N.W.2d 721 (1960)

[Action for injuries sustained when plaintiff was struck by some substance falling from above her as she walked on a public sidewalk adjacent to defendant's hotel where a convention was being conducted. The jury found for plaintiff. Defendant then moved for judgment notwithstanding the verdict. The trial court granted defendant's motion and entered judgment for the defendant, from which plaintiff appealed.

The accident occurred about midnight June 12, 1953, during the course of the National Junior Chamber of Commerce Convention at defendant's hotel. It was occasioned when plaintiff was struck in her left eye by a substance falling from above her as she walked on a public sidewalk adjacent to the hotel. The blow which struck plaintiff caused her to lose her balance but not to fall. Following the blow, she could not open her left eye. A dark substance which looked like mud was found imbedded in her left eye, as a result of which plaintiff lost the sight of her injured eye.

It appeared that during the course of the convention a mule was stabled in the lobby, and a small alligator was kept on the fourth floor. Guns were fired in the lobby. Broken bottles and broken glass were strewn on the sidewalk and it was necessary to clean the sidewalk at least twice a day during the convention. Property of the hotel was damaged on several floors; the window of the credit manager's office was broken, and so were chairs, screens, and doors. Carpets and walls were spotted with liquor and water; mirrors were pulled off the walls; lights, toilet bowls smashed, and in general the disorderly behavior of the hotel guests created a hazard to defendant's property.]

MURPHY, J.: 1. [The general rule is] that a hotel owner or innkeeper owes a duty to the public to protect it against foreseeable risk of danger attendant upon the maintenance and operation of his property [citations omitted]; and to keep it in such condition that it will not be of danger to pedestrians using streets adjacent thereto. [Citation omitted.]

". . . The plaintiff contends that the act which caused the injury was foreseeable and that the defendants failed in their duty to exercise reasonable care to restrain their guests or to prevent injury.

". . . It is recognized that one who assembles a large crowd of people upon his premises for the purpose of financial gain to himself assumes the responsibility for using all reasonable care to protect others from injury from causes reasonably to be anticipated. In the exercise of this duty it is necessary for him to furnish a sufficient number of guards or attendants and to take other precautions to control the actions of the crowd. Whether the guards furnished or the precautions taken are sufficient is ordinarily a question for the jury to determine under all of the circumstances.

"3. The common-law test of duty is the probability or foreseeability of injury to the plaintiff. . . .

"4. For the risk of injury to be within the defendants' 'range of apprehension,' it is not necessary that the defendants should have had notice of the particular method in which an accident would occur, if the possibility of an accident was clear to the person of ordinary prudence. . . .

"7. . . . That the dropping of objects from the hotel windows by certain of those occupying the premises was within the range of foreseeability is evidenced by the fact that the hotel company, prior to the convention, took the precaution of cutting the corners out of hotel laundry bags so as to prevent their use as water containers. Moreover, it seems to us that in light of what had happened prior to the accident the management of the hotel must have been aware of the fact that in the indiscriminate throwing of glasses, bottles, and other objects in and about the hotel they might expect as part of that course of conduct that objects might be thrown from the windows to the sidewalk below. It is our view that these facts and circumstances presented a question for the jury to determine as to whether the negligent act which caused the plaintiff's injuries was within the defendants' range of foreseeability.

"8. We turn next to inquire as to what precautions were taken by the defendants to protect the plaintiff as a member of the public from such foreseeable risk. It appears from the record that, after the hotel manager received the report that water bags had been dropped to the street, he said they patrolled the house and in rooms where they found 'they were doing entertaining we told them to be careful about throwing out anything.' He said that it wouldn't have done any good to try to find out the room from which the water bags were thrown, apparently for the reason that the convention was 'out of control. . . .'

"The record establishes that the defendants made no complaint as to the conduct of the guests and invitees to any responsible official of the Junior Chamber of Commerce. Had one been made, it may be assumed that the officers of the convention could have controlled their own members. Neither did the management of the hotel complain to the authorities or ask for additional police protection. . . . [W]e think that evidence of the defendants' failure to hire additional guards, to secure additional police protection, or to appeal to responsible officers of the convention presented a fact question as to whether the defendants exercised due care commensurate with the circumstances. The argument may well be advanced that by 'turning the other cheek,' to use an expression of the hotel's managing director, the defendants acquiesced in the misuse of their property and became for all practical purposes participants in such misuse.

"9. The defendants further contend that there can be no liability to the plaintiff for the reason that she was neither an invitee nor patron of their establishment. They argue that they cannot be held liable for the unauthorized acts of a third person who, while on their premises, causes injury to an occupant of a public sidewalk. It may be briefly said that, even though the plaintiff was not a patron or a guest of the defendants, a relationship existed between them at the time and place of the injury which gave rise to a legal duty on the part of the defendants. That relationship imposed an affirmative duty upon the defendants to guard the public from danger flowing from the use of their property by their guests and invitees, even though that use was not authorized by the defendants. There was a duty on the part of the defendants to members of the public at large to protect them from injury by forces set in motion as a result of the use which the defendants permitted to be made of their property. Here the plaintiff was a pedestrian within her rights as an occupant of the sidewalk on a street adjacent to the defendants' hotel. There was evidence from which a jury could find that she was injured as a result of disorderly conduct upon the premises, the risk of which was foreseeable and in regard to which the defendants after notice failed to take measures to protect her as a member of the public. . . .

"We think the authorities relied upon by the defendants may be distinguished. *Wolk* v. *Pittsburgh Hotels Co.,* 284 Pa. 545, 131 A. 537, 42 A.L.R. 1081, where it was held that an innkeeper is not liable for injuries caused by a transient guest's placing of objects on a window sill, which objects fell to the street injuring a person in an automobile, and *Larson* v. *St. Francis Hotel,* 83 Cal. App. (2d) 210, 211, 188 P. (2d) 513, 514, where a pedestrian was injured when a guest of the defendant hotel as 'the result of the effervescence and ebullition of San Franciscans in their exuberance of joy on V-J Day' tossed an armchair out of a hotel window, may be distinguished in that they deal with instances of sporadic or isolated acts of which the owner did not have notice and in regard to which he had no opportunity to take steps to remove the danger. We think that *Holly* v. *Meyers Hotel & Tavern, Inc.* 9 N.J. 493, 89 A. (2d) 6, may also be distinguished. Under the facts in that case the court concluded (9 N.J. 496, 89 A. [2d] 7): '. . . there was no occasion for any affirmative action' during the 2-hour period between the time the guests of the hotel who were responsible for the accident were warned by the hotel management and the time the accident occurred. These cases do not deal with facts establishing a course of disorderly conduct continuing over a period of days and under circumstances where the defendants admitted that they had lost control of the orderly management of their property and failed to do anything about it. . . .

"Reversed."

[Dissenting opinions omitted.]

CHAPTER 17

Responsibility Arising out of Sale of Food and Beverages

17:1 Liability for Serving Unfit Food

The law is now well settled that an innkeeper and a restaurant keeper both warrant to a paying guest or patron that the food served and consumed is "fit to eat." It has been held in *Temple* v. *Keeler*,[1] that "where a customer enters a restaurant, receives, eats and pays for food, delivered to him on his order, the transaction is the purchase of goods. . . . Consequently *there is an implied warranty that the food is reasonably fit for consumption* [emphasis supplied]."

Any lingering doubt as to the nature of the transaction between an innkeeper or restaurant keeper and the guest or patron in the dining room has been eliminated by the enactment of the Uniform Commercial Code, which is now law in all states but one (Louisiana). Section 2-314 of the Code specifically provides:

. . . (1) Under this section the serving for value of food or drink to be consumed either on the premises or elsewhere is a sale.

Section 2-314 also provides that:

. . . a warranty that the goods shall be merchantable is implied in a contract for their sale if the seller is a merchant with respect to goods of that kind.

(2) Goods to be merchantable must be at least such as

(c) are fit for the ordinary purposes for which such goods are used. . . .

In *Temple* v. *Keeler*, decided in 1924, the New York Court of Appeals held, for the first time, that the owner of a restaurant *sells* the food which he provides for his guests. The earlier prevailing common-

[1] 238 N.Y. 344, 346, 144 N.E. 635 (1924).

[249]

law rule governing the furnishing of food or drink to a customer was as stated in the opinion of the Supreme Court of Errors of Connecticut in *Merrill* v. *Hodson:*

In neither case does the transaction, insofar as it involves the supply of food or drink to customers, partake of the character of a sale of goods. The essence of it is not an agreement for the transfer of the general property of the food or drink placed at the command of the customer for the satisfaction of his desires, or actually appropriated by him in the process of appeasing his appetite or thirst. The customer does not become the owner of the food set before him, or of that portion which is carved for his use, or of that which finds a place upon his plate or in side dishes set about it. No designated portion becomes his. He is privileged to eat and that is all. The uneaten food is not his. He cannot do what he pleases with it. That which is set before him or placed at his command is provided to enable him to satisfy his immediate wants, and for no other purpose. He may satisfy those wants; but there he must stop. He may not turn over unconsumed portions to others at his pleasure, or carry away such portions. The true essence of the transaction is service in the satisfaction of a human need or desire—ministry to a bodily want. A necessary incident of this service or ministry is the consumption of the food required. This consumption involves destruction, and nothing remains of what is consumed to which the right of property can be said to attach. Before consumption title does not pass; after consumption there remains nothing to become the subject of title. What the customer pays for is a right to satisfy his appetite by the process of destruction. What he thus pays for includes more than the price of the food as such. It includes all that enters into the conception of service, and with it no small factor of direct personal service. It does not contemplate the transfer of the general property in the food supplied as a factor in the service rendered.[2]

In *Merrill,* the plaintiff visited the defendant's restaurant, ordered "creamed sweetbreads," ate them, and, as a consequence of the unwholesomeness of the food provided, became seriously ill. She sued on the theory that the transaction was a sale with an implied warranty that it was fit for human consumption. She neither alleged nor proved that the defendant had knowledge of the unwholesome character of the food served or that he was negligent in any particular in the premises. The judgment in her favor was, on appeal, set aside and a new trial ordered. The court ruled: The defendant was under a

[2] 88 Conn. 314, 317–318, 91 A. 533, 534–535 (1914).

duty only to use due care and was responsible only when negligent. The burden of proving negligence was on the plaintiff. Had the transaction been held a sale, the plaintiff would have prevailed on the facts found by the trial court.

17:2   What Is "Fit to Eat"?

In all food cases the problem is: Is what the innkeeper or restaurant keeper serves legally fit to eat? How are we to determine what is fit to eat? An upset stomach is not necessarily a cause of action even where the restaurateur had something to do with it. The injured patron must show that his discomfort was caused by something the law considers a defect. This is true whether the problem arises as one of "wholesomeness," "fitness," or "merchantability"; whether it arises under the Uniform Commercial Code or at common law; or arises in a suit for breach of warranty or common-law negligence.

The clearest case of legal defect is that of the generally unanticipated foreign object. A centipede in tomato soup, pebbles in canned beans, a piece of glass in a roll, are defects even though removing them would make the remainder edible. Obviously, this is not the kind of potential edibility intended by the law.

A common test of whether the injurious substance in food constitutes a legal defect is the test of "naturalness," that is, whether the substance is "natural" or "foreign" to the food.

WEBSTER v. BLUE SHIP TEA ROOM, INC.
347 Mass. 421, 198 N.E. 2d 309 (1964)

REARDON, J.: "This is a case which by its nature evokes earnest study not only of the law but also of the culinary traditions of the Commonwealth which bear so heavily upon its outcome. It is an action to recover damages for personal injuries sustained by reason of a breach of implied warranty of food served by the defendant in its restaurant. An auditor, whose findings of fact were not to be final, found for the plaintiff. On a retrial in the Superior Court before a judge and jury, in which the plaintiff testified, the jury returned a verdict for her. The defendant is here on exceptions to the refusal of the judge (1) to strike certain portions of the auditor's report, (2) to direct a verdict for the defendant, and (3) to allow the defendant's motion for the entry of a verdict in its favor under leave reserved.

"The jury could have found the following facts: On Saturday, April 25, 1959, about 1 P.M., the plaintiff, accompanied by her sister and her aunt, entered the Blue Ship Tea Room operated by the defendant. The group was seated at a table and supplied with menus.

"This restaurant, which the plaintiff characterized as 'quaint,' was located in Boston 'on the third floor of an old building on T Wharf which overlooks the ocean.'

"The plaintiff, who had been born and brought up in New England (a fact of some consequence), ordered clam chowder and crabmeat salad. Within a few minutes she received tidings to the effect that 'there was no more clam chowder,' whereupon she ordered a cup of fish chowder. Presently, there was set before her 'a small bowl of fish chowder.' She had previously enjoyed a breakfast about 9 A.M. which had given her no difficulty. 'The fish chowder contained haddock, potatoes, milk, water and seasoning. The chowder was milky in color and not clear. The haddock and potatoes were in chunks' (also a fact of consequence). 'She agitated it a little with the spoon and observed that it was a fairly full bowl. . . . It was hot when she got it, but she did not tip it with her spoon because it was hot . . . but stirred it in an up and under motion. She denied that she did this because she was looking for something, but it was rather because she wanted an even distribution of fish and potatoes. She started to eat it, alternating between the chowder and crackers which were on the table with . . . [some] rolls. She ate about 3 or 4 spoonfuls then stopped. She looked at the spoonfuls as she was eating. She saw equal parts of liquid, potato and fish as she spooned it into her mouth. She did not see anything unusual about it. After 3 or 4 spoonfuls she was aware that something had lodged in her throat because she couldn't swallow and couldn't clear her throat by gulping and she could feel it. This misadventure led to two esophagoscopies at the Massachusetts General Hospital, in the second of which, on April 27, 1959, a fish bone was found and removed. The sequence of events produced injury to the plaintiff which was not insubstantial.

"We must decide whether a fish bone lurking in a fish chowder, about the ingredients of which there is no other complaint, constitutes a breach of implied warranty under applicable provisions of the Uniform Commercial Code, the annotations to which are not helpful on this point. As the judge put it in his charge, 'Was the fish chowder fit to be eaten and wholesome? . . . [N]obody is claiming that the fish itself wasn't wholesome. . . . But the bone of contention here—I don't mean that for a pun—but was this fish bone a foreign substance that made the fish chowder unwholesome or not fit to be eaten?' . . .

"The defendant asserts that here was a native New Englander eating fish chowder in a 'quaint' Boston dining place where she had been before; that '[f]ish chowder, as it is served and enjoyed by New Englanders, is a hearty dish, originally designed to satisfy the appetites of our seamen and fishermen'; that '[t]his court knows well that we are not talking of some insipid broth as is customarily served to convalescents.' We are asked to rule in such fashion that no chef is forced to reduce the pieces of fish in the chowder to miniscule size in an effort to ascertain if they contained any pieces of bone. 'In so ruling,' we are told (in the defendant's brief), 'the court will not only uphold its reputation for legal knowledge and acumen, but will, as loyal sons of Massachusetts, save our world-renowned fish chowder from degenerating into an insipid broth containing the mere essence of its former stature as a culinary masterpiece.' Notwithstanding these passionate entreaties we are bound to examine with detachment the nature of fish chowder and what might happen to it under varying interpretations of the Uniform Commercial Code.

"Chowder is an ancient dish preëxisting even 'the appetites of our seamen and fishermen.' It was perhaps the common ancestor of the 'more refined cream soups, purées, and bisques.' Berolzheimer, The American Woman's Cook Book (Publisher's Guild, Inc., New York, 1941), p. 176. The word 'chowder' comes from the French 'chaudière,' meaning a 'cauldron' or 'pot.' 'In the fishing villages of Brittany . . . "faire la chaudière" means to supply a cauldron in which is cooked a mess of fish and biscuits with some savoury condiments, a hodgepodge contributed by the fishermen themselves, each of whom in return receives his share of the prepared dish. The Breton fishermen probably carried the custom to Newfoundland, long famous for its chowder, whence it has spread to Nova Scotia, New Brunswick, and New England.' A New English Dictionary (MacMillan and Co., 1893), p. 386. Our literature over the years abounds in references not only to the delights of chowder but also to its manufacture. A name-sake of the plaintiff, Daniel Webster, had a recipe for fish chowder which has survived into a number of modern cookbooks and in which the removal of fish bones is not mentioned at all. One old time recipe, recited in the New English Dictionary study defines chowder as 'A dish made of fresh fish (esp. cod) or clams, stewed with slices of pork or bacon, onions, and biscuit. "Cider and champagne are sometimes added." ' Hawthorne, in The House of the Seven Gables (Allyn and Bacon, Boston, 1957), p. 8, speaks of '[a] codfish of sixty pounds, caught in the bay, [which] had been dissolved into the rich liquid of a chowder.' A chowder variant, cod 'Muddle,' was made in Plymouth in the 1890's by taking 'a three or four pound codfish, head added. Season with salt and pepper and boil in just enough water to keep from burning. When cooked, add milk and piece of butter.' The recitation of these ancient formulae suffices to indicate that in the construction of chowders in these parts in other years, worries about fish bones played no role whatsoever. This broad outlook on chowders has persisted in more modern cookbooks. 'The chowder of today is much the same as the old chowder . . .' The American Woman's Cook Book, supra, p. 176. The all embracing Fannie Farmer states in a portion of her recipe, fish chowder is made with a 'fish skinned, but head and tail left on. Cut off head and tail and remove fish from back-bone. Cut fish in 2-inch pieces and set aside. Put head, tail, and backbone broken in pieces, in stewpan; add 2 cups cold water and bring slowly to boiling point. . . .' The liquor thus produced from the bones is added to the balance of the chowder. Farmer, The Boston Cooking School Cook Book (Little Brown Co., 1937), p. 166.

"Thus, we consider a dish which for many long years, if well made, has been made generally as outlined above. It is not too much to say that a person sitting down in New England to consume a good New England fish chowder embarks on a gustatory adventure which may entail the removal of some fish bones from his bowl as he proceeds. We are not inclined to tamper with age old recipes by any amend-ment reflecting the plaintiff's view of the effect of the Uniform Com-mercial Code upon them. We are aware of the heavy body of case law involving foreign substances in food, but we sense a strong distinction between them and those relative to unwholesomeness of the food it-self, e.g., tainted mackerel (Smith v. Gerrish, 256 Mass. 183), and a fish bone in a fish chowder. Certain Massachusetts cooks might cavil at the ingredients contained in the chowder in this case in that it lacked the heartening life of salt pork. In any event, we consider that the joys of life in New England include the ready availability of fresh fish chowder. We should be prepared to cope with the hazards of fish bones, the occasional presence of which in chowders is, it seems to us, to be anticipated, and which, in the light of a hallowed tradition, do not impair their fitness or merchantability. While we are bouyed up in this conclusion by *Shapiro* v. *Hotel Statler Corp.*, 132 F. Supp. 891 (S.D. Cal.), in which the bone which afflicted the plaintiff appears in 'Hot Barquette of Seafood Mornay,' we know that the United States District Court of Southern California, situated as are we upon a coast, might be expected to share our views. We are most impressed, however, by *Allen* v. *Grafton,* 170 Ohio St. 249, where in Ohio, the Midwest, in a case where the plaintiff was injured by a piece of oyster shell in an order of fried oysters, Mr. Justice Taft (now Chief Justice), in a majority opinion held that 'the possible presence of a piece of oyster shell in or attached to an oyster is so well known to anyone who eats oysters that we can say as a matter of law that one who eats oysters can reasonably anticipate and guard against eating such a piece of shell. . . .' (P. 259.)

"Thus, while we sympathize with the plaintiff who has suffered a peculiarly New England injury, the order must be

Exceptions sustained.

Judgment for the defendant."

In *Mix* v. *Ingersoll Candy Co.*,[3] it was alleged that a "chicken pie . . . contained 'a dangerous, harmful and injurious subject, to-wit, a sharp and pointed fragment and/or sliver of chicken bone . . . highly injurious to anyone eating said chicken pie,' " it was held as a matter of law that there could be no recovery "no matter how the pleading was drawn." [4] In the opinion by Curtis, N., it is said:

We have examined a great many cases dealing with the question of the liability of restaurant keepers which arose out of serving of food which was held to be unfit for human consumption, and we have failed to find a single case . . . in which a court has extended the liability based upon an implied warranty of a restaurant keeper to cover the presence in food of

[3] 6 Cal. 2d 674, 59 P.2d 144 (1936).   [4] *Id.* at 676, 681 and 145, 147.

bones which are natural to the type of meat served. All of the cases are instances in which the food was found not to be reasonably fit for human consumption, either by reason of the presence of a foreign substance, or an impure and noxious condition of the food itself, such as for example, glass, stones, wires or nails in the food served, or tainted, decayed, diseased, or infected meats or vegetables. . . . Although it may frequently be a question for a jury as the trier of facts to determine whether or not the particular defect alleged rendered the food not reasonably fit for human consumption, yet certain cases present facts from which the court itself may say as a matter of law that the alleged defect does not fall within the terms of the statute. . . . [A]s a matter of common knowledge chicken pies occasionally contain chicken bones. We have no hesitancy in so holding, and we are of the opinion that despite the fact that a chicken bone may occasionally be encountered in a chicken pie, such chicken pie, in the absence of some further defect, is reasonably fit for human consumption. Bones which are natural to the type of meat served cannot legitimately be called a foreign substance, and a consumer who eats meat dishes ought to anticipate and be on his guard against the presence of such bones. . . . [t]he application of the rule of implied warranty might impose a heavy burden upon the keeper of restaurants . . . but . . . considerations of public policy and public health and safety are of such importance as to demand that such obligation be imposed. This is true, but we do not believe that the onerous rule should be carried to absurd limits. Certainly no liability would attach to a restaurant keeper for the serving of a T-bone steak, or a beef stew, which contained a bone natural to the type of meat served, or if a fish dish should contain a fish bone, or if a cherry pie should contain a cherry stone—although it be admitted that an ideal cherry pie would be stoneless.[5]

In *Brown* v. *Nebiker*,[6] the court stated in sustaining a directed verdict for the defendant in an action for wrongful death caused by injuries received in swallowing a sharp bone while eating pork chops as a patron in defendant's restaurant:

There are bones in all pork chops. . . . [c]ertainly small bones in a pork chop are not a foreign substance to the pork chop. One who eats pork chops, or the favorite dish of spareribs and sauerkraut, or the type of meat that bones are natural to, ought to anticipate and be on his guard against the presence of bones, which he knows will be there. The lower court was right in directing the verdict.

[5] *Id.* at 681–682 and 148.
[6] 229 Iowa 1223, 1233–1234, 296 N.W. 366, 371 (1941).

In *Norris v. Pig'n Whistle Sandwich Shop, Inc.*,[7] the offending substance was bone in a barbecued pork sandwich. In sustaining a directed verdict for the defendant, the court said:

A particle of bone in a food prepared from meat is something which one might ordinarily expect to find in the food, and one should anticipate its presence and guard against possible injury from swallowing it. . . . [T]he defendant was not required, in the exercise of ordinary care, to discover and eliminate every single particle of bone from the barbecued-pork sandwich, and the mere presence of a particle of bone in the sandwich does not authorize an inference of negligence in preparing and furnishing the food to the plaintiff.

. . . Certainly it was not the intent of our lawmakers to deem an article of food, containing meat, adulterated merely because it contained portions of the animal which were inedible, but which did not render such food unfit for its intended consumption. Otherwise numerous articles of food which necessarily contain inedible portions of animal matter would be deemed adulterated. Numerous meats and fish are normally prepared which contain bone and other inedible matter indigenous to the animal from which the food is derived, yet these articles of food could not be deemed adulterated. . . . [D]efendant cannot be said to be guilty of negligence per se in violation of this statute so as to require the submission of the case to a jury.[8]

In *Cushing v. Rodman*,[9] the plaintiff stopped at a drugstore and ordered a cup of coffee and a roll. Defendant selected the roll from a tray behind the counter and served the plaintiff. The snack was paid for by the plaintiff. As he bit into the roll, he struck a pebble which had been hidden from view inside the roll. He broke a tooth and suffered pain, disfigurement, and dental expenses. The roll had been purchased from a confectionary in Washington, D.C., and there had been no negligence on the part of the defendant drugstore owner since the pebble could not have been found without tearing the roll apart. The plaintiff sued for breach of implied warranty of fitness for human consumption and also for breach of implied warranty of merchantable quality.

The question raised on the appeal was whether there is an implied warranty of wholesomeness when the food was not prepared by the

[7] 79 Ga. App. 369, 53 S.E.2d 718 (1949).   [8] *Id.* at 375–376 and 723.
[9] 82 F.2d 864 (D.C. Cir. 1936).

seller and the defect was not discoverable except by destruction of the goods. Judgment for defendant was reversed on appeal. The gist of the court's argument may be summarized as follows:

Courts holding against liability under this theory argue that the evil should be corrected at its source through pure food and drug laws and inspection laws at the production center rather than imposing insurer's liability to the dispenser. However, the dispenser of food and the consumer have a contractual relationship which must be considered. The consumer relies on the dispenser's experience and trade skill in preparing and serving food. There is no effective opportunity for the consumer to inspect or select the food as far as wholesomeness is concerned. In fact nothing will protect the consumer effectively except wholesome food.

Social interest in individual safety is the key here. If the courts were to require negligence on the part of the dispenser before liability was imposed, then plaintiffs simply would not be able to get the necessary proof. The burden on the dispenser is not really so great since he can pass it on to the public as part of his price of service. This is an incentive to the dispenser to protect the public. Inspection at the source of the food is not enough; the public should get double protection in this area. Just because the dispenser bought the food from someone else is no reason not to apply the warranty. Besides the dispenser can sue his vendor. Regardless of who bears the initial burden, the cost will be spread at large in the price of the goods. It would be altogether too difficult for the consumer to sue the source of supply, and there may well be privity problems.

17:3 *Privity of Contract*

Liability for breach of an implied warranty of fitness arises, if at all, by contract and a sale accomplished by the making of a contract. In the course of the development of the law of warranties a principle of law became established whereby recovery for breach of warranty was restricted to a plaintiff who had contractual relationship with the defendant. This relationship is known as *privity of contract*. Suppose a guest in a hotel invites a friend as her guest for luncheon and the guest of the guest is injured as a result of deleterious food served her. The food is ordered and paid for by the guest. Would lack of privity of contract be a good defense in a breach of implied warranty action by the injured guest of a guest? This was the issue in the following case.

CONKLIN v. HOTEL WALDORF ASTORIA CORP.
5 Misc. 2d 496, 169 N.Y.S.2d 205 (N.Y. City Ct. 1957)

STARKE (GEORGE), J.: "This case was tried with a jury. Plaintiff sued for breach of warranty and the defendant contended that there was a lack of privity between the plaintiff and the defendant.

"The following facts were conceded: Plaintiff was invited as a guest of a friend to lunch in the Peacock Alley Restaurant of the Hotel Waldorf. During the course of eating her lunch, plaintiff bit into a roll and sustained certain injuries due to a piece of glass concealed and imbedded in the roll. Plaintiff's friend signed the luncheon check and paid for the lunch for herself as well as for the plaintiff. Plaintiff did not reimburse her friend for the cost of the meal.

"Defendant rested at the end of plaintiff's case and moved for a dismissal of the complaint, which motion was denied. Both sides then moved for a directed verdict. The court directed a verdict for the plaintiff and asked the jury to assess damages, albeit in an advisory capacity, for by consent determination of the question of damages was left for the court. The jury recommended the sum of $1,415 in favor of the plaintiff, and the court took the recommendation under advisement. Decision was also reserved on the renewed motion by the defendant to dismiss the complaint as a matter of law, with 10 days for briefs to both sides.

"Defendant contends that plaintiff cannot be successful on the breach of warranty theory because there was no privity or contractual relationship between the plaintiff and the defendant under subdivision 2 of section 96 of the Personal Property Law. Defendant claims that plaintiff is not to be deemed the 'purchaser' because her friend paid the check. Defendant further urges that plaintiff's remedy was in negligence instead of in contract and that plaintiff has made the wrong election. . . .

"The sole issue is whether plaintiff should be barred from recovery in a breach of warranty action because her friend paid the check.

"Food consumed on or off the premises in New York is considered a sale of food and not merely a service provided by a restaurant. This was so held for the first time in New York in 1924, when the Court of Appeals, in *Temple* v. *Keeler* (238 N.Y. 344) decided that a restaurant sells the food which it provides for its guests. The court did not then rule as to 'when exactly does the contract of sale take place?'

"In order to determine whether there was privity between the plaintiff and the defendant, let us examine these questions: When was the contract formed? When were the obligations of the respective parties created?

"A contractual relationship existed between the plaintiff and the defendant long before payment of the restaurant check. The contract did not first come into being when the check was paid. An implied contract was formed when plaintiff and her friend became patrons of the restaurant, placed their orders for food and their orders were accepted. At that moment, an implied obligation on the part of both the plaintiff and her friend was individually created to pay for whatever was individually ordered. Simultaneously, the defendant impliedly agreed to serve each of them food fit for human consumption. The warranty arose then and ran to both of them. The warranty does not run only to the one who eventually pays the check. The actual payment of the check does not determine the time when the contract comes into being.

"Even if plaintiff's friend placed the order, the hotel knew it was serving an order for two persons. When one person undertakes to give the order for several people, that person is acting as the agent for the others. Which person pays the check and whether they reimburse each other or not is only a matter of private arrangement between the customers themselves. This is of no concern to the restaurateur as long as he is paid. The plaintiff and her friend relied on defendant's implied promise to serve each of them with fit and wholesome food. Consequently, it makes no difference whether the plaintiff or her friend paid the check. . . .

"The third-party beneficiary rule may very well be applied here. . . .

"Assume that plaintiff's friend had said to plaintiff: 'You paid for the lunch last week. So I'll pay today.' Or assume that the plaintiff, in accepting her friend's invitation to lunch, had said: 'All right, you pay for the lunch and I'll pay for the theatre tickets.' Would either of these suppositions change the respective obligations of both the patron and the restaurateur?

"Assume that plaintiff and her friend had taken violently ill in the middle of the meal as a result of harmful or contaminated food necessitating their removal to a hospital by ambulance and that the check was not paid at all. The nonpayment would not bar their action. Even if the check were not paid, it would not alter the obligation of each to pay, nor would it alter the obligation owed to each patron not to breach the warranty of fitness. In the event of a failure or refusal to pay the check, the defendant would not be without remedy. The restaurant could enforce collection against each person who ordered food, or assert a counterclaim with respect thereto in an action by the patron. In fact, it is a criminal offense not to pay for a meal in a hotel. (See Penal Law, §925.)

"A careful analysis of the makeup of the contract and the formation thereof can produce only one sensible conclusion. A patron impliedly obligates himself to pay when the order is taken by the waiter, at which time the warranty likewise commences. No less an authority than Dean Prosser says: When a customer orders food in a restaurant, 'the understanding certainly is that the guest owns the food and must pay for it *from the moment it reaches his table,* and is free to wrap it up in a newspaper and carry it away if he likes.' (27 Minn. L. Rev. 152.) (Italics mine.)

"The precise issue did arise in *Jensen v. Berris* (31 Cal. App. 2d 537) where the plaintiff, in company with other members of a card club, allegedly sustained injuries from the eating of unwholesome food in a restaurant, and was allowed a recovery as against the restaurateur for breach of warranty, *although she did not pay for the food herself.*

"The same issue also arose in *Coca-Cola Bottling Works v. Lyons* (145 Miss. 876). There the donee of a sub-vendee of food was given the right to recover for breach of warranty. The bottling company sold the bottled drink to the drugstore, where Mrs. Lyons and her friend procured two bottles. *The friend had ordered and paid for both. . . .*

"Defendant's counsel has overextended the use of the word 'privity' here. He has confused the restaurant situation with the store purchase as to when the contract is formed in each case. When a woman purchases food in a store, the contract of sale takes place when she either pays for the purchase or when the storekeeper permits a charge to her account.

"Consequently, I find that plaintiff is deemed to be a 'purchaser' even though her friend paid the check. The warranty ran to each from the time the order was placed and accepted. Aside from this finding, it is to be noted that the defendant admitted in its answer that plaintiff was a patron and did not deny this allegation in plaintiff's complaint; nor did defendant ever amend its answer.

"Viewed as a direct breach of contract, or under the theory of agency, or under the third-party-beneficiary doctrine, plaintiff is none-theless entitled to recover. . . .

"With respect to the jury's recommendation of $1,415, the court finds that this sum is inadequate and will not fairly and reasonably compensate the plaintiff. Plaintiff sustained the loss of her upper right lateral tooth which broke off irregularly at the gum line when she bit into the roll. The stump of the tooth was extracted. Another tooth was slightly damaged. . . ." [The court increased plaintiff's recovery to $3,000.]

17:4   Civil Liability for Injury Caused by Illegal Sale of Intoxicating Liquor—Dram Shop Acts

At common law the seller of intoxicating liquors was not generally liable for injuries resulting from intoxication of one of his customers were such injuries were inflicted on a third party through the action of the customer while inebriated or were sustained by the customer himself.[10] In reaching this result, the courts have held that the con-sumption of the liquor rather than its sale was the proximate cause of any damage resulting from the intoxication of the one who consumed it.

A notable exception is New Jersey, where it has been held that a tavern keeper who serves alcoholic beverages when he knows or should know that the patron is intoxicated, may properly be found to have created an unreasonable risk of harm, and to have thus en-gaged in negligent conduct on which a common-law claim for dam-ages may be grounded.[11]

Many states have abrogated the common-law rule by statute. These several civil damage or dramshop acts create a right of action against the sellers of intoxicating liquors although they vary significantly as to

[10] "Recent Developments," 60 Colum. L. Rev. 544 (1960).
[11] Rappaport v. Nichols, 31 N.J. 188, 202–203, 156 A.2d 1, 9 (1959).

who may bring the action and the type of conduct that will give rise to liability.

In New York, the statute (formerly Section 16 of the Civil Rights Law) is now part of the General Obligations Law, and reads as follows:

Section 11-101. *Compensation for Injury Caused by the Illegal Sale of Intoxicating Liquor*

1. Any person who shall be injured in person, property, means of support, or otherwise by any intoxicated person, or by reason of the intoxication of any person, whether resulting in his death or not, shall have a right of action against any person who shall, by unlawful selling to or unlawfully assisting in procuring liquor for such intoxicated person, have caused or contributed to such intoxication; and in any such action such person shall have a right to recover actual and exemplary damages.

2. In case of the death of either party, the action or right of action given by this section shall survive to or against his or her executor or administrator, and the amount so recovered by either wife or child shall be his or her sole and separate property.

3. Such action may be brought in any court of competent jurisdiction.

4. In any case where parents shall be entitled to such damages, either the father or mother may sue alone therefor, and recovery by one of such parties shall be a bar to suit brought by the other.

To maintain an action under Section 11-101, the following minimal factors must be present:

(1) An intoxicated person.

(2) Injury or damage either (a) caused by the intoxicated person or (b) arising out of the intoxication.

(3) Defendant seller whose illegal sale or furnishing of the liquor caused or contributed in whole or in part to the intoxication.

(4) Plaintiff victim of the injury or damage.

It has been held that Section 11-101 must be read in conjunction with Section 65 of the Alcoholic Beverage Control Law which prohibits the sale for which Section 11-101 affords the remedy.[12] Section 65 of the ABC Law provides:

---

[12] *Moyer* v. *Lo Jim Cafe, Inc.,* 14 N.Y.2d 792, 251 N.Y.S.2d 30 (1964); *Kinney* v. *1809 Forest Ave., Inc.,* 7 Misc. 2d 1, 165 N.Y.S.2d 149 (Sup. Ct. 1957) (memorandum opinions).

Section 65. *Prohibited Sales*

No person shall sell, deliver or give away or cause or permit or procure to be sold, delivered or given away any alcoholic beverage to

1. Any minor, actually or apparently, under the age of eighteen years;

2. Any intoxicated person or to any person, actually or apparently, under the influence of liquor;

3. Any habitual drunkard known to be such to the person authorized to dispense any alcoholic beverages.

Neither such person so refusing to sell or deliver under this section nor his employer shall be liable in any civil or criminal action or for any fine or penalty based upon such refusal, except that such sale or delivery shall not be refused, withheld from or denied to any person on account of race, creed, color or national origin.

MITCHELL *v.* THE SHOALS, INC.
19 N.Y.2d 338, 227 N.E.2d 21, 280 N.Y.S.2d 113 (1967)

FULD, C.J.: "On February 2, 1960, after having dinner together, the plaintiff, Yvonne Mitchell, her escort, Robert Taylor, and another couple drove to The Shoals, a restaurant on Staten Island, at about 9:00 P.M. for 'a few drinks' and some dancing. Between dances, they had their drinks. Miss Mitchell, after consuming several, passed out and remained asleep for the rest of the evening. Taylor, who was on a diet of 'double' bourbons 'straight,' became drunk and noisy. At one point, after he had fallen to the floor, the bartender was told not to let him have anything more to drink. Despite this admonition and Taylor's obviously intoxicated condition, the bartender—responding with 'Don't bother me; he is having a good time . . . let him enjoy himself'—served him three or four more double straight bourbons. The two couples left the restaurant at about 1 o'clock in the morning. The plaintiff, still asleep, was assisted to the car and placed in the front seat and Taylor, not to be dissuaded from driving, got behind the wheel and drove off. He apparently lost control of the car some nine miles from the restaurant; it left the roadway and crashed into a building. He was killed and the plaintiff was seriously injured. She brought this action for damages, under New York's version of the 'Dram Shop Act' (Civil Rights Law, §16, now General Obligations

Law, §11-101), against the defendant restaurant. The jury returned a verdict in her favor, and a divided Appellate Division affirmed the resulting judgment. [The verdict was for $30,000; however, since the plaintiff had settled her claims against Taylor's estate for $6,000, the judgment was reduced, by that amount, to $24,000.]

"The Alcoholic Beverage Control Law renders it a crime for any person to sell or deliver any alcoholic beverage to one who is intoxicated or under the influence of liquor (§§65, 130 subd. 3). . . .

"Although the statute—its forerunner goes as far back as 1873 (L. 1873, ch. 646; see Note, 8 Syracuse L. Rev. 252)—does not give the inebriated person a cause of action if he is himself injured [Citations omitted], it does entitle anyone else injured 'by reason of the intoxication' of such person to recover damages from the party dispensing the liquor. There is no justification, either in the language of the legislation or in its history, for exonerating the latter simply because he had also served, and brought about the inebriety of, the third person who was hurt. As long as the latter does not himself cause or procure the intoxication of the other, there is no basis, under the statute, for denying him a recovery from the party unlawfully purveying the liquor.

"In the case before us, the plaintiff had herself become drunk while with Taylor but she had not, in any sense, caused or procured his intoxication. She had neither purchased the drinks nor encouraged him to take more than he could weather. The plaintiff had simply had a few drinks and passed out before her escort's inebriacy became really serious. This did not amount to a guilty participation in his intoxication. To deny her a remedy because her own alcoholic capacity was limited would impair, if not go a long way toward defeating, the purpose of the statute.

"In two or three states [Illinois, Michigan], the courts have held that the plaintiff's mere participation in drinking with the person whose drunkenness caused the injury may be sufficient to prevent recovery under the Dram Shop Acts of those states. [Citations omitted.] We need not, and do not, go that far. It is our view that the injured person must play a much more affirmative role than that of drinking companion to the one who injures him before he may be denied recovery against the bartender or tavern keeper who served them. The plaintiff before us comes within the coverage of the statute and the defendant was properly held accountable. . . ."

[Affirmed.]

In the very recent case of *McNally* v. *Addis*,[13] the father of a 17-year-old boy who met his death in an auto accident sued defendant tavern keeper pursuant to §11-101 of the General Obligations Law, commonly referred to as the Dram Shop Act. Part of the cause of action was predicted upon the unlawful sale of liquor to the minor.

The deceased borrowed the family car and drove with parental consent ostensibly to a church social. He picked up a friend, twenty years old, whose military leave was about to expire and who was to celebrate his imminent departure.

After leaving the social, the two visited a bar where the deceased had at least one beer, and being unsuccessful in getting served at a second bar, decedent and his friend arrived at defendant's bar at about 11:30 P.M., where deceased was observed to consume at least one beer. In getting to defendant's place, decedent appeared normal, sober, and operated the vehicle without incident. At about 12:55 A.M., deceased was involved in a motor vehicle accident when the car driven by him struck two parked vehicles. Decedent was taken to a hospital where he was pronounced dead on arrival.

The court, sitting without a jury, found as a fact that beer was sold by the defendant to the decedent and consumed by him.

Neither the consumer nor his estate has a cause of action. Under the Dram Shop Act, the burden of proof rests with the plaintiff. He must establish that there was an unlawful sale of liquor to an intoxicated person which caused him injury. The key elements of recovery under the statute are: (1) unlawful sale; (2) of liquor; (3) to an intoxicated person; which (4) caused him injury.

The intoxication need not be the proximate cause of the occurrence which caused the injury. A remote proximate cause between the sale and the injury is sufficient to impose liability upon the vendor. Plaintiff must establish that the accident occurred while the consumer was intoxicated and that the sale contributed to the intoxication in the slightest.

The fact that the decedent had drinks in other establishments does

13 65 Misc. 2d 204, 317 N.Y.S.2d 157 (Sup. Ct. 1970).

not absolve a defendant vendor from full liability if his violation of the statute is established.

The sale of beer is the sale of an alcoholic beverage within the meaning of §65 of the Alcoholic Beverage Control Law. It is also a "liquor" within the meaning of §11-101 of the General Obligations Law (Dram Shop Act).

Although an autopsy established that the decedent was intoxicated at the time of his death, he appeared to be perfectly sober when he was served beer on defendant's premises. That the beer served by defendant may have contributed to decedent's subsequent intoxication is beside the point because liability is fastened upon the seller only where he sells to an intoxicated person, or to one actually or apparently under the influence of liquor.

The legislature did not intend to impose absolute liability without some notice having first been accorded the vendor regarding the dangers attendant upon a prohibited sale. The seller must have notice of a consumer's near intoxicated condition by means of objective outward appearances for the sale to be unlawful and hence within the Dram Shop Act.

The proof in the record indicated that decedent was not intoxicated or under the influence of liquor at the time of the sale and absent sufficient proof on this point signifying otherwise the complaint must be dismissed.

The court considered the question whether an unlawful sale to a minor must be read into the Dram Shop Act notwithstanding the condition of the consumer at the time of the sale; liability following, if the minor subsequently becomes intoxicated.

It has been held that in the absence of a statute creating liability, the violation of a provision prohibiting sale of liquor to minors does not create a cause of action in favor of third persons. This is merely a restatement of the general principle that the violation of a statute designed to protect the public-at-large, as concededly §65 of the Alcoholic Beverage Control Law is to be so classified, does not constitute negligence per se but must be the proximate cause of the accident to impose responsibility.

The court further held that a parent's cause of action for damages for unlawful sales to his minor child does not lie under the Dram Shop Act. Nor does a person standing in the shoes of a minor, sober when served, such as a parent suing essentially for loss of services, have a cause of action under the Dram Shop Act.

As to damages, under the act, plaintiff may only recover for injury to *his* person, property, means of support or otherwise, "otherwise" having been added to permit recovery for mental distress.

The action for damages under the Dram Shop Act is separate and distinct from the usual wrongful death action.

CHAPTER 18

Responsibility for Loss of or Injury to Guest's Property

18:1 Origin of Rule of Responsibility

The liability of the innkeeper for the goods of the guest has been enforced from the earliest times, and its nature can best be learned from a consideration of the original function of the innkeeper. Inns were established for the entertainment of travelers on their journey; and particularly to protect them against the bands of marauders and outlaws that infested the roads at night. The most important function of the innkeeper, therefore, after the furnishing of food and drink, was the protection which he offered to the weary traveler against nocturnal robbers. If a traveler were robbed at an inn, it was necessarily from defect of care of the innkeeper, since he undertook to protect against such misfortune.

It was, therefore, decided as early as the year 1367 that the innkeeper is responsible for the goods of his guest stolen from the inn. In the earliest case, the loss was alleged to be "for defect of guard of the innkeeper and his servants." [1]

With the march of civilization and the progress of commercial development, the conditions in which the common-law liability of the innkeeper to his guest originated have passed away; but other conditions exist, which render it wise and expedient that the modern hotel-keeper should respond for the loss of his guests' property while he is extending to the latter for compensation his hospitality, and there has consequently been no relaxation in the rule of his common-law liability, except as such liability has been modified by statute.

[1] Y.B. 42 Edw. 3, 11, pl. 13 (1367).

18:2 *Nature of Responsibility*

The innkeeper's responsibility for the goods of his guest has often been thought to depend upon the law of bailment; and, indeed, his responsibility is treated as one kind of bailment obligation in the treatises on the law of bailments, being treated, along with that of the common carrier, as an example of bailments where responsibility is exceptionally severe.

It is obvious, however, that the responsibility of the innkeeper is not that of a bailee of any sort; for the crucial test of bailment, delivery of possession to the bailee, is lacking. The innkeeper's responsibility does not depend in any degree upon delivery to him of the property for which he is held liable. In the earliest case in which he was held answerable for the goods stolen, he attempted to avoid liability by pleading that the guest had not delivered the goods to him, but had put them in the chamber; but judgment was given to the guest upon this plea.[2] The responsibility must therefore be rested upon the public undertaking of the innkeeper, rather than upon his position as bailee.

18:3 *Common-Law Rule of Insurer's Liability*

In the majority of jurisdictions, the courts have imposed upon innkeepers the liability analogous to that of common carriers. The rule has been well stated by Judge Porter of the New York Court of Appeals in the leading case of *Hulett* v. *Swift:*

An innkeeper is responsible for the safekeeping of property committed to his custody by a guest. He is an insurer against loss, unless caused by the negligence or fraud of the guest, or by the act of God or the public enemy. This liability is recognized in the common law as existing by the ancient custom of the realm. . . .

This custom, like that in the kindred case of the common carrier, had its origin in considerations of public policy. It was essential to the interests of the realm, that every facility should be furnished for secure and convenient intercourse between different portions of the kingdom. The safeguards, of which the law gave assurance to the wayfarer, were akin to those

[2] *Id.*

which invested each English home with the legal security of a castle. The traveler was peculiarly exposed to depredation and fraud. He was compelled to repose confidence in a host, who was subject to constant temptation, and favored with peculiar opportunities, if he chose to betray his trust. The innkeeper was at liberty to fix his own compensation, and enforce summary payment. His lien, then as now, fastened upon the goods of his guest from the time they came to his custody. The care of the property was usually committed to servants, over whom the guest had no control, and who had no interest in its preservation, unless their employer was held responsible for its safety. In case of depredation by collusion, or of injury or destruction by neglect, the stranger would of necessity be at every possible disadvantage. He would be without the means either of proving guilt or detecting it. The witnesses to whom he must resort for information, if not accessories to the injury, would ordinarily be in the interest of the innkeeper. The sufferer would be deprived, by the very wrong of which he complained, of the means of remaining to ascertain and enforce his rights, and redress would be well-nigh hopeless, but for the rule of law casting the loss on the party entrusted with the custody of the property, and paid for keeping it safely.

The considerations of public policy in which the rule had its origin, forbid any relaxation of its rigor. The number of travelers was few, when this custom was established for their protection. The growth of commerce, and increased facilities of communication, have so multiplied the class for whose security it was designed, that its abrogation would be the removal of a safeguard against fraud, in which almost every citizen has an immediate interest. The rule is in the highest degree remedial. No public interest would be promoted, by changing the legal effect of the implied contract between the host and the guest, and relieving the former from his common law liability. Innkeepers, like carriers and other insurers, at times find their contracts burdensome; but in the profits they derive from the public, and the privileges accorded to them by the law, they find an ample and liberal compensation. The vocation would be still more profitable, if coupled with new immunities, but we are not at liberty to discard the settled rules of the common law, founded on reasons which still operate in all their original force. Open robbery and violence, it is true, are less frequent as civilization advances; but the devices of fraud multiply with the increase of intelligence, and the temptations which spring from opportunity, keep pace with the growth and diffusion of wealth. The great body of those engaged in this, as in other vocations, are men of character and worth; but the calling is open to all, and the existing rule of protection should therefore be steadily maintained. It extends to every case, and secures the highest vigilance on the part of the innkeeper, by making him responsible for the property of his guest. The traveler is entitled to claim entire security for his goods, as against the landlord, who fixes his own measure of compensation, and holds the property in pledge for the payment of his charges against the owner.

In cases of loss, either the innkeeper or the guest must be the sufferer; and the common law furnishes the solution of the question, on which of them it should properly fall. In the case of *Cross* v. *Andrews*, the rule was tersely stated by the court. "The defendant, if he will keep an inn, ought, *at his peril*, to keep safely his guests' goods." (Croke's Eliz., 622.) He must guard them against the incendiary, the burglar and the thief; and he is equally bound to respond for their loss, whether caused by his own negligence, or by the depredations of knaves and marauders, within or without the curtilage. . . .

In the courts of this State, it has always been held that the innkeeper, like the carrier, is by the common law an insurer. [Citations omitted.] . . .

A shade of doubt has, at times, been thrown over the question, by the unguarded language of elementary writers, and especially by the suggestion of Judge Story, in his treatise on the law of bailments, that the innkeeper could exonerate himself from liability by proving that he was not guilty of actual negligence; and this view seems to have been adopted in two of the Vermont and one of the English cases. [Citations omitted.] The doctrine of these cases is opposed to the general current of English and American authority, and evidently had its origin in a misapprehension of the rule as stated by the judges in *Calye's Case*. It is true that the liability of the innkeeper, by the custom of the realm, was not unlimited and absolute, and that the loss of the goods of the guest was merely presumptive evidence of the default of the landlord. But this presumption could only be repelled, by proof that the loss was attributable to the negligence or fraud of the guest, or to the act of God or the public enemy. No degree of diligence or vigilance on the part of the innkeeper, could absolve him from his common law obligation for the loss of his guest, unless traceable to one of these exceptional causes.[3]

18:4 *Prima Facie Liability Rule*

In several jurisdictions a much less stringent rule is laid down, the innkeeper being held liable for loss of his guest's property in the inn only if the loss has occurred through his negligence. Under this rule, which prevails in Vermont, Texas, Indiana, Illinois, Maryland, and

[3] 33 N.Y. 571, 572–575 (1865).

a few other states, an innkeeper is only prima facie liable for loss or damage to the goods of his guest while in his possession, and he may exculpate himself by proof that the loss did not happen through any neglect or fault on his part, or that of his servants, for whom he is responsible. The justification for this rule has been stated by Judge Worden of the Supreme Court of Indiana in *Laird* v. *Eichold*, in the following language:

Innkeepers, on grounds of public policy, are held to a strict accountability for the goods of their guests. The interests of the public, we think, are sufficiently subserved, by holding the innkeeper *prima facie* liable for the loss or injury of the goods of his guest; thus throwing the burden of proof upon him, to show that the injury or loss happened without any default whatever on his part, and that he exercised the strictest care and diligence. And it is more in accordance with the principles of natural justice, to permit him to exonerate himself by making such proof, than to shut the door against him, and hold him responsible for an accident happening entirely without his default, and against which strict care and prudence would not guard.[4]

18:5 *Beginning of Responsibility for Guest's Property*

Where the goods are actually given into the possession of the innkeeper, his liability as innkeeper begins at the moment of delivery to the innkeeper; and, therefore, the innkeeper may become responsible for the goods of the guest even before the relationship of host and guest is established. This may well happen where the innkeeper sends a conveyance to an airport, railroad station, or steamship to bring guests to his inn. When, in such a case, a traveler gives his baggage to the porter or other person authorized by the innkeeper to take it, the innkeeper becomes liable for it at once, provided the traveler later becomes a guest.

[T]he liability of the proprietor commences from the time of delivery of the baggage or check to the porter. All that the traveler must do is to assure himself that the person representing himself as such porter, is in fact the porter of the house. Any private arrangement between the landlord and a carrier for the transportation of persons and baggage to his house, does not affect the traveler, who has the right to assume, without any knowledge to the contrary, that such carrier is in fact authorized by the proprietor of the

---

[4] 10 Ind. 212, 215 (1858).

house to safely and securely transport himself and his baggage; and when loss occurs by the negligence of such carrier, the proprietor of the house is liable to the traveler.

And this rule is founded, not upon the fact that the law gives to the landlord or proprietor of the house a lien upon the baggage or goods committed to his care, but upon the policy of the law that such should be the liability of the proprietor. In this case there never could have been any lien of the landlord upon the baggage at the time the loss occurred, but the liability of the landlord was the same notwithstanding no such lien existed. The lien of the landlord grows out of the indebtedness of the guest for his board during his stay at the house.[5]

It must clearly be seen, however, that in all these cases the responsibility of the innkeeper is conditioned on the owner of the goods becoming a guest within a reasonable time. Although at the time the goods are given to the innkeeper the owner bona fide intends to become a guest, still if he changes his mind and does not do so the innkeeper will be regarded as not responsible as such for the goods. So where the traveler gave his luggage to the porter of the inn at the railroad station, and the porter carried it to the inn, but the owner never became a guest, it was held that the innkeeper never became responsible for it as innkeeper.[6] And in a similar case where the traveler went to the office of the inn, but there found a telegram addressed to him, in consequence of which he did not register, but went to another place, the innkeeper did not become responsible.[7]

In both these cases it will be noticed that if the traveler had become a guest the innkeeper's responsibility for the goods would have dated from the moment when the porter took charge of them at the railroad station; but since the owner never became a guest, the innkeeper was not liable as such even during the time while the traveler was on his way to the hotel. In other words, during that period the responsibility is doubtful; and it is settled only by the event.

Where the check for the baggage is delivered to the porter of the hotel by one who does not intend to become a guest, it is obvious that the porter has no authority to accept the goods on behalf of the hotel, and the innkeeper would not be responsible for the goods even

---

[5] *Coskery* v. *Nagle*, 83 Ga. 696, 702–703, 10 S.E. 491, 493 (1889).
[6] *Tulane Hotel Co.* v. *Holohan*, 112 Tenn. 214, 79 S.W. 113 (1903).
[7] *Strauss* v. *County Hotel and Wine Co., Ltd.*, 12 Q.B.D. 27 (1883).

as bailee. Even if he deposited the goods in the hotel office, without calling the attention of the proper clerk to it, the innkeeper is not responsible as innkeeper or even as ordinary bailee. "It is the same as if the porter had gratuitously brought up the valise of a friend or a stranger, and put it down in the hotel office, without calling any attention to it, or giving the hotel employees any notice of it, and no occasion existing for them to take charge of it."[8] The porter individually is the bailee.

The case would seem, however, to be different if the owner, at the time he gives his goods to the porter bona fide intends to become a guest within a reasonable time. The porter's authority as distinguished from the innkeeper's responsibility, must be determined by the facts existing at the time he takes the goods; and at that time the facts are the same as in any case of the sort where the owner carries out his intention and becomes a guest. If the owner acts bona fide the porter has authority to receive the goods for the innkeeper and the latter is a gratuitous bailee. In *Tulane*, however, the owner intended, at the time he gave his valise to the porter, to become a guest; but the distinction indicated was not made by the court, and the innkeeper was held not to be even a bailee.

18:6 *Property in Transit to or from the Inn*

DAVIDSON v. MADISON CORP.
257 N.Y. 120, 177 N.E. 393 (1931)

Kellogg, J.: "The plaintiff had been a guest of the Madison Hotel in New York city, which was owned and operated by the defendant Madison Corporation. At the conclusion of a temporary visit to Norfolk, Va., she purchased a railroad ticket from the Pennsylvania Railroad and boarded one of its trains for New York city. Prior to leaving she had caused her trunk to be delivered to the railroad and had checked it to the same destination. On arrival, the plaintiff returned to her quarters in the Madison Hotel. The check for the trunk was delivered to the head porter with instructions 'to get the trunk in' promptly. The head porter handed the check to a licensed

---

[8] *Tulane Hotel Co.* v. *Holohan*, 112 Tenn. 214, 218, 79 S.W. 113, 114 (1903).

expressman, Peter J. Coen, with similar instructions. Coen delivered the check to a truckman employed by him, who obtained the trunk from the railroad and placed it on his truck. On the return journey to the hotel the truckman was required to pick up another trunk at the Hotel Buckingham. He parked his car at the curb in the vicinity of that hostelry; stopped his motor, leaving the ignition key in the lock; and went into the hotel, leaving the truck unattended. When he returned to the curb the truck had disappeared, and with it had gone the plaintiff's trunk. The car and the trunk had been stolen. The contents of the trunk, consisting of expensive furs and dresses, were worth $10,000, and for that sum the plaintiff has recovered a verdict against the Madison Corporation.

"'An innkeeper is an insurer of the safety of the property of his guest, brought *infra hospitium*. He is liable for its loss, whether by burglary, theft, fire or negligence, unless it arises from the neglect or misconduct of the guest, the act of God or the public enemies.' (*Wilkins* v. *Earle*, 44 N.Y. 172, 178; *Hulett* v. *Swift*, 33 N.Y. 571.) The innkeeper's liability, at common law, did not originally extend to cover property not within the walls of the inn, or the buildings used in connection therewith. 'So that the innholder, by law, shall answer for nothing that is out of his inn, but only for those things which are *infra hospitium*.' (*Calye's Case*, 4 Coke, part. 8, p. 63.) In several States of the Union, other than this, the innkeeper's liability has been greatly extended. The innkeeper has been held liable in respect to baggage never within the hotel precincts, lost in the course of transportation thereto from a railroad station, while in the custody of an independent transfer agent, to whom the innkeeper had delivered railroad checks, received from his guest, for the purpose of securing the baggage and bringing it to the inn. [Citations omitted.] The basis of the recovery in each of these cases was said to be the common-law liability of an innkeeper to his guest.

"We are not greatly impressed with the reasoning of these cases. Clearly the delivery of the railroad check to an innkeeper is not a symbolical delivery of the baggage which it represents. The baggage is then in the custody of the railroad, and while that custody continues the railroad, not the innkeeper, would be liable for a loss. When the baggage is received by a transfer agent, to whom the check has been delivered, the custody is that of an independent contractor, not the custody of the innkeeper or his agent. The whole theory of the inn-keeper's liability, that the things of his guest, which are within the walls of his inn, must be defended, at all costs, against attack from within or without against thievery by inside servants, or robbery by outside footpads, or highwaymen, against nearly all conceivable perils, fails of application where the circumstances are those of the cases cited. Never having had custody or possession of the things of his guest, never having assumed a relationship in the least degree resembling that of a bailee, it is difficult to see how the duty of an innkeeper to safeguard and defend the possessions of his guest may have arisen.

"In nearly all the cases cited the authority relied upon for the decisions is *Dickinson* v. *Winchester* (58 Mass. [4 Cush.] 114). In that case the facts considered were these: An innkeeper had engaged certain hackmen to attend at a railroad station to offer arriving travellers free transportation of themselves and baggage to his hotel, should they decide to become his guests. A traveller accepted such an offer from a hackman and entered his hack, to be transported to the hotel and become a guest of the innkeeper. The traveller's trunk was placed upon a rack near the driver, and was lost or stolen on the way to the inn. The traveller thereupon brought suit against the innkeeper to recover his loss. Chief Justice Shaw, who wrote the opinion of the court stated: 'The true ground, we are of opinion, on which the claim of the plaintiff rests, is that of an implied contract, and not the mere negligence of the driver of the coach as the defendant's servant.' He was undecided whether the obligation upon which the recovery must rest was that of an innkeeper or a carrier. Nevertheless, he said: 'When, therefore, such coach owner or his driver thus employed undertook to carry the plaintiff's son, and took charge of his baggage accordingly, such person became the agent of the defendants *pro hac vice*, and they became responsible that he should exercise due care and skill in performing the duty, which the defendants had undertaken to do for the plaintiff.' It would seem, therefore, that the basis of the recovery was the negligent performance of a contract to transport the baggage safely, not the breach of the absolute duty of an innkeeper at all hazards to safeguard the baggage of his guest received *infra hospitium*.

"The proprietor of the Madison testified that the hotel made 'charges for the transportation of baggage;' that 'if the porter receives instructions to go and get trunks, he makes his charge.' He was asked: 'Mr. Titze, you make a charge to your guests for the transportation of baggage, do you not?' and he replied, 'We do, yes.' We have, then, an innkeeper maintaining a system for the transportation of the baggage of his guests for which a charge is made, an order by the guest to the hotel porter to get her baggage and bring it to the hotel; an acceptance of the order and an undertaking to perform the service. How can it be gainsaid that the defendant, for a consideration, promised to obtain the baggage and transport it to the hotel, using at least ordinary care in the fulfillment of the promise? If the defendant chose to perform its contract through an independent contractor, it may have been within its rights. Nevertheless, it could not thereby escape liability for its nonperformance through the negligence of one to whom the contract duty was assigned. 'The performance in such a case is indeed in legal contemplation rendered by the original obligor, who is still the party liable if the performance is in any respect incorrect.' (1 Williston on Contracts, §411.) In this instance there was evidence to support the conclusion that the contract duty to transport was negligently performed and that there was no negligence on the part of the plaintiff. We prefer, therefore, to affirm the recovery upon this ground. We do not determine that the defendant was or was not liable for the breach of a duty owed by an innkeeper to his guest."

[Judgment affirmed, with costs. All concur.]

As a result of the *Davidson* case, the New York State Legislature enacted Sections 203-a and 203-b of the General Business Law, which limit a hotelkeeper's liability for property in transit to or from the hotel to the sum of $250, "unless at the time of delivering the same such value in excess of two hundred and fifty dollars shall be stated by such guest and a written receipt stating such value shall be issued by such keeper; provided, however, that where such written receipt is issued the keeper shall not be liable beyond five hundred dollars unless it shall appear that such loss or damage occurred through his fault or negligence."

A contrary view, namely, that delivery of a railroad baggage check is symbolical delivery of the baggage which the check represents so as to make the innkeeper liable as insurer for its loss, is held in Colorado.

In *Keith* v. *Atkinson,*[9] plaintiff and his wife arrived at defendant's hotel at about 11 P.M. on August 20, 1902, and were shown to a room which they occupied that night. The following morning plaintiff rang for a bellboy, gave him his railroad check for his baggage with instructions to give it to the clerk on duty so as to have it brought up from the depot, which the bellboy agreed to do. The trunk did not come. It was never found and the check was never returned to the plaintiff. Judgment in favor of defendant hotel was reversed on appeal.

The Colorado court held that "one who becomes the guest of a hotel, by giving his baggage checks into its possession, places the goods they represent into its custody, so far as to make the innkeeper responsible for goods which, by means of the possession of such checks, his representative or agent receives, although the baggage be never brought within the walls of the hotel." [10]

18:7 *Loss of Property Delivered to Innkeeper by Third Person for Guest*

In order to be responsible for a guest's goods as innkeeper, it is not necessary that the innkeeper receive the goods from the guest himself. The goods may be delivered to the innkeeper by a third person to hold for or to deliver to the guest; and in that case the responsibility for the goods is that of an innkeeper.

NEEDLES *v.* HOWARD
1 E.D. Smith (N.Y.) 54 (Ct. C.P. 1850)

[Action to recover the value of lace goods purchased by plaintiff at a local store and delivered to him at the Irving Hotel, of which the defendant was the proprietor. The goods in question were delivered to the receiving clerk of the hotel, and were lost. From a judgment below upon a verdict found for the plaintiffs, defendant appealed].

DALY, J.: "An innkeeper is not paid so much in money for taking charge of the property of his guest, but the custody of the goods is considered as *accessory* to, or following as a consequence of, the principal contract; . . . In the language of Sir William Jones, it comes within the class of cases, 'in which a man takes upon himself the cus-

---

[9] 48 Colo. 480, 111 P. 55 (1910).   [10] *Id.* at 481 and 56.

tody of goods, in consideration of *another gainful contract.*' [Citations omitted.] When an innkeeper, therefore, receives a traveller and his property, he is bound to take charge of the property, and though the guest pays but for his entertainment, what he thus pays, to quote again, in substance, from the same authority, is to be regarded as extending to the care bestowed upon his property. The care and custody of the property of guests constitutes a part of the innkeeper's business; and unless the parcel in question was received by the defendant, in the ordinary course of his business as an innkeeper, it was simply a bailment.

"The defendant is the proprietor of a large hotel in this city. He is in the habit of receiving small packages for his guests, while they are stopping at his house. It is not an incidental or casual thing, but an established practice. A book is kept in the office attached to the hotel, in which the packages are registered as they are received by the defendant's clerk. An entry is made of the date of the receipt of the package, the person to whom it belongs, the number of his room, and the servant to whom it was delivered. Thirty six packages were so received and registered upon the day when this package was delivered to the defendant's clerk. It is not necessary to inquire whether the defendant is bound to receive packages which his guests may send to his hotel, after they have taken up their abode there. He has himself adopted the practice of receiving them, and from the regulations he has established respecting them, I think he has made their receipt a part of the conduct and arrangement of his hotel. That is, that he has made it a part of his business as hotel keeper to receive and take charge of them for his guests. It is a practice which is adopted for the accommodation and convenience of his guests, as much so as the taking charge of the baggage of the guest when he arrives at the hotel. No direct compensation are [*sic*] received for either. They are both accessory to the principal contract. One, in my judgment, as much so as the other [*sic*]. The reason and inducement, on the part of the innkeeper, are alike in both cases. It is to render his hotel desirable and convenient to the traveller. It may fairly be presumed that he would not establish such a practice if he did not deem it his interest to do so. I would not say how far the casual acceptance of a package sent to an inn for a guest, who is stopping there, comes within the business of an innkeeper, but I have no doubt, that when he makes it his custom to receive such packages, when it enters into and forms a part of the general conduct and management of his establishment, that it is as much a part of his business as anything else he may do for the convenience and comfort of his guests."

[Judgment affirmed. Opinion of Woodruff, J., omitted.]

INGRAHAM, J. (dissenting): "A package left to be delivered to a lodger, constitutes simply a bailment, and the rule of liability is very different from that in the case of an innkeeper's liability for the goods of a guest."

PEET v. ROTH HOTEL CO.
191 Minn. 151, 253 N.W. 546 (1934)

STONE, J.: "The record is the story of a ring. Defendant operates the St. Paul Hotel in St. Paul. Mr. Ferdinand Hotz is a manufacturing jeweler. For 20 years or more he has visited St. Paul periodically on business, making his local headquarters at the St. Paul Hotel. He has long been one of its regular patrons, personally known to the management. Plaintiff's engagement ring, a platinum piece set with a large cabochon sapphire surrounded by diamonds, was made to order by Mr. Hotz. One of its small diamonds lost, plaintiff had arranged with him to have it replaced and for that purpose was to leave it for him at the St. Paul Hotel. November 17, 1931, he was a guest there on one of his seasonal visits. About four P.M. of that day plaintiff went to the cashier's desk of the hotel, wearing the ring. . . .

[She took off the ring and told the cashier that it was for Mr. Ferdinand Hotz. The cashier took an envelope, wrote the name of Mr. Hotz on it and plaintiff left. The cashier admitted that the ring was delivered to her. It was immediately lost, doubtless stolen, probably by an outsider. This action was commenced for the recovery of its value, fixed by the jury at $2,140.66]. . . .

"The jury took the case under the charge that there was a bailment as a matter of law. [Defendant contends] that there was at least a question of fact whether the evidence showed the mutual assent prerequisite to the contract of bailment which is the *sine qua non* of plaintiff's case. The supporting argument is put upon the cases holding that where the presence or identity of the article claimed to have been bailed is concealed from the bailee he has not assented to assume that position with its attendant obligation, and so there is no bailment. *Samples* v. *Geary* (Mo. App.) 292 S.W. 1066 (fur piece concealed in coat checked in parcel room); *U.S.* v. *Atlantic C.L.R. Co.*, 206 F. 190 (cut diamonds in mail package and nothing to indicate nature of contents); *Riggs* v. *Bank of Camas Prairie*, 34 Idaho, 176, 200 P. 118, Anno. 18 A.L.R. 83 (bailee of locked box supposed to contain only 'papers and other valuables' not liable for money therein of which it had no knowledge).

"The claim is . . . that plaintiff . . . failed to divulge the unusual value of her ring when she left it with [the cashier]. . . . [T]he stubborn truth remains that plaintiff delivered and defendant accepted the ring with its identity and at least its outward character perfectly obvious.

"The mutual assent necessary to a contract may be expressed as well by conduct as by words; or it may be manifested by both. [Citation omitted.] The latter is the case here. The expression of mutual assent is found in what passed between plaintiff and [the cashier]. The former delivered and the latter accepted the ring to be delivered to Mr. Hotz. Below that irreducible minimum the case cannot be lowered. No decision has been cited and probably none can be found where the bailee of an article of jewelry, undeceived as to its identity, was relieved of liability because of his own erroneous underestimate of its value. . . .

". . . The ring was accepted in the ordinary course of business by defendant in rendering a usual service for a guest, and so, plainly, it was for defendant's advantage, enough so, at least, to make the bailment as matter of law one for the benefit of both bailor and bailee.

"Defendant's liability, if any, is for negligence. . . ." [Here the court ruled that earlier decisions made it clear that the bailee had the burden of proving that the loss did not result from his negligence and that the doctrine that there are three degrees of negligence—slight, ordinary, and gross—was not recognized in Minnesota].

In *Van Cleef & Arpels, Inc.* v. *St. Regis Hotel Corp.*,[11] plaintiff, a well-known jewelry firm, sued defendant hotel in bailment and in negligence, for $19,000 for the loss of a pair of platinum and diamond earrings given to some unauthorized person by the hotel. Plaintiff moved

[11] 160 N.Y.L.J. No. 103, 2 (Sup. Ct. N.Y. Co. 1968).

to strike out the hotel's affirmative defense that its liability, if any, was limited to $500 by Sections 200 and 201 of the General Business Law. The court denied the motion on the ground that the question involved was a mixed one of law and fact properly determinable on the trial. The court stated:

Plaintiff left the earrings at the hotel to be delivered to a guest of the hotel, informing the hotel that the package contained jewelry. The hotel delivered the earrings to the guest. Plaintiff had agreed with the guest that, if he decided against the purchase, he would leave the earrings with the hotel to be picked up by plaintiff. The next day the guest returned the earrings to the hotel to be picked up by plaintiff, signed out of the hotel and left for Europe. The hotel put the earrings in its safe and recorded the package in its "Valuables Deposit" record, noting that it was for plaintiff firm. One week later plaintiff called and asked for the package. The hotel stated that it had turned it over to some unknown person, whose signed name was illegible in the valuable deposit record.

The statute provides that whenever a hotel has a safe in its office for the safekeeping of any jewels, &c., belonging to its guests and gives due notice thereof, the hotel shall not be liable for loss sustained by theft or otherwise if such property is not delivered to its office for deposit in such safe; and shall not be liable in excess of $500 for loss of any property, which is deposited, in the absence of special written agreement.

Plaintiff urges that the statute has no application to plaintiff's claim, that the statute regulates only the liability of a hotel to its guests, that the earrings did not belong to a guest, that the hotel was simply a bailee in this transaction and should be treated vis-a-vis plaintiff in the same manner as any bailee.

Defendant concedes that it was an ordinary bailee from the time it received the package from plaintiff and placed it in its safe up to the time it delivered it pursuant to plaintiff's instructions to its guest. It maintains, however, that on the next day, when it received the package from its guest and deposited it in its safe to be picked up by plaintiff, the statute applied, limiting its liability to $500 in the absence of a written agreement with the guest.

In the court's view the question rests on the hotel's knowledge of the nature of the transaction at the time that the guest delivered the package to it. If the hotel was informed that the package contained jewelry which belonged to plaintiff, not the guest, and that it was to be picked up by plaintiff because the guest had decided not to purchase the jewelry delivered to him the previous day through the hotel as bailee, then the transactions of the two days should be deemed to be continuous so far as the hotel's status is concerned. In such case the statute regulating the hotel's liability to its guest for the safekeeping of property belonging to him would not be applicable. Conversely, if the hotel merely was informed that a package being left by its guest and deposited in its safe would be picked up by plaintiff, the statute would appear to apply. Since the facts on this aspect of the case have not been fully established, the motion is denied.

18:8 Loss of Guest's Property in Private Custody of Hotel Employee

An innkeeper is not responsible for property lost in his house while in the private custody of an employee. Thus, in *Sneider* v. *Geiss*,[12] money was delivered to the defendant innkeeper's stepdaughter. It appeared that plaintiff was courting her at that time in marriage, and was in the habit of entrusting his money to her for safekeeping. The plaintiff having reposed his trust and confidence in her, instead of depending on the security of the inn, the defendant was held not responsible. Whether the guest deposits his money on the credit of the inn or not, is a question of fact for the jury and not a conclusion of law for the court.[13]

18:9 Property for Which Innkeeper Is Responsible

The general rule is that the innkeeper's responsibility is not confined to property of any particular kind, but subject always to statutory limitations, extends to money and all other personal property brought by the guest to the inn, and used by or suitable to the use of the guest.[14] The rule does not, however, apply to merchandise brought into the inn for sale or display by the guest.

MYERS *v.* COTTRILL
17 F. Cas. 1099 (No. 9985) (C.C.E.D. Wis. 1873)

[Action to recover the value of watches, chains, and various kinds of jewelry brought by plaintiff into defendant's hotel for the purpose

---

[12] 1 Yeates (Pa.) 34 (1791).   [13] *Houser* v. *Tully*, 62 Pa. 92 (1869).

[14] *Watkins* v. *Hotel Tutwiler Co.*, 200 Ala. 386, 76 So. 302 (1917); *Stoll* v. *Almon C. Judd Co.*, 106 Conn. 551, 138 A. 479 (1927).

of commercial exhibit and sale in one of the guest rooms therein, rented for such purpose. The articles were stolen from said room, used by plaintiff and his wife as a bedroom as well, while they were out for breakfast. It appeared that defendant failed to comply with the statute limiting his responsibility as an innkeeper.]

DRUMMOND, Cir. J. [charging the jury]: "I think this is the true rule on the subject. If a person, going into a hotel as a guest, takes to his room not ordinary baggage, not those articles which generally accompany the traveller, but valuable merchandise, such as watches and jewelry, and keeps them there for show and sale, and from time to time invites parties into his room to inspect and to purchase, unless there is some special circumstance in the case showing that the innkeeper assumes the responsibility as of ordinary baggage, as to such merchandise, the special obligations imposed by the common law do not exist, and the guest, as to those goods, becomes their vendor and uses his room for the sale of merchandise, and really changes the ordinary relations between innkeeper and guest.

"It is, we know, as a matter of experience, impracticable for the landlord to notice and vouch for every person who goes into the room. The guest permits them to stay as long as he pleases, and shows his goods and sells them to whomsoever he pleases. We must presume that it is not for that purpose that the innkeeper allows persons to come to his house and enter his rooms, and the fact that the vendor may sleep in the room I do not think changes the rule."

Whether a room is used for the exhibit or sale of merchandise and whether the articles lost constitute baggage or merchandise is a question of fact for the determination of the jury: "If a guest applies for a room in an inn, for a purpose of business distinct from his accommodation as a guest, the particular responsibility does not extend to goods lost or stolen from that room." [15]

Statutes in the various states should be consulted with respect to the obligations of innkeepers for merchandise and merchandise samples brought into their hotels. In New York, an innkeeper's liability for merchandise samples or merchandise for sale is conditioned upon the delivery to him by the guest of a "prior written notice of having the

[15] 2 Kent. Com. 596, cited with approval in *Fisher* v. *Kelsey*, 121 U.S. 383, 385–386 (1886).

same in his possession, together with the value thereof, the receipt of which notice the hotel-keeper shall acknowledge in writing over the signature of himself or his agent, but in no event shall such keeper be liable beyond five hundred dollars, unless it shall appear that such loss or damage occurred through his fault or negligence." [16]

18:10 *Property Brought by Guest into Inn after His Arrival*

In *Mateer* v. *Brown*,[17] the court stated:

One point further remains to be considered. It appears from the testimony that the bundle, which is claimed to have contained the gold dust, was not taken to the defendant's inn until several days after the plaintiff became his guest. As, in order to entitle the plaintiff to recover, it is necessary for him to establish the character of guest in the inn of the defendant, so also it is equally necessary that it should appear that his goods were taken there in the capacity of guest. [Citation omitted.] The liability of the innkeeper results from the relation of guest in which the traveller stands to him, and extends only to those things which properly pertain to him in that relation. [Citation omitted.] It does not necessarily follow that the strict responsibility can be imposed on an innkeeper for all property, which his guest may choose to bring into the inn after he has been received *infra hospitium;* or that the latter may make the former a compulsory depositary of any amount of goods or treasure, which, during his sojourn in the inn, he may desire to keep secure. The innkeeper is bound by law to receive the traveller and his goods, and, for his refusal, in case he has sufficient accommodations for him, he is liable not only to an action on the case for the private damage, but to indictment for the public wrong. [Citations omitted.] Inns are instituted for passengers and wayfaring men; and the keepers thereof can be held to the strict legal liability only for such goods as are brought into their inns by travellers in the character of guests. It would be too great a responsibility if that liability could be extended so as to cover any conceivable amount of money or gold dust, which the traveller, after he has become a guest, might be disposed to thrust into the custody of his host, and thus compel him to become the insurer of its safety. . . .

It is a question of fact for the jury to determine in what character goods have been taken into a hotel.

[16] Section 201, General Business Law.
[17] 1 Cal. 221, 230–231, adhered to on rehearing, 1 Cal. 231 (1850).

18:11 *Property in Possession of Guest*

In order for the innkeeper to become responsible for the property of his guest it is not necessary that possession thereof should be given up to the innkeeper. Thus, subject to statutory limitations, an innkeeper is responsible for the safety of the personal property of a guest in the room assigned to and occupied by the guest.

18:12 *Delivery by Custom*

Delivery may be made to the innkeeper by custom without an actual manual transfer. This is usually accomplished by putting apparel or baggage in a certain place in an open manner.

BRADNER *v.* MULLEN
27 Misc. 479, 59 N.Y.S. 178 (Herkimer County Ct. 1899)

[Action for the value of an overcoat lost in defendant's hotel. Judgment for defendant, and plaintiff appeals.

Defendant was proprietor of the Metropolitan Hotel in Little Falls, New York. On the evening of October 14, 1898 when plaintiff was a guest at defendant's hotel, plaintiff walked in behind the desk in the hotel office and in the presence of a hotel employee, who was apparently in charge of the office, hung up his overcoat on one of the hooks in said office provided for that purpose. The hotel management usually gave checks for umbrellas, but none for overcoats unless asked. The next day plaintiff discovered that his overcoat was missing.

Defendant takes the position that he is not liable for the loss of the overcoat and also set up a counterclaim for plaintiff's hotel bill. Defendant further claims that the overcoat was not specially entrusted to its care and relies on the protection of Section 201 of the General Business Law.]

DEVENDORF, J.: "The clerk in charge of the office says they gave no checks for overcoats unless asked for, yet at the same time back of the desk in the office was a row of hooks for the express purpose of hanging coats, and the guests about the house were accustomed to place their coats there; step behind the desk and hang their coats there themselves; it does not appear that any other place was provided.

"In this case the plaintiff obtained a check for his umbrella, stepped behind the desk and in the presence of the person there waiting on guests hung his coat on one of the hooks. That coat was afterwards lost from the hook.

"I think the defendant, as inn keeper, owed a duty to the plaintiff, his guest, to see that the articles of wearing apparel which were hung up in the place he had provided for them were protected from loss; it does not appear that he gave the guest any notice that they would place their garments there at their own peril, and I believe this act of maintaining the hooks for that purpose and permitting the guests to use them, carried with it a duty on his part to see that the property was safely cared for there.

"It is true he generally gave checks, but there is nothing in the statute that requires hotel keepers to give checks in return for baggage or clothing, but, as I understand it, the system of giving checks is largely for the convenience of the inn keeper, and not for the safety of the property.

"The defendant could have easily guarded against loss by having a person in charge of the property of his guests left in the office; or notice could have been given to each guest that no place was provided or would be provided for their overcoats, and in that way the safety of both the inn keeper and his guest from loss would have been assured.

"I do not think that a hotel keeper can absolve himself from a certain duty he owes his guests by providing for them a place to put their overcoats, hats, etc., and permit a custom to prevail for the use of that place in that way and then say in a case of loss that no obligation whatever rests on him.

"The above statute is to some extent in derogation of the common law, and I think it should not be construed too strictly as against the guest. . . .

". . . I have come to the conclusion that the judgment should be reversed, as I believe from the uncontradicted evidence in the case the inn keeper voluntarily assumed and was under obligation to his guest, which he failed to perform.

"The judgment is, therefore, reversed, with costs."

18:13 *Loss of Property Deposited in Hotel Lobby*

SWANNER *v.* CONNER HOTEL CO.
205 Mo. App. 329, 224 S.W. 123 (Springfield Ct. App. 1920)

[Plaintiff, a traveling salesman, went to the Conner Hotel in Joplin about 11:30 A.M. on a certain day in May, 1919, to obtain a room as a guest. Being familiar with the hotel, plaintiff went directly to the bell-boys' bench where it was the custom to leave grips, and set his grip by the bench. On previous occasions when plaintiff was a guest at this hotel he had seen the bellboy set his grip by this bench, and had seen the grips of other guests set by this bench. No room being vacant at the time, plaintiff had lunch at the hotel, went out and returned at about 5:30 P.M. Still there was no vacancy, but he was told there would be vacancies later. After 10:00 P.M. plaintiff succeeded in getting a room, registered, but by that time his grip was gone. None of the bellboys handled it or knew of it and plaintiff did not call anyone's attention to it. Defendant maintained a checkroom in the hotel, and plaintiff knew of this fact and could have checked his bag without any inconvenience. An attendant was present at all times in the checkroom. Plaintiff never looked for his grip, nor gave it any attention from the time he set it down until after 10 o'clock that night.

The cause was tried before the court, and at the close of the case defendant demurred to the evidence, and was overruled. The correctness of this ruling is the only question here. It was conceded or rather not questioned that the relation of innkeeper and guest was created and existed.

In Missouri, an innkeeper is liable for the loss of the goods of his guest not arising from the negligence of the guest, the act of God, or public enemies. *Batterson* v. *Vogel,* 10 Mo. App. 235.]

BRADLEY, J.: "Defendant urges that plaintiff's baggage was never *infra hospitium,* that is, in the care and under the custody of the innkeeper, and that, therefore, no liability attached. As stated, the fact that plaintiff was a guest is not questioned. He had put his baggage where it was customary to put baggage while a guest was registering and seeing about a room. . . . He was told there would be a room, and he waited for the room. His baggage was where it should have been at least up to the time he asked for and failed to get a room.

"In *Read* v. *Amidon*, 41 Vt. 15, 98 Am. Dec. 560, plaintiff laid down a pair of gloves and lost them, and discussing the case the court said: 'When the plaintiff entered the inn, and took off his overcoat and gloves, he did not deliver them to the defendant or to any of his servants, nor call the defendant's attention to them. . . . Story, in his work on bailments, says a delivery of the goods into the custody of an innkeeper is not necessary to charge him with them; for although the guest doth not deliver them, nor acquaint the innkeeper with them, still the latter is bound to pay for them if they are stolen or carried away. The loss will be deemed prima facie evidence of negligence. . . . The guest is not relieved from all responsibility in respect to his goods on entering an inn; he is bound to use reasonable care and prudence in respect to their safety so as not to expose them to unnecessary danger of loss. Whether the plaintiff was so careless, in laying down his gloves in the manner he did, as to exonerate the innkeeper is a fact to be determined by the jury, in view of all the circumstances.' [Citations omitted.]

". . . We do not think that plaintiff's negligence was any more than a question for the trier of the facts, and therefore we decline to sustain appellant on this feature.

". . . The judgment below is affirmed."

FARRINGTON, J. concurs.

STURGIS, J. [dissenting]: ". . . The innkeeper is an insurer only where the guest is not negligent in respect to his loss. The guest cannot recover if his negligence enters into the loss and the negligence on the part of the guest which will defeat his recovery is the want of that ordinary care which a reasonably prudent man would take under the circumstances of the case. . . .

". . . Certainly, if the plaintiff in making his case admits by his own evidence the facts showing his contributory negligence and such facts so clearly and unmistakably establish contributory negligence that reasonable minds cannot differ then the question is one of law and the court should direct a verdict for the defendant. This rule is so universal that citation of authorities is unnecessary.

". . . Certainly the defendant hotel had provided every reasonable means for caring for the baggage of the guests, all of which were

familiar to plaintiff and of which he could avail himself without cost
or inconvenience. . . .

"If plaintiff's own evidence does not show him guilty of negligence
in exposing his hand grip to peril without the slightest excuse for so
doing, I do not know what he could have done that would be negligence. Plaintiff has no one to blame for his loss except himself and
should not be allowed damages. The judgment should be reversed."

In *Widen* v. *Warren Hotel Co.,*[18] plaintiff applied for a room in defendant's hotel. The room plaintiff requested was occupied but plaintiff
was told that it would become vacant later in the day. The clerk told
plaintiff that he could check his baggage while waiting for a room or
leave it in the lobby and the bellboy would take it to his room when
he returned. The plaintiff left it in the lobby where it disappeared.

In conspicuous places throughout the hotel defendant posted regulations, one of which was: "Baggage may be left in charge of the
porter, for which checks will also be given; when sent for, a written
order must accompany the checks for the same. For articles not thus
checked the management will not be responsible."

It was held that the regulation was duly brought to plaintiff's notice,
that it was reasonable, and that the loss was caused by plaintiff's failure
to comply with the regulation. The clerk had no authority to waive the
regulation.

In *Clarke* v. *Hotel Taft Corp.,*[19] the plaintiff arrived at the hotel by
cab, was escorted to the lobby by a bellboy who also took the baggage (three suitcases) from the cab, carried them to the lobby and
deposited them in a portion of the lobby reserved for the baggage of
incoming and outgoing guests. The plaintiff registered, was assigned a
room and was ready to proceed when she found that the suitcases
were gone. They had never been found.

The defendant was held liable for $2,350, the full value of plaintiff's
loss, without benefit of the statutory limitation provided in Section 201
of the General Business Law as it then existed. The limitation then
applied only to property delivered "for storage or safekeeping in the
storeroom, baggage room or other place elsewhere than in the room
or rooms assigned" to guests. The court held that there was no such

[18] 262 Mass. 41, 159 N.E. 456 (1928).
[19] 128 N.Y.L.J. No. 53, 478 (N.Y. City Ct. 1952).

delivery for safekeeping or storage but that until plaintiff deposited them for storage or safekeeping, the statute did not apply.

The statute has since been amended so as to apply to property in the lobby, hallways, or in the room or rooms assigned to guests.

18:14 *Property Must Be within the General Control of Innkeeper*

While it is not necessary, in order to make the innkeeper responsible for the property of a guest that it should be delivered into his possession, still the property must be within his general care and control. If the guest himself undertakes the care of it, or if he makes a special arrangement by which the control of it is removed from the innkeeper, the latter is not liable. Thus, in an old case the innkeeper gave notice to a guest that he could not receive him because he was obliged to leave at once to serve on a jury. The guest then requested that he might himself take the keys and take care of the goods. The innkeeper gave him the keys, and went away; and the goods were lost. It was held that the innkeeper was not liable.[20]

18:15 *Loss by Accidental Fire*

Loss by accidental fire, where the innkeeper was not negligent, charges the innkeeper or not according to the rule prevailing in the jurisdiction concerned. In a state where the stringent liability is imposed, as in the state of New York, the innkeeper is liable for a loss by accidental fire. But in other states which hold the innkeeper liable only for negligence or breach of undertaking, he is not responsible where the goods were lost by accidental fire.

Whatever view is adopted, it is agreed that upon loss or injury to the property being shown the innkeeper is *prima facie* liable, and the burden is upon him to prove such facts as will exonerate him.

The liability of innkeepers for loss of or damage to property caused by fire is now limited in many states by statute. The New York statute (Section 201 of the General Business Law) provides that "no hotel or motel keeper shall be liable for damage to or loss of such property by fire, when it shall appear that such fire was occasioned without his fault or negligence."

[20] Y.B., 11 Henry 4, 45, pl. 18 (1410).

The property referred to in the quoted portion of the statute is wearing apparel or other personal property in the lobby, hallways, or in the room or rooms assigned to guests or deposited with the innkeeper for storage or safekeeping. As to whether the exemption applies to other property such as money, jewelry, and valuables required to be deposited in the hotel safe, or situated in other parts of the hotel building has not yet been the subject of judicial decision.

HYMAN v. SOUTH COAST HOTEL CO.
146 App. Div. 341, 130 N.Y.S. 766 (2d Dep't 1911)

[Action to recover the value of certain jewelry belonging to the plaintiff and lost after being deposited by her in defendant's hotel safe. Plaintiff appeals from a judgment in favor of defendant.

Plaintiff deposited some $2,000 worth of jewelry in the safe of the Long Beach Hotel while she was a guest there on July 28, 1907. At about 5 o'clock the next morning, the hotel was totally destroyed by fire. Before leaving the burning building, defendant's manager removed certain of the jewelry deposited by guests in the safe, put it in a bag, kept it under the mattress of his wife's bed for four days and then removed it to the Hotel Empire, where the bag was sealed. Plaintiff's jewelry was not in the bag, nor could it be found in the hotel safe when that was opened after the fire. It was conceded upon the trial that no jewelry was returned to plaintiff after the fire and that a demand therefor had been made.]

RICH, J.: "The plaintiff's cause of action was based solely upon defendant's negligence. . . . [Defendant set up a general denial and pleaded in partial defense that a safe was provided, notices were posted and no special agreement in writing was made.] When the plaintiff rested her case the learned trial judge granted defendant's motion to strike out all evidence of value over and above $250. The case was submitted to the jury as one of negligence. The court charged that 'the mere fact that it was lost does not entitle the plaintiff to a verdict. The plaintiff must go beyond that and show it was lost through negligence, and you must be able to put your finger on the negligence, point it out and say, "Yes, that is the act of the proprietor or of his employees which was negligent, therein did he fail to do his duty and because he thus failed he must pay." The question of fact submitted to you is: Was there such negligence? If so, plaintiff is entitled to recover $250. . . .' [Now $500. Ed.] The plaintiff's jewelry being in defendant's possession when the fire broke out, its liability for a return thereof continued after the destruction of the hotel. . . .

"This action is not based entirely upon the liability of the defendant as an innkeeper, but rests upon the affirmative negligence of its president and manager in the care of the jewelry after it was taken from the safe during the progress of the fire. If the plaintiff's jewelry was destroyed by fire while in the defendant's safe, its liability is limited under the provisions of the statute to $250 [now $500. Ed.], but if the jewelry was taken from the safe during the progress of the fire, in an uninjured condition, by defendant's president and manager, and he omitted upon demand made the morning of the fire to deliver it to its owner, the plaintiff, and thereafter so carelessly and negligently cared for it as to result in its loss, the statute invoked does not limit the liability of the defendant. The jury should have been so instructed, and the error of the trial court in limiting the defendant's liability to $250 [now $500. Ed.], presents reversible error."

[Reversed and new trial granted.]

[Jenks, P.J., Hirschberg, and Woodward, JJ., concurred. Burr, J. dissented.]

18:16 *Liability for Loss by Theft*

Loss of goods by theft on the part of the innkeeper's employees would clearly charge the innkeeper under any rule. And even if the goods are stolen by a stranger without actual negligence on the part of the innkeeper (unless they are stolen by someone for whom the guest is responsible) there is a breach of the innkeeper's obligation, and he should be held liable under any theory of liability.

In *Wies* v. *Hoffman House,*[21] the plaintiff and his wife registered at defendant's hotel and were duly assigned to a room. During their absence from the hotel, on the following evening, plaintiff's traveling bag and its contents, together with some wearing apparel, were stolen. Prior to their departure, the plaintiff had locked the room and handed the key to the night clerk. There was no proof of fraud or negligence on plaintiff's part. Plaintiff was allowed to recover for the loss, measured by the market value of the goods at the time of the loss.

[21] 28 Misc. 225, 59 N.Y.S. 38 (Sup. Ct. 1899).

DAVIS v. HOTEL CHELSEA
186 N.Y.S. 75 (Sup. Ct. 1921)

PER CURIAM: "Defendant appeals from a judgment in favor of plaintiff in an action brought to recover money deposited for safekeeping by plaintiff, a guest, with the defendant, as an innkeeper. Plaintiff has recovered a judgment for the full amount, $500, and defendant on this appeal invokes the statute limiting the amount of liability to $250 for money or other valuables placed for safe-keeping in the custody of an innkeeper.

"The evidence establishes that the theft was committed by a clerk who had been in defendant's employ for about 10 days; that he had been taken on for trial by defendant, and defendant had made inquiries and was making further inquiries concerning his references as to character and qualifications. The evidence showed that plaintiff's money was placed in an inside compartment of defendant's safe, that the compartment was locked, and that the keys to the inside and outside compartment were both in possession of the chief clerk, who was not in the hotel at the time of the theft, and that the clerk who did the stealing had no key to either the safe or the inside compartment.

"Plaintiff claims that the failure to make thorough investigations to the clerk's character established such negligence on defendant's part as to take him out of the protection of the statute [citation omitted] and that defendant was negligent in leaving a clerk, about whom it knew so little, in entire charge of the clerk's desk at night on the occasion of the theft. Neither of these facts constitutes proof of negligence, in view of the uncontradicted testimony that said clerk had no keys whatever to the safe; and negligence is not pleaded.

"It is also urged that defendant was negligent in not bonding said clerk; but there is no proof that a bond, if given, would cover anything but the legal liability of the innkeeper to his guest, so that it would have in no sense protected the plaintiff. The judgment must be reduced to conform to the statute.

"Judgment modified . . . and, as so modified, affirmed. . . ."

In *Millhiser* v. *Beau Site Co.*,[22] plaintiff, a guest in the Biltmore Hotel in New York City, left with the desk clerk jewelry of the value

[22] 251 N.Y. 290, 167 N.E. 447 (1929).

of $369,800, without notifying the clerk of its value, or in any way giving the hotel an opportunity of declining to accept the risk. When the plaintiff called for her jewelry and opened the safe deposit box in which it was deposited, it was found that jewelry of the value of $50,000 was missing. Thereafter the clerk who had received the package from the plaintiff was convicted of stealing the missing jewelry.

The court held that the hotel was entitled to the limitation of its liability under Section 200 of the General Business Law. "The act of the defendant's employee in stealing the jewelry was a wrongful act, outside the scope of his employment and for his own enrichment. It was not in any sense the act of the defendant." [23] The court made a distinction between a *theft by the hotelkeeper* from the guest where the statutory limitation would not apply, and a *theft from the hotelkeeper* of the guest's property. In the latter case, the court indicated, the statute would protect the hotel.

[23] *Id.* at 295 and 448.

CHAPTER 19

Responsibility for Property of Nonguests: Bailments

19:1 *Loss of Property from Tenant's Apartment*

The innkeeper may, and commonly does, provide accommodations not only for transient guests, but also for other persons who make their residence at the inn; such persons, whether they be tenants, boarders, lodgers, or roomers are not entitled to the exceptional responsibility of the innkeeper as insurer of the goods of his guests.

In the absence of negligence, there is no liability on the part of an innkeeper for loss of the property of such residents from the premises occupied by them.

In *Hackett v. Bell Operating Co.*,[1] the plaintiff occupied a suite of rooms in the Netherland Hotel in New York City, pursuant to a written agreement, for a term of six months and not to exceed a year, at a weekly rental of $90. During plaintiff's absence for two or three days from the hotel, certain tennis trophies were stolen from his room by some unknown thief. Plaintiff sued claiming liability on account of the duty he alleged was owing to him as defendant's guest. Defendant answered that plaintiff was not a guest, but a roomer or tenant, to whom defendant owed no duty other than that of reasonable care.

The court, in granting judgment for the defendant, said that "an innkeeper's liability, which is sought here to be enforced, exists only in the case of one who is a traveler and seeks the hospitality of the inn as a transient guest." [2]

In *Rosenbluth v. Jamlee Hotel Corp.*,[3] the jury awarded damages

[1] 181 App. Div. 535, 169 N.Y.S. 114 (1st Dep't 1918).
[2] *Id.* at 536 and 115.
[3] 122 N.Y.L.J. No. 103, 1439 (N.Y. County Civ. Ct. 1949).

to the plaintiffs because of the theft of their jewelry from the room rented to them by the defendant in its hotel. The rental was on a monthly basis. The cause of action of the plaintiffs was founded upon the theory that the defendant was negligent in not having changed the lock after a prior theft and that this negligence caused the theft of the jewelry involved in the case. The court, granting defendant's motion to dismiss the complaint on its merits and directing judgment in favor of defendant, said (per Capozzoli, J.):

It is well settled that where the original negligence of the defendant is followed by the independent act of a third person which directly results in injurious consequences to the plaintiff, the defendant's earlier negligence may be found to be the direct and proximate cause of those injurious consequences, if, according to human experience and in the natural course of events the defendant ought to have seen that the intervening act was likely to happen. But if this is not the case, if the intervening act which was the immediate cause of the injury complained of was one which it was not incumbent on the defendant to have anticipated as reasonably likely to happen, even though a high degree of caution would have shown him that it was possible, then he owed no duty to the plaintiff to anticipate such further acts. The chain of causation is broken, and the original negligence cannot be said to have been the proximate cause of the final injury. [Citations omitted.]

The proximate cause of the plaintiffs' loss was not the alleged failure of the defendant to change the lock, but, rather, the independent criminal act of a third person in the stealing of the property. . . .

A finding that the thief gained admittance to the room by the use of a key to the old lock is mere speculation, because there was no proof submitted as to how the thief gained admission. For all that is known, the thief might have stolen the property while defendant's servants were in and out of the room, engaged in its cleaning. As a matter of law, if an employee of the defendant, who had the right of entry into plaintiff's room, had stolen the property, the defendant would not be responsible (*Millheiser* [sic] v. *Beau Site Co.*, 251 N.Y. 290; *Castorina* v. *Rosen*, 290 N.Y. 445).

19:2 *Loss of Tenant's Valuables Deposited in Hotel Safe*

JACOBS *v.* ALRAE HOTEL CORP.
4 App. Div. 2d 201, 164 N.Y.S.2d 330 (1st Dep't 1957),
aff'd mem., 4 N.Y.2d 769, 149 N.E.2d 337 (1958)

FRANK, J.: "This is an appeal from a judgment in favor of the plaintiff, in an action predicated upon negligence. There is virtually no dispute upon the proven facts as they concern the question of liability. The problem arises from the inferences to be drawn from the proof with respect to reasonable care, causation and foreseeability.

"The defendant operated a hotel in the borough of Manhattan, occupied by permanent tenants and transient guests.

"On October 7, 1954, the plaintiff placed a quantity of her jewelry in a deposit box contained in a large safe which was located in the second room off a corridor behind the clerk's desk. The safe was not visible from the lobby. The safe-deposit box allotted to the plaintiff was one of 35, which could not be opened except by the use of two keys, one in the custody of the hotel clerk, the other in the exclusive possession of the person to whom the box was assigned. The method of access to and the appearance of the boxes were similar to those in the vaults maintained by safe-deposit companies.

"After placing her jewelry in her safe-deposit box, the plaintiff left the city and did not return for 11 days.

"On October 12, 1954, at approximately 4 o'clock in the morning, three unknown armed men entered the lobby and by a display of firearms, cowed the night clerk, a guest and his woman companion, trussed them with wire, gagged and confined them in a closet behind the desk. At the time the safe doors were open. No one actually saw the acts performed by the gunmen after they herded the persons whom they had subdued into the closet. After the robbery was completed and the perpetrators had left, it was found that a number of the individual boxes had been chiseled open and abandoned. A section of the safe which contained 15 boxes had been physically removed from the safe and the premises. The remaining section containing 20 boxes had also been removed from the safe but was abandoned on the hotel floor.

All of the plaintiff's jewelry was contained in one of the 15 boxes which were carted off by the criminals. The defendant, too, sustained a loss of about $2,000 of its own funds kept in the safe.

"The hotel manager testified in effect that the safe itself showed evidence of force having been applied to remove the sections. Through the testimony of one of its officers, the defendant's uncontradicted proof was that it had not been aware that the sections containing the boxes were not bolted or welded to the safe and could be physically removed therefrom.

"The trial court predicated its determination upon the finding that the safe doors were not kept locked and the sections were removable. There was no proof that the practice of leaving the safe doors open was not the customary and accepted method used by hotels, nor that the unlocked safe doors were the competent producing cause of the loss occasioned by the robbery. It cannot be urged that negligence would be imputed to the defendant, assuming that the doors were locked and the clerk had opened them at the direction of armed criminals capable of using force to compel acquiescence to their demands. We cannot therefore predicate negligence upon the distinction of locked or unlocked safe doors under the circumstances here present. The proximate cause of the loss was not the open safe doors but the robbery from which the loss resulted. The same consequence would have followed even if the doors were closed, so long as the clerk could have been forced to open the safe. The crime and the loss were cause and result. [Citations omitted.] The plaintiff might have been in a stronger position had she offered proof that the defendant knew that the sections of boxes in the safe were removable. But no such evidence was adduced.

"The facts here are quite different from those in the cases relied upon by the trial court and by the respondent, in which there was no one in attendance at the time the burglary or theft occurred.

"It cannot be said on the proven facts in this case that the defendant could have foreseen or should have been aware, in the exercise of reasonable care, that the plaintiff's property could be removed as it was. Nor can the inference be drawn that the defendant should have provided greater security. If a hindsight test were applied, the plaintiff's position might be sound. But the record is barren of any proof to indicate that prior to the occurrence the defendant could have foreseen the event and could have taken precautionary measures to prevent it.

"Essentially the basis of liability is the ability to reasonably anticipate the risk. Not included in such a premise is every possible occurrence due to unusual or unforeseeable situations. [Citation omitted.] Under ordinary circumstances no one is chargeable with damages because he has not anticipated the commission of a crime by some third party. [Citations omitted.]

"While the defendant is not a true bailee, its status being more in the nature of a warehouseman, nevertheless, even as a bailee it is not an insurer of the plaintiff's property. [Citation omitted.] It can only be held to the same degree of care as would be required from a reasonably prudent person under the same or similar circumstances. [Citation omitted.] Where a warehouseman accounts for the failure to deliver the property left in its possession by demonstrating that the loss resulted from theft, the burden of proving negligence and freedom from contributory negligence is upon the plaintiff. [Citation omitted.] The Court of Appeals expressly rejected the theory 'that sound principles of law and considerations of expediency combine to require that the bailee be held liable.' [Citation omitted.]

"Upon the facts in this case, it must be held that the plaintiff has failed to establish the negligence of the defendant. Under the circumstances, therefore, we are constrained to reverse the judgment and dismiss the complaint.

"We do not reach the other questions posed on this appeal in view of our determination with respect to liability.

"The judgment should be reversed and the complaint dismissed."

[Judgment reversed and the complaint dismissed. Settle order on notice. All concur except Botein, J.P., who dissents and votes to affirm in a dissenting opinion.]

BOTEIN, J.P. (dissenting): "Defendant hotel corporation permitted a safe containing the valuables of its guests to remain open at 4:00 A.M., the time when the robbery occurred. Access to the safe would seldom be required at that hour in a residential-type hotel which evidently did not cater to transient guests. Also, the section containing 15 safe-deposit boxes—one of which held plaintiff's valuables—was not in any way attached to the sides of the safe. The detective assigned to the case and an insurance company investigator both testified that there were no marks indicating that the section had been forced or pried out of the safe. It is evident that after hacking away and opening several boxes in the lower section, which consisted of 20 boxes, the holdup men found that the smaller upper section was readily removable, and they proceeded gratefully to walk away with it.

"These combined circumstances spell out a strong prima facie case of negligence on the part of defendant which it made no effort whatsoever to rebut. The only witness defendant produced was its officer, who testified to a technical compliance with the posting of notice required under section 200 of the General Business Law. Another officer, whose duties were never revealed, was examined before trial by plaintiff, and expressed surprise on learning that the upper section was removable. The conclusion is irresistible that if defendant did not know that the section was removable, then in the exercise of reasonable prudence it should have known that fact.

"Plaintiff has presented actual proof of negligent acts and omissions to act that combined directly to cause the loss of her jewelry—proof of facts not based on conjecture that amply justified the trial court's findings. We should not reject such findings on the basis of speculation as to what might have happened had the safe door been closed and the missing section attached to the safe itself. To illustrate how double-edged such speculation can be, it might be argued on plaintiff's behalf that since the holdup men had tried to pry open the boxes in the lower section, they would never have reached the upper section in which the plaintiff's box was located had that section been attached securely to the safe.

"The judgment should be affirmed." [4]

WALLINGA v. JOHNSON
269 Minn. 436, 131 N.W.2d 216 (1964)

ROGOSHESKE, J.: "This appeal concerns an action to recover the value of two diamond rings owned by plaintiff. They were delivered

---

[4] A provision of the lease exempting landlord from liability for the loss of tenant's property was held unenforceable by Section 234 of the Real Property Law. Nor was the landlord entitled to the benefit of the statutory limitation of liability in Section 200 of the General Business Law for the reason that the statute applies only to property losses of transients.

and accepted for safekeeping by the Commodore Hotel, operated by defendant partnership, and were subsequently taken from the hotel safe by robbery. Plaintiff had occupied an apartment in the hotel for some years. On July 9, 1960, having been confined in a hospital with a broken leg, she directed her son to take two rings from her apartment and deposit them with the hotel clerk for safe keeping. In accordance with customary practice in performing this service, the rings were exhibited to the clerk and placed in a sealed 'safety deposit envelope' used by the hotel for depositing valuables belonging to guests. A numbered stub attached to the envelope was signed by the clerk and plaintiff's son, and a 'depositor's check' containing the same number was detached from the signed stub and given to him. This 'depositor's check' was to be presented when the envelope and contents were called for, at which time the depositor was required to sign it so that the signatures could be compared. The envelope containing the rings was placed in a large safe located in the hotel's front office 4 or 5 feet behind the registration desk and about the same distance from the hotel switchboard. The safe was used not only to keep the valuables of guests, but also cash for use in the hotel's cafe, bar, and coffee shop. Although it was equipped with a combination lock, during the 16 years that defendants operated the hotel the safe door, while customarily closed, was never locked. A clerk was on duty at the registration desk at all times.

"On July 10 at 3:45 A.M., two armed men surprised the night clerk then on duty, rifled cash drawers in the registration desk, and took the contents of the unlocked safe, including the envelope containing plaintiff's rings. The rings have not been recovered.

"The question of defendants' liability was submitted to a jury upon the sole issue of whether defendants were negligent in failing to keep the rings safely locked up and, if they were, whether such negligence was the proximate cause of the loss. The jury returned a verdict for defendants, and plaintiff appeals from an order denying her motion for a new trial.

"The primary question presented is whether the court erred in refusing to hold as a matter of law that the relationship between plaintiff and defendants was that of bailor and bailee.

"Bailment is the legal relation arising upon delivery of goods without transference of ownership under an express or implied agreement that the goods be returned. [Footnote citations omitted.] The actions of plaintiff's son and the hotel clerk—inserting the rings in the safety deposit envelope, signing the numbered stub, detaching the companion presentation stub, and placing the envelope in the safe—plainly indicate that the parties intended the rings to be kept for safekeeping until called for. This was a bailment as a matter of law.

"The error at trial lay in assuming that *Asseltyne* v. *Fay Hotel*, 222 Minn. 91, 23 N.W. (2d)357, applied to the facts of this case. In that case, the plaintiff was a residential guest of the defendant hotel. Her personal property, located in her rented room, was destroyed by fire. The pivotal issue was whether plaintiff's relationship to the hotel was that of a residential lodger or a transient guest. Unlike this case, the owner did not surrender exclusive possession and control of the property to the hotel. Thus, a bailment was not created and the case is inapplicable. We agree with plaintiff that *Peet* v. *Roth Hotel Co.,* 191 Minn. 151, 253 N.W. 546, controls. There, plaintiff, who had no relationship to the hotel, left a ring with the hotel clerk for the purpose of delivering it to a jeweler, a guest of the hotel. We held that a bailment was established as a matter of law.

"Application of the *Asseltyne* case and the court's refusal to find a bailment resulted in its erroneously instructing the jury that plaintiff bore the burden of proving defendant's negligence. Since *Rustad* v. *G.N. Ry. Co.,* 122 Minn. 453, 142 N.W. 727, the rule in Minnesota has been that where the plaintiff has shown a bailment relationship to exist, the defendant must assume not only the burden of going forward with evidence to show lack of negligence but also the burden of ultimate persuasion. [Footnote citation omitted.]

"The record reveals that plaintiff's proof was not wholly consistent with her theory that defendants' liability was governed by the law of bailment. In addition to proving delivery and nonreturn of the rings, she went forward with evidence tending to establish defendants' negligence. Contrary to defendants' contention, however, she did not thereby waive any right to object to the erroneous instructions. At most, she may have waived the right to have defendants assume the burden of going forward with the evidence. The error in instructing the jury as to the burden of proof is one of fundamental law and controlling principle and was properly assigned in plaintiff's motion for a new trial. [Footnote citation omitted.] Moreover, it appears from counsel's affidavit in support of plaintiff's motion for a new trial that he made oral requests to charge the jury on the theory of a bailment which were refused. Clearly, plaintiff is not precluded from asserting the error on appeal. [Footnote citation omitted.]

"While the burden of proof in a bailment case rests on the defendant, the basis of his liability remains ordinary negligence. [Footnote citation omitted.] Failure to lock the safe, at least during the night, is very strong evidence tending to show negligence. The hotel, however, established that a clerk was on duty at all times and the unlocked door was, to some extent, a convenience for guests who wished to retrieve valuables without delay. This evidence, we believe, falls short of establishing defendants' negligence as a matter of law and the question is for the jury under proper instructions.

"Since the case must be retried, defendants' contention that their actions, even if negligent, do not result in liability because the robbery was a superseding cause should be put at rest. As a general rule, a criminal act breaks the chain of causation and insulates the primary actor from liability. [Footnote citation omitted.] A criminal intervening force, however, cannot be a legally effective superseding cause unless it possesses the attribute of unforeseeability. [Footnote citation omitted.] . . . The primary purpose of depositing the rings for safekeeping was to guard against theft; defendants must have, or at least should have, foreseen the possibility of their loss in the manner in which they were taken. We therefore hold that the robbery could not as a matter of law be a superseding cause.

" '. . . Only when there might be a reasonable difference of opinion regarding the foreseeability of the intervening act should the question of intervening cause be submitted to the jury.' " [Footnote citation omitted.]

"Reversed and new trial granted."

19:3 *Loss of Tenant's Property from Storage Room*

DALTON *v.* HAMILTON HOTEL OPERATING CO.
242 N.Y. 481, 152 N.E. 268 (1926)

HISCOCK, C.J.: "Plaintiff brought this action to recover the value of the contents of two trunks claimed to have been lost through the fault of the defendant. The facts which are claimed to sustain liability are as follows:

"The defendant operates an apartment hotel in the city of New York. In August the plaintiff desired to rent one of the apartments but the latter was then so occupied that possession could not be given to plaintiff until October 1, and a lease was subsequently made for the term of one year commencing on the latter date. Plaintiff had several trunks which she desired to store in the meantime and an oral agreement was made between her and the defendant under which the latter without compensation undertook to store said trunks until she should be entitled to possession of her apartment under the lease aforesaid. After this arrangement was made and after the execution of the lease the trunks were delivered to defendant, and the last seen or known of two of them was that they were sent to the basement of the apartment house where there was a room for the storage of such things. When the time arrived for the plaintiff to take possession of her apartment under her lease she sent word to the defendant to deliver her trunks at such apartment but two of them were not delivered and they have never been found. Defendant gave evidence to the effect that it had adopted a system covering the storage of baggage like that which prevailed in other similar buildings and under which articles were to be stored in the room above mentioned where they were under the custody and watch at all times of reliable employees. The only explanation of the loss of the trunks approaching definiteness was a statement said to have been made to plaintiff by one of defendant's officers in substance that the trunks must have been delivered at the apartment of some one other than the plaintiff.

"The lease contained a provision that the defendant should be under no obligation to accept or receive for safekeeping any property of the tenant, but in case any such property should be accepted or received it should be 'accepted, received and held entirely at the risk and hazard of the tenant and the landlord should [shall] not be liable or responsible for any damage thereto or loss or theft thereof whether arising from negligence or otherwise.' In addition to this the plaintiff received for each package delivered to defendant a check or receipt, which, in addition to describing the property, contained the following: 'Read conditions on the reverse side. . . . The property enumerated on the reverse side hereof being received and stored gratuitously it is expressly agreed by the guest that the said receipt and storage shall be entirely at the risk of the owner thereof and that the hotel shall not be liable for loss or injury thereto whether caused by negligence, fire, theft, or any other cause whatsoever. . . . Said hotel is further authorized to deliver said property to any person presenting said receipt without identification.'

"Upon these facts, which we do not understand to be disputed, the plaintiff recovered a judgment for the alleged value of the contents of her two trunks on the ground that defendant was a gratuitous bailee and was guilty of gross negligence, which judgment has been set aside by the Appellate Division both on the law and the facts with dismissal of the complaint and, thereby, several questions are presented to us for consideration.

"A majority of the court are of opinion that the complaint as a whole, notwithstanding various inapt expressions and allegations, does allege after a fashion the cause of action upon which recovery was had at the trial and this conclusion eliminates various questions discussed by counsel.

"We then come to the question whether the arrangement claimed to have been made by plaintiff with defendant for the storage of her trunks was one for gratuitous independent bailment as claimed by her, or was one incidental to and merged in the written lease so that the liability of the defendant is to be decided by the terms of that lease, especially including the exemption clause already quoted. We think that it was the former. The simple facts are that plaintiff rented an apartment but could not obtain possession thereof for several weeks; that she had several trunks which in the meantime must be stored, and that she made the arrangement with the defendant thus to store them until she could obtain possession of her apartment. Of course this arrangement for storage had a certain relation to her lease and undoubtedly never would have been made except for the fact that she made such a lease. But even so, the situation for which the arrangement provided was entirely separate and distinct from that which was covered by the lease. The lease covered occupation of the apartment from a certain future date. The arrangement for storage of the trunks covered the intervening period and the necessities for it and the rights secured were entirely different than those provided for by the lease. We are unable to see how either as a matter of technical law or as a matter of common sense it can be said that when a proposed tenant has rented a house or an apartment of which he cannot secure possession for the purpose of accommodating his property for some time to come, and says in effect that he wants to make another arrangement for storing such property until he can put it in his apartment or house, the latter agreement is covered by or merged in the former one. Therefore, we conclude that defendant accepted the lost trunks without promise of compensation and as a gratuitous bailee and, that being so, we encounter the question whether plaintiff's evidence has established any default in defendant's obligations as such bailee which entitles her to judgment.

"The obligations of defendant as gratuitous bailee are commonly described as involving the exercise of slight care and as being violated only when there has been gross negligence. The distinction between 'slight' and 'reasonable' care and between 'ordinary' negligence and 'gross' negligence is oftentimes shadowy and unsatisfactory. But the courts, however fortunate or otherwise they may have been in expressing that distinction, do recognize that it exists. In *First Nat. Bank* v. *Ocean Nat. Bank* (60 N.Y. 278, 295) it was said that: 'It [gross negligence] has been defined to be the want of that ordinary diligence and care which a usually prudent man takes of his own property of the like description. . . . This definition is given by a reference to the degree of care, rather than the degree of negligence which may be the easier and more intelligible mode of defining the extent of the obligation, and the measure of duty assumed. . . . A depositor of goods or securities for safekeeping with a gratuitous bailee can only claim that diligence which a person of common sense, not a specialist or expert in a particular department, should exercise in such department.' And in *Weld* v. *Postal Telegraph-Cable Co.* (210 N.Y. 59, 72) it was said: 'The cases cited recognize a distinction between ordinary and gross negligence, from which it may be said that gross negligence is the commission or omission of an act or duty owing by one person to a second party which discloses a failure to exercise slight diligence. In other words, the act or omission must be of an aggravated character as distinguished from the failure to exercise ordinary care.'

"When plaintiff demanded that her trunks be delivered to her at her apartment and the defendant failed to do this, a *prima facie* case was established against the latter even of gross negligence which amounted to a breach of its obligations and which called for an explanation. [Citations omitted.] And we do not think that defendant made such explanation as rebutted the presumption and destroyed the *prima facie* case. It attempted to do this by giving evidence of a system under which trunks were placed in a room under the constant watchfulness of competent and reliable employees. As a matter of fact there is no evidence that the plaintiff's trunks ever came within the operation of this system for they were traced no further than to show that they were taken to the basement of the apartment house. But if we assume that the trunks were placed in the proper depository under the watchfulness provided by the defendant, we do not think that this fact answers the presumption arising in favor of plaintiff on failure to deliver her trunks or satisfactorily explains their disappearance. Presumptively under this system the trunks should have been in defendant's possession and ready for delivery when called for and it is the failure of what was to be expected that defendant is called on to explain. So far as we can see their loss could naturally be accounted for on any one of three theories. They might have been abstracted by some external means not within the control of defendant, as larceny by an outsider. But there is no suggestion of any such occurrence as this. They might have been stolen by an employee whom the defendant had the right to regard as reliable and responsible. But again there is no suggestion of this, and the only remaining theory which occurs to us is the one that defendant voluntarily and without production of the appropriate checks delivered the trunks to some one other than the plaintiff or, as suggested by defendant's official, sent them to the wrong apartment when plaintiff called for them and wherefrom they were abstracted instead of being returned. Unless excused by special circumstances, a voluntary delivery of the trunks to a person other than plaintiff without production of checks, which at all times remained in possession of plaintiff, or the delivery of them to a different apartment than plaintiff's would not be a sufficient excuse for failure to deliver to plaintiff but would be affirmative evidence of a failure to exercise a very slight degree of care and would amount to gross negligence, if not willful misconduct.

"The exemption clauses in the lease and on the checks respectively do not become material elements in the disposition of the case. Regarding as we do the arrangement for storage of the trunks as an agreement outside of the lease, the provisions of the latter are not material. So far as concerns the exemption clause on the checks, independent of any other answer, we do not think it is to be assumed that it was the intention of the parties that it should relieve the defendant from its own gross negligence. Argument or authorities are not necessary to fortify this view, for defendant's counsel in his brief concedes its correctness. . . .

". . . [T]he judgment of the Appellate Division should be modified so as to provide for a new trial and as so modified should be affirmed, with costs to abide event."

[All concur except one judge not voting.]

19:4 *Authority of Employee to Accept Property from Nonguests*

Where goods are accepted by an employee from one who is not a guest the question of the innkeeper's liability for loss of the goods often depends on the authority of the employee to bind the innkeeper. The authority may be actual, or it may be apparent or implied from the position the employee occupies. The question of authority is one of fact for the jury to determine.

In *Coykendall* v. *Eaton*,[5] plaintiff attended a dance at defendant's hotel. Upon leaving the hotel premises, plaintiff's carriage was involved in an accident. Plaintiff returned to the hotel, where he checked a robe and a cushion seat from the carriage with the attendant in charge of the coatroom. There was conflicting testimony as to the authority of the attendant to accept property from persons other than those in actual attendance at the dance and as to whether the deposit was made on the authority of a bartender. Judgment in favor of defendant was reversed for failure of the trial court to submit the attendant's authority to bind defendant to the jury. Said the court, "The rule is that a bailee for hire, or a gratuitous bailee, who delivers the goods he has as such bailee, to a wrong party, or who, after they are demanded of him, does not in any way account for their loss, is liable to the true owner for their value." [Citations omitted.][6]

[5] 55 Barb. 188 (N.Y. Sup. Ct. 1869).   [6] *Id.* at 193.

BOOTH v. LICHTFIELD
201 N.Y. 466, 94 N.E. 1078 (1911)

COLLIN, J.: "During May, 1905, the defendants were the owners and proprietors of an apartment house or hotel in the city of New York in which a Mr. Lord had an apartment. The plaintiff on May 22, 1905, presented to the clerk of the defendants at the office of the hotel the letter of Mr. Lord, who was then in Chicago, addressed to the manager of the hotel, asking that plaintiff while in New York be afforded the use of his apartment, and, in response, he was immediately conducted and his suitcase, umbrella and overcoat taken to Mr. Lord's apartment. At about six o'clock in the afternoon of the following day, he told the clerk that he was going to leave the hotel and take his things with him; that he was going to Washington on the midnight train and had a dinner engagement for the evening and was pressed for time, and would like him to have his suitcase packed and brought with his overcoat and umbrella to the checkroom of the hotel ready for him when he called for them. The clerk stated to plaintiff the fact that the hotel had no checkroom and refused his request for a receipt for the goods and added, 'but I will keep them in the office here for you.' The office referred to was a space behind the desk or counter about three feet wide and eight feet long in which there was a small safe, a telephone switchboard and a telephone operator. The hotel valet went, at the direction of the clerk, to the apartment with the plaintiff, who instructed him as to the packing and that he should take the suitcase when packed, overcoat and umbrella to the office. Plaintiff then returned to the office and told the clerk that the valet would bring the things downstairs to him and that he would come for them on his way to the train at about eleven or eleven-thirty o'clock. No charge of any kind was made against or paid by the plaintiff. At about eleven o'clock he asked the clerk at the desk for the articles and was told by him they had been delivered to an uniformed messenger upon his demand for them, and such was the fact. Plaintiff brought this action in conversion for the recovery of the value of the articles and a judgment in his favor was rendered.

"During the trial the plaintiff's counsel stated to the court: 'We don't claim any innkeeper's liability, a statutory innkeeper's liability;

nothing further than it being a gratuitous bailee.' At the close of the entire evidence the defendants unavailingly asked that the plaintiff be nonsuited upon the ground, among others, that the clerk in the reception and care of the articles acted as agent and servant of plaintiff and not of defendants, such services not being within the scope of his duties. The trial court instructed the jury that they should first determine whether or not the act of the clerk in taking charge of the articles was reasonably within the scope of his employment, and if they resolved that in favor of the plaintiff they should determine whether or not he exercised ordinary care therein.

". . . The action must have as a support evidence that the delivery of the articles to the clerk was in legal effect a delivery to the defendants. It was not such unless they had authorized the clerk, either expressly or by implication, to accept under the conditions then existing, as their agent and for themselves, the goods. Under a fundamental rule of law the acts of the clerk cannot be deemed those of and chargeable to the defendants unless authorized by them. . . .

"The evidence does not permit the implication or inference that the act of the clerk in receiving and undertaking to keep for the plaintiff his goods, under the circumstances disclosed at the trial, was within the actual authority of the clerk or any authority indicated by the acts of the defendants. They were conducting the hotel and the relations of themselves and of the clerk as their agent with the plaintiff began when he presented the letter of Mr. Lord and ceased with the termination of his occupancy of the apartment. The defendants did not by their acts or the conditions created by them indicate that they would accept for safekeeping or would assume responsibility for the security of the goods of those who were not guests or occupants of the apartments of the hotel. The facts within the record show that the business of the defendants and the duties of their clerk therein were in relation to those persons only and not those who never became or had ceased to be their guests. The testimony of the plaintiff himself is, in effect, that when he went from the hotel to fulfill his engagement to dine, he had given up his room and had left his property in the charge of the clerk intermediate his leaving the hotel and calling for it on the way to the train. The result of the transaction between the plaintiff and the clerk was not different from what it would have been had the plaintiff surrendered his room, taken the articles to a taxicab waiting at the curb, and, reconsidering through his desire to be relieved of them while dining, returned to the hotel office and induced the clerk to place them in his care behind the desk while he met his engagement; or had he while walking along the street, carrying the articles, entered the hotel and obtained the same undertaking on the part of the clerk. Either of such transactions obviously would not have been within the real or apparent authority of the clerk. (*Coykendall* v. *Eaton*, 40 How.Pr. 266). The act of the clerk in receiving and assuming the care of the goods, after the plaintiff had ceased to be a guest at the hotel, was proven to be beyond the authority which the defendants by their words or acts had given or appeared to have given him, and as between the plaintiff and the defendants he and not they must sustain his loss. The motion for the nonsuit should have been granted.

"The judgment should be reversed and a new trial granted, with costs to abide the event."

[All concur.]

19:5 Liability for Misdelivery

A misdelivery of goods bailed is ordinarily held to make even a gratuitous bailee liable. This is obviously true if the misdelivery was negligent. So of a delivery to an apparent stranger who claims it without an effort to verify his claim.[7] Thus where the goods were wrongly delivered to an expressman who brought a slip of paper with the owner's name on it, the innkeeper was held liable.[8]

The facts of the case were as follows. The plaintiff had been a boarder at the defendant's inn, as a servant to other boarders, but she had departed from the inn, leaving her trunk behind. On November 18, 1895, the plaintiff left the order with Jackson's Express to call for her trunk. Manning, one of the drivers employed by that concern, called at the hotel for the trunk the next morning and demanded the trunk, but was told that it had been delivered to another expressman on the previous day. The defendant proved that a man with a wagon called on November 18, 1895, that he had a slip of paper with the plaintiff's name thereon, and that upon demanding the trunk he was allowed to take it. The defendant took no receipt for the trunk. Randolph, the hall man, who delivered it, testified that he had worked

[7] *Wear* v. *Gleason*, 52 Ark. 364, 12 S.W. 756 (1889).
[8] *George* v. *Depierris*, 17 Misc. 400, 39 N.Y.S. 1082 (Sup. Ct. 1896).

in hotels for six or seven years, and that in general they took receipts, but that "he did not think to take a receipt for help's trunks." He did not obtain the name of the man to whom he delivered it, or ascertain the license number of his wagon, or require him to leave the slip of paper containing the plaintiff's name; hence the defendant was unable to give any information concerning where the trunk had gone or where it could be found, except that it was given to an unknown expressman. The plaintiff testified that the delivery made was without her authority; and that, although she had consulted detectives and made efforts to recover her property, she had not been able to obtain it.

Under these circumstances the court held the defendant liable stating: "The delivery of the plaintiff's trunk . . . was not the exercise of that care which the law imposed upon the defendant . . . ; for the facts [showed] an indifference respecting the safety of the plaintiff's property and disregard of the usage as to taking receipts which excludes the idea that any diligence was used by the defendant to insure its delivery to her." [9]

The innkeeper is equally liable for a misdelivery the circumstances of which are unexplained. The burden is upon him to explain the loss.[10] And there is good authority and reason for the view that even a gratuitous bailee is liable in case of a misdelivery, however careful he may have been to secure a good delivery; for it is departing from the terms of his bailment.[11]

19:6 Goods in Bathhouse outside Inn

Where the goods of a guest are left in charge of the innkeeper outside the precincts of the inn, though the innkeeper is not as such liable for the goods, he is nevertheless responsible for the exercise of due care. So where an innkeeper provided bath rooms, outside the inn, for his guests, and the guest's goods were lost from the bath room, while the innkeeper is not liable on a declaration charging him as innkeeper [12] he is liable for loss by his negligence or misdelivery.[13]

[9] Id. at 402 and 1083.   [10] Murray v. Clarke, 2 Daly 102 (N.Y. Ct. C.P. 1886).
[11] Jenkins v. Bacon, 111 Mass. 373 (1873).
[12] Minor v. Staples, 71 Me. 316 (1880).
[13] Tombler v. Koelling, 60 Ark. 62, 28 S.W. 795 (1894). The defendant was the keeper of the bathhouse, not an innkeeper, but the same principle is involved.

CHAPTER 20

Responsibility for Automobiles and Their Contents

20:1 Introduction

At common law, the innkeeper was held to a strict liability for the loss of or damage to a guest's horse or carriage when placed within the confines of the inn, that is, *infra hospitium*. The innkeeper was excused from liability only if the loss, or damage, occurred by an act of God, an act of the public enemy, or the fault of negligence of the guest himself.[1]

As the horse and buggy were supplanted by the automobile, the common-law rule of strict liability was extended to cover this modern instrument of travel and transportation.[2] The rule required (1) that the claimant be a guest of the innkeeper, and (2) that the automobile be within the confines of the inn, *infra hospitium*.

20:2 Liability for Automobiles infra Hospitium

Although the early English cases had held that in order to qualify as a guest, the person had to be a "traveler," by the end of the nineteenth century the courts held that the relationship of innkeeper and guest "arises when a person goes to an inn for the purpose of receiving such accommodation and services as are ordinarily given to guests." [3]

The concept of what constitutes property *infra hospitium* has similarly been expanded by the courts. At first the *hospitium* was held to be merely the inn itself with its attendant buildings (such as

---

[1] *Hulett v. Swift*, 33 N.Y. 571 (1865).
[2] *Park-O-Tell Co. v. Roskamp*, 203 Okla. 493, 223 P.2d 375 (1950).
[3] *Orchard v. Bush & Co.*, [1898] 2 Q.B. 284.

stables and garages). However, the innkeeper might, by his actions, extend the confines of his *hospitium*. In *Calye's Case*,[4] it was held that if an innkeeper without direction from the guest, put a horse to pasture, he would be held strictly liable for its loss. The same principle applied to a guest's gig left by the innkeeper on a public street outside of the inn.[5]

In the much later case of *Aria* v. *Bridge House Hotel* (*Staines*) *Ltd.*,[6] the plaintiff, while a guest at defendant's hotel, parked his car in the parking lot adjoining the hotel, as he was directed by one of the defendant's employees. While plaintiff was at dinner in the hotel, his car was stolen. The court held that the insurance liability of an innkeeper for the goods of his guest extended also to the guest's automobile parked in a space adjoining the hotel, as directed by the porter, and that the defendant hotel was liable for the loss of the car stolen while the guest was at dinner.

The high point of English case law holding an innkeeper strictly liable as insurer for the loss of a guest's car was reached in the case of *Williams* v. *Linnitt*.[7] In that case the plaintiff, a local resident, called at defendant's inn for liquid refreshments only. He parked his car in an open lot provided free of charge for that purpose. The car was stolen. The court held that the plaintiff was a guest,[8] and that the parking lot was *infra hospitium*,[9] and that hence the innkeeper was strictly liable for the theft of the car. By providing the free parking space, the innkeeper extended an invitation [10] to the guest to park

4 77 Eng. Rep. 520 (K.B. 1584).

5 *Jones* v. *Tyler,* 110 Eng. Rep. 1307 (K.B. 1834).

6 137 L.T.R. (n.s.) 299 (K.B. 1927).   7 [1951] 1 K.B. 565 (C.A. 1950).

8 Asquith, L.J., felt that the broad construction given the term "traveler" to constitute plaintiff a guest did after all exclude, "for instance, (a) the innkeeper's family living in the inn; (b) the innkeeper's servants; (c) the innkeeper's private guests; (d) lodgers at the inn; (e) persons resorting to the inn for purposes unconnected with the enjoyment of the facilities it provides as an inn." *Id.* at 579.

9 The test applied by Lord Tucker in deciding whether the parking lot was *infra hospitium* was: "[I]s the place in question a part of the inn premises intended and suitable for user in connexion [*sic*] with some part of the innkeeper's business?" *Id.* at 577.

10 For a case drawing a distinction between an invitation which serves to extend the *hospitium* and mere permission, see *Watson* v. *People's Refreshment House Ass'n, Ltd.*, [1952] 1 K.B. 318. (Mere permission to park a motor coach on runway of hotel-owned gas station does not extend the *hospitium* and does not create liability for loss of motor coach.)

there, which invitation was sufficient to constitute the lot as within the *hospitium* of the inn. The court also held with one dissent, that the defendant innkeeper could not limit his liability by merely posting a notice to that effect.

In the New York case of *Lader* v. *Warsher*,[11] plaintiff, a traveling salesman, parked his automobile in a parking lot provided free of charge for that purpose for guests of defendant's hotel, the St. Charles, in Hudson, New York. Plaintiff locked his car and retired for the night. During the night the car was jimmied and plaintiff's sample case was stolen.

The court, in affirming judgment for the defendant, held that none of plaintiff's property was ever "within the walls of the inn," *infra hospitium*. Said the court:

> [T]he rule of absolute liability of an innkeeper for loss of property of a guest under the common law has always . . . been limited and applied to cases where the property was within the walls of the inn itself and not outside them; or if outside the walls the goods must have been in the care and under the charge of the innkeeper. [Citations omitted.]
>
> Where property is damaged or lost outside the inn itself the landlord's liability is measured by a different rule; it may be one of the many and various rules relating to contract or negligence or agency or bailment or what have you. . . .
>
> [Defendant], at the most, was a bailee, and his responsibility and liability must be measured by rules applicable to that relationship.
>
> If [defendant] was a bailee for hire on the theory that he derived some indirect benefit or profit in his business by providing a free parking place for automobiles belonging to his guests, he is held to the rule of ordinary care [citation omitted]; or if he was a gratuitous bailee he was liable only for gross negligence.
>
> In either case the burden of proof was on the [plaintiff]. [Citation omitted.] [12]

The majority of jurisdictions in the United States have adopted the strict rule of insurance liability of an innkeeper for the goods of his guest *infra hospitium*. In a few jurisdictions (Indiana, Kentucky, Texas, among them) the liability is not that of an insurer, but is predicated on negligence or wrongful acts. In these latter jurisdictions

11 165 Misc. 559, 1 N.Y.S.2d 160 (Columbia County Ct. 1937).
12 *Id.* at 561 and 162.

the loss or damage to the property creates a prima facie case against the innkeeper, which he can rebut by proving that the loss or injury was not due to any fault or neglect on his part. All states have enacted statutes limiting the innkeeper's liability for the goods of his guest.

Of the twelve jurisdictions which have passed on the problem of an innkeeper's liability for a guest's car and its contents, only two, Oklahoma and Utah, have imposed insurer's liability on the innkeeper. In most states the liability is predicated on a bailment relationship between the guest and the innkeeper.

Clearly, where no innkeeper-guest relationship exists, there is no case for imposing strict insurance liability. Nor has any jurisdiction in the United States been as liberal in construing the term "guest" as was the English court in *Williams* v. *Linnitt*. A person attending a banquet has been held not to be a guest of the hotel.[13] A bridegroom who entered the hotel solely for the purpose of getting married, without any intent of occupying a room, was not considered a guest.[14]

The two states that have held the innkeeper to an insurer's liability had no trouble deciding that the car in question was *infra hospitium*. In one case, decided by the Supreme Court of Oklahoma,[15] the car had been parked in the hotel garage, which garage facility was advertised as a special feature of the hotel. The court held that at common law as well as under the relevant statute it is not necessary, in order to render the innkeeper liable for their loss, that the goods be placed under his special care, or that notice be given of their arrival. It is sufficient if they are brought into the inn in the usual and ordinary way and are not retained under the exclusive control of the guest, but are under the general and implied control of the innkeeper.

In the other case,[16] the car had been parked at a loading platform situated in front of the hotel. The court found that the clerk had in-

---

[13] *Edwards Hotel Co.* v. *Terry*, 185 Miss. 824, 187 So. 518 (1939). Plaintiff's car was stolen from the hotel's free parking lot while he was attending a banquet held in the hotel. The court held that plaintiff was not a guest of the hotel.

[14] *Ross* v. *Kirkeby Hotels, Inc.*, 8 Misc. 2d 750, 160 N.Y.S.2d 978 (Sup. Ct. 1957).

[15] *Park-O-Tell Co.* v. *Roskamp*, 203 Okla. 493, 223 P.2d 375 (1950).

[16] *Merchants Fire Assurance Corp.* v. *Zion's Securities Corp.*, 109 Utah 13, 163 P.2d 319 (1945).

structed the guest to leave it there and the hotel would take care of it.

For the most part, the courts have refrained from facing the issue of whether or not a guest has placed his car *infra hospitium*. Where, on the facts, the innkeeper is liable under either a strict liability theory or as a bailee for hire, the courts have generally decided the case without passing on the issue of *infra hospitium*.[17]

Hallman v. *Federal Parking Services, Inc.*[18] was an action for loss of personal articles from a car parked in an independent parking lot under agreement with the codefendant hotel. The plaintiff sued both the hotel and the parking lot operator. The court held the innkeeper alone liable, on a bailment theory. Further, the court stated that the failure to redeliver the articles missing created a prima facie case of negligence against the bailee hotel, placing on it the burden of coming forward with an explanation. While notice of the presence in the car of the personal articles was necessary to create the bailment, constructive notice was deemed sufficient. The articles in question were clearly visible and of the kind which one would assume a traveler to have and even to leave in a car.

The court, summing up its review of the decided cases on the subject of *infra hospitium* stated:

The doctrine of *infra hospitium* has been applied in cases where a car or its contents are lost while *in the exclusive care and custody of a hotel.* [Footnote citations omitted.] *However, where the hotel takes custody of the vehicle, as here, and delivers it to a lot or garage not an integral part of the hotel* and thereafter a loss of the property occurs, the better rule imposes the liability of a bailee for hire on the hotel. [Footnote citations omitted.] [19]

20:3 *Liability as Bailee: Parking-Lot Transactions*

The existence of a bailment often turns on the degree of control exercised by the prospective bailee over the automobile. In cases in-

[17] See, for example, *Zurich Fire Ins. Co.* v. *Weil,* 259 S.W.2d 54 (Ky. 1953). The guest parked his car in front of the hotel, preparatory to its being sent to the garage. The bellboy took the key from the desk, and damaged the car. The court in holding the innkeeper liable stated: "We are not required to decide in this case whether the Hotel could be held liable as an innkeeper. . . . The [hotel] owed . . . at least the duty of a bailee for hire." *Id.* at 56.

[18] 134 A.2d 382 (D.C. Mun. App. 1957).

[19] *Id.* at 384. Emphasis supplied.

volving cars parked in parking lots a bailment is almost invariably held to exist,[20] and the operators found liable for loss or damage to the cars, where the attendant collects a fee and assumes control over the car. The control may be manifested by taking the car at the entrance of the lot, or by moving it to permit the entrance or exit of other cars. Usually the keys are left in the car and the owner is issued a claim ticket as a means of identifying the car for re-delivery.

On the other hand, a parking-lot operator is generally held not liable where the attendant merely collects a fee and the driver parks the car himself, without actual delivery to the proprietor, the car being locked or not, as the driver wishes.

If the parking area is fenced in and is subject to a high degree of control, the fact that the car owner is permitted to retain the ignition key in his possession does not necessarily prevent the existence of a bailment. The key, after all, merely signifies that the car cannot be moved. When a thief proves the fallacy of this assumption, the parking-lot operator may not be heard to say that he had not had adequate control to prevent the car from being moved, and was, therefore, not a bailee.

Where a bailment relationship does exist, the plaintiff must prove that the loss or damage to his car was due to the negligence of the bailee.[21] However, in many jurisdictions the mere failure to deliver the car, or its re-delivery in a damaged condition, constitutes a prima facie case against the bailee. He must then come forward with evidence, to show that the loss was not due to his negligence.[22]

These principles should apply as well in case of an innkeeper and his guest's car. Although the Tennessee case, *Andrew Jackson Hotel, Inc.* v. *Platt* did not reach the question of bailment, it seems apparent that there was insufficient delivery of the car to create such a relationship.[23] It would seem then that a hotel or motel may avoid liability by merely providing a parking area and permitting its patrons to park

---

[20] Jones, "The Parking Lot Cases," 27 *Geo. L.J.* 162, 178 (1938), contains an extensive review of cases supporting this contention.

[21] 8 C.J.S. Bailments §50 (c) (1962).

[22] *Hallman* v. *Federal Parking Services, Inc.*, 134 A.2d 382 (D.C. Mun. App. 1957).

[23] 19 Tenn. App. 360, 89 S.W.2d 179 (1935). The degree of delivery necessary to create a bailment would seem to be greater than that necessary to place an item *infra hospitium*.

there at will. Adequate notice warning the patron that he is parking at his own risk is most advisable.

The danger is that a court may conclude that, even though there was not a sufficient delivery to create a bailment, the car was placed *infra hospitium* and therefore an innkeeper's strict liability applies. This danger is most evident in the case of hotels and motels which handle guest cars in the regular course of their business. Moreover, where the parking area is an enclosed garage, the conclusion that the car has been placed within the control of the innkeeper becomes almost inescapable.

MALONE *v.* SANTORA
135 Conn. 286, 64 A.2d 51 (1949)

BROWN, J.: "The plaintiff in each of these cases sued the defendant to recover for damage to the plaintiff's automobile consequent upon its being stolen from the defendant's parking lot, where the plaintiff owner had left it and paid the required parking charge. In each case judgment was rendered for the plaintiff and the defendant has appealed.

"The essential facts are undisputed and may be thus summarized: The plaintiff Johnson's car was stolen on the evening of November 22, 1946, and that of the plaintiff Malone on the evening of November 29, 1946. Each was subsequently recovered in damaged condition. The defendant's parking lot, with a capacity of 150 cars, has a frontage of 70 feet on the north side of East Main Street in Waterbury and a depth of 270 feet. It is effectively inclosed except for two entrances, one, about 14 feet wide, at a rear corner, and the other, 59 feet wide, on East Main Street. About 8 P.M. on November 22 the plaintiff Johnson drove her car into the lot, paid the defendant or one of his attendants the customary twenty-five-cent charge and left the car with him in response to his statement, 'Leave your keys, I'll park the car.' She left her keys in the car and he parked it. For the purpose of identification she was given a ticket, a detached part of which he placed on the car. On it was printed: 'Liability. Management assumes no responsibility of any kind. Charges are for Rental of space. From 8 A.M. to 11 P.M. Not responsible for articles left in or on car. Agree to the within terms.' She read these words and understood their purport to be that the car owner agreed to the terms stated. There was also a sign on the premises which she did not notice and which read: 'Charges are for use of Parking space until 11 P.M. Not responsible for cars left open after 11 P.M. You may lock your car.' She left and when she returned for her car shortly before 11 P.M. it could not be found. It had been stolen meantime. Upon her return the defendant and two attendants were there on duty. In accepting this car as he did, the defendant acted in the ordinary course of his business as a parking lot operator and in accord with his practice as to the car of the plaintiff and as to those of many others, not only upon that evening but upon other occasions also. It was his policy to insist that no one claiming a car should be allowed to drive it off the lot without first presenting the identifying ticket, unless the claimant was known to the defendant or his employees.

"About 7 P.M. on November 29 the plaintiff Malone drove his car onto the parking lot, turned it over to one of the defendant's employees, paid the twenty-five-cent charge and received a ticket from the attendant, who placed the detached part of it on the car. The printing on the ticket was of the same purport as recited above. Malone put the ticket in his pocket without reading it and left. The attendant parked the car, leaving the key in the switch. Shortly before 10 P.M. Malone returned, presented the ticket to the attendant and demanded his car. It could not be found. Meantime a person had entered the lot and stated to one of the attendants that his brother was the owner of the car and that he had requested him to get the car for him. Malone had authorized no one to call for the car, and the person making the request was an imposter and a thief. One of the attendants delivered the car to him and he drove it away. On that evening at least three attendants were on duty.

"In each case the court concluded: There was a bailor and bailee relationship between the plaintiff and defendant; the wording on ticket and sign did not bar the plaintiff's right of recovery; on the ground of public policy the bailment was not subject to the limitation on liability therein set forth; the defendant was negligent in the discharge of his duty as bailee; the plaintiff is entitled to recover for the damage accruing to his car, that of the plaintiff Johnson being $168 and that of the plaintiff Malone $400. Whether these conclusions are justified is the question determinative of these appeals.

"In recent years there have been many decisions concerning the liability of operators of parking lots for cars parked thereon by customers. As has been well observed, cases of this nature may be divided into 'two types: first, those where the attendant merely collects the fee and designates the area in which to park, the driver himself doing the parking and retaining complete control over the car, locking it or not as he wishes; and second, those lots, usually enclosed, where the attendants take complete charge of the car at the entrance, park it, retain the keys and move the car about as necessary, giving the driver a check or ticket, upon presentation of which they deliver the car to him.' 27 *Geo. L.J.* 162, 163. As this article goes on to point out, situations of the second type have usually been held to give rise to liability on the ground that the transaction is a bailment, while liability has been denied in those of the first, the courts holding that the lack of the essential element of possession in the lot operator renders the relationship one of a license or of a privilege to park rather than of bailment. . . .

"Whether a car owner merely hires a place to put his car or has turned its possession over to the care and custody of the lot operator depends on the place, the conditions and the nature of the transaction. [Citations omitted.] Among the significant facts in each of the instant cases were these: The lot was inclosed; the defendant's attendants were present to attend to cars brought in to be parked; the plaintiff paid the parking charge to the attendant who gave him his claim ticket; the plaintiff left the switch key in the car at the request of the attendant who then took the car and parked it; no particular space for placing the car was either mentioned or contemplated. Under the principles which we have stated, it is clear that in each case these facts, without more, warranted, if in fact they did not require, the conclusion that the relationship between the plaintiff and the defendant was that of bailor and bailee.

"In neither case has the defendant assigned error in the court's finding that the plaintiff's car was stolen. He does, however, attack its conclusion in each that the theft of the car with the damage accruing to the plaintiff was due to the defendant's negligence. The court's conclusion was warranted on the record. The return of the car to the plaintiff in a damaged condition raised a presumption that this was due to the negligence of the bailee and prima facie established his liability; the presumption ceased to operate when the defendant had proven the circumstances of the theft of the car; and it was then for the trial court in the light of those circumstances to determine whether or not the bailee was negligent. [Citation omitted.] The finding, interpreted in the light of the memorandum of decision, makes clear that the court did find the bailee negligent.

"The defendant has assigned error in the court's conclusion that recovery was not barred by any limitation of liability in the ticket's provision or the wording of the sign. In so far as the Malone case is concerned, the fact that the plaintiff had no knowledge of the content of either shows that he did not assent to and could not have been bound by any such agreement. [Citation omitted.] In the *Johnson* case also there is good reason for concluding that one purpose for which the ticket was given and accepted was to afford a means of identification for the plaintiff in claiming her car and that it did not constitute a contract exempting the defendant from liability. The language of the ticket suggests that the defendant was charging the plaintiff only for rental of space and assumed no responsibility of any kind. Since the plaintiff read the ticket she knew its terms. Had she herself parked the car on the lot, left it there and paid the charge, the transaction might have been regarded as constituting a case of the first type referred to above, with consequent immunity of the defendant from liability for theft of the car. Even so, the court's conclusion that the defendant was responsible under a bailor and bailee relationship was not necessarily unwarranted. An existing contract may be modified or abrogated by a new contract arising by implication from the conduct of the parties. 4 Page, *Contracts* (2d ed.) §2471. So here the defendant's subsequent assumption of control of the car, acquiesced in by the plaintiff, was totally inconsistent with an agreement of the first type and afforded reason for concluding that the contract actually made was one of bailment of which the provision exculpating the defendant from responsibility was no part. Actions may be held to speak louder than words, and the defendant's assumption of control of the car may be held to have negatived any intent by either party that an agreement for a license upon the terms indicated by the ticket should in fact arise. Upon the facts, what was in form such a contract lacked that intent to make it effective without which no true contract could come into existence. [Citation omitted.]

"We must regard the transaction in the *Johnson* case as giving rise to a bailment, and the provision against liability printed on the ticket could not avail the defendant to bar recovery the plaintiff. This is so because of 'the well-recognized rule that the right of a bailee to limit his liability by special contract does not go to the extent of relieving him against his own negligence.' [Citations omitted.] The reason is that such a provision is 'revolting to the moral sense, and contrary alike to the salutary principles of law and a sound public policy.' [Citation omitted.] . . .

"There is no error in either case.

"In this opinion the other judges concurred."

PHOENIX ASSURANCE CO. *v.* ROYALE INVESTMENT CO.
393 S.W.2d 43 (St. Louis Ct. App., Mo. 1965)

WOLFE, J. (Acting Presiding): "This is an action by the plaintiff, Phoenix Assurance Company of New York, to recover from Royale Investment Company the amount the 'Assurance Company' paid to Roy M. Scott. The plaintiff sought recovery by right of subrogation after paying Scott $603.62 under a policy of insurance. This sum was for damages to Scott's automobile which had been stolen from a parking lot operated by the defendant Royale Investment Company. There was a judgment for the plaintiff, and the defendant prosecutes this appeal.

"The facts of the matter are that the Royale Investment Company operated the Ambassador-Kingsway Hotel in the City of St. Louis. Directly to the east of the hotel it maintained a parking lot which was generally used for hotel guests. The defendant corporation also maintained another lot about 100 feet east of the one mentioned, which was used for parking of cars belonging to persons who attended various functions at the hotel.

"Roy M. Scott carried a policy of comprehensive insurance with the plaintiff Phoenix Assurance Company of New York on his 1957 Buick. He came to St. Louis with his wife on September 27, 1960, in the automobile. They stopped by the main entrance of the Ambassador-Kingsway Hotel at about ten P.M. There a doorman took over the automobile and gave Scott a claim check. Scott kept the key to his car as the Buick ignition switch was made so that it could be turned and the motor started without the use of the key.

"Scott and his wife retired to their room in the hotel. At about 4:30 in the morning Scott was awakened by a phone call from a police officer who told him that his car had been involved in a wreck in south St. Louis. Scott dressed at once and went to the police station from which the call originated. The police gave him a release order to get his car, which had been taken to a parking lot. There he found his car damaged in the front end, including the hood, headlights, windshield, and right front fender. The car would still operate and he drove it away. The car was later taken to Yates Oldsmobile, Inc., and it was repaired there at a cost of $545.09. Scott was obliged to rent a car for a week, as he was in St. Louis on business, and for this he paid $50.00. He also paid a towing charge of $8.53. His insurance company, Phoenix Assurance Company of New York, the plaintiff herein, paid the damages that he had thus sustained in the total sum of $603.62.

"Scott remained at the hotel until October 4. He was charged and paid one dollar for the first night of parking. The claim check that he was given by the doorman had printed on the back of it: 'The Hotel assumes no responsibility for cars parked on this lot whether for the car or damages or contents therein. We do not have an attendant at all times. This ticket is not a receipt. It indicates our agreement concerning parking. All owners placing automobiles with the Hotel parking lot do so subject to the above terms and conditions.'

"The defendant's evidence chiefly consisted of the testimony of the bell captain of the hotel. He recalled that Scott and his wife arrived at the hotel and that he told Scott that he would park his car for him. He said that Scott kept the key, but he could operate the car without it and lock all of the doors. He said that he told Scott that he would park the car at Scott's own risk. He also said that he called Scott's attention to the 'writing on the stub.' He stated that he took the car, parked it on the lot, and that he closed all of the windows and locked the doors. The parking lot was lighted, but it was unattended from 1:30 A.M. to 8:00 A.M.

"The first point raised by the appellant defendant is that the court erred in refusing defendant's offered instruction C. This instruction stated that the automobile was parked at the owner's own risk if the owner's attention was directed to the printed statement, set out above, on the ticket given him, and that if his attention was so directed the defendant was not liable for the damage to the car.

"The respondent points out that its petition contained a general charge of negligence, and it contends that it is against public policy to permit one serving the public to exempt oneself from liability for one's own negligence. There is some support for respondent's contention in 8 Am. Jur. (2d), paragraph 131, p. 1026, wherein it is said: 'The courts, while recognizing that an ordinary bailee may contract to exempt himself from liability for loss of or damage to the goods, occasioned by his own negligence or that of his employee, exhibit a strong tendency to hold contracts of this character, when entered into by bailees in the course of general dealing with the public to be violative of public policy and this tendency becomes more pronounced in the more recent decisions. These bailees, who are termed "professional," as distinguished from "ordinary," bailees, are those who make it their principal business to act as bailees and who deal with the public on a uniform and not an individual basis, such as owners or proprietors of parcel checkrooms, garages, parking stations, and parking lots, carriers, innkeepers, and warehousemen. The basis for denying the right of such bailees to limit their liability for their own negligence is that the public, in dealing with them, lacks practical equality of bargaining power, since it must either accede to the conditions sought to be imposed or else forego the desired service. It is said that a bailee who is performing services for which the public has a substantial need should not be permitted to use this circumstance to coerce the members of the public into contracts of this kind.' . . .

"We are asked by the respondent to follow the foregoing pronouncements by holding that a contract such as this on a parking lot exempting the bailee from liability, is against public policy. . . .

"We do not reach the point raised by the respondent, on the facts before us, as to what public policy is or should be on the subject of such bailments. The established rule of construction of a contract containing provisions exempting one from liability will never be implied to extend to liability for one's own negligence unless such an intention is clearly and explicitly stated. [Citations omitted.]

"The general exculpatory clause does not meet the requirement set out above, and consequently cannot be construed to cover the negligence of the bailee. Nor is the bailee saved by the added statement, 'We do not have an attendant at all times,' for this does not exclude a conclusion that the defendant was negligent in leaving the entrance and exit of the lot open when the lot was not attended. The court therefore did not err in refusing the instruction offered by the defendant relating to the printed matter on the claim check.

"As stated, the petition charges general negligence. Under the pleading the proof of damage to the automobile raised a presumption of negligence, and the burden of going forward with the evidence then shifted to the defendant. [Citations omitted.]

"The fact that the car was stolen did not absolve the defendant, for it was incumbent upon it to present evidence that it had exercised ordinary care to safeguard the automobile from theft. [Citations omitted.]

"Another point raised is that the court erred in refusing to give defendant's offered instruction 'D,' which limited to $200 the amount of damages which the jury might award. This was offered under the theory that the loss came under 419.010, RSMo 1959, V.A.M.S., which limits innkeepers' liability for certain losses to $200. The statute relates to the loss of 'any money, jewelry, wearing apparel, baggage or other property of a guest.' It is contended that the words 'or other property' includes a guest's automobile.

"Under the common law, innkeepers were liable for the loss of their guests' goods, and this was to protect travelers against dishonest practices of innkeepers and their servants. [Citation omitted.] In so far as statutes of this nature are in derogation of the common law, they are to be strictly construed. [Citation omitted.]

"Under the rule or maxim of construction known as ejusdem generis, general words following the enumeration of particular classes of things will be construed as applying to things of the same general nature or class of those enumerated. [Citations omitted.] Applying that rule to the statute in question, the words 'or other property' obviously applied to things carried into the hotel by the guest. It would not include the guest's automobile. For this reason and for the further reason that the defendant under the evidence was nothing more than a bailee for hire, the statute has no application. The court did not err in refusing the offered instruction.

"Another point raised is that the court erred in admitting in evidence a photo copy of a draft by which the plaintiff Assurance Company paid Scott's repair bill. It is contended that this violated the best evidence rule. This assignment of error was not presented in the motion for a new trial, and it is therefore not before us for review. [Citation omitted.]

"The only remaining point which is not disposed of by that which we have heretofore said is that there was no evidence to support the measure of damages instruction as it related to the value of the automobile before and after the theft. We find the evidence of the cost of repairs which restored the automobile to the same condition in which it was prior to the theft sufficient to support the instruction. It should also be noted that there is no claim that the verdict is excessive.

"For the foregoing reasons, we affirm the judgment of the Circuit Court."

[Two judges concur, one not participating.]

In the recent New York case of *Klotz* v. *El Morocco International, Ltd.*,[24] it appeared that:

On Saturday, October 29, 1966, at about 1:00 A.M. plaintiff drove his specially equipped 1965 Cadillac up to El Morocco, the corporate defendant's night club. Other cars were parked at the curb, so plaintiff double-parked his car. A man wearing a French Foreign Legion type uniform, in front of the premises, helped plaintiff and his guests out of the car. Plaintiff testified the uniformed man said he would park the car and that plaintiff should "leave the keys in the ignition." Plaintiff left the car with the motor running and the keys in the ignition and entered El Morocco with his guests, after telling the uniformed man to be careful not to "nick" the car while parking it.

They remained in the club until about 3:00 A.M. When they emerged, the uniformed man handed plaintiff the car keys and said, "The car is gone. It's not here." Plaintiff went back into the club and complained to the *maitre d'*, at whose suggestion and in whose presence plaintiff phoned the police, who had not been previously advised of the car's disappearance. Plaintiff then went outside and walked around the block looking for the car.

On cross-examination plaintiff testified he had been at defendant's club on many prior occasions. In the courtroom, he identified the man with whom he had left the car. Plaintiff did not receive a claim check, nor did

24 56 Misc. 2d 319, 288 N.Y.S.2d 684 (New York City Civ. Ct. 1967).

he pay any fee. He did not tell the man where to park the car. Plaintiff testified without objection he "assumed it would be parked in front of El Morocco." When plaintiff came out of the establishment the uniformed man stated he had parked plaintiff's car on Second Avenue, between 54th and 55th Streets, around the corner from El Morocco, and that it was gone. After plaintiff notified the police, and before their arrival, he again talked to the uniformed man. Plaintiff then walked around the block with a man he described as the uniformed man's assistant, looking for the car without success. Later that night, plaintiff and a police detective toured the area looking for the car, which was never found. . . .

Defendant's witness, Vincent Di Giovanni, the person identified by plaintiff as the uniformed man in front of El Morocco, testified that he was the doorman at El Morocco. He greeted patrons of El Morocco, assisted them out of cabs and cars, called cabs and cars for patrons, and parked cars when asked to by patrons. He wore a uniform which he supplied. He worked several nights a week, always at the door, outside the club. He had no assistants and no one took his place on nights he was not there. No one else parked cars at El Morocco, although sometimes patrons' chauffeurs helped him. He parked about 30 to 35 cars on the night of the incident. He normally parked approximately 60 to 70 cars during a six-day week. Most of the cars were "classy" cars. He knew there was a public parking lot on the same block and a public garage in the area. However, he customarily parked the cars of El Morocco's patrons on 54th Street, west of Second Avenue, in the same block as the club, and also east of Second Avenue, toward First Avenue, and on the west side of Second Avenue, between 54th and 55th Streets. He also parked cars for the patrons of other restaurants in the area.

He confirmed plaintiff's testimony as to what had occurred on plaintiff's arrival at the club except that he testified plaintiff asked him to park the car. After assisting plaintiff and his guests into the club, Di Giovanni drove the car around the corner and parked it on the west side of Second Avenue, between 54th and 55th Streets, at a point which could not be observed from in front of the club. He locked the car, returned to El Morocco and put the keys on an unattended key rack inside the club, with other patrons' car keys. Sometime before 3 A.M., when he went around the corner for another patron's car, he observed plaintiff's car was gone. He thought plaintiff might have taken the car himself. Di Giovanni had been around the corner several times between 1:30 and 3:00 A.M. for other patrons' cars. He had not observed plaintiff's car was missing prior to 2:45 A.M. at the earliest. He returned to El Morocco and saw that plaintiff's keys were still on the rack. He took them off the rack and started looking for the car. When he could not locate it, he went back to El Morocco. Plaintiff was just emerging. He told plaintiff what had happened and gave him the keys. The man who helped plaintiff look for the car was a chauffeur whom Di Giovanni had asked to help because plaintiff was angry and doubted Di Giovanni's word as to what had happened and where he parked the car.[25]

The trial judge, a jury having been waived by the parties, gave judgment for the plaintiff, finding that Di Giovanni was negligent in having left the keys on an unattended rack, although there was no proof that the keys had been removed by anyone except Di Giovanni, and even though it had not been shown that such negligence was the proximate cause of the loss.

On appeal, the judgment for plaintiff was reversed, and judgment directed for defendant. Said the Appellate Term: "[D]efendant exercised that degree of ordinary care required of a bailee for mutual benefit." [26]

In *Continental Insurance Co. v. Meyers Bros. Operations, Inc.*,[27] plaintiff parked his car at Parking Lot Number 7 at Kennedy Airport at a fee of one dollar for each twenty-four hours of parking. The lot is surrounded by a fence, leaving a single opening for ingress and egress where an attendant is on duty at all times. On entry, a ticket is issued, which is to be surrendered by the driver upon leaving the lot. There are large printed signs conspicuously in evidence on the lot advising the customer to lock his car and that the defendant would not assume liability for loss due to theft. The ticket itself bears a more complete limitation and also alludes to the fact that defendant merely intends to grant a "license to park."

Upon returning to the parking lot after an absence of a week, he found his car missing. Defendant could offer no explanation for its disappearance.

The court found for the plaintiff, rejecting defendant's contention that the transaction was a mere license instead of a bailment. The use of a three-part ticket, a full-time attendant at a single point of ingress or egress, the obtaining of the license number on each ticket issued, the requirement for identification if the customer's portion of the

[25] *Id.* at 320–323 and 685–689.

[26] *Klotz* v. *El Morocco International, Ltd.*, 312 N.Y.S.2d 60 (Sup. Ct. 1968) (per curiam).

[27] 56 Misc. 2d 435, 288 N.Y.S.2d 756 (New York City Civ. Ct., 1968).

ticket is not returned, the six-foot wire fence; the provision for parking 3,500 cars for a fixed daily rate were held all to negate the theory
of a mere license.

See also *Liberty Mutual Insurance Co.* v. *Meyers Bros. Operations,
Inc.,*[28] where on facts similar to those in *Continental,* the court gave
judgment to plaintiff holding that the circumstances gave rise to a
bailment.

In Illinois, self-service parking lots have fared better in obtaining
immunity from liability for loss of automobiles. In *Wall* v. *Airport
Parking Co.,*[29] plaintiff car owner parked his car on an airport parking
lot and retained the ignition key. His only contact with the parking-lot
employee was on making payment upon leaving the lot. The court
held that there was no bailment, but merely a lease of land so that
although the plaintiff's car concededly disappeared the burden of
proof was on the plaintiff owner to prove defendant's negligence. The
court found that such negligence was not shown by the mere disappearance of the car.

20:4 *Liability for Loss of Articles Left in Automobiles*

In *Gresham* v. *Lyon,*[30] plaintiff, a guest in defendant's hotel, sued to
recover the value of luggage stolen from his car, which was parked in
the hotel garage, situated three hundred yards from the hotel. The
court denied plaintiff recovery on two grounds. While the garage was
infra hospitium with respect to the car, the court held it was not so
with respect to the luggage.

The court was of the opinion that the garage was not a place in
which a guest usually stores luggage and that the innkeeper at most
permitted (as distinct from having invited), the guest to leave his
baggage there. Permission is not an act which serves to extend the
hospitium of an inn.

As for a second ground, the court found that the plaintiff was contributorily negligent in leaving the luggage in the trunk of his car.

Generally, the liability of a bailee for hire for the loss or damage to
personal articles left in an automobile is made to depend on the

[28] 315 N.Y.S.2d 196 (New York City Civ. Ct. 1970).
[29] 40 Ill. 2d 506, 244 N.E.2d 190 (1969).
[30] [1951] 1 W.L.R. 1100 (D.B.).

presence of notice or knowledge of such articles.[31] The notice necessary need not be actual or express.

The courts have shown little hesitation in making an innkeeper liable for the loss of a car's contents. Where the car has been held to be *infra hospitium*, its contents have also been held *infra hospitium*, without need for specific notice.[32] Where the liability has been based on a bailment theory, the bailment has been held to include such items as a traveler may "reasonably be expected to leave in the car such accessories, equipment and baggage as they had no occasion to use while at the hotel." [33] The damages may even include cost of alternative transportation for the plaintiff.[34]

In the New York case of *Lader* v. *Warsher*,[35] the court held that, where a guest himself parked his automobile in the parking lot provided free of charge for that purpose, the car had not been placed *infra hospitium* and the hotelkeeper was not liable as insurer for personal articles rifled during the night from the automobile. The court suggested that the hotel's liability in such cases would have to be on a theory other than insurance liability, probably on a bailment theory.

In the more recent case of *Schibilia* v. *Kiamesha Concord, Inc.*,[36] the plaintiff's car was damaged while in the defendant hotelkeeper's garage. The court decided the case in favor of plaintiff on a theory of bailment and stated that the return of the car to plaintiff in damaged condition created a prima facie case of negligence, shifting to defendant the burden of coming forward with proof.

These cases are authorities for the proposition that in New York

---

[31] For a recent Canadian case dealing with this problem, see *George* v. *Williams*, [1956] 5 D.L.R. 2d 21, where the court held that a car parked by plaintiff in the hotel's parking lot was *infra hospitium* but its contents, which were stolen, were not. The only articles within a car for which an innkeeper was to be held liable were those associated with a car such as "cushions and knee-robes." For a criticism of this decision, see Comment, 34 *Can. Bar Rev.* 1203 (1956).

[32] Annot., 27 A.L.R.2d 796 (1953). See also *Hallman* v. *Federal Parking Services, Inc.*, 134 A.2d 382 (D.C. Mun. App. 1957).

[33] *Park-O-Tell Co.* v. *Roskamp*, 203 Okla. 493, 223 P.2d 375 (1950).

[34] *Campbell* v. *Portsmouth Hotel Co.*, 91 N.H. 390, 20 A.2d 644 (1941) (per curiam). This was an action for negligence in care of automobile left by plaintiff with defendant hotel company. The car was stolen. The court held that the contract of bailment included both the car and its contents.

[35] 165 Misc. 559, 1 N.Y.S.2d 160 (Columbia County Ct. 1937).

[36] 16 App. Div. 2d 504, 229 N.Y.S.2d 729 (3d Dep't 1962).

an automobile parked outside the hotel proper is not regarded *infra hospitium* and in the event of loss or damage do not subject the innkeeper to insurance liability.

In *Swarth* v. *Barney's Clothes, Inc.*,[37] a parking-lot operator was held not liable for the loss of a sum of money in a wallet which was left on the seat of a car and concerning which he had no notice. Said the court:

[A parking-lot operator who accepts an automobile for parking becomes its bailee and assumes the liabilities flowing from that relation.] It by no means follows, however, that [he] thereby also undertook the bailment of the wallet [containing $350 in cash], whose presence in the car was neither disclosed nor reasonably to be expected. Delivery, actual or constructive, to the person sought to be held as bailee is not enough to create a bailment; acceptance, actually or constructively, by the [bailee] is equally essential. [Citations omitted.] Acceptance is absent when the property is not such as is usually and customarily left with a custodian in like circumstances and no disclosure of this fact is made. In that situation, the person sought to be charged as bailee having no reason to suppose the property has been delivered to him, is liable only if on express notice, "for the bailee cannot by artifice be compelled to assume a liability greater than he intended." [Citation omitted.] Self-evidently valuable and easily stolen articles are not left in parked automobiles, and the operator of a parking lot, without notice that they have been so left, is not liable as bailee in respect to them. [Citations omitted.] [38]

20:5 *Apparent Authority of Hotel or Motel Employees*

A frequently litigated issue in these cases, whether the ultimate decision is based on a strict liability or on a bailee theory, is that of the extent of the "authority" of the employee who takes control of the car. Does a footman or bellboy who hands a guest a check for his car,[39] or suggests to him that the hotel has made arrangements for parking,[40] have the authority to do so, thus binding the hotel to a

---

[37] 40 Misc. 2d 423, 242 N.Y.S.2d 922 (Sup. Ct. 1963).

[38] *Id.* at 424 and 923.

[39] *Campbell* v. *Portsmouth Hotel Co.*, 91 N.H. 390, 20 A.2d 644 (1941) (per curiam).

[40] *Bidlake* v. *Shirley Hotel Co.*, 133 Colo. 166, 292 P.2d 749 (1956). The guest delivered his car keys to the night porter wearing the hotel's uniform. The porter

relationship in which the hotel is eventually held liable for the loss of or damage to the car? With but few exceptions,[41] the courts have stated that the "apparent authority" of such employees is sufficient to bind the hotel. The guest is under no duty to search behind the uniform to find whether or not the employee has actual authority.[42] Even the fact that the employee was expressly forbidden to take control of the car has been held not sufficient to save the innkeeper from liability.

---

took the car for a "joy ride," damaged it and also took some personal property from the glove compartment. The court held the hotel liable to the guest; the porter had at least apparent authority to accept the car. In *Todd v. Natchez-Eola Hotels Co.*, 171 Miss. 577, 157 So. 703 (1934), plaintiff left his car in care of the attendant in a parking lot operated by the defendant hotel. The attendant took the car for a ride and wrecked it. The court held that the defendant was the agent of the hotel even though he received his pay in tips. His taking the car from its place of safekeeping violated the hotel's duty as a bailee. See also *Zurich Fire Ins. Co. v. Weil*, 259 S.W.2d 54 (Ky. 1953).

[41] In *Smith v. Robinson*, 300 S.W. 651 (Tex. Civ. App. 1927), the guest's car was taken from the garage by a bellboy, and was damaged. In an action against the hotel for the recovery of the damage, the court held that the hotel doorman who was authorized to inquire as to the garaging of the car had not only apparent, but actual authority to store the car, and that the hotel was estopped from denying his authority. See also *Merchants Fire Assurance Corp. v. Zion's Securities Corp.*, 109 Utah 13, 163 P.2d 319 (1945).

[42] In *Andrews v. Southwestern Hotel Co.*, 184 Ark. 982, 44 S.W.2d 675 (1931), the plaintiff registered at defendant's hotel and inquired as to garage facilities. The clerk told plaintiff that a bellboy would take charge of the car and drive it to the garage. The bellboy damaged the car. The court held that in order to recover, the plaintiff had to prove that the clerk on duty authorized or directed the bellboy to take charge of plaintiff's car. In *Andrew Jackson Hotel, Inc. v. Platt*, 19 Tenn. App. 360, 89 S.W.2d 179 (1935), the guest arranged with defendant's doorman to have the guest's car sent to a garage to have the car repaired. While being driven back from the garage by one of the garage hands, the car was damaged. In an action against the hotel for recovery of the damage, the court held that the doorman acted as the agent of the guest in transmitting the latter's request that the car be repaired, and not as the hotel's agent. In *Smith v. Hotel Antler's Co.*, 126 Ind. App. 385, 133 N.E.2d 89 (1956), the guest's car was damaged while being driven by a bellboy. The car keys were given to the bellboy at a party to which he had been invited by the guest and while he was out of uniform. In an action against the hotel, the court held that the bellboy was acting as the guest's agent and not that of the hotel. Of the three cases, only the Arkansas decision is an exception to the general rule of imputing at least apparent authority to a bellboy, doorman, or porter. The other two cases can be limited to their respective fact situations.

20:6 Agreement between Hotel and Independent Garage

Where a hotel does not have its own facilities for parking a car, it usually arranges with a private garage or parking-lot operator for space in which to park its guests' cars. The private arrangement made by the hotel and the garageman in no way intrudes upon the relationship between the guest and the hotel. It is immaterial that only the garage's employees are permitted to collect the cars, or to take payment,[43] or whether the garage pays for this service or not.[44] The garageman is usually considered the innkeeper's agent in his relations with the guest.[45] Indeed, in one case where the plaintiff-guest sued both the innkeeper and the parking-lot operator, the court held that only the innkeeper was liable.[46]

20:7 Limiting Liability by Contract

The general rule in the United States is that a bailee of an automobile, whether he is a garage keeper, a parking-lot operator, or an innkeeper, cannot limit his liability for negligence by contract.[47]

[43] Bidlake v. Shirley Hotel Co., 133 Colo. 166, 292 P.2d 749 (1956); Smith v. Robinson, 300 S.W. 651 (Tex. Civ. App. 1927).

[44] Id.

[45] In most cases the hotel receives a payment for sending cars to a garage. See Kallish v. Meyer Hotel Co., 182 Tenn. 29, 184 S.W.2d 45 (1944). Even where no payment is made to the hotel the courts assume that a hotel derives some benefit from being able to extend a parking service to its guests. See Hallman v. Federal Parking Services, Inc., 134 A.2d 382 (D.C. Mun. App. 1957); Zurich Fire Ins. Co. v. Weil, 259 S.W.2d 54 (Ky. 1953). Often the hotel's employees are instructed that they are not to drive the cars to the garage, that the garage keeper will supply the drivers. These arrangements do not prevent the imposition of liability on the hotel, as the guest is not charged with knowledge of these "internal arrangements." See Bidlake v. Shirley Hotel Co., 133 Colo. 166, 292 P.2d 749 (1956).

[46] Kallish v. Meyer Hotel Co., 182 Tenn. 29, 184 S.W.2d 45 (1944). Private garage with which hotel had an arrangement to park its guests' cars turned plaintiff's car over to another person. The garageman was held to be the hotel's agent and therefore the hotel was held liable for damages caused by its agent's negligence.

[47] Hallman v. Federal Parking Services, Inc., 134 A.2d 382 (D.C. Mun. App. 1957).

In some states this prohibition is regulated by statute.[48] In any event, the courts have looked with disfavor upon contracts printed on the back of claim checks or notices on walls.[49] These prohibitions do not affect the applicability of statutes limiting such liability.[50]

20:8 Statutory Limitations of Liability

In the United States, all states have statutory provisions limiting the liability of an innkeeper for loss of his guest's property. A question arises as to the applicability of such statutes to a guest's car and its contents.

At the present time few states have dealt with this issue. The Oklahoma Supreme Court held that the language of the Oklahoma statute, declaratory of the common law, was broad enough to encompass both a car and its contents as "property." [51] Kentucky has held that a hotel statute limiting recovery for loss of or damage to a guest's property did not apply to any action based on negligence. This decision may be limited to the state, however, as it was based on a provision of the Kentucky constitution which prohibits limitations in negligence actions.[52]

[48] See 9 Williston *Contracts* 1069 (rev. ed. 1967) (semble); *Hallman* v. *Federal Parking Services, Inc.*, 134 A.2d 382 (D.C. Mun. App. 1957).

[49] *Klar* v. *H. & M. Parcel Room, Inc.*, 270 App. Div. 538, 61 N.Y.S.2d 285 (1st Dep't 1946), *aff'd mem.*, 296 N.Y. 1044, 73 N.E.2d 912 (1947).

[50] N.Y. Gen. Obl. Law §5–325 (McKinney 1964) disables garage keepers and parking-lot operators from making agreements exempting them from liability for negligence.

[51] *Park-O-Tell Co.* v. *Roskamp*, 203 Okla. 493, 223 P.2d 375 (1950). The relevant statutory language reads: "An innkeeper or keeper of a boarding house is liable for all losses of or injuries to, personal property placed by his guests or boarders under his care, unless occasioned by an irresistible superhuman cause, by a public enemy, by the negligence of the owner, or by the act of someone whom he brought into the inn or boardinghouse, and upon such property the innkeeper of a boarding house has a lien and a right of detention for the payment of such amount as may be due him for lodging, fare, boarding or other necessaries by such guest or boarder; and the said lien may be enforced by a sale of the property in the manner prescribed for the sale of pledged property." 15 Okla. Stat. Ann. §501 (1941).

[52] *Zurich Fire Ins. Co.* v. *Weil*, 259 S.W.2d 54 (Ky. 1953). The relevant statutory language reads: "*Injuries to person or property; recovery not limited—* The general assembly shall have no power to limit the amount to be recovered

The application of these statutory limitations to a car and its contents may be of increasing importance in light of the great increase in the number of motels. Thus far, none of the statutes has been made applicable directly to a guest's car.

---

for injuries resulting in death, or for injuries to personal property." Ky. Const. §54.

CHAPTER 21

Exceptions to the General Rule Governing Innkeeper's Responsibility for Property

21:1 Losses Chargeable to Guest

The innkeeper is not liable for losses chargeable in any way to the guest himself. Thus, the innkeeper is not liable for property of his guest stolen by the guest's own servant or roommate,[1] or by one authorized by the guest to handle the goods.

Similarly, where the guest gives explicit directions as to the care of the goods, and the loss happens through following such directions, the innkeeper is not liable. In *Owens* v. *Geiger*,[2] the facts, as stated by the court, were that the defendant was an innkeeper, and the plaintiff "delivered his horse to him to be kept till his return, as he was going to foreign parts; that Owens agreed with Geiger as to the feeding and keeping of the horse till his return, for which Owens was to pay a reasonable reward"; and "that Owens told Geiger that he wished his horse to run in his yard in the daytime, his leg being swelled." Owens' horse was put into the yard, jumped out and escaped, and was lost. The court held an instruction to the jury that "if they believed that Owens' horse was put into the defendant's yard by Owens' direction, and that the horse escaped therefrom without negligence on the part of Geiger, then they must find for the defendant," to be correct. And so where the guest gives the goods, not to the innkeeper or to his servant as such, but to another guest or other inmate in whom he reposes confidence, and the goods are embezzled, the innkeeper is not liable.[3]

---

[1] *Calye's Case,* 77 Eng. Rep. 520 (K.B. 1584).   [2] 2 Mo. 39 (1828).
[3] *Houser* v. *Tully,* 62 Pa. 92 (1869).

21:2 *Contributory Negligence of Guest*

The loss of goods is most commonly chargeable to the guest himself by reason of contributory negligence on the part of the guest. A guest cannot recover for the loss of his goods from an inn if his own negligence contributed to the loss. And the care required of the guest must not be such care as will cause him serious personal inconvenience; the innkeeper cannot call upon the guest seriously to inconvenience himself in such a matter.[4] A fortiori the guest cannot be called upon to run into danger.[5]

Whether the negligence of the guest did contribute to the loss is a question of fact; [6] and the burden of proof of this fact is on the innkeeper.[7] If the innkeeper might subsequently have avoided the effect of the guest's negligence but failed to do so, he cannot escape liability.[8]

In *Medawar* v. *Grand Hotel Company,*[9] the plaintiff sued the defendant innkeeper for the loss of certain jewelry. The plaintiff came to the inn and found it full, with the exception of one room which had been engaged in advance by another person. The plaintiff, however, was allowed to dress in the room, and keep it until the arrival of the person who had engaged it. He went to the room, opened his bag, and took out a stand which contained various implements for the toilet and the trinkets for the loss of which he sued. After he finished dressing he went out, leaving the stand on the dressing table and the door of the room unlocked, and left the inn to attend the races. While he was absent the person who had engaged the room arrived, and, in order to clear the room for his occupancy, the stand with the plaintiff's other luggage was placed in the corridor, where it remained until the plaintiff's return, that night. While the luggage was in the corridor the jewelry was stolen. The High Court held that the inn-

---

[4] *Maltby* v. *Chapman,* 25 Md. 310 (1866).

[5] *Jefferson Hotel Co.* v. *Warren,* 128 F. 565 (2d Cir. 1904).

[6] Of course the facts may be so clear that the court will decide the question without leaving it to the jury. *Lanier* v. *Youngblood,* 73 Ala. 587 (1883).

[7] *Jefferson Hotel Co.* v. *Warren,* 128 F. 563 (2d Cir. 1904).

[8] *Watson* v. *Loughran,* 112 Ga. 837, 38 S.E. 82 (1901) (discovered that the guest left door unlocked and yet did not lock it); *Medawar* v. *Grand Hotel Company,* [1891] 2 Q.B. 11 (C.A.) (discovered door unlocked and removed goods to public corridor).

[9] [1891] 2 Q.B. 11 (C.A.).

keeper was not liable, but the Court of Appeals reversed the decision. On the point here under discussion Lord Esher, Master of the Rolls, remarked:

[T]here was contributory negligence on the part of the plaintiff while the goods were in the room; but, when the defendants' servants went into the room and became aware of the plaintiff's negligence, they were bound to take reasonable care of the property. When they saw the negligence of the plaintiff they ought to have taken care not to be negligent themselves. If the jewellery was stolen while it was in the corridor, it was stolen not in consequence of the plaintiff's negligence, but by reason of the defendants' negligence.[10]

The negligence must of course have to do with the loss of the goods themselves; and evidence of careless conduct by the guest either before or after the time he was at the inn will not be received.[11]

It is obvious that the question is the same whether the owner of the goods is guest, boarder, or lodger, since contributory negligence will bar them all. The cases of all will therefore be considered together.

21:3   What Is Contributory Negligence?—Failure to Lock Door or Window

In accordance with the general doctrine, it is a question of fact in each case whether a failure upon the part of the guest to lock his door at night constitutes such negligence as to prevent him from recovering from the innkeeper the value of the goods stolen from his room; and it is a question for the jury unless the facts are so plain that the court will not leave it to the jury.

In one case a lodger in a city lodginghouse left his door unlocked, when he knew that the outer door was not locked so that anyone could enter the house. He was held to be barred by his own negligence from recovering for goods lost from his room.[12] This situation presents a weaker argument for recovery than the ordinary case for two reasons. First, since this involved a lodginghouse, the lodger could recover only on the ground of the landlord's negligence, viz., leaving the outer door unlocked, yet here plaintiff knew of and might have guarded against defendant's negligence. Second, in the situation

<hr>

[10] Id. at 22.   [11] Burrows v. Trieber, 21 Md. 320 (1864).
[12] Swann v. Smith, 14 Daly 114 (N.Y. Ct. C.P. 1887).

involving an ordinary inn where the outer door is unlocked, the innkeeper or his servant is usually on the watch to keep out thieves.

In a few cases the court has held, upon the whole evidence (usually
after a verdict for the plaintiff), that failure to lock a door was not
negligence.[13] And in one case where the innkeeper directed the guest
not to lock the door, as other persons were to go into the same room,
the court without leaving the question to the jury decided that the
guest who left the door unlocked was not thereby barred from recovery.[14]

In a case in Illinois (where the innkeeper is not responsible without negligence) it was held that a guest cannot recover where the
evidence shows that he probably left the door unlocked, and that he
failed to deposit his valuables in the office in accordance with the requirements of a notice which he saw.[15]

In most cases, however, it has been held that the failure to lock
the door is sufficient evidence of contributory negligence to go to the
jury; and that the jury is to determine the fact upon that and all
the other evidence,[16] and a dismissal of the suit by the judge on the
ground of contributory negligence, without leaving the question to
the jury, is erroneous.[17]

All the circumstances are to be considered by the jury in determining this fact; as, for instance, that the inn was a London inn,
where bad characters might be expected to seek entry,[18] or that the
valuable goods or money had been publicly displayed.[19]

In a Missouri case it was said:

The fact of the guest having the means of securing himself and not choosing
to use them, is one which, with the other circumstances of the case, should
be left to the jury. It should not be singled out and put to the jury as a

[13] *Mitchell* v. *Woods,* 16 L.T.R. (n.s.) 676 (Exch. 1867); *Buddenburg* v.
Benner, 1 Hilt. 84 (N.Y. Ct. C.P. 1856) (boardinghouse); *Cunningham* v.
Bucky, 42 W. Va. 671, 26 S.E. 442 (1896).

[14] *Milford* v. *Wesley,* 1 Wilson (Ind.) 119 (1872).

[15] *Hulbert* v. *Hartman,* 79 Ill. App. 289 (1898).

[16] *Oppenheim* v. *White Lion Hotel Co.,* L.R. 6 C.P. 515 (1871); *Ramaley* v.
Leland, 6 Robt. 358 (N.Y. Super. Ct. 1868); *Becker* v. *Warner,* 90 Hun. 187,
35 N.Y. 739 (Sup. Ct. 1895); *Shultz* v. *Wall,* 134 Pa. 262, 19 A. 742 (1890).

[17] *Classen* v. *Leopold,* 2 Sweeney 705 (N.Y. Super. Ct. 1870).

[18] *Filipowski* v. *Merryweather,* 175 Eng. Rep. 1063 (Nisi Prius, 1860).

[19] *Oppenheim* v. *White Lion Hotel Co.,* L.R. 6 C.P. 515 (1871); *Dunbier* v.
Day, 12 Neb. 596, 12 N.W. 109 (1882).

test of negligence. The question is, whether the loss would or would not have happened if the plaintiff had used the ordinary care that a prudent man might reasonably be expected to have taken under the circumstances. [Citations omitted.] The jury are not to be told that, if by reasonable care the plaintiff might have locked his door and did not do so, this is such negligence as to exonerate the inn-keeper, if the loss occurred through leaving the door unlocked.[20]

Failure of the guest, after locking the door, to bolt it, when he did not see the bolt nor have it called to his attention, is so clearly not contributory negligence that the court will not allow the jury to pass on the question, but will direct the jury that such failure will not defeat the action.[21] In a Massachusetts case the court said:

It must often depend much upon the circumstances of the case, the customs of the age and country, and the usages of the place, whether the plaintiff has been guilty of such negligence that the loss can be said to be attributable to it; and we cannot say, as matter of law, that, on the facts appearing in this case, if the plaintiff saw the bolt and did not use it, this was not some evidence of negligence to be submitted to the jury. The delivery of a key to a guest may be held to be an intimation to him that he is to use it in locking his door. The lock, however, is the only fastening which the guest can use when he is not in the room. A bolt, if seen, may itself suggest that it ought to be used. If, however, there are no regulations brought to the notice of a guest requesting him to bolt the door, and if it is not known to the guest that there is a bolt, and his attention is not in any way called to it, we are of the opinion that the fact that, after locking his door with the key, he does not search for a bolt and find it, is not evidence of negligence on his part.[22]

A new trial was granted, after a verdict for the defendant, by reason of the failure of the judge to direct the jury as the plaintiff requested.

On the other hand, where the guest saw the bolts, failure to use them was relied on as one element of negligence to bar his recovery.[23] Failure to notify the innkeeper that the lock is out of repair is not negligence on the part of the guest.[24]

[20] *Batterson v. Vogel,* 10 Mo. App. 235, 239 (1881).
[21] *Spring v. Hager,* 145 Mass. 186, 13 N.E. 479 (1887).
[22] *Id.* at 191 and 482.   [23] *Hulbert v. Hartman,* 79 Ill. App. 289 (1898).
[24] *Lanier v. Youngblood,* 73 Ala. 587 (1883).

COHEN v. JANLEE HOTEL CORP.
276 App. Div. 67, 92 N.Y.S.2d 852 (1st Dep't 1949),
rev'd mem., 301 N.Y. 736, 95 N.E.2d 410 (1950)

[Anna Cohen sued the Janlee Hotel Corporation for damages for loss of plaintiff's coat from a room that plaintiff occupied as a guest in defendant's hotel].

DORE, J.: "By the determination of Appellate Term appealed from, affirming judgment in plaintiff's favor after nonjury trial in the Municipal Court, defendant has been held liable in damages for loss of plaintiff's Persian Lamb fur coat from the room she occupied as a guest in defendant's hotel. The trial court granted plaintiff judgment on the merits for $250 and judgment with interest and costs was entered in plaintiff's favor for $315.75.

"At common law an innkeeper was liable as an insurer of the property of guests lost by theft unless the loss was occasioned by the negligence or fault of the guest. [Citations omitted.]

"Plaintiff admitted that on January 27, 1946, at 10:00 P.M. she undressed in her hotel room, suite 1206, and went to bed leaving the door of her room unlocked. She deliberately left the door unlocked so as to avoid the inconvenience of getting up to open the door for her girlfriend who shared the room with her and who was coming in later. Plaintiff had all the room lights lit and sat up in bed intending to read the papers while waiting for her friend, but later she fell asleep; and when she awoke about midnight, her Persian Lamb fur coat which she had in the closet of the room had disappeared.

"The hotel is a large metropolitan hotel, to the corridors of which thousands of persons necessarily have access. Defendant's evidence showed that there were 1,500 rooms in the hotel, accommodating about 2,300 guests at night; that in the month in question there was a check-out of 300 or 400 guests a day; that several thousand persons passed through the hotel during an average business day and ten or fifteen hundred persons used the ballrooms in the hotel; and that all of such persons had access to all the floors in the hotel. The hotel employed sixteen officers, seven in plain clothes and nine in uniform, and the latter patrolled the floors and observed hotel room doors after midnight; and if doors were found unlocked the guests were requested to lock them, and in the absence of the guest the doors are locked by the house officer.

"The action was for breach of contract of bailment, but there was no proof of bailment. The fur coat at the time of the loss was in plaintiff's room and in plaintiff's exclusive custody and control. [Citation omitted.] Under the circumstances disclosed, plaintiff in failing to take the simple ordinary precaution of locking the door of her room before she went to bed when she knew she had in the room a valuable fur coat, acted in a manner that facilitated the theft and was guilty of contributory negligence; on this record such negligence was at least a contributing cause of the loss. [Citation omitted.]

"In supplemental briefs requested by the court, both parties concede that Section 201 of the General Business Law is not herein applicable.

"Accordingly, we vote to reverse the determination of the Appellate Term and the judgment of the Municipal Court and to dismiss the complaint."

SHIENTAG, J. (concurring in result): "I concur in the result and vote for reversal and dismissal of the complaint on the ground that the implied finding of the trial court that the plaintiff was free from contributory negligence is against the weight of the evidence."

COHN and CALLAHAN, JJ. (dissenting): "Whether there was contributory negligence was a question of fact for the trial court. As there was sufficient evidence to sustain the findings of the trial court to the effect that plaintiff was not guilty of contributory negligence, we vote to affirm the determination of the Appellate Term."

[Van Voorhis, J., concurs with Dore, J.; Shientag, J., concurs in result in memorandum; Cohn and Callahan, JJ., dissent and vote to affirm the determination of the Appellate Term, in opinion.

The Court of Appeals reversed the Appellate Division on the ground that the question as to plaintiff's contributory negligence was one of fact and not of law and remitted the case to the Appellate Division for determination upon the questions of fact raised in that court. Thereupon the Appellate Division made the order and judgment of the Court of Appeals its own order and judgment, and reversed the determination of the Appellate Term and the judgment of the Municipal Court, and dismissed the complaint.]

21:4 *Failure to Deliver Valuables to Innkeeper*

In the absence of special circumstances, it is not negligence to leave the goods in a public room in the inn, if it is with the assent of the innkeeper or his servants, even though the innkeeper informed the guest that the goods would be safer elsewhere. Thus where the goods were left in the lobby of the inn and were lost, the innkeeper was liable.[25]

In one case an innkeeper, as his guest was about to go to bed, remarked to him that he had better take his valise to his room. The guest replied that it was not necessary that his valise would be safe in the barroom. The valise was allowed to remain in the barroom overnight but on the next morning was gone and could not be found. The court held that the keeper was liable for its loss.[26]

Where, however, the guest's act is not expressly permitted by the innkeeper, though known to him, the question of liability is for the jury. Thus where the guest laid down a valuable pair of gloves on a bench in a public room in the presence of the innkeeper, and they were lost, the question of contributory negligence might be determined by the jury.[27]

The fact that a custom exists to deposit valuables with the innkeeper does not render the guest negligent for not doing so, if the custom was unknown to him; though if he knew of it, it might be negligent for him to fail to comply with it.[28]

Where, however, the guest has express notice that he takes the risk of loss if he does not deposit his valuables with the innkeeper, he is negligent if he fails to comply with the notice.[29] Thus where a guest saw a notice to the effect that " 'The proprietor will be happy to take charge of any valuables,' " it was held negligent for the guest to leave money in a bag in his room, and he was not allowed to recover for the loss of it.[30] Piggott, B., said: "The invitation embodied in the notice was equivalent to a warning of risk. After that warning it was

25 *Clarke* v. *Hotel Taft Corp.*, 128 N.Y.L.J. No. 53, 478 (N.Y. City Ct. 1952).
26 *Packard* v. *Northcraft's Adm'r*, 59 Ky. (2 Met.) 439 (1859).
27 *Read* v. *Amidon*, 41 Vt. 15 (1868).
28 *Berkshire Woollen Co.* v. *Proctor*, 61 Mass. (7 Cush.) 417 (1851).
29 *Jalie* v. *Cardinal*, 35 Wis. 118 (1874).
30 *Jones* v. *Jackson*, 29 L.T.R. (n.s.) 399 (Exch. 1873).

negligent in the plaintiff to leave his property as he did"; and Bramwell, B., characterized the plaintiff's conduct as "most careless." [31] So where the guest asked if the goods would be safe in his room, and he was told he must leave them at the bar, but notwithstanding this warning he kept them in his room and they were lost, he was barred from recovery by his negligence.[32]

The notice, in order to impose the risk of loss upon the guest, must be clear; and other courts might perhaps have decided differently on the facts of the English case just stated. A notice that packages of value may be deposited in the office safe, and cautioning guests against leaving money or valuables in a guest's room, was held in a New York case insufficient to put the risk of loss of goods left in the room upon a guest:

This may very well have been understood, as Forbes appears to have understood it, as merely cautioning him against leaving money or valuables loose or exposed about his room. If the landlord, to enable him the more effectually to secure the property, requires something to be done by the guest, it must appear that what was required was in itself reasonable, and that the guest was distinctly informed of what was necessary to be done on his part. Whether the request was made orally or in the form of a printed notice, it should be in terms so clear and unmistakable as to leave room for no reasonable doubt as to what was intended. The traveller should know precisely what he is to do before he can be chargeable with negligence for not doing it; and as the notice did not apprize him that he was not to leave money locked up in his trunk, he cannot be regarded as guilty of negligence in so leaving it.[33]

21:5 *Failure to Inform Innkeeper of Value of Goods Deposited*

In the absence of a statutory requirement, it is not negligence to fail to inform the innkeeper that a package put into his possession or that of his servants contains valuables.[34]

[31] *Id.*   [32] *Wilson v. Halpin*, 30 How. Pr. 124 (N.Y. Ct. C.P. 1865).
[33] *Van Wyck v. Howard*, 12 How. Pr. 147, 150–151 (N.Y. Ct. C.P. 1856).
[34] *Sagman* v. *Richmond Hotels, Inc.*, 138 F. Supp. 407 (E.D. Va. 1956); *Stoll* v. *Almon C. Judd Co.*, 106 Conn. 551, 138 A. 479 (1927); *Fowler* v. *Dorlon*, 24 Barb. 384 (N.Y. Sup. Ct. 1856).

21:6 Publicly Exhibiting Money or Valuables

Opening or counting one's money or exhibiting valuable goods in a public place is not of itself such negligence as will bar recovery by the guest,[35] but it is one of the circumstances to be considered by the jury which may find the act negligent.[36] In *Armistead* v. *Wilde*,[37] the plaintiff was a guest at an inn, and had lost from a box which he brought to the inn a parcel containing several hundred pounds in bank notes. Upon the facts being examined, the evidence showed that the plaintiff had boasted of the sum which he possessed, and had ostentatiously rolled up the notes and put them in the box in the travelers' room in the presence of several persons, and had then left the box in the travelers' room, imperfectly secured. One of the persons to whom the plaintiff had shown the notes was probably the thief. The judge directed the jury to find a verdict for the defendant if they thought the plaintiff "had been guilty of gross negligence in leaving the money in the travellers' room"; and the jury accordingly found a verdict of not guilty. The plaintiff had the temerity to move for a new trial on the ground of misdirection, but the rule was discharged. Lord Chief Justice Campbell said:

Suppose a guest were to count out his money and leave it lying loose on the table of the public room; surely that might be such gross negligence as to be the cause of the loss. The facts here do not go so far as that; but there was evidence that the plaintiff's servant, in a public room, took out a large sum of money, counted it and shewed it, and then left it there in a box capable of being opened without using a key. These facts might or might not amount to negligence; but they were evidence of it; and it was a fair question for the jury.[38]

The court also noticed that the judge in his charge had spoken of "gross" negligence, and intimated that this was more favorable to the plaintiff than he had a right to ask.

---

[35] *Dunbier* v. *Day,* 12 Neb. 596, 12 N.W. 109 (1882); *Cunningham* v. *Bucky,* 42 W. Va. 671, 26 S.E. 442 (1896).

[36] *Cashill* v. *Wright,* 119 Eng. Rep. 1096 (Q.B. 1856); *Armistead* v. *Wilde,* 117 Eng. Rep. 1280 (Q.B. 1851).

[37] 117 Eng. Rep. 1280 (Q.B. 1851).   [38] *Id.* at 1281.

21:7 *Intoxication of Guest*

Intoxication of the guest is not in itself contributory negligence, but if it contributes in any way to the loss, it bars the recovery.

CUNNINGHAM *v.* BUCKY
42 W. Va. 671, 26 S.E. 442 (1896)

[Appeal from a judgment for $254.00 obtained by plaintiff against defendant in the Circuit Court of Randolph County.]

DENT, J.: "Plaintiff went to the defendant's hotel, called the 'Valley Hotel,' to stop for a few days at the most. His home was in Virginia. He had an arrangement with defendant to board the mail carrier at reduced rates, and, when stopping there, was accorded these rates himself. On this occasion, he had received payment of a draft; was drinking, and slightly intoxicated; exhibited his money freely; was arrested, fined, and paid the same. Mrs. Bucky, during the day, asked him to let her take charge of his money. This he declined to do, saying he was able to take care of his own money. At night he was assigned to a room which had two outside doors, both of which were locked and bolted. Another door opened in another small room, which communicated with the office through another door. There was no way of fastening the door between the rooms on plaintiff's side, but the door of the outer room which communicated with the office, had a lock on, with a key in it. The son of the proprietor says he gave the key of this door to the plaintiff, but the plaintiff says that he simply told him that the doors between the rooms could not be fastened, but that he would see that the office door was properly fastened, and relying on this statement, he (plaintiff) paid no more attention to the matter. He examined his pocketbook, to see that his money was in it, then placed it down in his coat pocket, and hung his coat on the bedpost, and retired for the night. On awakening in the morning, he noticed the pocketbook had been disturbed, and, on examining it, found his money gone. He got up, went out, found the colored porter, and acquainted Mr. Bucky with his loss. . . .

"It is plainly evident who committed this theft [the court recited testimony indicating that defendant's Negro porter was the thief]; and the sole question is, on whom does the law fix the loss? We have no statute on the subject, and must be governed by the common law. . . .

"There is no question that the plaintiff was a guest at the defendant's hotel, and that while there he was robbed in his room while asleep, from within the defendant's family, including his servants. That he had been drinking, was careless with his money and trusted in the honesty of defendant's household, and refused the services of Mrs. Bucky as to the care of his money, will not excuse the defendant from the dishonesty of those admitted to his employment. . . . As Judge Dixon says in *Jalie* v. *Cardinal,* above cited [35 Wis. 118 (1874)]: 'If drunk, the plaintiff might still have claimed the protection of his host, as did Falstaff when he fell asleep "behind the arras," and might say with him: "Shall I not take mine ease in mine inn, but I shall have my pocket picked?"' . . ."

[Judgment affirmed.]

In *Shultz* v. *Wall,*[39] plaintiff sued for the loss of money which had been stolen while he was a guest in defendant's hotel. It appeared that plaintiff was assigned to a room on the door of which was a lock with key upon the inside, and also an inside sliding bolt. A notice was printed at the head of each sheet of the hotel register, which read as follows: "Money, jewelry and other valuables must be placed in the safe. . . . Otherwise the proprietor will not be responsible for loss." Defendant claimed to have called plaintiff's attention to this notice.

Plaintiff testified that he both locked and bolted his bedroom door before retiring, but that the next morning he found it standing partially open. Plaintiff's vest was found downstairs carefully folded and laid between two lap blankets on the hat rack in the dining room, with the pocket book and everything intact, but the money gone. There was some testimony that plaintiff, though a sober man, was not a total abstainer, and had been drinking that evening. The trial court refused to submit the question of plaintiff's contributory negligence to the jury. On appeal, held, reversed and new trial granted. "[I]t is now held in our own case of *Walsh* v. *Porterfield* [87 Pa. 376 (1878)] that intoxication is no excuse for the negligence of a guest which contributes to his loss." [40]

[39] 134 Pa. 262, 19 A. 742 (1890).   [40] *Id.* at 275 and 744.

21:8 *Loss Caused by Act of God*

In *Wolf Hotel Co.* v. *Parker*,[41] plaintiff was a long-term guest in defendant's hotel. Defendant had stored several of plaintiff's trunks containing a quantity of clothing in a basement room of the hotel. One July evening there was a heavy rainfall, which caused the water from the streets and alleys in the vicinity of the hotel to back up into the basement of the hotel and into the room where the trunks were stored, thus damaging the clothing.

In an action to recover for the damages sustained, the complaint alleged that defendant was negligent in not having traps, valves, or shutoffs installed in the sewer and drain system of the hotel to prevent the street sewer from flooding the basement. The complaint also alleged that defendant was negligent in that it knew that its basement had been flooded several times previously and yet with such knowledge had placed plaintiff's trunks on the floor of the basement, where they were damaged.

Defendant contended that the flood was an act of God against which it could not guard with reasonable precaution; that defendant was merely a gratuitous bailee; and that the damage was due plaintiff's failure to open her trunk after the flood and unpack her apparel.

The trial court instructed the jury, *inter alia,* that an act of God which would excuse defendant from liability must not only be a proximate cause of the loss, but must also be the sole cause thereof; that if the damage was caused by an act of God commingled with the negligence of defendant and would not have occurred except for such negligence, defendant would be liable, unless plaintiff was contributorily negligent; "that if [defendant] knew, or by reasonable diligence could have known, the hotel basement flooded after heavy rainfall, and took no steps to prevent it by placing the usual and common devices to prevent such flooding, or if it placed the trunk of [plaintiff] on the basement floor with such knowledge, and that such devices would have prevented the overflow of the basement, the fact that there was an unusual rainfall would be no defense"; and that it made no difference whether plaintiff was a guest or a roomer, if the damage was caused by defendant's negligence.

[41] 87 Ind. App. 333, 158 N.E. 294 (1927).

After a judgment entered upon a jury verdict for plaintiff, defendant appealed. *Held:* affirmed. There was no error in any of the instructions.

The term "act of God," used to express the cause of loss or damage which will exonerate the innkeeper from all liability for the guest's property, means some casualty resulting from natural or physical causes without the intervention of any human agency. Thus, losses caused by lightning, earthquake, frost, rain, and snowstorms, tornadoes, freezing of canals and rivers, floods, etc., are due to acts of God.

The terms "inevitable accident" and "irresistible force" are sometimes used as synonymous with "act of God", but they lack the suggestion that the loss may be due to causes other than those of human agency, and are, therefore, unsatisfactory. Inevitable accident includes "act of God," but the term "inevitable accident" is not equivalent to "act of God," because inevitable accident may be due solely to human agency. Such are losses by incendiary or accidental fire, robbery, theft, etc.

It has been said that the act of God must have been the proximate cause of the loss. If there has been any intervention of a human agency, the innkeeper is not excused. The true test between these phrases seems to be the entire absence of any human agency in producing the loss.

21:9 *Loss Caused by Acts of the "Public Enemy"*

JOHNSTON *v.* MOBILE HOTEL CO.
27 Ala. App. 145, 167 So. 595 (1936), *cert. denied,* sub nom.
Johnston v. *Mobile Hotel Co.,* 232 Ala. 175, 167 So. 596 (1936)

[Action for loss of property by R. P. Johnston against the Mobile Hotel Company, Inc., from a judgment for defendant, plaintiff appeals.]

RICE, J.: "Appellant was, admittedly, a guest of the hotel; he testified that, while such guest, he was 'held up and robbed,' at the point of a gun, by two men, of the money and valuables on account of the loss of which he sues.

"Both parties submit that the decisive question in the case is 'whether or not an innkeeper . . . is liable at common law for a loss of money and valuables . . . of his guest, occasioned by *robbery* within the inn, without negligence on the part of the innkeeper or his responsible agents.' . . .

"The phrase 'public enemy' is universally understood to mean some power with whom the government is at open war. It does not include robbers. [Citations omitted.] . . .

"If appellant's testimony is to be believed, it is plain that his loss was neither caused by an 'act of God' nor by 'his own act.' And since we have declared a 'robber' not to be included in the phrase 'public enemy,' it appears that appellant is entitled to recover—should the jury believe his testimony. [Citation omitted.]

"Reversed and remanded."

CHAPTER 22

Limitation of Liability
for Loss of Property

22:1 *Limitation of Liability by Rules and Notices*

Like common carriers and others engaged in a public employment,
the innkeeper may make reasonable rules for the conduct of his
business. These rules cannot affect the nature or extent of his obligation, for instance, his liability for loss of goods, since it is imposed by
the common law. They may, however, so far as is reasonable, affect
the conduct of himself and his guests.

22:2 *Rule Requiring Deposit of Goods*

The commonest form of regulation is a rule that valuable packages
must be left at the office to be placed in the safe. So far as this may
be reasonably required of a guest, failure to do so will exonerate the
innkeeper from loss.[1] This is no more than just to the innkeeper; for
since the innkeeper can have no effective control over articles taken
by the guest into his room, he ought where the risk is great to be
allowed to exercise a more direct and efficient control. As Mr. Chief
Justice Day said in the case of *Fuller* v. *Coats:*

To enable the innkeeper to discharge his duty, and to secure the property
of the traveler from loss, while in a house ever open to the public, it may,
in many instances, become absolutely necessary for him to provide special
means, and to make necessary regulations and requirements to be observed
by the guest, to secure the safety of his property. When such means and

[1] *Stanton* v. *Leland,* 4 E.D. Smith 88 (N.Y. Ct. C.P. 1855); *Fuller* v. *Coats,*
18 Ohio St. 343 (1868).

requirements are reasonable and proper for that purpose, and they are brought to the knowledge of the guest, with the information that, if not observed by him, the innkeeper will not be responsible, ordinary prudence, the interest of both parties, and public policy, would require of the guest a compliance therewith; and if he should fail to do so, and his goods are lost, solely for that reason, he would justly and properly be chargeable with negligence. To hold otherwise, would subject the party without fault to the payment of damages to a party for loss occasioned by his own negligence, and would be carrying the liability of innkeepers to an unreasonable extent. [Citations omitted.] [2]

As will be seen in the next chapter, the defense of the innkeeper does not so properly rest upon the neglect of due care by the guest as upon neglect of a more specific duty, that is, the duty of acting in accordance with the innkeeper's directions. The notice of the innkeeper's reasonable rule for the conduct of the guest in this respect puts upon the guest the duty of abiding by the rule; and if the guest neglects the duty of abiding by the innkeeper's reasonable regulation the innkeeper is for that reason exempted from responsibility for the resulting loss.

Liability for the loss of money and valuables is now the subject of statutory limitation in most states. As will be seen in Chapter 23, a guest who fails to deposit his money or valuables in the hotel safe, always assuming that the innkeeper has complied with the statute, may not recover for their loss. An innkeeper is liable for the loss of everything deposited under this notice.[3]

22:3 How Far Deposit Can Be Required

The notice is effective only as to property which can conveniently be left in the safe, not as to property which the guest needs to keep by him; clothing and articles of daily use are not covered by it.[4] For it is obvious that the guest must have these things with him in his room. He cannot go to the innkeeper's office every time he needs an article of clothing to wear or a little money to spend, nor can he withdraw his watch from the safe whenever he desires to know the time. It is,

[2] 18 Ohio St. 343, 351–352 (1868).
[3] *Pinkerton* v. *Woodward*, 33 Cal. 557 (1867).
[4] *Johnson* v. *Richardson*, 17 Ill. 302 (1855); *Milford* v. *Wesley*, 1 Wilson (Ind.) 119 (1872); *Stanton* v. *Leland*, 4 E.D. Smith 88 (N.Y. Ct. C.P. 1855).

therefore, not reasonable to require him to surrender these things to the innkeeper.

It may of course be argued that he might be forced to exercise the option of surrendering them to the innkeeper or of taking upon himself the risk of losing them, as he would do if he carried them with him into the street outside the inn. But it is to be observed that if the innkeeper by means of his notice can force this alternative upon the guest, since the first course is impracticable, he is really forcing the guest to take the risk of loss, or in other words is limiting his own liability by notice, a thing which he is forbidden by law to do. A different problem is presented when a statute requires the guest to surrender goods to the landlord on notice, or else to take the risk of loss. The risk of loss may of course be placed upon the guest by statute, though it cannot be placed upon him by notice or contract of the innkeeper; and it is therefore a mere matter of interpreting the statute in order to discover whether the language of it covers the case. The question so far as it involves the construction of a statute will be discussed in Chapter 23.

22:4 Sufficiency of the Notice

The notice must be given reasonably. Notice given a year previous to the person's becoming a guest is not reasonable.[5]

Notice posted on the door of the guest's chamber was held not to be brought home to the guest unless it was found as a matter of fact that he either saw it or was negligent for not doing so.[6]

The notice must be construed strictly. Thus a notice that "valuables" must be put in the safe had been held not to extend to mineral specimens [7] or to money; [8] and a notice that the guest had better dispose of goods in a certain way is not notice that he must do so in order to hold the landlord responsible.[9]

---

[5] *Lanier* v. *Youngblood,* 73 Ala. 587 (1883).

[6] *Bodwell* v. *Bragg,* 29 Iowa 232 (1870).

[7] *Brown Hotel Co.* v. *Burckhardt,* 13 Colo. App. 59, 56 P. 188 (1899).

[8] *Stanton* v. *Leland,* 4 E.D. Smith 88 (N.Y. Ct. C.P. 1855).

[9] *Packard* v. *Northcraft's Adm'r,* 59 Ky. (2 Met.) 439 (1859).

STANTON v. LELAND
4 E.D. Smith 88 (N.Y. Ct. C.P. 1855)

[Action by plaintiff, as assignee of one Hugh Rose, against defendant innkeepers for the recovery of money lost in defendant's hotel.]

[Rose] became a guest at the Metropolitan hotel in the city of New York, of which the defendants were the proprietors. On reaching the hotel, he made the usual entry of his name in a book at the office, and a room was assigned to him, of which he received the key.

At the head of each page, in the book above mentioned, were plainly printed these words: "Money, jewels, and other valuable packages, must be placed in the safe in the office, otherwise, the proprietors will not be responsible for any loss." A similar notice was embodied in a list of regulations posted upon the door of the room, where there was also a conspicuous card, printed in crimson letters, as follows: "Notice. Money and valuables must be deposited in the office for safe keeping. If the above request should not be complied with, the proprietors will not be responsible. Simeon Leland & Co." Mr. Rose . . . admitted . . . that he observed the notices in the room, but was not certain that the words in the book attracted his attention. He made no deposit of money or valuables at the office, and gave no notice that there was money in his room.

. . . [T]wo days after his arrival at the hotel, he packed and locked his baggage, . . . and also locked his room, and delivered the key [to the desk clerk]. . . . He asked for his bill, stated that his baggage was ready for removal and [stated that he was ready to leave. . . . He was told that his conveyance would not be ready for some hours. He therefore had dinner in the hotel, at the conclusion of which he was apprised that his room had been broken into and that his money and valuables had been removed from his baggage.

The plaintiff recovered judgment in the court below, from which the defendants appealed to this Court.]

INGRAHAM, J.: "The defendants claim to be exempt from liability for money lost by robbery in the hotel, and on two grounds; first, because of the notice given to the guests that they will not be liable for valuables and money, unless deposited in the safe; secondly, because, without such notice, an innkeeper is not liable for money stolen out of a trunk, or for anything beyond necessary articles for a person who is travelling.

"That the carrier or innkeeper cannot limit his liability by a general notice, has been repeatedly adjudged. . . . Whether he may not, by a special agreement entered into by both parties, restrict such liability, it is not necessary now to inquire.

"In some cases of common carriers, the liability has been, both in the English and American courts, so far limited by a notice as to require from the owner a disclosure of the contents of the packages, and in cases of fraud or concealment, with a view to defraud the carrier of his hire, to relieve him from liability to the extent of the intended fraud. But these cases are based upon the supposed right of the carrier to a reward proportionate to the risk. . . .

"The notices in this case were, that the defendants would not be liable for anything of value, unless placed in the safe; and even admitting that they might, by such notice, require the traveller, while he was staying at the hotel, to keep his money in the safe of the establishment, which I do not mean to be understood as adopting as law, yet it could not be that the traveller, while preparing to start on his journey, should be required still to leave money in the safe until he actually leaves the hotel. It was not until he was packing his trunks for his journey that he placed the money in them, and as soon as it was so done, the key of the room was given to the proprietor, with the information that the baggage was ready. I think nothing contained in the notices would answer to limit the innkeeper's liability after he received the key, under such circumstances.

"It is contended that the innkeeper is not liable for money contained in the baggage, and so brought into the hotel without notice of the same being given by the owner. In the case of innkeepers, the liability in this respect is more extended than that of common carriers. They cannot refuse to receive, with the guest, any kind of goods he may bring, but they are bound to receive both, and they are equally liable for the goods while the guest remains. The innkeeper's compensation is his charge to the guest for his board and lodging, and he receives no additional compensation, whether the goods of the guest are of greater or less value. The ground, therefore, upon which a common carrier is not responsible for concealment of money, etc., in baggage, viz., that he is defrauded of his reward for the carriage, is not to be found in examining the liability of the innkeeper.

". . . It can hardly be necessary to cite authorities to show that the innkeeper is liable for money stolen from the guest, when we look at the necessity of the traveller having money with him in travelling, and the like necessity of taking it with him to the inn when he enters it. He is to be protected as to his property while he remains a guest; and as *no extra charge can be made, because he carries money, so no exemption from liability can be claimed,* if the fact of having money is not disclosed to the innkeeper. [Emphasis added.]

"The judgment should be affirmed."

"Daly, J., concurred in affirming the judgment, but filed no opinion."

WOODRUFF, J.: "I concur in the result to which the first judge has arrived in this case. . . .

"But the duty of the innkeeper to keep and protect such property, carries with it the right to provide such reasonable places of deposit within the inn as he may deem most secure; and if the guest will not give up the manual possession of the goods to the innkeeper, to be preserved by him during his stay, in my judgment the traveller takes the risk of loss from any cause happening without the actual fault or negligence of the landlord, or his servants or agents.

"And when it appears that the landlord had provided such place of deposit, and the guest had actual notice thereof, and notice that the landlord required valuables to be delivered into his actual custody to be deposited in such place, the guest was bound to conform to this reasonable requirement. . . .

". . . The protection of the innkeeper by reasonable rules respecting the custody of the goods of the guest while he remains at the inn, is not disfavored in the law, and it is eminently just that he upon whom the responsibility for the safety of the goods doth rest, shall have power to use such guards for that safe keeping as are consistent with the due comfort and convenience of the guest. The clothing of the guest, and articles necessary for his daily use and comfort while remaining, could not, of course, under this view of the subject, be removed from him, so as to interfere with or interrupt that use and convenience. But goods, merchandise and money, in trunks or packages, are, in my opinion, subject to the landlord's reasonable requirement in this respect.

"In the present case . . . the guest . . . saw and read the notices, he was bound to conform to the requirement contained therein, and deposit the package of money with the landlord.

"Had the loss then happened from the neglect of that precaution during his stay at the inn, and before he had given up his room and surrendered the key, and partially placed his trunks, etc., in the defendant's charge, I should have deemed the innkeeper free from responsibility, if free from fault or negligence.

"Judgment affirmed."

VAN WYCK v. HOWARD
12 How. Pr. 147 (N.Y. Ct. C. P. 1856)

[This was an action brought by one Van Wyck against Howard, proprietor of the Irving House, to recover the value of the property stolen from one Forbes while he was there as a guest.]

DALY, J.: "The only point, therefore, to be determined is, whether the plaintiff can recover for the money which was lost.

". . . [In] this case it is insisted that Forbes had notice of the fact that an iron safe was kept in the office of the defendant's hotel; . . . and it is further insisted that the liability of the hotel keeper extends no further than the care for such property as comes under the denomination of baggage; and that the money lost in this case formed no part of the baggage of the guest.

"It appears that Forbes had $450 in his portmanteau; that about 7 o'clock in the evening he locked his portmanteau, and quitted his room, locking the door, and putting the key in his pocket. He returned at 11 o'clock the same evening, and found the portmanteau broken open, its contents strewn about the room, and the money and jewelry gone. A printed notice or card was pasted on the inside of the door of the room, containing among other things, the following: 'Gentlemen are particularly requested to bolt their chamber-doors on retiring for the night, to prevent intrusion from strangers either by design or by mistake, and to lock their doors during the day, and leave the key at the office. They are also cautioned against leaving any money or valuables in their rooms. Packages of value, properly labeled, can be deposited in an iron safe kept in the office.'

". . . Forbes also testified that he had seen the notice, and . . . that he regarded it as merely cautioning lodgers not to leave things about their rooms, carelessly—not as warning them against leaving anything in their portmanteaus; and that he did not think it worth while to put anything downstairs, as it was his intention to leave immediately.

"There can be no doubt of the innkeeper's right to make such regulations in the management of his inn as will more effectually secure the property of his guests and operate as a protection to himself, and that it is incumbent upon the guest, if he means to hold the innkeeper to his responsibility, to comply with any regulations that is [sic] just and reasonable, when he is requested to do so. [Citations omitted.]

". . . And if the defendant in the present case had notified Forbes that he should not leave any money locked up in his trunk, but should deposit it in the iron safe, kept in the office, it may be that the defendant would not have been responsible for its loss. But the printed notice did not advise Forbes that he was not to leave money locked up in his trunk. It merely informed him that packages of value, properly labeled, might be deposited in an iron safe, kept in the office, and cautioned him against leaving money or valuables in his room. This may very well have been understood, as Forbes appears to have understood it, as merely cautioning him against leaving money or valuables loose or exposed about his room. If the landlord, to enable him more effectually to secure the property, requires something to be done by the guest, it must appear that what was required was in itself reasonable, and that the guest was distinctly informed of what was necessary to be done on his part. Whether the request was made orally or in the form of a printed notice, it should be in terms so clear and unmistakable as to leave room for no reasonable doubt as to what was intended. The traveller should know precisely what he is to do before he can be chargeable with negligence for not doing it; and as the notice did not apprize him that he was not to leave money locked up in his trunk, he cannot be regarded as guilty of negligence in so leaving it. . . .

"An innkeeper's liability is not limited, like that of a carrier of passengers, to the care merely of that species of property which comes under the denomination of baggage. The carrier of passengers performs a distinct employment. He undertakes to transport the passenger and his baggage. The baggage is what travellers usually carry with them, or what is essential or necessary to the traveller in the course of his journey. The care of it is incident to and forms a part of the contract for the carriage of the passenger, for which the carrier is compensated by the fare or rate agreed upon. But for anything beyond mere baggage the carrier is entitled to extra compensation; it is not embraced or compensated for in the fare paid by the passenger; and if he has anything with him, not coming under the denomination of baggage, of which the carrier is not advised, or for the carriage of which he receives nothing, it is at the risk of the passenger, and the carrier is not liable in the event of its loss. But the occupation of the innkeeper is different. He keeps a place of entertainment for the reception of all who travel . . . where provision is made, not merely for the personal entertainment of the guest, but for the housing and safekeeping of the property he brings with him, while he rests or reposes at the inn.

". . . The proprietors of such establishments . . . are under no obligation to receive a traveller with merchandise, and may, if they think proper, refuse to house or take care of it. But whatever may be the nature of the inn, or the kind of accommodation afforded, if the innkeeper receives the guest and his goods, he charges himself with their safe-keeping. The moment the goods are *infra hospitium,* the liability of the innkeeper attaches, and that liability extends to goods, chattels, and movables of any kind or description which the traveller brings with him. [Citations omitted.]

"The defendant, therefore, was chargeable with the safe-keeping of Forbes' portmanteau and all that it contained; and even if the defendant's liability extended no further than the care of the luggage of his guests, the money lost would come within what is usually known as baggage. . . .

"The plaintiff is entitled to judgment of $482."

Stanton v. *Leland* and *Van Wyck* v. *Howard* represent the common law as it existed prior to the enactment of Sections 200 *et seq.* of the General Business Law. The statute enacted in 1855 was not pleaded or referred to in either case.

In *Sanders* v. *Spencer:* [10]

One Spencer, an innkeeper . . . was sued . . . by one Sanders, for a piece of cloth stolen out of the inn by some delinquents. And he for his

[10] 73 Eng. Rep. 591 (Q.B. 1566).

excuse shewed that he gave warning to the plaintiff that he should lay his goods in packs in a certain chamber within the inn, under a lock and key provided for that purpose, and that if he would do so he would undertake to warrant them safe, otherwise not, but he, notwithstanding the said admonition, laid them in an outer court at large, where they were stolen by the default of the plaintiff himself, &c, upon which the plaintiff demurred in law. And the opinion of the court was against the plaintiff.

In *Wilson* v. *Halpin,*[11] the plaintiff was told by the chambermaid in defendant's hotel to take his baggage to the boy in the baggage room and give it into his charge. Instead of doing this, plaintiff put it under the bed in his room, in which other guests were also accommodated, and left the room. When he returned the bag was gone.

In an action for the recovery of the loss, *held,* for the defendant: "What [the chambermaid] told [plaintiff], therefore, was not merely a suggestion of her own, but the established regulation of the house, and where several persons who were strangers to each other were lodged in the same room, it was a reasonable and proper regulation to secure the safety of the baggage. . . . If the guest is notified to put his baggage in a particular place where it will be safely kept and he neglects to do so, the innkeeper, if it is lost, is not liable. [Citations omitted.]" [12]

In *Herter* v. *Dwyer,*[13] it appeared that plaintiff for some fifteen months had been a lodger in defendant's lodginghouse, where he paid twenty-five cents a night for a small room and bed. He left some clothes in the locker in the room when he went to work at 5:30 in the morning of November 21, 1910. On his return in the evening the clothes had disappeared. He had left the key of his room in the morning with the clerk. It is not clear whether he locked the locker, and, if so, what he did with the key; but no question was raised as to that point. In the locker was posted a notice in conspicuous type with the following words: "The proprietor will not be responsible for anything left in these closets, rooms, or hallways; his responsibility being only for goods and valuables left in the office."

The court found as a matter of fact that plaintiff had knowledge of the notice. In reversing judgment in favor of the plaintiff the Supreme Court, Appellate Term, said:

11 30 How. Pr. 124 (N.Y. Ct. C.P. 1865).   12 *Id.* at 125.
13 129 N.Y.S. 505 (Sup. Ct. 1911).

It is not pretended that the keeper of this lodging house can be charged with the peculiar responsibility attached to an innkeeper. *Cromwell* v. *Stephens*, 2 Daly, 15, 24. But even an innkeeper, though he has not complied with the act of 1855 (Laws 1855, c. 421) by posting a notice, may limit his responsibility by actual oral notice to a guest of a reasonable regulation. *Purvis* v. *Coleman*, 21 N.Y. 111, 113. It follows, therefore, that the notice posted by the defendant in this lodging house was a reasonable regulation, with which the plaintiff was bound to comply under all the circumstances of the case. *Schneps* v. *Strum*, 25 Misc. Rep. 168, 54 N.Y. Supp. 140. Defendant can, therefore, scarcely be charged, even as a bailee, with responsibility for clothing which has never been delivered into her care, either expressly or impliedly.[14]

In *Nesben* v. *Jackson*,[15] the Supreme Court of Appeals of West Virginia, in affirming a judgment entered upon a jury's verdict in favor of plaintiff guest, said:

An inn guest's actual knowledge that his host requires a deposit of his jewelry, . . . as a condition of liability, is obviously binding upon him. Actual notice is always more potent than merely constructive notice. The statute binding him by constructive notice simply extends a commonlaw principle, which exonerated the host in case of the refusal of his guest to make the deposit upon request, or his failure to do so with knowledge of a rule requiring it, and consequent loss of the property. Such failure is negligence, barring right of recovery. [Citations omitted.]

WIDEN v. WARREN HOTEL CO.
262 Mass. 41, 159 N.E. 456 (1928)

CARROLL, J.: "This is an action for loss of the plaintiff's baggage while he was a guest at the hotel of the defendant, a corporation duly licensed as an innholder. The action was brought in the District Court. The judge found for the defendant, and filed a 'memorandum' containing 'all the evidence material to the questions reported.'

"The plaintiff had been a guest of the hotel for more than two hundred times, and 'at least fifty times a year.' He generally occupied the same room. On the morning of January 19, 1925, he registered at the defendant's hotel and was told by the room clerk that his regular room was occupied but it was expected to be vacated before noon,

14 *Id.* at 506.		15 89 W. Va. 470, 473–474, 109 S.E. 489, 490 (1921).

'and that then the plaintiff could have it.' At the time of this conversation his baggage was in the custody of a bellboy, who had deposited it ten or fifteen feet away from the desk, near a sofa used 'by the bellboys to sit upon while waiting to perform their usual duties.' When the clerk told the plaintiff about the room, he also said he could check his baggage or leave it where it was and the bellboy would take it to his room when he returned. The plaintiff took a book from his bag and after closing it left the hotel. On his return the bag could not be found and it has never been returned to him.

"In conspicuous places in each room certain regulations and a printed copy of what is now [Gen. Laws, ch. 140, Secs. 10 to 13, inclusive] were posted. These printed regulations had been posted in a conspicuous place in the rooms of the hotel during all the years the plaintiff had been a guest; they were printed in good size blackfaced type and were so posted that they could readily be seen. One of the regulations was: 'Baggage may be left in charge of the porter, for which checks will also be given; when sent for, a written order must accompany the checks for the same. For articles not thus checked the management will not be responsible.'

"The judge found that a checking room was maintained; that the regulation was reasonable and proper; that the baggage was lost because of the plaintiff's failure to comply with the regulation; that the plaintiff although he had seen the notices posted in the room, had no actual knowledge of the terms of the regulation; and he ruled that, as required by [Gen. Laws, ch. 140, Sec. 17], the regulation was duly brought to the plaintiff's notice. The judge found that the room clerk waived the regulation; but he ruled that it was beyond his authority to do so. On report to the Appellate Division, the report was dismissed, and the plaintiff appealed.

"An innholder against whom a claim is made for loss by a guest may show under [Gen. Laws, ch. 140, Sec. 17], that the loss is attributable to the failure of the guest to comply with regulations of the inn, if they are reasonable and proper and are shown to have been duly brought to the notice of the guest by the innholder. The regulation in the case at bar was plainly printed and a copy was posted in a conspicuous place in each room. This was in conformity to the statute; the innholder was not required to show that each guest had actual notice. The plaintiff could read English, he had occupied the room in

which the regulation was posted on many occasions; his knowledge
could be inferred from the posted notice. . . .

"The regulation must be reasonable in order to excuse the innkeeper;
and if this regulation is to be construed to require a guest to remove
his baggage from his room and leave it in the charge of the porter,
whenever the guest is absent from the room, it would not be, in our
opinion, a 'reasonable and proper' regulation under the statute. But as
a regulation required a guest to place his baggage in the charge of the
porter, when a room had not been assigned to him, and the custody
of the baggage was not retained by the guest, it was a reasonable and
proper regulation, and in accordance with the statute. The innkeeper
having supplied a proper place for the keeping of baggage, it was not
unreasonable for him to call upon his guests to observe the regulation.
[Citations omitted.]

"The trial judge ruled that the clerk did not have authority to waive
the regulation in question. In our opinion this ruling was right. The
clerk, while acting within the scope of his employment, bound the
proprietor by his acts and words. He was in a position of authority,
reliance could be placed on his directions and his instructions followed.
In assigning rooms, in seeing to the comfort of guests, and in dealing
with them in their business as such, he represented the innkeeper. But
the printed regulations posted in the rooms were adopted, it is to be
assumed, by the directors or officers of the corporation. Frequent violations of these regulations with the knowledge of the officers would be
evidence that they were no longer valid, and they could be waived by
such officers. But they could not be waived, under the facts of this case,
by the clerk. He had authority to arrange for the care of the baggage
of a guest, and one who was ignorant of the regulations could follow
his directions and if loss resulted he would have an action against the
innkeeper. But in the case before us, the plaintiff must be held to have
been familiar with the printed regulations posted in his room, which
the clerk had no authority to waive. [Citations omitted.]

"Order dismissing report affirmed."

22:5 *Limitation of Liability by Contract*

Like other persons engaged in a public employment, for instance, the
common carrier, the innkeeper may not limit his liability for loss of

the guest's goods, as it is imposed by the common law, by a contract with the guest.[16] The same necessity of the guest who applies to be received which leads to the obligation to receive him, puts him at the mercy of the innkeeper who requires a consent to the limitation of liability as a condition of his being received. The parties are not on an equal footing, and public policy requires that the guest be protected. The contract therefore for limitation of the innkeeper's liability is void as against public policy.

For the same reason, the innkeeper cannot require the guest to take charge of his own goods, for that would in effect be a refusal to take them into the inn.[17]

MAXWELL OPERATING CO. v. HARPER
138 Tenn. 640, 200 S.W. 515 (1917)

Mr. Justice WILLIAMS delivered the opinion of the court: "The petitioner operates the Maxwell House, one of the leading hotels in Nashville and . . . has a checkroom near the lobby, where the overcoats and small baggage of its guests are kept. Harper, at the time a guest of the house, deposited his overcoat in this room for safe-keeping and received from the attendant a check . . . as follows:

"'Accommodation Check. Left at owner's risk. The management will not be responsible for loss or damage. No. 4554. [Signed] *Maxwell Operating Co.*'

"Harper had been a patron of the hotel . . . on numerous [prior] occasions; and . . . had been directed by the clerk and employees of the house to the checkroom as the place in which to deposit such articles. His overcoat in question was in some may misdelivered or stolen, and he brought this suit to recover its value. Both of the lower courts have given judgment in his favor.

"The defenses of the hotel company are that it maintained a baggageroom in the basement [operated] at its risk; also a place behind the clerk's desk where articles might be left, the company assuming responsibility; and, further, that the check received by Harper operated as a contractual limitation upon its common-law liability.

---

[16] *Stanton* v. *Leland*, 4 E.D. Smith 88 (N.Y. Ct. C.P. 1855); *Fuller* v. *Coats*, 18 Ohio St. 343 (1868).

[17] *Calye's Case*, 77 Eng. Rep. 520 (K.B. 1584).

[The common-law rule of liability is in force in Tennessee, and neither the baggage room, nor the safe were suitable repositories for wearing apparel.]

"A hotel which operates a checkroom in effect invites such use by its guests as Harper made of it; and the hotel company could not validly negative its common law duty or liability by any such regulation or stipulation. The stipulation in the check was void for unreasonableness, unsupported as it was by a consideration. . . ."

[Writ of certiorari denied.]

In an omitted portion of the opinion, the court stated that the exact legal question was one of first impression and noted that in the analogous cases of carriers it was pointed out that the liability of carriers was based on laws governing innkeepers which were already in existence. The rule thus laid down, holding stipulations releasing the innkeeper from liability for loss of his guests' property void, as unreasonable and contrary to public policy, must not be construed to deny to the innkeeper the power to make reasonable regulations governing the exercise of the rights of a guest. And when such reasonable rules and regulations to insure the safety of a guest's property are not observed by him, having been brought to his knowledge the innkeeper will not be responsible.

DALLAS HOTEL CO. v. RICHARDSON
276 S.W. 765 (Tex. Ct. Civ. App. 1925)

[Appeal from a judgment in the sum of $900 recovered by appellee (plaintiff) against appellant (defendant) in the district court of Dallas County. Appellant operates the Adolphus Hotel in Dallas. Appellee is a traveling saleswoman who has made the Adolphus her regular headquarters in Dallas. She had a large trunk in which she kept certain wearing apparel and household goods. She would leave this trunk in the hotel's baggage room, with the consent of the hotel management, whenever she was away on trips from the city. In May, 1921, she delivered her trunk to the baggage room, to remain there until she returned the following autumn and received the accustomed check evidencing such deposit. Said check had printed on it the following: "This baggage is left at the hotel at the risk of the owner and the hotel will not be responsible for same, inasmuch as we make no charge for checking baggage or trunks."]

JONES, C. J.: "When appellee returned in October or November and called for her trunk, it could not be found, and the trunk and its entire contents were lost. Appellee . . . did not pay any charge for the use of the baggage room during her absence from the hotel. She was considered by appellant as a 'permanent guest' of the hotel.

"The suit was to recover the value of the trunk and contents, alleged in the petition to have been $1,200. Appellee's petition was sufficient to authorize a recovery, either on the theory that the parties occupied the relation of innkeeper and guest, or the relation of mutual bailor and bailee, or that appellant occupied only the relation of a gratuitous bailee.

"Appellant defended the suit on the theory that, at most, it was only a gratuitous bailee, and that it received the trunk solely for the accommodation of appellee, placed it in its baggage room, and kept it in the same manner that other baggage stored in said room was kept, and that as appellee knew the conditions obtaining in reference to said baggage room and the manner in which baggage was kept in such room, and with such knowledge on her part voluntarily stored her baggage with appellant, she could not recover for the loss of same; also that the stipulation in the said receipt was binding on appellee and a bar to her recovery.

"The trial court evidently held the evidence insufficient to raise any issue on the first two theories above named, to wit, that of the relation of innkeeper and guest, and that of bailment for the mutual benefit of the parties, and submitted the issues solely on the law governing a bailment for the sole benefit of the bailor, requiring a finding of the jury that appellant was guilty of gross negligence as a prerequisite to recovery. . . .

"The limitation placed on the check for the trunk delivered to appellee at the time appellant received its custody cannot have the effect of relieving it against its own negligence, or the negligence of its agents and servants. 6. C.J. p. 1112, and authorities cited in note. The assignments in respect to this issue are overruled. . . .

"In view of another trial [Objections to the admission of certain testimony relating to the reimbursement of appellee by appellant for water damage to her trunk on a prior occasion having been sustained], we would suggest that, in our opinion, . . . the evidence does raise the issue of a mutual bailment. The test as to this issue in a given case is whether or not the bailee received anything of value for the undertaking. If there is such consideration, the courts will not stop to inquire as to its adequacy. Appellant was operating a hotel for the public, and, as an inducement to the public, it permitted the baggage of departing guests to be stored in its baggage rooms during the absence from its hotel of the guest, without any extra charge. In the particular case under inquiry the holding of appellee's trunk for her during her absence tended at least to make her a permanent guest of the hotel, a thing very much to be desired by any hotel, and we are of the opinion that this is a sufficient consideration to make the bailment one of mutual benefit to the parties.

"Because of the errors [of admitting objectionable testimony] . . . this case must be reversed and remanded."

In *Hotels Statler Co.* v. *Safier,*[18] plaintiff, by arrangement with defendant's assistant manager, left his trunk and contents in a special storage room in defendant's hotel, until plaintiff should return from a trip to an adjacent city. During plaintiff's temporary absence, his trunk disappeared.

The Ohio Supreme Court, in affirming judgment of the lower courts in favor of plaintiff stated, by way of *dictum:*

In a requested finding of facts in this case the trial court found that the relationship of innkeeper and guest did not exist. While technically a guest when the arrangement for storage was made, the transaction for the storage of goods covered a period when no such relationship existed, although such future relation was contemplated with advantage to both parties. We have held that this was a bailment for the mutual benefit of both, therefore the rigid rule of obligation between the innkeeper and guest gave way to the rule defining the rights and obligations between bailor and bailee for mutual benefit. As a bailee for hire impliedly contracts to use ordinary care it follows he may not contract against his own negligence or the lack of such care. Ordinarily in bailments the parties may diminish the liability of the bailee by special contract, provided the contract is not in violation of law or of public policy and does not relieve the bailee of negligence. (6 Corpus Juris 1112). But in the instant case no such special contract was made, and

18 103 Ohio St. 638, 134 N.E. 460 (1921).

in the absence of a special agreement the law of bailments fixes the degree of the bailee's liability.[19]

In *Ridgely Operating Co.* v. *White*,[20] plaintiff sued to recover for the loss of a trunk in defendant's hotel. There was no innkeeper-guest relationship and defendant denied the existence of a bailment or negligence on its part. Defendant further pleaded the exculpatory provision of a lease between it and plaintiff, which relieved defendant of any responsibility for plaintiff's property within defendant's premises. The Supreme Court of Alabama affirmed judgment in favor of plaintiff. Said the court: "[W]e pretermit altogether a consideration of the effect of an agreement by a bailee to relieve himself of the consequences of his negligence." [21]

In *Oklahoma City Hotel Co.* v. *Levine*,[22] plaintiff placed his baggage in defendant's hotel checkroom, paid his bill and checked out intending to return in a few days. The baggage was lost while in defendant's custody. In an action for the value of the baggage, it appeared that a statement was printed on the reverse side of the check delivered to plaintiff, as follows:

Contract Releasing Liability

In consideration of the receipt and free storage of the property (no value stated) for which this check is issued, it is agreed by the holder, in accepting this check, that the hotel shall not be liable for loss or damage to said property unless caused by negligence of the hotel, in which event only the hotel shall be liable for a sum not to exceed $25.00. The hotel shall not in any event be liable for loss or damage to said property by fire, theft or moth, whether caused by its own negligence or otherwise. The hotel is authorized to deliver property to any person presenting this check without identification. Not responsible for articles left over 30 days.

On appeal from a judgment in favor of plaintiff, *held*, affirmed. "Such alleged contractual limitations upon liability in such bailment cases in this jurisdiction are contrary to public policy and void. [Citation omitted.]" [23]

For the same reason, the innkeeper cannot require the guest to take charge of his own goods, for that would in effect be a refusal to take them into the inn.

[19] *Id*. at 646 and at 462.
[21] *Id*. at 464 and at 698.
[23] *Id*. at 333 and at 999.

[20] 227 Ala. 459, 150 So. 693 (1933).
[22] 189 Okla. 331, 116 P.2d 997 (1941).

What an innkeeper may well do and, profiting from experience, many are now doing, is to install coin lockers, similar to those at railroad and bus depots, for the convenience of departing guests who wish to leave baggage in the hotel intending to call for it later. The guest is courteously informed of the facility, the lockers are pointed out to him and upon dropping the required coin in the slot, the key in the lock becomes operative and the guest makes his own deposit. The innkeeper thus saves himself harmless as bailee.

CHAPTER 23

Statutory Limitations of Innkeeper's Liability for Money and Valuables

23:1 *Introduction*

At common law and in the absence of statutory limitation, an innkeeper is absolutely liable for the loss of a guest's property upon his premises to the full extent of the loss, except for losses or damage caused by the guest's own fault or negligence or by an act of God or of the public enemy.

In order to alleviate this extraordinary liability, legislatures have passed laws permitting an innkeeper who strictly complies with the law to protect himself by limiting his liability. At the present time such statutes are practically universal.

23:2 *Limited Liability for Money and Valuables*

In New York the statute was first enacted in 1855. As modified and amended, it is now part of the General Business Law. Separate sections relate to money and valuables, to personal property other than money and valuables, to property in transit to and from the hotel, and to property destroyed by fire.

Section 200. *Safes, Limited Liability*

Whenever the proprietor or manager of any hotel, motel, inn or steamboat shall provide a safe in the office of such hotel, motel or steamboat, or other convenient place for the safe keeping of any money, jewels, ornaments, bank notes, bonds, negotiable securities or precious stones, belonging to the guests of or travelers in such hotel, motel, inn or steamboat, and shall notify the guests or travelers thereof by posting a notice stating the fact that such safe is provided, in which such property may be deposited, in a public and conspicuous place and manner in the office and public rooms, and in the public parlors of such hotel, motel, or inn, or saloon of such steamboat; and if such guest or traveler shall neglect to deliver such property to the person in charge of such office for deposit in such safe, the proprietor or manager of such hotel, motel, or steamboat shall not be liable for any loss of such property, sustained by such guest or traveler by theft or otherwise; but no hotel, motel or steamboat proprietor, manager or lessee shall be obliged to receive property on deposit for safe keeping, exceeding five hundred dollars in value; and if such guest or traveler shall deliver such property, to the person in charge of such office for deposit in such safe, said proprietor, manager or lessee shall not be liable for any loss thereof, sustained by such guest or traveler by theft or otherwise, in any sum exceeding the sum of five hundred dollars, unless by special agreement in writing with such proprietor, manager or lessee.

23:3 *Notices Required to Be Posted*

In order to come within the protection of the statute, the innkeeper must strictly comply with the mandatory posting requirements of the statute. Posting requirements for hotels are prescribed in Sections 206 and 203-b; a posting requirement is also included in Section 201.

Section 206. *Rates to Be Posted, Penalty for Violation*

Every keeper of a hotel or inn shall post in a public and conspicuous place and manner in the office or public room, and in the public parlors of such hotel or inn, a printed copy of this section and sections two hundred and two hundred and one, and a statement of the charges or rate of charges by the day and for meals furnished and for lodging. No charge or sum shall be collected or received by any such hotel keeper or inn keeper for any service not actually rendered or for a longer time than the person so charged actually remained at such hotel or inn, nor for a higher rate of charge for the use of such room or board, lodging or meals than is specified in the rate of charges required to be posted by the last preceding sentence; provided such guest shall have given such hotel keeper or inn keeper notice at the office of his departure. For any violation of this section the offender shall forfeit to the injured party three times the amount so charged, and shall not be entitled to receive any money for meals, services or time charged.

See 12:9 for an application of this statute. The notice to be posted must be a printed copy of Sections 200 and 201 of the statute. The New York State Hotel and Motel Association has prepared a "Notice to Guest" card for use by hotels, which conforms to the requirements of the statute, and which is obtainable from the association at 141 West 51st Street, New York, New York 10019.

The required notice must be posted in the office or public room and in the public parlors of the hotel or inn. The "office" is the registration or reception office. A copy may also be posted in the front office or credit office, if there be one, the public rooms or public parlors for men and women, the ballrooms, function rooms, the elevator lobbies on the several floors, and the checkrooms and parcel rooms. Individual guest rooms are not public rooms and, except in motels, require no posting of notices. In case of doubt as to the nature or type of a room, err on the side of posting.

To "post," as used in the statute, means "to nail, attach, affix or otherwise fasten up physically and to display in a conspicuous manner, and not theoretically . . . and a posting is not made by printing or recording a notice in a book or on a card and keeping it on a desk." [1]

"Conspicuous" means what it says, plainly visible and obvious to the eye; not hidden.

Where a notice in a guest's bedroom merely warned guests to take care of their property and contained a statement that the innkeeper would not be responsible for valuables, money, or personal effects missing from guest's rooms and neither mentioned the availability of a safe nor suggested that valuables be turned over to innkeeper for safekeeping, it was not sufficient notice under the statute to protect the innkeeper from liability for the loss of a guest's undeposited valuables.

The fact that a safe is provided is not sufficient. Notice to that effect must be posted in conformity with the statute and posting in a bedroom is not sufficient where there has been no posting "in a public and conspicuous place and manner in the office and public rooms, and in the public parlors of" the hotel. [2]

[1] *Epp* v. *Bowman-Biltmore Hotels Corp.*, 171 Misc. 338, 342, 12 N.Y.S.2d 384, 388 (N.Y.C. Mun. Ct. 1939).
[2] *Slater* v. *Landes*, 172 N.Y.S. 190 (Sup. Ct. 1918).

It has been held, on the other hand, that an actual personal notice to a guest that a safe was provided for the safekeeping of the guest's money and valuables is equivalent to the constructive notice required to be posted by the statute. Where such a personal notice is given, the innkeeper's failure to post the statutory notice will not make him liable for the loss of the guest's undeposited valuables.[3]

The posting requirements for motels and motor courts are prescribed in Section 206-b:

Section 206-b. *Posting of Rates for Motels and Motor Courts*

Every person, firm or corporation engaged in the business of furnishing public lodging accommodations in motels and motor courts shall:

Post in a conspicuous place or manner in each and every rental unit, a printed copy of this section and section two hundred six-a and a statement of the rental unit charge or rate charged by the day for the rental unit. No charge or sum shall be collected or received by any motel or motor court keeper for any service not actually rendered or for a longer time than the person so charged actually remained at such motel or motor court, nor for a higher rate of charge for the use of said rental unit than is specified in the list of charges required to be posted by the last preceding sentence of this paragraph, nor for a higher rate of charge for the use of said rental unit than the maximum rate posted or maintained on any outdoor or outside advertising sign pertaining to such establishment, provided such guest shall have given such motel or motor court keeper notice at the office of his departure. For any violation of this section, the offender shall forfeit to the injured party, three times the amount so charged, and shall not be entitled to receive any money for services or time charged.

It should be noted that in motels and motor courts, the notices must be posted "in each and every rental unit." "Rental unit" means one or more rooms offered for rent as a unit for occupancy by one or more persons.

The distinction between a hotel and a motel is discussed in an earlier chapter. In case of any doubt as to the type of operation, the best practice is to post the notices conspicuously in every guest room, in addition to the office and public rooms. Posting on the inside of the bathroom door, or inside a closet, does not satisfy the requirements of the statute.

[3] *Purvis v. Coleman,* 21 N.Y. 111 (1860).

23:4 Safe Must Be Provided

The law does not specify the type of safe to be provided. The protective features of the various types of safes vary with the fire-resisting qualities of the hotel or motel property itself. The type universally favored in most hotels is the individual lock box type, also in use in the safe deposit vaults of banks. A significant protective feature of this type of safety box is that it can be opened only by the simultaneous application of a guard or master key in the possession of the hotel *and* the individual lock box key, in the possession of the guest.

The safe or the deposit boxes should be located near the cashier's section in the front office so as to be accessible to and in full view of guests so they may be eye-witnesses to every phase of the transactions involving their money or valuables. A separate vault room, adjacent to the front office providing safety and privacy, is most desirable. (See *Brodner: The Control of Guest's Safe Deposit Boxes in Hotels*, Harris, Kerr, Forster and Co., C.P.A.'s, 420 Lexington Ave., New York, New York 10017).

23:5 Instructions to Safe Clerks

Innkeepers who use the individual lock boxes of the double key type will find the following admonitions to safe clerks helpful:

1. Never, never, never, let any guest have access to the guard key.

2. Keep the guard key under the care and supervision of the safe clerk at all times.

3. When a guest requests access to the box, always ask his name, room number, and key number.

4. Always witness the guest's signature, compare the access signature with the guest's original signature, and always affix your initials to witness every access signature.

5. It is best that you let the guest remove his box from the safe; if you do it, be sure that it is done in the presence and in full view of the guest.

6. Afford the guest privacy to use his box, but be in a position at all times to observe the actions of the guest in the safe area.

7. Never use the guest's key; after you partially release the locking

mechanism with the guard key ask the guest to open the box with his own key.

8. Ask the guest to return the box into the safe and assist only with locking the safe.

9. If you are aware that the guest is checking out be sure to obtain his signature for the surrender of the box on the Safe Deposit Card and obtain the key.

10. Follow the standard procedure *every time with every guest.* Laxity is dangerous.

23:6 Articles Required to Be Deposited in Safe

An innkeeper who complies with the statute, posts the required notices, and maintains a safe is protected against liability for the loss of *money, jewels, ornaments, bank notes, bonds, negotiable securities* or *precious stones,* unless they are deposited in the hotel safe.

23:7 Deposit of Watch

The question has arisen whether a watch and chain come within the description "jewels and ornaments" as used in the statute. In New York it is held that they do not. In *Briggs* v. *Todd,*[4] the plaintiff, a guest, lost from his room in the inn a watch on the cover of which a state coat of arms had been engraved. The picture of the owner's mother was inside the case. The watch had been laid for a short time inside the owner's trunk. In spite of these facts the court held that the watch was not an ornament.

The reason for this interpretation of the words is forcibly put by Mr. Justice ALLEN in *Ramaley* v. *Leland:* [5]

Certain property, particularly valuable in itself, taking but small space compared with its value for its safe keeping, easy of concealment and removal, holding out great temptation to the dishonest, and not necessary to the comfort or convenience of the guest while in his room, is made the subject of the statutory exemption. Property of a different description, including all that which is useful or necessary to the comfort and convenience of the

4 28 Misc. 208, 59 N.Y.S. 23 (Sup. Ct. 1899).
5 43 N.Y. 539, 541–542 (1881).

guest, that which is usually carried and worn as a part of the ordinary apparel and outfit, or is ordinarily used, and is convenient for use, by travelers as well in as out of their rooms, is left, as before the statute, at the risk of the innkeeper. The words of the statute must be taken in their ordinary sense, in the absence of any indication that they were used, either in a technical sense or a sense other than that in which they are popularly used. A watch is neither a jewel or ornament, as these words are used and understood, either in common parlance or by lexicographers. It is not used or carried as a jewel or ornament, but as a time-piece or chronometer, an article of ordinary wear by most travelers of every class, and of daily and hourly use by all. It is as useful and necessary to the guest in his room as out of it, in the night as the daytime. It is carried for use and convenience and not for ornament. But it is enough that it is neither a jewel or ornament in any sense in which these words have ever been used. The question of negligence, and whether the plaintiff could and did bolt his door, were properly submitted to and passed upon by the jury.

A watch ornamented with diamonds is nevertheless regarded as an article of daily use and not a jewel, ornament, or precious stone, within the meaning of the statute. Nor would the fact that a broken clasp made it unsafe to wear the watch on the day of its loss change the nature of the article.[6]

23:8 Deposit of Valuables of Daily Use—Jewels and Ornaments

As regards money in possession of the guest, the innkeeper is not responsible for loss, howsoever small the amount and irrespective of the inconvenience of depositing it in the safe.[7] As regards jewels and ornaments, it has been held that a gold pen and pencil are not considered either jewelry or ornaments and need not be deposited.[8] Also, that a chain, a purse, and a rosary are all articles of use, and not of ornament.[9]

[6] Kennedy v. Bowman Biltmore Hotel Corp., 157 Misc. 416, 283 N.Y.S. 900 (Sup. Ct. 1935) (per curiam).

[7] Hart v. Mills Hotel Trust, 144 Misc. 121, 258 N.Y.S. 417 (N.Y.C. Mun. Ct. 1932).

[8] Gile v. Libby, 36 Barb. 70 (N.Y. Sup. Ct. 1861).

[9] Jones v. Hotel Latham Co., 62 Misc. 620, 115 N.Y.S. 1084 (Sup. Ct. 1909).

23:9 *Extent of Liability for Property Deposited in Safe*

CARLTON *v.* BEACON HOTEL CORPORATION
3 App. Div. 2d 28, 157 N.Y.S.2d 744 (1st Dep't 1956), *aff'd mem.,*
4 N.Y.2d 789, 149 N.E.2d 527 (1958)

BREITEL, J.: "Plaintiff, a guest of the defendant hotel, brought this action to recover for the loss of a package of jewelry and a package of foreign currency which she had deposited for safekeeping with the defendant's desk clerk. Defendant appeals from a judgment entered after a jury verdict in the amount of $10,000 in the plaintiff's favor. The judgment should be modified to limit the plaintiff's recovery to $500.

"At the time plaintiff registered as a guest at the defendant hotel, she asked the desk clerk whether he had a safe deposit box, as she 'wanted to put some things away.' The clerk replied that there were none presently available, but that he would store her valuables safely, until a safe-deposit box became vacant. He gave plaintiff an envelope specifically designed to receive guests' valuables. She placed her package of jewelry (worth $23,000, according to her verified bill of particulars) in the envelope but left blank the item 'Declared Valuation.' She then gave the clerk the sealed envelope. Plaintiff, during her six-weeks stay at the hotel, on five occasions utilized this procedure to deposit and redeposit her jewelry and on one occasion to deposit a package of English and French currency.

"The hotel had a large iron safe containing, among others, some 66 individual safe-deposit compartments and three larger compartments. One of the larger compartments, number 45, was used exclusively for envelopes containing guests' valuables. The desk clerk testified that according to the routine prescribed by the management, the envelopes were placed in compartment 45. He further testified that he could recall no deviation by him from this general practice. On the other hand, the clerk had no specific recollection of the several deposits of valuables made by plaintiff. Neither the packages of jewelry nor currency, nor even the envelopes in which they were deposited, were ever recovered.

"After both sides rested, defendant moved for a directed verdict in favor of plaintiff in the amount of $500. This motion was based on the provisions of Section 200 of the General Business Law. In denying the motion, the trial court stated that defendant had met two of the conditions imposed by that section, namely: (1) providing an adequate safe for the deposit of guests' valuables; and (2) posting effective notices to inform the guests that such a safe was provided. The trial court, however, went on to deny the motion, because it construed section 200 as requiring the hotel to actually deposit the valuables in the safe in order to take advantage of the limited liability provisions of that section. Accordingly, on the issue of liability, the trial court submitted to the jury the single question, namely, whether the defendant actually put the plaintiff's property in the safe.

"Even apart from the absence of any evidence in the record to indicate that in fact defendant did not deposit plaintiff's valuables in its safe, the verdict and judgment must be reduced. Section 200 of the General Business Law, in language that is quite clear, states that a hotelkeeper who provides a safe and posts requisite notices is not liable at all for the loss of guests' valuables unless the guest delivers the valuables for deposit in the safe. Where the valuables have been delivered to the person in charge of the safe 'for deposit in such safe,' the hotel's liability is limited to $500, unless it otherwise agrees in writing.

"Section 200 was enacted 'to relieve innkeepers of the heavy burden placed upon them by the common law. . . . The purpose of the section is to protect the hotel from an undisclosed excessive liability.' (*Millhiser* v. *Beau Site Co.*, 251 N.Y. 290, 293, 294). It is conceded in this case that the hotel complied with the posting requirements of sections 200 and 206 of the General Business Law. There is likewise no contention that the safe here provided by the hotel did not adequately comply with the statutory requirements.

"The trial court, however, read into the statute a further requirement that the hotel prove actual deposit of the valuables in the safe. Neither the language of the section or the precedents thereunder support that view. It has been held by the Court of Appeals that section 200 limits the liability of the hotel, even in instances when the loss is occasioned by a theft committed by an employee of the hotel. (*Millhiser v. Beau Site Co., supra.*) As construed by the trial court, the statute would not protect the hotel from unlimited liability when the desk clerk himself converts the valuables upon receipt from the guest. In the *Millhiser* case the court noted that the risk of loss by theft is greater as regards theft by employees than as regards theft by strangers. Similarly, the risk of theft by the employee receiving the property is greater than the risk of theft by other employees. (Of course there is no evidence in this case that plaintiff's loss was occasioned by a theft, or any implication that the loss was caused by the desk clerk.) The opinion in the *Millhiser* case indicates that the hotel's ability to claim the benefits of section 200 did not turn on whether the larcenous clerk perpetrated the theft before or after guests' valuables were placed in the safe.

"The record here demonstrates that plaintiff, with knowledge of the limited liability imposed on defendant by statute, deposited her jewelry and other property without making any declaration of value. Defendant, having complied with all the expressed conditions of section 200, is entitled to the benefit of the limited liability therein provided. . . .

"Judgment unanimously modified so as to limit plaintiff's recovery to $500 and, as so modified, affirmed, with costs to the appellant."

In *Hyman* v. *South Coast Hotel Co.*,[10] plaintiff deposited some $2,000 worth of jewelry in the safe of the Long Beach Hotel while she was a guest there on July 28, 1907. At about 5 o'clock the next morning, the hotel was totally destroyed by fire. Before leaving the burning building, defendant's manager removed some of the jewelry deposited by guests in the safe, put them in a bag, kept them under the mattress of his wife's bed for four days and then removed them to the Hotel Empire, where the bag was sealed. Plaintiff's jewelry was not in the bag, nor could it be found in the hotel safe when that was opened after the fire. It was conceded upon the trial that no jewelry was returned to plaintiff after the fire and that a demand therefor had been made.

The plaintiff's cause of action was based solely upon defendant's negligence. Defendant set up a general denial and pleaded in partial defense that a safe was provided, notices were posted, and no special agreement in writing was made. When plaintiff rested her case the

[10] 146 App. Div. 341, 130 N.Y.S. 766 (2d Dep't 1911).

trial judge granted defendant's motion to strike out all evidence of value over and above $250. The case was submitted to the jury as one of negligence. The court charged that:

[T]he mere fact that it was lost does not entitle the plaintiff to a verdict. The plaintiff must go beyond that and show it was lost through negligence and you must be able to put your finger on the negligence, point it out and say: "Yes, that is the act of the proprietor or of his employees which was negligent, therein did he fail to do his duty, and because he thus failed he must pay." The question of fact submitted to you is was there such negligence? If so, the plaintiff is entitled to recover $250.

Plaintiff requested the court to charge that, if negligence was found, she was entitled to a verdict for the value of her property lost, which was refused, and an exception taken. In revising and ordering a new trial, the Appellate Division said:

The plaintiff's jewelry being in defendant's possession when the fire broke out, its liability for a return thereof continued after the destruction of the hotel. . . .

This action is not based entirely upon the liability of the defendant as an innkeeper, but rests upon the affirmative negligence of its president and manager in the care of the jewelry after it was taken from the safe during the progress of the fire. If the plaintiff's jewelry was destroyed by fire while in the defendant's safe, its liability is limited under the provisions of the statute to $250; but if the jewelry was taken from the safe during the progress of the fire, in an uninjured condition, by defendant's president and manager, and he omitted upon demand made the morning of the fire to deliver it to its owner, the plaintiff, and thereafter so carelessly and negligently cared for it as to result in its loss, the statute invoked does not limit the liability of the defendant. The jury should have been so instructed, and the error of the trial court in limiting the defendant's liability to $250 presents reversible error.[11]

Since the decision in the *Hyman* case, the statutory limit has been increased to $500.

[11] *Id.* at 343–344 and at 768.

23.10 *Liability for Valuables in Guest's Possession Prefatory to Imminent Departure*

SPILLER *v.* BARCLAY HOTEL
327 N.Y.S.2d 426 (Civ. Ct. N.Y. 1972)

LEONARD H. SANDLER, J.: "Plaintiff, a guest of the Barclay Hotel, sues for the value of property, primarily wearing apparel and jewelry, lost on the steps of the hotel while she was in the process of leaving.

"Plaintiff testified that after her two bags were brought to the lobby floor, she asked a bellboy to take them to the cab area and to watch them while she checked out. When she came to the cab area, only one of her bags was there and the bellboy was not present. A search failed to disclose the missing bag or its contents. . . .

"Accordingly, I find that the property was lost through the actual negligence of the Defendant. No doubt the bellboy was under no inherent duty to watch the bags, and it may well be that his implicit undertaking to do so violated his instructions. Nonetheless, when he accepted the bags with the accompanying request to watch them, without explicitly declining the latter request, an obligation of care was assumed which quite clearly was not fulfilled.

"As to the claim for lost property other than jewelry, it is clear that the limitations of value set forth in Section 201 of the General Business Law, are not applicable because of the actual negligence of the Defendant. That section, relating to loss of clothing and other personal property, explicitly exempts from its coverage losses due to 'fault or negligence.' [Citation omitted.]

"The claim for the items of lost jewelry presents a more troublesome problem. Section 200 of the General Business Law excludes recovery by a hotel guest for loss of, among other categories enumerated, jewels, ornaments and precious stones where the hotel provides a safe for such items, gives appropriate notice of that fact, and the guest does not use that facility. It has conceded that the hotel maintained such a safe and had posted the required notice.

"Preliminarily, I find that the items of jewelry here involved, which included a necklace, a pendant, earrings and the like, come within the definition of 'jewels' and 'ornaments,' as those terms are used in Section 200. The distinction drawn in the leading case of Ramaley v. Leland, 43 N.Y. 539, 542 (1871), which has been consistently followed, is between articles 'carried for use and convenience' and articles worn as an 'ornament.' [Citation omitted.]

"Moreover, although the question is less clearly settled than one would have supposed, it now appears to be the law that a guest who has failed to deposit property for safekeeping in accordance with the requirement of Section 200 may not recover for the loss even if the hotel was actually negligent. [Citations omitted.]

"What seems to me decisive here is that Section 200 was not designed to apply to a loss occuring under the circumstances of this case. Section 200 clearly contemplates a procedure for safeguarding the specified categories of property during a guest's stay at a hotel. Its provisions do not seem to me to be reasonably applied to a loss that takes place when a guest is about to leave, has gathered together her property preparatory to an imminent departure, and is arranging for the transfer of luggage to a vehicle for transportation.

"Although that situation presents some conceptual difficulties, I am satisfied that the sensible and fair approach is to consider a loss occurring at that point in time neither in terms of the provisions of Section 200, nor in terms of the traditional common law liability of innkeepers, but rather on the basis of the presence or absence of actual negligence. [Citation omitted.]

"Having found that the loss here resulted from the negligence of a hotel employee, acting within the scope of his employment, I hold that Plaintiff is entitled to recover the value of the lost jewelry. . . ."

23:11 *Valuables Stolen from Safe by Hotel Employee*

An innkeeper is not necessarily liable in excess of the statutory limitation for valuables of a guest stolen by an employee from the hotel safe.

In *Millhiser* v. *Beau Site Co.*,[12] the plaintiff, Regina Millhiser, a transient guest in defendant's hotel, delivered to the clerk at the desk a package containing jewelry of the value of $369,800. She did not notify him of the value of the package. He gave her a key to a safety deposit box and placed the package in it. The box could only be

[12] 251 N.Y. 290, 167 N.E. 447 (1929).

unlocked by the use of a master key and the key given to the plaintiff, or a duplicate thereof. Later the plaintiff called for the package. When the box was opened, it was found that jewelry to the value of $50,000 was missing. Thereafter the clerk who had received the package from the plaintiff was convicted of stealing the missing jewelry.

The defendant had posted in the public rooms and guest rooms a notice which read: "A safe is provided in the office of this hotel for the use of guests in which money, jewels, or other valuables may be deposited for safekeeping." No other or different notice was posted.

The Appellate Division held that Section 200 of the General Business Law does not protect a hotel or limit its liability for the loss of jewelry stolen by its own employee.

The Court of Appeals disagreed. "The purpose of the section", said the court, "is to protect the hotel from an undisclosed excessive liability." [13] It was to enable hotels, without notice of value, to avoid liability in excess of $500; that the statute provides that if a guest desires to impose liability in excess of $500, he must give notice of value and obtain a written agreement making the hotel liable for more than $500.

However, the court continued, Section 200 is not intended to limit a hotelkeeper's liability to $500 where the articles deposited are stolen by the hotelkeeper from the guest. "We read the statute to mean a theft of the articles from the hotel keeper and not a theft by the hotel keeper from the guest. The act of the defendant's employee in stealing the jewelry was a wrongful act, outside the scope of his employment and for his own enrichment. It was not in any guise the act of the defendant. [Citation omitted.]" [14]

Notwithstanding the exculpation of the hotel from liability because of the theft of the jewelry by its own employee, the Court of Appeals agreed with the result reached by the Appellate Division holding the hotel liable, but on another ground, namely, that it failed and neglected to post the statutory notice required by Section 206 of the General Business Law.

23:12 *Statutory Exemption Applies Only to Property of Guests*

Sections 200 and 201 of the General Business Law were intended only as a limitation of the liability of an innkeeper as an insurer of the

[13] *Id.* at 294 and at 448.   [14] *Id.* at 295 and at 448.

property of his guest. It does not ordinarily apply to the relationship of landlord and tenant.[15]

23:13 Waiver of Statutory Limitation

The innkeeper may waive the statutory limitation in his favor and having once done so, he cannot afterwards ask for its protection.

FRIEDMAN v. BRESLIN
51 App. Div. 268, 65 N.Y.S. 5 (2d Dep't 1900),
aff'd mem., 169 N.Y. 574, 61 N.E. 1129 (1901)

[Action to recover the value of jewelry stolen from a hotel. From a judgment in favor of plaintiff, and from an order denying a motion for a new trial on the minutes, defendant appeals. Affirmed.]

WOODWARD, J.: "A review of this case discloses no sufficient reason for a reversal of the judgment or order appealed from.

"Bertha Myers, plaintiff's assignor, about August 1, 1898, applied to the hotel conducted by the defendant for board, and thereafter became a guest of the hotel. She had some jewelry with her, which at various times she deposited in the office safe, until upon a certain occasion, when she was about to leave the hotel for a few hours, at the suggestion of the clerk, the jewelry was left in her trunk in her room, the keys of the room and of the trunk being left in the custody of the clerk, who agreed to look after them, and who assured her that the jewels would be safe. There was some conflict of evidence upon this point, but the jury has decided that the plaintiff's version is true, and there is evidence to support the conclusion. Plaintiff's assignor was absent from the hotel from eight o'clock in the morning until about one o'clock in the afternoon, and on going to her trunk early in the evening the jewels were missing. This action was brought to recover the value of the jewelry, the jury found a verdict for the plaintiff, and from the judgment entered upon this verdict and from an order denying a motion for a new trial, appeal comes to this court.

"It is urged by the defendant that the clerk of the hotel had only limited authority; that he was merely a rooming clerk, who was not

15 Jacobs v. Alrae Hotel Corp., 4 Misc. 2d 665, 161 N.Y.S.2d 972 (Sup. Ct. 1956), rev'd on other grounds, 4 App. Div. 2d 201, 164 N.Y.S.2d 330 (1st Dep't 1957), aff'd mem., 4 N.Y.2d 769, 149 N.E.2d 337 (1958).

authorized to give plaintiff's assignor any assurance as to the safety of her jewels, except as they were deposited in the office safe; but there was evidence in the case from which the jury might properly find that the clerk was in fact the manager, and this question was submitted to the jury without exception on the part of the defendant, and the verdict is conclusive upon this point.

"We are of opinion that the provisions of chapter 421 of the Laws of 1855, as amended by chapter 227 of the Laws of 1883, and by chapter 284 of the Laws of 1892, have no relation to the facts presented by the record on this appeal. That statute was enacted for the protection of proprietors of hotels; but if the rooming clerk was the manager of the hotel, and authorized the plaintiff's assignor to leave her jewelry in her room, he must be deemed to have waived any rights which the defendant might have had under the law. It is well established in this State that a party may waive a statutory and even a constitutional provision made for his benefit, and that, having once done so he cannot afterwards ask for its protection. (*Matter of Cooper*, 93 N.Y. 507, 513, and authorities there cited.)

"The learned court at Trial Term refused to hold the defendant to the common-law liability as an insurer, but charged the jury that the defendant was only liable for negligence, which was as favorable to the defendant as the law would permit.

"The objection that the evidence of value was improperly proven does not seem to be sustained by the record. We think that, under the rule laid down in *Berney* v. *Dinsmore* (141 Mass. 42), it was competent for plaintiff to call attention to the ring worn by his assignor for the purpose of comparison with some of the jewels lost, and as a foundation for the opinion of an expert as to the probable value of the diamonds which were alleged to have been stolen. We are also of the opinion that the objection to the question 'Have you shown the diamonds in the ring you have on to Mr. Wise, an expert?' did not call the attention of the court to the point now urged, that Mr. Wise had not, at that time, been shown to be an expert. The objection was that the question was 'incompetent, irrelevant and immaterial,' and as the evidence was clearly competent as a means of comparison, and was not objected to because of its form, the ruling of the court will not be disturbed. The objections having been specified, the ruling must rest upon the objection stated, unless the evidence was in no aspect

of the case competent. (*Tooley* v. *Bacon*, 70 N.Y. 34, 37). In the case
at bar Mr. Wise was afterwards put upon the stand and testified as an
expert without objection upon that score, and no right of the
defendant was infringed by the form of the question under discussion
which would warrant interference on the part of this court.

"The judgment and order appealed from should be affirmed.

"All concurred.

"Judgment and order affirmed, with costs."

CHAPTER 24

Statutory Limitations of Innkeeper's Liability for Clothing and Other Personal Property

24:1 *Introduction*

Whereas Section 200 of the General Business Law limits the innkeeper's liability for money and valuables undeposited in the safe maintained by the innkeepers, Section 201 provides limitations of liability for loss of or damage to personal property other than money or valuables. As will be seen, the limitation depends on the nature and location of the property, as well as on the relationship between the owner of the property and the innkeeper.

24:2 *Limitations of Liability for Loss of Clothing and Other Personal Property*

Section 201. *Liability for Loss of Clothing and Other Personal Property Limited*

1. No hotel or motel keeper except as provided in the foregoing section shall be liable for damage to or loss of wearing apparel or other personal property in the lobby, hallways or in the room or rooms assigned to a guest for any sum exceeding the sum of five hundred dollars, unless it shall appear that such loss occurred through the fault or negligence of such keeper, nor shall he be liable in any sum exceeding the sum of one hundred dollars for the loss of or damage to any such property when delivered to such keeper for storage or safe keeping in the store room, baggage room or other place elsewhere than in the room or rooms assigned to such guest, unless at the time of delivering same for storage

or safe keeping such value in excess of one hundred dollars shall be stated and a written receipt, stating such value, shall be issued by such keeper, but in no event shall such keeper be liable beyond five hundred dollars, unless it shall appear that such loss occurred through his fault or negligence, and such keeper may make a reasonable charge for storing or keeping such property, nor shall he be liable for the loss of or damage to any merchandise samples or merchandise for sale, unless the guest shall have given such keeper prior written notice of having the same in his possession, together with the value thereof, the receipt of which notice the hotel or motel keeper shall acknowledge in writing over the signature of himself or his agent, but in no event shall such keeper be liable beyond five hundred dollars, unless it shall appear that such loss or damage occurred through his fault or negligence; as to property deposited by guests or patrons in the parcel or check room of any hotel, motel or restaurant, the delivery of which is evidenced by a check or receipt therefor and for which no fee or charge is exacted, the proprietor shall not be liable beyond seventy-five dollars, unless such value in excess of seventy-five dollars shall be stated upon delivery and a written receipt, stating such value, shall be issued, but he shall in no event be liable beyond one hundred dollars unless such loss occurs through his fault or negligence. Notwithstanding anything hereinabove contained, no hotel or motel keeper shall be liable for damage to or loss of such property by fire, when it shall appear that such fire was occasioned without his fault or negligence.

2. A printed copy of this section shall be posted in a conspicuous place and manner in the office or public room and in the public parlors of such hotel or motel.

DeBANFIELD v. HILTON HOTELS CORP.
35 Misc. 2d 967, 231 N.Y.S.2d 906 (N.Y. City Ct. 1962)

[Plaintiff sues defendant hotel to recover for the loss of his belongings which were taken by some unknown person during plaintiff's absence from his room.]

LEONFORTE (JOHN), J.: "It appears that while plaintiff was a guest of defendant's hotel and while he was away from his hotel room on April 22, 1959, someone unknown to the parties gained access therein and removed all of his belongings, valued by plaintiff at about $3,500.

"It is plaintiff's contention that, by reason of the fault, negligence and carelessness of the defendant, the property of plaintiff totally disappeared and was lost to plaintiff without any fault or negligence on his part and that plaintiff was thereby damaged in said sum of $3,500.

"The defendant denies its liability to the plaintiff and maintains that plaintiff invited Mr. Lyon, a stranger, to his hotel room; that plaintiff left this person alone in the room while plaintiff was dressing himself in a closet and that when plaintiff emerged from the closet he saw the said person bent over and looking at the lock on the door, and that plaintiff was therefore contributorily negligent in failing to report the said incident to the defendant. Defendant also claims that, in any event, even if plaintiff was not contributorily negligent, its liability under Section 201 of the General Business Law is limited to $500.

"After giving all of the evidence, including the exhibits, due and careful consideration, the court is of the opinion that the plaintiff was not guilty of contributory negligence in inviting Mr. Lyon to his hotel room. At the outset, even assuming the defendant's contention that Mr. Lyon was looking at the lock at the time plaintiff left him alone in the room, it certainly taxes one's credulity to believe that one can fashion a key to fit a lock merely by looking at the lock. Furthermore, no competent testimony was adduced to show that after Lyon left plaintiff's room he returned thereto. In any event, even if Lyon had been the miscreant who stole plaintiff's belongings, any misconduct on the part of plaintiff, in inviting a stranger to his room, had ceased before he met with his loss, and under such circumstances, plaintiff's rights and status as a guest in the hotel cannot thereby be affected. [Citations omitted.]

"As to the amount of plaintiff's recovery in this case, he is bound by the provisions of Section 201 of the General Business Law. . . .

". . . [T]he burden of proof is upon plaintiff to show defendant's negligence and . . . before any recovery can be made in an amount over $500 the negligence of the defendant must be established by plaintiff.

"It is plaintiff's contention that defendant's negligence has been satisfactorily shown by either or both of two factors which could have resulted in plaintiff's loss. First, plaintiff showed the possibility that a nonguest could obtain a key to a guest's room merely by going to the desk clerk and by posing as the guest, thus obtain the key. Secondly, plaintiff claimed that his hotel room was easily accessible to strangers and other guests since a balcony adjacent to plaintiff's room and upon which a window of plaintiff's room and those of 12 other adjacent rooms opened gave strangers and other guests the opportunity of entering plaintiff's room. Accordingly, plaintiff contends that the maintenance of the balcony under such conditions constituted negligence on defendant's part sufficient to warrant a recovery for the entire loss sustained by plaintiff.

"It is to be noted that neither plaintiff nor defendant testified as to how the alleged loss occurred. Therefore, assuming but not conceding that a nonguest could possibly obtain a key to plaintiff's room by posing as plaintiff, no evidence was submitted at the trial to show that Lyon or any other person did in fact obtain a key to plaintiff's room with the resulting loss. Nor was there any evidence to show that plaintiff's room was entered by way of the balcony. In fact, in the absence of proof of tampering with the window, if the court was of the opinion that the plaintiff's loss was occasioned because plaintiff's window was easily accessible from the balcony adjacent thereto, under such circumstances plaintiff's entire complaint would have to be dismissed because of the plaintiff's own contributory negligence in failing to close the window with the catch lock thereon contained.

"Accordingly, the court finds that plaintiff has failed to sustain the burden required of him under section 201 of the General Business Law and that he is therefore bound by the limitation of $500 provided thereunder. Judgment is therefore rendered in favor of the plaintiff and against the defendant in the sum of $500, with interest from April 24, 1959."

24:3 Loss from Storeroom or Baggage Room

Liability for loss of personal property entrusted to the innkeeper for storage or safekeeping in the storeroom, baggage room, or other place elsewhere than in the guest room is limited to $100, *unless* at the time of delivery the value in excess of $100 is stated and a written receipt stating such excess value is issued to the guest; even in such event, liability will not exceed $500 regardless of the value stated, unless the loss occurs through the negligence of the innkeeper.

If the guest fails to state value, he cannot recover in excess of $100. In no event will liability exceed $500, unless there is fault or negligence. If there is value stated and the loss occurs through negligence, then there is liability up to the value stated. These limitations remain unimpaired by the fact that the innkeeper made a reasonable charge for storage.

It was held in *Crosby* v. *20 Fifth Avenue Hotel Co.*[1] that "[a] hotel is not chargeable as a bailee for a valuable antique [silver porringer] left in a trunk where plaintiff did not give notice that the trunk contained anything but ordinary personal luggage."

24:4 *Loss from Parcel Room or Checkroom*

A parcel room or checkroom is a completely enclosed facility capable of being locked where personal articles may be deposited, *free of charge,* it being understood that any gratuities, not demanded or exacted, but voluntarily offered, are not considered a fee or charge. A checking facility consisting of movable racks in an open space in front of elevators or in a lobby or reception area, or at the entrance to a dining room, have been held not to constitute a "checkroom." [2]

24:5 *Limitation Not Available to Concessionaires*

Where the checking facility is operated by an independent concessionaire rather than by the innkeeper himself, the statutory limitations in Section 201 are not available to such concessionaire. As bailee, the concessionaire would be liable for the full value of the loss arising out of his negligence.[3]

24:6 *Innkeeper Liable for Loss Resulting from Concessionaire's Negligence*

The fact that a parcel or checkroom facility is operated by an independent concessionaire does not necessarily relieve the innkeeper

---

[1] 173 Misc. 604, 605, 17 N.Y.S.2d 498, 499 (Sup. Ct. 1940) (per curiam).

[2] *Peters* v. *Knott Corp.*, 191 Misc. 898, 82 N.Y.S.2d 650 (Sup. Ct. 1948) (per curiam); *Gardner* v. *Roosevelt Hotel*, 175 Misc. 610, 24 N.Y.S.2d 261 (N.Y. City Ct. 1940), *rev'd on other grounds per curiam,* 176 Misc. 546, 28 N.Y.S.2d 78 (1941), *rev'd on other grounds,* 263 App. Div. 268, 32 N.Y.S.2d 208 (1st Dep't 1942).

[3] *Jacobson* v. *Belplaza Corp.*, 80 F. Supp. 917 (S.D.N.Y. 1948), *aff'd,* sub nom. *Jacobson* v. *Richards & Hassen Enterprises, Inc.*, 172 F.2d 464 (1949); *Marks* v. *Planetary Recreations, Inc.*, 86 N.Y.S.2d 487 (Sup. Ct.), *aff'd mem.*, 274 App. Div. 993, 85 N.Y.S.2d 316 (1st Dep't 1948).

of liability where the guest has been led to believe that the facility was operated by the innkeeper himself.[4]

In view of the double exposure to liability of the concessionaire without limitation and of the innkeeper where the concessionaire's identity remains undisclosed to the guest, insurance covering the risk is a must. The concessionaire's coverage should include the innkeeper as coinsured.

24:7 *Loss of Merchandise Samples and Merchandise for Sale*

Note that under Section 201 the innkeeper is under *no liability whatsoever* for loss of or damage to merchandise samples or merchandise for sale (whether in the guest's possession or delivered to the innkeeper for storage) *unless* the guest shall have given him prior written notice, stating value, that he has such merchandise in his possession, the receipt of which notice the innkeeper shall acknowledge in writing over his signature or that of his agent. Even then, the limit of liability is $500, unless the loss occurred through the innkeeper's negligence, in which event the liability is the stated value.

The distinction imposed by the statute between business property and personal requirements of the guest received judicial approval in *Hagerstrom v. Brainard Hotel Corp.,*[5] where the loss was jewelry intended for sale and kept in a trunk without the knowledge of or notice to the innkeeper.

HONIG v. RILEY
244 N.Y. 105, 155 N.E. 65 (1926)

CARDOZO, J.: "Plaintiff, visiting defendant's restaurant on New Year's Eve, 1925, left a fur coat of the value of $850 at the checkroom, receiving the usual check therefor. She was not questioned as to the value, and did not state it. The court charged the jury in effect that the plaintiff should have a verdict for the full value of the coat if the jury believed that the defendant had been negligent in caring for it. The question is whether liability has been limited by statute.

"The case involves the construction of section 201 of the General Business Law. . . .

[4] *Grishman v. The Lincoln, Inc.,* 28 N.Y.S.2d 488 (1941).
[5] 45 F.2d 130 (2d Cir. 1930).

"The defendant maintains that where property is deposited in a parcel or check room without statement of value or delivery of the prescribed receipt, there is a limit of liability to $75 for loss from any cause. Disclosure of the value, if followed by a receipt, will extend liability for fault or negligence up to the limit of the value stated, though even then the liability, if any, as insurer will be $100 and no more. The plaintiff on her side maintains, and the courts below have held, that the exemption from liability in excess of $75 where the value is not disclosed is not to be read as a limitation of liability for loss from any cause, but is confined to losses not due to the fault or negligence of the proprietor.

"We think the defendant's construction is the true one, however clumsy and inartificial may be the phrasing of the statute. A limitation of liability affecting merely the measure of recovery is applicable, if not otherwise restrained, to loss for any cause. [Citations omitted.] The final words of the section, 'unless such loss occurs through his fault or negligence,' are to be confined to the limitation of $100 immediately preceding. They do not relate back to the beginning and modify all that follows. The sense of the words and the order of the clauses would lead to this conclusion as a matter of verbal or grammatical construction though the provision as to check rooms were one standing by itself. The construction is confirmed when the provision is read in conjunction with the provisions immediately preceding it as part of a connected plan. The guest at an inn who delivers goods to the innkeeper for storage or safekeeping in a place other than his room must state the value of the goods and procure an appropriate receipt. If he fails to do this, the liability of the innkeeper is limited to $100. In no event, however, is there to be liability in excess of $500 except for fault or negligence. There are similar provisions in respect of liability for merchandise samples or merchandise for sale. From the beginning of the section to the end, the exemption from liability in excess of the prescribed maximum is absolute where value is concealed. Only where value is stated and a receipt delivered is the exemption made dependent upon freedom from negligence or other fault.

"Argument is made that the statute is unworkable and meaningless. Proprietors of restaurants who are informed of the value and give a receipt are to have the benefit of a $100 limitation if fault or negligence is not established. In that contingency, however, they do not need a limitation. The common law does not charge them with an obligation approaching that of an insurer. The argument overlooks the fact that the statute is not aimed at the protection of proprietors of restaurants exclusively. Another purpose, and indeed the chief one, if we may judge from the preceding exemptions of the section, is the protection of innkeepers, whose liability to guests is absolute, with exceptions not here important, under the rule at common law. For the purpose of the new exemption, proprietors of inns and proprietors of restaurants are grouped as a single class. If they have been guilty of fault or negligence, they are liable for damages to the extent of the value stated. If free from fault or negligence, their liability, if any, as insurers, will not exceed $100, but within that limitation will be determined by the existing law. Negligence may indeed be inferred in the first instance from the delivery of the subject of the bailment and the failure to return it. Even so, the inference may be repelled through proof by the bailee that the thing, though not returned, has been lost without his fault (*Claflin* v. *Meyer,* 75 N.Y. 260). Whether liability will then survive must be determined by the character of the bailment and the liability assumed. The bailee now before us would not be liable in any amount if negligence were absent. Negligence being found, the statute preserves the liability, but limits the recovery.

"In one of the opinions at the Appellate Term the point was made that the statute, if read as the defendant read it, would permit the innkeeper or the proprietor of a restaurant to limit his liability to $75, in default of disclosure of the value, though he had stolen or willfully misused the thing confided to his custody. We have no thought by our decision to sanction such injustice. The statute is aimed at loss or misadventure. It has no application to theft by the defendant or his agents (*D'Utassy* v. *Barrett,* 219 N.Y. 420, 424). Very likely, the statute would be fairer if it charged a bailee with a duty to make inquiry as to value so as to put the owner on his guard. Those considerations are for the Legislature. They do not relieve us of the duty to enforce the law as it is written.

"The judgment of the Appellate Division and the determination of the Appellate Term should be reversed; and the judgment of the Municipal Court modified by reducing the amount thereof to the sum of $75 with interest and costs, and as so modified affirmed without costs of appeal in this or any court.

[All concur.]

"Judgment accordingly."

24:8 Loss by Fire

Section 201 also exempts an innkeeper from liability for loss of or damage to wearing apparel or other personal property by fire when the fire occurred without his fault or negligence. In case of loss or damage by fire, the burden of affirmatively proving freedom from fault or negligence is on the innkeeper. The reasoning is that he "is in a better position to prove the cause of the fire than is the guest. If the innkeeper would absolve himself of liability to his guest it is not too much to expect of him that he assume the burden of proving his freedom from negligence." [6]

24:9 Loss by Incendiary Fire in Outbuildings

It should be noted Section 201 exempts the innkeeper from liability for loss or damage by fire of wearing apparel or other personal property of a guest, "in the lobby, hallways or in the room or rooms assigned to a guest" provided the innkeeper can affirmatively prove his freedom from fault or negligence in causing the fire.

Section 202 exempts him from liability for the loss by fire of a guest's property stored with the guest's knowledge in a barn or outer building, where it appears that (1) the fire was the work of an incendiary; and (2) the innkeeper was not at fault in causing the fire.

Section 202. *Loss by Fire*
No inn keeper shall be liable for the loss or destruction by fire of property received by him from a guest, stored or being with the knowledge of such guest in a barn or other out-building, where it shall appear that such loss or destruction was the work of an incendiary, and occurred without the fault or negligence of such inn keeper.

24:10 Loss by Fire of Animals Belonging to Guest

Section 203 of the statute dates back to 1866 and is a relic of the horse and buggy days. It has no significant application today, but has

[6] *Steiner* v. *O'Leary*, 186 Misc. 236, 237, 59 N.Y.S.2d 729, 731 (N.Y. City Ct. 1945), *aff'd*, 186 Misc. 577, 64 N.Y.S.2d 529 (Sup. Ct. 1946).

remained on the statute books as harmless. It may be made to apply to valuable pet animals, should they be destroyed by fire while in a hotel or motel.

Section 203. *Value of Animals*
No animal belonging to a guest and destroyed by fire while on the premises of any inn keeper shall be deemed of greater value than three hundred dollars, unless an agreement shall be proved between such guest and inn keeper that a higher estimate shall be made of the same.

24:11 *Loss of Property in Transport*

Section 203-a. *Hotel and Motel Keeper's Liability for Property in Transport*
No hotel or motel keeper shall be liable in any sum exceeding the sum of two hundred and fifty dollars for the loss of or damage to property of a guest delivered to such keeper, his agent or employee, for transport to or from the hotel or motel, unless at the time of delivering the same such value in excess of two hundred and fifty dollars shall be stated by such guest and a written receipt stating such value shall be issued by such keeper; provided, however, that where such written receipt is issued the keeper shall not be liable beyond five hundred dollars unless it shall appear that such loss or damage occurred through his fault or negligence.

Section 203-b. *Posting of Statute*
Every keeper of a hotel or motel or inn shall post in a public and conspicuous place and manner in the registration office and in the public rooms of such hotel or motel or inn a printed copy of this section and section two hundred three-a.

CHAPTER 25

Responsibility of Restaurant Keeper for Patron's Property

25:1 *Difference between Restaurant and Inn*

The restaurant is a house for the entertainment of anyone, whether resident or traveler; and the entertainment furnished is food and drink, without lodging. It differs in this respect from inns and boardinghouses, which furnish lodging as well as food. An innkeeper may carry on, under the same roof, a restaurant, to which he invites all persons to come for food and drink only.

25:2 *Responsibility as Bailee for Patron's Property*

By the custom of the restaurant, the guest's coat and hat may be taken by a servant at the entrance to the restaurant. In that case there is an express bailment to the restaurant keeper, and the bailment is for hire, or, as it is sometimes put, for the mutual benefit of bailor and bailee. For though there is nothing specially paid to the restaurant keeper for taking charge of the goods, still it is done as a business matter: "for such a system might obviously add to the popularity of the establishment, and would probably be adopted with that very object in view." [1] The restaurant keeper in such a case is therefore liable for any loss caused by his neglect of reasonable care. [2]

The same principle is involved where the waiter takes the guest's coat and hat and hangs them on a hook when the guest sits at the table; then, too, there is held to be a bailment for mutual benefit, so

---

[1] *Ultzen v. Nicols*, [1894] 1 Q.B. 92, 94 (1893) (Charles, J.).

[2] *La Salle Restaurant & Oyster House v. McMasters*, 85 Ill. App. 677 (1899); *Buttman v. Dennett*, 9 Misc. 462, 30 N.Y. 247 (N.Y. Ct. C.P. 1894) (per curiam).

that the restaurant keeper is liable for a loss which happens by reason of his negligence.[3]

25:3 Responsibility on an Implied Bailment

An "implied bailment" may be established by less direct proof of delivery to the servant of the restaurant keeper; as, for instance, by evidence that an overcoat was necessarily laid aside under circumstances showing at least notice of the fact and of such necessity to the restaurant keeper or his servants.[4]

If there is a bailment the restaurant keeper is responsible for a loss caused by his negligence, even though the words "not responsible for hats and coats" are printed on the bill of fare, and the waiters are forbidden to take hats and coats. The customer may be affected by a rule of this sort only if it is properly published so as to be called to his attention.[5]

WENTWORTH v. RIGGS
159 App. Div. 899, 143 N.Y.S. 455 (1st Dep't 1913)

[Action by Reginald de M. Wentworth against Leon C. Riggs. From a Municipal Court judgment in favor of plaintiff, affirmed at the Appellate Term (79 Misc. 400, 139 N.Y. 1082), defendant appeals. Reversed, and complaint dismissed, with costs, on the following dissenting opinion of SEABURY, J., at the Appellate Term, 79 Misc. at 403–408, 139 N.Y.S. at 1085–1088.]

"I am unable to agree with the views expressed in the prevailing opinion.

"In view of the precautions taken by the defendant to police and care for the property of his patrons, I think it is evident that he cannot be held liable for the loss of the overcoat upon any theory of negligence unless there was a bailment. If the defendant is to be held liable at all, it can only be upon this latter theory. Confusion had been engendered by certain cases, which seem to discuss constructive bailment

---

[3] *Ultzen* v. *Nicols* [1894] 1 Q.B. 92 (1893); *Appleton* v. *Welch*, 20 Misc. 343, 45 N.Y. 751 (Sup. Ct. 1897).

[4] *Montgomery* v. *Ladjing*, 30 Misc. 92, 61 N.Y.S. 840 (Sup. Ct. 1899).

[5] *La Salle Restaurant & Oyster House* v. *McMasters*, 85 Ill. App. 677 (1899).

as if it were identical with constructive delivery. The two things are distinct. Formerly, delivery was regarded as the essence of a bailment. As this branch of the law has developed, cases of constructive bailment have been recognized covering cases where there had been no delivery either actual or constructive, as where one held the possession of a chattel under such circumstances that the law placed upon the person having the possession of the chattel the obligation to deliver it to another. The typical instance of such a constructive bailment is where one sells a chattel to another, who pays the price thereof, and the vendor refuses to deliver it to the vendee. Here the law implies the contract of bailment, and holds the vendor answerable as bailee. In such a case it is apparent that there has been no delivery by the bailor to the bailee, and yet the bailment exists constructively. All the other examples of constructive bailment which are given in the books, as in the case of a finder, of a captor, or salvor, of an attaching officer, are cases where the person having the *possession* of the chattel is held to be a bailee, although there has never been either an actual or a constructive delivery of the chattels to the bailee by the bailor. In other words, the essential fact of legal significance in all these cases is possession. It certainly is not delivery, for, in none of these cases of constructive bailment, is there either an actual or a constructive delivery. . . .

"In an actual bailment there must be a delivery of the chattels to the bailee or his agent. The delivery may be either actual or constructive.

"(a) An actual delivery consists in giving to the bailee or his agents the real possession of the chattel. [Citation omitted.]

"(b) A constructive delivery comprehends all of those acts which, although not truly comprising real possession of the goods transferred, have been held *constructione juris* equivalent to acts of real delivery, and in this sense includes symbolical or substituted delivery. [Citations omitted.]

". . . A constructive bailment arises where the person having the possession of a chattel holds it under such circumstances that the law imposes upon him the obligation of delivering it to another.

"From the definition of the two subdivisions of actual bailment, and from the definition of a constructive bailment, there ought to be no difficulty in determining whether there was in the case at bar a bailment of the plaintiff's overcoat. Neither the defendant nor his agents ever had the real possession of the overcoat, and, therefore there was not an *actual* delivery of the coat. The facts proved are inconsistent with the hypothesis that the plaintiff intended to transfer to the defendant or his servants such a possession of the coat as would exclude, for the time of the bailment, the possession of the owner. The overcoat hung upon a hook within two feet of where the plaintiff was sitting during the meal, and it does not seem to be capable of dispute that during that time the defendant did not have such a possession of it as to exclude the possession of the plaintiff. If the plaintiff had wished to reach his overcoat at any time during the meal, either to take something from one of the pockets of the coat or for any other purpose, he was entirely free to do so, without requiring any act on the part of the defendant or his servants. The presence of the hooks may be construed into an invitation to the patron to hang his coat upon them, but hanging the coat upon the hook cannot be reasonably held to constitute a delivery of the coat to the *exclusive* possession of the defendant. The hooks were obviously placed there for the convenience of the patron, provided he wished to retain possession of his coat. If he wished to deposit the coat in the exclusive possession of the defendant, he should have availed himself of the accommodations which the defendant provided for that purpose. If he had done this, the defendant would have been liable. *Buttman* v. *Dennett*, 9 Misc. Rep. 462. The frequency with which the plaintiff was accustomed to visit the defendant's restaurant leaves no room for doubt that he knew of the accommodations provided by the defendant for caring for the hats, coats, and other articles of his patrons. . . .

"The facts of this case, viewed in the light of the foregoing authorities, seem to me to establish that there was no actual bailment, because there was neither an actual or constructive delivery of the coat. That this is not a case of constructive bailment is apparent from the fact that the defendant never had the actual possession of the coat.

"It follows that there was neither an actual nor constructive bailment, and, as there is no other ground under the facts in this case upon which defendant's liability can be predicated, the judgment should be reversed and a new trial ordered, with costs to appellant to abide the event."

APFEL v. WHYTE'S, INC.
110 Misc. 670, 180 N.Y.S. 712 (Sup. Ct. 1920)

[Action by Isadore Apfel against Whyte's, Incorporated. From a judgment for plaintiff, after a trial by the court without a jury, defendant appeals. Reversed, and complaint dismissed.]

MULLAN, J.: "The plaintiff went to the defendant's restaurant, 'Whyte's,' on Fulton street, for lunch. He says he did not notice the hat-and-coat rack, in charge of a check boy, at the Fulton street entrance, by which he entered. He was escorted to a table, and either a waiter, or one of the assistants to the head-waiter, who have come to be known as 'captains,' helped him take off his overcoat, and took his hat and overcoat and hung them up on a hook on a post. The precise location of the hook in relation to plaintiff's chair was not fixed by the plaintiff. He did say, however, that it was 'nearby.' One of the defendant's 'captains' testified that plaintiff told him that the coat 'was hanging on the rack on the post at his right hand, right where he was sitting,' and there was no rebuttal as to that. It would seem as if plaintiff must have seen the coat and hat as they were put on the hook. At least, he knew somehow that the coat and hat were placed on the same hook. It would also seem to be beyond doubt that the coat was at all times within his reach, or within a few feet of him, and possibly within his view. The record is somewhat meagre and unsatisfactory in respect of these details. It was not even shown whether or not plaintiff was a frequent guest of the establishment, or whether he had ever before eaten there. I think it is clear, however, from what there is in the record, that the situation was the familiar one of a man sitting down to a meal in a restaurant, with his coat and hat hung up in close proximity to the seat he is occupying. When plaintiff finished his meal, and started to leave, he asked for his coat and hat, and his waiter brought the hat, but the coat was missing, and never was found. The judgment for plaintiff, for the value of the coat and a pair of gloves that were in one of the pockets, is assailed by the defendant, who cites Wentworth v. Riggs, 159 App. Div. 899, where the dissenting opinion of Seabury, J., at the Appellate Term (79 Misc. Rep. 40), was adopted by the Appellate Division. I can see no room for a valid distinction between that case and this. There a restaurant guest was seated near the hook on which his overcoat was hung. It did not appear whether or not there were any checking facilities. Judge Seabury, in writing for a reversal of the judgment for the plaintiff guest, stressed the point that the coat had not been placed in the exclusive possession of the restaurateur, and that the guest, had he at any time so desired was at perfect liberty to take down his coat for any purpose, or to take out anything there might have been in a pocket of the coat. That, it seems to me, is the controlling consideration. How can it be said that the restaurant people have been given control of something that the owner may freely take at any moment without asking leave to do so? Furthermore, we are dealing with a subject that is a matter of every-day experience with most of us, a commonplace of life in a large city, and we know that restaurant managers do not, and in the nature of things, cannot, station employees to stand guard over coats and hats, unchecked, and hung on hooks about the room. Even if there were such watchers, they would not know which coat belonged to a given guest. Nor can the waiter be expected to care for the coats and hats of the guests he is serving, for a large part of the time he is necessarily going to, coming from, and in, the kitchen. Checking stands or racks, with boys in charge, are provided in most restaurants of any size, except those that cater exclusively to persons seeking inexpensive meals, for the very purpose of relieving guests of the burden and worry of exercising care in respect of their coats, hats, umbrellas, sticks, hand-bags, and other things commonly carried into restaurants. Is it not a natural and instinctive thing for one whose coat has been hung up on a hook near his seat, occasionally to look in that direction to see that it is still there? I do not believe it enters into the head of such a guest to assume that he has thrown off all responsibility for the safety of his property; indeed, it seems to me that, on the contrary, he feels himself under a decided compulsion to guard it. A guest may, of course, enter into a special arrangement with a restaurant proprietor, by which the guest's property shall become the subject of special care; but there is no pretense of any such express bailment here.

"The respondent does not question the doctrine of the *Wentworth* case, but he seeks to have the distinction drawn that there the coat was at no time in the physical possession of an employee of the restaurant. I think the point is merely tenuous. Judge Seabury did, in the *Wentworth* case, refer to the fact there present that none of the restaurant people 'ever saw, much less received,' the coat. But that was observed in passing, as one of the facts of the case, and there is nothing in the opinion to warrant the belief that the decision was rested to any extent upon the ground. It seems to me to be quite clear that the act of the defendant's employee in helping plaintiff to hang his coat and hat was one of mere courtesy, an attention that is customary and familiar to us all and that it falls far short of showing such an intrustment of the plaintiff's property to the defendant's care as would constitute a bailment."

[Judgment reversed, with $30 costs, and complaint dismissed, with costs. All concur.]

25:4 *Loss of Overcoat in Self-Service Cafeteria*

WIELAR *v.* SILVER STANDARD, INC.
263 App. Div. 521, 33 N.Y.S.2d 617 (1st Dep't 1942)

GLENNON, J.: "The defendant was the owner of a self-service cafeteria at No. 38 Park row, borough of Manhattan, city of New York. The cafeteria consisted of two large dining rooms, one on the street floor and the other in the basement. A patron upon entering received a food check and went to a counter where food was selected and placed upon a tray. The tray was then carried to a table of the patron's own choice.

"Plaintiff entered the cafeteria on December 10, 1940, and was handed a food check. He testified, 'I selected some food, placed it on a table; took off my hat and coat, and hung my coat on a hook on a post, which was about three or four feet off my table.' In answer to a question of the court, he stated, 'I never checked it.' Further he testified, 'I got up to get a drink of some beverage. I was probably less than a minute getting the beverage, and when I turned around and went back to my seat, my coat was gone. I spoke to the manager, who is here in court. I told him of the loss of my coat. I went around with him thinking, perhaps, it might be found in some other place in the restaurant but which couldn't be found. I then asked—someone came up to me and spoke to me while I was walking around, and said that coats had been stolen before.' He brought this action on the theory of negligence to recover the value of the coat.

"The manager of the restaurant testified that in the cafeteria there were two different kinds of signs, one of which read, 'Not responsible for personal property unless checked,' and the other, 'Watch your overcoat, we are not responsible.' The following question was asked of him: 'Do you check coats of customers in that store?' to which he replied, 'Only if they are requested.'

"The case was tried in the Small Claims Part of the Municipal Court, Borough of Manhattan, by an official referee who, after hearing the evidence, directed a judgment in favor of the defendant. Upon appeal to the Appellate Term of the Supreme Court, the judgment was reversed by a majority of the court with one justice dissenting.

"Outside of the fact that the case now under consideration was tried on the theory of negligence, the situation here presented is similar to that which was before the Appellate Term of the Supreme Court, both in *Wentworth* v. *Riggs* (79 Misc. 400), which was reversed upon the dissenting opinion of one of the justices and reported in 159 Appellate Division 899, and *Apfel* v. *Whyte's Inc.* (110 Misc. 670). Both of those cases were tried on the theory of bailment. In the latter case, . . . [t]he restaurant there in question was located in the lower part of Manhattan. The food served was not inexpensive and it is fair to assert that during the winter months it was the common practice for each one of the diners to remove his hat and coat. We know from experience that in a self-service cafeteria, such as we are dealing with here, removal of overcoats by patrons while eating is by no means a common practice. Customers usually are in a hurry and the food is inexpensive. It would be well nigh impossible for the management to guard its customers' unchecked hats and overcoats during the rush hour periods without employing such a large force of special policemen or watchmen as to make the cost almost prohibitive.

"While there is evidence in the record to the effect that on a prior occasion in the month of October an overcoat had been stolen, still it seems to us that the failure of the management to detect the larceny of plaintiff's coat would not, in and of itself, under the circumstances constitute negligence. The referee properly could have found that if there were negligence on the part of the owner of the cafeteria, by the same token there was contributory negligence on the part of the customer.

"The determination of the Appellate Term should be reversed, and the judgment of the Municipal Court affirmed, with costs to the defendant in this court and in the Appellate Term."

[All concur.]

25:5   *Loss by Reason of Insufficient Supervision of Premises*

Finally, the restaurant keeper, though not a bailee in any sense, may be held responsible for loss of the goods of his guest if the loss happened by reason of the insufficiency of the general supervision exercised by the keeper of the restaurant for the protection of his customer's goods; and the burden of proving neglect of duty is on the plaintiff.[6] The kind and amount of supervision required of the restaurant keeper, and the question of his neglect of due care, depend of course upon the special circumstances of each case. "[I]t is well known that there are all kinds of restaurants. In some of them good taste and etiquette require that a customer should take his hat and overcoat off while taking a meal, while in others, especially the so-called quick-lunch establishments, customers frequently remove neither hat nor overcoat."[7] And where sufficient general supervision is exercised by the restaurant keeper, he is not liable when the guest himself hangs his overcoat on a hook, without calling the waiter's attention to it, and it is stolen from the hook.[8]

MONTGOMERY v. LADJING
30 Misc. 92, 61 N.Y.S. 840 (Sup. Ct. 1899)

FREEDMAN, J.: "This action was brought by the plaintiff to recover the value of an overcoat lost in a restaurant, kept by defendant, while

---

[6] *Harris* v. *Childs' Unique Dairy Co.*, 84 N.Y.S. 260 (Sup. Ct. 1903); *Montgomery* v. *Ladjing*, 30 Misc. 92, 61 N.Y.S. 840 (Sup. Ct. 1899); *Simpson* v. *Rourke*, 13 Misc. 230, 34 N.Y.S. 11 (N.Y. Ct. C.P. 1895).

[7] *Montgomery* v. *Ladjing*, 30 Misc. 92, 96, 61 N.Y.S. 840, 843 (Sup. Ct. 1899).

[8] See the three cases cited in note 6. In both *Harris* and *Montgomery* the guest had notice that articles might be deposited with the cashier; but the cases seem to have turned on the absence of a bailment.

the plaintiff was upon the premises as a customer. At the trial the plaintiff had judgment, and the defendant appealed. The defendant was not shown to be an innkeeper, but merely a restaurant keeper. As such, he cannot be subjected to the liabilities of an innkeeper. [J. Story, *Commentaries on the Law of Bailments*, 4th ed. (Boston, 1846).]

"In *Carpenter* v. *Taylor*, 1 Hilt. 193, it was held that a person who enters a restaurant to procure a meal or refreshments is not to be deemed a guest or traveller entitled to the protection which the law gives against innkeepers. In *Buttman* v. *Dennett*, 9 Misc. Rep. 462, it was held that a restaurant keeper in whose custody wraps and other articles of wearing apparel have been temporarily placed for safekeeping is liable as a bailee. This liability has been enforced where a waiter took the hat and coat of a customer when he entered the restaurant and seated himself at a table. *Appleton* v. *Welch*, 20 Misc. Rep. 343.

"But in *Simpson* v. *Rourke*, 13 Misc. Rep. 230, it was held that a restaurant keeper is not an insurer of the effects of customers who may have accepted the invitation held out by him, but at most is required to use only the ordinary care called for by the circumstances. In that case the plaintiff had not placed his overcoat in the physical custody of the defendant or his servant, but had it removed after having selected a seat and personally placed it on a rack, and it was, therefore, held that the question merely was as to the sufficiency of the general supervision exercised over the restaurant for the protection of the customers' property placed therein, and it not appearing that the size of the restaurant or any special conditions called for greater vigilance than was actually exercised, the judgment in favor of the defendant was affirmed.

"It is not necessary to multiply citations. The cases already cited sufficiently show the principles upon which the liability of a restaurant keeper for the loss of personal property of a customer depends. As to the other cases directly affecting restaurant keepers which may be found in the books, it will on examination be found that each of them depends upon an application of one or the other of the principles already stated to the peculiar facts of the case. . . .

". . . [B]efore a restaurant keeper will be held liable for the loss of an overcoat of a customer while such customer takes a meal or refreshments, it must appear either that the overcoat was placed in the physical custody of the keeper of the restaurant or his servants, in which case there is an actual bailment, or that the overcoat was necessarily laid aside under circumstances showing at least notice of the fact and of such necessity to the keeper of the restaurant or his servants, in which case there is an implied bailment or constructive custody, or that the loss occurred by reason of the insufficiency of the general supervision exercised by the keeper of the restaurant for the protection of the property of customers temporarily laid aside. After all, each case must largely depend upon its particular facts and circumstances, for it is well known that there are all kinds of restaurants. In some of them good taste and etiquette require that a customer should take his hat and overcoat off while taking a meal, while in others, especially the so-called quick-lunch establishments, customers frequently remove neither hat nor overcoat.

"In the case at bar the testimony on the part of the plaintiff is to the effect that, on the day of the loss, the plaintiff entered the restaurant kept by the defendant with a party of friends and removed his overcoat, which was a light spring overcoat; that he hung it on a hook fixed to a post near the table at which he seated himself; that the attention of neither the defendant nor of any of his employees was called to the coat in any way; and that some fifteen minutes later the coat was missing. The plaintiff testified that he would not say that the waiter who waited on him ever saw the overcoat. It was not shown how the loss occurred. These facts do not establish an actual bailment; for, as stated in Schouler on Bailments, §§1, 3, 9, 21, a bailment implies the delivery of a chattel, and to subject one to liability as a bailee, it is a constitutional element that he had voluntarily assumed or retained the custody of the chattel alleged to have been bailed. There was not even an implied bailment or constructive custody on the theory that the overcoat was necessarily removed under circumstances which gave notice of such fact and of the necessity to the defendant or his servants. The plaintiff seems to have been conscious of the necessity of proving that the defendant had assumed the custody of the overcoat, for in his bill of particulars he alleges his cause of action to be 'failure of defendant to exercise proper and lawful care of said coat while the same was in his care and custody,' but he utterly failed to show such assumption of custody.

"Neither actual nor implied bailment or constructive custody having been established, it remains to be seen whether the plaintiff sufficiently proved negligence on the part of the defendant in the general supervision exercised over the restaurant, such as it was, for the protection of customers' property in general. The burden of proof upon this point was upon the plaintiff, for it is only in the case of a bailment that the burden is cast upon a bailee to account for the loss of the goods. But the plaintiff rested his case, upon this point, upon the bare fact of the loss.

"The defendant, on the other hand, testified, and it was not disputed, that he had kept a restaurant for the past fifteen years; that this was the first loss that had ever occurred in his establishment; that the plaintiff had visited the place for about six months prior to the date of the loss; that he, the defendant, gave his personal attention and supervision to the restaurant and allowed no suspicious characters to enter, and that there was a place immediately behind the cashier's desk reserved for the care of the property of customers that might be given to him or to his employees for safekeeping. The plaintiff admitted that in this place he 'may have seen one of the other fellows leave a sample case.' Upon the whole case it did not appear that the size of the restaurant or any special conditions therein called for greater vigilance than was actually exercised, and the plaintiff wholly failed to show failure on the part of the defendant to exercise ordinary care in the general management of his establishment. In every aspect of the case, therefore, the defendant is entitled to a reversal of the judgment against him.

"Maclean and Leventritt, JJ., concur.

"Judgment reversed, new trial ordered, with costs to the appellant to abide event."

25:6 *Damage Caused by Negligence of Employees*

BLOCK *v.* SHERRY
43 Misc. 342, 87 N.Y.S. 160 (Sup. Ct. 1904)

GIEGERICH, J.: "This action was brought to recover the value of a dress, worn by the plaintiff in the defendant's restaurant on the evening of June 26, 1903, and claimed to have been ruined by the negligence of one of the defendant's waiters.

"On the trial the plaintiff gave evidence tending to show that while the plaintiff and her husband were dining on the veranda of defendant's restaurant, one of the waiters spilled part of a glass of water over her dress, which completely ruined it, the material being of such a character that it could neither be renovated nor repaired so as to be of further use, and that the water was spilled through the negligence of the servant, and that the plaintiff in no way contributed to the accident. The defendant's testimony tended to show that the water did not come from a glass, but came from a platter containing about a half a glass of water resulting from melted ice, and that as the waiter reached over for the platter the plaintiff moved her elbow back and knocked against it, causing it to fall on the dress. On this conflict of evidence the justice determined the issues in favor of the plaintiff, and while he might well have found from the evidence submitted, in favor of the defendant, yet there is not such a preponderance of evidence in favor of the defendant as would warrant us in reversing the judgment on that ground. The defendant strenuously contends that a restaurant-keeper is not an insurer of the effects of the customers who may have accepted the invitation held out by him, but at most, is required to use only ordinary care, and this is the well-settled law in this State. The strict rules governing the liability of hotel and innkeepers do not apply to the keeper of a restaurant. [Citations omitted.] But while this is so, they are still responsible for damages caused by the negligence of their servants while in the conduct of the business for which they are employed, under the well-settled rule of *respondeat superior*. [Citations omitted.]

"The appellant urges that the mere fact of the spilling of a glass of water in a crowded restaurant is not negligence. Whether it is negligence or not we think depends altogether upon the circumstances, and in this case the justice who tried the action and had the witnesses before him arrived at the conclusion that the spilling was through the negligence of the servant. . . ."

[Affirmed. Friedman, P.J., concurs. McCall, J. (dissenting).]

25:7 *Limitation of Liability for Articles Checked*

For articles of personal property accepted for safekeeping, the restaurant keeper is responsible as bailee, bound to exercise ordinary care in keeping and safeguarding the property. The measure of liability for loss through negligence is the reasonable value of the property. The parties to a bailment may, however, contract to diminish the bailee's common-law liability provided the contract is not in violation of law or of public policy. Such a contract must be a special contract spelling out the limitation in clear language and it must appear that the bailor (the customer) has had reasonable notice of the terms and that he has assented to them.

It has been held[9] that a parcel check of the usual cardboard type (3″ x 2½″) in size upon the face of which there appeared in legible red letters the word "Contract" together with terms and conditions limiting the parcel room owner's liability to $25, was not sufficient to charge the depositor with knowledge that he was contracting for a limitation of liability for loss. There was no proof in the case that there were conspicuous signs or large placards about the parcel room (nor any other form of notice) calling attention to the limitation of liability.

The parcel-room check with the usual legend printed either on its face or on the reverse side thereof that "the restaurant (or hotel, as the case may be), will not be liable for loss of or damage to the property as a result of fire, theft, ordinary or gross negligence, or otherwise, unless it shall appear that the loss or damage was caused by willful act or misappropriation by the restaurant (hotel) or its employees" is insufficient to limit liability *unless* there is adequate notice by a conspicuous large placard at the parcel room calling attention to the contract for limited liability.

In New York, Section 201 of the General Business Law does limit the restaurant keeper's liability, as it does that of an innkeeper, to $75 for articles checked in the checkroom or parcel room of any hotel *or restaurant,* the delivery of which is evidenced by a check or receipt therefor and for which no fee or charge is exacted. The posting re-

[9] *Klar v. H. & M. Parcel Room, Inc.,* 270 App. Div. 538, 61 N.Y.S.2d 285 (1st Dep't 1946), *aff'd mem.,* 296 N.Y. 1044, 73 N.E.2d 912 (1947).

quirements of the statute do not specifically refer to restaurants as they do to hotels.

25:8 *Summary*

A restaurant keeper is not absolutely liable as insurer for the safety of the property of his customers. He is liable for negligence as bailee, where he accepts the property for safekeeping either in a checkroom or elsewhere in the premises, and fails to return it when called for. He is also liable for losses occasioned by failure of adequate supervision of the premises. He is not liable for loss of an overcoat or hat left on a chair or hung on a hook by the customer himself. He is well advised to maintain a checking facility in the premises and to post adequate notices in conspicuous places in the establishment that he will be "Not Responsible for Personal Property Unless Checked with the Management." Disregard of such conspicuous notices may well charge the customer with contributory negligence.

CHAPTER 26

Lost and Found Property

26:1 *Introduction*

It is human to be careless at times and hotel guests are unexceptionally human. The number and variety of articles lost or misplaced by guests vary with the size and type of the hotel or motel. A fair estimate of articles found in a leading transient New York City hotel in a year's time is 5,000, of which about 1,800 are unclaimed and returned to the finder. Whenever an article is "lost" and "found" within a hotel or motel premises, a question arises as to the ownership of the article in question. It is the purpose of this chapter to acquaint the innkeeper with the legal principles applicable to lost property and to give him legal guidance for handling lost property.

26:2 *Title to Lost or Misplaced Personal Property*

At common law the principle was early established (1722) that the finder acquires a right to a found article good against the whole world except the true owner. Among the questions that developed in this area of the law was whether an article had been *lost, mislaid,* or *abandoned.* A loss is always involuntary or accidental; the owner never intends to part with the ownership of lost property. Property is never "lost" unless the owner parts with it unintentionally and does not at any time thereafter know where to find it. Mislaid property is that which the owner voluntarily and intentionally laid down in a place where he can again resort to it, and then forgets where he put it. Abandoned property is one which the owner voluntarily discarded with no intention of reclaiming. The law requires that title to the article must be in someone and as a practical matter, the finder, be he an employee or a stranger to the hotel, and the innkeeper on whose premises the property was found will each insist that he or she has title.

It is to be realized, of course, that except where a statute otherwise provides, title to lost or mislaid property remains with the true owner. But the true owner may never become known. It is, therefore, important to determine who is entitled to possession. The answer to this question may depend on the place where the property is found, that is, whether it is a private room or public place within the hotel. A chambermaid, who, in the course of cleaning, found three twenty-dollar bills in the public parlor of a hotel, was entitled to the possession of the money as against the innkeeper.[1] On the other hand, as between chambermaid and the hotel proprietor, the latter was awarded possession of eight one-hundred dollar bills concealed under the paper lining of a dresser drawer in a guest room, where it was found by the maid.[2] As a rule, a guest room in a hotel is considered to be a private rather than a public place and the innkeeper rather than the finder is entitled to the possession of articles found therein. On the other hand, lobbies, dining rooms, ballrooms, function rooms, halls and the like, to which the public has access, have been held public places. The cases generally hold that the finder, that is, the person who first discovers and takes possession, is entitled to articles found in public places. The obvious desire of the courts to safeguard the loser often leads to a finding that the property was mislaid rather than lost or abandoned. The right to mislaid property is generally held to be in the owner of the premises where the property is found.

26:3 *Statutes Governing Lost and Found Property*

Most of the states have enacted statutes imposing upon finders the duty of inquiring for owners of the found property and requiring the reporting of the loss and deposit of the property in a designated public office, usually the local police department.

Upon the recommendation of the New York State Law Revision Commission, the New York State Legislature enacted Article 7-B of

[1] *Hamaker* v. *Blanchard*, 90 Pa. 377 (1879).

[2] *Jackson* v. *Steinberg*, 186 Ore. 129, 200 P.2d 376 (1948), *rehearing denied*, 186 Ore. 140, 205 P.2d 562 (1949).

the Personal Property Law, effective September 1, 1958, to regularize procedures for dealing with lost and found property which will promote the return of the property to the owner and at the same time protect the expectations of the finder.

The law defines "property" as "money, goods, chattels, and tangible personal property," excluding instruments. "Lost property" for purposes of the law, includes both *lost* and *mislaid* property. The distinction between lost and mislaid property has been abolished. A "finder" is ". . . the person who first takes possession of lost property." *All* property which is found is presumed to be *lost* property unless it is established in an action or proceeding commenced within six months after the date of the finding that the property is not lost.

The statute prescribed the *procedure* for handling lost property. The finder of lost property of ten dollars or more in value must turn it over to the owner, if known; otherwise, to the local police department. Failure to do so is made a misdemeanor. A finder-employee may turn found property over to the innkeeper and relieve himself of further responsibility. The police will give the finder-depositor a receipt for the property which they will retain for six months (unless the owner will sooner claim it) where the property has a maximum value of five hundred dollars. If the property is valued at more than five hundred but less than five thousand dollars, it will be kept for one year, and if valued at five thousand dollars or more, for three years. If not claimed by the owner within the prescribed period, the property will be turned over to the finder, who then becomes entitled to possession against everyone *including the owner.* Instruments, as distinguished from property, will be retained in police custody; the finder will not acquire title thereto.

It should be noted that if "the finder is an employee under a duty to deliver the lost property to his employer, the employer shall have the rights of a finder . . . if, before the property is delivered to the finder by the police, he shall file with the police having custody of the property a written notice asserting such rights."

As to property under ten dollars in value, if the finder is unable, after reasonable effort, to find the owner, title vests in him one year after the date of finding.

26:4   *City Ordinances with Respect to Lost Property*

A representative example of city ordinances imposing duties on finders can be found in the Administrative Code of the city of New York, which provides as follows:

Section 435–4.1. Reporting and depositing lost money or property

(a) Any person who finds any lost money or property of or exceeding the value of ten dollars shall report such finding to and deposit such money or property in a police station house within ten days after the finding thereof. Such money or property shall thereupon be transmitted to the property clerk who shall make entry of such deposit in his records. Such money or property as shall remain in the custody of the property clerk for a period of three months without a lawful claimant entitled thereto shall be turned over to the person who found and deposited the same. If the person who so found and deposited such money or property shall not appear and claim the same within thirty days after notice by registered mail of the expiration of said three month's period, such money or property shall, in the case of money, be paid into the fund described in article one or title B of chapter eighteen of the code, and in the case of property be sold at public auction after having been advertised in "the City Record" for a period of ten days and the proceeds of such sale shall be paid into such a fund.

(b) Any person who shall violate, or refuse, or neglect to comply with any provision of this section, upon conviction thereof, shall be punished by a fine of not more than one thousand dollars or imprisonment not exceeding one year, or both.

The term "lost" used in the foregoing statute does not apply to baggage or personal property held by an innkeeper under the hotel lien; nor does it apply to property remaining unclaimed in storage at a hotel. Similarly, property found in a room vacated by a guest which appears to be the property of such guest cannot be considered "lost" in the first instance; it should be held for the account of such former guest, who should be notified of the facts.

If, however, money or property is found in the hallways, lobbies, elevators, stairs, or other public places in the hotel without any clue as to the owner of such property, it is undoubtedly in the category of "lost money or property," and if it is valued at $10.00 or more, must be turned over to the nearest police station within ten days after being found. The fact that this ten-day period is allowed by the law will give the hotel an opportunity to hold the money or property so found for this period and thus give the owner of the property a chance to reclaim it before it is delivered to the Police Department.

The local police stations in New York City are instructed to issue receipts to persons turning in lost money or property, and if no person claims the money or property within three months the Police Department will send a registered letter to the person depositing the property so that such person can appear and claim it within thirty days.

It is advisable and indeed is generally the custom for hotelkeepers to require of all employees contractual waivers of their rights as finders and to impose upon them the contractual duty of turning in to the hotelkeeper all property found within the hotel, irrespective of the place of finding. It is advisable under such circumstances, however, to recognize the rights of honest employees as finders after diligent search fails to discover the true owners.

26:5 Acquisition of Lost Property as Larceny

A finder who fails to take reasonable measures to return lost property to the owner may be guilty of larceny. In New York, Section 155.05 of the Penal Law specifically provides in pertinent part:

Section 155.05. *Larceny: Defined*

1. A person steals property and commits larceny when, with intent to deprive another of property or to appropriate the same to himself or to a third person, he wrongfully takes, obtains or withholds such property from an owner thereof.

2. Larceny includes a wrongful taking, obtaining or withholding of another's property, with the intent prescribed in subdivision one of this section, committed in any of the following ways: . . .

(b) By acquiring lost property. A person acquires lost property when he exercises control over property of another which he knows to have been lost or mislaid, or to have been delivered under a mistake as to the identity of the recipient or the nature or amount of the property, without taking reasonable measures to return such property to the owner.

26:6 *Internal Procedure for Handling Lost and Found Property*

Handling lost and found property produces no revenue. It is a service which, if properly performed, yields a wealth of good will; if neglected, it can cause vexation to host and guest, and, in extreme cases, may generate expensive law suits.

The large metropolitan hotels maintain lost and found departments. Every hotel or motel should have a proper system for handling lost and found property. All employees should be instructed to deliver articles found by them or turned in to them by a patron to a designated responsible person or office, *promptly*. A record is to be made in a lost and found record book of the date, the place where found, the description of the article, the name of the finder, and if found in a guest room, the name and address of the last occupant, together with any appropriate "remarks." The article should be deposited in a safe place, presumably in the hotel safe, until claimed by the owner or until delivered to the police according to law. Prompt efforts should be made to ascertain the owner. In corresponding with former guests who registered as "Mr. & Mrs." address the first letter to "Mr." and use his business address whenever possible.

HAMAKER *v.* BLANCHARD
90 Pa. 377 (1879)

"This was an appeal from the judgment of a justice of the peace. The material facts were these: Sophia Blanchard was a domestic servant in a hotel in Lewiston, of which the defendant was the proprietor. While thus employed, she found in the public parlor of the hotel, three twenty-dollar bills. On finding the money, she went with it to Mr. Hamaker, and informed him of the fact, and upon his remarking that he thought it belonged to a whip agent, a transient guest of the hotel, she gave it to him, for the purpose of returning it to said agent. It was afterwards ascertained that the money did not belong to the agent, and no claim was made for it by anyone. Sophia afterwards demanded the money of defendant, who refused to deliver it to her. Defendant admitted that he still had the custody of the money.

"In the general charge the court (Bucher, P.J.) inter alia, said: 'If you find that this was lost money, Hamaker did not lose it, and that it never belonged to him, but that it belonged to someone else who has not appeared to claim it, then you ought to find for the plaintiff, on the principle that the finder of a lost chattel is entitled to the possession and use of it as against all the world except the true owner. . . . The counsel for the defendant asks us to say that as the defendant was the proprietor of a hotel and the money was found therein, the presumption of law is that it belonged to a guest, who had lost it, and that the defendant has a right to retain it as against this woman, the finder, to await the demand of the true owner. I decline to give you such instructions; but charge you that under the circumstances there is no presumption of law that this money was lost by a guest at the hotel, and that the defendant is entitled to keep it as against this woman for the true owner.'

"The verdict was for the plaintiff for $60, with interest, and after judgment thereon, defendant took this writ and assigned for error the foregoing portions of the charge."

[Arguments of counsel omitted.]

Mr. Justice TRUNKEY delivered the opinion of the court, June 9th, 1879.

"It seems to be settled law that the finder of lost property has a valid claim to the same against all the world, except the true owner, and generally that the place in which it is found creates no exception to this rule. But property is not lost, in the sense of the rule, if it was intentionally laid on a table, counter or other place, by the owner, who forgot to take it away, and in such case the proprietor of the premises is entitled to retain the custody. Whenever the surroundings evidence that the article was deposited in its place, the finder has no right of possession against the owner of the building: *McAvon v. Medina*, 11 Allen (Mass.) 548. An article casually dropped is within the rule. Where one went into a shop, and as he was leaving picked up a parcel of bank notes, which was lying on the floor, and immediately showed them to the shopman, it was held that the facts did not warrant the supposition that the notes had been deposited there intentionally, they being manifestly lost by someone, and there was no circumstance in the case to take it out of the general rule of law, that the finder of a lost article is entitled to it as against all persons, except the real owner: *Bridges v. Hawkesworth*, 7 Eng. Law & Eq. R. 424.

"The decision in *Mathews* v. *Harsell*, 1 E. D. [*sic*] Smith (N.Y.) 393, is not in conflict with the principle, nor is it an exception. Mrs. Mathews, a domestic in the house of Mrs. Barmore, found some Texas notes, which she handed to her mistress, to keep for her. Mrs. Barmore afterwards intrusted the notes to Harsell, for the purpose of ascertaining their value, informing him that she was acting for her servant, for whom she held the notes. Harsell sold them, and appropriated the proceeds; whereupon Mrs. Mathews sued him and recovered their value, with interest from the date of sale. Such is that case. True, Woodruff, J., says: 'I am by no means prepared to hold that a house-servant who finds lost jewels, money or chattels, in the house of his or her employer, acquires any title even to retain possession against the will of the employer. It will tend much more to promote honesty and justice to require servants in such cases to deliver the property so found to the employer, for the benefit of the true owner.' To that remark, foreign to the case as understood by himself, he added the antidote; 'And yet the Court of Queen's Bench in England have recently decided that the place in which a lost article is found, does not form the ground of any exception to the general rule of law, that the finder is entitled to it against all persons, except the owner.' His views of what will promote honesty and justice are entitled to respect, yet many think Mrs. Barmore's method of treating servants far superior.

"The assignments of error are to so much of the charge as instructed the jury that, if they found the money in question was lost, the defendant had no right to retain it because found in his hotel, the circumstances raising no presumption that it was lost by a guest, and their verdict ought to be for the plaintiff. That the money was not voluntarily placed where it was found, but accidentally lost, is settled by the verdict. It is admitted that it is found in the parlor, a public place open to all. There is nothing to indicate whether it was lost by a guest, or a boarder, or one who had called with or without business. The pretence that it was the property of a guest, to whom the defendant would be liable is not founded on an act or circumstance in evidence.

"Many authorities were cited, in argument, touching the rights, duties and responsibilities of an innkeeper in relation to his guests; these are so well settled as to be uncontroverted. In respect to other persons than guests, an innkeeper is another man. When money is found in his house, on the floor of a room common to all classes of persons, no presumption of ownership arises; the case is like the finding upon the floor of a shop. The research of counsel failed to discover authority that an innkeeper shall have an article which another finds in a public room of his house, where there is no circumstance pointing to its loss by a guest. In such case the general rule should prevail. If the finder be an honest woman, who immediately informs her employer, and gives him the article on his false pretense that he knows the owner and will restore it, she is entitled to have it back and hold it till the owner comes. A rule of law ought to apply to all alike. Persons employed in inns will be encouraged to fidelity by protecting them in equality of rights with others. The learned judge was right in his instructions to the jury.

"Judgment affirmed."

[One judge dissented without opinion.]

The recommended rule is to require all employees to deliver to the management lost and found property. Such property is then either turned over to legal custody of the Police Department or other designated public authority, or held by the hotelkeeper in trust for the owner for a reasonable length of time, usually six months. If at the end of that time the rightful owner has not claimed it, the property is returned to the finder.

Employment contracts should require all employees to turn in, as a matter of course, all articles, whether lost, mislaid, abandoned, or temporarily forgotten.

FLAX v. MONTICELLO REALTY CO.
185 Va. 474, 39 S.E.2d 308 (1946)

[Plaintiff was a guest in defendant's hotel, the Monticello Hotel in Norfolk, Va. Immediately prior to checking out, he noticed on the dresser in his room something wrapped in tissue paper. Upon examination, it contained a pearshaped brooch, which plaintiff supposed at first sight to be a piece of worthless costume jewelry. Plaintiff took the article to the suite of some friends in the hotel, and later in the evening, at the suggestion of one of them, to a jeweler who appraised it as a genuine diamond brooch worth between $3,750.00 and $4,000.00.

The jewel was thereafter delivered to the hotel manager for custody until it should be called for by the true owner. Plaintiff called several times to ascertain if the owner had made claim for it and when he found that no such claim was asserted, he made demand for the jewelry. Upon refusal, he commenced this action. The jury returned a verdict for plaintiff which was set aside by the court as contrary to law and the evidence.

Investigation revealed the fact that the maid who was employed at the hotel, upon dismantling the bed in plaintiff's room, thinking that plaintiff was about to check out found the brooch wrapped in tissue paper, in the crevice of the margin of the mattress. In accordance with the hotel instructions and custom, as plaintiff occupant of the room had not actually departed, she placed the article on the bureau, on the supposition that it belonged to him.

It was plaintiff's contention (1) that the brooch was abandoned property and that he, as finder, was entitled to keep it as against everyone, except the true owner; (2) that his delivery of the brooch to the hotel manager constituted a bailment and that his bailee was estopped to deny his bailor's right to the possession of the brooch.]

BROWNING, J., delivered the opinion of the court: . . . "As to the contention that the brooch was abandoned property, the observation of the learned trial judge is sufficient to refute it. [The Court quoted from the opinion of the trial judge, as follows:]

" 'It is contrary to human experience that the owner of a $3,750.00 brooch would place it in a mattress in a hotel room and intentionally leave it there because of a desire no longer to possess it. On the other hand, the probability is so strong as to amount to proof that it was left at the hotel room as a result of inadvertence. Failure of the owner to make claim for it may be explained by a number of hypotheses more reasonable than that of voluntary abandonment.'

". . . The plaintiff in this case was not the finder of the jewel. He appropriated it and claimed it as his own. We may say at this time that the maid made no claim for it and does not do so. The claimant by mere coincidence found himself in an advantageous position to assert some sort of right thereto.

"In the adjudications which we have found a very controlling circumstance as to the rightful authority and custody of the article is the control over the *locus in quo* in which the thing is found. The *locus in quo* here is, of course, a private room in the hotel of the defendant.

"This court said in the case of *Crosswhite* v. *Shelby Operating Corp.*, 182 Va. 713, 30 S.E. (2d) 673, 153 A.L.R. 573: 'An innkeeper (as distinguished from a landlord) is in direct and continued control of his guest rooms.'

"Some of the cases have held that where money and bonds and packages of bills have been found in such public places as lobbies, dining rooms, halls and the like, to which the public has access, the finder is entitled to the property found, as against everyone except the rightful owner, but a private room in a hotel or an inn is a very different *locus in quo*. As to mislaid or forgotten property, which, we think this unquestionably was, the innkeeper, as the custodian, owed the duty to the owner of the chattel. He is treated in some of the cases as representing the owner and has the paramount custody, notwithstanding any agreement as that alleged. . . .

"The plaintiff in the case before us urged the contention that the defendant was his bailee and was thus estopped to deny his bailor's right to the possession of the brooch. It is probably enough to say that his contention was not made in the trial court. . . .

"If the rule of law on the subject of bailment is present at all, it is found in the fact that the defendant occupied the position as bailee, *in invitum,* for the true owner of the chattel, and if it made the agreement alleged, it would constitute a breach of trust and would have been unenforceable.

". . . A very pertinent excerpt is found in a passage in Pollack and Wright's Essay on Possession in the Common Law. . . . '. . . [T]he general principle seems to me to be that where a person has possession of house or land, with a manifest intention to exercise control over it and the things which may be upon or in it, then, if something is found on that land, whether by an employee of the owner or by a stranger, the presumption is that the possession of the thing is in the owner of the *locus in quo*.'

"The plaintiff, Flax, has no legal standing as a claimant to the brooch. Were he successful in his claim, in Biblical language, he would reap where he has not sown and would gather where he has not strawed, an abhorrent thought."

[Judgment affirmed.]

JACKSON v. STEINBERG
186 Ore. 129, 200 P.2d 376 (1948), *rehearing denied,* 186 Ore. 140,
205 P.2d 562 (1949)

[Action by Laura I. Jackson against Karl Steinberg, doing business as the Arthur Hotel, for money had and received. From an adverse judgment, defendant appeals. Reversed. The plaintiff, Mrs. Jackson, was employed by defendant innkeeper, as chambermaid in his hotel. On December 30, 1946, while cleaning one of the guest rooms, she found eight one-hundred dollar bills, U.S. currency, concealed under the paper lining of a dresser drawer. The bills were stacked neatly and her attention was drawn to them only by reason of their bulk having made a slight bulge in the lining. She removed the bills and delivered them immediately to the manager of the hotel, in order that they might be restored to the true owner, if he could be found, and subject to her claims as finder.

Defendant made an unsuccessful attempt to discover the true owner of the bills, by communicating, by mail, with each of the persons who had occupied this particular room from mid-October through December 31, 1946. Plaintiff then demanded of defendant that he return the money to her as finder, but he refused. This action for money had and received followed. Defendant's affirmative defense was that as innkeeper, he is required, both at common law and by the Oregon statute, to hold the bills as bailee for the rightful owner. Defendant's theory is that the bills constitute mislaid property, presumed to have been left in the room by a former guest of the hotel, and that, as innkeeper, he is entitled to custody of the bills and bound to hold them as bailee for the true owner. Plaintiff, on the other hand, claims the right to possession of the bills as treasure trove, as against all persons but the true owner.]

HAY, J. [after recital of facts]: "Lost property is defined as that with the possession of which the owner has involuntarily parted, through neglect, carelessness, or inadvertence. [Citation omitted.] It is property which the owner has unwittingly suffered to pass out of his possession, and of the whereabouts of which he has no knowledge. [Citation omitted.]

"Mislaid property is that which the owner has voluntarily and intentionally laid down in a place where he can again resort to it, and then has forgotten where he laid it. [Citations omitted.]

"Abandoned property is that of which the owner has relinquished all right, title, claim, and possession with the intention of not reclaiming it or resuming its ownership, possession or enjoyment. [Citations omitted.]

" 'Treasure trove consists essentially of articles of gold and silver, intentionally hidden for safety in the earth or in some secret place, the owner being unknown.' Brown, *Personal Property*, §13. . . .

"From the manner in which the bills in the instant case were carefully concealed beneath the paper lining of the drawer, it must be presumed that the concealment was effected intentionally and deliberately. The bills, therefore, cannot be regarded as abandoned property. [Citation omitted.]

"With regard to the plaintiff's contention that the bills constituted treasure trove, it has been held that the law of treasure trove has been merged with that of lost goods generally, at least so far as respects the rights of the finder. [Citations omitted.]

"The natural assumption is that the person who concealed the bills in the case at bar was a guest of the hotel. Their considerable value, and the manner of their concealment, indicate that the person who concealed them did so for purposes of security, and with the intention of reclaiming them. They were, therefore, to be classified not as lost, but as misplaced or forgotten property [citation omitted], and the defendant, as occupier of the premises where they were found, had the right and duty to take them into his possession and to hold them as gratuitous bailee for the true owner. [Citations omitted.]

"The decisive feature of the present case is the fact that plaintiff was an employee or servant of the owner or occupant of the premises, and that, in discovering the bills and turning them over to her employer, she was simply performing the duties of her employment. She was allowed to enter the guest room solely in order to do her work as chambermaid, and she was expressly instructed to take to the desk clerk any mislaid or forgotten property which she might discover. It is true that, in the United States, the courts have tended to accede to the claims of servants to the custody of articles found by them during the course of their employment, where the articles are, in a legal sense, lost property. [Citation omitted.] In *Hamaker* v.

Blanchard, 90 Pa. 377, 35 Am. Rep. 664, a servant in a hotel found a roll of bank notes in the public parlor. It was held that, as the money when found on the floor of a room common to all classes of persons, there was no presumption that it was the property of a guest and that, when the true owner was not found, the plaintiff was entitled to recover it from the innkeeper, to whom she had delivered it. In the case at bar, however, the bills were not lost property. [The court here called attention to the case of *McDowell* v. *Ulster Bank*, discussed in an article in 33 Irish Law Times 225 (1899), also noted in 60 Albany L.J. 346 (1899), in which it was held that the possession by a bank servant of a parcel containing 25 pounds on the bank's premises, was the possession of the bank itself and that therefore, the servant acquired no title as against the master.]

"On this branch of the case, the terse comment of a distinguished text writer will suffice to express our own view: 'In those cases where the servants are hired to clean up premises it seems that there might well be held that in finding things in the course of such cleaning the found property should belong to the master on this ground alone.' Aigler: Rights of Finders, 21 Mich. L. Rev. 664, 681 [1923] (footnote).

"The position of the defendant in the case at bar is fortified by the fact that, as an innkeeper, he is under common law and statutory obligation in respect to the found bills. 'When a guest gives up his room, pays his bill, and leaves an inn without an intention of returning, the innkeeper's liability as such for the effects of the former guest left in his charge ceases, and he is liable thereafter merely as an ordinary bailee, either gratuitous or for hire, depending upon the circumstances.' 28 Am. Jur. Innkeepers, section 94. Our statute (section 55–203, O.C.L.A.), in effect when the facts of this case transpired, provides that, when baggage or property of a guest is suffered to remain in an inn or hotel after the relation of guest and innkeeper has ended, the innkeeper may, at his option, hold such property at the risk of such former guest.

"Where money is found in an inn on the floor of a room common to the public, there being no circumstances pointing to its loss by a guest, the finder, even if an employee of the innkeeper, is entitled to hold the money as bailee for the true owner. *Hamaker* v. *Blanchard* (90 Pa. 377, 35 Am. Rep. 664, 665). It would seem that, as to articles voluntarily concealed by a guest, the very act of concealment would indicate that such articles have not been placed 'in the protection of the house' (Brown, Personal Property, section 14), and so, while the articles remain concealed, the innkeeper ordinarily would not have the responsibility of a bailee therefor. Upon their discovery by the innkeeper or his servant, however, the innkeeper's responsibility and duty as bailee for the owner becomes fixed. . . .

"The plaintiff in the present case is to be commended for her honesty and fair dealing throughout the transaction. Under our view of law, however, we have no alternative other than to reverse the judgment of the lower court. It will be reversed accordingly."

[All concur.]

ERICKSON v. SINYKIN
223 Minn. 232, 26 N.W.2d 172 (1947)

[Action to determine the ownership of $760 in currency. Defendants were the owners and operators of the Kenesaw Hotel in Minneapolis. They employed plaintiff to decorate several rooms therein. In the course of his work, plaintiff found it necessary "to raise up a rug which was on the floor, and under this rug he found $760.00 in the form of thirty-three old twenty-dollar bills around which was wrapped a new one-hundred-dollar bill."]

"Plaintiff reported his finding of this money to defendants, who informed him 'that they knew the true owner thereof, and that they would deliver said money' to the owner. Upon that representation, 'plaintiff delivered the money' so found to them. No evidence was offered at the trial that defendants knew who the true owner was or that they had made any effort to find him."

[As conclusions of law, the court determined that plaintiff was entitled to the money. Defendants' motion to vacate and set aside the finding or for a new trial was denied, and judgment entered for plaintiff.]

OLSON (JULIUS J.), J.: "[After recital of facts] . . . We are limited in this action solely to a determination of the rights and remedies of the parties to the cause. The original owner is unknown. He has made no appearance and is not a party to the action. This is a proceeding in personam, not one in rem. Therefore, until the actual owner appears and establishes his ownership, there can be no final determination of his rights.

"When plaintiff found this money under the circumstances we have related, he thereby came into physical possession of it. While that possession was a qualified one, he nevertheless had immediate dominion over the money. This possession and dominion as to any third person, including defendants, was adequate to sustain his cause until his adversary showed a better right. . . .

"In the instant case, the trial judge, in passing upon defendants' motion for a new trial, carefully reconsidered the matter of whether the money had been 'abandoned or lost,' characterizing the situation as a 'serious question.' After such reconsideration, he—'reached the conclusion that it was a question of fact for the court to determine. . . . In reaching the conclusion that it was abandoned, the court has taken into consideration circumstances existing since the finding of the money, that is, that the real owner has not stepped forth and claimed it. There is no way of knowing beyond the eighteen-month period how long this money remained under the carpet. It appears to the court that it is a reasonably clear case of an abandonment of the money.'

"Defendants challenge this finding as not sustained by the evidence. They take the view that since they were operating a hotel they owed a duty to their guests to see to it that property overlooked or forgotten by such guests is taken care of by them until such guest shall appear and demand a return of it. The case most heavily relied upon is *Flax v. Monticello Realty Co.*, 185 Va. 474, 39 S.E. (2d) 308, and the cases there cited. . . .

"The facts here are clearly distinguishable from those in the *Flax* case. Here, no one questions that plaintiff was the *finder* of this wad of old-style paper money. Nor was plaintiff's work at all comparable to the maid's work in that case. It is a matter of common knowledge that a chambermaid's work is nothing like that of a painter or decorator. Chambermaids frequently find articles which their employers' guests have forgotten. Ordinarily, their duty is to report and deliver to their employers the article so found, in order that restoration to the owner may be made. Here, the wad of currency which plaintiff found had obviously been placed under the rug by someone who wished to hide it. Not until the end of 1944 was it discovered, although the United States treasury department, on July 10, 1929, promulgated an order calling in, for cancellation and redemption, all paper currency then outstanding, and its reissuance in the new form. How long this money had remained under the rug in defendants' hotel no one knows. Unchallenged, however, by the record is the court's second finding:

"'That the plaintiff reported the fact of finding the money to the defendants, who told him that *they knew the true owner thereof and that they would deliver said money to the true owner; that upon that basis the plaintiff delivered the money to the defendants;* that there is no evidence to show that defendants knew the true owner or have ever delivered the money to the true owner or that they have reason to know [who] the true owner [is]; that defendants now retain possession of this money.' (Italics supplied [Supreme Court].)

"Defendants have done nothing to find the actual owner. Instead, they cling to it upon the theory that their possession of it as hotel proprietors now and ever since obtaining it from plaintiff is sufficient to defeat his cause. If their representation to plaintiff was truthful, then in the language we have italicized, it was their duty to comply with [Minn. Stat. (1945) and M.S.A. §622.11,] which provides: '*Every person who shall find lost property under circumstances which give him knowledge or means of inquiry as to the true owner,* who shall appropriate such property to his own use, or to the use of another person not entitled thereto, without having first made reasonable effort to find the owner and restore the property to him, shall be guilty of larceny.' (Italics supplied [by court].)

"The question whether the money found by plaintiff was abandoned by the person placing it in this peculiar and unusual hiding place is an important one. In a general sense, abandonment 'means the act of intentionally relinquishing a known right absolutely and without reference to any particular person or purpose.' 1 Am. Jur., Abandonment, §2. . . . Its characteristic element is the voluntary relinquishment of ownership so that thereby the property subject to such ownership becomes the subject of appropriation by the one who thereafter first takes it. *Id.* §3. . . . Thereby, the former owner of the title abandons whatever right or interest he had in it. . . . While mere lapse of time does not in and of itself establish abandonment, it nevertheless is of persuasive importance on the question of the former owner's intention. *Id.* §8. . . . And, since his intention is the important element to be considered, all relevant facts and circumstances may be shown, and considerable latitude is allowed in the taking of testimony. Generally, it is not necessary to support such a claim that there be any expressed declaration on the part of the former owner; rather, it may be inferred from the situation of the property and the conduct of the person who has placed it so as to lead to the conclusion that it has been abandoned. Thus, it has been held that if the conduct of the owner clearly shows an intention not to use the property for the purpose for which he acquired it, the facts in that regard may be shown. His intent in respect to the particular property claimed to have been abandoned 'may be inferred from' his conduct 'and the nature and situation of the property, without the positive testimony of the owner in affirmation of the fact.' *Id.* §13. . . . While, as we have said, lapse of time and nonuser may not be conclusive, such facts are competent evidence of an intent to abandon and in many instances 'are entitled to great weight when considered with other circumstances' shown in the particular case. *Id.* §15. . . .

"Initially, this money was neither lost nor abandoned. It was purposely hidden, for reasons which seemed adequate to the possessor— no doubt to keep it out of sight of subsequent users of the room so that he might later come back and repossess it. As to the respective rights and remedies of the parties to this case (and they are the only parties presently involved), we are of the view that in either case plaintiff's rights are superior to defendants' claim. . . . And here . . . the trier and finder of facts might conclude . . . 'that some of these transient people had left the money there designedly, and having gone away to sea or to some distant part of this or another country had found it inconvenient to return for the money, and so had abandoned it.' [*Roberson* v. *Ellis,* 58 Ore. 219, 225, 114 P. 100, 102 (1911)]. . . .

"In the light of adjudicated cases . . . we think that the question whether the money so found was abandoned or lost was a fact issue and that the evidence reasonably supports the conclusions reached by the trial court. A period of more than 15 years had elapsed since the time when our paper currency was changed until this money was found, and at least another two years have elapsed since then, yet no one claiming to be the actual owner has appeared. Defendants' silence and inactivity cannot be said to have been due to any excess of modesty on their part nor attributable to any good faith in their claimed interest in the original owner's rights. The judgment should be and is affirmed."

CHAPTER 27

Compensation of the Innkeeper

27:1 Innkeeper's Charges Must Be Reasonable

The innkeeper is not only obliged by law to receive all proper travelers for whom he has room, but is obliged to entertain them for a reasonable compensation. As was said by Chief Judge Simmons of the Supreme Court of Georgia,[1] "one who becomes a guest at an inn renders himself liable for his entertainment at the usual and customary rate of charges made by the innkeeper. . . ." The requirement that the compensation should be reasonable is a necessary corollary of the requirement that the guest should be received, for if it were open to the innkeeper to charge what he pleased he might exclude such applicants as he did not care to entertain by the mere device of demanding from them an unreasonable payment. "They do not deal upon *contracts* as others do, they only make bills, in which they cannot set unreasonable rates; if they do, they are indictable for extortion. . . ."[2]

The amount of the charge cannot easily be fixed by rule; nor is it usual to find the amount charged by an innkeeper disputed in court. The charge made by the innkeeper would, it seems, be upheld if it were not extravagant; "a person residing in a hotel cannot live so cheaply as at his own house."[3]

To prove the reasonableness or otherwise of a charge for board, the price of board at a similar inn in the neighborhood at about the same time may be shown. . . .[4]

[1] *Baldwin* v. *Webb*, 121 Ga. 416, 418, 49 S.E. 265, 266 (1904).
[2] *Newton* v. *Trigg*, 89 Eng. Rep. 566 (K.B. 1691) (Eyres, J.) (emphasis in original).
[3] *Proctor* v. *Nicholson*, 173 Eng. Rep. 30, 31 (K.B. 1835) (Lord Abinger, C.B.).
[4] *Cross* v. *Wilkins*, 43 N.H. 332 (1861).

27:2 *Amount of Charges May Be Fixed by Statute*

In earlier times it was more common than it is today to fix by statute the compensation to which an innkeeper should be entitled; for instance, as early as the year 1349, in one of the sections of the Statute of Laborers (23 ed. 3 c. 6), it was provided that the hostelers, that is, innkeepers, or other sellers of victuals "shall be bound to sell the same victual for a reasonable price, having respect to the price that such victual be sold at in the places adjoining, so that the same sellers have moderate gains, and not excessive, reasonable to be required according to the distance of the place from whence the said victuals be carried."

And in the year 1623 (21 Jac. 1, c.21) it was provided that "the hostelers or innholders shall sell their horse-bread, and their hay, oats, beans, peas, provender, and also all kind of victual both for man and beast, for reasonable gain, having respect to the prices for which they shall be sold in the markets adjoining, without taking anything for litter."

In most of the American colonies the regulation of the price of entertainment in general appears not to have been found necessary in earlier times. In Massachusetts and Plymouth colonies, for instance, the price of ale and liquor was regulated but not the price of food or other entertainment. Indeed, the Puritan colonists were rather more anxious to prevent than encourage miscellaneous travel, and they were interested to secure reasonable entertainment rather for themselves than for travelers who might be passing through. In some of the colonies, however, the price of entertainment in general was more carefully regulated.

As a result of the emergency created by World War II, the Congress authorized the creation of an Office of Price Administration (O.P.A.) and delegated authority to this federal agency to control and regulate prices of commodities as well as services. By virtue of its authority, the O.P.A. fixed prices for all hotel services, including room charges, food and beverage prices, etc., by selecting a so-called "freeze period," and by determining the maximum lawful charges at the highest level charged for the same commodity or service during the freeze period. Maximum prices or rates were required to be registered and were subject to inspection and certification by all those interested. Freeze periods differed in various sections of the United States. Thus, in the city of New York, hotel room charges were frozen at their maximum levels during the period January 31–March 1, 1943. Restaurant prices were frozen in the same city at their maximum levels during the period April 4–10, 1943. The administration of these regulations was rather complex and technical, and the regulations changed frequently.

These regulations were temporary for the period of the national emergency. Upon the termination of the emergency, they were repealed. States and municipalities acting under local emergencies have enacted local rent control laws of their own, patterned to some extent after the O.P.A. rent control laws and regulations. These local laws are similarly temporary in nature. An example is the New York City Rent Control Law, which became effective in July, 1947, and continues in effect today.

27:3 Innkeeper May Fix Rates

If no regulation of the innkeeper's charges is made by statute the innkeeper is entitled to frame a schedule of rates provided such rates are reasonable; or, without having framed a formal schedule, he may in any individual case make a reasonable charge. This may be a customary rate, or in the absence of a schedule of rates or any custom, it may be such amount as the innkeeper pleases to charge, subject to the provision that it be not more than the entertainment is reasonably worth. When once the rate of compensation has been fixed, it continues until a new arrangement is made.

27:4 Payment May Be Required in Advance

The innkeeper has a right, if he chooses, to demand payment in advance of his charges, *i.e.*, before he receives the guest.[5] This is of course a more awkward rule to utilize than payment in advance in the case of the carrier, and yet it is quite clear that this is within the

[5] *Mulliner* v. *Florence*, 3 Q.B.D. 484 (C.A. 1878); *Fell* v. *Knight*, 151 Eng. Rep. 1039 (Exch. 1841).

rights of the innkeeper. Whether the traveler applies for a room or for board he can undoubtedly be required, as a condition of his reception, to pay in advance for entertainment which he intends to receive for a reasonable time; that he must pay for one night's lodging at the time of being received is quite clear.

Doubtless he could be compelled to pay his board for a day in advance if the inn were conducted on the "American plan," but whether the innkeeper could demand payment for a longer period in advance than a single day is doubtful. A bill for entertainment at an inn accrues "de die in diem," and the day's charge would seem to be the unit of charge and the limit of the innkeeper's demand.

27:5 Compensation Due as Soon as Relation Is Established

The right to receive compensation for his services accrues to the innkeeper at the moment of the reception of a guest, and indeed the creation of the relation of host and guest and the right to make a charge for services performed are necessarily coincident. From this it would follow that as soon as the guest signs the register and is received into the inn he is bound to pay some compensation, even though he receives no further entertainment than the mere right of remaining in a common room; the liability to pay compensation continues until the guest ceases to bear that character. If he temporarily leaves the inn, intending to return and remaining meanwhile a guest, the innkeeper is entitled to make reasonable charge, even though neither food nor lodging is meantime furnished him.

In an English case a traveler on applying for a room at an inn was told that the inn was full, but that he might occupy a room which would not be needed until night. He went to the room and dressed there. The court intimated that the innkeeper was entitled to compensation, Bowen, L.J., saying: "I think that, as soon as he had taken the plaintiff's luggage up to the room, and had placed it in the room, the innkeeper became entitled to charge the plaintiff for the use of the room—a charge which would be expanded or contracted, according as the plaintiff's occupation of the room was prolonged or not." [6]

If the guest finally leaves the inn and ceases to be a guest the innkeeper's right to charge for his services as such comes to an end,

[6] *Medawar* v. *Grand Hotel Company*, [1891] 2 Q.B. 11, 26 (C.A.).

although circumstances may exist which would give the innkeeper a right to compensation for services rendered. Thus, if upon leaving, a guest desires that his room be reserved for him or for someone else whom he may send to the inn, he would be responsible for the rental value of the room. These services, however, are not innkeeper's services, and the amount of charge and the methods of enforcing the charge would be governed by the ordinary law of debtor and creditor, not by the law of innkeepers.

27:6 Services for Which Innkeeper Is Entitled to Compensation

The obligation of an innkeeper to his guest includes the obligation to render without extra charge the usual and reasonable personal attention to the health and comfort of the guest. For extraordinary services, however, the innkeeper is entitled to make a special, additional charge; for instance, if the guest is nursed by the innkeeper through a severe and protracted illness, compensation for the service as nurse is due the innkeeper.

The innkeeper must perform his entire obligation before he is entitled to any compensation. For instance, if he undertakes to furnish room and board he can make no charge for the room, although he furnishes it, if in point of fact he does not supply the guest with the reasonable board.[7] Where, however, there is a separate charge for separate articles of entertainment the innkeeper may be entitled to charge for some of the articles furnished, though he is not entitled to charge for others; for instance, if an innkeeper being unlicensed to sell liquor is unable to recover compensation for liquor furnished, he may, nevertheless, recover such amount as he is legally entitled to charge for board.

27:7 Who Is Liable for Payment?

Where a party of several persons dines together, and there is no agreement to give credit to any particular one, they are, it would seem, jointly liable for all the charges, not merely liable each for his own share.[8] If, however, the host knew that one member of the

[7] *Wilson* v. *Martin*, 1 Denio 602 (N.Y. Sup. Ct. 1845).
[8] *Forster* v. *Taylor*, 3 Camp. 49 (Eng. Nisi Prius 1811).

party had invited the others to dine with him he could hold only the one who is entertaining his friends. So in Rol. Abr., Action sur Case, 24, "As to the host both are liable to pay the reckoning, unless the host knew that B had been invited." And where the party forms a family, the head of the family is the person liable for the whole charge and not the separate members of the family; thus, where a father went to an inn with his daughter, it was held that the daughter was not liable for her father's entertainment, nor, it would seem, for her own.[9] And so where a husband and wife go to an inn together, the wife is not chargeable with any part of the bill, unless indeed it can be shown that the credit was extended to her and not to the husband.[10]

In such cases, it is well to render all bills not to the husband alone, but to "Mr. & Mrs.," so as to create a reasonable basis for the contention that credit was extended to both husband and wife and that a lien exists on the property of both.

Where two men or two women occupy a room together, they both should be required to register and all bills should be rendered to them jointly. Such procedure will help to make the lien applicable to the property of both persons.

27:8 "Necessaries" Furnished Married Women and Minors

A married woman may, by agreement, obligate herself for accommodations furnished to her. A husband is liable for the obligations of a wife where he has expressly agreed to pay or where apparent authority is given either from prior transactions which he had ratified or where the accommodations constitute "necessaries" furnished. In order that a husband be held liable for hotel accommodations furnished as "necessaries," it must appear that such accommodations are suitable in quality and character to the wife's station in life, the means of the husband, and the manner in which he permits her to live. It must further appear that the wife was not supplied with such necessaries by the husband.

A minor (a person under 21 years of age) cannot be held liable for accommodations furnished at his request unless they are "necessaries."

9 Clayton v. Butterfield, 18 S.C. 100 (1857).
10 Birney v. Wheaton, 2 How. Prac. (n.s.) 519 (N.Y. City Ct. 1885).

The principles of law just outlined with respect to the liability of a husband for accommodations furnished to a wife are equally applicable to the liability of a parent for necessaries furnished to a minor.

27:9 *Employees of Corporations*

Employees of corporations may incur hotel charges on their personal account, in which case they are treated as other individual guests are. They may also incur charges on the account of the employer corporation. In order to hold a corporation liable for charges incurred by an employee, it must appear that: (1) the corporation has specifically authorized such charges; (2) the employee has actual or apparent authority to bind the corporation. Apparent authority may be inferred from a course of prior dealings between the innkeeper and the corporation; (3) the accommodations rendered to the guest were in fact for corporate purposes and for the benefit of the corporation.

27:10 *Extension of Credit—Account Stated*

It is customary for guests who have established credit with the innkeeper to charge their hotel bill. It is advisable in such instances to request the guest, at the time of checking out, to sign a statement on the bill certifying to its correctness. Such procedure has been found to eliminate many a dispute and vexatious argument, and will avoid proof as to all details making up the bill, in case of a lawsuit. The statement may be printed or rubber-stamped on the guest's bill in the following form:

> The above account showing a balance due of
> $ _____ , is correct.
>
> Dates _____   _____
>   Guest's Signature
>
> In the presence of:
>
> _____

In the event the bill is not available at the time of check-out, the following statement, preferably in printed form, may be used:

Hotel _____

Having heretofore examined bills rendered by
Hotel_____ in due course, showing
accommodations rendered and payments on account,
I find there is a balance now due the hotel on my
account, in the sum of $ _____.

_____
Guest's Signature

In the presence of:

_____

27:11 Guarantee of Guest's Account

An innkeeper, as a condition of extending credit, or to insure collection where credit has already been extended, may insist upon a
guaranty of the guest's account by a reliable third party. It should be
remembered that a guaranty is a contract which, like other contracts,
requires a consideration in order to be enforceable and that it must
be in writing and signed by the guarantor.[11]

There are two kinds of guaranty; one is a guaranty of payment, the
other is a guaranty of collectibility. A guaranty of payment is an
absolute promise to pay the guest's bill when it is due, unless paid
by the guest. A guaranty of collectibility is a conditional promise, the
condition being that the innkeeper creditor first exhaust his remedies
against the debtor guest and if he fails, then and only then will the
guarantor pay. A statement that a check is "good and collectible" is a
mere guaranty of collectibility. On the other hand, a letter stating
"Cash his check; I'll make it good if it bounces" is a guaranty of payment. A guaranty of collectibility is obviously undesirable since it
involves the time and expense of an unsuccessful effort to collect
directly from the guest before action can be taken against the
guarantor.

The following are examples of enforceable guaranties: (1) a
guaranty of payment of an account for food, lodging and hotel
accommodations to become due *in the future;* (2) a guaranty of payment of an account for accommodations already furnished where, in
reliance upon said guaranty, the innkeeper waives his lien and permits

[11] N.Y. General Obligations Law §5–701.

the guest to remove his baggage from the hotel; (3) a guaranty of an account already due where, in reliance upon said guaranty, the innkeeper agrees not to institute suit for the amount due for a specific period of time. The following is suggested as a form of a guaranty of payment:

GUARANTY

Date _____

For value received and in consideration of the extension of credit for hotel accommodations by Hotel _____ to Guest _____ . I hereby waive notice of the non-payment of said account by said Guest _____ and consent to all extension of time that said Hotel _____ may grant to said Guest _____ and I agree to pay said account upon demand.

(Signed) _____
Guarantor

In the presence of:

_____

CHAPTER 28

The Innkeeper's Lien

28:1 *Nature of Innkeeper's Lien*

The innkeeper, being obliged by law to receive travelers and entertain them, is given, by law, not merely the right to compensation from the guest, but also a lien on the goods of the guest in the inn, to the extent of his charges. This lien differs in one respect from other liens created by the common law in that technical possession on the part of the innkeeper is not necessary for the enforcement of the lien. Although the goods remain in the possession of the guest, the innkeeper may prevent their being carried from the inn, take them into his own actual possession, and hold them as security for his charges. In other respects, this lien is in its nature and incidents like other liens given by the common law to persons carrying on a public employment, such as carriers and public warehousemen.

28:2 *General Rule*

By the common law, an innkeeper is entitled to a lien for the amount of his charges on all the goods of his guest which are found in the inn.[1] The charges which are secured by the lien include not merely compensation for entertainment, but also other charges connected with the guest's stay at the inn, as, for example, money lent to the guest by the innkeeper.[2] The lien is restricted to charges as between the innkeeper and the one who is his guest in the strict sense. Thus, an innkeeper at common law has no lien on the goods of a boarder,[3]

---

[1] *Waters* v. *Gerard,* 189 N.Y. 302, 82 N.E. 143 (1907).
[2] *Proctor* v. *Nicholson,* 173 Eng. Rep. 30 (K.B. 1835); *Watson* v. *Cross,* 63 Ky. (2 Duv.) 147 (1865).
[3] *Singer Mfg. Co.* v. *Miller,* 52 Minn. 516, 55 N.W. 56 (1893).

except of course by special agreement.[4] So an innkeeper taking horses to board for one who is not a guest has no lien at common law.[5] Nor can one who merely keeps a lodginghouse and lets rooms have a lien.[6]

28:3 Lien Does Not Require a Binding Contract

This lien is, properly speaking, not created by a contract, but by law; the innkeeper, being obliged by law to receive, is given by law the lien. Consequently, by the better view, an innkeeper may maintain his lien even against a guest who is incapable of making a binding contract. For example, one court has held "[I]t was his legal duty to receive appellee as a guest, and that being the case, the contract was, on his part, compulsory, and the law will not render such a contract on the other side either void or voidable, upon the simple ground of disability arising from infancy. . . . It would be a legal absurdity to compel a man to make a contract and, at the same time, permit the other party, who is the instrument of such compulsion, to avoid such contract." [7]

28:4 Lien Does Not Cover Prior Charges

The innkeeper's lien is not a general lien, in that it covers only charges accrued during the last period of entertainment. If the innkeeper once waives his lien by allowing the guest to depart and take away his goods without paying his bill, the charges then due can never afterwards be secured by a detainer of goods brought to the inn by the same guest on a subsequent occasion. This was established in the early case of *Jones* v. *Thurloe*.[8] This was an action of trover against an innkeeper for detaining and converting the plaintiff's horse. The defendant pleaded that the plaintiff owed him money for horse-meat at several times and that he detained the horse according to the custom for what was due. On demurrer the plea was held bad. The court said that if the innkeeper "give him credit for that time, and

---

[4] *Regina* v. *Askin,* 20 U.C.Q.B. 626 (1861).
[5] *Grinnell* v. *Cook,* 3 Hill 485 (N.Y. Sup. Ct. 1842).
[6] *Cochrane* v. *Schryver,* 12 Daly 174 (N.Y. Ct. C.P. 1883).
[7] *Watson* v. *Cross,* 63 Ky. (2 Duv.) 147, 148 (1865).
[8] 88 Eng. Rep. 126 (K.B. 1723).

let him depart without payment, then he has waived the benefit of that custom by his own consent to the departure, and shall never afterwards detain the horse for that expence [*sic*]. For this custom is founded on the hardship of the inn-keeper's case to sue for every little debt, or on a greater hardship, that he may not know where to find him who was his guest after he is gone; therefore when he has waived that privilege which the law gives him, he must rely on his other agreement."

28:5 *Property to Which Lien Extends*

Generally speaking, the lien extends to all property of every kind brought to the inn by the guest, or left at the inn for the guest, each article of property being security for the whole bill. There is one debt and one lien in respect to the whole of the innkeeper's charges. This proposition has almost never been questioned; it was, however, doubted and litigated in the case of *Mulliner* v. *Florence*.[9] In that case it appeared that a guest brought with him to the defendant's inn a pair of horses, wagonette, and harness. The guest left the inn owing over one hundred pounds for the keep of the horses. The horses belonged in fact to the plaintiff who tendered the amount due for their keep and demanded that they be given up to him. The court held that he must pay the whole charge. The Lord Justice Bramwell said:

[W]as it a lien on the horses for the charges in respect of the horses, and on the carriage in respect of the charges of the carriage and no lien on them for the guest's reasonable expenses, or was it a general lien on the horses and carriage and guest's goods conjointly for the whole amount of the defendant's claim as innkeeper. I am of opinion that the latter was the true view as to his lien, and for this reason, that the debt in respect of which the lien was claimed was one debt, although that debt was made up of several items. An innkeeper may demand the expenses before he receives the guest, but if he does not, and takes him in and finds him in all things that the guest requires it is one contract, and the lien that he has is a lien in respect of the whole contract to pay for the things that are supplied to him while he is a guest. If this was not the case a man might go to a hotel with his wife, and then it might be said that the innkeeper's lien was on the guest's luggage for what he had consumed, and on the

9 [1877] 3 Q.B. 484, 488.

wife's luggage for what she had had. The contract was, that the guest and his horses and carriage shall be received and provided for; there was one contract, one debt, and one lien in respect of the whole of the charges.

28:6 Goods in Inn Subject to Lien, Though Host Might Have Excluded Them

There was a tendency in the English cases at one time to restrict the lien to such goods only as the innkeeper is compelled to receive with his guests. Thus in *Broadwood* v. *Granara*,[10] Baron Parke said in the course of the argument: "An innkeeper has a lien on such goods only as he is compelled to receive with his guest. Could he be indicted for not receiving a pianoforte? It might be a nuisance to persons in his house." And again, later, the same judge said: "The principle on which an innkeeper's lien depends is, that he is bound to receive travellers and the goods which they bring with them to the inn." This notion, however, was unsound, and has been abandoned. The lien secures not merely compensation for care extended to the very goods over which it is exercised, but compensation for charges incurred by the guest for his own entertainment. The innkeeper is bound to receive and entertain the guest, and if he chooses to receive with him goods he is not obliged to receive, his right in those goods, after he chooses to receive them, is the same as his right in any other goods of the guest, "[T]hey are in the same position as goods properly offered to the innkeeper according to the custom of the realm. . . ." [11]

28:7 No Lien on Person of Guest

The lien is restricted to the goods of the guest; his person cannot be detained as security for the charges. In the case of *Sunbolf* v. *Alford*,[12] the plaintiff sued the defendant, an innkeeper, for assault and battery. The defendant pleaded that the plaintiff was a guest, and as such became indebted to the defendant, and would have left the inn without paying the debt, and for this cause the defendant detained

[10] 156 Eng. Rep. 499, 501, 502 (Ex. 1854).
[11] Lord Esher, M.R., in *Robins* v. *Gray*, [1895] 2 Q.B. 501, 504.
[12] 150 Eng. Rep. 1135, 1138 (Exch. 1838).

him. The court held the plea insufficient. Lord Chief Baron Abinger said:

If an innkeeper has a right to detain the person of his guest for the non-payment of his bill, he has a right to detain him until the bill is paid,—which may be for life; so that this defence supposes, that, by the common law, a man who owes a small debt, for which he could not be imprisoned by legal process, may yet be detained by an innkeeper for life. The proposition is monstrous. Again, if he have any right to detain the person, surely he is a judge in his own cause; for, he is then the party to determine whether the amount of his bill is reasonable, and he must detain him till the man brings an action against him for false imprisonment, and then if it were determined that the charge was not reasonable, and it appeared that the party had made an offer of a reasonable sum, the detainer would be unlawful.

He distinguished the case of lien on goods as an exception to the general law. The lien on goods is doubtless a survival of an ancient power of legally permitted self-help; however, in modern times it is an exceptional process, confined to certain classes of cases. This lien has never been extended at common law to any other class of property than tangible personal property, and there is not the slightest authority for extending it to the person of the debtor.

28:8 *No Lien on Goods Which Cannot Be Taken without Violation of Law*

No lien exists if it would be impossible to exercise it without violating the law. Thus, where horses, whether owned by an individual or the government, were employed in transporting the mails, the innkeeper could not hold the horses on lien in such a way as to interfere with the mail.[13] District Judge Winchester said on this point: "This law does not allow any justification of a *wilful and voluntary* act of obstruction to the passage of the mail. . . . Many exceptions might be introduced, and perhaps with propriety. For instance, *a stolen horse found in the mail-stage.* The owner cannot seize him. The driver being in debt, or even committing an offence, can only be arrested in such way as does not obstruct the passage of the mail.

---

[13] *U.S.* v. *Barney,* 24 F. Cas. 1014, 1016 (No. 14,525) (D.C. Md. 1810), emphasis added. But see *U.S.* v. *McCracken,* 26 F. Cas. 1069 (No. 15,664) (C.C.E.D. Va. 1878).

These examples are as strong as any which are likely to occur, but even these are not excepted by the statute."

Nor is there any lien on the clothing of a seaman, by reason of a federal law (46 U.S.C.A. §563) which provides: "[T]he clothing of any seaman shall be exempt from attachment, and that any person who shall detain such clothing when demanded by the owner shall be guilty of a misdemeanor, and shall be imprisoned not more than six months or fined not more than $500, or both."

The term "seaman" probably includes not only merchant seamen but also men in the U.S. Navy and Coast Guard. It should be noted, however, that the statute relates only to clothing; it does not seem to affect the hotel's lien upon other property belonging to or in the possession of a seaman in a hotel. The statute, being criminal, must be construed strictly. During World War II, the United States Attorney who enforces this law took the position on several occasions that this statute applied to a seaman even though he was temporarily detached from his ship.

28:9 *Wearing Apparel Worn by Guest*

For the above reason no lien can be exercised over clothes actually on the person of the guest, since they could not be detained without a breach of the peace and the risk, at any rate, of indecency. As Baron Parke once said: "[T]here is, at all events, no power to do what this plea justifies—namely, to strip the guest of his clothes; for, if there be, then, if the innkeeper take the coat off his back, and that prove to be an insufficient pledge, he may go on and strip him naked; and that would apply either to a male or to a female. That is a consequence so utterly absurd, that it cannot be entertained for a moment." [14]

28:10 *Property Exempt from Execution*

The above principle, however, does not extend so far as to cover property exempt by law from execution, and the lien may be exercised over such property. The privilege of exemption granted to a debtor

[14] *Sunbolf* v. *Alford,* 150 Eng. Rep. 1135, 1138 (Ex. 1838). One of Baron Parke's colleagues stated: "The consequence of holding otherwise might be to subject parties to disgrace and duress, in order to compel them to pay a trifling debt, which after all was not due, and which the innkeeper had no pretence for demanding" (Bolland, B., *id.* at 1138).

does not prevent him from voluntarily giving another an interest in such property or subjecting it voluntarily to a lien, as the guest does by taking it with him to an inn.[15]

28:11   *Goods of Third Person Brought by Guest to Inn*

The innkeeper's lien attaches to property brought to the inn by a guest ostensibly as his, though they were in fact the goods of a third person, unless the innkeeper knew or had notice that such property was not then the property of the guest.

WATERS *v.* GERARD
189 N.Y. 302, 82 N.E. 143 (1907)

CHASE, J.: "In 1898 and 1899, the defendant was the lessee and proprietor of a hotel . . . known as 'The Girard' in the city of New York. On August 23, 1898, one Carlisle came [to the] hotel as a guest, and so remained until March 15, 1899, inclusive. . . . On March 15, 1899, she owed the defendant [for board and entertainment] the sum of $161.24, a part of which accrued on March 13 to 15, inclusive, 1899.

"On March 15, 1899, she took a lease of certain apartments in said hotel for one year from that day, . . . and continued in the occupation thereof until June 25, 1899, . . . On June 25, 1899, she left said hotel owing the defendant $330.85, of which amount $161.24 accrued on and prior to March 15, 1899, . . . and the balance was due for rent under said lease and for food and incidentals furnished in the defendant's restaurant between March 15 and June 25, 1899. The lease of said apartments contained a proviso that the defendant should have a lien on all of the effects and property brought into said hotel by said Carlisle for any indebtedness accrued or accruing to her."

[The plaintiff sold a piano to Carlisle on March 13, 1899, under a conditional contract of sale. Carlisle never paid the full purchase price and on June 13, 1899 notified plaintiff to remove the piano. Plaintiff was prevented from removing the piano by defendant who claimed an innkeeper's lien thereon. The defendant did not know that Carlisle was not the real owner of the piano until demand was made therefor by plaintiff.]

---

[15] *Swan* v. *Bournes,* 47 Iowa 501 (1877); *Thorn* v. *Whitbeck,* 11 Misc. 171, 32 N.Y.S. 1088 (Greene County Ct. 1895).

"The provision in the lease by the defendant to Carlisle, by which Carlisle gave to the defendant a lien on all the effects and property brought by her into the hotel for any indebtedness accrued or accruing to the defendant, does not in any way affect the rights of the plaintiff herein, as it was in no way a party to it, and Carlisle could not, by contract with the defendant, transfer to her an interest in the property of a third person. . . .

". . . When the piano came into the possession of the defendant through her guest a part of the unpaid account had accrued; a part accrued thereafter while Carlisle remained a transient guest in the defendant's hotel, and the remaining part of the unpaid account accrued while Carlisle was the occupant of the apartments in the defendant's hotel as a guest at an agreed price per year. If the defendant had a lien on the piano for any part of the account claimed by her, she was entitled to retain possession of it, and the plaintiff's demand and claim for the possession of the piano cannot be sustained.

"It is only necessary to consider whether an innkeeper has a lien on the goods rightfully in the possession of a transient guest when such goods are the property of a third person.

"Two questions arise for our consideration: (1) Did the common law of England, on and prior to the 19th day of April, 1775, give to an innkeeper a lien on goods owned by a third person in the rightful possession of a guest for the value of his guest's entertainment? (2) Apart from the question whether such lien was so given by the common law is the act [Sec. 71 of the Lien Law] so far as it gives a lien upon goods owned by a third person in the rightful possession of the guest, a violation of our Constitution?

". . . The writers in encyclopedias and text books with singular unanimity have asserted that an innkeeper has a lien at common law upon all goods in the rightful possession of his guest for the value of the guest's entertainment. . . .

". . . From a time prior to 1775 the general lien of an innkeeper upon the goods owned by the guest has been conceded and it is not now disputed by the appellant. The reason for the general lien is as applicable against the property of third persons in the possession of the guest as against the property of the guest himself. Because the innkeeper was compelled to receive the traveler and accept the extraordinary liability which extends not only to the luggage and personal property owned by the traveler but to the luggage and personal property in his possession although owned by another, it was necessary to give to the innkeeper a compensatory lien for his charges to make the maintenance of inns desirable. The extraordinary liability and the lien are concurrent, and go hand in hand, and together make up the rule founded on public policy.

". . . The statutory rule adopted by this state in 1897 does not, in our judgment, extend the rule so far as it relates to the property of a third person in the lawful possession of a guest beyond the rule of the common law as it existed prior to 1775. [And since the common law prior to 1775 was the law of the land, the Lien Law giving an innkeeper a lien on the property of a third person does not deprive such third person of property without due process of law]. . . .

"The right which an innkeeper has to require payment in advance for the accommodation of a guest in view of the uncertain length of time that the guest may stay at the inn and the uncertainty in regard to what may be required by the guest in the way of accommodation from day to day is insufficient as a practical means of protection to the innkeeper. Unless the innkeeper's lien extends to all the luggage and goods which the guest brings to the inn, and for which the innkeeper becomes responsible as an insurer, an opportunity is afforded by which great fraud might be perpetrated upon the innkeeper through a relative or other person claiming the ownership of the luggage and goods in the possession of the guest. So long as public policy requires that an innkeeper be held to the extraordinary and severe responsibility prescribed by the common law, the same considerations of public policy require that the rule of the common law be retained in its entirety and that the innkeeper have a lien upon the luggage and goods in the possession of the guest for payment of his reasonable charges."

[Judgment for defendant affirmed.]

In Ohio, the innkeeper's lien does not extend to stolen property in possession of a hotel guest, whether or not the innkeeper had knowledge of the ownership of the property at the time he extended credit to the guest.[16]

16 *M. & M. Hotel Co.* v. *Nichols*, 32 N.E.2d 463 (Ohio Ct. App. 1935).

28:12 *Goods of Guest Who Is Not Responsible for Charges*

Where several people go together to an inn, but only one of them is responsible for paying the bill, only property which is really or ostensibly the property of the responsible party can be held on lien for the charges. Thus where a father and his daughter went to an inn, under such circumstances that the father alone was responsible for the bill, the host could not hold the daughter's goods as security for the payment of the bill.[17] And so where a husband and wife go together to an inn, the credit being extended to the husband, there is no lien on property evidently belonging to the wife,[18] though if the credit were extended to the wife her goods could be held, and not the husband's.[19] Where the wife goes alone to the inn, but the husband is liable, the wife's goods cannot be held.[20]

28:13 *Lien Attached When Charges Accrue*

The lien attaches as soon as the charge is incurred, that is, as soon as the guest is received, even if the time for payment has not arrived. So in a Massachusetts case it appeared that the defendant was a boarder at the plaintiff's house, paying his board by the week at the end of the week. A week's board would be due on Saturday night; on Saturday morning the defendant undertook, against the will of the plaintiff, and without paying anything for board during the week, to remove his baggage; and upon the plaintiff interfering, he forcibly removed her from the room. The plaintiff brought an action for assault and battery, and the defendant set up in defense his right to remove his property. The Supreme Court, however, held that the lien existed, and the plaintiff could recover. Mr. Justice Morton said: "Otherwise a guest who had obtained credit upon the strength of the

[17] *Clayton* v. *Butterfield*, 18 S.C. 100 (1857). In this case, the daughter tendered the amount of the charges incurred on her account; if she had not tendered this, the lien would not have been valid, as it seems, even to that extent, since she owed no debt.

[18] *Birney* v. *Wheaton*, 2 How. Prac. (n.s.) 519 (N.Y. City Ct. 1885); *McIlvane* v. *Hilton*, 7 Hun. 594 (N.Y. Sup. Ct. 1876) (a case of a boardinghouse keeper's lien).

[19] *Birney* v. *Wheaton*, 2 How. Prac. (n.s.) 519 (N.Y. City Ct. 1885).

[20] *Baker* v. *Stratton*, 52 N.J.L. 277, 19 A. 661 (1890).

lien, might destroy the security . . . by a sale or by removing the goods, at any time before the bill for board became payable by the contract; a result which is inconsistent with the nature of the lien." [21]

28:14 Sale of Goods by Owner Does Not Affect Lien

A sale of the property by the guest to a third person does not terminate the lien; the innkeeper may retain the goods against the purchaser for all charges accrued (even after the sale) until notice of the sale is received by the innkeeper.[22]

28:15 Removal of Goods to Another State Does Not Affect Lien

The lien is not lost by taking the goods into another state, even if no such lien would be created by the law of the latter state; the lien once having attached to the goods remains, wherever they may be taken by the innkeeper. In a New Hampshire case, the facts were that one S., in Massachusetts, held a trunk belonging to plaintiff's son under a lien for board; at plaintiff's request, she sent the trunk to him, in New Hampshire, by the defendant express company, C.O.D. The plaintiff tendered the charges for carriage only, and demanded the trunk; and upon the defendant refusing to give it up he brought this action of replevin. The Supreme Court gave judgment for the defendant, Mr. Justice Stanley saying: "In this case, there is an attempt to divest S. of her lien, and there is no reason why she may not defend her title as well as if she were the absolute owner residing in Massachusetts and a suit were brought to take the property from her. The lien of S. was as perfect as the lien under a mortgage made and executed in Massachusetts in accordance with their laws would be. In such cases the title under the mortgage could be shown, and would be a defence." [23]

---

[21] *Smith* v. *Colcord*, 115 Mass. 70, 71 (1874) (this was the case of a statutory boardinghouse keeper's lien; but the reasoning would equally apply to the common-law lien of an innkeeper).

[22] *Bayley* v. *Merrill*, 92 Mass. (10 Allen) 360 (1865).

[23] *Jaquith* v. *American Express Co.*, 60 N.H. 61, 62 (1880).

28:16 *Care of Goods Held on Lien*

An innkeeper holding goods on lien is bound to take due care of the goods, which is said to be the care which he takes of his own goods of a similar description. So where an innkeeper who was holding clothing and furs on a lien put them into a closet with similar goods of his own, and they were injured by moths and mice, it was held that that amount of negligence which would make an innkeeper liable had not been shown.[24] He may make reasonable use of the goods if such use is beneficial to the owner, as, for instance, in the case of live animals, but in that case he is bound to account for the value of the use. This question was discussed in a Vermont case, where an innkeeper, while holding a horse on lien, learned that the horse really belonged not to the guest but to someone from whom it had been stolen; under these circumstances he made use of the horse. The court held this action proper, saying that the right of the bailee to use the property depended, in the absence of express agreement, upon the circumstances. Thus, if the use would be for the benefit of the property, the consent of the owner might fairly be presumed, but not if it would be injurious or perilous; while, if the use would be indifferent, other circumstances might determine it, for:

It is generally not only the right, but the duty, of the bailee to use the property so far as necessary to its preservation. To this extent the assent of the owner may be presumed—as in case of the milking of a milch cow; and in case of a horse, exercise and moderate use to the extent necessary to the health and vigor of the animal. Again it is laid down by the elementary writers, that the right to use the property may depend on whether it is property of a nature that requires expense to keep it; and if so, the bailee may use it reasonably to compensate him for the charge of keeping.

Under the circumstances of this case it was reasonable to use the horse. The innkeeper did not know the owner, nor had he any reason to suppose that the owner would appear. Even though his lien was good against the owner, still he might hold the horse until it died without being paid, and then his only security for payment would be gone.

[24] *Angus* v. *McLachlan*, [1883] 23 Ch. D. 330.

Under such circumstances, the defendant had a right to use the property moderately and prudently, to the extent of compensating him for his charges, in the manner that the case shows he did use it. Whether the actual assent of the plaintiff in the meantime is presumed or not, it is fairly to be presumed that if the plaintiff had known the facts he would have assented. The use of the property has manifestly benefited the plaintiff, for, but for that, the expense of keeping for the four years would probably have exhausted the whole property.[25]

The value of the use must, however, be credited on the lien. "The defendant, having lawfully used the property, must account for the use upon his charges for trouble and expense of keeping the property; and the court having found that it is a full equivalent, the defendant had no lien upon the property."

28:17 End of Lien by Delivery of Goods to Guest

The lien is at an end when the innkeeper voluntarily delivers the goods to the guest.[26] But a mere executory agreement to give up the goods, made without consideration, does not put an end to the lien.[27]

28:18 End of Lien through Delivery Induced by Fraud

If the innkeeper is induced to give up the goods by fraud, the lien continues in spite of the delivery, or rather the innkeeper has the right to renew it; he may recover the goods by legal process, or otherwise, and the lien will again attach to them.[28]

28:19 End of Lien by Delivery for Temporary Use

The innkeeper may allow the guest to take the goods temporarily without parting with his lien; as, for instance, where a horse is put up at an inn and the guest drives it out from time to time, the innkeeper does not lose his lien.[29] In such a case the better view appears

---

[25] *Alvord* v. *Davenport*, 43 Vt. 9, 10, 11 (1870).

[26] *Jones* v. *Thurloe*, 88 Eng. Rep. 126 (K.B. 1723); *Danforth* v. *Pratt*, 42 Me. 50 (1856); *Grinnell* v. *Cook*, 3 Hill 485 (N.Y. Sup. Ct. 1842).

[27] *Danforth* v. *Pratt*, 42 Me. 50 (1856).

[28] *Manning* v. *Hollenbeck*, 27 Wis. 202 (1870).

[29] *Allen* v. *Smith*, 142 Eng. Rep. 1293 (C.P. 1862); *Huffman* v. *Walterhouse*, 19 Ont. 186 (C.P. 1890).

to be that the lien continues even during the temporary possession of the guest. In one case a creditor attached the horse of a guest at an inn while the guest was driving the horse in the neighborhood of the inn; the innkeeper's lien was held to have priority over the attachment.[30] But the opposite view has also been held.[31]

28:20 *End of Lien by Payment of Bill*

The lien is, of course, destroyed by payment of the debt. And so where the innkeeper owes the guest for labor more than the guest owes for food, and the guest has a right to set off the amount due him against his debt, there is no lien.[32] But a mere agreement to accept security for the bill if it is not inconsistent with the lien, does not put an end to it.[33]

28:21 *End of Lien by Conversion of Goods*

Conversion of the goods or wrongful dealing with them by the innkeeper while he holds them on lien puts an end to the lien. Thus, if the innkeeper refuses to give up the goods upon a good tender of the amount due, he is guilty of a conversion, but not where the tender is not a good one.[34]

28:22 *Extension of Time for Payment Is Not Waiver of Lien*

PEOPLE EX REL. KLAMT *v.* LOEFFLER
153 Misc. 781, 276 N.Y.S. 698 (Magis. Ct. 1934)

AURELIO, City Magistrate: ". . . Complainant seeks to hold the defendant for larceny for his refusal to return to her certain baggage belonging to her. The defendant is the manager of the Hotel Gladstone and claims a lien on the property under Section 181 of the Lien Law for an unpaid bill for accommodation and food furnished. . . .

[30] *Caldwell* v. *Tutt,* 78 Tenn. 258 (1882).
[31] *Crabtree* v. *Griffith,* 22 U.C.Q.B. 573 (1863). And see *Grinnell* v. *Cook,* 3 Hill 485 (N.Y. Sup. Ct. 1842).
[32] *Hanlin* v. *Walters,* 3 Colo. App. 519, 34 P. 686 (1893).
[33] *Angus* v. *McLachlan,* [1883] 23 Ch. D. 330.
[34] *Gordon* v. *Cox,* 173 Eng. Rep. 76 (Nisi Prius 1835).

"The evidence shows that before complainant was accepted as a guest she informed the defendant that she had no money, and that one Schlatter, a friend of hers, arranged with defendant to grant her at least one month's time to pay her bill while she was a guest as she was then expecting funds from some source, and said Schlatter also guaranteed the payment of the bill. Complainant remained in the hotel from April 6 to June 5, 1934, when she was locked out [for non-payment of the bill]. . . . Thereafter, complainant was arrested, tried and acquitted in the court of Special Sessions for a violation of section 925 of the Penal Law which deals with hotel frauds. The acquittal evidently was based on the ground that credit was extended, because the section also provides that: 'this provision shall not apply where there has been a special agreement for delay in payment.'

"There is some dispute as to whether the credit was extended for one month only or for the entire period. In view of the conclusion that I have reached I think it is immaterial as to how long credit was extended.

"When Schlatter arranged with defendant to give complainant time to pay her bill nothing was said about defendant waiving his innkeeper's lien on the baggage. The court cannot assume that the lien was waived without some evidence from which that inference may be drawn. Otherwise, every time a hotelkeeper allows a guest a few more days to pay he would run the risk of waiving his lien, 'a result which is inconsistent with the nature of the lien and which defeats the purpose of the statute.' (*Smith* v. *Colcord,* 115 Mass. 70). . . .

"Complainant also urges that the agreement made by Schlatter with defendant created the relation of landlord and tenant, and, therefore, the Lien Law does not apply, and cites the case of *Kuszewska* v. *Steiger Hotel Operating Co., Inc.* (152 Misc. 80) as authority for this proposition. . . . There is nothing before me indicating an intention to create the relation of landlord and tenant. All that defendant did was to grant complainant more time within which to pay her bill than was usual. This, in itself, did not operate to create the relation of landlord and tenant. Nor did the defendant by his act of kindness waive his legal right to the lien. True, payment was postponed, but this did not nullify the lien.

"The complaint is dismissed."

28:23 *Statutory Lien of Innkeepers*

The common law lien of innkeepers has been codified, with some modifications and extensions, by statutes in all states.

In *New York*, the applicable statute is Section 181 of the Lien Law.

Section 181. *Liens of Hotel, Apartment Hotel, Inn, Boarding, Rooming, and Lodging Housekeepers*

A keeper of a hotel, apartment hotel, inn, boarding house, rooming house or lodging house, except an emigrant lodging house, has a lien upon . . . his premises by a guest, boarder, roomer or lodger, for the proper charges due from him, on account of his accommodation, board, room and lodging, and such extras as are furnished at his request. If the keeper of such hotel, apartment hotel, inn, boarding, rooming, or lodging house knew that the property brought upon his premises was not, when brought, legally in possession of such guest, boarder, roomer, or lodger, or had notice that such property was not then the property of such guest, boarder, roomer or lodger, a lien thereon does not exist. An apartment hotel within the meaning of this section includes a hotel wherein apartments are rented for fixed periods of time, either furnished or unfurnished, to the occupants of which the keeper of such hotel supplies food, if required. A guest of an apartment hotel, within the meaning of this section, includes each and every person who is a member of the family of the tenant of an apartment therein, and for whose support such tenant is legally liable.

The statute grants a lien to the keepers of apartment hotels, and boarding, rooming, and lodginghouses in addition to common-law innkeepers. The statute does not, however, apply where the relationship is landlord and tenant.[35] In no event would the lien extend to property of *tenants* exempt from execution. Any lease or agreement for the occupancy of residential space which purports to grant the landlord a lien for unpaid rent is made void by Section 231 of the Real Property Law.

[35] *Kuszewska* v. *Steiger Hotel Operating Co., Inc.*, 152 Misc. 80, 272 N.Y.S. 659 (Sup. Ct. 1934); *Scott* v. *Browning Business Services, Inc.*, 175 Misc. 630, 24 N.Y.S.2d 227 (N.Y. Mun. Ct. 1941).

28:24 Statutory Lien as Disposition of Property without Due Process of Law

In *Klim* v. *Jones*,[36] the court invalidated the California innkeeper's lien law under the due process clause of the Fourteenth Amendment for its failure to provide any sort of notice or hearing prior to the seizure of the debtor's personal belongings. In making this determination the court relied heavily on the decision of the United States Supreme Court in *Sniadach* v. *Family Finance Corp.*,[37] in which the Court had held that the Wisconsin procedure for garnishing the wages of a debtor prior to judgment contravened constitutional due process because it failed to provide for notice and hearing prior to the freezing of the debtor's property. The *Klim* court noted that the lien procedure prescribed by the California statute had an even greater and more deleterious impact on the clan affected than the analogous Wisconsin garnishment procedures invalidated in *Sniadach:*

First, although Section 1861 applies as well to the thousands of more affluent patrons who stay at California's better lodging facilities, its primary impact appears to be on those who, like the plaintiff here, are either financially embarrassed or of extremely limited means. It is obvious that many of those who habituate hotels and rooming facilities of lesser light and who would be most oppressed by the procedure under Section 1861 are even less able to withstand such procedure than are wage-earners under prejudgment wage garnishment statutes. Many such boarders have no steady or significant source of income, much less regular wages.

Second, wage garnishment applies only to wages and only to a portion thereof, thus leaving the debtor's other property unencumbered. Under Section 1861, however, *all* of the boarder's possessions may be denied him if such possessions are all kept in his lodgings. With the probable exceptions of motels and inns, in each of the other rooming establishments covered by Section 1861 it is altogether likely that the occupant thereof keeps all his worldly goods there. This was the case with the plaintiff here, and nothing has been presented to this court to indicate that such is not a common situation.

Third, the lien of Section 1861, much like garnishment of wages, may well result in the loss of a boarder's job. This effect is exacerbated when, as in the present case, the imposition of a lien under Section 1861 denies

---

[36] 315 F. Supp. 109 (N.D. Cal. 1970).   [37] 395 U.S. 337 (1969).

the boarder access to his very tools of trade or other means of livelihood. In addition, the boarder will not even have access to personal identification papers, credentials, licenses and the like if these, too, are left in his quarters when the lien of Section 1861 is imposed.

Fourth, the lien procedure countenanced by Section 1861 results in economic leverage on the boarder at least as great as that stemming from the application of wage garnishment statutes. Here, too, the imposition of the lien may often result in dubious or fraudulent claims being paid by the harried boarder with valid legal defenses being relegated to the dustbin.

Fifth, and finally, Section 1861 provides for virtually no exemptions from its coverage, unlike the wage garnishment statutes in effect even before *Sniadach*. Section 1861, by its own terms, exempts only musical instruments used to earn a living and prosthetic or orthopedic appliances personally used by the boarder. While California attachment statutes provide for numerous exemptions, as for such obvious necessities as tools of trade, furnishings, and clothes, Section 1861 makes almost none. Without such exemptions, Section 1861 thrusts the allegedly defaulting boarder out onto the street without any possessions other than what he can manage to carry on his person. The two limited exemptions which are provided by Section 1861 bear little relationship to any rational policy and would seem to be aimed only at protecting people such as Benny Goodman and the late President Franklin D. Roosevelt.

In view of these harsh effects, the only possible way in which Section 1861 might be saved would be to find that it served some overriding "state or creditor interest" as expressed in *Sniadach*. No paramount state interest has been claimed before this court, and it does not appear that any such state interest is served by Section 1861. It is argued, however, that a significant creditor interest does exist, for without the innkeeper's lien the California proprietor would be unable to get in personam jurisdiction over the transients who often frequent California motels, hotels, and the like.

The court is not persuaded by this argument. The boarder who desires to leave the jurisdiction without paying his bill can easily do so and take all his possessions with him, so the threat of a lien is hardly an iron-clad safeguard for the California proprietor. A more practical consideration is that many if not most of the establishments which have resort to the lien of Section 1861 cater to lodgers who stay for significant periods of time, so the danger of a non-paying transient leaving the state just to avoid a lodging bill does not seem to be at all common.

The final point to be made here is that the innkeeper will not be left to the mercy of lodgers by the instant decision. The court is not purporting to abolish the innkeeper's lien, but only to require that it be conditioned by the procedural due process safeguards discussed by the Supreme Court in *Sniadach*. Moreover, a feasible if not entirely attractive alternative exists by which the California proprietor can guarantee that he will be paid, namely payment in advance. Innkeepers have long had the right to require payment in advance before receiving a guest, and nothing prevents today's innkeeper from doing the same.

In declaring Section 1861 unconstitutional for the reasons expressed, this court reaches a result contrary to that reached many years ago by the only other court which squarely faced the issue presented to this court today. In 1933 the Supreme Court of Missouri declared in *L. E. Lines Music Co.* v. *Holt,* 332 Mo. 749, 60 S.W.2d 32 (1933) that a Missouri statute declarative of the common law innkeeper's lien was not unconstitutional as a violation of due process. See Comment, 22 Geo. L.J. 101, 102 *supra*.[38]

In tackling the constitutional argument in *Holt,* the Missouri Supreme Court had said simply: "The common law is the law of our land unless abrogated by statute or Constitution. [The Missouri Lien Law] is no broader than the common law, therefore, it is not unconstitutional."[39]

[38] 315 F. Supp. at 122–124.

[39] 332 Mo. 749, 60 S.W.2d 34.

CHAPTER 29

Enforcement of Innkeeper's Lien

29:1 *Introduction*

An innkeeper holding goods on lien cannot sell the goods to reimburse himself without legal process, even though the care and keeping of the goods necessitates expense.[1] Nor can he pledge the goods.[2]

The proper method of enforcing the lien, in the absence of statute, is by a bill in equity to foreclose the lien; and on such a bill the court may order the sale of the goods.

29:2 *Statutory Sale of Property Held under Lien*

Most states have enacted statutes authorizing the sale by innkeepers of property held under lien. In New York, the applicable statutory authority is in Sections 207–209 of the General Business Law. Section 207 authorizes the immediate sale of property held under lien; it also authorizes the sale of property remaining unclaimed for six months. The statute, as amended, reads:

> Section 207. *Sale of Unclaimed Articles and Other Property Covered by His Lien*
>
> Any keeper of a hotel, motel, apartment hotel, inn, boarding-house, rooming house or lodging-house, except an immigrant lodging-house, who shall have a lien for fare, lodging, accommodation or board upon any goods, baggage or other chattel property, or, who, for a period of six months, shall have in custody any unclaimed trunk, box, valise, package or parcel, or other chattel property, may, in the manner provided by this section, sell the same at public auction to the highest bidder for cash, and out of the proceeds of such sale may, in case of lien, retain the amount of such lien and

---

[1] *Fox* v. *McGregor,* 11 Barb. (N.Y.) 41 (Sup. Ct. 1851); *Gildea* v. *Earle,* 2 City Ct. R. 122 (N.Y. 1885).

[2] *People* v. *Husband,* 36 Mich. 306 (1877).

the expense of advertisement and sale, and the expense of storage, advertisement and sale thereof. Not less than fifteen days prior to the time of the sale, a notice of the time and place of holding the sale, and containing a brief description of the goods, baggage and articles to be sold, shall be published in a newspaper published in the city or town in which such hotel, motel, apartment hotel, inn, boarding-house, rooming-house or lodging-house is situated; but if there be none, then in such newspaper published nearest such city or town; if the name and address of said guest, boarder, roomer or owner of such chattel articles and property, appears upon the records of such keeper, such notice shall also be mailed to said guest, boarder, roomer or owner, addressed to such address; such notice shall be mailed in the manner aforesaid at least fifteen days prior to the time of the sale.

In *Dajkovich* v. *Hotel Waldorf-Astoria Corporation*,[3] plaintiff deposited fifteen pieces of baggage with defendant's hotel. Some five years later, a friend of plaintiff called at the hotel to inquire about the baggage, and was told that it was still within the hotel intact and in good order, and that it would be held until plaintiff's return. Within two months after such assurance and promise, defendant sold the baggage at public auction, pursuant to Section 207, in the mistaken belief that it was abandoned by plaintiff. In an action by plaintiff for the conversion of the baggage, held, for plaintiff, the court stating:

Section 201 affords an innkeeper a limited liability, under certain circumstances, for the "loss of or damage to" a guest's property. There was no "loss" or "damage" in this case, and no misadventure of the kind which is contemplated by the statute. There was a sale and disposition of plaintiff's property as the voluntary, intentional and deliberate act of defendant as a matter of claimed right under section 207 of the General Business Law. This section of the law prescribes an innkeeper's rights under certain circumstances, in which defendant purported to act, and affords its own defined protection. The issue litigated at the trial was whether defendant was entitled, on the facts disclosed, to the protection of this statute. It has been held, and we affirm, that defendant did not bring itself within the statute and is, therefore, liable in conversion for its unlawful act.

We think there is no room for section 201 of the General Business Law then to come into play. It was not the contemplation of that section of

---

[3] 285 App. Div. 421, 137 N.Y.S.2d 764 (1st Dep't 1955), *aff'd mem.*, 309 N.Y. 1005, 133 N.E.2d 456 (1956).

the law to limit an innkeeper's liability for its own misappropriation of a guest's property, albeit without *animus furandi,* and to give the innkeeper a secondary protection of limited liability in those cases in which it has failed in its assertion of right under section 207.

The procedure for sale in compliance with Section 207 may be summarized as follows:

1. Contact a reliable licensed public auctioneer for the conduct of the sale.

2. Assemble the baggage to be sold in one place suitable for holding the auction. All articles should be tagged with the name of the guest, if ascertainable, from whom they have been detained or who left same unclaimed. Locked trunks, bags, valises and like containers should be opened for the auction so as to exhibit the contents to prospective buyers. Failure to do so may be negligence subjecting the innkeeper to damages in an action by the delinquent former guest.

3. Collate registration cards and other records, if any, relating to owners of property. If the address of a guest cannot be located, do not use this procedure; the sale should in such event be conducted under Section 209, *infra.*

4. Prepare *Notice of Sale,* and have it published at least fifteen days prior to the date of sale in a local newspaper. The following form may be used:

NOTICE OF SALE AT PUBLIC AUCTION

The Hotel _____ by _____,
  (name of hotel)   (name of auctioneer)
Auctioneer, will sell at public auction in Room_____ in said hotel at _____ the bags, suit-
        (name and location of hotel)
cases, brief cases, trunks, packages, boxes, wearing apparel and other like items, together with contents, if any, the nature of which is unknown, held as unclaimed property of, or for unpaid charges due said hotel from the following:

_____
(Here insert names of persons whose property is to be sold)

5. Obtain copy of the advertisement from the publisher together with his affidavit of publication and preserve same in your file of the auction.

6. Send a copy of the Notice of Sale, in the form published, to each person whose property is put up for sale at his address appearing on the records of the hotel. The person who mailed the notices should execute an affidavit of mailing in the following form:

_____, being duly sworn, deposes and says that he (or she) resides at _____ and is employed as _____ in the _____ Hotel; that on the _____ day of _____ deponent mailed in a sealed postpaid envelope at _____ (here insert place of mailing) in the City of _____ to each and every one of the persons named in the attached statement, at the address set forth opposite the name of such person, a notice of which the attached notice is a true copy.

_____
                                            (Signature)

Sworn before me this
_____ day of _____ 19 _____

Preserve the affidavit of mailing and attached list of names in your file relating to the auction.

7. The sale is to be conducted by a licensed public auctioneer and the property must be sold to the highest bidder for cash.

8. Out of the proceeds of the sale the innkeeper may retain the amount of his lien and the expense of advertising and sale.

9. The procedure set forth in the statute must be followed strictly. Failure to do so will expose the innkeeper to liability for damages to a guest returning at some future date, making claim for the property and offering to pay the charges. The damages would be the value of the property, less the amount of the lien.[4]

29:3 *Alternate Procedure for Sale of Property Held on Lien*

Section 209 of the New York General Business Law provides a simplified procedure for the sale of property held on lien. If the charges for which a lien is claimed have remained unpaid for a period of eighteen months, Section 209 applies. It reads as follows:

[4] *Lane* v. *Hotel Investors, Inc.,* 29 N.Y.S.2d 364 (Sup. Ct. 1941); *Crosby* v. *20 Fifth Avenue Hotel Co.,* 173 Misc. 595, 20 N.Y.S.2d 227 (N.Y. Mun. Ct. 1939), *modified,* 173 Misc. 604, 17 N.Y.S.2d 498 (Sup. Ct. 1940).

Section 209. *Certain Sales after Eighteen Months*

Any keeper of a hotel, motel, apartment hotel, inn, boarding-house, rooming-house or lodging-house, except an immigrant lodging-house, whose lien for fare, lodging, accommodation or board upon any goods, baggage or other chattel property, shall not have been paid for a period of eighteen months, may sell such property at public auction for cash to the highest bidder upon mailing a notice inclosed in a securely closed postpaid wrapper, directed to the person who left such property with such keeper, at the post office of the city, town or village where such hotel, motel, apartment hotel, inn, boarding-house, rooming-house or lodging-house is situated, such notice to contain a statement of the time and place when and where such goods, baggage or other chattel property will be sold and such notice shall be mailed at least fifteen days before such sale shall take place. Such keeper shall, out of the proceeds of such sale, retain the amount of his lien and the expense of selling such property, and, if there be any surplus, he shall, [if there is no demand for such by the person whose property was sold] . . . file with said treasurer, chamberlain or other chief fiscal officer a statement in writing containing the name of the person whose property was sold, the price at which it was sold, the date of such sale and by whom sold. Such surplus shall be kept and disposed of in the manner provided in section two hundred and eight of this chapter. Nothing contained in this article shall preclude any other remedy now existing for the enforcement and satisfaction of a lien of the keeper of a hotel, motel, apartment hotel, inn, boarding-house, rooming-house or lodging-house, except an immigrant lodging-house, nor bar his right to recover for so much of the debt as shall not be paid through such sale.

The procedure for sale under Section 209 is simpler than that outlined under Section 207 above, in that:

1. The Notice of Sale, in the form suggested above, may be mailed to the owner of the property whose address is unknown, *at the post office* of the city, town or village in which the hotel is located.

2. The sale need not be advertised in a local paper.

3. This section does not specifically apply to unclaimed property but only to property held in lien; if unclaimed property is sold the procedure outlined under Section 207 should be followed.

In selling *unclaimed property*, extreme caution must be used to make certain that the property has been held for at least six months and that no agreement, written or oral, was made to hold the property, as in the *Dajkovich* case (29:2). To be substantially safe, an innkeeper would be well advised to wait for six years before selling unclaimed property, whose owner's name and address were unknown to him.

29:4 *Disposition of Proceeds of Sale*

In the case of sales made under either Section 207 or 209, if any surplus remains after payment of the innkeeper's charges, the surplus must be disposed of in the manner prescribed in Section 208, which reads as follows:

Section 208. *Disposition of Proceeds of Sale*

Such keeper shall, out of the proceeds of such sale, retain the amount of his lien or storage charges and the expense of advertising and sale, and shall make an entry of the articles sold, the amount received therefor, the amounts retained by him as aforesaid, and if there be any surplus, he shall, within ten days after such sale, upon demand, pay over such surplus to such guest, boarder, roomer, or person whose property was sold. In case such surplus shall not be demanded and paid as aforesaid, within said ten days, then within five days thereafter, such keeper shall pay said surplus to the treasurer of the county or chamberlain or other chief fiscal officer of the city in which such sale took place, and shall, at the same time, file with said treasurer or chamberlain or other chief fiscal officer a statement in writing containing the name and place of residence, so far as they are known, of the guest, boarder, roomer or person whose goods, baggage or chattel articles were sold, the articles sold and the price at which they were sold, the name and address of the auctioneer making the sale, and a copy of the notice published. Said treasurer, chamberlain or other chief fiscal officer shall keep said surplus money for and credit the same to the person named in said statement as such guest, boarder, roomer or person, and shall pay the same to him or his executors or administrators, upon demand, and upon furnishing satisfactory evidence of identity to such treasurer, chamberlain or other chief fiscal officer.

CHAPTER 30

Crimes against Innkeepers

30:1 Fraudulently Obtaining Credit or Accommodation

In the early days of innkeeping, the protection of the traveler was the principal concern of the law. With the development of rapid means of travel, the increase in the type and number of travelers, and of the hotels and motels built to accommodate them, and with the discovery by criminal elements of the comparative ease of obtaining hotel accommodations on credit, the protection of the innkeeper became of vital concern to the state. With airplanes, railroads, and automobiles within easy reach to make a swift getaway, more and more innkeepers became victimized by "deadbeats," who would make free use of their hospitality and surreptitiously depart without payment of their bills. In the course of time, for the protection of an essential and growing industry, the legislatures of most states enacted penal statutes making criminal the fraudulent obtaining of credit, or lodging, food, or other accommodations and services in hotels, motels, inns, boarding, rooming, and lodginghouses. Such statutes are commonly referred to as hotel fraud acts, or "deadbeat" statutes.

30:2 New York Hotel Fraud Act

The revised New York Penal Code, which became effective September 1, 1967, classifies the crime of fraud on innkeepers as a type of larceny which does not, however, in law, amount to larceny, for the reason, among others, that the subject of the theft is not "property." It is an offense relating to theft and is now designated as "theft of services." It covers, in addition to hotel accommodations, restaurant services, credit cards, and a variety of other services, including transportation by railroad, subway, bus, air or taxi, telecommunications service, services compensation for which is measured

[467]

by a meter or other mechanical equipment, gas, electric, water, or telephone services and of commercial or industrial equipment or facilities.

Section 165.15. *Theft of Services*

A person is guilty of theft of services when:

1. He obtains or attempts to obtain a service, or induces or attempts to induce the supplier of a rendered service to agree to payment therefor on a credit basis, by the use of a credit card which he knows to be stolen.

2. With intent to avoid payment for restaurant services rendered, or for services rendered to him as a transient guest at a hotel, motel, inn, tourist cabin, rooming house or comparable establishment, he avoids or attempts to avoid such payment by unjustifiable failure or refusal to pay, by stealth, or by any misrepresentation of fact which he knows to be false. A person who fails or refuses to pay for such services is presumed to have intended to avoid payment therefor. . . .

Theft of services is a class A misdemeanor.

The statute applies only to *transient guests;* it may not be invoked against permanents, and certainly not against tenants. Unlike the earlier New York statute (Section 925 of the Penal Law), Section 165.15 applies to *restaurant patrons,* as well as hotel guests.

Section 155.00 *Larceny: Definitions of Terms*

The following definitions are applicable to this title:

"Credit card" means any instrument or article defined as a credit card in section five hundred eleven of the general business law.

"Service" includes, but is not limited to, labor, professional service, transportation service, the supplying of hotel accommodations, restaurant services, entertainment, the supplying of equipment for use, and the supplying of commodities of a public utility nature such as gas, electricity, steam and water. A ticket or equivalent instrument which evidences a right to receive a service is not in itself service but constitutes property within the meaning of subdivision one.

Section 165.17. *Unlawful Use of Credit Card*

A person is guilty of unlawful use of credit card, when in the course of obtaining or attempting to obtain property of a service, he uses or displays a credit card which he knows to be revoked or cancelled.

Unlawful use of credit card is a class A misdemeanor.

30:3 *Hotel Fraud Acts Are Not Collection Aids*

Innkeepers, in addition to their lien on the baggage of guests, are given further substantial protection by these penal statutes. Great care should be exercised, however, in the enforcement of these statutes, lest persons, who, without fraudulent intent, are temporarily unable to pay their bills, be unjustly arrested and prosecuted. The statute should not be utilized, in other words, as a weapon to force the prompt payment of hotel bills. The innkeeper must always be prepared to prove actual fraud in case the presumption arising out of nonpayment of the hotel bill on demand is rebutted. The courts are reluctant to be used as collection agencies and even more reluctant to imprison hotel guests for nonpayment of debts.

30:4 *Accommodations Must Be Actually Obtained*

The accommodations must be actually obtained in order to have an offense under the act; it is not enough that a contract for board has been made. Thus, where one has contracted to stay at an inn for a certain time and leaves before the time, paying for all the board he has had, the act cannot apply. In *Sundmacher* v. *Block*,[1] it appeared that the guest registered at night, and, on being asked how long he was to stay, said he should stay at least until after breakfast. He had notice of a rule that a guest staying until after the beginning of a meal must pay for that meal. The next morning, a few minutes after breakfast was served, he tendered to the clerk the amount due for his supper and room; the clerk, though he knew the guest had not eaten breakfast, demanded payment for breakfast under the rule, and, upon the guest's refusing to pay, caused his arrest and prosecution under the statute. The guest, having been acquitted, brought this action for malicious prosecution, and the court held that he might recover, there being no reasonable cause to suppose him guilty, Judge Pleasants said:

[H]e did not obtain the breakfast. Nor can it be held that there was a contract, as to either, that he would positively remain for any definite time. They were transients, whose present purpose in that regard, though

[1] 39 Ill. App. 553 (1891).

stated as represented, would not be contracts for the time mentioned, but lawfully changeable at their option for any reason thereafter arising. Nor, if they were contracts would it affect the question under consideration. This statute is not to be extended by any liberality of construction in favor of innkeepers; and we hold that in no proceeding under it is the civil liability of the guest for any accommodation not actually "obtained" at all pertinent. If he definitely contracted to remain for a week, and left without fault of the innkeeper, at the close of the first day, paying or tendering payment for all that he had actually obtained, evidence of his refusal to pay for the further time contracted for would not be admissible as tending to prove an offense, or probable cause for a prosecution, under this act. Nor should the jury be permitted, upon either of those issues, to consider whether or not the accommodation actually obtained was better, in view of what was further contracted for, than it otherwise would have been, if payment for it was made or tendered according to its actual value or regular price. The innkeeper will not be allowed to claim that if he had understood the guest was to remain only a day instead of a week, he would or might have been furnished a meaner room, any more than that there would or might have been less of benignity in the smiles of the clerk or of alacrity in the responses of bellboys or the movements of table waiters. Having peculiar rights they are subject to peculiar obligations.[2]

30:5 *Hotel Accommodations Must Have Been Obtained by Fraud*

There must be some element of fraud in obtaining hotel service in order to bring it within the statute. So where the only evidence was that the defendant, after being entertained for a week, was unable to pay; that the innkeeper forbade him to go until he paid; that he asserted that money was due him in a neighboring city, and the innkeeper allowed him to go get it; and that he did not return with the money, it was held that a conviction could not be supported.[3] Judge Ross said:

If an impecunious guest who has been guilty of no fraud except inability to pay, is unable to pay the amount of a board bill already incurred, it would seem from the contention of the complainant that he must either remain and increase his liability and the landlord's loss, or if he goes

    2 *Id.* at 563.
    3 *People* v. *Nicholson,* 25 Misc. 266, 55 N.Y.S. 447 (Onondaga County Ct. 1898).

away openly, and for the ostensible purpose of obtaining the money to pay the amount of the bill, that he is liable to arrest and conviction. This would amount practically to liability to conviction in every case of inability to pay a board bill. I do not think that the statute contemplates such a result. A hotel-keeper can require payment in advance from his guests; he has a common-law and statutory lien upon the baggage of his guest, and he is protected from actual fraud, and this is all. The mere fact of inability to pay a hotel bill is not made a crime.[4]

The statute is akin to the statues punishing one who obtains property by false pretenses, and is to be interpreted in the same way. The false pretense by means of which the board is obtained must therefore be made with reference to a past or existing fact; a promise to do something in the future is not such a false pretense as to justify a conviction under the statute, even if the promise was not kept. Thus, where a boarder promised to pay his board as soon as he drew his pay as clerk of the general assembly, but when he drew his pay he left the inn and the city without paying his board, the statute was not violated.[5] Judge Ellison said:

The statute upon which this indictment is founded cannot be distinguished in this respect from the sections relating to false pretenses, cheats, devices, etc. It simply places obtaining board in the same category with other things obtained by false pretenses. The matter charged here was a false representation, or statement, or pretense made by defendant, that in the future, *viz.*, when he drew his pay as clerk in the general assembly, he would pay his board. The indictment does not aver, nor is it pretended, that defendant made any representation as to any existing matter which was false. He was, at the time, a clerk in the general assembly, and his promise, representation, statement or pretense, that he would pay his board when he should, in the future, draw his money as clerk, was no more than if he had promised "to pay as soon as he should get the money." Every one who boards at a hotel or boarding house directly or indirectly promises to pay his board, and yet it would scarcely be thought such promise, though false, would subject the promisor to a criminal prosecution.[6]

[4] *Id.* at 267–268. [5] *State* v. *Tull*, 42 Mo. App. 324 (1890).
[6] *Id.* at 326.

30:6 *Fraud Must Have Been Committed for Purpose of Obtaining Hotel Accommodations*

The pretense must be made for the purpose of obtaining the accommodations. In a Missouri case, *State* v. *Kingsley,*[7] the defendant registered at the Southern Hotel on July 29 and was assigned to a room. On July 31, she sent for the manager, rented a room as a studio, stating that she was an artist, and inquired when the bills were payable. Being told that they were payable weekly, she said that it would be inconvenient to pay at the end of the week because she expected a remittance in two weeks, and asked that her bill might be payable then. The manager, without asking from whom she expected the remittance, assented. No remittance coming at the end of two weeks she was, after a few days, excluded from the hotel and indicted under the statute. The Supreme Court held that upon this evidence she should be discharged. Mr. Justice Thomas said:

We do not think it can be fairly inferred from the evidence that defendant in this case stated to the manager of the Southern Hotel that she expected a remittance, for the purpose of obtaining board. She registered at the hotel on June [*sic*] [July] 29, and without being questioned or making any statement she was assigned a room. In this manner she obtained board in the first instance. On June [*sic*] [July] 31, she sent for the manager, and upon inquiry she was informed that bills for board were payable weekly. She replied that she could not pay till the end of two weeks, at which time she expected a remittance. It appears, therefore, that she got board for two days, and she could have continued there for one week, at least, without saying a word about payment of the bills. Persons intending to perpetrate tricks or obtain money, property or other valuable thing[s] by means of a false pretense, do not ordinarily proceed in this way. They usually defer their false statements till they are forced to the wall. Here defendant made the statements voluntarily.[8]

30:7 *Surreptitious Removal of Baggage as Element of Crime*

Failure to pay the bill or absconding without paying the bill and surreptitiously removing or attempting to remove baggage is made prima facie evidence of guilt. This clause must be so interpreted as

[7] 108 Mo. 135, 18 S.W. 994 (1891).   [8] *Id.* at 141.

not to constitute practically an imprisonment for debt, since such imprisonment would be unconstitutional. It cannot therefore be so interpreted as to make the mere refusal to pay a bill sufficient reasonable cause for prosecution and imprisonment. The removal of the baggage surreptitiously must accompany the refusal to pay, in order to have such effect.[9]

A "surreptitious" removal of baggage involves some concealment; if done openly, though at a time when no one was watching, the removal would not be surreptitious, for "the fact that neither appellant nor any of his agents knew that he was going away, or taking his baggage away, does not, of itself, establish that the removal was surreptitious. He may have gone and taken his baggage in the most open and public manner, and yet neither appellant nor any of his agents seen the removal." [10] The approved definition of the word is "done by stealth, or without legitimate authority, made or produced fraudulently; characterized by concealment or underhand dealing; clandestine"; though one of the definitions mentions fraud, the fraud meant is obviously a fraud used to escape the notice of the person interested as, in an example given, the surreptitious edition of a book. The word, by derivation, means taken away secretly. It is therefore obvious that surreptitious removal is one which is done clandestinely so as to escape the notice of the innkeeper by reason of the method of doing it.

30:8 Rebutting the Presumption of Fraudulent Intent

In *People* v. *Dukatt*,[11] the complainants alleged that, with intent to defraud, defendants had registered as guests at the Hotel New Yorker in the city of New York and had failed, upon demand, to pay for room rent, restaurant, laundry, telephone, and valet service. There was evidence that each defendant, carrying baggage, had registered at the hotel with his wife and family; that neither had established credit; that when one defendant had been at the hotel for three days and the other for five days, demand had been made upon them for payment of their bills; that they had failed to make such payment but had tendered a check on the Riggs National Bank of Washington, D.C., to cover both bills, which the hotel refused to accept.

---

[9] *Hutchinson* v. *Davis,* 58 Ill. App. 358 (1895). [10] *Id.* at 363.
[11] 298 N.Y. 545, 81 N.E.2d 93 (1948).

Testimony that the hotel had learned by telephone that neither defendant had an account in the Riggs Bank was stricken as hearsay. The credit manager of the Waldorf-Astoria Hotel testified that the defendant Hillman had been a guest there on a number of occasions. Just prior to registering at the Hotel New Yorker, the defendant Hillman had been registered at the Waldorf-Astoria and upon failure to pay his bill upon demand had been "locked out" and his baggage withheld. The defendant Dukatt offered to go out and get the cash to pay his bill but was refused permission to do so. No attempt was made by either of the defendants to leave the hotel in an attempt to avoid payment of their bills.

The complaining witness was represented on the trial by counsel. No representative of the district attorney's office was present. The defendants contended that there were no violations of Section 925 of the Penal Law and that, in any event, the convictions were not authorized because the prosecution was not conducted by the People. The People contended on the other hand that the guilt of the defendants was established beyond reasonable doubt and that the fact that the district attorney did not conduct the prosecution was immaterial.

A memorandum decision by the court stated: "Judgments reversed and new trials ordered upon the ground that the undisputed evidence is that defendants tendered a check in payment for their lodging and other accommodations upon demand by the hotel; in the absence of competent evidence that the check was worthless, such tender overcomes the presumption created by Section 925 [Now Sec. 165.15 —Ed.] of the Penal Law."

30:9 *Abuse of Statute as Malicious Prosecution*

COOPER *v.* SCHIRRMEISTER
176 Misc. 474, 26 N.Y.S. 2d 668 (N.Y. City Ct. 1941)

MADIGAN, J.: "This is a non-jury action for malicious prosecution. The plaintiff was charged with a misdemeanor under Section 925 of the Penal Law, relating to frauds on hotelkeepers and others.

"He and his family occupied, under a lease for a term of six months, a small furnished apartment in a building at 305 West Eighty-eighth

Street, New York city, called the Hotel Oxford, owned and operated by the corporate defendant. The other defendant was in charge of the premises. . . .

"In the Court of Special Sessions it was held, in effect, that Section 925 of the Penal Law could not under the circumstances be successfully invoked inasmuch as the relationship between the corporate defendant and plaintiff was not that of hotel keeper and guest as these defendants assert. That court dismissed the charge at the end of the People's case. No evidence was taken from this plaintiff. No finding of fact was made as to any contest issue. . . .

"It is held that, so far as concerns the demise to this plaintiff, the premises did not constitute a hotel within the meaning of Section 925 of the Penal Law.

"As to plaintiff the corporate defendant was either the keeper of an apartment hotel or the landlord of an apartment house.

"For defendants it is urged that Section 925 of the Penal Law applied to apartment hotels; that as employed in such statute the term 'hotel' includes an 'apartment hotel.' . . .

"Defendants, however, are confronted with the fact that the Legislature has not inserted the term 'apartment hotel' in Section 925 of the Penal Law. This must be held deliberate in the absence of any expression or action on the part of the Legislature which might be deemed a sufficient basis for ascribing a different intent to the lawmakers.

"It is well to note, moreover, that statutes antecedent to the present Section 925 of the Penal Law apparently go back some sixty years, to a time when 'hotel' could not mean 'apartment hotel' inasmuch as the apartment hotel of this day was then unknown.

"As indicating the fraud which defendants charged in support of the prosecution under Section 925 of the Penal Law, they assert that plaintiff and members of his family removed their belongings, on a night in August, 1939, after nine o'clock, through a service exit without passing the desk near the main entrance. Plaintiff denies that anything was taken out surreptitiously. However, he had hired an apartment in another building and he had stipulated there for free occupancy until October 1, 1939. He apparently did not announce at the desk in the building conducted by the corporate defendant that he was leaving and he left no forwarding address.

"It is found that plaintiff departed from the 'Hotel Oxford' with his effects and those of his family without the knowledge or consent of defendants, though it had been suspected that he was about to leave somewhat as he did. It is also found that his purpose was to avoid paying his bill for rent, electricity and telephone service. . . .

". . . [E]lements in the evidence lead to the conclusion that defendants knew that it was venturesome to institute and prosecute the criminal charge and that nevertheless they proceeded in the hope that, by pressing plaintiff, they might bring him to pay his debt to them.

"Lack of probable cause and actual malice are found.

"Plaintiff is entitled to punitive damages.

"Plaintiff's motion to dismiss the defense set up in the answer is granted. . . .

"Defendants' motions to dismiss are denied.

"The claim as to humiliation has been considered, but it is believed that plaintiff suffered but very little humiliation.

"Judgment for $350 in favor of plaintiff and against defendants. That amount includes exemplary damages."

30:10 Bad-Check Laws

Statistics prove that the vast majority of checks in circulation are paid when presented to the drawee banks. Every so often it happens, however, that someone, who may well be an innkeeper, takes a loss upon a "bad check." He then learns that, although a check is a substitute for money, it is not money.

All states have enacted statutes making the issuing and passing of bad checks a punishable crime. Since the statutes vary from state to state, it is necessary to consult the statute of each particular state in relation to bad checks passed or accepted in that state.

30:11 Penal Law of New York Relating to Bad Checks

The revised New York Penal Law, effective September 1, 1967, classifies the issuing of bad checks as a species of fraud of the grade of misdemeanor, although the stealing of property by means of "committing the crime of issuing a bad check" is defined as larceny.[12] Four sections relate to bad checks:

[12] Section 155.05–2(c).

Section 190.00. *Issuing a Bad Check: Definitions of Terms*

The following definitions are applicable to this article:

1. "Check" means any check, draft or similar sight order for the payment of money which is not post-dated with respect to the time of utterance.

2. "Drawer" of a check means a person whose name appears thereon as the primary obligor, whether the actual signature be that of himself or of a person purportedly authorized to draw the check in his behalf.

3. "Representative drawer" means a person who signs a check as drawer in a representative capacity or as agent of the person whose name appears thereon as the principal drawer or obligor.

4. "Utter." A person "utters" a check when, as a drawer or representative drawer thereof, he delivers it or caused it to be delivered to a person who thereby acquires a right against the drawer with respect to such check. One who draws a check with intent that it be so delivered is deemed to have uttered it if the delivery occurs.

5. "Pass." A person "passes" a check when, being a payee, holder or bearer of a check which previously has been or purports to have been drawn and uttered by another, he delivers it, for a purpose other than collection, to a third person who thereby acquires a right with respect thereto.

6. "Funds" means money or credit.

7. "Insufficient funds." A drawer has "insufficient funds" with a drawee to cover a check when he has no funds or account whatever, or funds in an amount less than that of the check; and a check dishonored for "no account" shall also be deemed to have been dishonored for "insufficient funds."

Section 190.05. *Issuing a Bad Check*

A person is guilty of issuing a bad check when:

1. (a) As a drawer or representative drawer, he utters a check knowing that he or his principal, as the case may be, does not then have sufficient funds with the drawee to cover it, and (b) he intends or believes at the time of utterance that payment will be refused by the drawee upon presentation, and (c) payment is refused by the drawee upon presentation; or

2. (a) He passes a check knowing that the drawer thereof does not then have sufficient funds with the drawee to cover it, and (b) he intends or believes at the time the check is passed that payment will be refused

by the drawee upon presentation, and (c) payment is refused by the drawee upon presentation.

Issuing a bad check is a class B misdemeanor.

Section 190.10. *Issuing a Bad Check: Presumptions*

1. When the drawer of a check has insufficient funds with the drawee to cover it at the time of utterance, the subscribing drawer or representative drawer, as the case may be, is presumed to know of such insufficiency.

2. A subscribing drawer or representative drawer, as the case may be, of an ultimately dishonored check is presumed to have intended or believed that the check would be dishonored upon presentation when: (a) The drawer had no account with the drawee at the time of utterance; or (b) (i) The drawer had insufficient funds with the drawee at the time of utterance, and (ii) the check was presented to the drawee for payment not more than thirty days after the date of utterance, and (iii) the drawer had insufficient funds with the drawee at the time of presentation.

3. Dishonor of a check by the drawee and insufficiency of the drawer's funds at the time of presentation may properly be proved by introduction in evidence of a notice of protest of the check, or of a certificate under oath of an authorized representative of the drawee declaring the dishonor and insufficiency, and such proof shall constitute presumptive evidence of such dishonor and insufficiency.

Section 190.15 *Issuing a Bad Check: Defenses*

In any prosecution for issuing a bad check, it is an affirmative defense that:

1. The defendant or a person acting in his behalf made full satisfaction of the amount of the check within ten days after dishonor by the drawee; or

2. The defendant, in acting as a representative drawer, did so as an employee who, without personal benefit, merely executed the orders of his employer or of a superior officer or employee generally authorized to direct his activities.

Cross–Reference Table, Sherry to Beale

The below-listed sections in the present book draw upon material in the corresponding sections of Joseph Henry Beale's *The Law of Innkeepers and Hotels* (1906).

Sherry	Beale	Sherry	Beale
1:1	1	7:2	68
1:2	2	7:3	68
1:3	3	7:4	67
1:4	4	8:1	82
1:5	5	8.2	83
1:6	6	8.3	84
2:1	11	8:5	86
2:2	12	8:7	88
2:3	13	8:8	89
2:4	14	9:1	91
2:5	15, 16	9:2	92
2:6	18, 19	9:3	65
2:7	21	9:4	94
3:1	31	9:5	96
4:1	51	9:8	97
4:2	52	10:1	101
4:3	53	10:2	102
4:4	54	10:3	103
4:5	55	10:4	104
4:6	56	10:12	105
4:7	57	11:1	111
4:8	58	11:2	112
5:1	61, 62	11:3	113
5:2	63	11:4	114
5:3	64	11:5	121
5:4	66	11:6	122, 123
7:1	69	11:7	124

Sherry	Beale	Sherry	Beale
11:8	125	23:7	431
12:1	131	25:1	301
12:2	132	25:2	304
12:3	133	25:3	305
12:4	134	25:5	306
12:5	135	27:1	241
12:6	136	27:2	242
12:7	137	27:3	243
13:1	161	27:4	244
13.5	166, 167	27:5	245
14:1	170	27:6	247, 248
14:3	162	27:7	249
14:4	164	28:1	251
16:1	171	28:2	252
16:2	172	28:3	253
16:6	175	28:4	254
18:1	181	28:5	255
18:2	182	28:6	256
18:4	186	28:7	257
18:5	142, 143	28:8	258
18:7	146	28:9	259
18:8	147	28:10	260
18:14	149	28:11	261
18:15	189	28:12	264
18:16	188	28:13	266
19:5	206	28:14	267
19:6	207	28:15	268
21:1	221, 222	28:16	269
21:2	223	28:17	270
21:3	224	28:18	271
21:4	225	28:19	272
21:5	226	28:20	273
21:6	227	28:21	275
21:7	228	29:1	276, 277
22:1	212	30:4	447
22:2	213	30:5	444, 445
22:3	214	30:6	446
22:4	215	30:7	449, 451
22:5	211		

Law Review Articles

A subject index to these articles is on page 489.

1. "Bailments—Innkeeper—Liability for Damage to Automobile of Guest." 80 *U. Pa. L. Rev.* 122 (1931).
2. "Bailments—Innkeepers—Liability for Loss of Baggage." 30 *Mich. L. Rev.* 1107 (1932).
3. "Bailments—Innkeepers—Limited Liability under General Business Law." 11 *Fordham L. Rev.* 209 (1942).
4. "Bailments—Statutory Limitation of Liability of Innkeeper Where Value of Goods, Deposited for Safe-Keeping, Has Not Been Revealed." 3 *Temp. L.Q.* 316 (1929).
5. "Basis for Liability of a Restauranteur for Serving Unwholesome Food." E. B. Quint. 8 *N.Y.U. Intra. L. Rev.* 77 (1953).
6. "Boardinghouses: Liability for Loss of Guest's Property." 19 *N.Z.L.J.* 89 (1943).
7. "Can an Innkeeper Contract out of His Common Law Liability?" 179 *L.T.* 116 (1935).
8. "Club Visitors as Innkeepers' 'Guests.'" 43 *L.J.* 748 (1908).
9. "The Common Lodging House." 110 *Just. P.* 551 (1946).
10. "Constitutional Law—Due Process of Law—Innkeeper's Lien—Appellate Jurisdiction." 22 *Geo. L.J.* 101 (1933).
11. "Construction of the Illinois Dram Shop Act Imposing Liability upon Tavernkeeper and His Lessor for Injuries Caused by Intoxicated Persons." J. R. Vicars. 14 *Notre Dame Law.* 295 (1939).
12. "Damaged Goods at the Inn." A. L. Diamond. 19 *Modern L. Rev.* 408 (1956).
13. "The Duty of Business to Serve the Public: Analogy to the Innkeeper's Obligation." H. L. Molot. 46 *Can. B. Rev.* 612 (1968).
14. "Fraud on the Innkeeper: The Need for Legislative Reform." 16 *U. Fla. L. Rev.* 622 (1964).
15. "Guests and Lodgers at Inns." G. Sawer. 17 *Modern L. Rev.* 272 (1954).
16. "Guests at an Inn." 70 *Albany L.J.* 317 (1908).

17. "Holiday Bookings." A. Samuels. 106 *Sol. J.* 499 (1962).
18. "Holiday Problems." V. Powell-Smith. 115 *L.J.* 379, 397 (1965).
19. "Hosts and Guests." 185 *L.T.* 202 (1938).
20. "Hotel Garage Accommodation." 75 *Sol. J.* 186 (1931).
21. "The Hotel—[In the Event of Fire] Always the Insurer?" E. Steinfeld. 1947 *Ins. L.J.* 316 (1947).
22. "Hotelkeepers Liability for Negligent Loss of Property of a Guest." 57 *Dick. L. Rev.* 348 (1953).
23. "Hotel Keeper's Liability—Property in Transport." 6 *Fordham L. Rev.* 489 (1937).
24. "Hotel Law in Virginia." 38 *Va. L. Rev.* 815 (1952).
25. "Hotels: Liability of Innkeepers for Property of Guests and Tenants." H. A. Carrington. 1 *U. Fla. L. Rev.* 283 (1948).
26. "The Illinois Innkeeper and the Goods of His Guests." 7 *DePaul L. Rev.* 102 (1957).
27. "Implied Warranty and the Sale of Restaurant Food." 63 *W. Va. L. Rev.* 326 (1961).
28. "Innkeeper and Guest." 188 *L.T.* 91 (1939).
29. "Innkeeper and Guest's Motor Car." 171 *L.T.* 90 (1931).
30. "An Innkeeper and His Guest's Car." 75 *Sol. J.* 68 (1931).
31. "The Innkeeper and His Lien." 91 *Sol. J.* 488 (1947).
32. "Innkeeper-Guest Relationship—Statutory Limitation of Liability." 23 *Fordham L. Rev.* 209 (1954).
33. "Innkeeper—Liability for Loss of Goods Left in Car of Guest—Whether Goods Left by Guest in Car Parked in Hotel Parking Lot Are Infra Hospitium—Innkeepers Liability Acts." R. G. Murray. 34 *Can. B. Rev.* 1203 (1956).
34. "Innkeeper—Liability for Loss of Guest's Car—Traveller—*Infra Hospitium*—Contracting out of Liability—Innkeepers Liability Act." R. G. Murray. 29 *Can. B. Rev.* 768 (1951).
35. "Innkeeper—Liability—Injury to Guest's Goods—Insurer—Negligence." 9 *Can. B. Rev.* 750 (1931).
36. "Innkeeper—Liability of Innkeepers for Employee's Theft of Guest's Automobile." 29 *Rocky Mt. L. Rev.* 136 (1956).
37. "Innkeeper: Status or Contract?" 114 *Just. P.* 233 (1950).
38. "Innkeeper—Statute Limiting Liability for the Property of Guests." 52 *Harv. L. Rev.* 334 (1938).
39. "Innkeepers." 92 *Sol. J.* 4 (1948).
40. "Innkeepers and Parked Cars." 163 *L.T.* 465 (1927).
41. "Innkeepers and Parked Cars." 31 *Law Notes* 112 (1927).

42. "Innkeepers—Assault by One Guest on Another—Liability of Landlord." 3 *Wash. L. Rev.* 194 (1928).

43. "Innkeepers—Definition for Purpose of Statutory Provision." 37 *Yale L.J.* 265 (1927).

44. "Innkeepers—Duties to Guests: §200 and §206 of New York General Business Law." 7 *N.Y.U.L.Q. Rev.* 536 (1929).

45. "Innkeepers—Duty to Guests—Liability for Servant's Tortious Conduct on Basis of Implied Contract—*Crawford* v. *Hotel Essex Boston Corp.*, 143 F. Supp. 172 (D. Mass. 1956)." 32 *Notre Dame Law.* 542 (1957).

46. "Innkeepers—Failure of Guest to Disclose Character of Contents of Baggage as Negligence." 44 *Mich. L. Rev.* 1148 (1946).

47. "Innkeepers' Guests: Their Personal Safety." G. H. L. Fridman. 29 *N.Z.L.J.* 43 (1953)

48. "Innkeepers—Hotel Providing Lodging Only—Liability for Valuables Deposited." 21 *Colum. L. Rev.* 95 (1921).

49. "Innkeepers—Injury to Person of Guest." 11 *U. Cin. L. Rev.* 536 (1937).

50. "Innkeepers—Injury to Property of Guest—Care Required of Innkeeper." D. A. Gelber. 12 *Notre Dame Law.* 463 (1937).

51. "The Innkeeper's Legal Obligations." 85 *Ir. L.T.* 285 (1951).

52. "Innkeepers' Liability." 83 *Sol. J.* 615 (1939).

53. "Innkeepers' Liability." P. S. James. 14 *Modern L. Rev.* 352 (1951).

54. "Innkeepers' Liability." 101 *Sol. J.* 137 (1957).

55. "Innkeeper's Liability and the Hospitium of the Inn." 4 *Chitty's L.J.* 231 (1954).

56. "Innkeepers—Liability as Modified by Statute." 28 *Mich. L. Rev.* 345 (1930).

57. "Innkeeper's Liability at Common Law and under the Statutes." J. J. Hemphling. 4 *Notre Dame Law.* 421 (1929).

58. "Innkeeper's Liability at Common Law—What Amounts to Carelessness by a Guest." 13 *Austl. L.J.* 358 (1939).

59. "Innkeepers—Liability for Acts of Servant without the Scope of Employment." 24 *Albany L. Rev.* 433 (1960).

60. "Innkeepers—Liability for Damage to Automobile of Guest." 14 *Tenn. L. Rev.* 289 (1936).

61. "Innkeepers' Liability for Guests' Lost Goods." A. Stirling. 4 *Austl. L.J.* 319 (1931).

62. "Innkeepers—Liability for Guest's Personal Property—Automobiles." 15 *Albany L. Rev.* 236 (1951).

63. "Innkeepers—Liability for Guest's Property." 24 *S. Cal. L. Rev.* 319 (1951)

64. "An Innkeeper's Liability for Infection of Guest." 73 *Sol. J.* 49 (1929).

65. "Innkeepers—Liability for Injuries to Guest Caused by Defective Premises." 22 *Miss. L.J.* 246 (1951).

66. "Innkeepers—Liability for Loss of Guest's Property—Effect of Statutory Limitation." W. H. Skipwith, Jr. 26 *Texas L. Rev.* 541 (1948).

67. "Innkeepers—Liability for Loss of Property of Guest—Ohio Statutes Limiting Liability." 19 *U. Cin. L. Rev.* 531 (1950).

68. "Innkeepers—Liability for Negligence of Porter in Transporting Guest's Baggage." 1 *Brooklyn L. Rev.* 120 (1932).

69. "Innkeepers—Liability for Property of Guest." 9 *N.Y.U.L.Q. Rev.* 237 (1931).

70. "Innkeepers Liability for Safe Custody of Goods of Guest." 74 *Sol. J.* 697 (1930).

71. "An Innkeeper's Liability for the Safety of His Guests—Some New Considerations." 74 *Ir. L.T.* 123 (1940).

72. "Innkeepers' Liability for Thefts from Cars." 89 *L.J.* 80 (1940).

73. "Innkeeper's Liability—Negligence of Guest." 4 *Austl. L.J.* 293 (1931).

74. "Innkeepers' Liability: The Need for Reform." 23 *Ir. Jur.* 5 (1957).

75. "Innkeepers' Liability—Theft of Jewellry from Room." W. J. Bryden. 50 *Jurid. Rev.* 194 (1938).

76. "Innkeeper's Liability to a Permanent Guest for Loss of Goods by Fire." 32 *Iowa L. Rev.* 95 (1946).

77. "Innkeepers—Liability to Guests." 93 *Cent. L.J.* 156 (1921).

78. "The Innkeeper's Lien at Common Law." J. C. Hogan. 8 *Hastings L.J.* 33 (1956).

79. "An Innkeeper's Lien on Letters Addressed to His Guest." 55 *Sol. J.* 199 (1911).

80. "Innkeeper's Lien on Stolen Goods Brought into His Hotel by a Guest." L. A. Boxleitner. 10 *Ohio. Op.* 199 (1938).

81. "Innkeepers—Lien on Stolen Property Brought to Hotel by Guest: *M. & M. Hotel Co.* v. *Nichols,* 32 N.E. (2d) 463 (Ohio)." F. G. Mehlman 21 *B.U.L. Rev.* 559 (1941).

82. "Innkeepers—Limitation of Liability for Loss of Guests' Property—Article 2971, Louisiana Civil Code of 1870." 22 *Tul. L. Rev.* 333 (1947).

83. "Innkeepers—Loss of Customer's Goods—Common Law—Motor/Car Stolen While Owner Dining at Hotel—Innkeepers Act 1863 (26 & 27 Vict. c. 41), s.3." 163 *L.T.* 470 (1927).

84. "Innkeepers—Negligence—Insurer's Liability—*Davidson* v. *Madison*

Corporation, 177 N.E. 393 (N.Y.)." N. F. Smith. 11 *B.U.L. Rev.* 585 (1931).

85. "Innkeepers—New York General Business Law, Section 201, Applicability of Statute Where Guest Has Merely a Right to Possession." 31 *Colum. L. Rev.* 166 (1931).

86. "Innkeepers—Personal Property—Innkeepers' Relationship with Clientele." 11 *Baylor L. Rev.* 329 (1959).

87. "Innkeeper's Remedy against Unruly Guest." 94 *Just. P.* 649 (1930).

88. "An Innkeeper's 'Right' to Discriminate." 15 *U. Fla. L. Rev.* 109 (1962).

89. "Innkeeper's Right to Exclude or Eject Guests." 7 *Fordham L. Rev.* 417 (1938).

90. "Innkeepers—Statutory Limitation of Liability Effect of Maximum Liability Clause When Guest's Property Is Stolen by Servant." 13 *Minn. L.Q.* 615 (1929).

91. "Innkeepers—Statutory Limitations of Liability—Application Where Valuables Deposited by Guest Are Stolen by Employee of Innkeeper." 14 *Minn. L. Rev.* 419 (1930).

92. "Innkeepers—Statutory Limitation of Liability—Necessity of Strict Compliance as a Condition Precedent to Exemption." 33 *Mich. L. Rev.* 127 (1934)

93. "Inns and Innkeepers—Innkeeper's Lien—An Innkeeper May Not Enforce a Statutory Innkeeper's Lien Unless the Lodger Is Given Notice and Has an Opportunity to Test the Validity of the Seizure at a Hearing—*Klim* v. *Jones,* 315 F. Supp. 109 (N.D. Cal. 1970)." 39 *U. Cin. L. Rev.* 815 (1970).

94. "Landlord and Tenant—Innkeeper—Liability of Proprietor for Injury to Occupant." 21 *St. Louis L. Rev.* 91 (1935).

95. "Legal Effects of Serving Impure Food by a Restaurant Keeper to His Guests." 24 *Yale L.J.* 73 (1914).

96. "Legislation—Innkeepers—Limitation of Liability for Loss of Guest's Vehicle." D. C. Fraser and J. G. Fogo. 32 *Can. B. Rev.* 1149 (1954).

97. "The Liabilities of Innkeepers." 5 *Austl. L.J.* 21 (1931).

98. "Liability of an Innkeeper for Damage to Goods." 102 *L.J.* 284 (1952).

99. "Liability of an Innkeeper for the Loss of His Guest's Goods." 99 *Sol. J.* 51 (1955).

100. "Liability of an Innkeeper in Recent Cases." W. H. D. Winder. 1952 *S.L.T.* 58.

101. "The Liability of an Innkeeper to Supply Reasonable Refreshment." 82 *Ir. L.T.* 59 (1948)

102. "Liability of Hotel to Pedestrian for Misconduct of Guests." 44 *Minn. L. Rev.* 584 (1960).

103. "Liability of Innkeeper for Damage to Goods of Guest." 171 *L.T.* 115 (1931).
104. "Liability of Innkeeper for Offensive Acts of Employees." 69 *Albany L.J.* 313 (1907).
105. "Liability of Innkeeper to Guest Insulted by Employee." 13 *Bench & Bar* 90 (1908).
106. "The Liability of Innkeepers." 203 *L.T.* 287 (1947).
107. "Liability of Innkeepers." 79 *L.J.* 146, 166, 185, 201 (1935).
108. "Liability of Innkeepers." 170 *L.T.* 318 (1930).
109. "Liability of Modern Innkeepers." 71 *Sol. J.* 395 (1927).
110. "Liability of Restaurant Owner for Fitness of Food Served." A. B. Armstrong, 10 *S. Cal. L. Rev.* 188 (1937).
111. "Liability of Tavern Owners under the New York State Dram Shop Act." 30 *Albany L. Rev.* 271 (1966).
112. "Liens—Innkeepers—Lien of Innkeeper on Stolen Goods Brought into His Hotel by Guest." 10 *U. Cin. L. Rev.* 495 (1936).
113. "Limited Liability of Innkeepers under Statutory Regulations." S. H. Hirsch. 76 *U. Pa. L. Rev.* 272 (1928).
114. "Luggage Trouble." A. Samuels. 106 *Sol. J.* 660, 681 (1962).
115. "A Modern Innkeeper's Liability." 101 *L.J.* 143 (1951).
116. "The Modern Innkeeper's Liability for Injuries to the Person of His Guest." E. L. Eyerman. 19 *St. Louis L. Rev.* 232 (1934).
117. "Modern Liability of Innkeepers—Under Virginia Statute." 1 *Wm. & Mary L. Rev.* 121 (1957).
118. "The Motorist and the Innkeeper." 95 *Sol. J.* 53 (1951).
119. "Negligence—Innkeeper and Lodger—Lodger Giving False Name for Immoral Purpose—Whether Invitee or Trespasser." 19 *Austl. L.J.* 372 (1946)
120. "Negligence—Innkeepers—Liability for Loss of or Injury to Goods of Guest." 6 *Texas L. Rev.* 545 (1928).
121. "A New Look at the Liability of Inn Keepers for Guest Property under New York Law." G. A. Navagh. 25 *Fordham L. Rev.* 62 (1956).
122. "Non-Liability of an Innkeeper for Damage." 106 *L.J.* 341 (1956).
123. "Note." 5 *Law Q. Rev.* 481 (1939).
124. "Offenses and Quasi-Offenses—Innkeepers—Liability for Objects Thrown into Streets Causing Injury." 26 *Tul. L. Rev.* 394 (1952).
125. "Personal Property—Bailee—Innkeeper—Damage to Guest's Car— Injury by Frost—Liability of Innkeeper." 4 *Camb. L.J.* 376 (1932).
126. "Personal Property—Innkeeper—Liability for Loss of Guest's Property by Theft—Question of Guest's Negligence." 7 *Camb. L.J.* 271 (1940).

127. "Personal Property—Innkeeper's Liability for Loss of—Burden of Proof under Modifying Statute." W. Montague. 13 *S. Cal. L. Rev.* 164 (1939).

128. "Personal Property—Innkeepers—Liability for Loss of Guest's Property—Question Whether Loss Caused by Guest's Negligence." 9 *Camb. L.J.* 246 (1946).

129. "Personal Property—Innkeeper's Liability in Oregon for Loss of Guest's Property." M. J. Wormser. 22 *Ore. L. Rev.* 95 (1942).

130. "Personal Property—Innkeeper's Lien—Lien over Stolen Property—Held: Innkeeper Entitled to Exercise Right of Lien over Such Property." 9 *Camb. L.J.* 122 (1945).

131. "Personal Property—Statutory Liability of an Innkeeper for Personal Property of a Guest." W. P. Hamilton. 1 *Ark. L. Rev.* 86 (1946–1947).

132. "Personal Safety of Innkeepers' Guests." G. H. L. Fridman. 102 *L.J.* 689 (1952).

133. "Public Accommodations in New Mexico: The Right to Refuse Service for Reasons Other than Race or Religion." 10 *Natural Resources J.* 635 (1970).

134. "Refusal of Reasonable Refreshment by Innkeeper." 81 *Ir. L.T.* 193 1947).

135. "Registration of Visitors at Hotels." 72 *Sol. J.* 358 (1928).

136. "The Status of Hotels under the Federal Housing and Rent Act." 16 *U. Chi. L. Rev.* 554 (1949)

137. "Statutory Limitation of Innkeepers' Liability." G. M. Martin. 14 *Wash. L. Rev.* 217 (1939).

138. "A Summary of Rights and Liabilities of Innkeepers Regarding Property of Guests." W. D. Arnold. 1 *S. Tex. L.J.* 63 (1954).

139. "Theft by Hotel Servant." 72 *Sol. J.* 127 (1928).

140. "Theft of Motor-Car—Hotel Parking Ground—Liability of Hotel Company." 5 *Can. B. Rev.* 440 (1927).

141. "Tort—Innkeeper—Refusal to Receive Guest—Action on Case—No Need to Prove Special Damage." 9 *Camb. L.J.* 123 (1945).

142. "Tort—Negligence—Innkeeper's Liability for Customer's Goods Stolen Whilst in Custody—Customer Not a Guest at Common Law—No Liability." 6 *Res. Judicatae* 537 (1954).

143. "Torts—Innkeeper's Liability for Personal Injuries of Guest." 25 *Geo. L.J.* 200 (1936).

144. "Torts—Liability of an Innkeeper for Personal Injuries to Guests." 28 *Fordham L. Rev.* 559 (1959).

145. "Torts—Liability of Hotel Keeper for Refusing Dining Service to

Person Not Lodging in Hotel [Virginia]." R. B. Spindle, III. 4 *Wash. & Lee L. Rev.* 107 (1946).

146. "Torts—Negligence—Liability of Innkeeper for Acts of Transient Guests." 3 *Mercer L. Rev.* 351 (1952).

147. "Tourist Homes and Cabins as Inns." L. H. Cole. 13 *Ind. L.J.* 242 (1938).

148. "Unwarranted Refusal by an Innkeeper." 94 *Ir. L.T.* 245 (1960).

149. "Innkeeper's Lien and Due Process." 5 *U. Richmond L. Rev.* 447 (1971).

150. "Innkeeper's Lien in Missouri." 36 *Mo. L. Rev.* 431 (1971).

151. "Innkeepers' Liens and the Requirements of Due Process." 28 *Wash. & Lee L. Rev.* 481 (1971).

152. "Tax Aspects of Organizing and Operating Hotels and Motels." Albert B. Ellentock. 29 *N.Y.U. Inst. on Fed. Tax.* 887 (1971).

Subject Index to
Law Review Articles

The index numbers refer to the list on pages 481–488.

Table of Cases

The numbers refer to chapter and section.

Index

The numbers refer to pages.

THE LAWS OF INNKEEPERS

Designed by R. E. Rosenbaum.
Composed by Vail-Ballou Press, Inc.,
in 10 point linotype Caledonia, 3 points leaded
with display lines in monotype Bulmer.
Printed letterpress from type by Vail-Ballou Press
on Warren's Olde Style, 60 pound basis,
with the Cornell University Press watermark.
Bound by Vail-Ballou Press
in Columbia Sampson Buckram
and stamped in All Purpose foils.

Library of Congress Cataloging in Publication Data
(For library cataloging purposes only)

Sherry, John Harold.
  The laws of innkeepers.

  Bibliography: p.
  1. Hotels, taverns, etc.—U. S.—Law.   I. Title.
KF951.A7S5   343'.73'078   76-37780
ISBN 0-8014-0702-8